# A History of Russian Music

*The publisher gratefully acknowledges the generous contribution to this book provided by the Carol Franc Buck Foundation and by the Music Endowment Fund of the Associates of the University of California Press.*

# A History
# of Russian Music

From *Kamarinskaya* to *Babi Yar*

## Francis Maes

TRANSLATED BY
Arnold J. Pomerans and Erica Pomerans

UNIVERSITY OF CALIFORNIA PRESS
*Berkeley · Los Angeles · London*

Originally published as *Geschiedenis van de Russische muziek: Van Kamarinskaja tot Babi Jar*, © 1996 Uitgeverij SUN, Nijmegen. The translators would like to thank John Colleer for his expert advice and assistance.

University of California Press
Berkeley and Los Angeles, California

University of California Press, Ltd.
London, England

Library of Congress Cataloging-in-Publication Data

Maes, Francis, 1963–
    [Geschiedenis van de russische muziek. English]
    A history of Russian music : from Kamarinskaya
to Babi Yar / Francis Maes ; translated by Arnold J.
Pomerans and Erica Pomerans.
        p.   cm.
    Includes bibliographical references (p.) and
index.
    ISBN 0-520-21815-9 (alk. paper)
    1. Music—Russia—History and criticism.
    2. Music—Soviet Union—History and criticism.
    I. Pomerans, Arnold.   II. Pomerans, Erica.
    III. Title.

ML300.M1313   2002
780'.947—dc21                          2001027617

Manufactured in the United States of America
11   10   09   08   07   06   05   04   03   02
10   9   8   7   6   5   4   3   2   1

The paper used in this publication meets the minimum requirements of ANSI/NISO Z39.48-1992 (R 1997) (*Permanence of Paper*).♾

*For Katia and Anton*

# Contents

# Plates

# Preface

When Fyodor Mikhailovich Dostoyevsky said, "We are all sprung from under Gogol's cloak," he was referring to the influence of Gogol's short story "The Overcoat" on the course of literary realism in Russia. Pyotr Chaikovsky applied a similar dictum to Russian music. On 27 June 1888, he noted in his diary that the whole Russian symphonic school was there in *Kamarinskaya,* a relatively short and unpretentious orchestral piece by Mikhaíl Glinka, "just as the whole oak is in the acorn." Many objections can be raised to Dostoyevsky's and Chaikovsky's statements, which, indeed, are oversimplifications. Yet both reflect a longing for a cohesive national tradition. In that sense, we can consider *Kamarinskaya* a symbol of the beginning of a Russian art-music tradition; that is, "art music" in the western European sense, as distinct from the folk and liturgical music that had existed in Russia for many centuries.

*Babi Yar,* for its part, might be considered a symbolic end point in the history of Russian music. This work—*Babi Yar* being the name by which Dmitry Shostakovich's Thirteenth Symphony is popularly known—exemplifies the difficult relationship between music and art on the one hand and the Communist regime on the other, a relationship that largely shaped the history of twentieth-century Russian music. Because what came after Shostakovich is still history in the making, I conclude my analysis with him. The time for a historical analysis of contemporary music, it seems to me, has not yet come.

Over the past few decades, ideas on the history of Russian music have been stood on their head. The Western view used to be based largely on the ideas of Vladimir Stasov. As the friend and confidant of leading nine-teenth-century Russian composers, Stasov was a privileged witness of the early development of Russian music. The picture he presented in his writings, however, was above all a portrayal of his own ideals; Stasov was not so much a historian as a propagandist. In the West, nevertheless, he was taken at his word, and in the Soviet Union his history was officially approved, thanks to the importance he attached to progressive and pop-ulist ideals. Stasov's opinions still make themselves felt—as recently as 1994, in the case of Dorothea Redepenning's *Geschichte der russischen und der sowjetischen Musik* (History of Russian and Soviet music).

A completely different picture has emerged over the past two decades, however, one that makes short shrift of Stasov's authority. American writers such as Richard Taruskin, Malcolm Brown, and Caryl Emerson have exposed Stasov's ideas as so many tendentious and prejudiced assertions. With the deconstruction of Stasov's interpretation, the old picture of Russian music history has collapsed. Students are now at liberty to dismiss all dogma, to take a critical view of all clichés, and to return to the sources with no preconceptions. The result is a historical conception that has very little in common with the old. It is less uniform and schematic, and its greater subtlety renders it infinitely more interesting.

The old picture rested on a black-and-white distinction between artists reaching out for freedom on the one hand and a repressive state machin-ery on the other. Musical renewal, folklorism, and nationalism were gen-erally seen as expressions of resistance to repression and a longing for emancipation. That, in any case, had been the view of Stasov, who prof-fered his wishful picture as the reality. In the new picture, that simple di-chotomy has disappeared, and as a result, the relationship between mu-sic and ideology has become less unequivocal. Many musicians were in fact closely associated with official, conservative, and even reactionary cir-cles. In the new picture, therefore, more attention is paid to the personal development of composers against the complex background of their times and to inconsistencies in their work that reflect those complexities. Mu-sorgsky, for instance, has been transformed from a straightforward com-poser with a well-defined program into a rich figure full of contradictions.

The two historical viewpoints outlined are so contradictory that they cannot possibly be reconciled. Any author wishing to provide an account of Russian music must accordingly make a choice. This book attempts to sum up the new historical picture, a picture that stretches, symbolically speaking, from *Kamarinskaya* to *Babi Yar*. In this regard, it may be con-sidered the converse of Dorothea Redepenning's history of Russian music mentioned earlier. That I identify myself completely with the new approach, elaborated above all by American musicologists, will be obvious. For a more detailed account of my choice, I would refer the reader to my article "Modern Historiography of Russian Music: When Will Two Schools of Thought Meet?" in the *International Journal of Musicology* (1997).

This book would never have become what it now is without the experiences I had as a visiting scholar at the University of California, Berkeley. My stay there was rendered possible by the Fulbright Scholar Program, and I should like to express my most cordial thanks to the J. William Fulbright Foreign Scholarship Board and the Commission for Educational Exchange between the United States of America, Belgium, and Luxembourg, who were kind enough to nominate me for a Fulbright grant.

I am most grateful to Wilfried Uitterhoeve of the SUN Publishing Company in Nijmegen, Netherlands, for the enthusiasm with which he has supported this project from the start. His professional advice proved of great help to the inexperienced author I was when I started writing this book. Geertje De Winter and Gerrit Tyberghein kept a watchful eye on the readability of the text. They went through the manuscript patiently and carefully, tracking down mistakes and infelicities.

The Slavist Xavier Verbeke was my indispensable philological adviser and a most appreciated authority on the subject of Orthodox liturgy.

Most invigorating were my discussions with leading specialists on the history of Russian music. I had brief but stimulating contacts with Malcolm Brown, Laurel Fay, Alexander Poznansky, and Anne Swartz. I also enjoyed the privilege of the attention and support of Professor Richard Taruskin of the University of California, Berkeley. Without exaggeration, he may be called one of the pioneers of modern Russian music studies and a foremost protagonist of contemporary musicology. He was always ready to answer my questions. In addition, he was kind enough to let me see the text of his future publications in typescript. As a result, I was able to use his groundbreaking, monumental study of Stravinsky before it appeared in book form. Taruskin's conspicuous presence in this book will escape no one. The large number of backnote references to his publications are homage in themselves. I am particularly grateful to him for the new prospects his work has opened up for my own understanding of the subject and of the musicological field as a whole.

This book originally appeared in Dutch. I was playing it safe—no comprehensive survey of Russian music was available in that language.

I feel particularly honored that a number of people have gone out of their way to bring my book to the notice of a wider readership through the present version. I am indebted above all to Richard Taruskin, David Fanning, Margarita Mazo, and Lynne Withey. My heartfelt thanks go to my translators, Arnold Pomerans and Erica Pomerans, for their enthusiastic collaboration and the care they have bestowed upon my work.

I consider the publication of my book by the University of California Press a recognition of my motive in writing it, namely that insights gained by leading scholars are too important to remain confined to a small circle of specialists and deserve being made accessible to a wider public.

Between the publication of the original version and that of the English edition I met my dear wife, Katia, who, through her grandmother, is of Russian descent. The period during which the book was being translated will always remain associated with the birth of our son, Anton. I have dedicated the book to both of them.

Every book on Russia needs a double clarification: of the dates used and of the transliteration.

In Russia, the Julian calendar—also known as the "Old Style"—was used until 1 February 1918. It continues to be the calendar of the Russian Orthodox Church. In the nineteenth century, Russian dates were twelve days behind those of the Western—the Gregorian or "New Style"—calendar; from 29 February 1900 to 1 February 1918, the Julian calendar lagged thirteen days behind the Gregorian (because 1900 was a leap year in the Julian but not in the Gregorian calendar). For all dates given in this book, I have used the original chronology. Practically speaking, this means that events that took place in Russia are given in the Old Style. In cases of possible confusion, I specify which style I am using.

The transliteration of Russian words always encounters specific problems. The best systems involve a compromise between phonetic transliteration and legibility in the target language. In this book, I follow the system developed by Gerald Abraham for the *New Grove Dictionary* (one based on English orthography) and later modified by Richard Taruskin. (For a detailed account, the reader is referred to "A Note on Transliteration" in Taruskin's *Stravinsky and the Russian Traditions*.) This system involves careful phonetic rendering but also respects the accepted spelling of a number of names that, through common usage, have become so established that a different spelling might merely confuse the English-speaking reader.

## CHAPTER ONE

# Introduction

## *Natasha's Dance,*
## *or Musical Nationalism*

In book 2 of *War and Peace* Tolstoy transports us to the Russia of our dreams in his delightful account of the hunt in the copse at Otradnoe and of the nocturnal outing in the troika—the moonlight over the snow-covered plain, the wintry silence broken by the jingle of the bells, the swish of the runners, and the crunch of the snow. After the hunt, "Uncle," a congenial distant relation of the Rostovs, invites Nikolai and Natasha to his country house. They spend the evening savoring tempting delicacies, vodka, and balalaika music. "Uncle" picks up his guitar. The two young Rostovs are entranced by his playing. And then:

> "Uncle" rose, and it was as though there were two men in him, one of whom smiled a grave smile at the merry fellow, while the merry fellow struck a naïve, formal pose preparatory to a folk-dance.
>
> "Now then, niece!" he exclaimed, waving to Natasha the hand that had just struck a chord.
>
> Natasha flung off the shawl that had been wrapped round her, ran forward facing "Uncle," and setting her arms akimbo made a motion with her shoulders and waited.
>
> Where, how and when could this young countess, who had had a French *émigrée* for governess, have imbibed from the Russian air she breathed the spirit of that dance? Where had she picked up that manner which the *pas de châle*, one might have supposed, would have effaced long ago? But the spirit and the movements were the very ones—inimitable, unteachable, Russian—which "Uncle" had expected of her. The moment she sprang to her feet and gaily smiled a confident, triumphant, knowing smile, the first tremor of fear

which had seized Nikolai and the others—fear that she might not dance it well—passed, and they were already admiring her.

Her performance was so perfect, so absolutely perfect, that Anisya Fiodorovna, who had at once handed her the kerchief she needed for the dance, had tears in her eyes, though she laughed as she watched the slender, graceful countess, reared in silks and velvets, in another world than hers, who was yet able to understand all that was in Anisya and in Anisya's father and mother and aunt, and in every Russian man and woman.[1]

Tolstoy is a masterful writer. His powers of persuasion sweep us along. The charm of the above scene is so compelling that we barely notice that the writer has conjured up something highly improbable. How can the graceful countess possibly perform a dance she has never learned, that is not part of her social milieu? It is true that from the beginning of the nineteenth century folk music and folk dancing had become part of urban life in St. Petersburg and Moscow, a great many peasants having moved into the cities, bringing their customs with them. But the aristocracy had kept its own culture distinct from theirs. The gulf is well illustrated in Chaikovsky's opera *The Queen of Spades*. In the second act several aristocratic young ladies make so bold as to dance to the strains of a folk tune, whereupon their governess rebukes them sharply: "Fi, quel genre, mesdames!" For Tolstoy, however, the question of how Natasha might have come to know the dance she performed is moot. As he puts it, her movements were "inimitably, unteachably Russian." In the passage quoted above, Tolstoy thus introduces the reader not only to the welcoming warmth of a Russian country house, but also to the very heart of an ideology.

Tolstoy was voicing his faith in the Russian communal spirit. Book 2 of *War and Peace* revolves around the deep-rooted communal ties of the Russian family. In books 3 and 4 he extends these ties to embrace the entire Russian nation. This national spirit is adumbrated in the scene described above. Natasha and Anisya belong to different social worlds: the first is a young countess, the second a housekeeper. Yet the difference in their social and cultural backgrounds does not affect their deep affinity. In her dance, Natasha reveals her bond with her compatriots.

This is precisely the crux of the nationalist idea: all members of the nation share a single national identity. They are related. Their solidarity is more fundamental than the etiquette and values their social status bestows on them, and is clearly reflected in language, music, and dance.

For Tolstoy, national identity is no cultural artifact but a basic reality, a product of nature, one might say. And although the scene above refers to dancing, Tolstoy thinks in the same way about music, as is shown by a slightly later passage: "'Uncle' sang as the peasant sings, with the full and naïve conviction that the whole meaning of the song lies in the words, and that the tune comes as a matter of course and exists only to emphasize the words. This gave the unconsidered tune a peculiar charm, like the song of a bird."[2]

"The song of a bird" equates with the voice of nature and is therefore "good." Tolstoy calls folk music naive and unconsidered. Peasants do not think about how their tunes ought to sound; that takes care of itself. Nature alone can create music of any worth, simply by doing her work. There is therefore no such thing as musical creation by man. It is well known that in his later, moralistic phase, Tolstoy rejected Beethoven's and Schumann's music. His short story "Kreutzer Sonata," based on Beethoven's violin sonata by the same name, is a poisoned tribute to be sure, suggesting nothing less than that art music can unleash criminal passions. Tolstoy thought infinitely more of the song of the Volga boatmen. No wonder, then, that tears filled his eyes when he heard Chaikovsky's First String Quartet.[3]

That folk music springs straight from nature and that Russian music "can be breathed in with the Russian air" is a nineteenth-century idea. Folk music seemed a world apart from everything that European art music stood for. It went without saying that the two should be considered fundamental opposites, their difference reduced to the simple distinction between nature and culture.

What do we think about this matter nowadays? Modern people tend to take a more global view of music than was true in the 1800s. Although profound differences of opinion still prevail about what is natural in music and what is culturally determined, it now seems clear that the division does not lie where it was drawn in the nineteenth century. Folk music cannot be reduced to a natural expression of feelings, in opposition to the more formally fashioned art music. Folk music, too, is the result of structural thinking. It has its own rationale. A case in point is the Russian *protyazhnaya*, a splendid form of melismatically decorated song set to poetry of great expressive power and lyrical intensity. There is no doubt that the *protyazhnaya* was the type of folk song that Tolstoy had in mind when he wrote the above passages.

Tolstoy's view of folk music was not original; rather, it echoed the realistic and utilitarian vision of art presented by Nikolai Gavrilovich Chernïshevsky in his influential *The Aesthetic Relations of Art to Reality* (1855). A work of art, Chernïshevsky said, must be an objective rendering of reality. But how can music satisfy that demand? According to Chernïshevsky, by allowing itself to be guided by natural song. Chernïshevsky equated folk song with "natural singing," which wells up spontaneously from the emotions. "Artificial singing," by contrast, is the province of the prima donna.

> In what relation does this artificial singing stand to natural singing? It is more deliberate, calculated, embellished with everything with which human genius can embellish it. What comparison can there be between an aria of an Italian opera and the simple, pale, monotonous melody of a folk song! But all the training in harmony, all the artistry of development, all the wealth of embellishment of a brilliant area, all the flexibility and incomparable richness of the voice of the one who sings it cannot make up for the absence of the sincere emotion that permeates the pale melody of a folk song and the ordinary, untrained voice of the one who sings it not from a desire to pose and display his voice and art, but from the need to express his feelings.[4]

The idea that folk music is a product of nature played an important part in the rise of musical nationalism, and it was part of the complex of ideas at the root of romantic nationalism. In the German Romantic movement, the folk song was considered an expression of the "purely human." Instead of being universal, however, that expression was thought to vary from one nation to the next. Folk song was considered a reflection of the particular mystical characteristics of a people and to go back to times immemorial. In this scheme, the division of mankind into nations was a natural fact. Every nation was said to have its own deep-rooted identity, its "national soul." Folk music was believed to be the clearest expression of the national character, a typical feature enshrined in every nation.

This interpretation of the meaning of folk music became dogma for nationalistic music ideologists. A natural outgrowth of this way of thinking was the idea that a nation's music is not created but "discovered," inasmuch as music reflecting the national character has always existed in folk song. Composers simply have the task of unveiling that character, of refining it, and of raising it to a higher artistic level. Their main concern must be to listen carefully and to polish the rough musical voice of their people.

Nationalistic musical thought had a strong influence on the historical picture of nineteenth-century music. This is particularly true of the music that appeared outside the dominant musical nations, that is, outside Germany, France, and Italy. The label "national schools," which was generally applied to the peripheral musical countries, is a sign of nationalist thinking in itself. These "national schools" were for a long time judged almost exclusively by nationalist criteria; even today this habit continues, in that we spontaneously expect to discover the "typically Spanish" or "typically Russian" in the music of those countries.

Romantic nationalism has become firmly rooted in our listening habits, and this quality applies especially to Russian music. The persistence of this historical view, which colors the reception and critical evaluation of Russian composers to this day, stems from the fact that we associate the idea of national character with folklorism and authenticity, which in turn are associated with liberal, "progressive" values. The resulting picture is highly idealized; it is based on the belief that the interest of composers in folklore reflects their concern with the lot of the common man. The music taken to be the most typically Russian is thus spontaneously associated with progressive social ideas: the bridging of the enormous gulf between the elite and the broad masses of the Russian people. This basic idea is prominent not only in Soviet aesthetics but also in Western music historiography.

In the Soviet version, nineteenth-century composers belonged to the progressive intelligentsia. Glinka, Borodin, and Rimsky-Korsakov were turned into advocates of social and national emancipation, and Musorgsky was called a musical populist and a protorevolutionary. Even as conservative a composer as Chaikovsky was dragged into the progressive camp—Chaikovsky of all people, a man who had expressed his revulsion of communism quite unequivocally in a letter to Nadezhda von Meck:

> What you have said about communism is entirely true. It is impossible to imagine a more senseless utopia, something more discordant with the natural qualities of human nature. And how dull and unbearably colorless life will surely be when this equality of wealth reigns supreme (if ever it does). Indeed, life is the struggle for existence, and if it is permitted that this struggle not be [i.e., if we allow that this struggle may cease to be]—then neither will there be life, merely senseless proliferation.[5]

The national element (what the Russians call *naródnost'*) was assigned a central place in Soviet ideology, according to which art had to be socialist in content and national in form. Ever since, the folklorism of the nineteenth-century masters has been dogmatically associated with progressive ideas.

In the West, the artificial character of this picture was clearly appreciated, and the most blatant distortions—the obvious way in which Chaikovsky's character had been twisted, for instance—were ironed out.

Yet even Western musicologists have continued to identify the idea of national character with progressive thought. In particular, Russian music with a "national color" is still associated with the emancipation of the Russian people. Cosmopolitan music, in contrast, is treated as the elitist, alien culture of the aristocratic minority.

Musorgsky, for example, was traditionally counted among the populists, as in this characterization by Michael Russ: "Musorgsky was the only true musical Populist. . . . The emancipation rendered him penniless . . . but he bore the common people no malice, and concern and interest in their character and qualities helped shape his unique musical style."[6] Cosmopolitan traits in the work of such composers as Chaikovsky, however, were branded as conservative and un-Russian. A typical example of that attitude is this comparison of Musorgsky with Chaikovsky:

> The abandonment of bourgeois in favor of epic-popular themes thus appears as the unavoidable way out for the "Russist" Musorgsky, as his utopian and outsider's cultural decision, spurning identification with the European culture of Petersburg, with its classical and salon melodies, with the line of development that led from Glinka to Chaikovsky and saw its showpiece in *Eugene Onegin*. . . . The contrast is one between the Russia of the millions of souls and that of a million cultured people.[7]

Even in the recent textbook by Dorothea Redepenning we still read:

> I have tried to take seriously the national character and also the role of folklore in art music and to treat it as a central phenomenon of the musical development in nineteenth-century Russia. . . . Only in that way can it be made clear that the composers of the "Mighty Little Heap" [the circle of composers around Balakirev], and Musorgsky in particular, were not the "classicists" into which Soviet musicology had turned them; rather did national subjects and folklore in about 1860 to 1880 have a socio-critical, mutinous, and political dimension that the tsarist state considered a threat.[8]

That view is hardly tenable. If a direct link indeed exists between national character and progressive liberalism, how then can we explain that a nationalistic work such as *Rogneda* earned its composer, Alexander Serov, a life annuity from the tsar? And how can we reconcile the fact that the impetus for Chaikovsky's most folkloristic opera, *Vakula the Smith*, came from court circles? Or how is it that Musorgsky's *Khovanshchina* has the reputation of being an opera about the people when the people do not play even the most minor role in it?

We cannot endow music with an ideological content unless we have a clear picture of the context in which it originated and was expected to function. The ideological development of a composition such as Balakirev's Second Overture on Russian Themes (1864) is a good example that ought to prevent us from jumping to hasty conclusions. The composer himself gave at least three ideological explanations of this work, a powerful piece of symphonic music based entirely on Russian folk-music themes. Musical nationalism in its purest form, you might think. But what did the work really signify? During its composition Balakirev was under the spell of the radical populist Alexander Herzen. From his London exile, Herzen tried to infuse Russian youth with political awareness through his journal *Kolokol* (The bell). His portrayal of the tidal wave of social unrest flooding across Russia and his slogan "to the people!" were famous. That slogan expressed precisely what Balakirev himself did by transcribing folk songs directly from the mouths of the people and then elaborating them symphonically. In 1869 he published the result, now with the programmatic title of *1,000 Years*—a reference to the millennium in which the Russian state had emerged and established itself. A sound commercial ploy? Not altogether. For, in fact, the millenary existence of the state had been celebrated in 1862 (to mark the supposed foundation of Novgorod in 862 by the Varangian prince Rurik). From a letter of his friend Stasov of 17 December 1868 we gather that Balakirev and Stasov had given the work a fresh meaning. It was no longer the flood of social unrest they wished to portray, but three stages in Russian history: the ancient, the medieval, and the modern (the last illustrated on the title page with locomotives and telegraphs). In other words, the work was glorifying progress, painting an optimistic and melioristic picture of Russian history. No vestige of a revolutionary message was left. In 1884, Balakirev revised the overture, and four years later he published the work anew, now under the title of *Rus*, the Old Slavic name for Russia. "Rus" was a central concept of Slavophiles, who used it to refer to the old Russia before the reforms of Peter the Great—the Russia they considered as their ideal, and a romantic idealization strongly opposed by liberal and progressive thinkers. Now Balakirev spelled out his message quite specifically. The clash between three elements—the pagan period, the Muscovite state, and the autonomous republican system of the Cossacks—he said, had culminated in "the fatal blow dealt all Russian religious and national aspirations by the reforms of Peter I." In a letter to a Czech Slavophile, Balakirev wrote that he was trying "to depict how Peter the Great killed our native Russian life." He had effected a 180-degree turn from left populism via optimistic meliorism to pessimistic, right-wing reaction.[9]

The example of Balakirev's Second Overture on Russian Themes makes it clear that there is no direct link between his music, which remained relatively unchanged, and his ideology, which changed dramatically. Of course, it is always possible to argue that Balakirev himself did not grasp the significance of his work or, worse still, was guilty of opportunism. However, the significance of a composition never lies in its musical characteristics alone; it lies above all in the link between the composition and its context. The incorporation of musical folklore is not automatically bound up with liberal and democratic ideas: the impact of nationalism can also be conservative or even reactionary, with the romantic glorification of the people having a role-affirmative function. In the historiography of Russian music this distinction is too often neglected. Dorothea Redepenning, for instance, refers to a restorative nationalism, but places it entirely in the generation of composers working after 1880 (such as Glazunov, Lyadov, and Arensky). For the generation of Balakirev and Musorgsky she does not challenge the progressive picture—with the exception of Borodin's *In the Steppes of Central Asia,* which she considers the exception that proves the rule.

However important the role assigned to folk song by nationalistically inspired historians of music, the national character of Russian music does not stop there. The picture of what is typically Russian in music must be filled in with other characteristics. What these are has been defined largely by the views of Vladimir Stasov, one of the most powerful spokesmen of the New Russian School. It was Stasov who created the myth of the "Mighty Little Heap," a nickname for the five composers of the Balakirev circle (also known as the Mighty Five), namely Balakirev himself, Musorgsky, Cui, Borodin, and Rimsky-Korsakov, a cohesive group that was said to have remained loyal to liberal ideals—which, in fact, were merely Stasov's. Stasov's characterization of the New Russian School has made history; until recently, it had an almost exclusive hold on historiography.

According to Stasov, the New Russian School embodied the following four characteristics: the absence of preconceptions and of blind faith; an oriental element; a pronounced preference for programmatic music; and the quest for a national character.[10] The first point implied the rejection of academicism and of fixed musical—that is, Western—forms. The second sprang from contacts with eastern nations inside the Russian empire. The third reflected an aesthetic approach that was considered progressive and anti-academic at the time. The last point involved the incorporation of folk music.

Russian music history was marked by a simple split between a national camp—as defined by these four points—and a cosmopolitan camp. The national camp consisted of the Mighty Five; the cosmopolitan camp included Rubinstein, Chaikovsky, and Rachmaninoff. Chaikovsky, for example, was considered to be less Russian than the Mighty Five inasmuch as his work followed classical forms, contained few oriental elements, and left little scope for programmatic musical treatment, and national character did not seem to be his greatest concern.

Stasov created his system in defense of the group with which he was associated. His view of the Russian national aspect of music must therefore be taken with a pinch of salt.

What, for instance, are we to make of orientalism? Is it truly a national characteristic, an inherent feature of Russian musicality? Hardly. In fact, the treatment of orientalism as a Russian national characteristic is as much the result of Stasov's *magister dixit* as it is the natural outcome of the success of orientalizing works by Russian composers in Paris during the first decades of the twentieth century.

Now, the fate of "oriental" Russian music had an ironic aspect. In 1909, when Sergey Diaghilev, the founder of the Ballets Russes, devised the program for his first Paris season, he was playing things safe. Shrewd businessman that he was, he came to Paris with a repertoire that was bound to appeal to the Parisians. From the work of Russian composers he chiefly selected oriental music, tying it to ideas of Eastern luxury and eroticism: the dance of the Persian slave girls in Musorgsky's *Khovanshchina,* Borodin's *Polovtsian Dances,* Rimsky-Korsakov's *Sheherazade,* complete with visual fantasies about Cleopatra and harem scenes.[11] The Parisians were delighted, the money rolled in, and orientalism quickly came to be considered one of the national characteristics of Russian music—first in France and then throughout western Europe. That response was understandable. French culture had long had a strong penchant for orientalism, together with its ideological accompaniment: the sense that French ways were greatly superior to the admittedly brilliant but nevertheless barbaric customs of the remote and different world inhabited by distant Asiatic peoples. And to the French, Russia herself was quite distinctly part of that mysterious East. The irony of the situation is that the St. Petersburg composers, for their part, identified themselves with the European sector of their immense country: the feeling of superiority vis-à-vis the East played the same role in their culture as it did in western Europe. In their eyes, European Russia had reached a much higher level of civilization than the primitive Asiatic region of Russia. Thus Diaghilev was portraying Russian culture in a light these composers and the impresario himself did not condone.

Such relativizing comments, however, must not lead the reader to conclude that nationalism had been superseded, in Russia as well as in western Europe. Nationalism continued to be a powerful element of nineteenth-century intellectual life. Moreover, because music is an art form
that often deliberately seeks bridges to existing cultural currents, music
demanded a preeminent place in nineteenth-century culture. Musicians
no longer accepted that their discipline was nothing more than a noble
pastime. In Germany in particular, consistent attempts were made to have
music treated as an independent form of high art. Although in Russia music did not at first enjoy an elevated cultural standing—Western music
was considered an upper-class pastime, a sign of social status, no more—
that situation altered in the 1860s, when Russian composers began to
demand that the cultural significance of their music be recognized. They
did so in part by associating their work with important cultural currents—
including nationalism. A composer's civic sense was thus reflected in work
that somehow expressed national feelings or aspirations. Nationalism also
became a useful propaganda weapon: the most effective means of dis-
crediting an opponent was to deny the national relevance of his music.
If we plumb genuine motives for the conflicts between rivals, however,
we find that they often lie at quite a different level: in musico-aesthetic
differences, in professional rivalry, even in downright personal antipathy.

Russian music is no longer judged exclusively in terms of its national character. Such judgments constitute a form of essentialism, in that they reduce critical evaluations to a few fixed formulas. The idea that nationalism and progressive values go hand in hand has also been abandoned,
a fact that sometimes leads to unpleasant surprises, for instance when
we discover reactionary tendencies in works by Glinka and Musorgsky.
A different, more complex approach, however, one that leaves behind
the nationalistic clichés, gives rise to considerable gains, clarifying the
real creative issues that were at stake and providing a more detailed in-
sight into the relationship between music and society. Nothing is simple
in Russian culture; its context is specific and unusual. To be sure, the
charm of Natasha's dancing serves as a symbol: not of the Russian national character, but of the fascination that Russian music continues to
exert.

## CHAPTER TWO

# "I'm Finished
# with Russian Music"

## *Mikhaíl Glinka*

For a long time Mikhaíl Glinka was considered the father of Russian music. With his two operas, *A Life for the Tsar* and *Ruslan and Lyudmila,* he made music part and parcel of Russian culture. Music historians proclaimed him the first composer able to express the Russian national spirit and Russian ambitions in music, thanks especially to his imaginative treatment of Russian folk song. Later ideologists went further still, calling Glinka the first musical populist. *A Life for the Tsar* is about the common people, with whom Glinka is said to have identified. From that it is not a big step to the conclusion that his work had progressive ideological content.

If we treat Glinka as a populist, however, what are we to make of this statement about *Kamarinskaya,* an orchestral fantasy based on two folk songs (and which, of all things, Chaikovsky was to declare the foundation of the entire Russian symphonic school): "I can assure the reader that I was guided in composing this piece solely by my innate musical feeling, thinking neither of what goes on at weddings, nor of how our orthodox populace goes about celebrating, nor of how a drunk might come home late and knock on the door so that he might be let in." Again, in a letter Glinka wrote in 1850, we read: "I have decided to shut down the Russian song factory and devote the rest of my strength and sight to more important labors." And his comment to the poet Nestor Kukolnik beats them all: "I'm finished with Russian music, as I am with Russian winters."[1] These comments sound very odd indeed coming from the mouth of the "father of Russian national music." Had the laurel crown perhaps been bestowed on someone unworthy? In any case, there is good reason to wonder whether the portrait that came down to us of Glinka was not painted largely with the benefit of hindsight. To understand Glinka's art, we must place it in its proper historical context. Failure to do so will cause his work to remain an enigma.

## THE IDEOLOGICAL BACKGROUND

The idea of a national identity shared by the entire population was, to say the least, at odds with reality. For where was the class structure of the *ancien régime* applied more rigorously than in Russia? The institution of serfdom, indeed, rendered part of the population the property of a small minority; that the peasantry and their landlords constituted a single nation was simply unfathomable. The Russian language reflects the strength of that class consciousness. Until the eighteenth century, no word existed for peasants, nor were they called Russians. They were simply "Christians" (*krest'ianye*) or "Orthodox" (*pravoslavnye*).

Russian national consciousness sprang not from the people but from the aristocracy. Educated and well traveled, the elite classes were influenced by the Enlightenment, a western European movement with pronounced ideas about nationality and national values. Thus inspired, Russian writers felt impelled to seek out a national literary language, as distinct from the archaic Church Slavonic. Others collected folk songs or studied popular customs. Interest in national history grew. Nikolai Karamzin's monumental *History of the Russian State* (1818–26), commissioned by the tsarist government, was the right work at the right moment. It met a great need for historical understanding—or, more accurately, a longing for national self-affirmation: the assurance that Russia had a solid history and played an active role on the international stage.

The social content of the nationalist idea assumed many guises. The Decembrists, pioneers of the emancipation of the serfs, owed their name to an abortive liberal uprising of December 1825—abortive because it lacked popular support. The subsequent accession to the throne of Nicholas I ushered in thirty years of stagnation in Russian society. Nicholas made the national idea part of his ideology, but in a very special form: his political thought was dominated by the doctrine of Official Nationality, promulgated on 2 April 1833 by Sergey Uvarov, the minister of education. Uvarov decreed that all Russians must adopt three inseparable and immutable principles: orthodoxy, autocracy, and nationality. According to this model, orthodoxy was the basis of the emergence of the Russian people, while autocracy was the political means for ensuring the survival of that people. The combination of orthodoxy and autocracy constituted the essence of Russian nationality.

Official Nationality was conservative ideology; its task was to frustrate the call for change. Adherents presented the existing order as if it were God's own, reinforced by faith—meaning that autocracy, the absolute rule of the tsar, had likewise been instituted by God. Only a strong will, inspired by God himself, could keep the vast territory of Russia intact and prevent the Russian people from being swallowed up by other nations. Loyalty and obedience to the tsar were inseparable from the love of God, an article of faith with every Russian. National consciousness, finally, was the ultimate seal of the moral, social, and political system. Every Russian was expected to support the order of the Russian state, not merely by virtue of faith and conscience, but also out of national sentiment.

The third element of the dogma, nationality, was the most difficult to define. Nicholas I, who equated national sentiment with patriotism, interpreted it in its dynastic sense: all subjects of the legitimate tsar constituted the Russian nation, pure and simple. However, not even his own ideologists were agreed on the subject. Some clung to the romantic idea of nationhood, with its emphasis on native character, a character that had to be protected. Herein lay an aggressive form of nationalism, entailing the forced Russification of ethnic minorities and national expansion at the expense of other peoples.

The repressive policies of Nicholas I kept Russia outside the main current of a rapidly changing Europe. Thought, however, did not stand still, but found an outlet in literature and cultural discussions. The central conflict in Russia's intellectual life was that waged between the *Zapadniki* (pro-Westerners) and the Slavophiles. Their differences were quite clear: the *Zapadniki* argued that Russia must adopt the innovations of western Europe; the Slavophiles disagreed.

The crucial distinction in this debate was not the national question but the definition of the human personality. *Zapadniki* such as Belinsky and Herzen championed the autonomy and the rights of the individual. The Slavophiles for their part, such as Kireyevsky, Khomyakov, and Aksakov, rejected these, stating that humans could be happy only in a community, one that grew organically and was not allowed to be disrupted by outside intervention. They believed that this ideal state had been attained in Russia prior to the reforms of Peter the Great, and particularly through the Orthodox religion and the *mir*, the Russian peasant commune. Paradoxical though it might seem, the Slavophile devotion to the Russian people also had Western influences: the Slavophiles based their views largely on those of the German Romantic movement.

The progressive ideals of the *Zapadniki* were naturally at odds with the rigid doctrine of Official Nationality. The Slavophiles, too, were opposed to it, but for different reasons. To them, Nicholas I was an exact replica of Peter the Great, the destroyer of traditional Russia. Their opposition was therefore little more than a late form of boyar anti-absolutism. Members of the old hereditary nobility, they were determined to protect their interests, by elevating and universalizing the old values and the social status quo.[2]

## MUSIC IN RUSSIA BEFORE GLINKA

The history of art music in Russia goes back to the second half of the seventeenth century. Before that time it lacked a fertile breeding ground, the Church having invariably denounced secular music. As contacts with the West grew, however, so did interest in European music.

The reforms of Peter the Great (1682–1725) opened the doors wide to all sorts of western European imports. Music was one of these, although Peter I himself did not have much of an ear for it. Military music alone appealed to him, and that was only because of his passion for modernization. More important for the musical life of Russia was the founding of St. Petersburg. The European character of that city demanded European music, and Western musicians—who, invited by the tsarist court and the greater nobility, soon took the place of local artists—felt immediately at home in the new environment.

During the reign of the three empresses, Anne, Elizabeth, and Catherine II, music enjoyed a real breakthrough, and the Russian court entered the mainstream of eighteenth-century Europe. Italian opera became the predominant genre. Opera seria, which played the same role in Russia as it did in the West, namely the glorification of the legitimate rulers and the self-representation of the aristocracy and its values, was given a place in court ceremonial. Prominent musicians and composers, from Francesco Araja to Paisiello, Cimarosa, and Martín y Soler, were wooed with financial rewards they could not refuse. The spirit of the times in any case encouraged cosmopolitan ambitions, and they were pleased to add St. Petersburg to their itinerary.

Only when Locatelli first staged an opera buffa, however, did opera begin to appeal to the aristocracy more generally. Rich aristocrats then founded their own companies. French comic opera, introduced under Catherine II, served as a model for Russian ventures in this genre.

Musical life in St. Petersburg was dependent upon foreigners. Meanwhile, Russian music continued to develop outside official circles. Growing urbanization had lured countless peasants and artisans into the city, and with them they brought their folk song. In the urban environment of St. Petersburg, traditional music came under heavy pressure from all kinds of new influences, among them arias and songs from European operas and French and Italian dances. This cultural amalgam gave rise to a new genre called *rossiyskaya pesnya,* or "Russian song," so called because they had Russian words. The accompaniment of these urban songs, however, differed from that of genuine folk songs. In authentic practice, folk songs were harmonized by the *podgoloski*—"undervoice"—principle: an intriguing tradition of heterophonic folk harmonization that followed simple but effective principles. In the towns, by contrast, the Western form of chordal accompaniment came into vogue.

Russian music also drew on another source: *kantï,* songs in a simple three-part setting. Of Polish-Ukrainian origin, *kantï* had initially served a religious purpose, but they were quickly appropriated by the secular realm. *Kantï* were used, for instance, to celebrate the glorious deeds of Peter the Great.

The first collections of folk song appeared at the end of the eighteenth century. The most important were those of Vasiliy Trutovsky (published 1776–95) and of Nikolai Lvov (1790–1815); later came the collections of Ivan Rupin (1831) and Daniyil Kashin (1833–34). Lvov's collection exerted an especially great influence, outside as well as inside Russia. For foreign composers in search of Russian or unusual melodic material, it was the preeminent source. In addition to Rossini, Hummel, and Sor, no less a person than Ludwig van Beethoven drew upon it (for the Russian themes in the *Razumovsky* Quartets, op. 59).

The collectors went wherever they thought folk songs could be found. Lvov's collection was, above all, a compilation of "Russian songs," that is, of folk songs transformed in an urban environment. Lvov's collaborator, Ivan Pratsch, provided the piano accompaniment to them. As a result of their labors, folk song gained access to the salons of the aristocracy and played a part in awakening the national consciousness. Because the accompaniment was based on Western models, it pointed ahead to a future step in the evolution of Russian song, the "salon romance" (*bïtovoy romans*). This type had two important characteristics: it used the patterns of Western dance forms (especially the waltz and the polonaise), and it employed a sentimental melodic style that made exaggerated use of sixths. For that reason, Russian musicologists tend to refer to it as *sekstovïy romans,* or "romance in sixth-style."

Folk song also found its way onto the stage. The first Russian comic operas were not true musical dramas; based on the French *comédie mêlée d'ariettes,* they were, rather, comical plays with brief musical numbers. The players were not real singers, but actors who could sing. The music was rarely set down in a score. Contributions from several composers were often combined, or songs that happened to be in vogue were included. Generous use was made of folk songs, sometimes as part of popular genre scenes such as the country wedding.

The milieu of peasants and serfs was a favorite subject and was generally treated with a relatively open mind. Criticism of social abuses was tolerated, provided only that serfdom as such was not placed in question. Pieces of this sort involved a Russification of the French portrayal of the lower classes, with the comedies of Charles-Simon Favart, Jean-Jacques Rousseau, and Michel-Jean Sedaine serving as models. A popular example of the genre was *The Miller Who Was a Wizard, a Cheat, and a Matchmaker* (1779). The author was Alexander Ablesimov; Mikhaíl Sokolovsky brought the tunes together, and Yevstigney Fomin later revised the score. Folk songs accounted for the lion's share of the music. Another successful comic opera was *The Bazaar of St. Petersburg* (1782; rev. 1792), by Vasiliy Pashkevich, which took place in a middle-class milieu.

Russian composers had limited musical skills. The most fortunate among them—Fomin, Maxim Berezovsky, and Dmitry Bortnyansky, for instance—were sent to Italy for further training. From 1803 to 1812, the French musician François-Adrien Boieldieu held the post of imperial bandmaster in St. Petersburg. The Venetian Catterino Cavos was a strong advocate of Russian opera. He had been on the staff of the Imperial Theaters since 1798 and was named musical director of the Italian theater in 1803. He was also in charge of Russian-language opera at the *Bolshoy kamennïy* theater. He wrote all his mature operas to Russian librettos. His *Ivan Susanin* (1815) dealt with a patriotic Russian subject: the story of the peasant, Ivan Susanin, who saved the first tsar of the Romanov dynasty from the Poles—the very subject that Glinka would resurrect two decades later in his *A Life for the Tsar.*

The leading opera composer apart from Glinka was Alexey Verstovsky, whose great model was Carl Maria von Weber. *Pan Tvardovsky* (1828) and *Askold's Grave* (1835) were his most important works. The first is a Polish variant of the Faust legend; the second, based on the novel by Zagoskin of the same name, is set in the tenth century and confronts the old pagan Russia with the Christian. The most powerful vocal part in *Askold's Grave,* which bears the telltale marks of Slavophile conservatism, is that of the mysterious "Stranger," who bemoans the decline of the old Russia.[3]

Enthusiasm for folk song was given a fresh impetus between 1820 and 1850, when the cultural elite discovered the special beauty of the *protyazhnaya,* a lyrical folk-song style marked by astonishing poetry and musical originality. It immediately became an important model for the writers of the Golden Age of Russian lyrical poetry; not only Pushkin, but also Anton Delvig, Nikolai Tsïganov, and Alexey Koltsov made considerable contributions to this genre. After some delay, enthusiasm for the musical possibilities opened up by the *protyazhnaya* followed, musical taste proving, as so often, more conservative than literary taste. The intriguing originality of the popular model was soon adapted to the style of the Italian aria and the French romance.

The *protyazhnaya* was too unusual for the musical milieu of St. Petersburg, however. This was not surprising: the irregular rhythm, variable tempo, abundant melismas, and unstable tonality were far removed from anything Western music had to offer at the time. Yet the lyrical folk song did find its way into Russian solo song. In the romances of Alyabyev, Varlamov, and Gurilyov, the *protyazhnaya* model was elaborated (or, in the eyes of the purists, mangled) and, in the best cases, sensitively adapted to Western listening habits.[4]

## AN ARISTOCRATIC DILETTANTE

On 27 November 1836 an event occurred that the Russian intelligentsia had been expecting for a long time: the première of the first fully composed opera, with no spoken dialogue, to a Russian text on a lofty national subject. Mikhaíl Glinka's *A Life for the Tsar* had its first staging and was given a glowing reception. Apart from a few derogatory comments (the folk music included in the score was belittled by some as no more than "coachman's music"), the cultural elite stood behind Glinka almost unanimously. Gogol was particularly enthusiastic as he dreamed aloud about the future:

> What an opera one could make out of our national motifs! Show me a people that has more songs. Our Ukraine rings with song. Along the Volga, from

source to sea, on all the drifting trains of barges the boatmen's songs pour forth. To the strains of song huts are carved from pine logs all over Russia. To the strains of song bricks are thrown from hand to hand and towns spring up like mushrooms. To the sound of women singing Russian man is swaddled, married, and interred. All traffic on the road, whether noble or commoner, flies along to the strains of the coachman's song. By the Black Sea the beardless, swarthy Cossack with resined moustaches sings an ancient song as he loads his pistol; and over there, at the other end of Russia, out among the ice floes, the Russian entrepreneur drawls a song as he harpoons the whale. Do we not have the makings of an opera of our own? Glinka's opera is but a beautiful beginning.[5]

Gogol's admiration is not surprising: opera had for some time inspired his literary work. His short story "St. John's Eve," for example, has a good deal in common with Carl Maria von Weber's *Der Freischütz.* For his "A May Night, or the Drowned Maiden," he used an idea from Stepan Davïdov's *Lesta, or the Mermaid of the Dnieper,* a Russian version of Ferdinand Kauer's singspiel *Das Donauweibchen.*[6]

Glinka's road to *A Life for the Tsar* was a winding and unusual one. He was not the kind of single-minded artist who sacrifices everything to reach his lofty goal. As an aristocrat freed from the struggle to earn a living, he had no pressing responsibilities and all the time in the world to devote himself to his interests. Music was one of these, together with card games and amorous intrigues.

Mikhaíl Glinka was born on 20 May 1804 in Novospasskoye near Smolensk, into a family of landowners. His uncle retained an orchestra made up of serfs, which brought Mikhaíl into contact with music at an early age. While a pupil in St. Petersburg, he continued to indulge this interest. Once he had left school, he frequented St. Petersburg salons, where he was a welcome guest behind the piano. After a trip to the Caucasus in 1823, he returned to Novospasskoye, where he became deeply involved in the rehearsal of his uncle's orchestra—a luxury available to few young composers. During the 1820s he took up a minor official post in St. Petersburg and was able to continue following his own musical devices. He became acquainted with such leading literary figures as Pushkin and Delvig. At one stage he found himself in hot water when he was suspected of having aided Wilhelm Küchelbecker, a Decembrist on the run. Glinka retired to the countryside until the storm had blown over.

The music Glinka composed during this time, mostly fashionable drawing-room pieces, was lacking in individuality. He imitated what he heard, be it works by Rossini, Haydn, Mozart, or Beethoven, or merely dance music. That was all he needed to entertain his high-society public. Glinka, however, had long harbored the wish to study Italian opera in its country of origin. His father was opposed to the idea and, in general, looked askance on his son's musical activities. However, thanks to a doctor's orders—he needed a warm climate to restore his failing health—Glinka was able to leave Russia in 1830 in pursuit of his heart's desire.

In Italy he met Bellini and Donizetti and had ample opportunity to hear Italian opera. (In his own publications he had not yet ventured into operatic music, preferring to avoid competition by concentrating on piano pieces.) Studies at the Milan Conservatory quickly bored him, however: society life was more to his taste. Because his health did not improve, he left Italy in 1833 and traveled to Berlin, where he stayed with his sister Natalya.

In Berlin, Glinka made the crucial decision to improve his musical skills by systematic study. The teacher he chose was a man of some consequence, Siegfried Dehn, one of the most respected musical theorists of the time. For five months Glinka worked daily at exercises in counterpoint, fugue, and choral harmony. The immediate result was the composition of two new works, an unfinished Symphony on Two Russian Themes (or rather, an unfinished first movement with a slow introduction) and a Capriccio on Russian Themes for piano duet.

In May 1834, Glinka's stay in Berlin was cut short by the news of his father's death. Back in Russia, he felt the time was right to embark on a bigger project. He had in mind an opera, if possible one based on a national theme. His first idea was to adapt "Marina roshcha" (Mary's grove), a short story by Vasiliy Zhukovsky. That author, however, suggested that he use the story of Ivan Susanin instead. Glinka was enthusiastic, and had already completed some of the music by the time an acceptable libretto was found. Collaboration with Zhukovsky, Sologub, and Kukolnik having proved unproductive, Baron Rozen (Rosen), the final choice, appeared just the right man to fit words to the music.

Baron Rozen was of German descent, and, as the secretary of the tsarevich, the future Tsar Alexander II, he had important connections. During work on the opera, moreover, Glinka often kept company with the ideological champions of Official Nationality. Baron Rozen's daughter later declared that the suggestion to entrust the libretto to her father had come from the tsar himself. A "national" opera was very much to the liking of the ideologists. Nicholas I backed the project and agreed to have the opera dedicated to himself. Although the first title suggested for the work had been *A Death for the Tsar,* the eventual title—*A Life for the Tsar*—was thought to be more acceptable: after all, "living for the tsar" was, according to the official doctrine, the religious, civil, and national duty of every Russian.

## A LIFE FOR THE TSAR

The opera opens in the village of Domnino in the early seventeenth century. Russia is emerging from a dark phase in her history: the "Time of Troubles," a period marked by anarchy and Polish occupation. In 1612 the *zemski sobor* (literally, "Assembly of the Land") elected a new tsar, Mikhaíl Fyodorovich Romanov. A year later, the Kremlin was retaken from the Poles and the new tsar crowned, thus beginning the 304-year reign of the Romanov dynasty.

Although Glinka's opera deals with the foundation of the Romanov dynasty, the telling of that historical event was not its main concern, but rather the ideological significance of the story. *A Life for the Tsar* focuses on the *idea* of dynasty, which was one of the pillars of Official Nationality. It is, indeed, a patently ideological work, one that underscores a basic message: without the welfare of the state there can be no personal happiness. In the opera, the election of the new tsar is seen through the eyes of Russian peasants, though the result is far from realistic. We are not given a faithful picture of the common man; rather, people react as the official doctrine decrees. They welcome the news of the coronation as a sign from heaven: Russia is saved because God himself has appointed his tsar. The tsar alone can ensure the happiness of his subjects. The hero of the opera, Ivan Susanin, identifies himself with the destiny of his country. In the first act, he does not think the time is right for his daughter Antonida to marry. How can such a happy event take place when one's country is in mourning? Instead he wants to wait until Russia has a tsar. Soon, though, his future son-in-law, Sobinin, brings news of the election of Mikhaíl Romanov. Let the wedding feast begin, then, and all Russia share in the joy!

In the third act, Susanin talks to Vanya, his adopted son. He tells him the great news and enjoins him to serve the tsar loyally. Vanya says that he dreams of a life as a soldier in the tsar's service. The villagers come out to greet and congratulate Susanin. What follows is a glorification of family values, virtue, and domestic happiness. This accords with the rules of Official Nationality, whose ideologues instructed the people to nurture the Christian virtues in the bosom of their family. Public welfare, according to them, rested on moral education. As Nicholas I put it in a declaration justifying the execution of five Decembrists,

> Let parents turn their entire attention to the moral education of their children. Not enlightenment, but mental idleness, more noxious than physical idleness, but the absence of firm principles must be held accountable for this wilfulness of thought, the source of violent passions, this destructive luxury of semiknowledge, this urge towards fantastic extremes, the beginning of which is the decline of morals, and the end perdition. All the efforts, all the sacrifices on the part of the government will be in vain if home education does not prepare the character and does not cooperate with the purposes of the government.[7]

Act III of *A Life for the Tsar,* in particular Susanin's homely chat with his children and with the villagers, has sometimes been criticized for delaying the dramatic development unnecessarily. But while the scene may be dramatically superfluous, it is of great ideological importance. Not only does Ivan Susanin embody the patriarchal values of Russian society, but the link between personal happiness and the preservation of the autocracy receives considerable emphasis as well, as, in the midst of the wedding preparations, Susanin and his family pray for the welfare of the tsar.

Ivan Susanin is soon offered the chance to prove his loyalty when a group of Polish knights invades his home and forces him to lead them to the hiding place of the new tsar. Susanin tells them not to delude themselves: God's own stronghold protects the tsar, and that stronghold is surrounded by the might of all Russia. The Poles threaten him. He quickly devises a plan to thwart them: he will lead them into the forests and swamps and make them lose their way. Vanya is instructed to warn the tsar. In Act IV, while Sobinin goes off in search of his father-in-law, we follow Vanya to the monastery where the tsar is hiding. We next see the Poles in the forest, frozen and exhausted. Susanin wakes up at daybreak; the sunlight tells him that the tsar is safe and beyond the reach of the Poles. The Poles grow suspicious. Susanin tells them that he is the instrument of God's justice; they will all perish of hunger and cold. The Poles hurl themselves upon him, killing him.

The epilogue follows immediately. On the Red Square in Moscow, crowds are awaiting the arrival of the tsar. They pay homage to him and praise the heroic deed of Ivan Susanin. The final chorus—to words by Zhukovsky, the so-called "Slavsia"—is an abridged version of the doctrine of Official Nationality: orthodoxy, autocracy, and nationality:

Glory to you, our Russian tsar!
Our Sovereign, given us by God!
May your royal line be immortal!
May the Russian people prosper through it!

As an opera, *A Life for the Tsar* was novel in two respects. For one thing, it was the first tragic opera in the Russian repertoire, the first in which the hero dies. Catterino Cavos had worked on the theme earlier, but he spared Susanin at the last moment. Susanin's death in Glinka's version adds extra weight to the patriotism that the opera celebrates. The second innovation was the absence of spoken dialogue—it was an entirely sung opera, something that stunned the critics.

Prince Vladimir Odoyevsky praised Susanin's monologue in Act IV, in which "the melody achieves the highest tragic style, while—something unheard of up to now—preserving in all its purity its Russian character."[8] That monologue is indeed remarkable. First, there is the setting. It is night; the Poles, bivouacked around the campfire, are trying to catch some sleep. Ivan Susanin is alone with his thoughts. He sings a dignified, solemn aria in which he meditates upon his action and prays to God for help in the trial that awaits him. The music reflects the gravity of the situation particularly well. Susanin does not complain. He proves to be a true tragic hero, a man who grasps and accepts the consequences of what he has done.

What follows is, if possible, even more impressive. In a long recitative, Susanin recalls that a short while earlier he was making preparations for a wedding. He allows his thoughts to dwell on his children, then takes leave of them with deep emotion. The orchestra underlines Susanin's memories with motifs from the previous acts: there are no fewer than eight musical reminiscences. The happy nature of these musical references contrasts sharply with Susanin's fate. His own song is full of feeling but in no way lugubrious or sentimental. The long period of reflection adds greater dramatic effect to the denouement, which follows soon afterward.

Susanin's monologue combines many motifs of the opera. It is an ingenious device, musically as well as dramatically. In *A Life for the Tsar*, Glinka made a deliberate effort to create a coherent whole, largely through a complex system of musical references. Thus the "Slavsia" chorus of the epilogue is foreshadowed throughout, especially in connection with the dynastic ideal. The material of the overture, too, is used in the rest of the opera to good effect.

While folk song enters into the characterization of the vocal parts, it does not play a major role in the opera. Only a few numbers are based directly on actual folk songs. An important theme in Act IV, for instance, is modeled on the folk song "Downriver on the Volga." And although the bridesmaids' chorus in the third act is Glinka's own creation, he does use the quintuple meter of actual folk wedding songs. Most of the vocal numbers, however, are modeled on urban salon romances, with the Russian character lying in two elements taken from westernized *protyazhnaya* stylizations: irregular phrasing and an alternation between major and minor. A good example is Antonida's cavatina and rondo in Act I. The schema (slow-fast) is Italian. The first section is closest to the italianized form of the *protyazhnaya:* long, irregular phrases, extensively embellished with melismas reminiscent of Italian coloratura. The second section is even more obviously Italian. Yet no real break in style can be discerned, because both sections have Russian as well as Italian characteristics.

The dramaturgical structure of the opera employs two contrasting styles: Russians are characterized by "Russo-Italian" music, whereas the Poles are musically identified by their national dances. The Polish act (Act II) is almost entirely a "ballet divertissement," with a polonaise, a krakowiak, and a mazurka. On the basis of these dance rhythms, Glinka decided to have the Poles sing in triple meter, or occasionally in the syncopated binary rhythm of the krakowiak. The Russians sing in characteristic duple meter. The clash between the two types of rhythm, which is even found in the overture, is very effective at indicating the Russo-Polish conflict.

The opera has several beautiful Russian genre scenes. Act I opens with a peasant tableau, in which the required rural atmosphere is created most compellingly. The spatial effect in particular is neatly presented by several songs that are intoned in the distance. First we hear the typical question-and-answer song of the Russian folk tradition, in unaccompanied solo phrases. Choral song then transports us directly to the Russian countryside. A group of women approaches from afar, their bright song contrasting with the solemn phrases of the male chorus. A little later we hear the song of the boatmen on the river. Balalaika players bid them welcome. It was probably this very scene that provoked Gogol's enthusiastic remark about Russians as a song-loving people.

A second genre tableau, in the third act, is set in a Russian peasant home. A group of girls comes out to greet Antonida as a bride. Their song is reminiscent of the bridal chorus in Weber's *Der Freischütz,* but the elaboration is original. The quintuple meter captures the verse structure of Russian bridal songs. Glinka was the first to use half-lines of five syllables each in a composition, without adaptations to a conventional meter.

The epilogue is the last genre scene: a crowd sings the praises of the tsar in Moscow's Red Square. The hymnlike character of the music is derived from the older genre of *kanti.* A peal of bells reinforces the formal, ritualized nature of the scene.

## RUSLAN AND LYUDMILA

It took Glinka six years to write another opera. While his admirers looked forward to a work in the elevated style of *A Life for the Tsar,* Glinka chose instead to write a fantasy along the lines of Mozart's *Die Zauberflöte* and Weber's *Oberon.* He found the subject in the mock-epic poem *Ruslan and Lyudmila,* with which the young Pushkin had made his name in 1820. The idea was probably suggested to Glinka by the playwright and theatrical official Alexander Shakhovskoy. In his memoirs, Glinka later wrote that he had hoped to work with Pushkin in person, until the poet was unexpectedly killed in a duel. Perhaps this hope was no more than wishful thinking in retrospect, a reaction to the negative reviews the opera elicited.

It was the fantastic element in Pushkin's story that stirred Glinka's musical imagination. Once again he wrote many of the numbers before a libretto came to hand. In the end he found his librettist in Valerian Shirkov.

Glinka was forced to make frequent interruptions in his work. From 1837 to 1839 he served as director of the imperial chapel, a responsibility that was not to his liking. Another obstacle was his marital crisis. Glinka had married Maria Petrovna Ivanova in 1835, but their relationship had quickly soured; they separated at the end of 1839. In 1840, Nestor Kukolnik asked Glinka to write the music for his new play, *Prince Kholmsky.* Glinka came up with an overture, four intermezzi, and three songs, including a "Hebrew Song" he had composed previously. The play was badly received and Glinka's musical contribution vanished from the repertoire.

In the winter of 1841 he worked hard on *Ruslan and Lyudmila.* When it finally had its public première on 27 November 1842, however, the audience was not overly enthusiastic. The growing success of Italian opera in St. Petersburg gave this Russian-inspired work little chance. In 1843 Nicholas I—in an act that was above all diplomatic, an investment in European prestige—established an Italian opera company in the *Bolshoy kamennïy* theater. As a result, the Russian opera company lost its home. *Ruslan and Lyudmila* was the main victim. The opera quickly disappeared from the program in St. Petersburg, to be performed in Moscow alone.

Act I of the opera opens with the celebrations in Kiev prior to Lyudmila's marriage to Ruslan. Two of Ruslan's rivals are present, Farlaf and Ratmir, both of whom refuse to give up their claims to Lyudmila. Suddenly, darkness descends and Lyudmila vanishes. The Grand Prince Svyetozar, Lyudmila's father, then promises the hand of his daughter and half his duchy to any man who brings her back. The search begins. In Act II, Ruslan is advised by the good wizard Finn, who confides that Lyudmila is being kept in the palace of the dwarf Chernomor and warns Ruslan against Naína, an evil enchantress. Naína has taken Farlaf under her wing; she instructs him to wait at home and do nothing: she will take care of everything. Ruslan, meanwhile, does battle with a giant's head and captures the magic sword with which he can defeat Chernomor. Act III is set in Naína's enchanted palace. There, Ratmir succumbs to the charm of the maidens who dwell in her garden, which displeases Gorislava, one of Ratmir's former lovers, who is full of woe because Ratmir has deserted her. Then Ruslan enters, and at once falls in love with Gorislava. The two knights are saved by Finn, who breaks the spell of the enchanted palace. Ruslan moves on, and Ratmir becomes reconciled with Gorislava.

In Act IV, Lyudmila bemoans her fate in Chernomor's palace. Ruslan appears and overcomes the dwarf in the only way he can: by cutting off his enormous beard with the magic sword. But Chernomor has taken precautions. He has cast a magical spell over Lyudmila and put her into an enchanted sleep. Ruslan decides to take her back to Kiev. His plans go awry in Act V, though, when Farlaf steals Lyudmila and arrives with her in Kiev first. But he is unable to awaken her. Finn hands Ratmir the magic ring that can restore Lyudmila to consciousness. Having been united with Gorislava, however, Ratmir has ceased to be Ruslan's rival, and he hands the ring to Ruslan. To loud acclaim Ruslan awakens his bride, and the wedding feast can resume.

The plot of the opera differs considerably from Pushkin's original. Gorislava does not appear in Pushkin's version, nor does the scene in the magic garden. Pushkin's text is a racy *jeu d'esprit*, an ingenious parody of Ariosto. Glinka preferred magical scenes and a surfeit of romantic images. The prophetic song of the bard Bayan in the first act introduces the epic tone and the Ossianic spirit of the work, the dramatic rhythm of which is slow and irregular. The colorful amalgam of fairy-tale scenes is formally held together by Acts I and V. Only when the circle is closed can the celebration continue from where it was cut short. Musically, too, the formal framework is adumbrated by the thematic relationship between the opening and final scenes, with the finale harking back to the overture.

To portray the various characters, Glinka used different national idioms. The Italo-Russian style of *A Life for the Tsar* becomes the distinguishing characteristic of Ruslan and Lyudmila. Finnish folk music influences the music used for Finn. Farlaf is given an Italian buffo part: Rossini *à la Russe*. Oriental styles characterize Ratmir and Naína's and Chernomor's retinues.

Orientalism in the score has little to do with local color, serving instead to define musical atmosphere, in this case one of languorous sensuality. Although the source of the melodies is relatively unimportant, the "Persian Song" that casts a spell over Ratmir in Act III may indeed have been of Persian origin. Johann Strauss was to use it in 1864 for the middle section of his "Persian March." Glinka's treatment, however, conjures up a completely different atmosphere from what Strauss created. The secret lies in the chromatic oscillation of the bass, the chromatic passing notes between the Vth and VIth degrees in the middle voices, and the sound of the women's chorus. This is the music that the sorceress Naína uses to entice male heroes and render them harmless. Her first victim, Ratmir, is a model of languishing hedonism. Pushkin calls him an incurable daydreamer. Ratmir's is a travesty part, his lack of "masculine qualities" betrayed by the alto voice. Unable to play a heroic role, he easily falls prey to temptation. His great aria, with sighing melismas in the melody and an English horn as an obbligato instrument, reflects his sensual character. The melody is assumed to be of Tartar origin. Its precise provenance does not matter; what counts is the sensuality of the expression. In any case, the aria turns into a western waltz in the end.

The third idiom in the score—next to the diatonic folk-song style and the oriental element—can be qualified as "artificial." It represents the supernatural characters and their world of black magic. The typical code is a chromatic idiom, based partly on the whole-tone scale, as in Chernomor's leitmotif, or on chord progressions through common notes, as in Chernomor's grotesque march.

Glinka's orchestration is rightly famous, with tone colors set off one against the other. The mixture or clash of sonorities renders the orchestration particularly brilliant. A telling example of his ability to create an atmosphere with sound is the cradle song in Act IV. Chernomor's *rusalki* (water nymphs) lull Lyudmila to sleep with their song, accompanied by harp, glass harmonica, and slowly swaying chords in the wind section. Add the tone color of a woman's chorus and the illusion is complete. In Bayan's archaizing song, Glinka evokes the tone color of the *gusli* (a Russian psaltery) by a combination of piano and harp. The dances in Act IV evoke the East in all its sensual splendor and Dionysiac intoxication. The sparkling orchestration is enhanced with quick percussion effects (based on Turkish janissary music) and a spatial impression obtained by the interplay of a wind ensemble on the stage and the orchestra in the pit.

## KAMARINSKAYA

*Ruslan and Lyudmila* drained Glinka. The public had not reacted as he had hoped they would. Professional admiration, though, came from no less than Franz Liszt, who heard *Ruslan* during his Russian tour of 1843 and transcribed Chernomor's March for piano as a tribute to the composer. In 1844 Glinka left for Paris, where he met Berlioz. The great French composer was enthralled with Glinka's music; he included it in his concert programs and praised it highly in the *Journal des débats*.

Berlioz's music greatly appealed to Glinka in turn. He therefore conceived the plan of writing orchestral music with different national characteristics, based on the example of Berlioz's *Hungarian March* and his *Le carnaval romain*. This led to two Spanish pieces, *Jota aragonesa* (1845) and *Recuerdos de Castilla,* or *Souvenir d'une nuit d'été à Madrid* (1848), and a Russian piece, *Kamarinskaya*. For the first two, Glinka stayed in Spain from 1845 to 1847, the better to savor the atmosphere. *Jota aragonesa* was composed during that stay. The second and third pieces were written later, during Glinka's sojourn in Warsaw in 1848.

*Kamarinskaya* is famous because it is an orchestral work based entirely on Russian folk music. Nevertheless, the two Spanish pieces make it clear that Glinka had no nationalistic Russian objective. *Kamarinskaya* is what Glinka himself called picturesque music, and in this case the national element lends no more than local color. The origin of the material again does not matter; all that Glinka intended was to convey its typical nature. This goal can be seen clearly in the two Spanish pieces, with their use of castanets and imitation of guitars by harp and pizzicato in the strings. Music with a national color was fashionable in the early nineteenth century; the decorative treatment of national styles did not yet differ in essence from what it had been in the eighteenth century.

*Kamarinskaya* is based on two melodies. The first is a bridal song, "Izza gor" (From beyond the mountains); the second is the instrumental dance "Kamarinskaya"—a *naigrïsh,* a dance to an ostinato melody that is repeated for as long as the dancers can keep it up.

The piece begins with the slow bridal song, which contrasts with the quick dance that follows. Next Glinka uses a transition leading back to the wedding song and revealing a relationship between the two themes. Then there is another transition, once again to the dance theme, now with the help of motifs from the bridal song. The piece ends with the "Kamarinskaya" dance.

The introductory and transitional motifs are derived from the first theme. The treatment of the dance melody is highly original. It is an ostinato melody that allows of no motivic development without distorting the character of the piece. Glinka repeats the theme some seventy-five times. What he changes is the background: orchestral color, harmonization, counterpoint. In this way he is able to preserve the original character of the dance, but complemented with brilliant variations in the orchestral treatment.

*Kamarinskaya* is a work of modest format, one to which Glinka attached no high-flown nationalistic significance. He hit by chance upon what later nationalists were to pursue deliberately: a fully fledged instrumental work based solely on folk-song material.[9]

With *Kamarinskaya* Glinka's creative life largely ended. Between 1848 and 1851 he still wrote a few songs, and in 1851 he revised *Recuerdos de Castilla,* to which he gave the new title of Second Spanish Overture (*Jota aragonesa* becoming the First). He lived in St. Petersburg, Toulouse, and Paris but wrote little music. A plan to compose a Ukrainian Symphony came to nothing. After 1855 he stopped writing music altogether, immersing himself instead in the works of the great classics: Bach, Handel, and Gluck. He returned to Berlin, where he died on 3 January 1857 (dated in the Old Style; 15 January according to the New Style).

Glinka was the first Russian composer to gain the ear of the West, as witness the admiration of Liszt and Berlioz. An eclectic composer, one whose artistic development was far from straightforward, he drew on all the Western styles he knew. The Russian element in his music, limited as it is, has been given far too much emphasis by nineteenth-century Russian historiographers and, in their wake, in twentieth-century reference works. The use of the folk-song style in *A Life for the Tsar*—the nationalism of which is wholly bound up with the prevailing official ideology—was meant to reflect the presence of popular characters in the opera. In no sense was it part of a concerted plan to turn folk song into the basis of a new form of Russian art music.

## CHAPTER THREE

# "There's Petersburg for You!"
## The Birth Pangs
## of a Music Culture

His sister Lyudmila tells us that when Glinka left Russia for good, he spat on the ground and expressed the hope "never to see this vile country again."[1] His bitterness followed the poor reception of his opera *Ruslan and Lyudmila,* which had become the first victim of a new fashion introduced by Nicholas I: Italian opera, performed by an Italian troupe that the tsar installed in 1843 in the prestigious *Bolshoy kamenniy* theater. Glinka's disenchantment caused him to abandon what further opera plans he may have had. Meanwhile, Italian opera came to monopolize the musical life of St. Petersburg to such an extent that the social elites of the city were hardly aware of the existence of Russian composers. Some of the latter, highly placed dilettantes such as Alexey Lvov, attempted to supply imitations of Italian operas themselves, but their works could not challenge the cherished pieces by Bellini, Donizetti, or Rossini. The situation was especially difficult for those Russian composers who had to work at their art for a living. After all, aristocratic men of leisure, like Glinka, Lvov, and Alexander Dargomïzhsky, had the luxury of devoting time to their art, without depending on it for an income. The case was different for young composers like Alexander Serov, Anton Rubinstein, and Miliy Balakirev, all of whom had professional ambitions. Their struggle to succeed and survive as Russian composers would change the course of Russian music dramatically.

That Russian musicians experienced St. Petersburg as a thankless place is movingly illustrated by the comments of Alexander Serov, a musical autodidact who in 1851 was brave enough to sacrifice a safe legal career for his beloved art. He could not afford to follow Glinka's example and study abroad, so to keep body and soul together he chose to work as a music critic. Within a very short time, his had become the most powerful critical voice in St. Petersburg. He had loftier ambitions, however, and in the 1858–59 season he organized a series of public lectures on music. It quickly became embarrassingly clear how much he had overestimated the musical interest of the people of St. Petersburg: "My circumstances are abominable! Since the middle of the series (since the ninth lecture) there are only about forty listeners! Not a half-kopek profit; I am paying for the lights at the lectures with articles! There's Petersburg for you!"[2]

At the time, indeed, music played only a modest role in the public life of the Russian capital. There were no flourishing concert societies, no large orchestras, no broad musical education, no critical press, and above all no public eagerly anticipating every new composition, every new talent on the platform. The reason was simple: music was still a privilege of the aristocracy. Money could buy anything, including musical excellence.

And there was no lack of money: St. Petersburg was a rich city. The nobility and the imperial family accordingly spent large sums on sumptuous musical performances. It was a token of wealth and prestige to be able to lure the leading European musicians to the city, which became an obligatory stop on the itineraries of distinguished virtuosos. In 1862 the Imperial Theaters paid Giuseppe Verdi a handsome fee to compose an opera for St. Petersburg. He wrote *La forza del destino,* and no expense or effort was spared to make it a spectacular production, performed by soloists of the highest international renown.

Opera was at the center of the musical life of St. Petersburg. The city boasted two opera companies, the Italian and the Russian Opera. The Italian Opera performed at the *Bolshoy kamennïy* theater (where the Conservatory now stands) and was held in high esteem. Here the best Italian singers appeared, and the quality of the orchestra was unequaled. Nicholas I lavished large sums on the Italian Opera, mainly for diplomatic reasons. Faddey Bulgarin, the tsar's chief spokesman, put it as follows:

> Let's admit it: without an Italian opera troupe it would always seem as if something were missing in the capital of the foremost empire in the world! There would seem to be no focal point for opulence, splendor, and cultivated diversion. In all the capitals of Europe the richest accoutrements, the highest

tone, all the refinements of society may be found concentrated at the Italian Opera. . . . Consequently, [the Italian Opera] not only satisfies our musical cravings but nourishes our national pride.[3]

The two companies were under the management of the directorate of the Imperial Theaters, a division of the Ministry of the Imperial Court. For them, looking after the Italian Opera was a point of honor. Members of high society and of the diplomatic corps frequented its productions. The Russian Opera, however, was no more than a subsidiary interest of the directorate, which spent little money on it. Its singers were poorly trained, and the orchestra was no match for its outstanding rival at the Italian Opera. For a long time, the Russian Opera even lacked a proper home, having been forced to leave the *Bolshoy kamenniy* theater in 1843. It was first accommodated in a building originally intended to house a circus (Plate 1): a telling sign of the disregard in which it was held. In 1859 the Theater Circus burned down, and the Russian Opera was temporarily assigned the Aleksandrinsky Theater, which it had to share with the stage company established there. Meanwhile, the Mariyinsky Theater (Plates 3 and 4) was built on the site of the old Theater Circus, opening its doors in 1860. However, its audience was not in the same league as that of the Italian Opera. It consisted of civil servants, businessmen, officers, and students—people who could not afford a seat at the Italian Opera. The Russian Opera did not perform Russian works alone but also—indeed, above all—foreign operas in Russian translation.

Symphony concerts were also in a difficult situation. Controlled by the directorate of the Imperial Theaters, they were put on only when the Imperial Theaters were closed—during Lent, for instance, when opera performances were not allowed.

The oldest concert organization was the St. Petersburg Philharmonic Society, founded in 1802. From 1850 onward, however, the standard of its productions declined noticeably as the repertoire was reduced to popular numbers, mainly taken from Italian operas. In 1850 a new body was founded: the Concert Society, which organized three concerts during the forty days of Lent. The program was more demanding than that of the Philharmonic Society, but rarely included any composers more modern than Beethoven and Mendelssohn. In 1859 the theaters directorate started its own series of Lenten concerts, with a program of both serious and popular works.

The musical life of St. Petersburg was rounded off with guest performances by important virtuosos, including Robert and Clara Schumann,

Liszt, and Berlioz. Robert Schumann, incidentally, was not yet treated as a serious composer in Russia. The 1844 concert tour was organized for Clara: Robert was no more than the husband of the great pianist.

A single organization ran concerts during the entire winter season: the University Concert Society. It was the only one of its kind to play outside the period of Lent. The orchestra was made up of university students, and the performances attained at best a good amateur standard.

Although modern concert performances were gradually making headway in western Europe, the symphony remained considerably less popular than opera in St. Petersburg. Professional orchestras were few, and the repertoire remained confined to popular opera extracts or bravura passages. Contemporary European music was virtually unknown. The works of Schumann, Wagner, or Liszt found their way into Russia only after a considerable delay. This state of affairs can be explained in part by the special characteristics of nineteenth-century Russian social structure, which proved a serious obstacle to the development of musical life.

"For in our country," as Gogol explained in his story "The Overcoat," "you must state a person's rank first." In the remarkable Russian system of social precedence, everyone occupied a fixed rank, or *chin*, that depended on one's family, education, and profession. Originally the system, which Peter the Great introduced to encourage people to enter the service of the state, relied on personal merit as the means to join the hierarchy and to rise within it. However, the system grew more complicated as titles were given to the higher ranks and became hereditary for the highest ranks. In the nineteenth century, the resulting hierarchical system was responsible for fierce bureaucratic rivalry, a situation that Gogol ridiculed with unrivaled wit.

The stratification of Russian society had repercussions in music. Not only did musicians belong to the lowest rank, but their calling had no official status, no place in the hierarchy. Whereas painters, sculptors, and actors could lay claim to the title of "free artist," a title that carried a number of privileges, including exemption from the poll tax and from military service, musicians had no more rights than peasants.

There were only two ways of living as a musician. The first was to be an affluent member of the nobility. The second was to become a teacher in an academy or to play an instrument in an imperial theater. In both cases, the musician entered the service of the state, and then on the lowest rung of the hierarchical ladder. Because of this low status, no aristocrat would ever have dreamed of making music his career.

In view of these circumstances, the sorry state of Russian musical life

at the time was hardly surprising. There was no decent musical education. In St. Petersburg, admittedly, private music lessons were available,
but the teachers were badly trained. Anyone looking for something better had no choice but to go abroad.

## A FRESH MOMENTUM: ANTON RUBINSTEIN

In 1855 the Viennese journal *Blätter für Theater, Musik und Kunst* published a scathing article on the state of Russian music. The predominance
of opera, the amateurism, the lack of both professional training and social status—all were mercilessly criticized. Mikhaíl Glinka was furious
when he read the article, and the nationalists, who stood solidly behind
him, were dismayed. Yet the writer of the article was plainly someone
who took his subject seriously, someone who thought that Russia de-
served a better musical life than the lamentable one with which she had
to content herself. That writer was Anton Grigoryevich Rubinstein.

Rubinstein was a famous pianist. Born in 1829, he had taken his first
piano lessons at an early age. In 1844 the family moved to Berlin, where
he studied composition with Siegfried Dehn, the great authority whom
Glinka had consulted. Rubinstein liked to spend his spare time with the
Mendelssohn family. It was not long before he began composing his own
works.

The experience of German musical life not only influenced Rubinstein's
development as a composer, but also shaped his views on the place of
music in society. In Germany, music enjoyed a prestige inconceivable in
Russia. It was treated as great art, as an exalted expression of the human spirit—something Rubinstein was never to forget. He also came to
realize how essential serious professional training was to any good musician. Amateurism might well produce results with a genius like Glinka,
but it was not the basis for a flourishing musical life. Rubinstein became
convinced that higher musical education was a prerequisite for the building of a music culture.

Rubinstein's experiences in Germany—specifically, his contacts with
Mendelssohn and Schumann—had yet another consequence, one that determined the contours of his musical taste. As a result, he failed to appreciate the new music of the generation of Liszt and Wagner. Indeed,
he did not count their work as real music.

On his return to Russia in 1848, Rubinstein's disillusionment was extreme. Abroad he had seen how things could be. He had visited conservatories in Paris, Berlin, and Leipzig. Musical life flourished everywhere.

Composers were held in high regard. Musicians were devoted to their art, heart and soul. When it came to music, Russia was a desert compared to the rest of Europe.

In Europe, Rubinstein had been fêted as a pianist, but in Russia he was a nobody. He experienced his lack of social status as a humiliation. Moreover, he was unable to find work. His opera, *Dmitry Donskoy,* composed in 1849–50, was not performed until 1852 and then proved a complete failure. The subject was not to blame, for what could be more patriotic than the story of the first Russian victory over the Mongols in the fourteenth century? There was no hope either of any appointment as a conductor in the Imperial Theaters. His only option, therefore, was a career as a piano virtuoso. This he embarked upon with reluctance and against his principles, since under the influence of so powerful a personality as Robert Schumann he had gained a thorough loathing for musical acrobatics. But when needs must. . . .

In 1852 he was offered a post in the household of the grand duchess Yelena Pavlovna, the tsar's aunt, who asked him to run her musical soirées. Despite the brilliance of his new surroundings, Rubinstein felt that he was no more than an entertainer. That same year he conceived a plan for a conservatory. He had a dual objective in mind: good professional training and the granting of the title of "free artist" to the graduates. However, his plan came to nothing.

In 1854 he went abroad again, hoping to improve his standing. A year later, during his travels, he published the article mentioned above in Vienna. In the west he could voice views that he had to keep to himself in Russia.

The reign of Nicholas I came to an end in 1855. The new tsar, Nicholas's younger brother, Alexander II, was determined to support national talent. In 1858, therefore, Rubinstein returned to Russia, having finally managed to arouse the interest of influential people in his plans, including Grand Duchess Yelena Pavlovna and Count Matvey Wielhorsky.

His first step was to found the Russian Musical Society, in 1859. Its objectives were clearly defined: "The development of music education and the taste for music in Russia and the encouragement of native talent."[4] The grand duchess took the society under her wing, and Rubinstein became its artistic director.

A few weeks after the first concert, Rubinstein started to organize music classes. In the light of subsequent developments, the following anecdote is worth recalling. A young man turned up one day to observe the classes, a friend having drawn his attention to them. The young man—

his name was Pyotr Chaikovsky—seemed to have talent. But Rubinstein told the young man to choose: either he must take a serious interest in music or he should not come again. It is not certain who actually conveyed this message to Chaikovsky, Rubinstein or his assistant, Nikolai Zaremba. However, it clearly reflected Rubinstein's credo: music is a serious form of art and does not allow half measures. Chaikovsky had just graduated from the Imperial School of Jurisprudence—more a finishing school than an institute of law—and was part of the typical social round of young nobles in the service of the state. His attitude was that of the dilettante, which Rubinstein abhorred. The young man did not come back—not immediately, at any rate.

Rubinstein continued to devote himself to the struggle for a proper conservatory. He tried at first to raise public support, but his stern critique of Russian amateurism had alienated many people. Once again Yelena Pavlovna came to his aid. Although the Ministry of Education had made short shrift of Rubinstein's plans, the grand duchess brought her influence to bear on the Ministry of the Imperial Court, and in 1862 the St. Petersburg Conservatory opened its doors. Pyotr Chaikovsky, whose awareness of his talent and his musical vocation had developed at precisely the same time as the founding of the institute, entered the conservatory. He would be among the first crop of graduates, in 1865, together with Gustav Kross and Vasiliy Bessel, followed one year later by Hermann Laroche. The St. Petersburg Conservatory had presented Russian musical life with an instant and notable new generation. In 1866 the conservatory in Moscow opened, with Nikolai Rubinstein, Anton's brother, as its director and Chaikovsky and Laroche as instructors.

Anton Rubinstein had given Russian music a fresh momentum. He was a forceful personality, deeply convinced of the seriousness of his mission. His efforts met with resistance, however. To begin with, he was attacked for his alleged lack of patriotism, his criticism of Russian amateurism having been badly received in nationalist circles. The composition of the teaching staff, too, aroused objections. Rubinstein's stand was unequivocal: quality came first; nationality was of secondary importance. Only good musicians would be considered. As a result, most of the teachers came from abroad, immediately branding the conservatory with the reputation of being a foreign institution.

Another problem was Yelena Pavlovna. She was undoubtedly a brilliant woman, but as a member of the imperial family she wished to exercise her authority to the full and was used to having her every whim satisfied. She did not approve of many of the ideas put forward by Rubinstein, who had to learn the uncomfortable lesson that he was completely dependent upon her. He also had to put up with the fact that she treated the teachers and students of the conservatory like members of her own household, taking it entirely for granted that they should play at her soirées. Without her, however, nothing could be achieved. As a private aristocratic enterprise rather than an official institution, the conservatory relied on the grand duchess to ensure its continued ability to issue officially recognized diplomas. As a result, the grand duchess's approval was indispensable; the whole institution existed by the grace of aristocratic patronage.

Things were not very different in the Russian Musical Society, although here Rubinstein had other opponents. He regularly came into conflict with the board, an advisory committee that helped to determine artistic policy and included such influential figures as Prince Vladimir Odoyevsky and the composer Alexander Dargomïzhsky. Rubinstein took little notice of their advice, and tensions ran high. Compromise was not Rubinstein's forte; without exception he considered it a surrender of his artistic integrity. In 1867 he gave up the struggle, resigned his two posts, and left Russia again.

From 1859 to 1867 Rubinstein had managed to lay a sturdy foundation from which serious music in St. Petersburg could develop. Moreover, he had been the only person in the Russian capital to make a professional career of music. In a place with few opportunities for such a calling, he had held an enviable position. And envied he was. His bitterest opponents, who, like him, had professional ambitions in the music world, included Miliy Balakirev and Alexander Serov.

## OPPOSITION: MILIY BALAKIREV

At around Christmas 1855 Glinka was paid a visit by Alexander Ulïbïshev, a rich amateur critic, who had come to present a protégé, Miliy Balakirev, an eighteen-year-old youth from Nizhniy Novgorod. The young man was well on the way to becoming a great pianist. To please Glinka, he played him a virtuoso fantasy he himself had composed on themes from *A Life for the Tsar*. Glinka was pleasantly surprised and praised the young man as a real musician with a brilliant future.

Balakirev had been trained as a pianist and had had to find his own way to becoming a composer. He laid the foundations of his technique by sifting through the scores of the great musicians—an empirical approach that had filled him with a revulsion for theories of all kinds. Exercises in musical technique were not for him. He mistrusted all forms of academic education and was skeptical about Rubinstein's plans for a conservatory.

In order to spread his ideas and gain a following, Balakirev surrounded himself in the years from 1856 to 1863 with a group of musicians whom he proposed to train as composers in accordance with his own principles. A striking feature of this group was that every one of them, except for Balakirev, looked upon music as a pastime. They were all in a position to indulge this luxury: César Cui was an engineer and officer, Alexander Borodin was a chemist, Modest Musorgsky served in the famous Preobrazhensky guard, and Nikolai Rimsky-Korsakov was a naval cadet. Vladimir Stasov set himself up as their aesthetic adviser. He had no wish to compose music himself but only to propagate his ideals and shape the creativity of others accordingly. A good picture of the way in which the members of the Balakirev circle approached music is conveyed in the sketch Borodin drew of Musorgsky in 1856: "Modest was then still very boyish, extremely elegant, the very picture of a young officer. . . . Ladies all made a fuss over him. He would sit down at the piano, and smartly lifting his hands in the air, play excerpts from *Trovatore*, *Traviata*, etc., very sweetly and gracefully, while all around him murmured together, 'charmant, délicieux,' and so forth."[5]

Balakirev had the experience his disciples lacked. They listened avidly to his views and followed his advice punctiliously. However, his influence varied from one disciple to the next. He was on very friendly terms with César Cui and placed great hopes in Musorgsky—until Musorgsky began to stray from the narrow path, thus forfeiting Balakirev's sympathy. Balakirev had little hold over Borodin. Three years older than Balakirev and a man of science, Borodin kept his distance, making no secret of the fact that music would always remain a pastime for him. Balakirev's authority was strongest over Rimsky-Korsakov, who was still a tractable adolescent when he joined the circle. The young musician's admiration for Balakirev was boundless:

> From the very first, Balakirev produced an enormous impression upon me. A magnificent pianist, playing everything from memory; endowed with bold opinions, new ideas, and, last but not least, a gift of composition, which I already revered! . . . He was obeyed absolutely, for the spell of his personality was tremendous. Young, with marvellously alert fiery eyes, with a handsome beard; unhesitating, authoritative, and straightforward in speech; ready at any moment for beautiful piano improvisation, remembering every music bar familiar to him, instantly learning by heart the compositions played for him, he was bound to exercise that spell as none else could. Though valuing the slight-

est proof of talent in another, he still could not help feeling his own superiority; nor could that other, too, help feeling it. His influence over those around him was boundless, and resembled some magnetic or mesmeric force.[6]

Balakirev opposed academicism with tremendous vigor. He considered academic training to be of no help, indeed to be a threat, to the musical imagination. This attitude, a mere rationalization of his own lack of technical training, sufficed to make him Rubinstein's sworn opponent. The fervor with which he fought Rubinstein reflected his anger at the enviable niche Rubinstein, as the only Russian musician able to live on his art, had carved out for himself. The conflict between these two men, then, was above all one of personal rivalry. Their ideological quarrels disguised the real stakes: a viable musical career. (For despite their differences, the men did see eye to eye on two counts: both were pianists who abhorred professional virtuosity and who sought recognition as conductors or composers, and both were convinced of the high cultural value of music.) Balakirev had no other source of income than his music lessons and his piano recitals in the salons of the aristocracy. He was therefore determined to take the wind out of Rubinstein's sails, for in St. Petersburg a conductor or composer had no other alternative professionally than to become artistic director of the Russian Musical Society.

Balakirev attacked Rubinstein on two flanks: for his conservative taste and for his advocacy of professional training. Balakirev had many followers who were not afraid to speak out bluntly. Musorgsky, for example, called the conservatory a place where Rubinstein and Zaremba, dressed "in professional, antimusical togas, first pollute their students' minds, then seal them with various abominations."[7]

Balakirev's dislike of Rubinstein also had a petty personal side. He had not forgotten how hurt Glinka had been by Rubinstein's critical article of 1855. Glinka had expressed his anger in a style that was unreservedly anti-Semitic—an attitude that Balakirev and Musorgsky both ardently shared. As his personal situation became more difficult, Balakirev's nationalism turned into undisguised xenophobia. As far as he was concerned, Rubinstein, of German and Jewish descent, was an alien, and the Russian Musical Society was little more than a German club, founded, according to the rumor that he helped to spread, for the express purpose of benefiting Germans. One of Rubinstein's anonymous supporters summed the situation up as follows:

> We still have here, you see, such fiery patriots, such ardent zealots of Russianness, who deny the right of being a great Russian artist to anyone whose

name does not have the good fortune of ending in "ov" or "in." On such grounds these fiery patriots, "hating the alien sound" in Mr. Rubinstein's name, not only do not allow him to call himself their compatriot but even make the most out-of-date allusions to his foreign origin.[8]

## THE THIRD PARTY: ALEXANDER SEROV

There was yet a third party to the dispute: Alexander Serov. Nowadays Serov's work is as good as unknown; as a composer, he has vanished from the repertoire, and as a critic he was until recently largely dismissed.[9] Vladimir Stasov did his best to belittle Serov's importance, having ample opportunity to do so because he outlived his opponent by a few decades. Yet Serov and Stasov had been good friends for a time. Serov, born in 1820, had attended St. Petersburg's Imperial School of Jurisprudence, where he met Stasov, who kindled his interest in music.

Serov began his career as music critic in 1851. His reviews were well received from the outset—no one could match his breadth of vision or professional knowledge—and by the end of the 1850s Serov was the most important critic in St. Petersburg. In 1858 and 1859 he organized public lectures on music, but (as we have seen) the public showed little interest in them. On his fortieth birthday he came to the painful realization that he had no real musical achievements to his credit; he therefore made the decision to try his hand at opera, the genre preferred by St. Petersburg and one he had spent considerable time thinking about. Between 1861 and 1865, then, he devoted himself to two opera projects, *Judith* and *Rogneda*.

Serov perceived Anton Rubinstein's position as a real threat, aware that Rubinstein had the potential to monopolize musical life in St. Petersburg. Serov's opposition to Rubinstein was as virulent as Balakirev's; his pronouncements, too, were interlarded with anti-Semitic and anti-German tirades (this despite the fact that Serov's own maternal grandmother was Jewish). Also like Balakirev, he was an opponent of academic training and of fixed formal schemas and a champion of progressive music.

However, Serov soon turned on Balakirev as well. Although he was enthusiastic about Balakirev early on and was in regular contact with the Balakirev group in the 1850s, subsequently their differences grew, probably owing to a personal quarrel with Vladimir Stasov, but also influenced by Serov's growing passion for Wagner. When Balakirev fiercely attacked Serov's opera *Judith* in the press, there was no holding back Serov, who now focused his criticism on Balakirev. Their alliance in the fight against Rubinstein was broken. Serov became the third party in the dispute, the opponent of both Rubinstein and Balakirev.

## THE CONFLICT

The opponents of the Russian Musical Society and of the St. Petersburg Conservatory used two strategies: they published critical press reviews and they looked for an alternative organization.

Serov's press campaign was merciless. He attacked the repertoire of the society, calling it "German, conservative, and old-fashioned." He maintained that Rubinstein lacked experience as a conductor and that he did not count as a composer. The man's oeuvre, he said, was unworthy of the name of music.

His attack on the conservatory was, if anything, even more stinging: in his view, its Russian patrons were supporting a foreign charlatan. Moreover, he contended that no great art could flow from academic training. The tone of his reviews was unusually offensive. In 1863 Richard Wagner visited St. Petersburg and was taken aback by the sharp manner in which his Russian admirer attacked Rubinstein. Serov is said to have replied: "I hate him and can make no concessions."[10]

Serov's hostility cannot be attributed solely to a difference in artistic attitudes: personal feelings came into it as well. It rankled Serov that he was not asked to join the advisory committee of the Russian Musical Society or the teaching staff of the conservatory. Perhaps he felt that Rubinstein's strictures against Russian amateurs not only were justified but applied to him as well. In any case, he was all the more determined to prove his worth. By failing to acknowledge Serov as a full-fledged musician, Rubinstein had touched a sore spot.

As for the opposition to Rubinstein from the Balakirev group, it was first voiced by Vladimir Stasov. Originally, he restricted his attacks to artistic objections, but the nationalistic barbs were not long in coming.

When César Cui became a critic on the authoritative newspaper the *Sankt-Petersburgskiye vedomosti* in 1864, the Balakirev group gained an influential mouthpiece. More outspoken than Stasov, but temperate in comparison with Serov, Cui lent unwavering support to Balakirev and his associates. His reviews focused in the main on the themes of progressive versus conservative music and of creative freedom versus academicism. He made less free with nationalistic slogans than Serov and Stasov did; as the son of a French father and a Lithuanian mother, he probably knew xenophobic prejudice firsthand.

Rubinstein's reaction was judicious: he refused to react. Why should he? His concerts and his classes at the conservatory were well attended. He even forbade his students to take sides. This strategy bore fruit, for it was not long before Serov and the Balakirev group began to fight among themselves, provoked by disagreement over Glinka's importance in Russian music. Serov had been impertinent enough to question the dramatic merit of *Ruslan and Lyudmila,* thus, in the view of his opponents, betraying Russian music. His liking for Wagner was also held against him.

Both Serov and Balakirev, meanwhile, looked for alternative ways of making their names as composers. Serov played it safe in pandering to public taste by composing operas. He had even hoped to have his *Judith* performed in the prestigious Italian Opera. How ironic that the man who called himself Wagner's apostle in Russia, as well as an enemy of foreign domination of Russia's musical life, based his first opera on an Italian text! Nothing came of this project, however, and *Judith* had to be translated into Russian. In 1863 the work enjoyed a triumphant première, Stasov's and Cui's acerbic attacks notwithstanding. Encouraged by his success, Serov began work on a second opera, *Rogneda,* based on a legend from pre-Christian Russia. Again the public was enthusiastic. At long last, Serov received the recognition he had sought for so long.

For Balakirev, who cared less for opera than did Serov, the road to public recognition was considerably more arduous. In 1862 the Free Music School opened, a philanthropic institution aimed at fostering the musical education of a wide public. Its director, Gavriyil Lomakin, hoped to provide a good basic training through the teaching of choral singing. He asked for Balakirev's assistance, and Balakirev obliged by working with the school's small orchestra. He was able to raise its performance to a fairly high standard, molding it into a suitable ensemble for performing his own work and that of his supporters.

In May 1867 a great event took place. During a visit to St. Petersburg by Czech, Serbian, and Croatian delegates to a Slavic ethnographic congress being held in Moscow, Balakirev organized a concert of Slavic music. Included were works by Glinka, Dargomïzhsky, Rimsky-Korsakov, Balakirev, Lvov, Moniuszko, Liszt (the Hungarian Fantasy), and Berlioz (the Hungarian March). (Stasov considered the last two works Slavic because he imagined that "Hungarian" was synonymous with "Slovak.") Cui and Stasov praised the concert in extravagant terms. Stasov used the following words: "May God grant that our Slavic guests never forget today's concert, may He grant that they preserve forever the memory of how much poetry, feeling, talent, and ability there is in the *small but already mighty handful of Russian musicians.*"[11]

Serov immediately seized upon Stasov's ludicrous encomium and turned "the mighty handful" into a mocking nickname for the Balakirev circle. He let no opportunity pass to use the term pejoratively. As a result, the "Mighty Handful" or "Mighty Little Heap" (*moguchaya kuchka*) has entered history as the name for the main members of Balakirev's circle, otherwise known as "The Five": Balakirev, Cui, Borodin, Rimsky-Korsakov, and Musorgsky. Because the Russian term is difficult to render precisely, musicologists prefer simply to refer to the group as the *kuchka*.

In 1867 the situation suddenly changed: Anton Rubinstein resigned and withdrew from Russian musical life, taking up an existence as a traveling virtuoso and conductor. (He would return to Russia only in 1887–89, and finally die there in 1894.) With this act he was succumbing not to the pressure of a hostile press, but to tensions in both the Russian Musical Society and the conservatory. Serov and Balakirev, however, remained convinced that they had forced him to resign and that they had thus attained their objective.

## BALAKIREV'S PYRRHIC VICTORY

Rubinstein left a vacuum. In the search by the board of the Russian Musical Society for a new conductor, Balakirev's name was mentioned. Yelena Pavlovna agreed to his appointment for one season, provided Nikolai Zaremba and a leading foreign composer were engaged as well. The choice fell on no less a person than Hector Berlioz, whose visit in 1847 was still warmly remembered. The 1867–68 season thus appeared promising.

Berlioz's appointment was widely applauded. Enthusiasm for Balakirev, however, was less wholehearted. Serov resumed his caustic press campaign. Within the Musical Society, Balakirev's uncompromising nature also did not please everybody. Behind the scenes, Yelena Pavlovna started to lobby for Balakirev's replacement by the German Max Seifritz. Balakirev hung on for the 1868–69 season, but tensions continued to increase.

The Balakirev circle encountered another formidable opponent in Alexander Famintsïn, professor of music history and aesthetics at the St. Petersburg Conservatory. At Rubinstein's request he had not entered the fray before, but he now found himself able to speak out freely in the reviews he contributed to *Golos* (The voice). In these writings Famintsïn attacked the very essence of the aesthetics of Balakirev and his circle. In particular, he argued that folk song was not the appropriate means of creating a national musical tradition.

Meanwhile, Serov failed to consolidate the success of his *Rogneda* in 1865 with a new opera. In 1867 he and his wife had founded a specialized journal for music and drama, but for lack of subscribers it enjoyed no more than a short life. The greatest blow, however, came in 1868 when Serov staged *Lohengrin*. The performance, a complete fiasco, was greeted with derision by the *kuchka*. Serov had had enough. Going over to the camp of the Russian Musical Society, he made common cause with the conservative wing by demanding Balakirev's dismissal.

In 1869 Yelena Pavlovna informed Balakirev that his services were no longer required. However, her choice of a successor proved to be a mistake, and Seifritz was quickly replaced by the Czech conductor Eduard Nápravník.

Balakirev's two-year term as conductor of the Russian Musical Society had not brought him the breakthrough he had hoped for. His influence over his followers began to wane. Musorgsky and Rimsky-Korsakov refused to countenance his continued high-handed meddling with their work. A distance also grew between Stasov and Balakirev. The more fanatical Balakirev's nationalism became, the less the two men saw eye to eye.

In urgent need of new disciples, Balakirev turned to Pyotr Chaikovsky, who had just graduated from the conservatory. It did not worry Balakirev that Chaikovsky had trained in the enemy camp; he was, after all, still young and malleable. In 1868 Chaikovsky had sent some instrumental fragments of his opera *Voyevoda* to the Russian Musical Society. Balakirev had presented them to the directorate of the Imperial Theaters and been able to arrange the opera's production. He offered to help Chaikovsky develop his talent further. When Chaikovsky wrote a favorable review of Rimsky-Korsakov's Serbian Fantasy, he was welcomed into the circle, despite reservations about his academic education.

Balakirev and Chaikovsky corresponded frequently. Balakirev's harsh critique of the symphonic poem *Fatum* was humbly accepted by Chaikovsky. Balakirev then offered Chaikovsky his help in the creation of a masterpiece, the overture-fantasia *Romeo and Juliet* (1869), for which Balakirev not only provided the idea but even proposed the details of the composition: Chaikovsky had only to follow his instructions. By this time, however, Chaikovsky had developed sufficient backbone to avoid such slavish compliance.

## THE FINAL CONFLICT

Having been dismissed by the Russian Musical Society, Balakirev devoted his attention once more to the concerts of the Free Music School. In order to attract the public, he decided to recruit popular soloists and found the great pianist Nikolai Rubinstein ready to help. Yelena Pavlovna was furious and went on the counterattack: she would raise the concerts of the Musical Society to a higher social plane by attending in person together with her court.

The rivalry between the two concert societies caused financial difficulties for both. The membership of the Russian Musical Society declined, while the Free Music School was no better off financially. Balakirev soon found himself in straitened circumstances. Not even the Free Music School could pay him any longer, and in the 1870–71 season the current concert series had to be cut short.

The Russian Musical Society now entrusted its programming policy to Mikhaíl Azanchevsky, a champion of progressive music who gave modern and Russian music greater prominence. In the 1871–72 season the Russian Musical Society presented the first public performance of Chaikovsky's *Romeo and Juliet* and the polonaise from Musorgsky's *Boris Godunov*. Balakirev's concert series could no longer be justified; his program had ceased to be original. Even César Cui could summon no objections to the concerts of the Russian Musical Society and had to admit that Nápravník was an outstanding conductor. Beyond that, the Russian Musical Society had acquired some social status. Balakirev's last season with the Free Music School proved a financial disaster. He withdrew from the music world. The rivalry was over.

From 1872 to 1877 Balakirev vanished from the scene. Financial distress forced him to take a post as a clerk on the Warsaw railroad line, and he suffered bouts of deep depression. Exhausted and disillusioned by the last phase of the fight, he sought solace in the strictest form of Orthodox religion. The liberal atheist had turned into an uncompromising Slavophile and religious fanatic. He wanted nothing more to do with his former circle.

## OPERA

At the end of the 1860s the focus of interest of Balakirev's disciples shifted. The success of Serov's operas had given them food for thought, but although opera still reigned supreme over musical life, Balakirev himself was not interested in it. His circle therefore looked for another mentor. They found one in Alexander Dargomïzhsky.

Dargomïzhsky, a dilettante with an opera or two to his credit, had gained some renown from his *Rusalka*. At the time Balakirev's followers sought him out he was at work on an unusual project, having decided to set one of Pushkin's plays, *The Stone Guest*, to music and to reproduce the text word for word without first turning the original into a libretto. This experiment aroused the group's interest. His example inspired Musorgsky to set to work on the composition of *Marriage,* based on Gogol's farce, though he soon put this project aside and started instead an opera based on Pushkin's *Boris Godunov.* Cui wrote the opera *William Ratcliff,* and Rimsky-Korsakov *The Maid of Pskov (Pskovityanka).* Borodin followed quickly with *Prince Igor,* but for the spare-time composer he always remained, the project was too much; he would leave *Prince Igor* uncompleted at his death eighteen years later.

These four composers hoped to reach the general public more readily with their operas than with their symphonic work. The aristocratic and intellectual elite, however, remained faithful to the Italian Opera until the 1870s, while Russian Opera continued to play to an audience made up of merchants and bureaucrats. As a result, the first operas by Cui and Serov, and the last by Dargomïzhsky, went virtually unnoticed by the most influential circles in the city. Russian composers had to content themselves with a passive and rather unadventurous public whose voice went largely unheard in the intellectual world.

*William Ratcliff* was produced in 1869. Dargomïzhsky did not live to see the production of his *Stone Guest;* he died in 1869, and the opera was not given its première until 1872. Although the members of the Balakirev circle praised it to the skies, the reactions of other critics and of the public were overwhelmingly negative. Rimsky-Korsakov's *Pskovityanka* opened in 1873—but only after the composer pulled some strings. Ivan the Terrible appears in the opera, and when Rimsky-Korsakov applied to the censors for permission to stage the production, he was told bluntly that it was not permitted to use Ivan the Terrible as a character. In reply to his question "Why not?" he was told, "And suppose the tsar should suddenly sing a ditty; well, it would be unseemly."[12] Behind this ruling was a law dating back to 1837 which stipulated that the historical figures of tsars could not be represented in an opera. (In the case of spoken drama, the position was slightly different: here the prohibition applied solely to tsars of the Romanov dynasty.) But Rimsky-Korsakov had powerful friends, and through the grand duke Konstantin, the tsar's brother, an exception to the rule was made. There was another difficulty, however: the opera depicted the old republican traditions in the town of Pskov. Rimsky-Korsakov had to change the scene showing an authentic republican council into one of a neutral meeting.

Rimsky-Korsakov's lobbying also smoothed the path for a production of *Boris Godunov*, with the proviso that Musorgsky change his monks into hermits or vagabonds, since clerical characters were protected by the same prohibition as tsars. Musorgsky had submitted the first version of *Boris Godunov* to the Imperial Theaters directorate in 1870. They rejected the opera on the grounds that it lacked a prima donna role. By 1872 Musorgsky had finished a second version, three scenes of which were performed in the Mariyinsky Theater on 5 February 1873.[13] The public reaction was unexpectedly favorable. Even the critics were forced to admit the opera's potential and value. Hermann Laroche, though a staunch opponent of the *kuchka*, wrote appreciatively: "*Boris Godunov* is a most portentous event. The opera reveals that the circle that forms the *extreme left* of our musical world has a quality for which it has not until now been known: original invention, independent content. In union with bold and original talent the party of our musical radicals can go far without faltering."[14]

On 27 January 1874, the entire second version of *Boris Godunov* was staged—with some cuts—by the conductor Eduard Nápravník. He had the habit of streamlining every opera he conducted to produce what he felt was the maximum theatrical effect. Musorgsky had agreed to Nápravník's cuts; he also had no difficulty with the decision by the Mariyinsky Theater in 1876 to scrap the great revolutionary scene. This decision infuriated Stasov, however, who accused Musorgsky of being spineless. Later he went so far as to claim that the mutilation of the opera was the cause of Musorgsky's escape into alcohol, and hence of his death in 1881. This is the origin of a legend that persists to this day. In truth, Stasov was defending his own ideal of socially committed art at a time when Musorgsky had distanced himself from it.[15]


## CHANGE

Serov died on 20 January 1871. He had no followers. In 1872, Balakirev retired from public life. The protagonists of the conflict had gone.

The St. Petersburg Conservatory was headed by Nikolai Zaremba until 1871. Following Rubinstein's departure, he had continued the latter's conservative policy, though the conservatory still had to deal with the Achilles' heel of contemporary musical life in Russia: its dependence on noble sponsors. The disadvantage of this situation became painfully obvious when Yelena Pavlovna demanded a change in the training program: in future, she decreed, the conservatory would teach the playing of orchestral music only, since fostering musical originality clearly served no useful purpose. Her decision was in line with the reactionary education policy adopted after the abortive attempt on the life of Alexander II in 1866. Free thought was once again restricted, and Yelena Pavlovna contributed her might to this policy. Nikolai Zaremba protested and was dismissed. The conservatory remained a private institution, with the grand duchess having the last word.

Zaremba was succeeded by Mikhaíl Azanchevsky. To curry favor with the grand duchess, he professed acceptance of the new charter, though in fact he did not much care for it. He was determined to modernize the program. The appointment of Hermann Laroche as teacher of music theory was a first step. More daring still was his choice of a new teacher of composition, a modern composer whom he attracted with a particularly generous financial offer: Nikolai Rimsky-Korsakov.

Rimsky-Korsakov, though enthusiastic, was extremely nervous about his lack of technical knowledge. He consulted Chaikovsky, and in a heroic attempt to make up for his deficiencies, he devoted himself wholeheartedly to exercises in harmony and counterpoint.

On 9 January 1873 Yelena Pavlovna died, and the last obstacle to the modernization of the conservatory disappeared. The government assumed financial responsibility for the institution, now renamed the Imperial Conservatory, and took charge of the Russian Musical Society as well.

The kuchka broke up. Musorgsky considered Rimsky-Korsakov's capitulation in taking a job at the conservatory a form of treason. He himself fell under the sway of the reactionary aristocratic circle embracing the poet Golenishchev-Kutuzov. Rimsky-Korsakov distanced himself from the dilettantism of his former circle. Cui's development came to a standstill and he no longer played any more than an insignificant role as a composer. Borodin was unable to finish his opera project. Stasov alone continued to uphold the ideals of the kuchka and to maintain the illusion that the group remained a cohesive whole.

## CHAPTER FOUR

# The Clash of Ideas
## The Quest for the Essence
## of the New Russian Music

The tangle of personal conflicts, many of them conflicts of interest, in the musical life of Russia during the 1860s and 1870s does not make for a peaceful picture. Let us, however, take a more elevated view of the subject and look at the clash of ideas that accompanied the conflicts of interest. This clash cannot be reduced to a conflict between nationalism and cosmopolitanism, between the Balakirev group (the *kuchka*) and Rubinstein and Chaikovsky. To do that is to oversimplify the issue. Although that conflict did play a part, it was not nearly as clear-cut and persistent as the traditional view suggests. The real differences lay elsewhere, spread across three separate camps, each championing a different aesthetic ideal, a distinct conception of the essence and function of music. At stake was a conflict between conservative and progressive musical ideals: specifically, the distinction between abstract and program music and between a music-oriented and a realistic opera aesthetic.

In his *Culturhistorische Bilder aus dem Musikleben der Gegenwart* (1860), the German music historian August Wilhelm Ambros suggested that the musical hegemony of central Europe was coming to an end and that it was high time for the periphery, America and Russia, to take up the torch. This view was warmly welcomed in Russia. In 1867, Hermann Laroche wrote with youthful enthusiasm that Russia had already produced a savior of music: "Ambros never guessed that long ago a Russian musical genius finished his career, one whose works, so fresh and healthy, contain within themselves the elements of renewal, capable of fertilizing new musical developments and laying the foundations of a new musical school."[1] That savior was, of course, Mikhaíl Glinka.

This unbridled enthusiasm for Glinka demonstrates how shortsighted and provincial Russian musical thinking still was. Until about 1860, Glinka remained the center of critical attention and the object of highest public esteem. While no one doubted that Glinka was the leading light of Russian music, however, opinions differed as to the path he had taken. After all, his oeuvre comprised so many conflicting elements that it was difficult for up-and-coming musicians to know which aspects of his work warranted further pursuit, and which would lead to a dead end. The exact meaning of Glinka's legacy thus became the basis of a real controversy.

## THE GLINKA CONTROVERSY

The war of words revolving around Glinka hinged on the difference between *A Life for the Tsar* and *Ruslan and Lyudmila,* operas so distinct that disagreement as to their merits was virtually guaranteed.

At its première, *A Life for the Tsar* was greeted as a milestone in Russian music. Prince Vladimir Odoyevsky enthused about Glinka's treatment of Russian melody. Folk song, he observed, was no longer purely decorative, but had been upgraded by Glinka from the "lower" style of comedy to the exalted realm of tragedy.

The admirers of *A Life for the Tsar* felt that Glinka took a step back with his *Ruslan and Lyudmila,* a series of disjointed episodes rather than a coherent drama. Its musical style is not exclusively Russian; Glinka culled the folk music in his score from a variety of sources, turning his back on the fusion of national music and exalted drama. The folk-song elements are once more purely decorative. The music as such was appreciated, however, so much so that the critics were forced to praise *Ruslan* even while rejecting it. A common view was that as music, the work was the best thing Glinka had done, but as opera it was *une chose manquée.*[2]

Prince Odoyevsky defended Glinka's second opera by stressing its fantasy element. In his view, lack of drama in a fantasy opera could not be considered a fault: since the fairy-tale world does not involve conflicts between ordinary people, it necessarily lacks a dramatic element. Rather, it is a metaphor for human life. Odoyevsky also argued that while the fairy-tale world had no place on the dramatic stage, it did have one in opera, because music underlines the poetic dimension and makes it seem convincing.

In 1857, Stasov produced a more spirited defense. On the occasion of Glinka's death he devoted a monograph to the composer in which he tried to change the relative importance commonly attached to the two operas. For Stasov, *Ruslan* was the masterpiece and *A Life for the Tsar* a mistake. Glinka, he said, had been misguided in trying to make folk music an integral part of his first opera. According to Stasov, it was impossible to create new art from old material. Trying to do so could only result in monotonous melancholy.

*A Life,* however, did have one decisive quality, in Stasov's view. In writing that opera, Stasov remarked, Glinka had continued along the path of the revolutionary operas of Cherubini and Beethoven (*A Life for the Tsar* was a successor to Beethoven's *Fidelio*), in which the characters matter less than the moral of the story. Stasov found theatrical productions that portray individuals risible and outmoded. More important was the rendering of high morals and idealistic sentiment. In short, opera must be more like an oratorio. And that, Stasov believed, was nowhere better done than in *Ruslan and Lyudmila*. He considered that work great poetry, its aim being the profound expression of Glinka's own soul.

Alexander Serov, for his part, had placed high hopes in *Ruslan and Lyudmila* even before its première. In 1841 he wrote:

> Russian opera needs a magical subject—so as to uncover all the riches of our mythology and express the true Russian view of nature. If such a subject were to be developed with a true knowledge of the Russian spirit, with burning enthusiasm and if it were to meet today's criteria for theatrical music—then a real path would be laid and the fate of Russian music would be decided![3]

But *Ruslan* did not turn out to be what Serov had expected. For him the work was a model to be eschewed. His disappointment convinced him that opera can never dispense with the dramatic element. Serov's new axiom was that musical theater must be drama first and foremost. He became, as it were, reconverted to *A Life for the Tsar,* an opera he had originally rejected for its narrow patriotism. Serov kept his new opinion to himself until Glinka, whom he revered, was dead and *Ruslan* was again included in the repertoire—something for which Serov himself had worked hard. Although the musical merit of the opera could not be denied, he made short shrift in 1858 of the arguments defending *Ruslan.* For what must opera be—music or drama? "All that is given on the stage is drama, a living dramaturgical organism, or else it would be better never to raise the curtain. . . . What kind of opera is this, if its music produces a greater effect in the concert hall than on the stage? What kind of artistic creation is this, which gains when performed piecemeal rather than in its entirety?"[4]

Stasov replied in 1859 with an article entitled "A Martyr of Our Time" (an allusion to Lermontov's novel *A Hero of Our Time*). In it he dismissed *A Life for the Tsar* as an exhibition of ludicrously narrow patriotism and tried to demonstrate that *Ruslan and Lyudmila* was in fact a genuine dramatic creation, thus going back on his previous view that *Ruslan* was an attempt to give poetic expression to Glinka's soul. In order to defend his new idea, he introduced a distinction between "scenic" and "dramatic" effects, arguing that although Glinka was no master of the first, he excelled in the second. However, Stasov failed to define his concepts clearly. His line of reasoning had to disguise the fact that he had capitulated before Serov's view that opera must always be drama.

Soon afterward, however, Stasov was given another chance at confounding Serov. Serov began openly to declare his interest in the ideas and the work of Richard Wagner. He now averred that *Ruslan* lacked the mythical and mystical basis that rendered Wagner's work such convincing spiritual drama. Yet in *A Life for the Tsar,* he said, Glinka had come very close to the Wagnerian ideal. Stasov immediately mobilized every Slavic sentiment to pillory Serov as a traitor, capitalizing on the prevailing pan-Slavism to insinuate a conspiracy by a subversive German party. Together with Rubinstein and the St. Petersburg Conservatory, Serov was labeled an alien enemy of Russian culture.

## CONSERVATIVE VS. PROGRESSIVE

Anton Rubinstein had only just managed to bring the Russian Musical Society into being and to found the St. Petersburg Conservatory when a sharp difference of opinion broke out between a conservative and a progressive camp. Rubinstein himself was the champion of the first. The progressives split into two wings: the Balakirev circle, inspired by Liszt, and Serov, who chose Wagner as his mentor.

In addition to Rubinstein, the conservative current was represented by his followers, Nikolai Zaremba, Alexander Famintsïn, and Hermann Laroche. Although the term "conservative" is readily given a negative connotation, it must be stressed that Anton Rubinstein could not be accused of the slightest lack of artistic integrity. He fought for change and progress in musical life. Only his musical taste was conservative, harking back to the Viennese Classics and the early Romantics. His appreciation extended therefore to Schubert and Chopin, but not to Liszt and

Wagner. In his memoirs, written in 1889, he contended that the history of genuine music was over: Chopin had written the last note.[5] That said, it must also be noted that Rubinstein took care not to foist his personal preferences on his students. In his orchestration classes he included the new techniques used by Liszt and Wagner, allegedly saying that he "wished the students to have the chance to hear various opinions and become acquainted with varying trends."[6] Rubinstein's musical approach was grounded in tradition. Many new ideas struck him as absurd, including the idea of national music. For Rubinstein, national music existed exclusively in folk song and folk dance. In larger works there was no room for the national element, and certainly not in opera. His own use of folk music in operas such as *Dmitry Donskoy* and *Children of the Steppes*—an opera with a German libretto originally intended for Liszt and in which Rubinstein exchanged the Hungarian *puszta* for the Ukrainian steppe—remained within the limits of what was usual in early Romantic works: local color, characteristic music as a decorative allusion to a particular milieu.

After Rubinstein's departure in 1867, Alexander Famintsïn became the spokesman of the conservative current. He rejected the formlessness and the nationalism of the Balakirev group, and in particular was opposed to their use of folk song:

> Many people seem to think that we already have Russian instrumental music and even call it "national." But is music national just because it uses as themes for composition trivial dance tunes that automatically remind one of disgusting scenes in front of a saloon? . . . This only shows that our composers have completely failed to distinguish between national music and rustic folk music. . . . If the kernel from which an entire composition grows is not refined, then the work itself cannot be refined. . . . In no case can it serve as a model or ideal of instrumental music in general. But then today most of our composers scarcely seek the higher ideals.[7]

What were these higher ideals? In 1869 Hermann Laroche raised them in connection with Chaikovsky's symphonic poem *Fatum,* advising Chaikovsky to abandon his mistaken approach to music. Instead, he would do well to return to the great masters of the past, "when petulant programs and formless rhapsodies were equally unknown, when musical compositions did not present such profound philosophical ideas as today, but showed more musical polish, when composers did not seek the resolution of problems of existence but always found the resolution of a dissonance."[8] In other words, for the conservative party, music had to accord with the formal principles developed and perfected by the tra-

dition. Laroche looked askance at program music and opera. Adhering to
the position of the authoritative Viennese aesthetician Eduard Hanslick,
whose fundamental *Vom Musikalisch-Schönen* (Of musical beauty) he
translated into Russian, Laroche argued that the essence of music is to
express what would always remain "inexpressible" in words.

Laroche's defense of Glinka's *Ruslan and Lyudmila* ran along the same
lines as Hanslick's critique of Wagner. He treated the work as a kind of
anti-Wagnerian manifesto, precisely because the music never sacrificed
its intrinsic value to an external scenic logic, never aimed at dramatic illusion. Glinka did not overlook the least musical detail; all his numbers
strove for inner musical beauty.[9] Like Hanslick, Laroche thus stripped
opera of its *raison d'être*. Even so, he found Glinka's *Ruslan* very nearly
acceptable: an effective dam against the Wagnerian flood.

The progressive current was represented both by the circle around Balakirev (the *kuchka*) and by Alexander Serov, in two distinct ways.

At the time, progressive music meant works by Berlioz, Liszt, and
Wagner—though Balakirev did not include the last. His great models
were Berlioz and Liszt. In them he discovered a new musical ideal, which
can be briefly defined as "free form," music that had shaken off the traditional formal patterns. The form of each work had to be unique and
inspired by its content; each content had to create its own form. Balakirev
was a fervent advocate of program music and dismissed music without
a program as devoid of content. In his view, music needed a content to
develop into a full-fledged form of art.

The crucial issue for him, therefore, was the link between music and
content. Balakirev thought that this link must be "realistic." For him,
music was not abstract but the faithful portrayal of a concrete content.
From the correspondence between Balakirev and Chaikovsky on the
composition of Chaikovsky's fantasy overture *Romeo and Juliet,* a work
that Balakirev had, so to speak, supervised, we see how seriously Balakirev took the reality content of the music:

> I don't know how your compositional process works, but with me it goes as
> follows. I'll cite you an example that is appropriate for you—how I composed
> my overture to *Lear.* First, after reading the play, I was inflamed with a de-
> sire to write the overture . . . , but having as yet no materials, I fired myself
> by means of a ground plan. I projected a maestoso introduction, and then
> something mystical (Kent's prophecy). The introduction fades away, and there
> begins a stormy, passionate allegro. This is Lear himself, already uncrowned,
> but still a strong lion. The characters of Regan and Goneril were made to act

as episodes, and finally the quiet and gentle second subject personified Cordelia. Further on the development (the storm, Lear and the Fool on the heath), then the recapitulation of the allegro. Regan and Goneril finally outdo him, and the overture ends with a dying-down (Lear over Cordelia's body). Then follows a repetition of Kent's prophecy, now fulfilled, and then a calm, solemn death. I'll tell you that at first, [even] with this plan, no ideas formed themselves, but then afterwards ideas did begin to come and fit themselves into the frame I had created.

When Chaikovsky sent him the themes of his *Romeo and Juliet,* he replied:

> The first theme is not at all to my taste. Perhaps when it's worked out it achieves some degree of beauty, but when written out unadorned in the way you've sent it to me, it conveys neither beauty nor strength, and doesn't even depict the character of Friar Laurence in the way required. Here there ought to be something like Liszt's chorales (Der nächtliche Zug in F-sharp, Hunnenschlacht and "St Elizabeth") with an ancient Catholic character resembling that of Orthodox [church music]. But instead your E-major tune has a completely different character—the character of quartet themes by Haydn, that genius of petty-bourgeois music, who arouses a strong thirst for beer. . . . On the other hand, it's possible that in its working out your theme gains a completely different character—and then I'll recant my words. . . .
>
> The first D-flat theme is very beautiful, though a bit overripe, but the second D-flat tune is simply delightful. I play it often, and I want very much to kiss you for it. Here is tenderness and the sweetness of love. . . . When I play [it] then I imagine you are lying naked in your bath and that the Artôt [Balakirev was referring to Désirée Artôt, with whom Chaikovsky had had a brief flirtation] herself is washing your tummy with hot lather from scented soap. There's just one thing I'll say against this theme; there's little in it of inner, spiritual love, and only a passionate physical languor (with even a slightly Italian hue)—whereas Romeo and Juliet are decidedly not Persian lovers, but Europeans.[10]

These passages are self-explanatory. For Balakirev music was inextricably bound up with extramusical ideas. Musical inspiration, according to him, only came once identification with the subject matter was intense enough. He judged music by the perfection with which it expressed a particular content. Without a specific content, music could have no value.

The Balakirev circle turned the link between music and content into an aesthetic that could be called a musical form of realism, an offshoot of Russian realistic philosophy. For realists such as Belinsky and Chernïshevsky, beauty was not an immutable, absolute idea. To them empirical reality was the sole reality. Beauty, accordingly, had to be sought in reality, not in intellectual abstractions. And because reality kept changing, the standards of beauty kept changing as well. Chernïshevsky's definition of beauty was: "A beautiful object is one that expresses life or reminds us of life."

Art mirrors life. The artist speaks of that fact, thinks about it, and produces a vision of concrete reality in his work. In other words, an artist's task is not to portray beauty but to discover and reveal reality. Musorgsky called the simple reproduction of beauty in art an infantile endeavor: "The subtlest aspects of human nature . . . the intensive exploration of these uncharted regions and their conquest—there you have the true calling of the artist."[11]

Realism discovered a suitable path to follow in Russian literature, in the work of Dostoyevsky, Tolstoy, and Chekhov. But to what extent could that theory be applied to music? The *kuchka* drew their arguments from Chernïshevsky's *Aesthetic Relations of Art to Reality* (1855), in which the author proves to be a pioneer of a positivistic aesthetic. Art's purpose is to unveil reality. The subject of art is not some abstraction of the intellect (in that respect, realism is a reaction to the then influential idealism of Hegel) but objectively observable reality. Because the imagination invariably falls short of the riches of reality, art can aspire to beauty only if it imitates reality. But the artist's vision is always a selection from the profuse supply proffered by life and nature. This ability to select is what reveals artistry, as the artist becomes a thinker, someone who puts reality to the scalpel and comments upon it.

What about music? Chernïshevsky maintained that music was itself a product of nature. To him, singing was a natural expression of feeling. He did not consider formal elaboration a part of music. Chernïshevsky put it as follows: "It is strange . . . that nobody has drawn attention to the fact that singing, being, in essence, an expression of joy or sorrow, does not by any means spring from our striving for beauty. Is it to be expected that a person under the overwhelming influence of emotion will think about attaining charm and grace, will concern himself with form? Emotion and form are opposites."[12] Folk song fit into this theory as the paradigm of natural singing. It was part of nature. The task of the composer accordingly was to imitate nature. Art music, or "artificial singing," has the same relationship to folk music as a copy has to an original.

Autodidacts often present their shortcomings as positive qualities. Hence we should not be surprised that the Balakirev circle adopted the realist doctrine with such enthusiasm, for it legitimized their lack of technical knowledge. What point was there in acquiring technique, in learning to apply formal schemes? According to Chernïshevsky, all that was quite superfluous. Technique merely prevented the spontaneous expression of emotion. The support of so great an authority stoked the flames of contempt for any form of academic training, allowing the Balakirev circle to elevate their empirical approach to the chosen method of musical realism.

The realist theory had its most important application in opera. The Balakirev group greeted the Italian operas that were proving so triumphant in St. Petersburg as examples of what to avoid. These operas were nothing but models of artificial, decorative virtuosity and of stereotyped forms. César Cui described realism in opera thus:

> The new Russian school is striving musically to project the character and type of the *dramatis personae* in the boldest possible relief, to model each phrase of a role to an individual and not a general pattern, and lastly, to portray truthfully the *historical epoch* of the drama, and to depict the *local color*, the descriptive as well as the picturesque aspects of the action, in its poetic as well as exact sense.

About the traditional operatic forms, Cui wrote: "The Russian school understands all the falsity of these immutable, stereotyped forms. It is convinced that the musical development of an opera demands a complete independence of forms, and is governed only by the text and the dramatic situation."[13]

Dargomïzhsky's *The Stone Guest* (1866–69) was considered the realization of this ideal. According to Stasov, that opera was the ultimate victory over threadbare Italianism. As an illustration he drew a parallel with Mozart's *Don Giovanni*, an opera with the same subject: "*Don Giovanni* is simply an amusing and entertaining child's babble (added to the fact that most of the time it is boring beyond belief) in comparison to Dargomïzhsky's creation of *genius*."[14]

César Cui praised *The Stone Guest* highly as well but did not hold it up as an example. He held that the opera, the success of which rested solely on Dargomïzhsky's genius, highlighted no more than one facet: melodic recitative. The future of Russian opera, he said, had to be more ambitious and comprehensive, more certain about the contribution of the chorus:

> An opera in which the movement of the people would unite directly with the action of the principal characters of the drama, where the people would be depicted in colors as vivid and true as those Dargomïzhsky employed to animate each of the individual figures of his opera, would make an even more profound impression than the beautiful creation of dramatic music we call *The Stone Guest*.[15]

Cui's operatic theories were not free of contradiction. In 1878, for example, he wrote that the works of great poets did not lend themselves to being set to music. A composer, he suggested, would do better to look for texts that could easily be turned into vocal melodies—a viewpoint that might seem to challenge the very raison d'être of *The Stone Guest*. Yet he continued to consider Dargomïzhsky's opera a masterpiece. For him, *The Stone Guest* was a milestone as well as an aberration.[16]

## ALEXANDER SEROV

The other champion of the progressive current was Alexander Serov, who paid special attention to opera. Serov voiced his ideas for the first time in 1852, in an article on Spontini, in which he wrote: "The major criteria [of musical drama] are the same as those of spoken drama, that music drama must be, in fact, and above all, *drama*."[17] Shortly afterward he wrote to Stasov:

> We must get together and talk about a certain Richard *Wagner*, whose work in three little volumes, *Oper und Drama*, has been *very much* on my mind lately. This is a *terribly intelligent* man—he understands many things completely contrariwise to the *popular* view. Just the fact that he hates Meyerbeer and considers the Ninth Symphony the *crowning glory of all music* was enough for me to love his outlook and his whole nature. But despite all these *good things*, one must *renounce* the joy of considering him "one of us." . . . He does not pay respect where it is due and either goes too far a priori . . . or is simply talking through his hat, seeking theoretically to "justify" his unsuccessful practical ambitions in composition. (He himself writes operas—without the least aptitude for musical beauty.)[18]

Serov's attitude toward Wagner remained cool until 1858. Then, in Dresden, he attended a Wagner opera—*Tannhäuser*—for the first time. From that time on he was wildly enthusiastic:

> In the face of Wagner's creation, I was seized with the most *naive* astonishment, as if I had never before had any inkling of what theatre is, or drama, or opera! So stunningly new was this inspired solution of the great problem of fusing three separate arts. . . . Of all other operas which I know in actuality, that is, on the stage, not one can compare with *Tannhäuser* in "wholeness" of impression.[19]

Wagner's work convinced Serov that the ideal of dramatic music was attainable. But although Serov became a great champion of Wagner in Russia—a position he was alone in defending for a long time—he was anything but a slavish follower. His ideas retained a number of strikingly unique features.

He formulated these most clearly in 1856 in his critique of Dar-gomïzhsky's opera *Rusalka*. In it he defined opera as an art with three components: (1) the poetic framework, that is, the content and underlying idea of the opera as drama; (2) the musical element, that is, the expression of the idea through music; and (3) the scenic, or theatrical, element, that is, the implementation of the idea of the text and the music by means of visible plastic images on the stage.

Each of these three elements (text, music and staging) might dominate a given opera or certain of its parts to a greater or lesser extent, but in the complete absence of any of them the idea of "opera" is vitiated. From such a division of elements it is clear that, for example, the blatant incongruity of music and text (as in certain Italian operas of the "bravura" school) destroys the ideal of opera; but no less (even more, perhaps) is it destroyed by contradiction between that which is demanded by the nature of the play and the music, and that which we actually see on the stage (in the production and in the acting).

Serov then looked more closely into the first category of his theory:

One must definitely distinguish three stages in the text of an opera—stages of extremely unequal importance—which are often not distinguished but confused, and this confusion is inimical to true judgment of opera. These stages are:

1. The plot, as a poetical invention (la fable de la pièce, die Fabel des Stückes).
2. The musico-poetical disposition of the operatic ground plan—the "scenario" of the opera.
3. The words—the rhymed or unrhymed verses of the text.

The *first* of these stages is the most important one, both in relation to the opera as a dramatic composition and in relation to the opera as a theatrical presentation or spectacle, and even with regard to music. On the first stage depends the ability of the text to "inspire" the musician; on this same factor, together with the music and production, depends the interest and attraction of the opera and its whole fate.

The *second* stage . . . must be strictly and equally balanced between the requirements of the poet and those of the musician. This is often a very difficult task, and because of this there are so few operatic libretti with completely successful scenarios.

The third stage is altogether subordinate to the music. The music is written to a given set of "words," to be sure, but the musician writing the opera is inspired, of course, not by words, but by the situation of the given character or characters. This situation is in turn dependent upon the "plot" and "plan." Consequently, even for the composer himself, the "words" are not of primary importance. In them one need only observe a few conditions demanded by the music, that is, that the words be so adjusted as to assist, and never impede, the "musico-scenic impression."

For the listener, the words in most cases disappear behind the music, drown in an ocean of vocal and instrumental sounds. In keeping with this virtually inescapable evil, the libretto of an opera must be so made that the plot in its broad outlines be consistently clear and understandable almost without the assistance of words; that it be almost as simple and graphic as that of a ballet.[20]

This passage contains several original ideas that differ from other theories on opera as theater. In Wagner's conception, for instance, it is precisely the text, the *Dichtung,* that drives the entire work. For Serov, in contrast, the contents of an opera are determined by the dramatic constellations—the actual words sung are of secondary importance. Serov's ideas also differ from the realism of Dargomïzhsky and of the Balakirev circle, precisely because they focus on the musical reproduction of concrete, distinct words.

Serov did not believe that every story lent itself to operatic treatment. Intellectual plays, with a host of arguments and a concrete background, struck him as being unmusical (as an example he cited Pushkin's *Boris Godunov*). The plot of an opera must instead be based on strong and elementary emotions, expressed by one-dimensional characters. For Serov, psychological complexity was the domain not of opera but of spoken drama.

According to Serov, the composer must be his own librettist—in the sense only of plot and scenario, however, which had to be devised in close connection with the music. Filling in the actual words could be left to others.

Strangely enough Serov, though a passionate defender of Wagner, took a view of opera closer to French *grand opéra* than to Wagner's music drama. For Serov, the dramaturgy of an opera rests on the compression of dramatic situations into musical units or blocks, the combination or contrast of which in turn allows for the development of the dramatic conflict. That definition applies more to the static conception of a Meyerbeer than to the flexible, carefully composed music drama of a Wagner. How, then, could Serov consider himself a Wagnerian? His Wagner remained essentially the composer of *Tannhäuser* and *Lohengrin*—operas that in their turn were indebted to the model of the *grand opéra*—and less the composer of the *Ring* or of *Tristan und Isolde*. What Serov thought typical of Wagner was his ability to link musical blocks with great flexibility, in keeping with the needs of the dramatic development, without elaborating them into rounded "numbers." In *Tannhäuser,* Wagner used all the traditional ingredients—monologues, duets, and

choral numbers—but joined them together in what Serov called an "uninterrupted finale." By that he was referring to the structure of the finales
in Mozart's operas, great dramatic edifices from which the "number"
structure is absent and the musical episodes succeed one another in accordance with the complications of the dramatic action. Serov believed
that Wagner had applied that principle to operas as a whole and that this
constituted his most important innovation.

## FOLK SONG AND NATIONALISM

Musically, nationalism was traditionally associated with the adaptation
of folk song. Despite the reputation of the *kuchka* as musical nationalists and folklorists, they were not agreed on treating folk song as a national symbol. Balakirev, who held that it did serve such a function, tried
to use folk song to convey national character in monumental orchestral
music. Stasov and Cui, in contrast, saw no national significance in folk
song. Their opera aesthetic, centering as it did on the question of realism, allowed the use of folk song only if it satisfied their realist criteria.
In an opera, folk songs—which they considered so many objective
facts—were thus appropriate only when the situation demanded it: as a
means of depicting a specific setting or period. At most, folk songs could
be used in situations that also occurred in reality, and had to be sung by
characters representing the folk. Thus César Cui thought that Rimsky-
Korsakov had been quite wrong to include a folk song in a love duet in
*Pskovityanka:*

> One can give a folk song to a chorus representing the folk; one can give it
> also to individuals who are singing a song; but individual feelings cannot be
> poured forth in the sounds of a folk song. Here Olga and Tucha are speak-
> ing of their own love, of their own feelings; in such a spot the sounds of a
> folk song are altogether out of place on their lips.[21]

A folk song, according to the nay-sayers, can only represent itself; it
can never denote such ideological concepts as the "folk" or national
character.

The approach differs fundamentally from Glinka's in *A Life for the
Tsar.* Glinka used folk song to characterize Ivan Susanin—not to depict
him as an individual, but to make him an expression of *narodnost'* (national character), for Ivan Susanin represents the entire Russian nation.

The link between folk song and *narodnost'* was renewed by Alexander Serov when he fell under the sway of *pochvennichestvo,* an intellec-

tual movement which maintained that every nation must develop organically from the "soil" (*pochva*) of its own traditions. In their view, moreover, folk song was one key expression of the national tradition, the national spirit. The *pochvennik* poet Apollon Grigoryev compared it with a plant: "A song comes to birth we know not when and where, is created by we know not whom, thrives as a plant thrives, yes, precisely like a plant, which vegetates luxuriantly in congenial soil."[22]

*Pochvennichestvo* caused an about-face in Serov's views. His belief had been that great music must be cosmopolitan, that the expressive possibilities of folk song were too limited for music that tried to reach this highest spiritual goals. After 1868, however, he adopted Grigoryev's view: "Folk song is a plantlike product purely of the soil."[23] From that time on, he searched for a way to turn folk song into the basis of a national opera style. His opera *The Power of the Fiend* was the result.

## CHAPTER FIVE

# The Theory in Practice
*Musical Creation*

An account, work by work, of musical contributions during this crucial period in the history of Russian music not only would prove unwieldy, but would also fail to throw much light on the subject. More useful is an analysis of the themes employed by composers at the time. The following discussion, therefore, rather than being exhaustive, will be selective, for the purpose of illustrating the options open to different composers. Our analysis will cover Russian style and form at large, Chaikovsky's individual path, orientalism, harmonic explorations, realism, and vocal lyricism.

## RUSSIAN STYLE AND FORM AT LARGE

At first, Rubinstein—whose symphonies were the first monumental orchestral works by any Russian composer—reigned supreme over Russian symphonic form. His rivals could not help being impressed by him. Balakirev was fascinated by his second symphony, known as the *Ocean Symphony*, op. 42 (the original 1851 version in four movements, followed later by a version with seven movements), notwithstanding the patronizing reviews published by his disciples. However, with his idea of basing Russian music on folk song, Balakirev was challenging Rubinstein's view that national style and symphonic form were incompatible. To that end he had first to prove that he was not inferior to Rubinstein.

The anti-German propaganda of the Balakirev circle almost leads us to forget the extent to which Balakirev himself was grounded in the German symphonic style. The fact that he was self-taught makes his achievement all the more striking, as witness his *King Lear* Overture (1859), an impressive work indeed for a young man of twenty-two. *King Lear* is not a symphonic poem on Liszt's model, but a tragic overture in sonata form along the lines of Beethoven's overtures. These rely more on the dramatic qualities of the sonata form than on any literary program. In other words, the literary content is reduced to its dramatic essence, while the themes of the sonata form are associated with the opposing forces involved in the conflict. Thus Balakirev transformed *King Lear* into an instrumental drama. In it, the first theme of the sonata form is already replete with conflict as the Lear theme, derived from a motif Balakirev first uses in the introduction as a symbol for Kent's prophecy, is combined in counterpoint with the threatening motifs of Goneril and Regan. The second theme reflects the gentler character of Cordelia. The development leads to a clash of themes and at the same time portrays the storm in which Lear loses his sanity. The recapitulation marks the dramatic climax. The Cordelia theme turns into the tragic portrayal of Lear mourning over the dead body of his devoted daughter. The sorrowful epilogue tells of Lear's death and rounds the piece off with a return of Kent's prophecy motif.

Balakirev's composition, with its motivic development and a tonal strategy that purposefully stresses the dramatic climaxes, is a typical model of a sonata form after Beethoven. The approach does not differ essentially from that in comparable compositions by Rubinstein, such as *Dmitry Donskoy* (1852) or the "musical character sketch" *Ivan the Terrible* (1869). Compared with Rubinstein's treatment of the sonata form, however, Balakirev's shows great daring and fantasy. Nevertheless, it was Rubinstein, not Balakirev, who drew on national themes: *Dmitry Donskoy* deals with the highly patriotic subject of the Russian victory over the Mongols in 1380; *Ivan the Terrible* introduces a national figure that appeals strongly to the Russian imagination. Balakirev's overture, by contrast, is cosmopolitan in both style and content.

As early as 1858, however, with his First Overture on Russian Themes, Balakirev took a step toward an independent Russian style. It was his first attempt at a genuine symphonic work with a Russian character. (In this context, the Fantasia on Themes from *A Life for the Tsar*, for piano, and the *Grande fantaisie sur des airs nationaux russes,* for piano and orchestra, can be ignored. They are bravura pieces of a type common in the nineteenth century.)

Balakirev chose his themes from folk-song collections available in 1857, apparently referring to Glinka's *Kamarinskaya* as his model. In keeping with that work, he took a slow song for the introduction, in this case a *bilina* (an epic song); then for the fast section he chose two songs comparable in structure with the ostinato pattern (the continuous reiteration of musical phrases) of the *Kamarinskaya* dance-song. The use of two songs in the allegro section as well was an important departure from the model. Balakirev introduced them for a clear purpose: to link the symphonic process of the sonata form with Glinka's variations on an ostinato pattern. However, where Glinka had relied on his skill in decorative variation, Balakirev aimed at symphonic treatment. In so doing, he departed resolutely from Glinka as well as from Dargomïzhsky, who in his *Fantaisies pittoresques* simply copied the Glinka model. The works by Glinka, Dargomïzhsky, and Balakirev mentioned here make up the complete repertoire of orchestral music with a Russian character before 1864.[1]

For Balakirev, the First Overture on Russian Themes could not have been an end point, for the Russian style did not yet penetrate all layers of the composition. After the First Overture, Balakirev was the first Russian composer actively to go in search of folk song, on a trip along the Volga in the summer of 1860. He worked the material he discovered into a groundbreaking collection of folk-song arrangements (1866) and into the Second Overture on Russian Themes (1864). He paid particular attention to the *protyazhnaya*—literally, "drawn-out song," or melismatically elaborated lyric song. The hallmarks of this type of song are extreme rhythmic flexibility, asymmetrical phrase structure, and tonal ambiguity. The last term is also referred to as *peremennost'*, or modal mutability. One of its characteristics is that the lower neighbor to the tonic often serves as a second tonic. Even earlier, the *protyazhnaya* had exerted an influence on Russian music, but in mutilated form, adapted to Western listening habits, as in the songs of Alyabyev, Varlamov, and Gurilyov. In contrast to the advocates of the mixed style, Balakirev focused his attention on what distinguished the *protyazhnaya* from Western sound. In the Second Overture on Russian Themes he showed how the new material could be given symphonic dimensions. In particular, he tried to use the structural characteristics of the *protyazhnaya* for the elaboration of a large-scale work. In concrete terms, that meant importing the tonal instability of folk song into larger structures by relying on the principle of tonal indeterminacy. The structure of the Second Overture thus departs from the classical tonal relationships, based on the tonic and dominant and appropriate major and minor modes. In using a different approach Balakirev came close to the tonal experiments of Schubert and Liszt, who also tried to break the shackles of the dominant. This explains Balakirev's interest in Liszt and also his aversion to Wagner, whose harmonic language was ultimately based on the consistent use of dominant tension.

In the Second Overture, Balakirev combined his newly discovered harmonic freedom with a symphonic—Beethovenian—approach. The form is tripartite: an allegro in sonata form is framed by a slow introduction and its final recapitulation. The middle movement plays two themes off against each other, with the motivic development becoming even more intense than it is in the First Overture. The treatment is subtle and indeed worthy of Beethoven. In the incorporation of folk music, the Second Overture still follows the example of *Kamarinskaya*, but outstrips it by far. Through the intermediate stage of the First Overture, Glinka's ostinato variations make way for true symphonic drama. With the Second Overture, however, Balakirev boldly refuted Rubinstein's theory: he showed that Russian music did not have to remain confined to genre pieces à la Dargomïzhsky, but could hold its own against German symphonic works.

Balakirev, realizing that his Second Overture was an important new step, aimed also at endowing it with ideological significance. During its composition he had been under the spell of the populist writer Alexander Herzen, who, from his exile in London, was addressing impassioned appeals to the Russian intelligentsia and to Russian students in his journal *Kolokol* (The bell). Vladimir Stasov was a great admirer of Herzen and passed his enthusiasm on to Balakirev. Herzen used powerful images and slogans to persuade Russian students to engage in revolutionary acts, a well-known example being the slogan "To the people!" It is highly probable that Balakirev considered his Second Overture an answer to Herzen's appeal. After all, "to the people!" was precisely where Balakirev had gone during his journey of exploration along the Volga. Herzen also used another celebrated image, that of a tidal wave of unrest among the people. In his article "The Giant Awakes" he wrote: "From all sides of our enormous fatherland, from the Don and from the Urals, from the Volga and the Dnepr a moan is growing, a rumble is rising—it is the beginning of a tidal wave which is boiling up, attended by storms, after a horribly fatiguing calm."[2] This image probably explains the dramatic qualities of Balakirev's overture. He published the work in 1869, changing the title to *1,000 Years* and calling it no longer an overture but a "musical picture." Its ideological meaning had changed as well: it had ceased to be an expression of social unrest and had become an optimistic view of Russian history. In accordance with his new approach, he used *1,000 Years* to depict three historical periods: the pagan, the medieval, and that of modern Russia. In 1882 Stasov stated that the fourth theme—the only one that was not derived from folk song—reflected the glittering future of Russia: "The emerging new life is expressed in an enchanting, truly inspired melody of wondrous beauty," Stasov crowed in ecstasy.[3]

A chronological study shows that—contrary to Balakirev's advocacy of program music—a literary program was not the guiding principle of his compositions. The musical form came first; the literary explanation followed later. Without exception, Balakirev's work was based largely on internal musical principles. Despite all his attacks on German academicism, his technique continued to reflect the symphonic approach of the German tradition.

Balakirev's overtures did, however, play a crucial role in the emergence of Russian symphonic music, for with them he introduced the musical style that we tend to consider "Russian"—even though that aspect was of Balakirev's making and not a spontaneous expression of Russian national musicality. His style was then adopted by his followers to such an extent that it acquired the aura of a national characteristic. Balakirev's influence was impressively far-reaching, as may be gathered from just a few examples: the opening of Musorgsky's *Boris Godunov* is a *protyazhnaya* stylization that bears a close resemblance to the first theme of Balakirev's Second Overture; Borodin's *In the Steppes of Central Asia* begins with a dominant pedal extending over ninety bars in the upper register of the violins, a formula used in Balakirev's First Overture; the texture of sustained notes in the wind section combined with a quicker pizzicato in the strings is another quotation. Not even Chaikovsky escaped Balakirev's influence, as witness the beginning of his Second Symphony and the song with which the peasants pay their respects to Madame Larina in the first act of *Eugene Onegin*.

Balakirev returned to the design of the Second Overture in his Overture on Czech Themes (1866–67). He revised the work later, called it a symphonic poem, and published it in 1906 under the title of *In Bohemia*, having foisted a high-flown romantic and national content upon it in tribute to the Czech brother nation. Balakirev's Second Overture served other composers as model and guide. Rimsky-Korsakov's Overture on Russian Themes (1866) is a virtual plagiarism. Even in Rimsky-Korsakov's later works, Balakirev's influence is palpable, for instance in the "Russian Easter" Overture (1888). Borodin's *In the Steppes of Central Asia* bears a formal resemblance to Balakirev's model. Borodin described that piece as a "musical picture," on the analogy of Balakirev's "musical picture" *1,000 Years*.

After the Second Overture, Balakirev had felt able to tackle the monumental form and had begun work on the First Symphony. He cut that project short, however, when he started on the Overture on Czech Themes, resuming it only thirty years later. Indeed, he did not finish his First Symphony until 1897, when his original intention to bestow symphonic status on Russian music had long been abandoned. We cannot tell how far the work had progressed before the interruption took place. From letters to Stasov and Cui we know that two-thirds of the first movement had been broadly sketched out. The planned scherzo was later incorporated into the Second Symphony (1900–1908). The new scherzo and the third movement came in the 1890s. The fourth movement had been sketched out, but had a new theme added to it later. For an idea of the state of Balakirev's symphonic development in the 1860s, therefore, we have to rely entirely on the first movement.

From the plan of the symphony it appears that Balakirev reserved the adaptation of folk songs for the finale. Yet he was anxious to incorporate some Russian characteristics into the first movement, which, as he wrote to Cui, introduced a new Russian element, somewhat religious in nature.[4] In the introduction, the diatonic harmonic color of his folk-song elaborations regularly makes itself felt, although the "Russian character" is rather discreet. More important is the highly original symphonic design. The slow introduction introduces the motif on which the allegro vivo is based, and the first phrase includes the basic motifs of both the first and the second themes. The allegro vivo has a three-part structure, but differs from the sonata form. Instead of the exposition-development-recapitulation pattern, it consists of an exposition, a second exposition, and a development. This means that after the actual exposition, the thematic material is developed in two phases. What we can schematically call a second exposition is in fact an elaboration involving a variation of the first. The true development is the next step. All the while, the music moves further and further away from the starting point; it does not end in a recapitulation, but in the final confirmation of the main motif, whereupon the piece ends in the main key (C major). The formal process is one of continuous development, divided into three stages of increasing complexity.

Balakirev consistently applied the symphonic principle of motivic work and deliberate climaxes in a most original way. If it was really planned in 1864, then Balakirev's First Symphony merits a prominent place in the history of the genre. Indeed, the principle of progressive development in several phases points ahead to the late symphonies of Jean Sibelius. The scant "Russian character" of the work pales before the impressive contribution to international symphonic thought.

Balakirev had difficulty completing large-scale works because he was always weighed down by practical cares. Even during the later period of his life, when he was no longer involved with the musical world, he apparently needed excessive amounts of time to produce major works. Thus he interrupted work on his Piano Concerto in E-flat Major, begun in 1861, and resumed it only in 1906. He still failed to finish it: the work was finally completed in 1910 by Sergey Lyapunov, after Balakirev's death.

Balakirev encouraged his disciples to produce major works. Between 1862 and 1865 (between the ages of eighteen and twenty-one) Rimsky-Korsakov wrote his First Symphony under Balakirev's supervision. In 1884 Rimsky-Korsakov revised the score and published it as a study for amateur and student orchestras. The work is more reminiscent of Schumann than of Russia, despite the inclusion of folk songs in the first and second movements. That did not prevent César Cui from extolling it, in a flagrant snub to Rubinstein, as "the first Russian symphony."[5]

In 1866 Borodin completed his First Symphony, on which he had worked for four years and in which he went further, as far as Russian character is concerned, than Rimsky-Korsakov. The introduction has a striking modal color as the opening melody stylizes the twists and turns of the *protyazhnaya*. Other folk-song stylizations are the Phrygian second theme of the first movement and the trio in the scherzo. The form is based on the German model, but lacks the original variations Balakirev used in his First Symphony. Motivic thinking was Borodin's basic principle; thus, the first theme of the sonata form is derived from the opening phrase of the introduction. Typical of Borodin, too, are the many repetitions and transpositions of motifs, which often appear as ostinati. The scherzo resembles the shadowy scherzi used in German symphonies after Beethoven's *Eroica*. The finale is close to Schumann in its rhythmical vitality.

Borodin's Second Symphony took longer to complete, occupying the composer from 1869 to 1876. In it, Borodin drew on melodic material from *Prince Igor*, an opera he no longer hoped to complete. The trio of the scherzo refers back to the chorus of the Polovtsian maidens, the end of the third movement links up with Igor's aria, and the festive scenes of the opera are echoed in the finale. The references to the heroic world of *Prince Igor* suggested the nickname of *Bogatïrskaya simfoniya* (Heroic symphony) to Stasov. Because *Prince Igor* was modeled in almost every detail on Glinka's *Ruslan and Lyudmila*, it is not surprising that this symphony, too, should keep recalling Glinka. Examples are the oriental-sounding trio of the second movement (with wind, harp, and triangle), the use of the harp in the third movement—strongly reminiscent of Bayan's aria—and the asymmetrical rhythms in the finale. The splendidly evocative third movement refers back most powerfully to the mythical, imaginary world of both *Ruslan* and *Prince Igor.*

The first movement of the Second Symphony is an unusual construction. The main theme consists of two contrasting parts: a concise motif and a melody in the wind with a different tempo. The actual second theme is a *protyazhnaya* stylization, but this plays hardly any part in the development. The lion's share of the thematic development is based on the principal theme and cannot really be called motivic work. Rather, it is a compulsive repetition of the motto, in sequences, diminutions, and augmentations. The contrast effect, inherent in the theme itself, is continued throughout the structure and amplified by the orchestration (with intensive use of the low brass). An additional peculiarity is the frequent change of tempo. All this turns the first movement into a montage of contrasts rather than into a developing sonata form.

Another unusual interpretation of the sonata form can be found in Rimsky-Korsakov's Third Symphony (1873), where he combined the normal scheme with the principle of third-rotation: the mirroring of keys in their major or minor upper and lower thirds. The usual third relationships are diatonic: in C major, for instance, they are E minor and A minor. In the finale, Rimsky-Korsakov completed the third relationships with consistent rotations and reflections in major and minor thirds, as in the following schema:

> *Exposition:*    C major / E minor / A minor: diatonic mediant
>                  and submediant
>
> *Development:*   C major / E minor / A-flat major (C major):
>                  complete circle of major thirds
>
> *Recapitulation:* C major / E-flat major / A major: mirroring of
>                  tonic in minor thirds

An extension of Balakirev's Beethovenian approach can be found in Rimsky-Korsakov's programmatic works *Sadko* and *Antar.* The history

of *Sadko* (1867, revised in 1869 and 1892) begins with Balakirev's fascination with Rubinstein's *Ocean* Symphony. That work made him think
of creating a Russian alternative, whereupon Stasov drew his attention
to the legend of Sadko, a *gusli* (a form of psaltery) player from Novgorod who, transported to the realm of the King of the Sea, accompanies the dance celebrating the marriage of the king's daughter. The dance
grows so wild that the great expanse of water begins to billow and surge,
endangering the ships. To calm the sea, Sadko smashes his *gusli*. The
storm abates.

Stasov produced the program for this work. Balakirev replayed it to
Rimsky-Korsakov, trusting in the former sailor's love of the sea. Rimsky-
Korsakov, however, relied more on Liszt's example than on his own mar-
itime recollections; in his memoirs, he mentioned Liszt's *Ce qu'on entend sur la montagne* as his source of inspiration. The main structure is
framed by two dazzling sketches of the calm, gently rippling sea. The
central section is formed by an evocative passage portraying Sadko's
underwater journey and the Russian dance that leads the work to its
climax.

In *Antar* (1868, revised in 1875 and 1897), Rimsky-Korsakov returned
to the idea of a loosely structured "musical tableau," but on a larger scale.
Berlioz's program symphonies were his starting point. *Antar* is in four
movements. The first tells the major part of the story, an "Arabian fairy
tale" by Osip Senkovsky, and constitutes the basis of the program. In the
story the poet Antar withdraws from the world, disillusioned by man's
sinfulness. In the ruins of Palmyra he comes across a gazelle cornered by
a bird of prey. Antar kills the bird. The gazelle later appears to him in a
dream and reveals herself as Gul Nazar, a peri, or winged Persian fairy.
She promises him three of life's pleasures. The second, third, and fourth
movements are devoted to these: the pleasure of revenge in the second;
the pleasure of power in the third, and the pleasure of love in the fourth.
Once Antar has enjoyed the last, he dies in the peri's arms. From Berlioz,
Rimsky-Korsakov took the principle of the idée fixe, a melody associated with the main character and recurring in all the movements. The
form of the work bears a vague resemblance to symphonic formats
(sonata form in the first movement; rondo form in the fourth movement)
but lacks the dialectic associated with these forms in symphonic music.
Instead, the music is developed by variations, repetitions, and gradations
of timbre. Rimsky-Korsakov originally called *Antar* his Second Symphony. Later he reconsidered and described the work as a symphonic
suite.

No other member of the *kuchka* identified himself so openly with the
ideal of absolute music as did Borodin in his two string quartets. A cellist himself, Borodin was an enthusiastic chamber-music player, and his
interest deepened during a stay in Heidelberg from 1859 to 1861. This
early period thus yielded, among other chamber works, a string sextet
and a piano quintet. In the structure of his themes and in the development of his texture Borodin based himself patently on Mendelssohn. That
he clung to his preference even in the company of the *kuchka,* so hostile
to chamber music, speaks for his independence of mind. In 1875 he
started on his First String Quartet, much to the displeasure of Musorgsky
and Stasov. From the first quartet on he displayed mastery of the quartet style, a fact worthy of respect in a part-time composer. His Second
String Quartet followed in 1881.

Borodin used the "chamber-music tone," which once had been the hallmark of good quartet style in many German centers. In concrete terms,
that meant laying stress on the melody, on clarity of texture, and on a
subtle but aurally clear use of the motivic work. In the nineteenth century, standards differed from those that came to prevail in the twentieth.
Beethoven's late quartets did not yet enjoy their present status as models of good quartet writing. What Russian traits there are in Borodin's
quartets are completely incidental. Strictly speaking, they occur exclusively in the folk-song paraphrase found in the second movement of the
First Quartet, and in the Glinka-like technique of varying the background
in the finale of that work. The First Quartet is richest in changes of mood.
The Second Quartet has a more uniform atmosphere and expression. The
sonority of both works is subtly graded. A brilliant effect, for instance,
is the combination, in the trio of the scherzo of the First Quartet, of har-
monics in the first violin with the subdued sounds of the viola.

## CHAIKOVSKY'S PERSONAL PATH

Chaikovsky's individual approach becomes immediately apparent when
the wide range of his oeuvre is surveyed. Even if we confine ourselves to
the major instrumental works he wrote between 1866 and 1880, the list
is impressive: four symphonies; five programmatic orchestral works
(symphonic poems or overtures); three concertos (two for piano and one
for violin); the Variations on a Rococo Theme, for cello and orchestra;
the ballet *Swan Lake;* an orchestral suite; three string quartets; and such
occasional works as the Festival Overture on the Danish National An-
them and the Slavonic March. The list even includes genres for which

the young Chaikovsky had once declared loathing. From Kashkin's memoirs we know, for instance, that he had vowed never to write a piano concerto, and that on listening to Beethoven's late quartets he had to struggle to keep awake. Whence, then, the self-imposed discipline needed to explore every genre?

Chaikovsky thought of himself as a professional composer and considered his professionalism the crucial difference between him and his colleagues in the *kuchka*. He shared a number of their ideals—certainly not excluding the emphasis on national character—but his aim was a professional standard that would satisfy the highest European norms. In this regard, the first version of the Second Symphony and the First Piano Concerto are good demonstrations of the linkage between the national ideal and international standards of structural perfection. Professionalism also implies the wish to reach a broad public. Given the tepid popular attitude toward Russian music at the time, it is understandable that Chaikovsky should have tried to reach potential audiences along every accessible front. But his ambitions stretched further still: he wanted to prove himself on the international plane, and ultimately did so with the triumphant première of his First Piano Concerto in Boston on 25 October 1875, with Hans von Bülow as soloist.

On the aesthetic plane, Chaikovsky was open to all aspects of St. Petersburg musical life. He was impressed by Serov, by Balakirev, and by the classical values upheld by the conservatory. Both the progressive and the conservative camps made attempts to win him over. In response to his symphonic poem *Fatum* (1868), Balakirev and Laroche alike decided to help cure the composer of his weaknesses. Unfortunately, they differed on the nature of these shortcomings. Balakirev judged the composition not meticulous enough, calling it a makeshift collection of loose parts. Laroche, for his part, believed that Chaikovsky had taken the wrong path in opting to compose in free form. He advised him urgently to immerse himself once more in the work of the classical masters.

In the overture-fantasia *Romeo and Juliet* (1869, drastically revised in 1870 and 1880), Chaikovsky allowed himself to be guided by Balakirev (though not slavishly so, as we earlier observed) and modeled the work on Balakirev's overture to *King Lear*. He reduced the plot to one central conflict, combining it with the binary structure of the sonata form. The two opposing currents in *Romeo and Juliet* are the quarrel dividing the city of Verona, on the one hand, and the love of Romeo and Juliet, on the other. Chaikovsky's resolution of the conflict is a refined example of musical dramaturgy.

The introduction is a portrayal of Friar Laurence, the understanding outsider, based on Kent's prophecy in the prologue to Balakirev's *King Lear.* The exposition presents the two contrasting elements of the plot. The first theme stands for violence and conflict, reflected in the bitter outbursts, the emotional turmoil, and above all the violent irregularities of the rhythm. The second theme represents the world of love. It consists of two parts: the broad love theme—generally associated with Romeo in the commentaries—framed by a theme of gently oscillating chord combinations, generally associated with Juliet. The two major themes are placed side by side. The love theme is tonally remote from the first theme (D-flat major as against B minor), serving as a kind of peaceful oasis in a world of violence. The development plays out the first theme against the melody of the prologue and culminates in the partial recapitulation of the first theme. The second theme is not used in the development: Chaikovsky saved the confrontation of the two themes for the second half of the recapitulation. In the exposition, the love theme remains shielded from the violence of the first theme. In the recapitulation it is strongly influenced by the latter and ultimately destroyed. Chaikovsky thus shifted the real musical conflict of the two themes from the development to the recapitulation, where it culminates in the dramatic catastrophe. The coda first seeks a consoling tone in a chorale-like passage, but then grows into a passionate recall of the love theme, to end with four measures of powerful final chords in the minor.

Chaikovsky arrived at this musico-dramatic approach after only two radical revisions. On the advice of Balakirev he replaced the original prologue with the far more evocative one we know today. The effective transposition of the thematic conflict to the recapitulation was also absent from the first draft. The development of the 1869 version was entirely in keeping with what could be expected of an academically trained composer: an opening with a fugato and a confrontation of the two themes. In the 1870 revision Chaikovsky cast off the traditional straitjacket. In 1880 he perfected the new draft and extracted even more dramatic energy from his themes.

In view of this fascinating process of revising and polishing, it is all the more difficult to understand why Chaikovsky is so often called a spontaneous—and by some even a naive—composer, one who relied entirely on his inspiration and his flair for lyric invention. Indeed, before the recent discovery of the importance of structural planning and motivic cohesion in his music it was assumed that Chaikovsky attained the motivic cohesion of his compositions unconsciously. The lyric spontaneity seemed too great to allow suspicion of the presence of a meticulously planning, calculating intellect. The consistency of his approach, however, suggests nothing less. Typical of Chaikovsky is precisely his ability to make complicated structural innovations look like spontaneous insights. In his best moments Chaikovsky knew full well how to hide his craftsmanship behind a façade of naïveté.

The clearest example of the combination of lyrical spontaneity and structural planning is the famous First Piano Concerto in B-flat Minor, op. 23 (1874–75). Until the nineteenth century piano concertos were chiefly the province of the virtuoso composer, intended in the first place for the composer's own use. Such was the case during the time of both Mozart and Beethoven. Nor was it any different in Chaikovsky's day, though Chaikovsky himself was anything but a masterful pianist. He felt motivated, however, to take advantage of the high regard in which virtuosos were held by the public, and planned a concerto for the virtuoso closest to hand, Nikolai Rubinstein, director of the Moscow Conservatory. Perhaps he was even then thinking of Hans von Bülow as a possible alternative, having in 1874 become well acquainted with this great German pianist and conductor. Bülow took an extremely positive view of Chaikovsky's music, and it was he, in fact, who gave the first performance of the concerto after Rubinstein, overcome by jealousy of Chaikovsky's talent, refused to do so.[6]

Unfamiliar as he was with virtuoso piano technique, Chaikovsky had quite a few problems with the concerto. The combination of piano and orchestra being new to him, a considerable part of the creative process was taken up with attempts to strike the correct balance between these two instrumental partners. The concerto reached its final form only after two revisions in consultation with the prominent pianists Eduard Dannreuther and Alexander Siloti.

The famous opening section is a fine example of the balance between piano and orchestra at which Chaikovsky aimed. To appreciate this, we must look at the concerto in the form in which Chaikovsky originally conceived it, which differs somewhat from the version we are accustomed to hearing today. For the work had another beginning: instead of having chords struck forcefully across the entire keyboard, Chaikovsky gave the melody to the strings, accompanied by arpeggios over a limited range of the piano.[7] This is understandable because the melody is sounded only in mezzo forte; the piano does little more than add color. Where the full chords we usually hear come from is in fact a mystery. They first appeared in the third edition (1889), and may have been suggested by Siloti. The theatrical pose of the new piano part is most inappropriately treated by many soloists as an acrobatic tour de force. Such an approach often destroys the unique character of that famous page, the particular middle way between grandeur and elegiac lyricism. It would be interesting to restore the original beginning as an alternative in concert practice, if only to discover what Chaikovsky originally had in mind.

For a long time, the introduction posed an enigma to analysts and critics alike. What was the link between it and the rest of the concerto? Why should Chaikovsky have introduced melodic material and then left it alone? That question has been posed most trenchantly in a famous review by Eric Blom: "The great tune's strutting upon the stage at the rise of the curtain, like an actor-manager in a leading part, and then vanishing suddenly and completely, leaves the hearer disconcerted and dissatisfied. He feels as though he were witnessing a performance of *Hamlet* in which the Prince of Denmark is killed by Polonius at the end of the first scene."[8]

The key to the link between the introduction and what follows is once again Chaikovsky's gift of hiding motivic connections behind what appears to be a flash of melodic inspiration. The opening melody comprises the most important motivic core elements of the entire work, something that is not immediately obvious, owing to its lyrical quality. However, a closer analysis shows that the themes of the three movements are subtly linked. Chaikovsky presents his structural material in a spontaneous, lyrical manner, yet with a high degree of planning and calculation.[9] The use of folk-song material is particularly subtle. The first theme of the sonata form of the first movement uses the Ukrainian folk song "Oy, kryatshe, kryatshe. . . ." The middle section of the second movement is based on a French *chansonnette*, "Il faut s'amuser, danser et rire." A Ukrainian *vesnyanka*, or greeting to spring, is the basis of the first theme of the finale, while the second theme is motivically derived from the Russian folk song "Podoydu podoydu vo Tsar-Gorod." A strong motivic link ties all the songs together. Because they are known songs and not newly conceived themes, the relationship between them is often attributed to chance. However, it is likely that Chaikovsky chose these songs precisely because of their motivic affinity, deploying them wherever necessary. The selection of folkloristic material went hand in hand with the planning of a large-scale structure.

Nowhere is Chaikovsky's characteristic course—between the paths followed by Rubinstein and Balakirev, respectively—as clear as it is in his early symphonies. He composed his First Symphony in 1866, but revised it twice, later that same year and again in 1874. Begun under the academic influence of Rubinstein, the First Symphony has the formal characteristics of the German model. In the development of the themes, however, Chaikovsky hewed more closely to Balakirev, whose influence is most obvious in the first movement, titled "Daydreams on a Wintry Road." It is the symphonic elaboration of a well-known type of folk dance, the *naigrïsh*, structured in units of three measures, which Chaikovsky knew from Glinka's *Kamarinskaya* and from Balakirev's Overture on Russian Themes. Thus, what on first hearing seems to be asymmetrical sentence structure in the first movement of Chaikovsky's First Symphony becomes transparent when we hear the movement in broad triple measure.

The second movement ("O land of gloom, O land of mist") is based on a folklike air of Chaikovsky's own making. It is a magnificent *protyazhnaya* stylization, helping to create considerable tension by means of subtle variations.

The third movement is a Mendelssohnesque scherzo with a symphonic waltz as its central section. The finale is based on a folk song ("Shall I plant, then, little sweetheart"), in line with a tradition going back to the eighteenth century: the inclusion of picturesque or rustic material in the finale of a symphony, sonata, or concerto.

The Second Symphony was composed in 1872 but thoroughly revised in 1879 and 1880, when the first movement was almost completely rewritten. The symphony owes its nickname, the "Little Russian," above all to the finale. Here Chaikovsky openly adopted the plan of Glinka's *Kamarinskaya*—ostinato patterns projected onto a constantly varied background—applying it to a Ukrainian folk song, the dancing song (*gopak*) called "The Crane." The symphony also contains echoes of famous examples from the symphonic tradition. The framing of the opening movement with a melodic introduction and its recapitulation as a coda, for example, recalls Schubert's Great Symphony in C Major—an affinity that is brought home by the initial horn solo. The introduction to the finale recalls the finales of Beethoven's First (in the step-by-step structure of the main theme) and Fifth (in the majestic use of the brass). The first movement is full of Beethovenian energy and reflects a feeling for musical construction based on concentrated motifs. The second movement is a short march recycled from a discarded early opera, *Undine*. The third movement quotes a folk song ("Spin, My Spinner") in the trio.

The Third Symphony (1875) received little praise from the critics, who took exception to Chaikovsky's strict adherence to the German model, saying that by neglecting his personal lyricism he arrived at uninspired hackwork. The argument is typical of the traditional critics of Chaikovsky: inspiration is judged by the presence of lyrical charm, and formal complexity rejected as incompatible with the alleged lyrical personality of the composer. Yet not only is the high degree of motivic and polyphonic intricacies in the Third Symphony impressive in its own right, but it also contributes significantly to the astonishing dynamism of the first movement. The motivic interplay is underlined by the brilliant orchestration.

The Third Symphony as a whole is related to another Third: Schumann's. They share their five-movement structure and their exuberant optimism. Another parallel between the two works is their rhythmic complexity: in his first movement, Schumann uses the contrast between hemiolas and the normal rhythmic pattern; Chaikovsky works with asymmetrical phrases, clearly defined in the first theme and exceptionally flexible in the second. However, that is where the similarity stops. Chaikovsky's themes cannot easily be confused with Schumann's.

In the Third Symphony, Chaikovsky's feeling for the magic of sound is revealed for the first time, in combination with capricious rhythms and fanciful manipulation of musical forms. The sensual opulence of the Third Symphony points ahead to the composer's later orchestral suites.

In the first movement we already notice the presence of dance rhythms, and these will be dominant in the following movements. The introduction is based on the rhythm of a *marcia funebre,* the second theme on the bolero rhythm, and the codetta on the polka. The rest of the symphony resembles a dance suite, playing mainly on the contrast between the waltz and the polonaise.

The last movement of the Third Symphony, an exuberant polonaise, was responsible for a misunderstanding. Ever since Sir August Manns performed it in England in 1899, the work has been known as the *Polish* Symphony, the finale being treated as an expression of the Polish longing for freedom and national resurgence. The real meaning was the precise opposite, as becomes clear when we remember the special function of the polonaise in the Russian context. The dance owed its prominent place to Osip Kozlovsky (1757–1831), a Polish composer who served in the Russian army, and who had his greatest success with his polonaises. For the celebration of the Russian victory over the Turks in the Ukraine he wrote a triumphal polonaise on a text by Derzhavin: "Thunder of Victory, Resound!" After that, the polonaise became the preeminent Russian ceremonial genre, an expression of tsarist patriotism and imperialism. The polonaise in the finale of the Third Symphony, therefore, was intended to appeal to the patriotic sentiment of the aristocracy; its remoteness from Polish nationalism could not have been greater.

Chaikovsky wrote his three string quartets between 1871 and 1876. The first is famous for its folk-song quotation in the second movement. In design this quartet is closely related to the First Symphony. The Second Quartet does not use folk-song quotations and is better known for its strict thematic logic. The most surprising element in the Third Quartet is the reference to the Orthodox service in the slow movement—with an imitation of the "gospodi pomiluy" (Lord have mercy) prayer and of the monotonous recitation by the deacon. The piece was written in memory of the violinist Ferdinand Laub.

Following the programmatic overture to *Romeo and Juliet*, Chaikovsky tackled programmatic music on a few other occasions. By adding the symphonic poem *The Tempest* (1873) and an overture to *Hamlet* (1880), he created a three-part Shakespeare cycle. Perhaps his most fascinating symphonic poem is *Francesca da Rimini* (1876). It came from a passage that appealed strongly to the imagination of nineteenth-century listeners: the story of Francesca da Rimini, taken from the fifth canto of Dante's *Inferno*. Francesca was a patrician woman who was discovered by her tyrannical husband in the act of betraying him, put to death, and condemned with her lover to be tossed about through hell for eternity by a whirlwind. To romantics, this bizarre punishment was a fitting simile for insatiable longing. In addition, the idea of a somber fate appealed to their sense of tragedy. The story was tragic in two senses. First, Francesca was forced into marriage with the authoritarian Giacotto when she was really in love with his brother, Paolo. Furthermore, she had the misfortune of being discovered during an unguarded moment of passion, without any chance of atonement or hope of divine forgiveness. This story is consequently a tragedy of fate at its most extreme, one that is likely to strike the modern reader as manifestly unjust.

Chaikovsky was not the first to exploit the material musically: it is also used in Liszt's *Dante* Symphony. Although the story of Francesca da Rimini accounts for the largest part of Chaikovsky's symphonic poem, while in Liszt's work it is but one theme among others, Chaikovsky's work is closely related to Liszt's model. This is seen especially in the passages dealing with the descent into hell and the whirlwind. The middle section is a detailed portrait of Francesca. In it Chaikovsky returns to the concept he developed in the adagio of his First Symphony: an essentially monothematic structure, based on subtle variations and gradations of a single, sweeping, lyrical melody. The love theme in *Francesca da Rimini* is an "Unending Melody" that has few equals. The insatiable longing is reflected in the fact that the melody never reaches a cadence, Chaikovsky thus creating a passionate climax. After this hint at Francesca's erotic awakening, the story is abruptly cut short by a passage telling of her death. Then the whirlwind starts up anew, to carry the work to its conclusion.

## ORIENTALISM

In Russian literature the oriental tradition goes back to the Caucasian campaign of Nicholas I. As the Russian empire spread to the south and east, so the importance of Islamic themes in literature grew. Russian orientalism is nevertheless not confined to interest in the East. It is, rather, an ideology, one colored by a typically Western view. Hence orientalism tells us more about Western than it does about Eastern cultural values.

Orientalism was able to fulfill several functions. It could, for instance, serve as a safety valve for subjects unmentionable in one's own culture. Thus it helped to disguise political themes in the eighteenth century, and erotic fantasies in the nineteenth. During the colonial period orientalism was, moreover, a means of expressing Western feelings of superiority, as the entire non-Western world was made to play the role of "the other." While the rule of reason prevailed in the West, irrationality and barbarism were seen to reign supreme in the East. This dualism was the basis of a misogynist symbolism: the West was the civilization of the male—rational, active, and moral; the East of the female—irrational, passive, and immoral. As an expression of Western feelings of superiority, orientalism was the ideology of the colonizing nations. France and England led in this field, but when it came to imperialism Russia yielded pride of place to no other country. The Caucasian conquests gave the impetus to the introduction of the oriental fashion into literature. In Russian music, orientalism reached its peak during the eastward expansion of the empire under Alexander II.

In the West, orientalism is among the best-known aspects of Russian music, so much so, in fact, that it is widely considered a feature of the Russian national character, a view that was firmly held by Stasov and has been one of the dogmas of traditional historiography ever since. There is yet another reason why orientalism is so readily identified with the Russian national character. At about the turn of the twentieth century, Russian music first came to the attention of the Western public in Paris. Presented chiefly with oriental works, the Parisians, unprompted, considered them to be "typically Russian." Understandably so: to them Russia herself was part of the mysterious East, of oriental "otherness." This misconception proved persistent, surviving even in recent publications.[10] The attitude of the Russian composers of St. Petersburg was essentially the same as that of the Western public: the East was a culture with which they could not identify. For them, too, orientalism was a sign of otherness. Soviet ideologists liked to present Russian composers as preachers of brotherhood among all the peoples of the empire. But that is Soviet propaganda, which, strangely enough, was often swallowed by the West.

The foremost orientalist work is Borodin's *Prince Igor* (1869–87), which draws freely on Glinka's *Ruslan and Lyudmila*. The erotic scenes in Glinka's opera (Naína's magical garden, Ratmir's lasciviousness, the dance of Chernomor's slave girls) served as models for the pervasive sensuality of Borodin's music. Best known in the work are the Polovtsian dances, which betray the ideological content of orientalism. The Russian prince, Igor, is the prisoner of the khan of the Polovtsi, a race of nomadic warriors. Khan Konchak wants Prince Igor to enter into an alliance with him, since the support of the Russian prince would leave him free to pursue his conquests. One of the means he uses to achieve this acquiescence is erotic seduction. In the Polovtsian dances he shows Igor his slave girls "from across the Caspian Sea" and invites him to choose one. Despotism, erotic fantasies, sensual temptation as a threat to the rationality and vigor of the Western male—all these oriental themes are present here. *Prince Igor* is the classical example of an ideology legitimizing the military drive to the East: the theory of Western superiority, on racial grounds, over the Eastern nations, giving Russia the right (or the duty) to subdue them.[11]

Another well-known example is Borodin's orchestral work *In the Steppes of Central Asia* (1880–81). Although the peaceful character of the music does not immediately suggest an underlying aggressive ideology, the work appears in a new light when we recall the occasion for which it was intended: the twenty-fifth anniversary of the reign of Alexander II. *In the Steppes of Central Asia,* in short, is a tribute to the tsarist policy of conquest. The work once again plays up the orientalist polarity: the Russian melody is active, bright, and rationally presented; the Eastern is passive, sensual, and hedonistic. The languorous tone of the English horn is a frequently used code. The idea that orientals with their passivity were no match for the decisiveness of the Russian people is expressed even more overtly in the orchestral work Musorgsky wrote for the same occasion, *The Capture of Kars* (1880), a commemoration of one of the rare episodes of Russian success against the Turks in the Crimean War. The outer movements are energetic, martial, and triumphant, the middle movement again an exemplification of oriental sensuality.[12]

The musical characteristics of orientalism are not confined to the use of authentic Eastern melodies. Nor, indeed, is that an essential feature. Thus, while Glinka's "Georgian Song" does use an authentic melody, that does not make the song more "oriental." More crucial are the musical conventions these composers added to the oriental material. For them, orientalism involved the use of very specific musical codes, which fall into two groups: those representing Dionysian intoxication, on the one hand, and those representing hedonistic sensuality, on the other. The first group relies on obsessive rhythms, note repetitions, climactic effects, and accelerating tempi, an example being Balakirev's piano fantasy Islamey (1869). In orchestral works, percussion instruments with an Eastern sound are added, for instance the Turkish drum or the tambourine. The codes for sensual longing follow a different course. The rhythm is unpredictable, with numerous metrical irregularities, often masking the meter and blurring the pulse, and composite rhythms; the phrasing is irregular and based on long passages with many repeat notes, augmented and diminished intervals, motifs revolving around frequently recurring notes, and extensive decorations or, in vocal music, melismas. The texture combines pedal harmonies with chromatic movement, often in the middle voices, and more particularly chromatic passing notes in both directions between the Vth and VIth degrees. In the instrumentation, sonorities with a languorous, sensual association predominate, with the English horn given pride of place. This type of musical hedonism is so strongly associated with sexual desire that Balakirev criticized Chaikovsky for his use of the oriental code in the love theme of Romeo and Juliet, arguing that the Veronese lovers were European, not Persian. In other words, their love had a spiritual dimension and was not purely sexual.[13]

Two great orchestral works are wholly dominated by orientalism: Rimsky-Korsakov's Antar and Balakirev's Tamara. In Antar, which is set in the Eastern (Arabian) world, Rimsky-Korsakov highlights two different styles, one Western (Russian), the other oriental. The first represents the male protagonist, Antar; the second his female counterpart, the peri Gul Nazar. Although the work does not involve a major struggle between the two, the female sensuality exerts a paralyzing, indeed destructive, influence on the male. In the end the peri takes Antar's life in a last embrace.

Balakirev gives free rein to a misogynous view of oriental women in

*Tamara.* Originally he intended to write a *lezginka,* a Caucasian dance, modeled on Glinka (*Ruslan and Lyudmila*), but he later fell under the spell of a poem by Mikhaíl Lermontov about the beautiful Tamara, who entices travelers to her tower beside the gorge of Daryal and allows them to savor a night of sensual delights, only to kill them and fling their bodies into the River Terek. Balakirev finished the draft in 1869 but did not complete the work until 1882. In 1898 he revised the orchestration once more, using oriental codes to the full—those of Dionysian intoxication and of sensual lust. *Tamara* is one of the masterpieces of the musical portrayal of dark, demonic eroticism. Rimsky-Korsakov's better-known symphonic suite, *Sheherazade* (1888), is greatly indebted to it.

## HARMONIC EXPLORATIONS

In the harmonic field, the *kuchka* developed two distinct idioms: the diatonic harmonization of folk song or of folk-song imitations, on the one hand, and chromatic or "fantastic" harmony, on the other.

The diatonic style was Balakirev's own creation. Following his trip along the Volga in 1860, he looked for a method of harmonizing Russian folk songs without destroying their distinguishing features. In his folk-song collection of 1866 he applied this idea consistently. To preserve the songs' tonal ambiguity he avoided dominant chords and modulations as much as possible. The leading note was seldom used. The unpredictable rhythm of the *protyazhnaya* was underlined by an unpredictable harmonic rhythm. Chords were kept static for a time, only to spring into sudden movement. Pedal notes give the harmony a floating impression, making the melodic contours more obvious. This aspect is complemented with a fanciful use of textures. Balakirev's folk-song arrangements served as a model for those of Rimsky-Korsakov, Lyadov, and Chaikovsky. The diatonic style also dominated the folk-song imitations of Musorgsky, Borodin, and Rimsky-Korsakov.

The other idiom was chromatic harmony, developed in the footsteps of Glinka and Liszt. In *Ruslan and Lyudmila* Glinka had used the whole-tone scale as the leitmotif of the evil dwarf Chernomor. This kind of "artificial" harmony was later continued with precisely the same function: as a code for the fantastic, for the demonic, and for black magic. We rediscover the whole-tone scale, for instance, in Dargomïzhsky's *The Stone Guest,* in Borodin's song "The Sleeping Princess," in Rimsky-Korsakov's *Antar,* down to Chaikovsky's *Queen of Spades,* where it is particularly noticeable during the appearance of the dead Countess's ghost.

Rimsky-Korsakov extended the harmonic arsenal with the octatonic scale, in which half tones alternate with whole tones. He found the model in Liszt's *Ce qu'on entend sur la montagne,* and first used it himself in *Sadko.* The harmonic functions of the whole-tone scale and the octatonic scale are comparable. Both originate in the nineteenth-century use of sequences of thirds, prevalent in the work of Schubert and Liszt. In a descending sequence of major thirds, the whole-tone scale originates in the passing notes in the bass. If the descending sequence uses minor thirds, the passing notes give rise to the octatonic scale.[14] As soon as he had discovered this functional parallel, Rimsky-Korsakov was able to use the octatonic scale as an alternative to the whole-tone scale in the representation of fantastic subjects. Examples are *Sadko,* the symphonic poem *Skazka* (The tale), and the many magical moments in his later fairy-tale operas.

Another famous innovation was the association of unexpected chords by means of common notes. Once again Glinka provided the model with Chernomor's grotesque march in *Ruslan and Lyudmila.* Musorgsky carried the process furthest, especially in his imitation of the sound of bells in *Boris Godunov.* Here he used the alternation of two dominant-seventh chords, with the tonics a tritone apart. The resulting curious sonority is due to the fact that the two chords share two notes, which in their turn constitute the tritone. The formula (which Musorgsky did not invent: the prototype occurs in one of Serov's works, the hunting scene in the third act of his opera *Rogneda*)[15] was copied on countless occasions.

In nineteenth-century Russian music, the two harmonic systems were used side by side. Each had its own function: the portrayal of the national character, on the one hand, and of fantastic subjects, on the other. The two idioms were never confused. This polarity can be seen in numerous works, the clearest example being Musorgsky's piano cycle *Pictures at an Exhibition,* in which each picture belongs unequivocally to one of the two types.

## REALISM

"These are the witches glorifying Satan—as you can see, stark naked, barbarous and filthy": that is how Musorgsky described one of the themes in his orchestral work *Night on Bald Mountain* (1867).[16] We can speak of realism in instrumental music when it is associated with visual representations. *Night on Bald Mountain* is one of the best examples of visual suggestion in music. The subject matter is hardly realistic at all, dealing rather with the realm of the fantastic and the demonic. However, Musorgsky's music is meant to convey as vividly as possible the visual images attached to the scene. If we can call the music realistic, it is precisely because its suggestive quality is developed to perfection.[17] Musorgsky started with a plan for an opera about witches, the inspiration for which was Matvey Khotinsky's *Witchcraft and Mysterious Phenomena in Modern Times*. Nothing came of the opera. Instead Musorgsky produced an orchestral piece, which he tried twice to insert into an opera, the first time into *Mlada*—a collective project on which the entire *kuchka* (with the exception of Balakirev) would collaborate in 1872, but which was eventually abandoned—and the second time into his own unfinished *Fair at Sorochintsï*. Although Gogol's story by the same name did not, strictly speaking, provide any justification for including a witches' Sabbath, Musorgsky got around the obstacle by casting *Night on Bald Mountain* as the hallucinatory dream of one of the characters.

The orchestral version of 1867 is divided into four episodes, corresponding to the four stages of a witches' Sabbath, which Musorgsky detailed as the assembly of the witches, the cortege of Satan, the "black mass," and the actual Sabbath, or *sabbat*. He described the succession of scenes as follows:

> If [my] memory has not played me false, the witches used to assemble on this mountain . . . gossiping, playing lewd pranks, awaiting their superior—Satan. Upon his arrival, they, the witches, would form a circle around the throne, where he sat in the guise of a he-goat, and would carol glory to their superior. When Satan became frenzied enough at the witches' glorification, he would order the start of the sabbat, whereupon he would select the witches that caught his fancy to satisfy his needs.—So this is the way I did it. In the title of the composition I have indicated its plot. . . . Actually, the witches' sabbat starts from the appearance of the little imps, because the unholy glorification, according to the legends, was included in the body of the sabbat, but I have given the episodes separate titles for greater ease in conveying this musical form—because it is new.[18]

The form follows the narrative sequence of the scenes, with the structure reflecting a process of continuous development. Motifs are constantly varied and regrouped; the orchestral effects, which constitute an integral part of the narrative process, are bold. The portrayal of visual effects is achieved in several ways. The music imitates the behavior of the witches, their chatter and gossip, their procession and wild dances. The crude harmonies and rough sounds suggest the witches' ugliness, their filthy and repulsive appearance, by association. The chaotic plan, finally, reflects the barbaric disarray of the scene. Musorgsky mentioned Franz Liszt's *Totentanz* as the model for his composition, but a more obvious model could be found in the Russian repertoire: the bacchanalia of the Assyrians in Serov's *Judith*. As ever, Musorgsky refused to acknowledge Serov's influence, but it is too obvious to be fortuitous. In the use of empirical crudities as a means of depicting ugliness and barbarity, Serov was Musorgsky's unacknowledged but indisputable master.

The imitation of visual impressions and actions is the basis of another well-known study in musical realism as well: Musorgsky's *Pictures at an Exhibition* (1874). This work—an extensive piano cycle, a succession of characteristic miniatures—might have been modeled on comparable cycles by Schumann, such as *Papillons* and *Carnival*. What renders Musorgsky's work unique, however, is that all the numbers are based on concrete visual representations, namely drawings or watercolors by the painter Victor Gartman (Hartmann).

Some of the "pictures" are as bizarre as *Night on Bald Mountain*: "Gnomus," for instance, or "The Hut on Hen's Legs." Gnomus is a fantasy character—a limping gnome with bandy legs, presented by Gartman in the form of a nutcracker. The hut on hen's legs is the abode of a well-known fairy-tale character, the witch Baba-Yaga; the hen's legs help her to face and attack anyone who ventures near. Lost children thus come to a sad end. The large stone mortar in which the witch grinds up the bones of the children is also her carriage. Gartman used the motif of the hut in the design of a clockwork mechanism. It was Musorgsky's idea to include the ride in the stone mortar. "The Ballet of the Unhatched Chicks" was originally a scene for which Gartman had designed the sets and the costumes. "Il vecchio castello" is a more poetic image of a medieval castle, complete with a troubadour singing a serenade under a balcony.

Realistic pictures are "The Tuileries," which portrays a noisy squabble between children; "Bydlo," a huge Polish ox-cart; "Limoges le marché" or "La grande nouvelle," a scene with women gossiping in the market; and "Catacombae, sepulcrum romanum," a visit to the Paris catacombs. "'Samuel' Goldenberg and 'Schmuÿle'" is a crude example of Russian anti-Semitism. It used to be thought that it portrayed two Jews, one rich and the other poor. That interpretation goes back to Vladimir Stasov, who discovered that Gartman had never made a drawing of two Jews. He accordingly assumed that Musorgsky had based his piece on two separate portraits. Yet the form of the title indicates that "Samuel" and "Schmuÿle" are one and the same person. The first name is European, the second is Yiddish. If that interpretation is correct, then the underlying anti-Semitic meaning is shocking, to say the least, the piece reflecting, on the one hand, the respectable outward behavior of the character and, on the other, his contemptible inner nature. In other words, no matter how civilized, how European, he may seem to be, he remains an inferior Jew under the skin. Unfortunately, the many manifestations of anti-Semitism in Musorgsky's correspondence support this interpretation.[19] "The Knight's Gate (in the Ancient Capital, Kiev)," finally, was based on Gartman's design for a triumphal gate in Kiev. When Alexander II escaped an assassination attempt in 1866, a competition was launched for a monument to honor the tsar. The design Gartman submitted incorporated the representation of an ancient Slavic helmet and a woman's headdress, or *kokoshnik*, within the domes of a triumphal gate.

In the overall design of *Pictures at an Exhibition*, Musorgsky presented bizarre and poetic pictures in turn. He fused the parts into a coherent whole by means of a recurring piece, which he named "Promenade." The music was intended to evoke the spectator at the exhibition. The formal tension of the cycle is due in large part to the inventive manner in which Musorgsky used the theme. At the start of the piece, it is presented at length. It thereafter appears in abbreviated form. At the fifth repetition it is again used in extended form, thus serving as an important signpost in the overall scheme. After that it no longer appears, save when motivically incorporated into the pictures themselves. This is a discerning move, indicating that the spectator has ceased to be an outsider and has entered the world portrayed in the music.

In the presentation of the bizarre pictures, Musorgsky uses every possible harmonic code representing the world of the fantastic: whole-tone motifs, octatonic scales, modal or mixed keys, juxtaposition of unexpected chords. The diatonic style of the poetic tableaux and of the "Promenade" serves as a clear contrast, the "Promenade" being one of the most beautiful *protyazhnaya* stylizations in the Russian repertoire. In "The Knight's Gate," Musorgsky imitates the festive sound of Russian bells.

Insofar as the term "realistic" is applicable at all to *Night on Bald Mountain* or *Pictures at an Exhibition,* it refers more to the close relationship between music and visual representation than to the portrayal of everyday life. The musical portrayal of real life is, however, present in a small but important number of Musorgsky's songs, whose realism relies on two principles: dramatization and imitation of the spoken language.

Dramatization is the basis of several of Musorgsky's character sketches, some of which are drawn from life. The scene found in "Darling Savishna" (1866) is something Musorgsky is said to have seen with his own eyes: a *yuródivïy* (holy fool or village idiot) pleading vainly for a young girl's love. In "The Ragamuffin" (1867), we are made witness to the caustic scorn with which street urchins mock passersby. Here an old woman is their target. Other examples are "The Seminarian" (1866) and "Gathering Mushrooms" (1867). In the first, a seminarian recites his Latin exercises while his thoughts stray to the priest's daughter and to the scolding he can expect for having looked too long in her direction during the service. (This song was banned by the censor, an obstacle Musorgsky tried to overcome by having it published in Leipzig. However, the copies were confiscated at the border.) In the second song a young woman gives free rein to her fantasy of making love to her young friend and of helping her aged husband out of this world, by wondering what would happen if she were to serve the husband a broth of poisonous mushrooms.

Poverty is the subject of "The Orphan" (1868) and of "Yeryomushka's Cradle Song" (1868). What social concern there is to be found in Musorgsky's songs—an aspect the commentators tend to play up—lies in these two examples. Musorgsky's other portraits of the common people (for instance, his "Kalistratushka" of 1864) often have a distant, ironical tone.

Some of his songs are downright sarcastic. In "A Society Tale" (1867)—better known under Stasov's title of "The Billy Goat"—Musorgsky berates the stupidity of a young girl who takes to her heels on seeing a billy goat but does not shrink from marrying a wizened hunchback: an old goat in human form. Laughter at the girl has even been written into the vocal part. A similar mocking tone can be found in "Mephisto's Song of the Flea" from Goethe's *Faust* (1879).

Musorgsky was not the first to write satirical songs. He followed the course set out by Dargomïzhsky. In his genre sketches, however, Dargomïzhsky aimed his shafts particularly at injustices of military or social rank (for instance in "The Worm," "The Miller," and "The Old Corporal"), while Musorgsky extended his character sketches to all sections of the population.

In some of his songs, Musorgsky uses musical parody as a satirical tool. In "The Seminarian" he parodies motifs from church music. In "The Classicist" (1867) he pokes fun at Famintsïn, the conservative critic, with the help of a dry-as-dust classical style, using classical stereotypes at their dullest. The middle section serves to interpret the way conservatives experience contemporary modern music: as chaotic noise. The musical opponents of the *kuchka* are given a dressing-down in "Rayok" (The peepshow, 1870). A *rayok* was a fairground attraction in which the spectators were shown pictures on a roll while being treated to a satirical commentary by a *rayoshnik*. Musorgsky parades all his opponents: Zaremba, Rostislav, Famintsïn, Serov, and Yelena Pavlovna. "Rayok" was not Musorgsky's own idea: it was a commission from Stasov, and it reflects his views rather than Musorgsky's. Stasov's wish above all was to strike out at Serov.[20]

Mimicry of the spoken language—of the varieties of speech patterns and their context, including such features as age, character, and social class—is the second principle of Musorgsky's songs. Such close imitation necessarily means that the music differs from one character to the next. In "Svetik Savishna," for example, he uses an uninterrupted 5/4 pattern, without any breathing pauses, to portray the monotonous, chanting, pleading tone used by the *yuródivïy*. The 5/4 rhythm is an ironic parody of a wedding song. Because of the absence of breathing pauses, this song is generally said to be both unsingable and a poor composition. But that is the whole point: the more breathless the singer becomes, the better he succeeds in portraying the *yuródivïy*'s voice. In "The Orphan," Musorgsky imitates an imploring, begging tone. In "Yeryomushka's Cradle Song," an ordinary Russian mother is characterized by slow, irregular phrases, while the motif "*bayu bai*" is closer to the sound of weeping than to the soothing tones of a lullaby.

The height of virtuosity in the reproduction of the spoken language is the song cycle *The Nursery* (1870). In it, Musorgsky portrays the behavior of a child, with its typical turns of speech, games, desires, and mischief. The child's relationship to the *nyanya*, or nurse, is paramount, a factor that shows that the scenes are played out in an aristocratic milieu. Together with the opera fragment *Marriage*, *The Nursery* marks the high point of Musorgsky's realism, based on the observation and imitation of the spoken language and reflecting its variability.

## VOCAL LYRICISM

In 1872, when Musorgsky fell under the spell of the aristocratic poet Count Arseniy Golenishchev-Kutuzov—a relationship that would lead to their sharing a home for fourteen months from the end of March 1874—he came face to face with an aesthetic that was the antithesis of the *kuchka*'s. Stasov was highly suspicious of this new influence. Golenishchev-Kutuzov was an opponent of realism and of social commitment in art, valuing aristocratic aestheticism and subjectivism in their stead. When Musorgsky began to show signs of sharing that philoso-phy, Stasov accused him of betrayal. Later Stasov would blame the ob-vious change of direction in Musorgsky's work for an alleged decline in the quality of his oeuvre, attributing both to the influence of drink. By then, however, Musorgsky's confidence in his compositions no longer de-pended on Stasov's approval. The phase of consistent realism—Stasov's aesthetic—was no more than transitory with Musorgsky.

Musorgsky's later songs did bear witness to a fundamental change in direction, which has not always been recognized as such, partly because Musorgsky went to great trouble to present his development as a coherent logical process. He called his new vocal style "rationally justified melody," describing it as a melodic manner of writing that reflected the intona-tions of speech. What was new was the fact that his songs were thence-forward conceived far more melodically. The close tie that had previously existed between melody and such linguistic characteristics as stress, speech rhythm, and manner of speaking became considerably looser. Ab-stract melodic style gained the upper hand over realism both in prosody and in the use of idiom. The importance of stress decreased; the rhythm was simplified and became the subject of an autonomous musical style. Strictly realistic declamation made way for lyricism and cantability.

Great though Musorgsky's reputation as a musical realist may be, his change in direction need not surprise us. From the beginning of his ca-reer he had been writing lyrical songs, some of them even along the lines of the salon romances, with their typical waltz rhythms and other fash-ionable formulas. A good example is the romance "Tell Me Why, Fair Maiden" (1858). Well-known examples of early lyrical songs are "Night" (two versions, 1864) and "The Wish" (1866). A model of *protyazhnaya* stylization is the early song "Where Art Thou, Little Star?" (1857). The poetry of the lyrical songs is romantically subjective. The other composers in the *kuchka* were equally interested in vocal lyricism. Before he started exploiting Glinka's oriental model, Balakirev worked in the style of the salon romances of Varlamov and Gurilyov. Most of the early songs of Rimsky-Korsakov and Borodin are lyrical in conception. Some employ melodic recitative, without, however, drawing the conclusions Mu-sorgsky did in a work such as *The Nursery*.

In Golenishchev-Kutuzov, Musorgsky found the ideal partner to ex-press the lyrical and subjective side of his personality. The two most im-pressive results of this partnership are the song cycles *Sunless* and *Songs and Dances of Death*.

Despite the greater abstraction of the melody, *Sunless* (1874) is as uncompromising in content as Musorgsky's more realistic songs. The cycle is a reflection of subjective introspection. Golenishchev-Kutuzov's poems are extremely pessimistic, with piece after piece expressing disillusionment and hopelessness. Every recall of past joy causes pain and deepening despair. It is the poetry of a morbid world-weariness. The vocal style often has a marked motivic concentration. The piano texture is applied sparingly. In the last two songs the only form of coloration is found in the accompaniment: in "Elegy," in the evocation of the bells of grazing horses and the sound of the death knell; in "On the River," in the portrayal of the undulating movement of the water. For the rest, the strict piano accompaniment reinforces the sense of world-weariness and abandonment.

The dark content of *Sunless* is often associated with Musorgsky's own life. It is usually asserted that the disappointments he encountered in the creation of *Boris Godunov* had embittered him and driven him finally into alcoholism. But that is a Stasovian myth. It is far more probable that Musorgsky's pessimism stemmed from the impoverishment of his aristocratic family in the wake of the Emancipation, when they were badly hit economically by Alexander II's abolition of serfdom. Musorgsky's contacts with Golenishchev-Kutuzov increased his aristocratic nostalgia.[21] In 1877, Musorgsky continued the somber atmosphere of *Sunless* in five songs with texts by Count Alexey Tolstoy.

The cycle *Songs and Dances of Death* (1875–77) reflects a different approach. The poetry is no longer introspective but a balladlike mixture of storytelling and drama. Like the realistic songs, this cycle portrays different characters, although the portraits are not drawn from life but are based on fantasy. The central theme of the four songs, the omnipotence of death, is elaborated with the help of the various characters. Each poem has its own poetical framework, its own atmosphere. The variations in the expression of the theme are a model of the Golenishchev-Kutuzov aesthetic approach. In each of the four situations, Death appears in a different human form. In the first, he comes to the aid of a mother who is rocking her feverish child in vain, and promises to lull the child to sleep. The mother takes fright but cannot prevent Death from singing his final lullaby. In the second scene Death appears as a knight serenading an ailing girl. He tempts her into a fatal embrace. In the third song an exhausted and drunken peasant stumbles through a snow-covered forest. Death dances the *trepak* with him before burying him in a bed of snow. The last song takes us to a battlefield, on which Death appears in the shape of a triumphant field marshal addressing his fallen soldiers. The ending is especially gruesome: Death announces that he will dance on their graves and stamp the earth down so hard that they will never again be able to rise from the ground. There is not even a glimmer of transcendental hope in this cycle.

The first song, "Lullaby," comes closest to Musorgsky's more realistic scenes. In the others, Musorgsky evinces a greater poetic distance, which is also reflected in the musical interpretation. The second number has a regular rhythm, evoking the accompaniment to a serenade. The third uses the dance rhythm of the *trepak*. In the last song, the melodic style is highly expansive. The abstraction in the vocal line contributes to the superhuman, apocalyptic character of the vision. In the previous songs there was a degree of intimacy promising solace and deliverance, all of them involving the relationship of one individual to another. The last song, in contrast, reflects the ultimate victory of Death over a whole group and hence points to his ultimate rule over mankind as a whole.

Plate 1. The Theater Circus in St. Petersburg in 1849. It was the home of the Russian Opera until 1859, when it was destroyed by fire. The Mariyinsky Theater was then built on the site.

Plate 2. The Bolshoy Theater in Moscow, about 1856.

Plate 3.   The Mariyinsky Theater in St. Petersburg at the beginning of the twentieth century. The statue on the left is of Glinka.

Plate 4.   The interior of the Mariyinsky Theater.

Plate 5. Musorgsky's *Khovanshchina:* the confrontation between Golitsïn, Khovansky, and Dosifey in the 1950 production at the Moscow Bolshoy Theater.

Plate 6.　A scene from Act II of *Swan Lake* by Pyotr Chaikovsky, at the first performance in Moscow in 1877.

Plates 7a–b.   Carlotta Brianza as Aurora and Pavel Gerdt as Désiré in the first performance of Chaikovsky's *Sleeping Beauty*, 1890.

Plate 8.   Nadezhda Zabela-Vrubel as Volkhova in *Sadko* by Rimsky-Korsakov, in the production by Savva Mamontov's Private Opera Company, ca. 1898.

Plate 9.    Fyodor Ivanovich Chaliapin in 1913 as Boris Godunov
in Musorgsky's opera.

Plate 10.   Tamara Karsavina as Zobéide in the ballet version of Rimsky-Korsakov's *Sheherazade*, choreographed by Mikhaíl Fokine in 1910. The role was originally danced by Ida Rubinstein.

Plate 11.   A scene from Act II of Rimsky-Korsakov's *Snegurochka* in the 1978 Bolshoy Theater production.

Plate 12.   Prince Vsevolod and the Maiden Fevroniya in a Bolshoy production of Rimsky-Korsakov's *The Legend of the Invisible City of Kitezh* in 1983. The costumes are based on the neonationalist style (cf. Plate 17).

Plate 13.   Sergey Rachmaninoff working at his Ivanovka
country estate, 1910.

Plate 14.  Design by Nikolai Roerich for the Polovtsian Dances in Borodin's
*Prince Igor* for the performance in Paris in 1909.

Plate 15.    Tamara Karsavina in the title role of Stravinsky's *Firebird*, 1912.

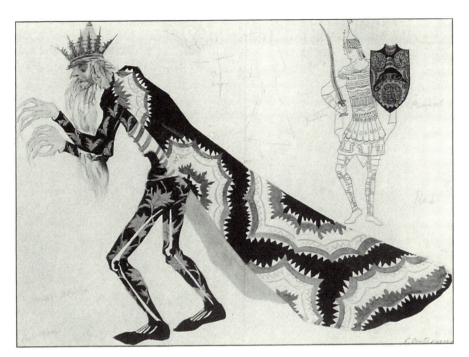

Plate 16.   Costume design by Natalya Goncharova for Kashchey in
*The Firebird*, 1926.

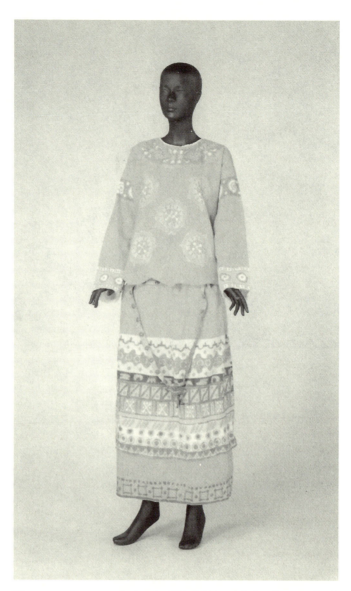

Plate 17.   Costume design by Nikolai Roerich for the sacrificed
maiden in the original production of Stravinsky's *Rite of Spring*
in 1913.

## CHAPTER SIX

# "Truth in the Realm of the Pseudo"

## Russian Opera

"Operatic matters now stand with us on a higher plane than in western Europe"—with this declaration of 1889 César Cui looked back on a period of intense activity in the world of opera.[1] The assertion certainly lacks modesty, and it is evidence of a good share of provincial self-importance: such shameless disavowal of the innovations of Wagner and Verdi could only take place in an isolated milieu. Yet Cui's statement reveals something else as well, namely, that Russian composers took opera very seriously. At the time, Russian artists were expected to be morally as well as socially committed. Composers were anxious to prove that they, too, could discharge that responsibility, not least in their operas.

As long as Italian opera continued to dominate the repertoire, Russian composers were unable to force an entry into the establishment. Their breakthrough was a long and laborious process, and their difficult situation explains the extreme views they propounded. As against the predominant Italian model, they embraced a different opera aesthetic. Music historians have long appreciated the important role of Dargomïzhsky's reformist opera *The Stone Guest* in this process, and in the emergence of Musorgsky's opera style in particular. Less well known is the influence of Serov and Cui, composers who were to become mere footnotes in the history of music. The historical importance of their work is, however, beyond any doubt.[2] Dargomïzhsky, Serov, and Cui were the indispensable links between *A Life for the Tsar* and such masterpieces as *Boris Godunov* and *Eugene Onegin*.

Opera has never been the work of composers alone. In Russia as elsewhere, writers and historians, too, helped shape the profile of a national opera. For lovers of Russian literature it will perhaps come as a surprise to learn that such literary figures as Fyodor Dostoyevsky and Alexander Ostrovsky were involved in the process of the creation of operas.

The history of Russian opera in the 1860s and 1870s begins with the work of Dargomïzhsky, Serov, and Cui, whose contributions may be called "experiments in realism." The subsequent "classic" Russian opera can be divided into two genres: historical opera and Gogolian comedy. Both genres are to be found in the work of Musorgsky, Rimsky-Korsakov, and Chaikovsky, the first in *Boris Godunov, Pskovityanka, The Oprichnik,* and *Khovanshchina,* and the second in *Vakula the Smith, May Night,* and *Sorochintsï Fair.* We will end this chapter with an opera sui generis: Chaikovsky's *Eugene Onegin.*

## EXPERIMENTS IN REALISM

### ALEXANDER DARGOMÏZHSKY

Dargomïzhsky was not a member of the *kuchka* when he started work on *The Stone Guest* (1866–69). He belonged to an older generation and, like Glinka, was an aristocratic dilettante. He already had two conventional operas to his credit, *Esmeralda* (1839) and *The Triumph of Bacchus* (1847), when he scored his greatest success with the national opera *Rusalka* in 1855. His fame was short-lived, however, and, somewhat disillusioned, he decided to make a private experiment, one not intended for performance on the big stage: the setting of Pushkin's play *The Stone Guest* to music. Rather than fashioning the tragedy into a traditional operatic libretto, he would use the text verbatim, as Pushkin had written it. When the members of the *kuchka* heard of his plan, they started to take interest. It was not long before they declared that a major revolution was afoot. What Dargomïzhsky had started by way of a pastime, they saw as the implementation of their ideals.

*The Stone Guest,* one of Pushkin's "little tragedies," is a retelling of the Don Juan legend. Pushkin focused on the relationship between Don Juan and Donna Anna and on the Commendatore's revenge, the essential difference from the *Don Giovanni* of Mozart and Da Ponte being that, in Pushkin's version, the Commendatore is not Donna Anna's father but her husband. A second difference is that in the cemetery scene, Don Juan does not invite the Commendatore for supper but instructs him to keep watch while he himself makes love to Donna Anna. The two operas end the same way, however: the Commendatore arrives for the appointment and consigns Don Juan to the depths of hell.

Dargomïzhsky's score follows Pushkin's text closely in an arioso vocal style. The composer, hoping to avoid any reference to existing musical forms, tried to devise a new musical idea for every phrase in the text. That in itself, however, does not render the declamation of the vocal parts realistic. The vocal line, which remains lyrical in essence, is no copy of the spoken language. Realism therefore lies not in the text setting as such, but rather in the avoidance of traditional musical forms. In this Dargomïzhsky's style recalls the carefully composed romances of his last period.[3] This quality did not escape the keen eye of Hermann Laroche, who wrote: "*The Stone Guest* is an excellent study in recitative, but [it is] that particular recitative-in-song, which is much closer to cantilena than to the Italian recitative, and constitutes a peculiarity of the Russian school (its first examples appeared in *A Life for the Tsar*)."[4]

The orchestra plays a subordinate role in Dargomïzhsky's work. It accompanies the singers and to some extent controls the flow of the music, thus creating a measure of musical regularity, but it develops no themes of its own. For Dargomïzhsky, opera remained the singers' province. He absolutely rejected symphonic treatment of the orchestra based on Wagner's model. He viewed abstract musical logic as a straitjacket that unnecessarily restricts the expressive possibilities of vocal music. To him, music had to be able to respond freely to every word and to every emotion.[5]

If we call Dargomïzhsky's opera realistic, we must specify on what that realism is based. It cannot be on subject or style: *The Stone Guest* is a romantic tale with supernatural and fantastic elements (a talking statue, for example), and the style is lyrical, indeed elegant. No, the realism lies in the method: the building of an opera upon an existing play, with the musical drama obeying the same laws as the spoken play. The composer thus interprets the literary text but adds no operatic conventions. This type of composition has entered history under the name of *opéra dialogué*.

Musorgsky adopted Dargomïzhsky's librettoless method in *Marriage* (1868), but took a different approach to it, as may be seen in his choice of subject. Pushkin's *The Stone Guest* still had ties with the world of opera, not least of which were those with Mozart's *Don Giovanni*. If *The Stone Guest* was a reformist opera, then *Marriage* was true anti-opera. In Gogol's play by the same name, Musorgsky found a subject that differed as much as possible from everything connected with traditional opera. It is a curious comedy of a man who is not sure whether

he should get married but, persuaded by a friend, finally makes a pro-
posal. However, he is then seized by terror and leaps from a window.
Gogol's prose is a grotesque exaggeration of natural speech. For Musorgsky, this was an additional challenge.

The speed with which he worked on this project is a measure of his
enthusiasm. He started on 11 June 1868 and finished the first act (the
only one he was to compose) on 8 July. He described the score as "an
experiment in dramatic music in prose." The term "experiment" had a
scientific ring to it. Indeed, Musorgsky's approach was almost positivistic: "My music must be the artistic reproduction of human speech in all
its subtlest twistings; that is, the sounds of human speech, as the exte-
rior manifestation of thought and feeling, must, without exaggeration
or strain, become music—truthful, accurate, *but* (read: which means)
artistic, in the highest sense artistic."[6]

Musorgsky no longer relied on a lyrical impulse, but on the intonation of human speech. While Dargomïzhsky tried to give every word its
own musical shape, Musorgsky attempted to copy the intonation, stress,
rhythm, and tempo of the spoken language with scientific precision—
which certainly did not simplify the vocal parts. Musorgsky worked at
length with augmented and diminished intervals (the very intervals that
are generally considered to be "unsingable"). The rhythm and tempo of
the delivery change continually, making the rhythmic complexity of some
passages difficult to follow in every detail.

Musorgsky never turned his back on *Marriage* and nursed hopes of
completing the opera. Yet he felt trapped by the severe limitations he had
imposed on himself. "*Marriage* is a cage in which I am imprisoned until tamed, and then on to freedom," he wrote to Lyudmila Shestakova,
Glinka's sister.[7] He found that freedom in Pushkin's *Boris Godunov*. In
this extension of *Marriage*, Musorgsky relied once again directly on the
literary text, without first molding it into a traditional opera libretto. But
the road to *Boris Godunov* did not run through *Marriage* alone. We can
see this in a scene that does not occur in Pushkin's play: the madness of
Boris following his dramatic encounter with Prince Shuisky. The madness scene had a specific model: the delirium of Holofernes in *Judith*,
Alexander Serov's first opera.

### ALEXANDER SEROV

Serov was not a great composer. His inspiration was shallow, his style
was eclectic, and his inadequate trial-and-error technique rendered him

unable to translate his ideas into music of lasting value. Yet *Judith* (1861–63) is not without merit.[8] The music-drama conception is strong and contains moments of great dramatic force.

The opera deals with the biblical story of Judith, the Hebrew woman who saves her people from the Assyrians by seducing their king, Holofernes, and then killing him. Serov's opera is based on two sources: *Giuditta,* a play by the Italian writer Paolo Giacometti, and Friedrich Hebbel's tragedy *Judith.* Yet Serov's version differs from both. Unlike *Giuditta,* Serov's opera dispenses with all melodramatic elements (Judith has no lover, and her relationship with Holofernes is not threatened by a jealous odalisque), from which it seems clear that he tried to avoid stock opera melodramatics. Compared with Hebbel's characters, Serov's lack psychological subtlety. Hebbel's Judith is a tragic figure: She has an inner struggle to wage, and her psyche suffers as a result. Instead of savoring her triumph, she begs the elders to kill her. She would sooner die than bear Holofernes a child.

Serov loved and admired Hebbel's play, yet he reduced his characters to cardboard figures because he believed that the laws of spoken drama were not the same as those of music drama. Serov's Judith waged no inner struggle but rather acted in full accord with her mission. Serov thought that opera lent itself better to capturing the biblical simplicity of the story than a stage play, which must take psychological nuances into account.

Unlike Dargomïzhsky, Serov attached no importance to individual words. Instead he allowed the musical effect to determine the drama. In that sense his conception of opera was closer to the traditional approach than to Dargomïzhsky's realism. The crucial departure from traditional opera lay in Serov's rejection of self-contained musical numbers. To him, intrinsic musical worth was not an end in itself. Music had to adapt directly to each dramatic situation. Moreover, he eschewed musical beauty if the drama did not warrant it. The choruses of the starving Hebrews in no way resemble the elegiac refinement with which they sing of their plight in Verdi's *Nabucco.* Serov wanted to depict exhaustion and so kept the choruses rough and unmelodic.

Serov's dramatic gifts are best appreciated in the crucial scene of the confrontation between Holofernes and Judith—neither of whom has anything in common with Glinka's bel canto roles. Holofernes, significantly, is the first dramatic bass part in the Russian repertoire. In his dialogue with Judith, Holofernes continually alternates expressions of cruelty and of sensual desire. Stupefied with drink, he becomes delirious and finally falls asleep. At that point the musical action stops. To the accompaniment of sustained chords, Judith first consults Bagoas, the king's confidant, and then Avra, her own servant. This moment of musical stasis constitutes the background against which Judith musters courage for her deed. Out of this protracted stagnation there gradually emerges the energy that will lead to the denouement. From the manner in which Serov depicts her, it appears that Judith is not swayed by personal hatred but is following the directives of a higher power. The composer sustains this exalted emotion to the climax, the moment when Judith kills Holofernes. There follows no jubilant aria or any other expression of triumph. Instead the women simply retreat, immediately and hastily. Serov reserves the victory jubilation for the grand finale of the fifth act.

*Judith*, though warmly received in St. Petersburg, did not bring Serov the international recognition he had hoped for. Wagner and Liszt greeted the score with scorn. The Russian intelligentsia advised Serov to turn his attention to a national subject. "Write an opera about your own people, Sashka! You have the talent for it. Something about your own people, something of your own, has more vitality than anything foreign," the poet Apollon Grigoryev advised.[9] That was also the view of his fellow *pochvenniki,* such as Dostoyevsky, Ostrovsky, and Yakov Polonsky, who believed that Russia had to continue growing in an organic way, that old traditions such as autocracy and orthodoxy were essential for the good of the nation. In Serov they saw the composer who could carry their views onto the stage. Polonsky therefore drew Serov's attention to the possibilities of another, Russian, story, that of Rogneda, and Dostoyevsky and Apollon Maikov helped him with the libretto.

The action takes place during a period beloved of Slavophiles and *pochvenniki:* the old Kiev dominion, which flourished in an age into which the origin of all Russian traditions was projected. Christianity was first brought to the country in 988, during the reign of Prince Vladimir. The story of *Rogneda* (1865) deals with the contrast between bloodthirsty paganism and peace-loving Christianity. Rogneda is a Varangian princess who is forced into marriage to Prince Vladimir. She bears him a son, but later assaults her husband. Vladimir spares her life out of Christian charity, which he had experienced himself when a Christian saved his life during a hunt; he forgives her and becomes converted to the new faith. Because Vladimir's conversion is looked upon as the beginning of the history of the Russian state and of the Russian nation, *Rogneda* is a paean of praise to the unity of "orthodoxy, autocracy, and nationality," the three pillars of Official Nationality, an ideology that is even more patent in *Rogneda* than it is in *A Life for the Tsar.* The opera was approved by the tsarist court and earned the composer a life annuity from the state.

In *Rogneda* the intrigue threatens to disappear under the vast number of genre scenes: idol worship, visits to witches' caves, royal hunts and feasts, the plaintive cries of captured maidens, the song of pilgrims, and so on. The result is a static representation piece far removed from Serov's own ideal of opera as drama. His opponents thus had sufficient cause to dwell on his shortcomings. Some scenes, for instance "the offering to Perun," nevertheless made a great impression and would serve as models for scenes in Rimsky-Korsakov's later fairy-tale operas.

In his third opera, *The Power of the Fiend* (1867–71), Serov abandoned romantic heroism, not least because his opponents missed no opportunity of parodying *Rogneda*. Borodin, for example, in his operetta *Bogatïri* (The heroic warriors, 1867), mercilessly mocked the world of ancient Russian warriors, demons, and gods. *The Power of the Fiend* portrays a different world: the milieu of Moscow merchants as it had become known through the realistic plays of Ostrovsky. The opera is based on a play by that author whose title may be translated as "Live Not the Way You'd Like." Ostrovsky himself was involved in writing the libretto, although his collaboration with Serov ultimately foundered. Among opera lovers, Ostrovsky owes his reputation above all to *Kát'a Kabanová,* the pioneering opera by Leoš Janáček, which is based on Ostrovsky's play *The Storm.* Had he been able to attend the première, however, Ostrovsky would not have approved of that opera, something we can deduce from the libretto he wrote for the composer Vladimir Nikitich Kashperov. For Ostrovsky, who admired Italian singing, reduced his play to a number-opera on the Italian model, with all its banalities. The fact was, Ostrovsky did not consider opera the equal of spoken drama.[10] It was for that very reason that Serov fell out with him. A disagreement over the conclusion of the opera (it required a happy ending, according to Ostrovsky; a tragic dénouement, according to Serov) put an end to their collaboration. Serov asked Peter Ivanovich Kalashnikov to finish the libretto.

*The Power of the Fiend* is a play about infidelity and jealousy against the background of the *maslenitsa,* the Russian Shrovetide carnival. The opera was an expression of *pochvennichestvo* ideals, but the treatment was different from that in *Rogneda.* The new opera did not trace the origins of Russian traditions back to mythical times, but drew on current customs, in particular on those elements that have become part of the standard image of Russia: balalaikas, the bells of Orthodox churches and monasteries, sleigh rides, snowstorms, the carnival with its street vendors and bear trainers, and so on. To convey the close links between the characters and the Russian tradition, Serov based his vocal style on the intonation of Russian folk songs. No such consistent attempt to fuse folk song into the style of an opera had been made since *A Life for the Tsar*. In *The Power of the Fiend*, folk songs serve as the representation of national identity.

The most important genre tableau was the Shrovetide carnival scene, an exuberant rendering of urban folklore and at the same time the prototype of a scene that was to become world famous in Stravinsky's *Petrushka*. In his portrayal of drunkards and street vendors, Serov dispensed with all aesthetic embellishments. The empirical harmony portraying the unpolished character of the common man points ahead to Musorgsky. Still unsurpassed is the evocative description Boris Asafyev gave of the scene:

> The archaic quartal harmony (plus minor seventh) of Russian folk songs, the E♭ clarinet tunes, the witty tracery of the piccolos over the heavy tread of the trainer and his bear, the motley mixture of rhythms, the vividly characteristic and colorful phrases of the tavern drunks, the lurching *muzhiks,* the cries of the street vendors hawking their wares—spiced mead, hot rolls, honey cakes, *bliny*—the women's shrieks and the boisterous song of strolling couples against the background of shrill commotion, alcoholic fumes, intoxication, high spirits, alongside the exuberant, joyous, buzzing stream of lively, healthy revelry. It all hums, jangles, wails and culminates dazzlingly in the wild Shrovetide procession.[11]

## CÉSAR CUI AND HIS INFLUENCE

The *kuchka* mocked Serov's operas. For them, César Cui was a greater authority in both theory and practice. Nonetheless, the two operas Cui wrote in the 1860s and 1870s demonstrate how far apart theory and practice really are. In his polemical writings, namely, Cui appeared as a champion of realism. His musical world, however, was conventional. *William Ratcliff* (1861–68) was meant to be the first opera to implement the *kuchka*'s reformist ideas to the full, but the result differed only in detail from an ordinary romantic opera. The subject, taken from a play by Heinrich Heine, is a romantic tragedy, set in a Scotland plagued by ghosts. The occasional naturalistic touch does not blend with the conventional style of the whole. Cui had little eye for the overall structure. He lost himself in detail, and the result was shallow eclecticism. Neglect of the general design for the sake of a characteristic detail was to become a typical *kuchka* failing. Rimsky-Korsakov and Musorgsky were quick to spot the danger, just as Chaikovsky did in *Vakula the Smith*. Cui's next opera, *Angelo, the Tyrant of Padua* (1871–75), also had a romantic setting. The opera, based on a drama by Victor Hugo, was composed at a time when *Boris Godunov* and *Pskovityanka* had already been written. Cui's reviews had shown he was not very taken with such works, but in *Angelo* he was unable to escape their influence. The result was a score stylistically even more incoherent than *Ratcliff*'s.

At first, Musorgsky and Rimsky-Korsakov lacked the self-confidence to question the authority of their leaders. Musorgsky echoed Cui's opinions, in particular his mocking remarks about Serov. In reality, however, Musorgsky was under Serov's spell. Influenced by *Judith*, he began work on an oriental opera of his own, *Salammbô* (1863–66, revised 1874), based on Flaubert's novel of the same title, but laid that project to one side to take up the naturalistic experiment of *Marriage*. Serov's influence on Musorgsky is clearest in the choral work *The Destruction of Sennacherib* (1866–67, revised 1874), based on a text by Byron. The subject is related to that of *Judith*: the war between the Assyrians and the Hebrews. Musically, too, there is a parallel: the first theme of the chorus is a direct copy of Holofernes' war song. No matter what his fellows in the *kuchka* claimed, Serov's example was crucial for the direction Musorgsky was to take. The combination of the dual influence of Dargomïzhsky and Serov—and here and there of Cui—was to lead to the creation of Musorgsky's first masterpiece, *Boris Godunov,* the earliest in the series of famous Russian operas that deal with historical subjects. This opera was composed in two stages, the first version being finished in 1869.

## HISTORICAL OPERA

### MUSORGSKY: *BORIS GODUNOV* (FIRST VERSION)

Historical drama gained in popularity in Russia following the publication of Karamzin's monumental *History of the Russian State,* which yielded a surfeit of historical material. During the Emancipation, interest in history was considered an intellectual duty. Historiography and historical plays served to test political and social ideas. As Vissarion Belinsky put it, "We question, nay, we interrogate the past for an explanation of our present and a hint of our future."[12] In Russian history, the reign of Ivan the Terrible (1533–84) and the Time of Troubles (1605–13) that followed held a special and irresistible attraction. The link between the two was Tsar Boris Godunov.

Boris Godunov ascended the throne in 1598, when the line of the Rurikovid dynasty, which had ruled over Russia since the ninth century, died out with Fyodor I. Upon the death of Ivan IV in 1584, his son Fyodor had been the legitimate heir to the throne. He was feeble-minded, considered unfit to rule, however, and the boyar Boris Godunov, Fyodor's brother-in-law, acted as regent. Fyodor had a half-brother, Dmitry, the son of Ivan IV and his seventh wife, Maria Nagaya. Upon being crowned, Fyodor banished Dmitry with his mother and entire family to the cathedral town of Uglich, where the boy died in 1591 following an epileptic fit—though his family insisted that the child had been murdered. When Fyodor died in 1598, Boris Godunov had himself elected tsar by the *zemsky sobor* ("Assembly of the Land"), the result of intense lobbying and manipulation of the gullible populace. The absence of a legitimate heir was without precedent in Russian history. To endorse his election as the tsar, Boris felt impelled to demand clear signs of loyalty and to install an efficient secret police service.

So much for the history as reconstructed by modern historians. Musorgsky's opera tells another story, based on Karamzin's version. In it, Boris Godunov is held responsible for the death of the tsarevich Dmitry. This version was created by rivals of Boris Godunov, including the Romanovs, who, no sooner had they themselves ascended the throne in 1613, branded Boris Godunov a murderer. There are, however, no serious grounds for that accusation, if only because the murder of the tsarevich would not have enhanced Godunov's chances of acceding to the throne. Dmitry's claim to the crown was negligible (canon law recognized just three marriages, and Maria Nagaya was Ivan's seventh wife). Moreover, Fyodor could still have fathered an heir in 1591 (the year of Dmitry's death). In any case, thanks to Karamzin, the story that Boris Godunov smoothed his path to the throne with the murder of a child became the classic literary version.

Modern historians consider the reign of Boris Godunov a relatively successful one, at least until 1601, after which Europe was afflicted by successive years of climatic cooling. For a northern country such as Russia, the result was catastrophic. A series of natural disasters resulted in harvest failures and starvation. The suffering peasants held the tsar responsible. In the midst of the social unrest a pretender to the throne appeared in Poland, claiming to be none other than the tsarevich Dmitry and supported by members of the Polish nobility. It is probable that the Romanov family, Boris's rivals, were also behind this dubious enterprise.

Against all expectations, the false Dmitry succeeded in usurping the Russian throne in 1605, a few months after Boris Godunov's death. The success of the false Dmitry was short-lived; he was murdered a year later. Then came the Time of Troubles, a period of civil war that continued until 1613 and the election of Mikhaíl Romanov as tsar.

The story of Boris and Dmitry was popular in European literature, and grew quickly into a dramatic genre of its own, with Dmitry for the most part taking the leading role. As far as music is concerned, two contributions are of particular importance: Schiller's *Demetrius* fragment (1805), which was to serve as the basis for Antonín Dvořák's opera *Dimitri;* and Alexander Pushkin's tragedy *Boris Godunov* (1825), the source of Musorgsky's opera. The role of Boris is not as prominent in Pushkin's work as the title suggests; the writer was in fact following the model used by Shakespeare in his histories, where the names of sovereigns provide the titles.

Pushkin, using Karamzin's interpretation, portrayed Boris as a just tsar, but with a crime on his conscience. Boris is smitten with guilt, a romantic anachronism introduced by Karamzin. Even had Boris been responsible for the murder, it would have been absurd to suppose that a sixteenth-century monarch would have felt "guilty" about the elimination of a political rival. The Boris of Karamzin and Pushkin considers the false Dmitry a sign of God's wrath.

There is, however, a marked difference in the ways Karamzin and Pushkin tell the story. Karamzin preaches a moral lesson, telling us that the reign of an "unlawful monarch" has disastrous consequences for his country. What positive achievements that ruler may have to his credit are no more than a hypocritical veil drawn over the criminal foundations of his reign. In Pushkin, this moralizing tone is lacking. He tells the story by snatches, in almost deliberately fragmentary form, and leaves it an open question where the truth lies. The essential motor of the story is fueled by rumor, with the murder in Uglich serving as a pretext for any who need it. The pretender to the throne is a brilliant creation by Pushkin. Like a chameleon, Grigory Otrepev, Pushkin's false Dmitry, knows how to adapt himself to any given situation. He nowhere betrays even a hint of his own character, never ceasing to sound out what others expect of him and acting accordingly.

Though Pushkin's version abounds with the common people, they play no role of any importance. As in Shakespeare, they are there largely to provide comic relief. They observe the events and comment on them, but do not influence them. "That is the boyars' affair and does not concern us," says one of the characters in the scene in which the crowd is enjoined to implore Boris to accept the crown.

In Pushkin's play, Boris Godunov does not take a prominent part. It was Musorgsky's idea to focus on him instead of on the false Dmitry. Musorgsky's opera was written in two stages, the first version being completed in 1869, the second in 1872. He conceived the original version as an *opéra dialogué* and, continuing his experiment with Gogol's *Marriage,* adopted the play as it stood, concentrating on the scenes in which Boris himself appeared. Two scenes—at the monastery and in the inn—he took over word for word. Others he compressed into five scenes, retaining as much as possible of the original dialogue. The seven resulting scenes do not constitute a balanced whole. Those at the monastery and the inn, in particular, seem somewhat out of place. In them, Musorgsky enters at length into the early fate of the Pretender, only to lose sight of him completely in the end: having leapt out of the window of the inn on the Lithuanian border, he disappears from the opera for good. It has been suggested that Musorgsky originally planned to continue the Dmitry plot with the interpolation of the "Polish scene," but he dropped the idea.[13]

The seven scenes that make up the first version of *Boris Godunov* are arranged in four acts:[14]

ACT I

First scene:     outside Novodevichy monastery
Second scene:    the coronation of Boris

ACT II

First scene:     a cell in Chudov monastery
Second scene:    an inn on the Lithuanian border

ACT III

The Terem (the tsar's apartments in the Kremlin)

ACT IV

First scene:     the square outside St. Basil's Cathedral
Second scene:    Granovitaya Palace (death of Boris)

In his first version of Boris, Musorgsky used the opera aesthetic with which he had experimented in *Marriage:* the transposition of a play directly into music, without the intermediate step of a libretto and with the minimal number of traditional opera elements, that is, without musical numbers, love duets, or divertissements. Pushkin's play, in fact, was so out of keeping with opera convention that Alexander Serov had declared it unfit as an operatic subject, not least because of the lack of love interest. That sort of subject was, however, precisely what Musorgsky needed for his frontal attack on the established genre.

In *Boris Godunov,* Musorgsky found a wealth of characters and situations that had been absent from *Marriage.* All strata of the population are represented, from the tsar to the illiterate policeman, from the patriarch to the drunken vagabond of a monk. The two scenes taken straight from Pushkin, the monastery cell and the inn, provided Musorgsky's realism with a wide range of possibilities. The music of the cell scene radiates monastic peace. The old monk, Pimen, is characterized by a singing style reminiscent of the emotionally exalted tone in which Russian poetry is often recited.[15] The gently undulating lines in the orchestra reflect the detached way in which Pimen is writing his chronicle. The ragged vagabond monks in the inn scene, Varlaam and Missail, and the obtuse policeman are sharply contrasted with the dignity of Pimen. The musical declamation of the prose text is close to normal speech. All in all, the scene is a tour de force of musical realism. Consider, for instance, Grigory's conversation with the hostess of the inn, which takes place against Varlaam's drunken rantings in the background. Grigory questions the woman about the secret route to Lithuania, and the policeman then interrogates the monks. When the policeman asks for someone to read out the tsar's warrant of arrest, which he himself is unable to do, Grigory volunteers to do so. The warrant fits his description, but he tries to throw suspicion on Varlaam by making it match the vagabond's appearance. Driven into a corner, Varlaam takes hold of the paper and tries falteringly to decipher what is written on it. When it becomes clear that the warrant is meant for Grigory, the latter jumps out of the window and escapes. The two monks and the policeman go in pursuit of him. Their voices disappear in a fade-out, a technique Musorgsky had learned from Serov.

The chorus scenes were new in comparison with those in *The Stone Guest* and *Marriage.* The opera opens with a crowd scene in which the people are being ordered to implore the tsar to accept the crown. Anything but interested, they have not the slightest idea of the importance of what is happening. Pushkin does not spare the crowd his contempt, as the following dialogue shows: "'They're all crying here. Come on, we'd better join in.'—'I'm trying to, but I can't manage it.'—'Me neither. You don't have an onion, do you? . . .'" With Musorgsky, the people fare no better. They are represented by the stupid Mityukha and the clumsy, boorish policeman, who forces the people to pray with his knout. Musorgsky portrays the scene musically by having the choruses engage in a dialogue. The scene is relieved by interruptions of the conversations by several musical "numbers": the crowd's supplication, an address by the boyar Shchelkalov on Boris's behalf, and the hymn of the crippled pilgrims. This scene, too, ends in a fade-out; the crowd disperses to the repetition of the marvelous *protyazhnaya* stylization with which the opera began.

Boris's portrait is based on three great monologues, the first delivered on the steps of the cathedral, the second in the Kremlin, and the third shortly before his death. Musorgsky's Boris is an even more tortured character than Pushkin's. In the first monologue, Boris has a premonition of threatening disaster, while with Pushkin he merely gives voice to the humble sentiments expected from a tsar upon his accession to the throne. The central monologue in Musorgsky's Kremlin scene is taken almost verbatim from Pushkin. In it the tsar, sensing great danger, voices his disappointment at the ingratitude of the people. Musorgsky moves the last lines of Pushkin's monologue to the end of the scene, which he rounds off with a gripping hallucination of his own invention in which Boris sees the murdered child before him and tries to drive it away. For the hallucination scene and the discussion with Shuisky, Musorgsky's music owed much to the model of Serov's Holofernes. The last monologue carries the theme of Boris's guilty conscience to an extreme. In this it differs strongly from the wise counsel Pushkin's Boris gives his son when he receives his tonsure—the custom associated with a tsar's surrender of his office and preparation for death. Musorgsky's Boris, in contrast, is crushed by mortal fear when he succumbs. The death knell is sounded. A chorus of monks has already started to intone the requiem, but the scene then switches to a vision of a murdered child. Boris cries out that while he still has breath he remains the tsar, and then falls dying in their midst.

Musorgsky brings out the theme of the tortured conscience more strongly than Pushkin. In his portrayal of Boris, the music goes far beyond a realistic declamation of the text, instead intensifying the expression of psychological dread and impotence. The guilt is emphasized musically in the treatment of the opera's central motif, the Dmitry motif. Musorgsky uses it twice in the cell scene, the first time as a reference to the real Dmitry—the child who had died in Uglich—and the second time to refer to Grigory Otrepev, the false Dmitry. As the motif of the real Dmitry, it is mostly in the minor; as the motif of the Pretender, it is in the major. The motifs are then interspersed throughout the scenes in which Boris appears. By virtue of the ambiguity with which Musorgsky treats them, they become a token of the deep fears the Pretender unleashes in Boris. For Boris, the distinction between what is true and what he fears becomes blurred.

Another assault on Boris's conscience comes from the *yuródivïy,* the Holy Fool. A *yuródivïy* was a kind of mendicant monk who applied the Christian commands given in the Sermon on the Mount literally, including the stipulation "Blessed are the poor in spirit." He enjoyed the privilege of being able to say everything that ordinary people had to keep to themselves. In the scene outside St. Basil's Cathedral, therefore, he flings the truth in Boris's face, calling him a Herod, someone for whose salvation the Mother of God herself does not permit anyone to pray. Here the *yuródivïy* is not a spokesman of the people, who believe that Dmitry is alive, for he knows that the tsarevich truly is dead. Instead he stands outside the people and serves, just like the Pretender, as the embodiment of Boris's guilty conscience.

Folk songs figure in the score only inasmuch as *kuchka* realism allows: they are sung by the common people and in real situations. The first version of *Boris Godunov* employed them on but two occasions: Varlaam's second drinking song (the first uses no more than the text of a folk song, but the second is an authentic melody, although originally not connected with the text), and "Slava," the song with which the people salute the tsar. That song has an unexpected source. Although it sounds perfectly fitting as a tribute to the tsar, originally it formed part of a game with which young girls predicted the future at the New Year and wished one another good luck.[16]

### RIMSKY-KORSAKOV: *PSKOVITYANKA*

Karamzin's historical approach remained unchallenged into the 1850s, when it began to attract criticism as the Hegelian philosophy of history altered attitudes about Russia's past. Ordinary moral accountability was considered less important than the historical patterns to which an individual's actions contributed. According to the new historical ideology, these patterns all pointed toward the Russian national state to come. Russian historians looked on the reign of Ivan the Terrible as the ultimate test of their ideas, either justifying Ivan's excesses and brutality or playing them down. In this new light, Ivan gained the status of a far-sighted statesman, a proto–Peter the Great, a ruler who laid the foundations of Russia's later power. His means may have been morally objectionable,

but his ends were judged to be historically justified. The reign of Ivan
the Terrible seemed dictated by the laws of progress.

The new interpretation was elaborated by Konstantin Kavelin and
Sergey Solovyov. The writer Lev Alexandrovich Mey brought Solovyov's
ideas to the stage with the plays *Pskovityanka* (The maid of Pskov) and
*The Tsar's Bride*. Rimsky-Korsakov embarked upon a musical version
of *Pskovityanka* in 1868, completing it in 1872.

Mey's play was a demonstration of the new ideology, according to
which the continued existence and development of the Russian state
served as a yardstick of historical progress. As Mey put it, not even the
tsar could alter the historical laws. In illustration, Mey devised a plot
that combined historical events with romantic fiction. The historical background of his play was a campaign by Ivan the Terrible in 1570 against
two important Hanseatic towns in the north, Novgorod and Pskov, both
of which had a long tradition of autonomy. Ivan's campaign was part of
his determination to strengthen the Muscovite autocracy. Although he
destroyed Novgorod, oddly enough he spared Pskov—one of the many
mysteries surrounding his reign. Mey sought an explanation in Ivan's alleged personal links with Pskov. He created the character of Olga, Ivan's
daughter by the love of his youth, the boyarinya Vera Sheloga. This
fictional character provided Mey with a figure who could embody the
fate of Pskov. The relationship between Ivan and Olga symbolizes the
tsar's love for Pskov and at the same time his ruthless determination to
sacrifice its autonomy to higher, historical ideals.

The story goes as follows: the inhabitants of Pskov learn of the fall of
Novgorod and weigh their best course of action. Opinions differ: while
some are ready to open the gates of the town to the tsar, others advise
resistance. The leader of the second group is Mikhaíl Tucha, Olga's fiancé.
He leaves the town with his partisans. When Ivan nears Pskov, he recognizes Olga as his own daughter and decides to spare the town. He is torn
by conflicting emotions; he wants the best for Olga, but must also punish
her lover. While Ivan talks to Olga in his tent, Tucha and his men attack
the camp and are killed by the guards. When Olga hears the news, she
stabs herself. (In the opera, the plot is slightly amended: during Tucha's
attack, Olga rushes out to her lover and is felled by a shot meant for
him.) The tsar calls for his personal physician, who tells him that only
the Lord can raise the dead. Ivan the Terrible weeps beside the body of
his dead daughter. An epilogue immediately follows in which the events
receive a historical interpretation: the fall of Pskov was inevitable; it was
God's will. The laws of history cannot be altered by the acts of men. The

chorus here does not play the usual role of a group of bystanders, but rather serves as the collective voice of reflection.

The play had previously been turned into an operatic libretto by Vsevolod Krestovsky. Rimsky-Korsakov, however, decided to abandon that libretto and to apply Dargomïzhsky's method by working directly on Mey's text. Faithful to the *kuchka* approach, he avoided such traditional formulas as arias or ensembles. His realistic dramaturgy was reflected, for instance, in the denouement in the last scene. Rather than placing the musical climax where it might be expected, at the deaths of Tucha and Olga (an event that barely serves as a dramatic element in the music: a salvo fired by the guards is enough to eliminate the rebels), he saved the musical climax for the tsar's emotional outburst beside Olga's dead body.

The rich psychological complexity of Ivan's character was a challenge to musical realism. Ivan's monologues are taken word for word from the play. The tsar muses about his historical role in a dignified recitative reminiscent of Musorgsky's Pimen. In the scene with Olga, he manages to reassure his daughter by convincing her that his image as a cruel tyrant does not tally with his true nature. Rimsky-Korsakov's aim was to portray Ivan as a complex but humane character: a Machiavellian prince on the one hand but a sensitive man—lover and father—on the other.

Rimsky-Korsakov's greatest achievement in the score is the scene portraying the *veche,* a gathering open to all the citizens of the town. (The republican traditions of old Russia incited keen interest in the nineteenth century.) In *Pskovityanka,* the *veche* portrayed in action by Mey is the assembly called after the fall of Novgorod at which the citizens consider their best way forward. There are two parties: Prince Tokmakov and his followers are prepared to open the gates to the tsar, while Mikhaíl Tucha urges resistance. He does not trust Ivan and does not want Pskov to surrender its freedom. Tokmakov tries to dissuade him, but Tucha assembles a band of rebels, who leave the town to the sounds of a folk song.

Rimsky-Korsakov begins this scene with the peal of the *veche* bell. Although intended to provide greater authenticity, it is in fact an anachronism: by the time the action takes place the *veche* bell had been removed on orders issued by Ivan III several decades earlier. What follows in the opera is a brilliant adaptation of Dargomïzhsky's realism to the treatment of the chorus. Musorgsky had aimed at a similar effect in his Novodevichy and St. Basil scenes, but Rimsky-Korsakov went much further. He tried to portray true chaos in his music. In opera, choral numbers usually constitute complete blocks, the chorus appearing as a whole or divided into two groups. Rimsky-Korsakov devised a free texture, in which the choral parts enter into dialogue with each other and with the soloists, in asymmetrical and unpredictable patterns. The *veche* scene is a portrayal of a crowd of people in action. The chorus, no longer a mere spectator or commentator, has become a protagonist. It is itself the action. Technically, Rimsky-Korsakov left the chorus parts to declaim freely by transferring the musical continuity to the orchestra. In its realism and treatment of the chorus, *Pskovityanka* holds a unique position in the history of opera.

### MUSORGSKY: *BORIS GODUNOV* (SECOND VERSION)

Musorgsky completed the first version of *Boris Godunov* on 15 December 1869 and submitted the score to the directorate of the Imperial Theaters. Their decision came on 10 February 1871: they rejected the work. There has been much speculation about the reasons for this decision. Subsequent statements by Stasov and Rimsky-Korsakov (the latter thirty-five years after the event and wrong in several details) have contributed to the picture of the board of directors as Philistines with no understanding of the originality of the score. The next step in the establishment of the widespread *Boris* legend was the implanting of the firm belief that Musorgsky then revised the opera under pressure from the directorate and from the censors. The new score was thus declared to be a compromise, a concession to the prevailing taste.

If we examine the sources, it appears that there is a more or less reliable document capable of throwing light on the decision of the directorate: a memoir by Lyudmila Shestakova, Glinka's sister. She asked two members of the board, the conductor Eduard Nápravník and the chief *régisseur* Gennady Kondratyev, "'Is *Boris* accepted?'—'No,' they answered me, 'it's impossible. How can there be an opera without the feminine element?! Musorgsky has great talent without doubt. Let him add one more scene. Then *Boris* will be produced!'"[17] Lyudmila Shestakova conveyed the news to Musorgsky in person. To her great surprise it did not upset him. "I told them [Musorgsky and Stasov] what I heard, and Stasov with heated enthusiasm began talking over with him the new parts to be inserted into the opera; Musorgsky began playing over some themes, and the evening passed in a very lively fashion."[18] In a letter to Alexandra Purgold, Rimsky-Korsakov wrote: "[Musorgsky] knows everything concerning *Boris*'s fate and reacted completely differently from how one might have expected, and therefore, completely differently from how we all had predicted."[19]

If we take these statements seriously, we have to dismiss the idea that Musorgsky revised his opera under external pressure. It was his own decision. There is no evidence that the directorate ever asked him for more than the addition of a female role. There is even less evidence that the censor placed any obstacle in the opera's way.[20] Indeed, Musorgsky's eventual revision of *Boris Godunov* went so much further than the demand of the directorate that it can only have reflected his own artistic development, which entailed the renunciation of his earlier extreme viewpoints.

The revision of *Boris Godunov* began with the call by the directorate for a scene with a female character. Pushkin supplied that character: Marina Mnishek, the daughter of a Polish nobleman and a wily schemer who uses the false Dmitry to further her own ambitions. In Pushkin, Marina plays no great part. She delivers no monologues. As a result, Musorgsky was obliged to write his own text. In his "Polish act," therefore, he turned his back on the ideal of the *opéra dialogué,* assigning ample room to the most established formulas of romantic opera, giving Maria a proper aria, inserting a polonaise, and incorporating a true love duet.

In Pushkin, Dmitry and Marina are two cynical, calculating schemers. Their great dialogue in the fountain scene is more of a verbal sparring match in mutual manipulation than a love scene. When it is over, Dmitry says that one would do better dealing with Godunov or with a Jesuit than with a woman. Musorgsky's characters are altogether different: they are true denizens of opera. Passion rules their lives, and their scene ends with a genuine love duet. But while the composer simplified the characters of Dmitry and Marina, he retained the fundamental ambiguity of their encounter, the characteristic mixture of eroticism and political intrigue. To that end he distilled the cold, political calculation in the two characters and projected it into a figure of his own making, the Jesuit Rangoni, who wants to use the relationship between Dmitry and Marina to introduce his religion to Moscow.

In the Polish act, Musorgsky found a way of employing traditional operatic dramaturgy. Musically, too, he retreated from his strictly naturalistic vocal style. The music is now arranged in large blocks, which are used several times as self-contained musical numbers. Short, characteristic responses have been replaced by broader phrases. In the roles of the Pretender and of Marina, Musorgsky again leaves ample space for passionate lyricism.

Musorgsky then applied the stylistic and dramaturgical innovations of the Polish act to the rest of the opera, and particularly to the Kremlin scene. The new design of this act differs fundamentally from the old. In the first version, Boris's monologue fails to bring out his character. In the second version, Musorgsky uses a different monologue based on a text of his own. A disquisition on power makes way for an emotional expression of a moral dilemma, and naturalistic recitative for a genuine aria in broad musical periods. For the new monologue, Musorgsky borrowed musical material from his *Salammbô*. The rhythmical complexities—in the first version of *Boris* still a legacy from *Marriage*—disappear almost completely from the vocal writing. With the new exalted tone of Boris's monologue, the dramaturgy of the act also changes. In the older version the Kremlin scene was lacking in contrast. In the second version Musorgsky overcomes that by setting off Boris's tragedy with a variety of genre scenes: Xenia's lament on the death of her betrothed, the little songs and games the tsarevich sings and plays with the nurse, and the comical incident involving the parrot. A chiming mechanical clock serves as the linking musical and dramatic motif.

The new Kremlin scene is no longer a verbatim rendering of Pushkin's play, the dramaturgy being based on contrasts between larger musical blocks, not to speak of musical "numbers." Musorgsky thus took quite a long step backward to traditional opera, finding the model for the Kremlin scene in César Cui's *William Ratcliff*. The second act of Cui's opera has a similar construction: a long divertissement is suddenly interrupted by the entrance of the tragic protagonist, who pours out his heart in a great monologue that is followed in turn by a comic contrast.[21]

Enhancement of the dramatic and musical contrast was also the reason for two further additions to the opera: the monks' chorus in the monastery-cell scene and the song of the hostess in the inn scene. In addition, Musorgsky scrapped passages from the older version: in the Novodevichy scene, he omitted the realistic choral setting following the pilgrims' hymn; in the monastery-cell scene, he dispensed with Pimen's account of the tsarevich's murder, and he also dropped Shchelkalov's monologue in the scene depicting Boris's death. The most striking change was the omission of the St. Basil scene and its replacement with the new Kromy scene. The rumor that Musorgsky dropped the St. Basil scene under pressure from the censor is unfounded. It used to be thought that the confrontation between the tsar and the people in that scene went beyond what was ideologically permitted. However, the replacement scene was ideologically even more questionable. It depicts the people in open revolt against the tsar—a tragic uprising, indeed, for the same allegiance paid by the people to Boris at the beginning of the opera is paid here to an impostor. The scene takes us to Kromy forest and portrays several incidents during the Pretender's march into Russia: the mocking homage paid to the boyar Khrushchov, the teasing of a *yuródivïy* by a group of children, the arrival of Varlaam and Missail (the down-at-heel monks we know from the inn scene), the maltreatment of two Jesuits, the Pretender's procession, Khrushchov's acceptance of the Pretender as the tsarevich, and finally—on an empty stage—the *yuródivïy*'s lament over Russia's tragic fate.

Nothing like the Kromy scene is present in Pushkin. Nor did Karamzin provide the material for it; the idea that the people could sway the course of history was no part of Karamzin's ideology. Musorgsky took the material from a contemporary historian, Nikolai Kostomarov. For this populist, the people were the driving force behind all historical processes. In his study of the Time of Troubles he attributed the success of the false Dmitry to the spontaneous intervention of the people. Large groups of hungry serfs were overrunning the countryside in their attempt to escape the famine, giving their support to anyone who could rid them of the hated Muscovite regime. The incidents mentioned by Kostomarov include the very episodes found in Musorgsky's libretto, such as the mocking of the boyars and of Boris's followers, and the defection to the Pretender's camp of Khrushchov (dispatched by Boris to rouse the Don Cossacks against the false Dmitry).[22] Musorgsky took the two passages with the *yuródivïy* from the St. Basil scene and inserted them bodily into his new one.

The replacement of St. Basil with Kromy was an ideological modernization. In the earlier version the role of the populace was insignificant. Only with the inclusion of the Kromy scene did the confrontation between tsar and people become a central theme. Apart from an ideological impetus, there was also a musical one: the example of the *veche* scene from *Pskovityanka*. When Rimsky-Korsakov composed that scene, Musorgsky was looking over his shoulder.

The *veche* scene filled him with particular enthusiasm. In a letter to the Purgold sisters, Musorgsky wrote: "Before [Rimsky-Korsakov's] departure from Petrograd I went to see him and experienced something extraordinary. This something is none other than a milestone in Korsinka's talent. He has realized the dramatic essence of musical drama. He, that is, Korsinka, has concocted some magnificent history with the choruses in the *veche*—just as it should be: I actually burst out laughing with delight."[23] The combination of free declamation and musical logic, though still absent from the first version of *Boris Godunov,* is present

throughout *Pskovityanka*. The chaotic declamation in the chorus parts
of the second version's Kromy scene, then, was taken from Rimsky-
Korsakov, rendered musically by a melodic or motivic continuum in other
choral voices and in the orchestra. Folk song plays a major role, with
authentic melodies being used; to wit, the song mocking the boyar, the
song of Varlaam and Missail, and the middle section of the revolutionary chorus.

While the first version of *Boris Godunov* was a relatively disconnected
succession of scenes, the second is a balanced drama, with the Kremlin
scene as its pivot. The character of Boris is the linchpin of the whole opera.
The Kremlin scene is framed by two acts in which the Pretender plays
the main role. The structure begins and ends with direct confrontations
between the people and Boris.[24]

> *Outline for* Boris Godunov
>
> PROLOGUE
>
> 1. Outside Novodevichy monastery          The people
> 2. The coronation of Boris                 Boris
>
> ACT I
>
> 3. A cell in Chudov monastery        ⎫
> 4. An inn on the Lithuanian border   ⎬ The Pretender
>
> ACT II
>
> 5. The Terem in the Kremlin                 Boris
>
> ACT III
>
> 6. Marina's boudoir            ⎫
> 7. A garden by the fountain    ⎬ The Pretender
>
> ACT IV
>
> 8. Granovitaya Palace                       Boris
> 9. A clearing in the forest near Kromy      The people

Musorgsky's use of large structures in the second version of *Boris Godunov* marks the distance he had traveled from his previous *opéra dialogué* ideals. The new *Boris* is a synthesis of Musorgsky's realism and
the dramaturgical principles of seasoned opera composers. Verdi's
influence makes itself felt in the structure of large sections and in several
details, such as the dramatic use of tonalities and reminiscence motifs.
The subtle treatment of the Dmitry motif, for its part, is a tribute to
Berlioz's idée fixe. In the second version, all the ambiguity of the Dmitry

motif has gone. It is applied exclusively to the false and no longer (as in the first version) to the real Dmitry, except in the title character's terrified imagination—a masterstroke of dramatic irony.

Musorgsky laid down the final version of the opera in the vocal score published by Bessel in 1874. Nowadays that version is rarely, if ever, performed. Indeed, the opera's modern-day reception, based as it is on a persistent confusion of the two versions, merits closer consideration. For a long time *Boris Godunov* was played in Rimsky-Korsakov's adaptation (discussed in chapter 8). Today people tend to revert to Musorgsky's own score, but in a conflation of the 1869 version and that of 1872 (published in 1874). The *Boris Godunov* that is nowadays held to be authentic therefore differs considerably from Musorgsky's own intentions: the sound of the original may have been preserved, but the overall structure and the dramatic rhythm have been lost. The misunderstanding arose when Pavel Lamm published the two versions in 1928 in a single continuous score in which all the passages deleted by Musorgsky were restored. This approach gave rise to an overelaborate *Boris,* which David Lloyd Jones then treated as the standard in his modern edition.

The reason for the misunderstanding is not a lack of familiarity with the sources but the widespread legend according to which Musorgsky was thwarted from all sides: by the Imperial Theaters directorate, the press, and the censor. The published vocal score was consequently considered a compromise, not the expression of Musorgsky's artistic will. According to this reasoning, it was essential that the composer's original intentions be restored. Hence the overelaborate *Boris,* which then, of course, proves too long for a normal night at the opera and has to submit to arbitrary interventions by the interpreters. *Boris Godunov* has been wretchedly transformed into a "self-service" score, from which everyone can choose what he pleases. Even to this day Musorgsky is considered an artist in need of a firm correcting hand.[25]


CHAIKOVSKY: *THE OPRICHNIK*

*The Oprichnik* (1870–72) was Chaikovsky's third opera. Having destroyed his two earlier operas, *The Voyevoda* (1867–68) and *Undine* (1869), Chaikovsky looked for a play with comparable scenes in order to recycle the music from *The Voyevoda.* He found suitable material in Ivan Lazhechnikov's tragedy *The Oprichnik* (1834). As a historical opera, Chaikovsky's *Oprichnik* is the very opposite of *Boris Godunov* and *Pskovityanka,* being quite conventional in both content and dramaturgy.

Like *Pskovityanka*, Chaikovsky's opera is set during the reign of Ivan the Terrible. The picture of that tsar is still based on Karamzin's classical portrait: the bloodthirsty and unpredictable tyrant surrounded by his hated *oprichniki*. The word *oprichnik* comes from *oprichnina*, the personal domains of Ivan IV, which he established in 1565 as a separate administrative entity distinct from the *zemshchina*, the rest of Russia. The land in the *oprichnina* was not held by the traditional landed gentry, but by a special class of men bound to the tsar by an oath of loyalty: the *oprichniki*. They lived a quasi-monastic life and served as a secret police force, their special task being to hunt down and eliminate traitors. The fanaticism and extreme violence with which they went about their duties caused the Russian people to loathe them, and Karamzin's evocative descriptions made them a splendid subject for romantic melodrama.

Lazhechnikov's *Oprichnik* is not a historical play in the sense that Pushkin's *Boris Godunov* is, or Mey's *Pskovityanka*. The historical theme merely serves as a background for a romantic tragedy of fate, in which Ivan and the *oprichniki* are the tools of a destiny that threatens and eventually destroys two innocent lovers.

Chaikovsky's work thoroughly satisfied the traditional operatic criteria, an aspect all too often used as evidence of Chaikovsky's ingrained conservatism. However, if we look at *The Oprichnik* in the proper context and without prejudice, it appears that his recourse to convention was a deliberate move and certainly not a sign of ignorance of modern developments. The young composer's aim in *The Oprichnik* was to display his ambitions to the full. To that end he used the opera model that enjoyed the greatest renown at the time: French *grand opéra* as found at its most complex in the librettos of Eugène Scribe. Setting out to compose an opera that would meet the most stringent international standards, Chaikovsky reduced Lazhechnikov's intrigue to a series of basic situations, which he then rearranged in accordance with Scribe's model.

Few grand operas are subtle psychological studies; rather, they portray a clash of conflicting forces, ones generally beyond the control of the onstage characters. The musical dramaturgy works with coded forms, related to one another hierarchically. The broad trend in this type of work is a gradual buildup of tension, so that the whole culminates in an inextricable dramatic tangle and inevitable catastrophe.

In *The Oprichnik*, the young boyar Andrey Morozov is caught in a web he himself has spun. To take his revenge on Prince Zhemchuzhnïy—who has reduced the Morozovs to poverty by fraud—he decides to become an *oprichnik*, in the hope of gaining power over his adversary. Andrey's mother is, however, so appalled at this decision that she curses her son. Andrey then decides to revoke his oath to the tsar, who agrees but insists that Andrey remain an *oprichnik* until after his wedding. During the feast the tsar claims the *ius primae noctis* and orders Andrey's bride to repair to his royal apartments. The young man is out of his mind with rage and curses the tsar. This is all the excuse the *oprichniki* need to murder him. In order to make their perverse pleasure complete, they invite Andrey's mother to a "splendid celebration": her son's execution.

The opera proceeds in the slow rhythm characteristic of grand opera. Acts I and II prepare the audience for the actual drama. Act I is largely a divertissement (the scene with Natalya, Andrey's fiancée, and her nurse and girlfriends); Act II ends with Andrey's fatal oath to the tsar. In Act III the tension is heightened when the mother curses her son. The act meets the strictest demands of Scribian dramaturgy. Act IV begins with a deceptive decrease in dramatic tension by a divertissement of wedding songs and dances. Then the tragedy is led to its inescapable climax.

Musically, the score uses all the ingredients of dramatic opera. Yet the tone is strikingly Russian, something that is especially true of the charming genre scenes in Act I (taken from *The Voyevoda*) and the mockecclesiastical choruses of the *oprichniki*. In the characterization of the various roles, that of Andrey's mother is particularly impressive. In her great aria and duet with Andrey in Act II, Chaikovsky proves that he is a dramatic composer of rank.

*The Oprichnik* has little to offer those looking for true-to-life psychology or historical analysis. Those, however, who are prepared to enter into the spirit of the game—of grand opera as formalized dramatic architecture, and of drama as romantic horror story—will find *The Oprichnik* one of the best examples of the genre.

## MUSORGSKY: *KHOVANSHCHINA*

In addition to the reign of Ivan the Terrible and the Time of Troubles, Russian historians discovered yet another test case of historical ideologies in the reign of Peter the Great. In 1872, when the bicentenary of his birth was celebrated, official Russia did not doubt for one moment the positive significance of his rule. His policies were said to have ushered in the birth of modern Russia. Against this background of almost unanimous public acclaim, Musorgsky conceived the plan of writing a critical opera about the celebrated tsar. From a letter to Stasov, it is clear that he was not prepared to join in the game of public optimism: "'We've *gone forward'*—you lie. *'We haven't moved!'* Paper, books have gone forward—we *haven't moved.*"[26]

The new opera was *Khovanshchina,* begun in 1873 and left unfinished at Musorgsky's death in 1881. Peter the Great does not appear on the stage—the censor would not have allowed that—nor does the opera deal with Peter's actual reign; instead, it focuses on the turbulent times in which he rose to power.

*Khovanshchina* came into being in a disorganized manner. It would seem that Musorgsky "improvised" the plot, the libretto, and the score without any preconceived plan, leaving us a musical fragment from which no definitive version can possibly be distilled. The confused state of the sources even makes it difficult to determine what precisely Musorgsky had in mind. Any attempt at an explanation must therefore take account of all the source material that has come down to us. This material consists of a series of manuscripts in the form of piano arrangements (1873–80), some orchestrated numbers, an incomplete sketch of the last scene, Musorgsky's correspondence with Stasov, and a notebook from 1872 in which Musorgsky recorded historical—mainly seventeenth-century—quotations. In 1932, a new document was found among the papers left by Golenishchev-Kutuzov: a libretto in prose, recorded in a blue notebook. In all probability it reflects the last phase of Musorgsky's work on *Khovanshchina.* Although the libretto does not tally exactly with the music manuscripts, it suggests that Musorgsky had decided on a definitive version of what was still an unorganized music drama.

The term *Khovanshchina* means the "Khovansky affair," or the intrigues of Ivan Khovansky, the leader of the Muscovite Streltsï (musketeers). Musorgsky's opera is not, however, an account of this historical event alone. Rather, it combines three great historical facts in a single fictional plot. Though Musorgsky's own invention, the story refers back to real events and characters; its purpose was to reveal the historical essence that lay concealed behind the events in question.

The relevant incidents were the first Streltsï revolt in 1682, which started as a plot by Peter's half sister Sophia to have her feeble-minded brother Ivan declared joint sovereign with the ten-year-old Peter, while she herself became regent; the Khovansky affair followed, with Ivan Khovansky's attempt to have the church reforms abrogated, and possibly also his plot to have his own son Andrey crowned. After Khovansky's defeat, the Streltsï turned against Sophia, who forgave them and placed the boyar Fyodor Shaklovitïy, her accomplice in Khovansky's downfall, at their head. In 1689, the second Streltsï revolt took place. This time Sophia;

her confidant, Vasiliy Golitsïn; and Shaklovitïy intrigued against the seventeen-year-old Peter. The third Streltsï revolt, finally, came in 1698 and was again directed against Peter, who happened to be abroad at the time. That revolt was put down with unprecedented severity. In Musorgsky's version all these characters except Sophia appear, but in anachronistic situations. A typical example of the amalgamation of historical facts in the opera is the pardon the Streltsï are granted by Peter, just before their execution. Musorgsky took this incident (although the pardon was granted by Sophia and not by Peter) from the history of the first Streltsï revolt.

Another historical event recalled in the opera was the revolt of the Old Believers, Christian communities that had broken with the Orthodox Church in the seventeenth century in protest against the reforms of the patriarch Nikon. They were severely persecuted by Peter's father, Alexey, and by Sophia—by the latter above all because of the links between the Old Believers and the Khovanskys. Indeed, so harsh was the persecution during her regency that many Old Believers chose mass suicide, and Musorgsky's opera ends with the self-immolation of one such community. To represent the Old Believers in *Khovanshchina,* Musorgsky created the fictional character of Dosifey, an amalgam of such distinct historical personages as the archpriest Avvákum, Nikita Pustosvyat, and Prince Mïshetsky.

In the revised *Boris Godunov,* the Kromy scene was the most progressive component, both musically and ideologically. In this scene, the people take the initiative in an event of historical importance, even though the lament of the *yuródivïy* makes it painfully clear that their actions are futile. In *Khovanshchina* the people are no longer at the center of history; in fact, they are barely present at all, and those that do take center stage in the opera—the Moscow immigrants, or the Streltsï—play anything but positive roles. Every character of any importance is an aristocrat, right down to Dosifey. This was enough to make Stasov protest: "What is this finally to be, *an opera of princes,* while I thought you were planning an opera *of the people.* After all, who among your characters will not be a *prince* or an *aristocrat,* who will come directly *from the people?*" He called it "a chronicle of princely *spawn!!*" and deplored the fact that Musorgsky had departed from his (Stasov's!) populist ideal. Musorgsky himself called *Khovanshchina* a "*narodnaya muzïkalnaya drama,*" which is generally translated as "musical folk drama." The term can equally well mean "national music drama," or, better still, a "music drama about national history."[27] This last definition fits the work we know, which is an aristocratic tragedy first and foremost.

In *Khovanshchina* freedom of action does not exist. This is perhaps the central theme of the work. No initiative ever leads anywhere. Everyone—aristocrats and people alike—is confronted with the inadequacy of the human will. The opera is not about revolutionary acts, but about loss and impotence. The historical ideology of *Khovanshchina* is unrelievedly pessimistic. Change—let alone progress—appears out of the question. No new dawn follows upon the nightmare.

In musico-dramatic terms, *Khovanshchina* projects the concept of the Kromy scene onto a wider scale. That scene was a collage of disparate elements: folk songs, hymns, ariosos, processional music. Compared with the rest of *Boris,* there recitative was firmly sidelined. The scene brimmed over with action but served as a single great tableau in the opera. Minor events passed in review, but the whole did not follow any clear narrative direction. *Khovanshchina* is based on many different sources (historical documents, folk songs, hymns of the Old Believers). Musorgsky paints powerful portraits but provides no central dramatic conflict. This feature aptly captures the sense of fate and damnation with which the opera is replete. Conflicts, rather than being resolved, are temporarily assuaged. All the characters are caught up in the cogs of their own perdition. A good example of their impotence is the magnificent scene in which the Streltsï call on Ivan Khovansky to lead them against the troops of Peter the Great. But Khovansky tells them: "Things are different now: Tsar Peter is an awesome man! Go home and calmly await what fate has in store for you! . . . Farewell!" Instead of heeding their leader, who has left them in the lurch, the Streltsï resort to prayer, imploring God for his protection. It is a brilliant portrayal of men who no longer believe in the possibility of action.

In this story about human inability to influence the course of history, the Old Believers play a central role. "Be patient a little longer and serve our old and holy Russia," is the advice Dosifey gives Marfa, an Old Believer. But the holy Russia of the Old Believers does not lie in the future. From their eschatological perspective, the holy existence they seek is possible only outside secular history. Time no longer exists for them, and holy Russia is likewise timeless. Their escape from worldly life is thus the logical outcome of their religious outlook. It is also the logical outcome of an opera in which doubts about the future are voiced uncompromisingly. Commentators on *Khovanshchina* have always had difficulty with the prominent role of the Old Believers and their mystical pessimism, and have often dismissed them as incomprehensible and exotic or as dangerous fanatics, sworn opponents of any reform.[28] A fascinating counterinterpretation, however, placing the Old Believers at the center of the historical fatalism of *Khovanshchina,* has been given by Caryl Emerson:

> Fate-based operas are common enough, of course, especially with libretti drawn from fairy-tale or myth. But what is peculiar in *Khovanshchina* is the implacability of fate combined with a concreteness of historical event. Even more startling is the absence of any genuine, sustained dramatic resistance—of the sort we get in *Boris*—to what fate has decreed. Characters do not confront their destiny so much as fuse with it. The crucial concepts in the libretto are those favorite words of Marfa and Dosifei: *sud'ba* and *nevolia,* fate and unfreedom (or "non-will"). "In God's will lies our non-will," Dosifei consoles Marfa, and all the characters still alive by the end of the opera come around to this truth. The passage of time neither adds nor removes. . . . We sense here Musorgsky's own passion and terror for human history as a powerful but blind force.[29]

In musical terms, Musorgsky moved a long way in his *Khovanshchina* from the old *kuchka* ideal of recitative based on natural speech. The score now gives prominence to broad, contiguous musical phrases, often periodically divided—in other words, to lyric ariosos, or even to arias, as in Shaklovitïy's monologue. Musorgsky's vocal style becomes much more melodic as a result, and the melody has a greater abstract quality. Its close links with the personality of individual characters is partly abandoned. A fine example is the part of Marfa, which Musorgsky himself called an illustration of his new melodic style.[30] Marfa regularly uses phrases that come straight out of Russian folk songs or are derived from the lyrical folk-song style, especially when she appears as a prophet. Folk song functions as an impersonal voice, as the expression of ideas transcending the powers of individual characters. Marfa's part serves as a musical reproduction of the otherworldly or suprahistorical longings of the Old Believers.

The other characters also participate in this exalted melodic style. An obvious example is Shaklovitïy's aria, which reflects his reactionary yearnings for a strong hand able to restore order in Russia. The splendid political argument between Golitsïn, Khovansky, and Dosifey in Act II clearly demonstrates the distance Musorgsky has traveled from his earlier practice (Plate 5). In this scene, compared with one such as the discussion between Boris and Shuisky, all the characters make far more frequent use of exalted lyrical phrases, with the role of recitative remaining confined to brief utterances. The scene culminates in the solemn song of the Old Believers passing in procession. The melodic style of *Khovanshchina*

serves above all to express such suprapersonal ideals as mystical yearning (Marfa, Dosifey), purity of faith (the choruses of the Old Believers),
and aristocratic status (Khovansky, Golitsïn, Shaklovitïy).

Upon Musorgsky's death in 1881, Rimsky-Korsakov examined all of Musorgsky's manuscripts and prepared the ones he thought interesting for
publication. He started his editorial work on *Khovanshchina* in December 1881, completing his version of the opera in 1883. From Rimsky-
Korsakov's redaction, however, we gather that he could not swallow the
overt pessimism of the work. We see that most clearly in two passages
that Musorgsky had left uncomposed, ones that might have shed some
light on the meaning he wanted to give to the portrayed events. Rimsky-
Korsakov filled in these gaps according to his own views, thereby clarifying the work's ideological stance. However, it is highly unlikely that
Rimsky-Korsakov's interpretation came close to Musorgsky's intentions,
as far as these can be known from the material he left behind.

The crucial gaps occur at the end of Act II (the announcement of the
arrival of Peter's troops) and of Act V (the suicide of the Old Believers).
In the version Rimsky-Korsakov elaborated, Act II concludes with a
reprise of the theme of the orchestral prelude entitled "Dawn over the
Moskva River." At the end of Act V, he added a choral number of his
own in which he brought back the musical representation of Peter the
Great, the Preobrazhensky march from Act IV. These interventions radically altered the content, for with them the reign of Peter the Great was
again shown in a favorable light; by the conclusion, the tsar had solved
all the problems of the old Russia and ushered in a new dawn for the
nation. In 1958, when Dmitry Shostakovich produced a new orchestration based on Musorgsky's piano arrangement, he adhered to the same
concept: he ended the second act with a foreshadowing of the Preobrazhensky march, and retained Rimsky-Korsakov's chorus at the end
of Act V but rounded it off with a reprise of the "dawn" theme from the
prelude.

To produce a version that would be more in keeping with Musorgsky's ideas, it is advisable to abandon Rimsky-Korsakov's and
Shostakovich's additions, to restore cuts (wherever possible following the
guidelines laid down in the "blue notebook"), and to conclude Act V
with the chorus that Igor Stravinsky wrote in 1913 for a production by
Diaghilev in Paris.[31] Although Diaghilev's version was even further from
Musorgsky's ideas than Rimsky-Korsakov's, and was aimed simply at
providing a star role for the great basso Fyodor Chaliapin as Dosifey,

Stravinsky's final chorus serves the purpose well. Not only did he base it on the Old Believers' melody, chosen by Musorgsky himself, but it also makes a particularly effective fade-out, which was probably also Musorgsky's intention. Thus Musorgsky's custom of bringing scenes and acts to an end with a musical fade-out is carried to its logical conclusion: the exit of characters from the stage serves as an image of their departure from history.

## GOGOLIAN COMEDY

"I am well acquainted with the Gogol subject. I gave it some thought two years or so ago, but it doesn't go well with the path I have chosen— it takes in too little of Russia in all her openhearted breadth." So went Musorgsky's reply (3 January 1872) to Alexandra Purgold's suggestion that he write an opera based on "The Fair at Sorochintsï," the first story in Gogol's collection called *Evenings on a Farm near Dikanka*.[32] That collection is made up of both humorous and ghost stories set in a Ukraine populated by witches, demons, and common folk. Musorgsky thought the subject matter too narrow, too trifling.

Some clarification is called for here. Musorgsky had already composed a fragment of a Gogol opera, as an experiment in strict realism. The *Dikanka* stories, however, bring out an aspect of Gogol very different from that found in *Marriage*. In the latter, he is the acute observer and satirist of life in the Russian capital; in the *Dikanka* stories, he is the master of unbridled fantasy. These stories contain no realistic observations, but are an amalgam of folklore, stock characters, and conventional situations, translated into a bizarre, imaginary world. The characters come straight from the Ukrainian puppet theater, the plots from romantic plays and such operas as Weber's *Der Freischütz*, which inspired "St. John's Eve," or Ferdinand Kauer's *Das Donauweibchen*, which provided the theme for "A May Night." For a committed composer such as Musorgsky, the *Dikanka* stories were not a suitable source of material. "It's shameful to take pen in hand to depict nonsense words like 'Sagana, chukh!' and suchlike folderol," he wrote to Stasov in 1872, when expressing his dissatisfaction with the collective *Mlada* project.[33] The *Dikanka* stories are filled with exactly this kind of "folderol." Small wonder that Musorgsky rejected them.

Even so, he started in earnest on *Sorochintsï Fair* in 1877, a paradoxical situation that commentators generally resolve with a large dose of wishful thinking. For Soviet reviewers, *Sorochintsï Fair* was a realistic (and hence progressive) picture of the people, and Western critics generally take the same line. Thus Gioacchino Lanza Tomasi wrote:

> For Musorgsky, true culture is based above all on national character, the concerted action of a community that ritually lays down its own manifold, historical deposits and achieves its identity solely by virtue of this liturgical conservation and fixation. "I prefer to lie as little as possible, and to speak the truth as much as I can," he writes to the singer Lyubova Ivanovna Karmalina in connection with *The Fair at Sorochintsï*.[34]

Tomasi, however, confuses the romantic concept of national character (*Volkstum*) with Musorgsky's idea of truth. The quotation he gives is misleading, for the context shows that Musorgsky was explaining why he had decided *not* to compose the opera! Dorothea Redepenning likewise adduces no convincing argument in support of her contention that *Sorochintsï Fair* is a continuation of *Marriage* transposed from the small stage to the big one.[35] Such commentaries ignore the artificial nature of the story, the abundant arguments with which Musorgsky originally rejected the idea, and the characteristics of Gogolian comedy as a special genre.

### CHAIKOVSKY: *VAKULA THE SMITH*

Comedy with a Ukrainian background was introduced into Russian opera with *The Zaporozhian Cossacks across the Danube* (1863), a singspiel by Semyon Gulak-Artemovsky. However, the genre only attained artistic importance with Chaikovsky's *Vakula the Smith* (1874). The literary source was Gogol's "Christmas Eve." The libretto, written by the poet Yakov Polonsky, was commissioned by the grand duchess Yelena Pavlovna, who had intended it for Alexander Serov. When his untimely death left her without a composer, the grand duchess, determined to bring the libretto onto the stage at any price, organized a competition for the best setting.

*Vakula the Smith* was a political creation, reflecting the official propaganda line. In Gogol's tale there is a scene in which Ukrainian Zaporozhian Cossacks swear submission and loyalty to Catherine the Great. The scene has little historical credibility, because Catherine the Great had abolished the autonomy of the Ukrainians in general and of the Cossacks in particular. By making it appear, however, as if the Ukrainians, unable to dispense with Russian support, submit to her voluntarily, Gogol confirms the idea of the unity of the tsarist state. That was precisely what the court needed at a time when Ukrainian separatism was assuming dangerous forms. From 1861 onward, in fact, romantic nationalism had expanded greatly in the Ukraine, eliciting severe repression from St. Petersburg. With *Vakula the Smith,* Yelena Pavlovna commissioned a libretto in which the idea of Ukrainian nationalism was bound up directly with loyalty to the crown—an aspect that Polonsky magnified beyond anything conceived by Gogol. Chaikovsky entered the competition, winning both first and second prize. *Vakula the Smith* was given its first performance in 1876.

With his conservative and monarchist political convictions, Chaikovsky was quite comfortable with the message in Polonsky's libretto. He was, however, dissatisfied with the dramatic structure, and so revised the work himself in 1885, giving it the new title of *Cherevichki* (Ukrainian for "women's boots").

In no other work by Chaikovsky does folk music play so prominent a role, a direct result of his having chosen a popular subject. *Vakula the Smith* is the story of the love of Vakula for Oxana, the Cossack girl. She rejects him and mocks him by ordering him in public to bring her the tsaritsa's *cherevichki.* If he does, she will marry him. Vakula tames the Devil and flies on his back to St. Petersburg. There he mingles with a delegation of Zaporozhian Cossacks, to whom Catherine the Great has granted an audience. When the empress asks the Cossacks if they have any wishes, Vakula seizes his chance and asks for her boots. Catherine is so charmed by his unaffected manner that she promptly grants his wish.

In Gogol this simple story is complicated by a loose, episodic structure and a quantity of narrative elements that render the action unpredictable. In his libretto, Polonsky introduced some structural clarity. The first and second acts comprise two scenes each. In the first scene, the Devil and the witch Solokha (Vakula's mother) are the central characters; in the second, Vakula and Oxana. In the second act, the pattern is the same, but with the addition of other characters. The Devil's flirtation with Solokha is expanded in Act II by the entrance of village notables who come to pay court to Solokha. Vakula and Oxana, too, are no longer alone in Act II, but surrounded by village youths. It is in their presence that Oxana makes her mocking request to Vakula. The contribution of the chorus is gradually stepped up. In Act I we hear the young people in the background singing *kolyadki,* the carols they perform outside the villagers' houses on Christmas Eve. From time to time, these carols interrupt the dialogue between Vakula and Oxana. In Act II, however, the chorus comes into its own in the great *kolyadki* scene, where it carries the confrontation between the two leading characters to a dramatic climax.

Act III also consists of two scenes: Vakula beside the river, and the palace reception, this last scene being the most resplendent of the whole opera. Because of the censor, an unidentified "Excellency" takes the place of Gogol's Catherine the Great. The scene includes an elaborate panegyric to the autocracy—according to custom, set to a polonaise, the musical code for the autocracy, together with a ballet divertissement, and the first rococo pastiches to be found in Chaikovsky's oeuvre. Act IV brings the final reconciliation between Oxana and Vakula, and culminates in a hymn of praise to bride and groom, accompanied on the *gusli*.

Vakula and Oxana are assigned the most lyrical parts. Vakula is a romantic lover, and Oxana is more sympathetic in Chaikovsky's version than in Gogol's. Solokha's love for her son is given greater emphasis than her witchcraft. The minor characters of Chub, Panas, the mayor, and the schoolteacher are drawn from the people. The Devil is cleverly portrayed in a caustic, devious role reflecting the comical versatility of the character.

Gogol's story provides rewarding opportunities for the creation of musical and visual atmospheric effects. The dramatic buildup to Act II is accompanied by a masterly intensification of the atmosphere. Act I opens with a snowstorm in the dark. When the storm abates, the first *kolyadki* singers make their entry. In Act II, the moon has reappeared. The great *kolyadki* chorus gives a splendid musical rendering of what Gogol describes so evocatively:

> Everything was flooded with light. It was as though there had been no snowstorm. The snow sparkled, a broad silvery plain, studded with crystal stars. The frost seemed less cold. Groups of boys and girls appeared with sacks. Songs rang out, and under almost every hut window were crowds of carol singers.
>
> How wonderful is the light of the moon! It is hard to put into words how pleasant it is on such a night to mingle in a group of singing, laughing girls and among boys ready for every jest and sport which the gaily smiling night can suggest. It is warm under the thick pelisse; the cheeks glow brighter than ever from the frost, and the devil himself prompts to mischief.[36]

## RIMSKY-KORSAKOV: *MAY NIGHT*

"A May Night" is less ideologically charged than "Christmas Eve." It is a simple love story, in which father and son desire the same girl, with all the turmoil that entails. The narrative line is interspersed with a gruesome story about a haunted house, a witch, and *rusalki* (Slavic water nymphs). In Rimsky-Korsakov's oeuvre, the opera *May Night* (1878–79)

marks a turning point in two ways: the abandonment of dramatic realism and a change of course in musical dramaturgy.

The vocal hallmark of realism was recitative or arioso. In *May Night*
both make their return. Folk song and folk-song intonation grow in importance. The stress is shifted from realistic portrayal to romantic idealization of the people. The comic characters, such as the mayor, the charcoal burner, and the brandy distiller, are true buffo types. In the finale
of Act II there is even an undisguised parody of *Boris Godunov:* the town
bailiffs, preferring to stay at home rather than go on a nocturnal mission, beg the mayor to revoke his order, and do so to the tune of the supplication of the people in the Novodevichy scene.

The musical dramaturgy exchanges the word-bound, formless composition for a clear arrangement of numbers and ensembles. This volte-
face was the result of Rimsky-Korsakov's academic retraining. In his
memoirs he described the change of course not as a capitulation but as
an important step forward and as a release from his previous inexperi-
ence. He based his orchestration on Glinka's transparent timbres. Many
of the details come straight out of *Ruslan:* the combination of piano
and harp in imitation of the *gusli,* the buffo role of the mayor (comparable to Glinka's Farlaf), and the use of the whole-tone scale at alarming moments.

*May Night,* which makes full use of calendar songs—that is, folk songs
associated with particular ritual events—marked the beginning of Rimsky-
Korsakov's interest in popular customs. In *May Night,* the customs in
question are those of *Rusalnaya* week, the "Green Christmas," a tradition in which the Christian feast of the Trinity is coupled to the celebration of burgeoning plant life.

## MUSORGSKY: *SOROCHINTSÏ FAIR*

*Sorochintsï Fair* (1874–81) outdoes *May Night* in the number of authentic
folk songs it contains, with folk song replacing recitative, as in Serov's
*The Power of the Fiend.* The musical characterization of the parts is less
individualized than we might expect of Musorgsky. Rather, he proffers
us a romantic view, one in which the characters represent the "popular
soul." The instrumental prelude is a "musical picture" suggesting the famous beginning of Gogol's story: "How intoxicating, how magnificent
is a summer day in Little Russia [the Ukraine]." Vladimir Stasov, the
unswerving champion of the *kuchka* ideal of realism and committed art,
was clear and unequivocal in his response to the work: he protested

against "this whole unfortunate Little-Russian undertaking" and referred bluntly to the music Musorgsky composed for it as "rubbish."[37]

Musorgsky was aware that he had moved a long way from the principles of the *kuchka*. On 10 November 1877 he wrote to Golenishchev-Kutuzov:

> I'll begin with the fact that at the first showing of the second act of *Sorochintsï* I became convinced of the basic lack of understanding of Little-Russian comedy on the part of the *musici* of the disintegrated "kuchka." Such a deep freeze radiated from their view and demands, that "my heart did congeal," as Archpriest Avvakum would say. . . . It's annoying to have to talk to the *musici* of the disintegrated "kuchka" from across the barrier behind which they have remained.[38]

Yet it had taken Musorgsky himself a long time to cross that barrier. His correspondence indicates that from 1872 to 1877 he was constantly plagued by doubt. Time after time he put the Sorochintsï project to one side, as he explains in a frequently quoted letter written in 1875:

> I have given up the Little-Russian opera. The reason for this renunciation is the futility of a Great-Russian trying to pretend he's a Little-Russian, and consequently, the futility of trying to master Little-Russian recitative—that is, all the shades and peculiarities of the musical contour of Little-Russian speech. I prefer to lie as little as possible, and to speak the truth as much as I can.[39]

This was the credo of Musorgsky the realist, the composer of *Marriage*. Yet in 1877, no more than two years later, he started in earnest on his "Little Russian" opera.

His reasons for composing *Sorochintsï Fair* in the end remain unclear. In the first place, he probably wished to use certain pieces of music once again: the market scene from the collective *Mlada* project and extracts from *Night on Bald Mountain*. The market-scene music fitted perfectly into the *Sorochintsï* plans, but *Night on Bald Mountain* was a peculiar choice, there being no reason in the story to introduce a witches' Sabbath. Musorgsky got around this by using the music for the dream of the character Gritsko.

A second reason was perhaps Musorgsky's wish to accommodate certain singers, such as Osip Petrov, Anna Vorobyova-Petrova, and Darya Leonova. There are grounds for assuming that the Petrov couple, who were themselves of Ukrainian origin, persuaded Musorgsky to compose this work.[40]

A third reason is that Ukrainian—or Little Russian, in the terminology of the time—comedy was an officially approved genre, as the production of Chaikovsky's *Vakula the Smith* in 1876 proved. In addition, Musorgsky was moving in circles that had ties with reactionary groups and personalities, among them the "aristocrat par excellence" Golenishchev-Kutuzov and the folk-song connoisseur Tertiy Ivanovich Filippov. As imperial controller, the latter combined romantic devotion to folk song with the reactionary politics of Official Nationality. The anti-Semitism of these circles left its traces in the score. As with Gogol, the portrayal of Jews is denigrating and caricatural—an aspect played down in Pavel Lamm's edition and in Vissarion Shebalin's completed version.

## CHAIKOVSKY: *EUGENE ONEGIN*

> Dargomïzhsky wrote *The Stone Guest* near the end of his life, fully believing that he was demolishing old foundations and was building on their ruins something new, colossal. A pitiable delusion! I saw him in his last period of his life and in view of his suffering (he had heart disease) it was not, of course, the time for arguing. But if anything is more hateful and *false* than this unsuccessful attempt to introduce *truth* into a branch of art where everything is based on *pseudo* and where *truth* in the usual sense of the word is not demanded at all—I do not know it.[41]

These words come from a diary note by Pyotr Chaikovsky for 23 July 1888. They may sound strange in light of the opera that Chaikovsky had composed in 1877–78 and that has entered the world repertoire as a tour de force of realism in opera: *Eugene Onegin*. Chaikovsky had, however, developed his own way of introducing truth in the realm of the pseudo.

Pushkin's "novel in verse" *Eugene Onegin* is a tour de force of narrative art. With a sidelong glance at Byron, it tells a simple story set among provincial landowners in about 1820. The plot is deliberately minimal: Tatyana, the young daughter of Madame Larina, falls in love with Eugene Onegin, from St. Petersburg. He rejects her. Her marriage to an eminent general then makes her a princess and a prominent member of St. Petersburg society. Onegin encounters her again in the highest St. Petersburg circles, but now it is his turn to be rejected. Running through this basic story is a subplot involving Onegin's relationship with his friend Lensky. When Onegin is bored at a ball to which Lensky has dragged him, he flirts with Lensky's fiancée, Olga, infuriates Lensky, is challenged to a duel, and kills his friend.

The attraction of *Eugene Onegin* does not lie in the story, but in the inimitable way in which Pushkin tells it, with detailed descriptions, intriguing digressions, and above all ubiquitous irony. The solid construction of the poem is masked by the flowing, improvised impression it makes.

In few literary works are style and content as closely interwoven as they are in *Eugene Onegin*. A transposition to the stage carries a high risk of ending up with nothing but a banal plot, which is, in fact, a criticism often leveled at Chaikovsky's opera. Some critics even speak of the fundamental incompatibility of the opera with its literary source. Chaikovsky is taken to task for ignoring Pushkin's irony as well, a point that defenders of the opera are quick to grant. In their estimation, however, the quality of the score springs from Chaikovsky's identification with the characters, and with Tatyana in particular. According to this view, the story is no more than a basic scheme onto which Chaikovsky has projected his own emotions. Both sides ignore the special role music plays in this opera, for in transforming Pushkin's detached and ironic narrative voice into music Chaikovsky unquestionably succeeds. The opera is closer to the original than is generally thought, the secret lying in a meticulous use of musical conventions, echoing the virtuosity with which Pushkin handled literary codes.

Early sketches of the opera indicate that Chaikovsky first considered taking examples from existing operas: a quintet à la Mozart; an ensemble divided into two pairs, as in Gounod's *Faust*. Not mentioned in the first scenario, but clearly present, is the typical Verdian scene of a party that ends in conflict: the ball in Act II. To lead this scene to a dramatic climax, Chaikovsky had to alter the story slightly. In Pushkin, Lensky does not challenge Onegin until the following day, and by letter, "in precise form, cold, lucid, with the deference befitting a gentleman." With Chaikovsky he does this at the ball itself in a paroxysm of rage.

Chaikovsky sets the opera very precisely in its own social milieu and period. The two ballroom scenes—the first at the country estate of the Larina family, the second in St. Petersburg—are easily distinguished by their dance music: a rustic waltz played by a military band as against a polonaise, the symbol of autocracy and high aristocracy. The characters, too, express themselves in the musical conventions of their milieu. This applies not only to the peasants and the old nurse, who sing in folk-song style, but also to the main characters. Their vocal style is based on the preferred genre of the bourgeoisie and the lower aristocracy, the salon romance. The intonation faithfully follows this idiom, called *sekstovïy* in Russian, because of the central importance of intervals of a sixth. That idiom dates the opera precisely in respect to time: the style is typical of the first quarter of the nineteenth century. The most important numbers in the score use the intonations of the salon romance. The best example is Tatyana's letter scene—in which, ignoring social norms, she declares her love for Onegin in a letter. Her great monologue is a concatenation of four romances, joined by recitatives. The music refers extensively to the opening number of the opera, the sentimental romance Tatyana and Olga sing in duet.[42] Pushkin draws the reader's attention to the artificial character of Tatyana's letter—"poignant nonsense," or "the *Freischütz* on the piano by a girl who cannot do it properly. . . ." Chaikovsky does exactly the same. Both show that Tatyana expresses herself in formulas she knows only from literature or from music. Her feelings have been filtered by the conventions of her background and upbringing.

In his treatment of Onegin, Chaikovsky transposes Pushkin's irony into music. Thus, in Act III, Onegin declares his love for Tatyana using the same motifs with which he had rejected her earlier; again, on recognizing Tatyana, he chooses a melody from the letter scene. Both examples are like asides by the composer, a musical commentary on Onegin's lack of character.[43]

The final scene between Onegin and Tatyana is once more a string of romances. Chaikovsky designed it with a very clear model in mind: Act III of Rubinstein's *The Demon* (1871), from which Chaikovsky learned how salon romances can be transformed into great, passionate love dialogues. The conventional idioms in the scene show that even the most fervent feelings of the characters are influenced by social conventions.

*Eugene Onegin* is one of the finest examples of musical realism. But its realism is based no more on *opéra dialogué* than it is on Musorgsky's naturalistic recitative. It is based, rather, on the choice of the subject and the careful use of codes in the characterization of persons and their milieu. Chaikovsky considered *Eugene Onegin* more as a chamber opera than a work for the big stage. He did not even call it an opera, but referred to it as "lyrical scenes." Generally considered to be a composer of passionate music, Chaikovsky reveals himself in this score as an exceptionally keen observer of daily life. The scenes with Tatyana and her nurse are splendid examples of this, constituting a unique portrait of two figures drawn from life: the emotionally confused adolescent girl and a clumsy old nurse unable to cope with such emotions.

## CHAPTER SEVEN

# "The Musician-Human"
## Pyotr Chaikovsky

"I have decided that one cannot avoid one's destiny and that in my encounter with this girl there is something fateful."[1] Chaikovsky wrote these lines to his patron Nadezhda von Meck, in a situation that had much in common with the story of *Eugene Onegin*. He, too, had received a passionate letter from a young girl, Antonina Milyukova, who declared her love for him and threatened suicide if he rejected her. The end result was that Chaikovsky married her in 1877, but left her again some two months later, fleeing from Russia. Because this biographical episode ran an almost parallel course to his work on the opera, it seems reasonable to link the two. Indeed, Chaikovsky himself helped to foster that connection. To the outside world he explained that his disastrous marriage had been influenced by his involvement with *Onegin,* and implied that he had been so troubled by Onegin's behavior that he resolved not to repeat his heartlessness. This explanation was recorded forty years after the event by Nikolai Kashkin, Chaikovsky's colleague at the Moscow Conservatory, and has since been part and parcel of all standard interpretations of Chaikovsky's life and work.

Myths about artists rarely stand up to careful biographical study, however. The chronology of Chaikovsky's story in fact does not tally, for his relationship with Antonina started well before he even considered writing an opera based on the *Onegin* story. Alexander Poznansky puts it as follows:

> It seems evident, then, that Tchaikovsky, consciously or not, later falsified to some extent the course of events in order to fit them into a Pushkinian liter-

ary framework. Betraying the inherent romanticism of his mind, this wishful reversal reshaped events to accord more completely with artistic notions of coincidence and destiny. Fate, not his own folly, became for him the instrument of his undoing.[2]

For a long time, Chaikovsky biographers have relied on such accidental and romanticized parallels between the composer's life and his work. Chaikovsky was proclaimed the prototype of the romantic composer: the "typical musician of the nineteenth century," as Vladimir Fédorov called him in an influential essay from 1970. In the standard account, Chaikovsky was a neurotic introvert, an artist entirely wrapped up in himself, whose inspiration depended on the extent to which he could release his emotions in his work, someone who needed music to keep his mental composure; he was "a composer who not only never ceased writing . . . but who no longer knew how to live, or to ward off the melancholy and emptiness that overwhelmed him when he was not composing."[3] The portrait we have of him today, one that has been academically underpinned by David Brown's four-volume critical study, is thus of the quintessential tortured artist, racked with emotional misery, a man who fought suicidal tendencies all his life.[4] As a "typical romantic" composer, Chaikovsky was applauded and maligned at one and the same time. The mystery surrounding him added to the popular appeal of his work, though on music critics, by contrast, his reputation had the opposite effect. As soon as the romantic norms came under review, Chaikovsky's artistic stature tumbled.

The romantic interpretation of Chaikovsky's work is misleading. Although the allegedly inseparable links between his life and his work, for instance between his marriage and *Onegin*, cannot be detected in the rest of his music, so strong was the image that it was projected into his entire oeuvre. The resulting absurd discrepancies forced commentators to come up time and again with explanations or rationalizations. How, for instance, can Chaikovsky's interest in eighteenth-century styles be reconciled with a romantic need for self-expression? According to David Brown, the retrospective style of the Rococo Variations or of the orchestral suite *Mozartiana* was for Chaikovsky a means to escape from himself into an artificial paradise of peace and harmony. He allegedly sought refuge in these earlier styles for his anguished emotions, which were to erupt with full force in the Fourth and Sixth Symphonies. In Brown's line of reasoning everything is put neatly into place: retrospection becomes a negative pole in the paradigm of self-expression.

Brown and most other biographers draw a thoroughly pathological picture. Chaikovsky's manifestations of his feelings are magnified into emotional excesses, the better to reconcile them with the rapt expression of his music. The reception of his work was, moreover, hampered by a long tradition of homophobia among influential critics. Chaikovsky's homosexuality had never been a secret, but his sexuality was seen as something destructive, a deviation against which he would struggle all his life, an obstacle Fate had placed in the way of a "normal" and happy existence. In this context, it did not take much for all sorts of rumors of suicide to gain credence. In 1981, Alexandra Orlova, an émigrée Soviet musicologist, presented the world with a bizarre suicide fantasy, which has since become an integral part of the Chaikovsky legend.[5] She suggested that Chaikovsky had been driven to attempt suicide by his former classmates at the School of Jurisprudence following a homosexual liaison. Although without a shred of reliable evidence, the story was nevertheless widely believed. It was exactly what people expected to hear.

Orlova's preposterous story has since been comprehensively refuted. Thus Poznansky has shown that her version is based on a false view of the attitudes regarding homosexuality in Chaikovsky's circles. Russian society was in fact less repressive than is generally believed.[6] The suicide theory is all the more remarkable in that we have more detailed information about Chaikovsky's death than about that of any other composer. From the plethora of daily newspaper reports about the progress of his illness, from the doctors' bulletins, and from the correspondence of relatives and friends, we can reconstruct the fatal course of his cholera with great precision.[7] The reason for the stream of rumors directly afterward was largely that cholera was considered a disease of the lower classes. It seemed inconceivable that someone of Chaikovsky's social rank would succumb to it.[8]

Alexander Poznansky's ground-breaking study of Chaikovsky, based as it is on a wealth of documentation and a thorough knowledge of Russian mores and habits at the time, overturned this traditional picture.[9] Chaikovsky emerges as a perfectly ordinary man, with many weaknesses and neuroses, but with a healthy enough common sense and sound inner balance. With the help of loving friends he came to terms with his homosexuality. The "Victorian" morality of Russian society at the time was in any case little more than a thin veneer, sexual mores having been in reality looser and more tolerant than elsewhere. Highly placed persons were quite able to display their homosexuality openly (as Chaikovsky never did) without endangering their position.

A revision of his biography thus challenges the romantic concept of the unity of Chaikovsky's life and work. Our starting point, the story of Chaikovsky's marriage in 1877, is a good illustration. To explain his decision to marry we do not need the notion of a malign destiny or a guilty conscience about homosexuality. The extant letters betray no trace of the latter, although the composer was understandably eager to quash rumors. The most probable explanation of the marriage is that Chaikovsky was anxious to acquire a normal social image. He had been plagued his whole life long with rumors about his private affairs, and not in the sexual sphere alone. Having noticed that among his friends homosexuality did not necessarily preclude marriage and family life, he decided to copy their example. He chose a wife whom he thought he could dominate and suggested to Antonina Milyukova that they live together "like brother and sister," believing he could arrange matters in such a way that his wife would not interfere with his sex life. Antonina Milyukova worshiped him and agreed to all his conditions. Though not very mature, she was a normal woman in all respects, certainly not the dim-witted virago Chaikovsky made her out to be later. She was, however, too naive to grasp the situation. From the correspondence it appears that it was not until 1880 that she realized what Chaikovsky had meant by his conditions.

It is a sad story. Chaikovsky bore the marriage with the courage of desperation. He tried for over two months to live with Antonina, but then he fled abroad. Once abroad, he found solace and support in his entirely platonic relationship with Nadezhda von Meck, a wealthy businesswoman who set herself up as his patron. There never was a formal divorce because of the intricacies of Russian law, and for years Antonina followed him and tried to regain his love, which regularly drove Chaikovsky to despair.

The story is hardly romantic, let alone heroic. It is a tale of painful human error. Quite patently Chaikovsky brought his misfortune upon himself. His lack of frankness and clarity, his conscious or unconscious abuse of the feelings of a young woman, inflicted grave hurt upon the both of them. But there was one positive result: Chaikovsky became acutely aware of his sexual identity following his crisis of 1877 to 1878 and came to terms with it. "Only now," he wrote to his brother Anatoly, "especially after the incident of my marriage, have I finally come to understand that there is nothing more fruitless than wanting to be other than what I am by nature."[10]

The work that is generally taken for the direct expression of Chaikovsky's spiritual crisis of 1877 to 1878 is his Fourth Symphony. However, all the programmatic explanations became attached to the work after the fact, whereas the chronology tells us that the Fourth Symphony was conceived in outline before the crisis it is alleged to portray. We may put it that the symphony in its final form bears traces of Chaikovsky's emotional crisis, but they are—as Chaikovsky himself explained—little more than echoes. In no sense can biographical considerations do justice to the artistic complexity of the work. On the other hand, it is absurd to transpose the idea of a romantic fate which Chaikovsky later tried to read into the symphony—or rather, which he copied from the program that was being foisted upon Beethoven's Fifth at the time—into his life. If we adhere to such identification of his life and work, the Chaikovsky portrait simply becomes a caricature. For how else can the following interpretation be viewed?

> Beginning with the Fourth Symphony and *Eugene Onegin,* Tchaikovsky's music now reflects all the indulgent yearning and the garish exteriorisation of a composer who can never refrain from wearing his heart on his sleeve. . . . It was no accident that such music was conceived by a warped neurotic, shy and tortured. . . . [Climactic passages in the Fourth and Fifth Symphonies] do more than tear the heart (as indeed they are meant to do) but also affect the nerves like an exhibition of hysteria (with which they are very possibly related). . . . There is something quite unbalanced and, in the last resort, ugly, in this dropping of all restraint. This man is ill, we feel: must we be shown all his sores without exception? Will he insist on us not merely witnessing, but sharing, one of his nervous attacks?[11]

In more recent literature the exaggerations have been somewhat scaled down, but the message has remained unchanged.

The assessment of Chaikovsky's artistic achievement is in need of radical revision. To reach beyond the clichés, we must look at the context of his art. What did Chaikovsky himself aim to achieve with his work, what were his aesthetic principles, and in what social milieu was his music set?

## CHAIKOVSKY'S PROFESSIONALISM

"As for me personally, to tell the truth I have only one interest in life: my success as a composer." From this comment, made in 1872, it appears that Chaikovsky was by no means averse to success and fame. He wrote boastfully to his brother Modest, "The time is drawing near when Kolya, Tolya, Ippolit, and Modya will no longer be the Tchaikovskys but merely the brother of *the Tchaikovsky.*" To Nadezhda von Meck he wrote on 28 July 1877, during the darkest period of his life: "I have the weakness (if it can be called a weakness) of loving life, of loving my work, of loving my future successes."[12] Do these remarks betray even the slightest trace of the romantic artist? Contempt for social success was alien to Chaikovsky. He had no sympathy with the idea of the artist as outsider, with the "Davidsbündler" mentality of a Schumann, or with the expanded ego of a Wagner. For Chaikovsky, there was no conflict between the artist and his public. He was highly sensitive to external circumstances and expectations, and searched constantly for new ways of reaching the public, seeing no harm in playing on the taste of particular audiences. The stylization of eighteenth-century melodies and the patriotic themes in his work are bound up with the values of the Russian aristocracy. We have already mentioned the role of the polonaise as a code for the Russian dynastic state, the musical symbol of Russian patriotism. The polonaise as a finale was one of Chaikovsky's recipes for success. His phenomenal triumph on 12 January 1885 in St. Petersburg with the première of his Third Suite was due in large part to the polonaise with which it concluded. That success exceeded even Chaikovsky's own high expectations. He wrote to Nadezhda von Meck: "Never before have I experienced such a triumph; I saw the whole mass of the audience stirred and grateful to me. These moments are the best adornments of an artist's life. For their sake, living and toiling are worthwhile."[13]

In discussing Chaikovsky's work in the 1860s and 1870s, we have already referred to the large number of genres he employed, and the professional approach that distinguished his work from that of the *kuchka*. In the 1880s he continued along the same lines. Chaikovsky's predominance became so great that Rimsky-Korsakov remarked with some envy:

> At this time [1892] there had begun to be noticeable a considerable cooling-off and even a somewhat inimical attitude toward the memory of the Five in the time of Balakirev. On the contrary, a worship of Tchaikovsky and a tendency toward eclecticism were growing stronger. Nor could one help noticing the predilection (which sprang up in our circle) for Italian and French music of the era of the wig and the farthingale [that is, the eighteenth century], music introduced by Tchaikovsky in his *Queen of Spades* and *Iolanta*.[14]

## AESTHETICS

We must look to the cursory comments scattered in his correspondence in order to distill Chaikovsky's aesthetic conception. His ideas were not always consistent, and particularly when it came to his own oeuvre, he could be self-contradictory. Of some of his works we can prove by

Chaikovsky's own words that he counted them among the best and the worst he had ever written, for instance the Fifth Symphony and the *Manfred* Symphony. The critiques he wrote from 1871 to 1876, moreover, are not always representative of what he really thought. His review of Wagner's *Ring* in Bayreuth, for instance, was balanced enough, but we know from a letter to his brother Modest that he could not stand the work. The reason for his aversion can be summed up in the famous comment: "And so this is what Wagner's reform seeks to achieve! Before, music strove to delight people—now they are tormented and exhausted."[15] Chaikovsky thought that the high demands Wagner made of the audience were in conflict with the true function of music: the provision of aesthetic pleasure.

His objections to Brahms were of a similar kind. He thought that Brahms "never expresses anything or, when he does, he fails to express it fully. His music is made up of fragments of some indefinable *something*, skillfully welded together."[16] As far as Chaikovsky was concerned, Brahms lacked what was most important: beauty. Brahms, he believed, considered structural complexity an end in itself, a learned pose.

From that we may take it that Chaikovsky sought the expressive value of music in its immediately appreciable and comprehensible qualities—in what, in the wake of a long tradition of structural music analysis, used to be referred to rather deprecatingly as "surface phenomena." Chaikovsky's admiration of Bizet's *Carmen* was fully in line with that attitude: "This music has no pretensions to profundity, but it is so charming in its simplicity, so vigorous, not contrived but instead sincere, that I learned all of it from beginning to end almost by heart."[17]

Mozart aroused an enormous fascination in Chaikovsky. From his statements, it appears that Mozart was a mystery to him, especially in the way in which he combined simplicity with profundity. For a long time Chaikovsky remained alone in this admiration, since neither the *kuchka* nor Nadezhda von Meck found anything but superficiality in Mozart.

Responsiveness to beauty, the importance of musical surface phenomena, aesthetic enjoyment as a final end, veneration of Mozart—all this is far from the Promethean artistry generally associated with the nineteenth century. Indeed, Chaikovsky's idea of music was to a large extent based on its aesthetic impact. That view was reinforced by the interest in his work shown by Ivan Vsevolozhsky, director of the Imperial Theaters since 1881. Connoisseur, aesthete, lover of classical art (at the end of his life he became director of the Hermitage), a keen Francophile,

Vsevolozhsky was responsible for the first flowering of the Mariyinsky Theater. He paid the utmost attention to the aesthetic perfection of opera performances. In addition, he extended the ballet program appreciably, finding an ideal partner in the French ballet master Marius Petipa. Vsevolozhsky was the driving force behind such operas by Chaikovsky as *The Queen of Spades* and *Iolanta* and such ballets as *The Sleeping Beauty* and *The Nutcracker*. The collaboration of Vsevolozhsky, Chaikovsky, and Petipa was one of the earliest manifestations of Russian aestheticism.

Self-expression was not as central to Chaikovsky's aesthetic as is generally believed. While Chaikovsky had a great deal of sympathy for his subjects, sympathy does not necessarily mean identification. To treat all his works with a literary inspiration—the operas, *Manfred*, and *Francesca da Rimini*—as confessional music is unwarranted. Although the demonic figure of Hermann in *The Queen of Spades* has occasionally been considered an expression of Chaikovsky's morbidity and suicidal tendencies, the sources make it clear that Chaikovsky did not identify himself with this character. Hermann's obsession simply aroused Chaikovsky's compassion. His diary entry on 2 March 1890, following the completion of the opera, reflects a characteristic mixture of empathy and detachment: "Wept terribly when Hermann breathed his last. The result of exhaustion, or maybe because it is truly good."[18]

Chaikovsky's perception of music is perhaps best summed up in a declaration to Nadezhda von Meck in which he described music as heaven's best gift to humanity: "It alone clarifies, reconciles, and consoles. But it is not a straw just barely clutched at. It is a faithful friend, protector, and comforter, and for its sake alone, life in this world is worth living."[19]

## THE SOCIAL CONTEXT

In all the above-mentioned respects, Chaikovsky differs from the leading nineteenth-century composers. His art is closer to the principles of Mozart and Mendelssohn than to those of his contemporaries. That is hardly surprising when we consider that Chaikovsky worked under conditions much like those that prevailed in the eighteenth century. Russia, indeed, was "the last eighteenth-century state," and Chaikovsky created his oeuvre in circumstances that Mozart and Beethoven would have considered ideal. He enjoyed an extensive system of aristocratic patronage, his most noted sponsor being Nadezhda von Meck, the rich widow of a railroad entrepreneur who set aside a considerable part of her fortune for the patronage of artists. She was a forceful personality who did not support artists out of vanity but from conviction. She sustained Chaikovsky financially from 1876 to 1890, enabling him to give up his teaching post at the Moscow Conservatory and devote himself wholly to writing music. The relationship between Mme von Meck and Chaikovsky is documented in an impressive body of correspondence, one that provides a wealth of information about Chaikovsky's work. This oft-quoted source material has contributed appreciably to the romantic image of the composer; that view, however, is somewhat misleading, because the picture Mme von Meck formed of Chaikovsky was strongly colored by her own romantic ideas—a picture with which Chaikovsky, in his turn, tried to comply.

His patron's personality reflected an unusual combination of realistic utilitarianism and passionate romanticism. Nadezhda von Meck was a sober businesswoman who ran a large financial empire with efficiency, and yet found an outlet for her deep romantic longings in Chaikovsky's music. To her, Chaikovsky was both a musical genius and also the embodiment of the highest moral good: "I cannot convey to you what I feel when I listen to your compositions. I am prepared to give up my soul to you, you become deified for me; everything conceivable of that which is most generous, pure, and sublime rises up from the depth of my soul."[20] She saw Chaikovsky as a realization of the ideal unity of musician and human being: "I regard the musician-human as the supreme creation of nature."[21]

Chaikovsky's temperament differed radically from his patron's. He lacked the rebellious ego of the romantic, having a sentimental rather than passionate character. There has been much speculation as to why Mme von Meck ended their relationship in 1890. Uncritical biographers, who prefer rumor to verifiable sources, claim, of course, that she discovered the secret of Chaikovsky's homosexuality and hence rejected him, but it seems probable that she had come to know about that at an earlier stage. The reason must perhaps be sought in the pressure her family exerted on her to give up her eccentric art patronage.

Chaikovsky also enjoyed the favors of other sponsors, who, if anything, were even more interesting because they were connected to the court: Ivan Vsevolozhsky, Prince Meshchersky (a leading politician and counselor to Alexander III), and Grand Duke Konstantin Konstantinovich (a cousin of Alexander III).

In Russia's paternalistic society it was customary for members of the higher estates to patronize those of the lower. Thus Chaikovsky could count on the support of the higher reaches of the aristocracy, while he himself acted as patron to young people of lower rank. An essential feature of this artistic patronage was the equal footing of patron and artist. In their correspondence, Chaikovsky and Nadezhda von Meck discussed all sorts of subjects as equals: art, philosophy, politics, religion. Nowhere does he evince the slightest trace of subservience or flattery. With Konstantin Konstantinovich, too, Chaikovsky had a straightforward relationship. Dedications of works to patrons were expressions of artistic partnership rather than of humble gratitude. The Fourth Symphony is known as the seal of Chaikovsky's friendship with Mme von Meck. His relationship with Konstantin Konstantinovich bore artistic fruit in the Six Songs, op. 63 (1887), for which the grand duke himself wrote the words.

From 1884, Chaikovsky enjoyed the patronage of Alexander III, who bestowed the Order of St. Vladimir upon him. The tsar asked personally for a new production of *Eugene Onegin* to be performed in St. Petersburg. Previously, the work had been staged only in Moscow, by a student ensemble from the conservatory. Alexander III had *Onegin* put on, not in the Mariyinsky Theater, but in the *Bolshoy kamenniy* theater, an indication that Chaikovsky's music would henceforth take the place of Italian opera as the official, imperial art. Thanks to the intercession of Vsevolozhsky, moreover, Alexander III granted Chaikovsky a lifetime pension of three thousand rubles a year, thus making Chaikovsky the premier court composer, in practice if not in name.

As his career advanced, Chaikovsky increasingly became the embodiment of the artistic values of the aristocracy. His art gave unequaled expression to the transition from the artistic ideal of the 1860s and 1870s—with its emphasis on civil responsibility—to the aestheticism of the 1880s and 1890s. The retrospective and international character of his art was the symptom of a nostalgic revival of the aristocratic spirit in an age when the aristocracy was being forced to make way gradually for a new capitalist elite.[22]

## EXAMPLES OF PROFESSIONALISM: CHURCH MUSIC AND BALLET MUSIC

Since the two genres seem to have little in common, it is not customary to consider Chaikovsky's church and ballet music under a single heading. Could there be a greater contrast than that between the ascetic gravity of the one and the exuberant sensuality of the other? Yet there is a link between them. In both, the composer is expected to heed specific norms, and in neither is there much room for personal creative contributions. Then too, Chaikovsky brought all his professional skill to bear upon both: his sensitivity to audience expectations, his respect for institutions, and his willingness to adapt himself to these. Professionalism marks Chaikovsky's entire oeuvre, but it is nowhere as manifest as in his church and ballet music. The fact that he worked in both genres is in itself a correction of the cliché that he was a "self-expressing composer." On listening to his music, it would not immediately occur to one that the two genres sprang from the same hand.

CHURCH MUSIC

Chaikovsky's church music reflected his dissatisfaction with the prevailing Orthodox mode, dictated by the Court Chapel in St. Petersburg and amounting to the perpetuation of the style of its director from 1796 until 1825, Dmitry Bortnyansky. When Bortnyansky became director of the Imperial Court Chapel, he obtained the exclusive right to publish Russian church music. His powers to decide what might be sung in the Russian Church were absolute, this monopoly passing into the hands of his successors after his death.

In 1878, Chaikovsky composed his Liturgy of St. John Chrysostom. Jurgenson published the score in Moscow in 1879, having circumvented the monopoly of the Court Chapel by a direct appeal to the church censor. Although the Court Chapel immediately took legal proceedings against him, Jurgenson won his case, following which the approval of the church authorities sufficed to have liturgical music published. This decision smoothed the path for the renewal of Russian church music, in which Muscovite composers were to play a pioneering role. Chaikovsky wrote to Mme von Meck: "This is of importance not so much for my *Liturgy,* which may not even be all that worthy, as for the victory of the principle of liberty in the composition of church music."[23]

The first performance of Chaikovsky's Liturgy took place in the Kiev University church, excerpts of the work being played on 21 November 1880 before a closed circle of members of the Moscow Conservatory and on 18 December at a public concert. Now it was the church authorities' turn to protest. The bishop of Moscow condemned such use of ecclesiastical texts outside the context of a church service, using the anti-Semitic argument that even Jewish composers would now feel entitled to make use of the liturgy.[24] Although Chaikovsky had genuinely intended the work for church use, observing all the rules—the demand for homophonic and text-bound recitation without musical embellishments—his Liturgy was no longer authorized for performance in church after this intervention.

Immediately after the disappointing experience with his Liturgy, Chaikovsky started work on his most important piece of church music, the "Vsenoshchnoye bdeniye" (usually abbreviated to "Vsenoshchnaya") or "All-Night Vigil" (1881–82). The vigil, held on the eve of every Sunday and of all important church feasts, is one of the most important elements of Orthodox practice. In strict monasteries it is performed throughout the night, whence the name. In normal practice it is shortened into an extended service, consisting of a combination of vespers and matins. The liturgical principles of the service are relatively complicated, in part because the texts are derived from several sources. Chaikovsky's composition was accordingly preceded by a long study, for which the composer consulted various clerics. "If even the priests don't know, how am I, a poor sinner, to resolve it!" was his comment when a priest of his acquaintance admitted that his sexton arranged every service as he saw fit.[25] However, Chaikovsky did obtain help from Dmitry Razumovsky, an authority on the history of Russian church music.

Unlike his Liturgy, Chaikovsky's "Vsenoshchnaya" was based on the original liturgical melodies. He was not the first to do this. In St. Petersburg, Gavriyil Lomakin had used a similar approach, as had Nikolai Potulov in Moscow. Chaikovsky, though, did not consider their solutions very satisfactory. He was strongly aware of the stylistic gulf between modern harmony and the old style based on the church modes. His ambition, in fact, was confined to a tentative attempt to do something about this discrepancy; by basing his work on the old church chants, he hoped to help reduce the modern European influence on Russian church music. He had no illusions about the eclectic nature of his method. Some of his liturgical pieces were based more closely on the European model, others on Russian chant. He saw his work as a middle path between Bortnyansky's and Potulov's. The strict note-for-note harmonization of Potulov's old chants struck Chaikovsky as being too extreme. He felt that some adaptation to the modern taste was unavoidable: "It is equally impossible to restore the chants Ivan the Terrible must have heard in the Uspenski cathedral, as it is to change the modern visitors to this cathedral with their overcoats, uniforms, chignons and German dress back into boyars or suburban *oprichniki*."[26]

Chaikovsky's "Vsenoshchnaya" gave a crucial impetus to the flowering of Russian church music that was soon to begin. In 1884 and 1885, at the behest of Alexander III, he composed another nine liturgical pieces, including three versions of "Cheruvimskaya" (the "Hymn of Praise of the Cherubim" from the Liturgy).

## BALLET MUSIC

On first seeing *Swan Lake,* Hermann Laroche responded with amazement: "With an ease which no one would assume the learned author of so many symphonies, quartets, and overtures to have, Mr Tchaikovsky noticed the peculiarities of the ballet style, and, adapting himself to it, once again manifested that versatility which constitutes one of the most treasured properties of his compositional talent."[27] This reaction seems astonishing to those who are accustomed to look upon Chaikovsky as a ballet composer by nature. A privileged witness such as Laroche had a different impression. Ballet music was not part of Chaikovsky's normal development; his use of the genre was anything but the result of a spontaneous process. Ballet music made special demands upon a composer and called for precise working conditions, so much so that Chaikovsky at first declined to work in the field: "They tell me that during the production of a new ballet, balletmasters treat the music very unceremoniously and demand many changes and alterations. To write under such conditions is impossible."[28]

In the production of a ballet, the composer was subordinate to the balletmaster, a relationship that was sometimes contractually stipulated. The balletmaster's wish to have a say in the composition was due not so much to a lack of respect for the music as to a fundamental quality of the ballet: dance is preeminently a "living" art, and subject as is no other discipline to the demands of the moment. Nowadays, classical ballets such as Chaikovsky's have such a long tradition of artificial preservation that they are all too readily associated with rigid conventions. At the time when it emerged, however, this art form was as "living" as modern dance is today. Productions underwent continual change in order to tailor them to the abilities of new dancers. They were constantly being shortened or lengthened, the dances were rearranged, and the libretto was altered in accordance with changes in cultural preferences and philosophical ideas.

Before Chaikovsky applied himself to this genre, it had been the exclusive province of specialists, composers such as Ludwig Minkus and Cesare Pugni, who wrote nothing else and who knew all the tricks of the trade. Expected to satisfy the demands of the moment, they were given little room for individual creativity. It was an absolute rule that the visual aspect took pride of place in ballets. Music that was too demanding, or that vied for the attention of the audience, was dismissed as unsuitable. The second criterion ballet music had to satisfy was its *qualité dansante,* its ability to give emphasis to dance movements. Dancers demanded a regular meter and stereotyped phrasing. In Chaikovsky's day, the stylistic clichés of French ballet music of half a century earlier were still in vogue, and familiarity with the musical patterns gave dancers a sense of security. Only in the orchestration could the composer let himself go to any extent. Auditory appeal was part of the sensory richness of the performance. An anonymous critic put it as follows: "As the best woman is the one of whom nothing is said, the best music for ballet is that which passes almost unnoticed."[29] Not surprisingly, ballet music did not rank high with ambitious composers for these very reasons. That Chaikovsky nevertheless chose this genre bears witness to his professionalism; not only that, but he strove in his ballet music to extend the boundaries of the genre and raise its artistic standing.

Chaikovsky's first experience in this field came with the production of *Swan Lake* in Moscow (composed in 1876, premièred on 20 February 1877; Plate 6). The choreographer was Julius Reisinger. The ballet tells the story of Odette, a girl turned into a swan whose bewitchment can be broken only by the faithful love of a man. When the man appears in the person of Siegfried, he proves to be not faithful enough, with the tragic death of both lovers following as the result. The libretto makes use of standard elements from the world of romantic ballet. Enchanted girls are almost obligatory, whether they be swans, Wilis (in *Giselle*), or Sylphides. Wagner's influence in the libretto of *Swan Lake* is unmistakable. Not only does the man, whose name is Siegfried, share with his namesake the weakness of denying his true love under the influence of magical deception, but the death of the protagonists is accompanied by a flood, as it is in *Götterdämmerung;* the medieval German setting is reminiscent of *Lohengrin,* not by chance an opera in which a bewitched swan also appears; and the famous swan theme in Chaikovsky's score contains a quotation of the motif by which Lohengrin utters his warning to Elsa.

Unfamiliar as he was with the rules of ballet music, Chaikovsky took his cue from the specialists. In the score of *Swan Lake,* we can easily distinguish their formulas from Chaikovsky's own. The variation schemes are traditional. The codas of the dance numbers make use of the clichés and the lavish orchestration of traditional ballet music, in a manner very unlike Chaikovsky's personal style. In the music of the dances themselves he greatly simplified his style rhythmically, minimizing the rhythmical subtleties found in his other work. The orchestration is more refined than in the average ballet score and at times suggestive. In the work as a whole, Chaikovsky aimed for closer than the customary structural links. There is a marked motivic unity, the central conflict being reflected in the arrangement of the keys.

Little is known about Chaikovsky's collaboration with Reisinger. It does seem, however, that during the composition Chaikovsky was given an unusually free hand—which does not mean that his score was treated with greater respect than the work of his specialist colleagues. His score, like theirs, was abridged, revised, and rearranged. The version of *Swan Lake* with which we are familiar today is not based on the original production, but on Marius Petipa's revision for St. Petersburg in 1895. Modest Chaikovsky adapted the libretto for that production, and Riccardo Drigo and Eduard Langner the music.[30]

*Swan Lake* was well received by the public, but press reactions were divided. There were nationalistic objections to the "German theme," to what one critic called "*Kartoffelnmusik*" (German potato music). The main complaint, however, was the unsuitability of such music for a ballet: "Is the ballet written for the music, or, on the contrary, the music for the ballet?" Despite the concessions Chaikovsky had made to convention, his score was considered "too learned." One critic parodied the opening scene in a pointed manner:

> A magnificent green park. In one of its glades Mr Gilbert II (also the noble prince Siegfried) celebrates his coming of age, and on account of this orders the villagers to dance. Nothing can be done; grudgingly, but putting on a happy appearance, they begin to jump clumsily.
>
> "But why do you dance so badly?" Mr Vanner (the Prince's tutor) asks them sternly.
>
> "Ah, forgive us! To do otherwise to Mr Tchaikovsky's music is impossible; it is worse than marching in 3/4."[31]

*Sleeping Beauty* (1889) was begun under more auspicious circumstances, as a prestigious production by the Mariyinsky Theater in St. Petersburg, staged on the initiative of Ivan Vsevolozhsky. The work reflected his artistic vision in the glorification of seventeenth-century French court culture, the Versailles of Louis XIV, the heyday of absolute monarchy. It was an expression of Vsevolozhsky's aestheticism and at the same time tailored to the taste of the Russian court and the higher ranks of the aristocracy.

*Sleeping Beauty* is a *ballet-féerie,* loosely based on the model of the seventeenth-century French *comédie-ballet.* The subject is the well-known fairy tale by Charles Perrault, *La Belle au bois dormant.* The scenario was expanded with an elaborate divertissement: the concluding wedding celebration, which takes up the entire third act and is at the same time a parade of Perrault's well-known fairy-tale figures, all of whom are guests at the party. Neither time nor money was spared for the visual effects, although the aestheticism of the project did not mean that Vsevolozhsky was intent on providing entertainment with little substance. The fairy tale has rich allegorical possibilities. Perrault's nameless "Beauty" was given the name of Aurora, with all its appropriate connotations—morning, renewal, spring, the regeneration of life, and so on. The awakening of the Sleeping Beauty after the prince's kiss is one of the classical poetic images of the burgeoning of sexuality. Chaikovsky saw the theme above all as an expression of the struggle of Fate against the forces of life. The message is optimistic, because Fate (represented by the curse of Carabosse, the wicked fairy) turns out to be powerless in the end.

*Sleeping Beauty* is not a drama in the strict sense of the word, since by the end of the prologue we know what will happen in the following acts. Accordingly, Chaikovsky eschewed the dramatic opposition of keys he had used in *Swan Lake* in favor of related keys in large tableaux. The third act, for instance, does not contain a return to the opening key; rather, the musical link is established by simple motivic references to the preceding acts. The undramatic structure of the score contributes appreciably to the impression that the story is ageless. Not governed by the laws of place and time, the ballet seems wholly situated in the autonomous world of the imagination.

In *Sleeping Beauty* Chaikovsky was given the opportunity of collaborating with one of the greatest balletmasters of the time, the Frenchman Marius Petipa. The artists treated each other with the utmost respect. Petipa, for his part, left Chaikovsky an exceptionally free hand. He also worked to convince the dancers of the music's worth, because they perceived the score as unusually complicated (Plate 7). The belief that Petipa laid down what he wanted from Chaikovsky to the smallest detail rests on a misunderstanding, one arising from the confusion of two distinct sources: Petipa's sketchy and general instructions to Chaikovsky, and his detailed choreographic plan. Although the second has been mistaken for a set of instructions to the composer, in reality it reflected Petipa's changing thoughts as preparations for the production proceeded.[32] Petipa's respect for Chaikovsky was in fact so great that he hardly ever demanded changes, something he certainly did with other ballet composers.

Chaikovsky's score was a crucial step in the aesthetic revaluation of ballet music. He aimed at an overall impression of noble simplicity, while leaving room within that framework for musical invention. Hence rhythm and texture are richly varied, and the clichés of *Swan Lake* have largely disappeared. Even where Petipa asked for standard dances (polkas, waltzes, galops, and so on), Chaikovsky toned down the rhythmic stereotypes. In the fine-tuning of the music to the dramatic situations, too, *Sleeping Beauty* left all rivals far behind. The piece as we know it represents Chaikovsky's score in its ideal state. For the first production, however, it was abridged and rearranged, as was customary in ballet practice.[33]

The success of *Sleeping Beauty* led Vsevolozhsky to plan a new collaboration without delay between Chaikovsky and Petipa. As its subject he chose *The Nutcracker,* based loosely on a tale by E. T. A. Hoffmann, in an Alexandre Dumas adaptation. When Petipa had to withdraw for health reasons, he was replaced by Lev Ivanov.

*The Nutcracker* (1892) was conceived as a ballet in which children would play the leading roles, to which end the virtuoso dance parts were given to the supporting characters. The structure of the ballet was exceedingly free and original for the time. The story starts with a Christmas party and ends in a fairy-tale world. The girl Clara is attracted to a Nutcracker, a small wooden figure given to her by her eccentric uncle Drosselmeyer. At night she witnesses a battle between the Nutcracker and the King of the Mice. The Nutcracker, saved by her from death, then changes into a Prince, and as a token of his gratitude takes her with him to the Kingdom of Sweets. In this form, the story has little to do with Hoffmann's. The typical combination of reality and demonic fiction so characteristic of that writer has been abandoned, and the story transformed into a fairy tale in which the links with reality are adumbrated but not elaborated. Petipa had retained Drosselmeyer's demonic character, but Ivanov softened this aspect.

Chaikovsky's score combines a calculated naïveté with concern for detail and characterization. An example of this studied artlessness is found in the simple descending scales, most conspicuous in the great pas de deux of the second act, but subtly marking all the important stages of the tale. Sound color plays a significant part in the characterizations, for example in the grotesque study of Drosselmeyer, in the sound illusion that paints the atmosphere of the fantasy world (with flutter-tonguing in the flute, for instance), or the use of the celesta in the "Sugar-Plum-Fairy" variation. (Chaikovsky had become familiar with this instrument in Paris and had it brought over in the greatest secrecy lest it fall prematurely into the hands of Rimsky-Korsakov or Glazunov.) The portrayal of the snowstorm in the pine forest is a splendid example of sound suggestion.

The unusual structure of the ballet provoked much criticism, as did the "nonsense" of the story. Paradoxically enough, these two "failings" ultimately profited the ballet. The vagueness of the content became an advantage as soon as choreography was treated more as an abstract art. What is essential for the appeal of *The Nutcracker* is not the story itself, but the possibilities it offers for creating a visual atmosphere. Throughout the plot there is also a clear choreographic development in the transition from mime to pure dance, or, as Margarita Mazo puts it, in "the development of the main character, Clara, along the path from an unhappy and dance-less world into a world where she finds the inspiration of expressing herself in dance."[34]

## OPERA

Chaikovsky used Rubinstein's *The Demon* as the model for the third act of *Eugene Onegin*. His next opera, *The Maid of Orléans* (1878–79), was a response to another opera by Rubinstein, *The Maccabees*. The creative answer of a historical *grand opéra* responded directly to the tremendous international success of Rubinstein's opera. Chaikovsky's starting point was Schiller's play *Die Jungfrau von Orleans,* but he expanded on this with borrowings from other sources: Jules Barbier's *Jeanne d'Arc,* Auguste Mermet's opera by the same name, and details from Henri Wallon's biography of the saint. Chaikovsky centered his version on Joan of Arc's love for the Burgundian knight Lionel, a worldly, sexual passion that renders her unfit for her mission in the eyes of God and of men. She is unmasked by her own father as an impostor and dies her historical death at the stake—while Schiller preferred to have her killed in battle. The opera is constructed with broad musical gestures and relies on the contrasting effects of large blocks of music. Because of the consistent simplification of the historical and psychological contents, *The Maid of Orléans* is not one of the most interesting elaborations of the Joan of Arc story. It nevertheless contains impressive passages, for instance the robust, ecstatic hymn at the end of the first act, where Joan is engaged in a dialogue with a chorus of heavenly voices.

In *Mazepa* (1883), Chaikovsky chose another historical subject but restructured it to form an essentially personal drama. The literary source was Pushkin's epic *Poltava,* a panegyric to Peter the Great in his fight against the Ukrainian separatist Ivan Mazepa in 1709. In the opera, Chaikovsky applauds Peter's victory with a symphonic intermezzo representing the battle of Poltava. The Russian victory is expressed by the "Slava" melody, which Musorgsky had raised into a symbol of tsarism in *Boris Godunov.* In the rest of the opera the historical background plays hardly any part. There is no meaningful link between personal drama and historical context in *Mazepa,* as there is, for instance, in *Boris Godunov* or in Verdi's *Don Carlos.* That is no reason, however, for dismissing the work: it is a feature rather than a fault. The personal interaction of the characters in fact yielded several powerful pages of opera, the best example being the impressive scene between Mazepa and Maria in the second act. Mazepa is married to the much younger Maria, whose father, Kochubey, is opposed to the marriage and betrays Mazepa's plan for an independent Ukraine to Peter the Great—who, however, has no reason for doubting Mazepa's loyalty. Mazepa takes his revenge on Kochubey, having him seized, tortured, and condemned to death. He worries, though, about Maria's reaction. His aria shows that he is deeply in love with his wife. He makes her privy to his ambitions, and Maria, in turn, declares herself prepared to stand by him. But he does not have the heart to tell her what that will entail for her personally, and she has no idea of what is going on in the castle dungeons. The music signals a fundamental break in relations; the two voices are given no chance of becoming reconciled. Mazepa abruptly breaks off the conversation. After his departure, Maria's mother confronts her with the truth. Hastening to the place of execution, they arrive too late, and Maria loses her reason. Chaikovsky allows the music to die out at the end with a forlorn lullaby that Maria sings in her madness. *Mazepa* is an opera of uncompromising gloom. In the scenes that follow, things go from bad to worse. The opera betrays the influence of Musorgsky and Serov, for instance in its declamatory choral style and in the role of the drunken Cossack during the execution scene. The fade-out at the end of Maria's lullaby is comparable to the lament of the *yuródivïy* at the end of *Boris Godunov.*

In 1885 Chaikovsky made a radical revision of his Gogol opera, *Vakula the Smith.* The new title, *Cherevichki,* is generally mistranslated as "the little shoes" or "the little slippers." In fact it designates the women's boots that are part of the Ukrainian national dress. The title refers to Vakula's quest for the boots of Catherine the Great to satisfy his flirtatious beauty, Oxana. Chaikovsky was dissatisfied with the first version, believing that he had lost himself in detail and had neglected the crux of the story. In his revision, he simplified the harmony, added several musical numbers, and enhanced the spectacular impact of the reception scene in the palace. The revision may be considered an artistic criticism of the earlier *kuchka* aesthetic—not its folklorism, but its demand for realism in every detail. Lack of articulation and of attention to the overall structure was the result. Both Musorgsky and Rimsky-Korsakov, as well as Chaikovsky, later broke out of the *kuchka* straitjacket through the study of international examples.

*Charodeyka* (The enchantress, 1885–87) is based on an undistinguished melodrama by Ippolit Shpazhinsky. Set in the fifteenth century, it concerns Natasha, a beautiful widow who keeps an inn and has a loose reputation. No man can escape her spell, not even the local prince and his son. A tangle of jealousies and vengeful feelings sows death and destruction. The story is extremely unconvincing, but Chaikovsky was obviously fascinated by the theme of feminine allure. He explained that his choice of the plot had been inspired by "my soul's radical need to express in music what was called by Goethe *das Ewig-Weibliche zieht uns hinan* [the Eternal Feminine draws us upward]. The fact that with Natasha the *powerful beauty of femininity* is for so long concealed in the shape of a *loose woman* rather intensifies her theatrical appeal."[35] Chaikovsky saw *The Enchantress* as a kind of remake of *La Traviata* or of *Carmen,* works he interpreted as reflecting ideal femininity in characters with a provocative manner. Although the opera foundered on the preposterous libretto, the erotic tension of the best scenes suggests that the idea might well have worked with a better text.

*The Queen of Spades* (1890) was Chaikovsky's third Pushkin opera, the source being the short story by the same name, a masterpiece of irony and literary conciseness. Pushkin tells the story of Herman, an impoverished officer who dreams of making his fortune at the gaming table. When he discovers that an elderly countess knows which three cards will always win, he becomes obsessed with wresting the secret from her. By feigning love for Liza, the countess's poor niece, he gains entry into the countess's house. He seeks the old lady out in her bedroom and asks about the three cards, but the countess dies of fright. She later appears

to him as a ghost and imparts the secret to him: "Three, seven, ace!"
At the gaming table, Herman wins with the first two cards. The third
time, however, the queen of spades is turned up instead of the promised ace. Overcome by the shock, Herman passes the rest of his life in
a madhouse.

The libretto, originally intended for the unknown composer Nikolai
Klenovsky, was written by Modest Chaikovsky at the request of Ivan
Vsevolozhsky. The arrangement links the story to a number of opera
conventions (including a blatant plagiarism from Bizet's *Carmen,* the
children playing at soldiers). The relationship between Herman and Liza
is turned into pure romantic love, and Liza becomes the countess's
granddaughter, so that socially she is out of Herman's reach. In the opera,
love is the mainspring of Herman's obsession: he wants to learn the secret of the cards to gain social advancement and hence be entitled to ask
for Liza's hand. The libretto also provides him with a rival in the person of Prince Yeletsky, Liza's fiancé. Liza for her part is carried away by
Herman's passion. Yet the moment she realizes that Herman has lost his
mind and become monomaniacally obsessed with the secret of the cards
and the fortune he is going to make, she commits suicide. At the gaming table, Prince Yeletsky asks to play against Herman in the ultimate,
fatal game. The transposition of the story to the eighteenth century was
Vsevolozhsky's winning formula. The period is highlighted in the second act, where the guests at a palace in St. Petersburg are treated to a
pastoral divertissement before Catherine the Great honors the company
with a visit.

Chaikovsky composed the opera in the unusually fast time of forty-
four days. His score strikingly transcends the melodramatic conventions
of the libretto. The changes to Pushkin's text enabled him not only to
compose impassioned love music but also to portray different social mi-
lieus. A splendid example is the second scene of Act I, in which a governess reproves Liza and her friends for singing folk songs, something
unbecoming in people of their rank. The portrait of Liza has an interesting social dimension: in her aria in the same act she sings of how dis-
enchanted she has become with her belief in conventional happiness.
Though she ought to be happy about her betrothal to a leading prince,
she feels confused by her fascination with the foreign admirer.

One of the greatest qualities of the opera is the manner in which the
supernatural gradually takes possession of the characters. Act I begins
in a carefree way with a day out in the park, but the atmosphere changes
during the very first meeting of the leading figures. In a short but intense

quintet they give voice to their anxieties and presentiments. Count Tomsky tells the countess's story in the form of an old ballad. His song introduces the central motifs that will recur throughout the opera. A storm blows in, magnificently anticipated by the grotesque orchestral effects at the end of Tomsky's song. During the reunion of the girls in the second scene, Pauline sings a song (to a poem Konstantin Batchukov wrote in 1810) about a dead young girl. When Herman declares his love for Liza soon afterward, he echoes the melody of Pauline's song. Malevolent fate intervenes, and the process of Liza's perdition is begun. When she shows Herman the way to the countess's bedroom in Act II, we again hear the threatening motifs from Tomsky's song. Herman now realizes that fate has taken control of his life.

In the bedroom scene reality is finally abandoned. In the orchestral introduction, and in Herman's monologue, Chaikovsky obliterates time by means of ostinato patterns in ever-changing combinations. All the opera's central motifs are combined after the countess's death, when Liza drives Herman out to the accompaniment of harrowing double-bass ostinato patterns. The orchestral color contributes greatly to the unreal character of the scene, starting as early as the instrumental introduction, with its original division of the strings and its fragile *divisi* sound in the violins. The sound magic is continued in the special wind instrument combinations that dominate Herman's monologue and in his concluding dialogue with Liza. The combination of the incantatory double-bass motif with trombones and bass tuba contrasts with the gloom of the combined alto and bass clarinets, bassoons, and horns.

The hallucination is complete in the first scene of Act III. In his army barracks, Herman is plagued by the memory of the countess's death. The requiem music is first played softly in the strings—at times interrupted by the bugle call bringing Herman back to reality—and then with great emphasis in the chorus. The sound magic is stepped up on the appearance of the countess, announced by the whole-tone scale obligatory in scenes of ghostly apparitions in Russian music. By avoiding the expected cadence at the end of that scene, Chaikovsky is indicating that Herman will never be rid of his obsession. In the rest of the opera Chaikovsky gives free rein to his inventive genius. Liza dies to an extravagant distortion of the fate motif, with the melody in the horns and trombones and the accompanying chords in the trumpets. The final scene in the gaming house begins with contrasting gaiety, but as Herman plays his hand the central motifs carry the opera through to its inevitable catastrophe. *The Queen of Spades* exceeds all romantic demonic operas in meta physical horror, a characteristic for which the term "surrealist" has rightly been suggested.[36]

The large number of eighteenth-century pastiches in the score can be interpreted in two ways. They may first be read as "period style," as indications of the time and social context of the action. However, the style quotations also play an alienating role, adding to the overwhelming impression of unreality. In that interpretation the numerous deformations of the classical models become important, as for instance the saraband in 4/4 instead of 3/4, or the almost grotesque allusions to the peasant chorus from *Don Giovanni* or to the sentimental popular song "Plaisir d'amour" in the pastoral scene in Act II.

Chaikovsky's last opera, *Iolanta* (1891), is a short one-act work, originally intended as a double bill with *The Nutcracker*. Like that ballet, *Iolanta* is set in a fairy-tale dream world. It is the story of a blind princess and her cure through love. By Chaikovsky's standards the score is a fairly stereotyped lyrical work, enlivened, however, by his evocative treatment of the sound color.

## INSTRUMENTAL MUSIC

In a letter to Nadezhda von Meck dated 5 December 1878, Chaikovsky explained that there were two kinds of inspiration for a symphonic composer, a subjective and an objective one:

> In the first instance, [the composer] uses his music to express his own feelings, joys, sufferings; in short, like a lyric poet he pours out, so to speak, his own soul. In this instance, a program is not only not necessary but even impossible. But it is another matter when a musician, reading a poetic work or struck by a scene in nature, wishes to express in musical form that subject that has kindled his inspiration. Here a program is essential. . . . Program music can and must exist, just as it is impossible to demand that literature make do without the epic element and limit itself to lyricism alone.[37]

This explanation is new only for those who consider Chaikovsky nothing but a "self-expressing composer." Such program music as *Francesca da Rimini* or the *Manfred* Symphony was as much a part of Chaikovsky's artistic program as the expression of his "lyrical ego." And yet this dichotomy did not stretch to his entire oeuvre. A whole group of compositions falls outside it, music that is rarely assigned a place in interpretations of Chaikovsky's art but that nevertheless belongs to the core of his mature work. This group comprises the orchestral suites, the Italian Capriccio, and the Serenade for Strings. Even such popular works as the

Violin Concerto and the Variations on a Rococo Theme are seldom treated as "essential Chaikovsky" by the commentators.

Few compositions are as far removed from the cliché of "confessional romantic music" as Chaikovsky's orchestral suites. Judged by symphonic standards, they are hybrid mixtures of every possible genre and characteristic, from scholarly counterpoint to salon style, folk music, bizarre scherzos, and character pieces. From a letter to Nadezhda von Meck we know that Chaikovsky valued this genre precisely because of "the freedom it leaves the composer not to be bound by all sorts of traditions, conventional techniques and fixed rules."[38] The orchestral suite was the sphere of unrestricted musical fantasy.

The genre originated in Germany, in the wake of the rediscovery of Bach's orchestral suites. Chaikovsky found his models in the suites of Franz Lachner, Joachim Raff, and Jules Massenet. The aim was not to restore baroque dance forms, but to capture the sensual charm of the imaginative use of archaizing and pseudomodal keys. Chaikovsky probably went further than anyone in expressing unbridled fantasy. The First Suite (1879) followed Lachner's neobaroque model in the first (prelude and fugue) and the last movements (gavotte). Between them we find a scherzo with special orchestral effects, daring rhythmical contrasts, and hemiolas; an intermezzo; and a *marche miniature* for high-pitched instruments, triangle, and glockenspiel. Subsequently Chaikovsky added a divertimento of the waltz type as a second movement. This combination of archaizing stylization with dance music and character pieces reached its peak in the Second Suite (1883). The first movement, Jeu de sons, is an almost satirical game of musical structures, with its combination of the sonata form, fugue, a burlesque distortion of the folk-music style, sentimentality, and unexpected rhythmical and orchestral contrasts. The composition does not aim to provide a cohesive formal development but is a collage of musical qualities. In addition, the work combines a waltz, the character piece "Rêves d'enfant," a burlesque scherzo, and an archaizing "Dance baroque." The scherzo contains Chaikovsky's most radical treatment of Russian folk music, with the imitation of street music by an accordion quartet; in the trio, Chaikovsky relies on the primitive folk technique of harmonization. Street music and folk heterophony are both assigned a place in this parade of contrived and surprising effects. Unlike the earlier suites, the Third Suite (1884) begins with an intimate touch, with a character piece ("Elegy"), a "Valse mélancolique," and a rather overstylized scherzo. The last movement provides a counterweight to the first three in length and content. An impressive series of variations reveals a surfeit of musical characteristics, culminating finally in a triumphal polonaise—a tribute to Alexander III in gratitude for the special support he had granted Chaikovsky since 1884.

Like the suites, the Italian Capriccio (1880) is a montage of musical characteristics or pittoresque pieces. A form of genre tableau, it evokes Italian urban folklore. Chaikovsky shared the incorporation of music from various social circles with the Viennese classical composers. Haydn and Mozart, too, had employed musical codes of every possible origin, without the nationalistic implications typical of the nineteenth century. As in pre-Romantic aesthetics, Chaikovsky's music represents a stable world in which everything has been assigned its proper place.

The link to pre-Romantic aesthetics is most clearly seen in such retrospective works as Variations on a Rococo Theme (1876) for cello and orchestra and *Mozartiana* (1887), a collection of orchestrations based on Mozart piano pieces: a Gigue in G (K. 574), a Minuet in D (K. 355), and the Variations on a Theme by Gluck. The third movement is the famous "Ave verum," which Chaikovsky knew in the Liszt transcription under the title of *Preghiera*. After Chaikovsky's death, *Mozartiana* was added to his orchestral suites as No. 4.

The reference back to pre-Romantic aesthetics is more subtle in the Violin Concerto (1878) and in the Serenade for Strings (1880). The Violin Concerto does not follow the classical pattern. In particular, the usual double exposition in the first movement is missing. After a short orchestral introduction, the thematic material is presented by the soloist. The work is also a far cry from the "symphonic" concerto. The tone of the orchestral introduction is almost "classicist," as is the transparent texture in which the solo part keeps the upper hand. All the material is introduced and developed by the solo violin, the role of the orchestra being confined to accompaniment and to a few ritornellos. In virtuosity the solo part goes quite a long way beyond the classical models, but it does not satisfy the characteristic functions of nineteenth-century concertos: virtuosity for virtuosity's sake (as with Paganini) or virtuosity as a means of expressing a symphonic concept (as in Brahms's Violin Concerto). With Chaikovsky, virtuosity has above all a playful function (as in the double-stop variation of the first theme at the start of the development) or provides a dynamic impetus and the climactic effect needed to round off the structure (at the end of the exposition or in the coda). The second movement is a deliberately simple canzonetta. The third movement relies on a scintillating, dynamic part for the solo violin. The second theme is of folkloristic inspiration. The treatment of the ostinato pattern of a Russian folk dance is based on the technique of background variation à la *Kamarinskaya*.

The Serenade for Strings was intended as a tribute to Mozart, the genre of the serenade being a clear allusion to a quintessentially eighteenth-century type of music. With its beginning more reminiscent of Handel, present-day listeners may find that surprising; however, the reference to Mozart lies in the first movement, Pezzo in forma di sonatina, with its sometimes remarkably tenuous texture (above all in the second theme). The Serenade is certainly no copy of any style. It is an attempt to convert the special spirit of the classical approach into Chaikovsky's own idiom, one marked by spontaneity, attention to the expressivity of surface phenomena, and clarity of texture. As in the classical model, folkloristic elements are reserved for the finale. The opening of the latter with a Tema russo was probably borrowed from Beethoven's *Razumovsky* Quartets. The unique tone of the Serenade is the result of a subtle balance between Chaikovsky's lyrical sentimentality and his attention to classical measure and clarity.

The Trio for piano, violin, and cello, op. 50 (1882), is one of Chaikovsky's most beautiful compositions, despite the fact that it has been criticized for its alleged lack of organic coherence. The second movement (Tema con variazioni) is a collection of divergent musical characteristics, just like the variation form of Beethoven's *Kreutzer* Sonata (which is generally attacked for the same reason). Playful heterogeneity is an essential characteristic of this type of music. In Chaikovsky's Trio, it is framed with music of an elegiac tone (in memory of Nikolai Rubinstein) in the first movement and its reprise in the coda of the second movement.

Between 1877 and 1893, in addition to revising the Second Symphony (1879–80), Chaikovsky wrote the Fourth, Fifth, and Sixth Symphonies. These three works, which are generally taken for an autobiographical trilogy, have had an ambiguous reception. As assumed models of extreme psychologization, they are both admired and decried, depending on the value listeners or critics attach to emotional expression. The autobiographical dogma is so strong that nearly all discussions are confined to attempts at uncovering its meaning. Structural analysis is then expected to show to what extent Chaikovsky succeeded in translating the intended content into symphonic structures. Edward Garden's critique of the Fourth Symphony is characteristic:

> All the frustrations of his endemic homosexuality and bottled-up emotions, further engendered rather than released by the fiasco of his marriage, are set loose in this symphony. . . . Nevertheless the conflict between escapism and

reality is not entirely convincing and, for all the great contrasts and the emotional involvement, in the final analysis Tchaikovsky protests too much and in so doing fails to achieve that complete identification with his material that is the crowning glory of *Eugene Onegin.*

Analysts of the Fifth Symphony are generally agreed on the greater thematic cohesion of that work, which Chaikovsky achieved by the return of a single motto in all movements. The problems start, however, with the evaluation of the role of the motto in the finale. The ultimate "triumph" of the theme in *ffff* in the brass sounds to many like hollow rhetoric. Garden came up with this rationalization:

> The hysterically overstated endeavour to produce "triumph," which in the end only sounds "hollow" and false, leaves the impression of the inescapably overwhelming power of "Fate" and the uselessness of the fight against it, however hard that fight may be and however successful the apparent outcome. The effect of the Fifth Symphony is therefore one of failure to resist the inevitable power of Destiny in spite of monumental struggle and even temporary success.[39]

These two quotations typify the manner in which the discussion of Chaikovsky's late symphonies is generally conducted. Psychosexual interpretation is the latest trend. Susan McClary, for instance, considers the structural deviation from the German symphonic model in the first movement of the Fourth Symphony a token of Chaikovsky's homosexual deviation from the "patriarchal model" of society.[40]

The Sixth Symphony bears the entire weight of the suicide myth, an interpretation that emerged at the time of Chaikovsky's death. Because the composer died unexpectedly a mere nine days after the première, the public was almost bound to look for a connection between the two. While the work had been received with some bewilderment at its first hearing, it suddenly came to be taken for Chaikovsky's own requiem: an expression either of a longing for death or else of the fear of death, of a tragic presentiment. Reception of the Sixth Symphony (*Pathétique*) was further colored by the fact that the composer's death prevented him from adding to it. Such a composition tends all too quickly to acquire the status of a final work, the composer's death being, in pure romantic style, endowed with an inescapable aura, as if it were the culmination of an artistic destiny. David Brown puts it as follows: "In the Sixth there had been no compromise; the method, the form, the ethos were as personal as the musical invention and the expressive experience which shaped its structure. Had he lived, it is impossible to imagine any direction he could have taken beyond this. But the matter never arose. Within nine days of conducting its première he was dead."[41] Luckily so, Brown seems to insinuate. It was as though Chaikovsky had completed his artistic mission and had been allowed to depart according to the rules of Fate.

Hard evidence for all these interpretations is difficult to find, since most of them rely on the unwarranted emphasis of minimal events. In connection with the Fourth Symphony, great attention has been paid to Chaikovsky's much-quoted letter to Nadezhda von Meck in which he presents a program for the work. In fact, what he puts forward is no program in the strict sense of the word; it is not a guideline that Chaikovsky followed. On the contrary, the music had long been finished when Chaikovsky produced the program. Nor is the program very original, being clearly copied from the program that contemporary music critics were unanimously attributing to Beethoven's Fifth Symphony. (Everyone with a musical background spontaneously associated the powerful mottolike beginning of the Fourth *in unisono* with the beginning of Beethoven's Fifth and the idea of Fate knocking at the door.) Chaikovsky's program is in fact quite banal, only the interpretation of the first movement as a struggle against destiny having any weight. As for the other movements, commonplaces were the rule: nostalgic daydreams in the second movement, brief impressions in the scherzo, and a popular festival in the fourth. More important are Chaikovsky's comments at the end of the letter:

> Just as I was about to put this letter in its envelope, I reread it and was taken aback by the vagueness and inadequacy of the program I am sending you. For the first time in my life I had to convert musical ideas and musical images into words and sentences. I failed to do that as it should have been done. Last winter, when I wrote this symphony, I was terribly depressed, and it serves as a true echo of what I went through then. But it is no more than an echo. How can you put that into words clearly and precisely? I cannot do it, I would not know how to. And also I have forgotten a lot. I have retained general memories of the abyss and the terror of the emotions I experienced.[42]

Eighteen months later, in a letter to Mme von Meck dated 25 September 1879, he struck a different note. Whereas the program had originally been couched in general terms, it now became autobiographical, the emphasis shifting to the positive outcome of the crisis. He called the symphony "a *memorial* to a time when, after a long-evolving spiritual illness and after a whole series of unbearable agonies of anguish and despair that had all but driven me to utter madness and ruin, there suddenly shone a dawn of rebirth and happiness in the person of her to whom the symphony is dedicated [Nadezhda von Meck herself]."[43] The autobiographical interpretation thus appeared long after the facts and was partly an expression of gratitude to Mme von Meck for all she had meant to him at a difficult period.

It is undeniable that the Fourth Symphony was written in a charged emotional context. However, it is equally certain that the biographical background cannot provide an adequate explanation or interpretation of a work of such complexity.

As for the Fifth Symphony (1888), Chaikovsky told Konstantin Konstantinovich that it had no program. Even so, most commentators see a general indication of the contents among Chaikovsky's earliest notebook sketches: "Intr[oduction]. Complete submission before Fate, or, which is the same, before the inscrut[able] predestination of Providence. Allegro. (1) Murmur of doubt, complaints, reproaches to XXX. (2) To leap into the embrace of *Faith???* A wonderful program, if only it can be carried out."[44] The notebook entries reflect the spiritual climate in which Chaikovsky began work on the symphony. Poznansky links its origins to the composer's emotional distress at the death of his friend Nikolai Kondratyev in 1887. However, Chaikovsky traveled a long road from the initial idea to the final result.

The situation is more complex in the case of the Sixth Symphony (1893). Chaikovsky started its composition after becoming disillusioned with a symphony in E-flat major, which he had intended as a "symphony with a secret program" but which he destroyed after its completion in 1892, although he used material from it in the Third Piano Concerto. From his notes, we know that Chaikovsky thought of naming it *Life,* using a program that staked out the most important stages of human existence. The Sixth Symphony was strongly associated with this project, the major difference lying in its more subjective program. To his nephew Bob Davïdov, Chaikovsky declared that the program was highly subjective and that he had been reduced to tears when he composed it in his thoughts.[45] The Sixth Symphony, therefore, was probably the result of an interaction between the abstract philosophical program of the symphony in E-flat major and Chaikovsky's personal recollections.

Poznansky suggests that Chaikovsky was beset with a strong fear of death and that he tried to dispel it by surrounding himself with young people. The quotations in the work from the requiem mass and the final adagio are probably expressions of sadness about man's mortality rather than of a longing for, or a presentiment of, death. In any event, the tone of sublime suffering in the Sixth Symphony cannot be explained by the circumstances in which the work was composed. Chaikovsky wrote it during what was perhaps the happiest period of his life, at the height of his fame, full of plans for the future, surrounded by friends he loved, and, as his letters make clear, having come to terms with himself. On 1 August 1893 he wrote to the poet Daniil Rathaus: "In my music I claim utter candour and although I too have a predilection for songs of wistful sadness, yet, in recent years at least, I, like yourself, do not suffer from want and can in general consider myself a happy person!"[46]

The Sixth Symphony has also been mistaken for Chaikovsky's last composition. The work, apart from the orchestration, was finished on 24 March 1893, that is, before the composition of the Eighteen Pieces for piano; Six Songs, op. 73; the Third Piano Concerto; the Andante and Finale for Piano and Orchestra; the vocal quartet "Night"; and an uncompleted duet from *Romeo and Juliet*.[47] The Sixth Symphony is generally known as the *Pathétique,* a misguiding translation of the Russian *Pateticheskaya simfonia,* which translates roughly as "impassioned symphony," with no overtones of mental suffering. Modest Chaikovsky claimed the honor of having come up with the title, but a letter from Chaikovsky to Jurgenson dated 20 September 1893 shows that the title was his own idea.[48]

Great symphonic music tends to convey the impression that it "signifies" something important—but to specify just what that "something" is generally proves impossible. The usual autobiographical approach to Chaikovsky's symphonies glosses over many facets that should be taken into consideration when interpreting the works. Instead of looking for an alternative explanation (which might again prove inadequate and incomplete), therefore, we might do better to stress the musical riches of the work, to dwell on facets that are not mentioned in most commentaries.

It has been agreed for some time now that Chaikovsky's sonata form differs from the German symphonic model; it relies less on transformations of themes and linear tonal developments and more on block-like juxtapositions of tonalities and thematic groups. Depending on the critic's preferences, that aspect is considered either a fault or a sign of originality. More important, however, is the special way in which structure is defined in Chaikovsky's work. In his compositions, melody, tonality, rhythm, and sound color constitute an indivisible whole. This is clearly shown by the first movement of the Fourth Symphony, which is dominated by a powerful and highly rhythmical motto in the brass. That motto marks off the different stages of the structure, which consists of a complete series of rotating thirds (from F via A-flat, B, D, back to F, with the recapitulation of the first theme in the "wrong" key of the third below the tonic). To obtain dramatic impact from that structure, Chaikovsky relies largely on his characteristic treatment of rhythm, texture, and sound color. The actual first theme is rhythmically complex. Chaikovsky increases the impression of instability by the shrewd use of accompanying notes. During the forte recapitulation of the theme, he creates a new rhythmic movement by means of chromatically descending lines in the woodwinds. The second theme involves sinuous motifs in the wind section, combined with a lyrical melody in the cellos. The rhythmic pattern of the accompaniment, however, is now regular, with occasional supporting notes. The impression of regularity is enhanced further in the exchanges between the violins and the woodwind group. Complexity makes way for a static passage, in which a single chord is maintained for twenty-two measures in a regular rhythmic pattern. This passage of tonal and rhythmic stasis serves as a preparation for the rhythmically confused episode that follows, in which the orchestral groups converse by complex hemiola structures. That passage wipes out the sense of meter, rendering the reappearance of the motto all the more dramatic. In the development, the complexities of the exposition are further increased.

The dramaturgy of the first movement of the Fourth Symphony is not based on the transformations of themes in the German sense. The crux is the rhythmic opposition between the motto and the first theme. The motto employs the rhythm of the polonaise, not in its triumphant, but in its provocative and aggressive aspect. The first theme is marked "in movimento di valse": a waltz expressing sentiment and vulnerability. At first, the two elements are contrasted; in the development they are thrown together remorselessly. In the coda, the waltz is brought back in augmented note values, so that the phrasing agrees with the structure of the polonaise and the two thematic elements become fused.

The first movement of the Fifth Symphony relies on the same link between tonality, rhythm, and sound color. The sonority is almost monochromic, with the combination of clarinet, bassoon, and low strings in the introduction providing the basic color of the entire movement. The allegro begins with the melody in clarinet and bassoon. When the violins take over the theme, the basic color is retained in the accompanying passage-work of clarinet and bassoon. The color is intensified, downward with the low brass and upward with the oboe and now and then with the flute (as in the subtle highlighting of the second part of the first theme). The horns are sounded at important articulation points. The unity of the sound color goes hand in hand with highly self-contained melodic material. The first theme, for instance, uses a tonic-subdominant pattern and continues to revolve around the tonic. This theme does not allow of a great deal of expansion. The climax is produced by the juxtaposition and accumulation of sound blocks, full of rhythmic complications. The entire first movement relies on the tension between the descending, darkening tendency of the themes and expansion by accumulation and contrast. The tension comes to a head in the lyrical melody that concludes the second group of themes, a melody that tries constantly to offset the downward pull. The end of the first movement, with the descent in diminuendo to the darkest regions of the orchestra, is the logical outcome of the downward tension that dominates the entire movement.

The Fourth and Fifth Symphonies differ radically in their second movements. The slow movement of the Fourth is an emotionally well balanced lied form; that of the Fifth looks more like an instrumental translation of an opera scene. From the Fifth it appears that Chaikovsky considered symphonies less as fixed forms than as general frames of reference. This explains the addition of the operatic style and the replacement of the usual scherzo with a waltz.

The third movements of both the Fourth and the Fifth Symphonies are startling. The giddy pizzicato of the scherzo in the Fourth is a real treasure, thanks in particular to the breathtaking rhythmic transpositions and the contrast effect produced by the shrill high woodwinds. The third movement of the Fifth is a symphonic waltz, though its waltzing character is often left uncertain. During the first introduction of the melody, the accompaniment eschews the heavy downbeat, so that the listener loses sense of the meter. Only during the normalized repetition does the waltz character become clear. This movement ends with a subtle allusion to the motto theme from the first movement.

The finales of the two symphonies are generally judged by their success in rounding off the symphonic cycle into a cohesive whole. In the Fourth, Chaikovsky manages to do this by repeating the motto of the first movement; in the Fifth, with a version of the opening melody of the introduction in the major. In comparison with a strict cyclical symphonic model, the two solutions are generally considered inadequate. Admittedly, the reprise in the Fourth is highly artificial and the end of the Fifth tends to be bombastic. The two finales only make sense if we do not judge them in terms of the strictly organic symphonic model. Both also gain considerably if we do not take them for the result of this or that psychological process, but simply for what they probably are: an appeal to the heroic and patriotic sentiments of the public and—in the case of the Fifth—an example of the imperial style Chaikovsky developed in the 1880s. That makes the finales very much the products of their time, perhaps more so than any other music in his symphonies.

The Sixth Symphony demonstrates most clearly that Chaikovsky treated the genre as a general frame of reference and not as a strict model. The most patent deviation from the tradition is the slow last movement (adagio lamentoso—andante). The two central movements are equally remarkable. The second resembles a waltz, but in quintuple meter. The unique character stems from the combination of an asymmetrical meter with very regular phrasing. Only occasionally does one gain the impression of subtle rhythmic disruptions. The third movement is a highly original combination of a scherzo and a symphonic march, using two distinct sections in an A-B-A-B pattern. The remarkable feature is that the two sections are superposed as separate layers. The A-section is scherzolike and relies on a *moto perpetuo* in triplets. The B-section is a march in a distinct duple time with a dotted rhythm. After the introduction of the A-section, the B-section is gradually superposed upon it. This process is repeated until the march finally gains the upper hand, with the exception of the closing notes, in which the triplet rhythm brings the movement to its conclusion.

The outer movements constitute the emotional core of the symphony. The opening movement is more emotionally balanced than the reputation of the symphony would lead one to suppose. The exposition has a noble pathos. However, the real emotional outburst is deferred until the development, which is in stark contrast to the restrained and lyrical second theme. The dramatic development (with a quotation from the Orthodox requiem) culminates in an emotionally charged reprise of the first theme. The music then proceeds to an unmistakable crisis, a low point articulated by a descending line spanning more than two octaves. The movement does not end there, however, for Chaikovsky uses the second theme to relieve the tension. The lyrical melody has a solacing and conciliatory effect. Chaikovsky continues the process for only as long as it takes to restore a final sense of peace. The famous adagio lamentoso that concludes the Sixth Symphony may be one of the most intense pieces of music Chaikovsky ever wrote. The pathos of the two melodies ends in a gentle stroke on the gong. With the elegiacally sad second melody the low strings carry the symphony to complete silence.

In addition to the series of six symphonies, Chaikovsky also wrote a programmatic symphony based on Byron's *Manfred*. The initiative came from Balakirev, true to his habit of directing the creativity of others. Balakirev had been given the program by Stasov, who had written it while under the influence of Berlioz's *Harold en Italie*. In 1882 Balakirev handed the program on to Chaikovsky, who took a few years to warm to the idea. In outline, the program involved the following elements (Chaikovsky switched the second and third movements around): (1) Manfred in the Alps, dreaming of his fair Astarte, obsessed with thoughts and memories; (2) the Alpine fairy appears to him in the rainbow over a waterfall; (3) a visit to the hunters and mountain dwellers; and (4) Manfred at Arimanes's subterranean palace, where a bacchanal is being held and the phantom of Astarte appears before him; Manfred's death and apotheosis.

The *Manfred* Symphony is Chaikovsky's most romantic work. No other is so close to Berlioz, Liszt, and—in sonority—Wagner. Aesthetically, *Manfred* is perhaps the least typical of Chaikovsky's oeuvre, though that does not detract from its high quality. The music gives an outstanding impression of the epic scope of the subject, developed with the help of striking sound pictures. A splendid example is the coda of the first movement, with its massive melody in the strings against a rhythmic ostinato background in the woodwinds. Perhaps the greatest surprise is the scherzo, in which the outer movements conjure up the waterfall, and the trio presents the entry of the Alpine fairy. The portrayal of nature is particularly effective. Chaikovsky uses what is almost a pointillist style, with motifs that run to a bare few notes. Moreover, except for the trio, the whole structure has been rhythmically shifted by half a beat, in order to do away with any rigid sense of metrical division: a brilliant effect, but a nightmare for the conductor.

Chaikovsky was the most outstanding Russian composer of the 1880s. In the decade that followed, too, his work continued to hold its place in public esteem against few challengers. Unlike the *kuchka*, Chaikovsky had no difficulty adapting himself to the conditions of his surroundings. His music was considered the starting point of a Russian tradition that was no longer bound up with folk music. Laroche's review of *Sleeping Beauty* sums it up clearly:

The Russian way in music . . . is the issue at hand. . . . The point is not in the local colour, which is beautifully observed, but in an element deeper and more general than colour, in the internal structure of the music, above all in the foundation of the element of melody. This basic element is undoubtedly Russian. It may be said, without lapsing into contradiction, that the local colour [in *Sleeping Beauty*] is French, but the *style* is Russian. . . . One may thank Peter Ilyich that his development has coincided with a time when the influences of the soil became stronger among us, when the Russian soul was inspired, when the word "Russian" ceased to be a synonym of "peasant-like," and when the peasant-like itself was recognized in its proper place, as but *part* of being Russian.[49]

## CHAPTER EIGHT

# "A Musical Conscience"

## Rimsky-Korsakov and the Belyayev Circle

When Balakirev resumed his musical activities in the 1880s, he began by revising his earlier work. In 1884 he retouched the "symphonic picture" *1,000 Years,* which Bessel & Co. published in 1890 as a "symphonic poem" under the title of *Rus.* The use of the Old Slavonic name for Russia was a clear sign of Balakirev's ideological change of direction: from a tribute to progress, the work had been turned into a Slavophile glorification of Russia's idealized past. In the preface we can read:

> As the basis of the composition I selected the themes of three folksongs from my own anthology, by which I wished to characterize three elements in our history: the pagan period, the Muscovite order, and the autonomous republican [*udel'no-vechevoi*] system, reborn among the Cossacks. Strife among these elements, expressed in the symphonic development of these themes, has furnished the content of the instrumental drama, to which the present title is far better suited than the previous one, since the author had no intention of drawing a picture of our thousand-year history, but only a wish to characterize some of its constituent elements.[1]

In the 1907 edition, Balakirev put it even more strongly: "Their strife, culminating in the fatal blow dealt all Russian religious and national aspirations by the reforms of Peter I, has furnished the content of the instrumental drama."[2] The progressive champion of the 1860s had been transformed into a reactionary Slavophile, a xenophobic advocate of the old religious and social traditions and a fanatical foe of liberalism. When we consider that Balakirev's Second Overture in its original form had been composed under the influence of Herzen's radical populism, we gain some idea of the ideological distance Balakirev had traversed.

Gradually Balakirev started to compose again. In 1882 he completed *Tamara.* Between 1895 and 1910 he finished his First Symphony (1897), composed his Piano Sonata (1905) and his Second Symphony (1908), republished his folk-song arrangements, and nearly completed his Piano Concerto (1908–9; the finale was finished after his death by Sergey Lyapunov). Balakirev worked in isolation, for the younger composers now looked upon his style as an old-fashioned curiosity. In his later years Balakirev became his own epigone.

Balakirev's ideological turnabout is a clear sign that by the end of the century the days of the old *kuchka* were finished. He had lost contact with its earlier members: from 1872 until his death in 1881 Musorgsky had moved in the circle of reactionary aristocrats around Golenishchev-Kutuzov; at his death in 1887, Borodin had not succeeded in completing his *Prince Igor;* César Cui no longer counted as a composer. Only Vladimir Stasov clung to the *kuchka,* keeping the legend alive and canonizing it in countless articles. This was not an easy task. Musorgsky's position caused him the greatest difficulty, for he viewed Musorgsky's friendship with the poet Golenishchev-Kutuzov—a member of the aristocracy who harbored an aestheticist attitude to art—with regret. Musorgsky had introduced his new friend to Stasov in 1873, writing in a letter:

> Since Pushkin and Lermontov I have not encountered what I encountered in Kutuzov: this is no simulated poet like Nekrasov, and without Mey's sense of strain (though I prefer Mey to Nekrasov). . . . It is noteworthy that in his university days (at a time when, etc. [i.e., when students were politically active and protests followed by reprisals were the order of the day]) our youthful poet (and he is *very* youthful) was not carried away by civic themes, that is, he did not submit to fashion and ape Mr. Nekrasov's grimaces, but hammered into verse those thoughts that occupied *him,* and those longings that were inherent in *his own* artistic nature. This *lordliness of mind* especially pleased me when I glanced at Kutuzov's notebooks (here in pencil, there in pen, there a blank page—a photograph of an artist's mental activity).[3]

Stasov was anything but ecstatic about this tribute to Golenishchev-Kutuzov's "lordliness of mind"; he took it for a betrayal of the social and liberal ideas they had once shared, and justifiably so, as Musorgsky's work after *Boris Godunov* no longer reflected the old ideals. *Khovanshchina* is an aristocratic tragedy, an expression of aristocratic doom-mongering at the time of the Emancipation; *The Fair at Sorochintsï* is a nostalgic return to romantic nationalism. As Richard Taruskin puts it:

> [Musorgsky] was not a "civic" artist. The voice that speaks from the *Sunless* cycle is that of a neurotically self-absorbed, broken-down aristocrat. That was Musorgsky by 1874. The voice that speaks from *The Nursery* is that of a pampered gentry brat. That, too, was a self-portrait, and a very nostalgic one. The peasant types that abound in his songs and operas of the 1860s are objectively drawn life-portraits motivated by Musorgsky's peculiar scientistic views of the period, not by any hint of sentimental identification. The portrayal of the crowd in *Boris* and (especially) *Khovanshchina* is unflattering. His reputation as a *narodnik* or radical democrat notwithstanding, the composer's correspondence gives no hint of any such involvement. Belinsky, Chernïshevsky, Pisarev—these names will be absent from the index to any collection of Musorgsky's letters (save, of course, the editorial commentary).[4]

That Musorgsky attached little importance to the political and social message found in his earlier work is reflected most clearly in his agreement to have the Kromy scene cut from *Boris Godunov,* a step the Mariyinsky Theater decided to take in 1876. Stasov reacted furiously in the press, calling the decision a "castration" of the work. Musorgsky, for his part, applauded the decision. We know from the memoirs of Golenishchev-Kutuzov that "Musorgsky not only approved this cut, he was particularly pleased with it." Golenishchev-Kutuzov wrote that he was amazed at this reaction and asked for an explanation. Musorgsky answered him: "In this act, and for the only time in my life, I lied about the Russian people. The people's mockery of the boyar [Khrushchov]— that's untrue, that is an un-Russian trait. An infuriated people may kill, may execute, but they do not mock their victim."[5]

After Musorgsky's death, Stasov tried to shape the memory of the composer in accordance with his own ideals. The result was the picture of Musorgsky as a populist, the myth of official opposition to *Boris Godunov,* the idea of his artistic decline in his late work, and the legend that Musorgsky turned to alcohol because he was embittered by his fate. In reality he shared that fate with many members of the impoverished nobility who lost their income in the wake of the abolition of serfdom. The Stasovian line enjoyed much success and until recently determined the general view of the composer.[6]

The coup de grâce to any justification of the *kuchka*'s continued existence was the academic conversion of Rimsky-Korsakov. In 1871, when he was invited to help strengthen the St. Petersburg Conservatory, he was supported by Balakirev, who thought it useful to infiltrate the enemy camp. But instead of playing a subversive role, Rimsky-Korsakov engaged in an impressive course of technical self-improvement and became the staunchest defender of academic training. In his later memoirs he attacked Balakirev's teaching methods:

> But with all his native mentality and brilliant abilities, there was one thing he failed to understand: that what was good for him in the matter of musical education was of no use whatever for others, as these others had not only grown up amid entirely different surroundings, but possessed utterly different natures; that the development of their talents was bound to take place at different intervals and in a different manner. Moreover, he despotically demanded that the tastes of his pupils should exactly coincide with his own. The slightest deviation from his taste was severely censured by him. By means of raillery, a parody or caricature played by him, whatever did not suit him was belittled—and the student blushed with shame for his expressed opinion and recanted for ever or for a long time to come. . . . Was Balakirev's attitude to his pupil-friends right? In my opinion absolutely wrong. A truly talented pupil needs so little. It is easy to show all that is necessary in harmony and counterpoint to put him on his own feet in that respect, it is easy to direct him in understanding the forms of composition, if only the thing is properly undertaken.[7]

Rather shamefacedly Rimsky-Korsakov recalled the thoughtless way in which he had accepted the invitation to join the staff of the conservatory:

> Had I ever studied at all, had I possessed a fraction more of knowledge than I actually did, it would have been obvious to me that I could not and should not accept the proffered appointment, that it was foolish and dishonest of me to become a professor. But I, the author of *Sadko, Antar* and *The Maid of Pskov,* compositions that were coherent and well-sounding, compositions that the public and many musicians approved, I was a dilettante and knew nothing. This I frankly confess and attest before the world. I was young and self-confident; my self-confidence was encouraged by others, and I joined the Conservatory. And yet at the time I could not decently harmonize a chorale; not only had I not written a single counterpoint in my life, but I had hardly any notion of the structure of a fugue; nay, did not even know the names of augmented and diminished intervals, of chords (except the fundamental triad), of the dominant and chord of the diminished seventh, though I could sing anything at sight and distinguish chords of every sort. . . . Of course, to compose *Antar* or *Sadko* is more interesting than to know how to harmonize a Protestant chorale or write four-part counterpoint, which seems to be necessary for organists alone. But it is shameful not to know such things and to learn of their existence from one's own pupils.[8]

Rimsky-Korsakov's retraining led to a number of chamber works in which he adhered strictly to the classical models: the String Sextet and the Quintet for flute, clarinet, horn, bassoon, and piano (1876). Later he was to add a piano trio (1897) to his oeuvre, only to decide that chamber music did not really appeal to him. The two central movements were completed by Maximilian Steinberg.

Unlike Chaikovsky's, Rimsky-Korsakov's technique was not developed in a straightforward or cohesive manner. His early work was often diametrically opposed to the fruits of his new technical proficiency, which did not help his self-confidence. On several occasions his creativity was paralyzed, and from 1881 to 1888 his progress came to an almost complete standstill. He saved himself from that impasse by doing editorial work on the legacy of Musorgsky and by completing Borodin's *Prince Igor.* In 1888 he reemerged with his three best-known orchestral works: *Sheherazade, Capriccio espagnol,* and the overture *Svetliy prazdnik* (literally, "The radiant festival," but better known as the "Russian Easter" Overture). Lack of self-confidence and scrupulous attention to technical perfection were the causes of the continual revisions to which he subjected his work. He revised all his earlier compositions, reworking *Sadko* and *Antar* more than once. He "improved" *Pskovityanka,* first in 1876–77, and again in 1891–92. In the last version he had, in his own words, at last "closed accounts with the past."[9] During his creative periods his output was considerable, which distanced him even further from the former *kuchka.* For instance, he wrote to his friend and confidant Semyon Kruglikov, anticipating his reaction to his high productivity:

> You are no doubt amazed? Well, there's nothing to be amazed at; that's the way it ought to be. Already thirty years have passed since the days when Stasov would write that in eighteen-sixty-so-and-so the Russian School displayed a lively activity: Lodïzhensky wrote one romance, Borodin got an idea for something, Balakirev was planning to rework something, and so on. It's time to forget all that and *travel a normal artistic path.*[10]

In 1892 Rimsky-Korsakov's creativity came to a halt once more, and he decided to give up composing for good. However, the death of Chaikovsky in 1893 suddenly opened up new prospects. Chaikovsky's privileged relationship with Vsevolozhsky had left Rimsky-Korsakov few opportunities to make his mark in the Imperial Theaters. His next opera, *Christmas Eve,* was a deliberate alternative to Chaikovsky's *Cherevichki.* Thereafter, Rimsky-Korsakov completed an opera every eighteen months on average, composing no fewer than eleven between 1893 and 1908.

## NEW CONDITIONS:
## BELYAYEV, MAMONTOV, AND DIAGHILEV

In the last decades of the nineteenth century, capitalist entrepreneurs set themselves up as patrons of Russian culture. In sociological respects, they had no links with the traditional nobility; rather, they had sprung up from the old merchant estate, mainly established in Moscow. For successful businessmen, art patronage meant investing in public prestige, a means of bolstering their own rather modest status. In order to avoid competition with the nobility, they concentrated on art forms that lay outside the aristocratic sphere of interest, collecting modern art, for instance, rather than works by the classical masters. Pavel Tretyakov promoted Russian realism in art, while Savva Mamontov supported neonationalism. Two capitalist entrepreneurs set their stamp on musical life: Belyayev in St. Petersburg and Mamontov in Moscow.

Mitrofan Belyayev had made his fortune as a timber merchant. An amateur viola player and a chamber-music enthusiast, from the 1880s he regularly invited musicians to his home, his Friday night quartet sessions becoming a tradition. Rimsky-Korsakov was a frequent guest, as were Glazunov, Borodin, Anatoliy Lyadov, and many others. Rimsky-Korsakov has left us a colorful description of the carpe diem mentality that presided over these gatherings:

> The music over with, supper was served at one in the morning. The suppers were generous and laced with abundant libations. Occasionally after supper Glazunov or somebody else played on the piano something new of his own, just composed or just arranged for four hands. Adjournment was late, at three A.M. Some, finding insufficient what they had imbibed at supper, would, after parting with the host, repair—to use a mild term—to a restaurant "to continue." At times after supper, during the music-making, a bottle or two of champagne appeared on the table, and was opened to "baptize" the new composition.[11]

The Friday night gatherings provided an extra stimulus for chamber-music composers. The gregarious spirit typical of these gatherings also gave rise to collaborative efforts by several composers, for instance the String Quartet on Belyayev's Name, a work based on the motif B-la-F. Rimsky-Korsakov wrote the first movement, Lyadov the scherzo, Borodin a Spanish serenade as the third movement, and Glazunov the finale. Other examples are Variations on a Russian Theme for String Quartet and the *Pyatnitsi* (Fridays) collection. Apart from work by the composers mentioned above, these collections also contain contributions from Artsïbushev, Scriabin, Vitols, Sokolov, Kopïlov, and others.

One amusing curiosity is the *Parafrazi* collection of twenty-four variations and fifteen pieces on an unvarying theme (the children's piece "Tati-tati," or "Chopsticks"), "dedicated to young pianists who can play the theme with one finger of each hand," as the dedication specifies. The first edition contained contributions by Rimsky-Korsakov, Borodin, Cui, and Lyadov. In the second edition the series was completed with pieces by Liszt and Nikolai Shcherbachov and new compositions by Borodin and Rimsky-Korsakov.

Belyayev's ambitions went further, however. In 1884 he established an annual Glinka prize, and in 1885 he set up his own publishing house in Leipzig and published music by Glazunov, Lyadov, Rimsky-Korsakov, and Borodin at his own expense. Young composers also appealed for his help. To make a selection of their offerings he established an advisory council consisting of Rimsky-Korsakov, Glazunov, and Lyadov. In 1885 Belyayev started his own concert series, the Russian Symphony Concerts, open exclusively to Russian composers. Many symphonic works were written especially for this series, among them Rimsky-Korsakov's three best-known compositions: *Sheherazade,* the "Russian Easter" Overture, and *Capriccio espagnol.* In 1889 Belyayev arranged two Russian concerts in Paris, and in 1891 he founded the Russian quartet evenings: public concerts devoted exclusively to Russian string quartets. In 1892, finally, he established an annual chamber-music competition. Belyayev's financial empire was so great that after his death in 1903 provision was made for the continuation of his patronage in perpetuity.

However, Belyayev's patronage also had a negative side. Under the control of Rimsky-Korsakov, Glazunov, and Lyadov, the Belyayev circle was reserved for those who worked in a style of which the circle approved. Rimsky-Korsakov's style thus became the preferred academic style, the model that young composers had to follow if they were to have a career. The opponents of the circle did not fail to notice this situation, as may be seen from a review by Alfred Nurok:

> Mr. Beliaev's Maecenas activities bear a very special imprint. His undeniably lavish patronage of Russian music of the newest variety does not, unfortunately, so much facilitate the development of the talents of gifted but as yet unrecognized composers, as it encourages young people who have successfully completed their conservatory course to cultivate productivity come what may, touching little upon the question of their creative abilities. Mr. Beliaev encourages industry above all, and under his aegis musical composition has assumed the character of a workers' collective (*artel*), or even a crafts industry.[12]

Savva Mamontov was a railroad entrepreneur who devoted his fortune to the support of neonationalism, that style in the fine and applied arts which sought its inspiration in the decorative patterns of folk art. Mamontov set up an art colony on his estate at Abramtsevo, an initiative that was not so much philanthropic as commercial. He opened studios for applied art, appointing Victor Gartman (Hartmann), the artist who became known through Musorgsky's *Pictures at an Exhibition*, as director, and had peasants trained to produce quantities of folk art, icons, and embroidery. Gartman died soon afterward and was followed in turn by Victor and Apollinariy Vasnetsov; Vasiliy Polenov and his wife, Yelena; and Valentin Serov, the son of the composer.

In 1882 the crown monopoly on theaters was abolished, and three years later Mamontov established his own opera company. The productions staged during the first phase of the company's existence (1885–87) included Rimsky-Korsakov's *Snegurochka* (The snow maiden), for which Victor Vasnetsov designed the sets and costumes. With all the visual motifs borrowed from folk art, the performance was intended as a Slavic *Gesamtkunstwerk*. In 1896 Mamontov's Private Opera Company made a fresh start, though its collaboration with Rimsky-Korsakov did not begin properly until 1897, with *Sadko* (Plate 8). (This opera had been turned down by the Imperial Theaters on the personal orders of Nicholas II, who preferred "something a bit merrier.")[13] Following *Sadko*, the company staged another five operas by Rimsky-Korsakov, as well as his reworking of *Boris Godunov*. Fyodor Chaliapin acquired his early experience in Mamontov's company, singing the part of Boris for the first time there. In 1899 Mamontov went on a downhill slide. He was arrested for fraud and was not acquitted until he had already spent nine months in custody. The opera company continued without him until 1904.

The impresario Sergey Diaghilev was adroit in channeling the capital of the new entrepreneurs into prestigious artistic projects. In 1898 he launched the journal *Mir iskusstva* (World of art) and founded an exhibition society by the same name, as well as the concert society Evenings of Contemporary Music. In 1906 he introduced Russian paintings to the outside world at a major exhibition in Paris. The next year he was back with a series of Russian "historical concerts." And then it was the turn of Russian opera when, in 1908, Diaghilev organized the Parisian (and Western) première of *Boris Godunov*, in Rimsky-Korsakov's orchestration. That was the first step in the international career both of the work and of the bass Chaliapin (Plate 9). One year later Diaghilev staged the Polovtsian dances from *Prince Igor* and Rimsky-Korsakov's *Pskovityanka,* the latter under the title of *Ivan the Terrible* (by analogy with *Boris Godunov*), again with Fyodor Chaliapin in the title role. In 1913 he produced an idiosyncratic version of *Khovanshchina,* in a revision with a disproportionately large role for Dosifey—another star part for Chaliapin. Rimsky-Korsakov's *The Golden Cockerel* became known through Diaghilev's Parisian production of 1914. The Diaghilev enterprise enjoyed the financial support of such leading capitalists as Mamontov and Morozov and attracted in addition a whole series of new sponsors, who, however, were less interested in artistic merit than in commercial publicity. Finally, Diaghilev was able to combine these private funds with state assistance, thanks largely to the mediation of Grand Duke Vladimir, although after the grand duke's death Diaghilev lost the support of the court. His last enterprise, the Ballets Russes, was run entirely on commercial lines.

## CONTINUATION OF, AND DETACHMENT FROM, THE *KUCHKA* IDEAL

It is difficult to detect a straight line in Rimsky-Korsakov's development after his retraining. His oeuvre comprised a continuation of *kuchka* trends and also growing detachment from the past. A continuation of the *kuchka* ideal can be seen first of all in the *Svetliy prazdnik* Overture (1888) mentioned above, which, in its arrangement of liturgical themes, follows the design and structural plan of Balakirev's Second Overture. *Capriccio espagnol* is based on folk song, but the structure is more rhapsodic. The work can pass for a continuation of Glinka's Spanish *Fantaisies pittoresques,* although the sparkle of the orchestration far outshines that of the model. This work became the best-known example of Rimsky-Korsakov's gift for orchestration: more than any other of his works, *Capriccio espagnol* is calculated for effect. It went down in history as the model for Ravel's *Rhapsodie espagnole.*

Russian orientalism received its best-known expression in *Sheherazade* (1888). The work is based on *A Thousand and One Nights,* the story of the sultana Sheherazade, who keeps her husband, the sultan Shakriar, from his intention of killing her by telling him stories for one thousand and one nights. The encounter between barbarous despotism and feminine seduction (Plate 10)—a contrast that Rimsky-Korsakov's work emphasizes from the start—renders the story an oriental paradigm par excellence. The sultan is introduced with a robust theme in the brass, whereupon Sheherazade appears in the arabesques of a violin solo. This famous theme, a near plagiarism of Balakirev's *Tamara*, betrays the link between *Sheherazade* and the orientalism of the *kuchka*. The sensual aspect of orientalism is clearest in the dreamy third movement. The composer told Glazunov that the work did not have a specific program and, accordingly, gave the four movements no titles. The first movement was a prelude, the second a tale, the third a reverie, and the fourth "an Oriental feast, a dance, in short a kind of carnival in Baghdad."[14] Listeners have to decide for themselves which tales they associate with the music. Modern editions tend to do that for them: the first movement is generally associated with "the sea and Sinbad's ship"; the second with "the tale of Prince Calendar"; the third with the romance between "the young prince and the young princess"; and the fourth with "the festival in Baghdad, the sea, and the shipwreck on a rock dominated by a bronze warrior." Another exercise in orientalism is the symphonic poem *Night on Triglav Mountain* (1899–1901), a symphonic rearrangement of Act III of the opera *Mlada*. The original is a motley mixture of conventional romantic music (a ballet of wandering souls à la *Giselle*), a Slavonic witches' Sabbath in the spirit of *Night on Bald Mountain,* and a vision of Cleopatra as destructive seductress of the hero. The entry of the Egyptian queen is accompanied in the opera by a whole range of exotic instruments: piccolo clarinets, *timpano piccolo,* "lyres" (small autoharps), and brass panpipes. In the symphonic poem, the instrumentation is reduced to the normal symphonic set of instruments.

In his operas Rimsky-Korsakov continued to use a number of types. He took the model of *Ruslan and Lyudmila* to new heights in *Mlada* (1889–90) and *Sadko* (1895–96). *Mlada* is a mythological opera-ballet, filled with every conceivable fantasy figure: Slavic princes, pagan priests, Vikings, Orientals (a Moor, Cleopatra, and her train), the evil wizard Kashchey, the "black god" Chernobog, spirits, werewolves, witches, and much more. It is the exuberant fantasy of *Ruslan* carried to the extreme. Several parts are modeled on characters from Glinka's opera: the bard Lumir is a copy of Bayan; Chernobog and Kashchey recall the Gigantic Head; and the evil goddess Morena bears a close resemblance to the sorceress Naína. The musical dramaturgy, too, follows the recipe of *Ruslan:* people are characterized by various national styles, supernatural beings by artificial harmonies. To Glinka's whole-tone scale as a code for black magic, Rimsky-Korsakov added the octatonic scale (the modern term for scales alternating whole and half tones in regular succession). *Mlada,* moreover, harks back to another model: Wagner's *Ring.* For a long time persona non grata with the *kuchka,* Wagner nevertheless impressed Rimsky-Korsakov when the *Ring* was first performed in St. Petersburg in the 1889–90 season. Although the intrigue in *Mlada* bears similarities to the *Ring,* Rimsky-Korsakov was mainly interested in Wagner's orchestration and in the expressive force of his music. He designed the orchestration of *Mlada* in a Wagnerian spirit, complete with a thirteen-piece brass section and twelve horns or tubas on the stage. The introduction to Act III has more than superficial parallels with the prelude to *Das Rheingold.*

*Sadko* tells the story of a merchant from Novgorod, a character based on a twelfth-century historical figure around whom a cycle of epic songs (*bïlinï*) had sprung up. A simple *gusli* player, Sadko prospers and becomes a rich merchant. He is helped by the Sea King and the latter's daughter, Volkhova. The opera reaches its climax in the opposition of diatonic and chromatic idioms as reflections of human and fantasy worlds. In addition to the *Ruslan* model, the opera is also reminiscent of *Prince Igor* (the two minstrels are based on Skula and Yeroshka) and of Serov's operas (the songs of the Viking and Indian merchants originate in *Rogneda* and *Judith*). The recitatives based on folk song are an inheritance from *The Power of the Fiend.* In *Kashchey the Deathless* (1901–2), a one-act opera, Rimsky-Korsakov went furthest with the exploration of artificial scales in the portrayal of black magic, stimulated by his renewed acquaintanceship with Wagner's *Siegfried.*

Dargomïzhsky's *The Stone Guest* served as a model for Rimsky-Korsakov's *Mozart and Salieri* (1897). Both were based on a "little tragedy" by Pushkin, the two plays having also been conceived as fantasies on Mozartian subjects. Rimsky-Korsakov followed Dargomïzhsky's model in the word-for-word setting of the text to music, and expressly dedicated the work to Dargomïzhsky's memory. He developed that composer's ideal once again in the short opera *The Boyarinya Vera Sheloga* (1898). The libretto is based on the first act of Mey's play *The Maid of Pskov.* The opera, which may be considered a prelude to *Pskovityanka,* serves as prologue to that greater historical opera in the revised version of 1891–92.

Following *Pskovityanka,* Rimsky-Korsakov turned his back on historical or civic subjects almost completely. For him, the time of socially committed art was largely over. His sole historical opera after that was *The Tsar's Bride* (1898), like *Pskovityanka* based on a play by Lev Mey, though the content is completely different. Instead of being a historical reflection, *The Tsar's Bride* is a personal tragedy set in a historical context, closer to Chaikovsky's *Oprichnik* than to *Pskovityanka.* In both cases, Ivan the Terrible and his *oprichniki* have a destructive effect on the lives of individuals. It is a somber play with every kind of romantic element: jealousy, murder, magical potions, and madness.

Rimsky-Korsakov exchanged historical subjects for fables partly for practical reasons. Following the assassination of Alexander II in 1881, liberalism had had its day in Russia. Censorship became stricter once again, and the ban on assigning voice parts to historical tsars was reintroduced, Ivan the Terrible being allowed to appear in *The Tsar's Bride* only in a silent role. Satisfying the censor became a tragicomedy in the case of the opera *Christmas Eve*. Although Rimsky-Korsakov altered the role of Catherine the Great to that of a nameless tsarina in order to avoid trouble, the censor refused to consider her as a fictional character. Everyone was familiar with Gogol's tale, he insisted, and would therefore know who was meant. Once again, Rimsky-Korsakov had to appeal to his influential friends. The tsar finally gave his approval, to the great relief of Ivan Vsevolozhsky, who was anxious to make the most of his formula for success based on Catherine's eighteenth-century court. Despite these proscriptions, Vsevolozhsky saw to it that the singer resembled the historical Catherine the Great. When the grand dukes Vladimir Alexandrovich and Mikhaíl Nikolayevich attended the rehearsals, they were outraged. They railed at the singer for having the impertinence to pass herself off as their great-grandmother, and the tsar subsequently withdrew his approval. The performance was ultimately saved by the same ruse that had saved Chaikovsky's *Cherevichki*: the role was assigned to a baritone representing some vague "Excellency."

However escapist his operas may have been, Rimsky-Korsakov remained true to his liberal ideas, as may be gathered, for instance, from his support for the uprising of the conservatory students during the 1905 revolution—an attitude that earned him a temporary suspension of his professorship and a ban on the performance of his works. In his last opera, *The Golden Cockerel* (1906–7), he returned to a political theme. With its portrait of the grotesque, blundering Tsar Dodon, the opera is a razor-sharp satire of the autocracy, of Russian imperialism, and of the Russo-Japanese war. There was little chance of getting the work past the censor, and it was finally staged only after Rimsky-Korsakov's death, in an adapted version. The writing of *The Golden Cockerel* was an impromptu response to the prevailing political conditions; Rimsky-Korsakov had not planned the work in advance, looking on his next to last opera, *The Legend of the Invisible City of Kitezh and the Maiden Fevroniya* (1903–4), as the rounding-off of his oeuvre. This opera was intended as a farewell not only to his own style, but also to a tradition he considered to be of the past.

The Legend of the Invisible City of Kitezh is a retrospective work. It tells of the miracle that saved the city of Kitezh from destruction during the Mongol invasion, and has occasionally been interpreted as a synthesis of historical and fantastic opera. This view is an exaggerated one, however, since the ostensibly historical element is largely imaginary. The Mongol invasion is not presented in a historical context, but transformed into an epic or even fairy-tale motif. The Mongols in the opera, who spring up suddenly out of nowhere, are little more than mythical personifications of Evil. The Legend of the Invisible City of Kitezh is wholly in the line of fairy-tale operas. It also harks back not only to Rimsky-Korsakov's own work but also to the Russian opera tradition as a whole. Most elements in the story and in the musical dramaturgy have a precedent. The opera once again uses the contrast between two musical idioms to express the clash of two peoples, as in A Life for the Tsar, complete with the contrast between duple and triple rhythms. The Mongols force a Russian to lead them to Kitezh, just as the Poles forced Ivan Susanin to lead them to the tsar. The role of the drunkard Grishka Kuterma is reminiscent of Musorgsky's declamatory style in Boris Godunov, while Prince Yuri recalls the character of Boris. Other musical references are the ringing of the church bells and the melody sung by the people in the third act, which recalls the Pretender's leitmotif. The role of the visionary maiden Fevroniya bears similarities to that of Marfa in Khovanshchina. In the second act, we witness a folk wedding reminiscent of the Shrovetide scene in Serov's The Power of the Fiend. The idea for the battle of Kerzhenets, portrayed in a symphonic intermezzo, comes straight out of Chaikovsky's Mazepa. All these features help to make Kitezh a nostalgic testimony to half a century of Russian opera.

In contrast to this tendency to build upon the past, Rimsky-Korsakov was also inclined to distance himself from his earlier oeuvre. This was particularly noticeable around the turn of the century. In 1897 he composed an impressive total of forty-three romances and duets, in an attempt to train himself in vocal lyricism in preference to declamation, a by-product of his overall effort to dissociate himself from the kuchka ideal. The new lyrical style was something he then elaborated on a larger scale in The Tsar's Bride, an opera based on number structure and thus amounting to a late tribute to Verdi. Featuring the same lyrical romance style that dominates the entire work, the vocal score is closer to Chaikovsky's than to Rimsky-Korsakov's own former style. The composer's aim was to shake off his image of fairy-tale opera composer as well as his *kuchka* past. Rimsky-Korsakov pursued this path further in *Servilia* (1900–1901) and in *Pan Voyevoda* (The commander, 1902–3), even abandoning the Russian background in both operas: *Servilia* is set in ancient Rome during Nero's reign, *Pan Voyevoda* in seventeenth-century Poland. The distance he had traveled from the earlier realistic ideal can be discerned from the preface he wrote to the score of *Servilia*:

> In the performance of his operas the composer does not admit devices, reckoned as dramatic, that lie outside the realm of musical art, as for example: speaking, whispering, laughing, shouting and so on. He demands singing exclusively, with clearly defined pitch, whether the music be "arioso" or declamatory, since he is convinced that only in this way can a truly musical-dramatic effect be achieved. In the lyrical moments of the opera, those artists on stage who are not occupied with singing must in no way distract the audience from the singing with superfluous acting or gestures, since *an operatic work is above all a musical work*.[15]

Rimsky-Korsakov's distance from the past is not always as extreme as it is in the three operas cited. He continued to be interested in harmonic experiments and the exploration of new idioms, although his progressive ideas always went hand in hand with a dislike of excess. Following the examples of Glinka and Liszt, he went very far in the use of whole-tone and octatonic scales, developing both idioms in the fantastic sections of such operas as *Mlada, Sadko,* and *Kashchey the Deathless.* In the last of these operas his aim was to drive the harmonic possibilities to the limit. By devising strict rules of voice-leading, he tried to prevent his music from becoming chaotic. In this he saw an essential difference from what was happening in the West, which he called "d'Indyism," after the French composer d'Indy, not least as a pun on dandyism:

> In the works of French d'Indyism there are many brusque harmonies and modulations, just as there are in *Kashchey*. But despite that I have absolutely nothing in common with this d'Indyism. And the difference lies not only in rhythm, but in the implacable logic of my [harmonic] combinations, in the *invisible presence* of the tonic at all times, and in my impeccable voice-leading. In d'Indyism the sharp combinations are linked for the most part with artistic thoughtlessness and caprice.[16]

Rimsky-Korsakov was at once a progressive and a conservative composer. He kept his tendency to experiment under constant control. The more radical his harmonies became, the more he subjected them to strict rules. He called this need for control his "musical conscience," as is shown in his own comparison of his method of work with that of Wagner, written on the occasion of his study of *Siegfried* in 1901:

> As always after a long interval, Wagner's music has become alien to me, and I had to get used to it. Now that I'm a little used to it, I started to like it, but then I again experienced something akin to disgust. I began to grow indignant at all his *blunders of the ear*, and his *constant crossing of the boundary of what is possible in harmony*—to put it simply, the nonsense and the falseness that you find strewn about *Siegfried* at every step. . . . Could my musical ear be better than Wagner's? . . . No, of course, not better; maybe even worse; but I have a *musical conscience*, to which I am obedient, and Wagner frittered his conscience away in his quest for grandiosity and novelty. . . . It's terribly hard to define the limits of what is *possible* in music; it's a much too complicated question, into which everything must be reckoned: not only harmony, but melodic and rhythmic considerations. I could not hope to solve it, but I feel that I am right.[17]

The same "musical conscience" was Rimsky-Korsakov's guide in his completion and arrangement of the work of others, particularly of his former *kuchka* colleagues.

## ORCHESTRATION, REARRANGEMENT, OR RECOMPOSITION: RIMSKY-KORSAKOV AND THE LEGACY OF THE *KUCHKA*

Rimsky-Korsakov revised not only his own work from his *kuchka* period, but also the scores of other composers. He undertook these projects partly out of necessity, since many unfinished pieces would otherwise have proved unplayable. Before Dargomïzhsky died, for instance, he asked Rimsky-Korsakov to orchestrate *The Stone Guest*, realizing that he himself would not live long enough to complete it. When Borodin lacked the time needed for *Prince Igor*, Rimsky-Korsakov offered to help. He was willing to take on any kind of routine work—orchestration, transposition, writing out sketches—with the categorical assurance that he would impose none of his own ideas. When Musorgsky died in 1881, Rimsky-Korsakov looked after his legacy, for which he decided to provide playable editions rather than philologically correct ones:

> In the majority of cases, these compositions showed so much talent, so much originality, offered so much that was new and alive, that their publication was a positive obligation. But publication without a skilful hand to put them in order would have had no sense save a biographico-historical one. If Moussorgsky's compositions are destined to live unfaded for fifty years after their author's death (when all his works will become the property of any and every

publisher), such an archaeologically accurate edition will always be possible, as the manuscripts went to the Public Library on leaving me. For the present, though, there was need of an edition for performances, for practical artistic purposes, for making his colossal talent known, and not for the mere studying of his personality and artistic sins.[18]

The first major task was the completion of *Khovanshchina*. Rimsky-Korsakov was faced with the need to bring some order into the rather confused content of the opera. As was pointed out earlier, he chose a melioristic interpretation: the presentation of the reign of Peter the Great as a new phase in the history of Russia, a new beginning for which all that had gone before had to stand aside. He gave this interpretation shape by reprising the "Dawn" theme at the end of the second act, and by composing a new triumphant finale, with a quotation of the Preobrazhensky march, following the death of the Old Believers, thus re-adopting the teleological interpretation of history he had used in his own *Pskovityanka*.

He put *The Fair at Sorochintsï* to one side, probably because it contained a caricature of a village priest that the censor was most unlikely to pass. He did, however, orchestrate *Songs and Dances of Death* and *Pictures from an Exhibition*. As for *Night on Bald Mountain*, Rimsky-Korsakov considered the work impossible in the form in which Musorgsky had written it. Rimsky-Korsakov's own version, therefore, cannot be fitted into the category of redactions and orchestrations; it is, rather, a radical recomposition, loosely based on the same thematic material but wholly different in structure, orchestral coloring, and expression, so much so, in fact, that Musorgsky can no longer be considered its author.

### PRINCE IGOR

After Borodin's death in 1887, Rimsky-Korsakov, assisted by Glazunov, turned his attention to *Prince Igor*, which Borodin had left in an even more sketchy and truncated state than *Khovanshchina*. Only the second act had a more or less definite form; all the rest consisted of unconnected fragments. Together, Rimsky-Korsakov and Glazunov produced a performable edition. Although the individual contributions of the two composers are difficult to distinguish, it is generally assumed that Rimsky-Korsakov edited and orchestrated the existing fragments, while Glazunov composed and added missing sections. Most of the third act is Glazunov's work, and it is probable that the overture is as well. An analysis of Borodin's manuscripts by Pavel Lamm has shown that Rimsky-Korsakov and Glazunov dispensed with nearly a fifth of Borodin's score. In the form in which we know the opera, then, *Prince Igor* is more the collective work of three composers than a true presentation of Borodin's intentions. However, the chaotic state of Borodin's material renders it extraordinarily difficult to come up with an acceptable alternative.[19]

Unsatisfactory though the reconstruction by Rimsky-Korsakov and Glazunov may be, it does give some indication of Borodin's own aims. He began with an 1869 scenario of Stasov's based on the twelfth-century epic "Lay of Igor's Campaign," which tells of the struggle between Prince Igor and the Polovtsi, a nomadic eastern tribe. The opera was modeled from the outset on Glinka's *Ruslan and Lyudmila,* the oriental idiom of the Polovtsi being based on the music accompanying the scenes in Naína's garden and in Chernomor's castle and that used in the characterization of Ratmir. Melodic turns based on folk-song models govern the style of the Russian characters.

The story deals with Igor's captivity in the Polovtsian camp and the attempt by Khan Konchak to win him over as an ally. Igor demurs. He also refuses to agree to the marriage of his son Vladimir to the Khan's daughter, Konchakovna. With the help of the Christian Ovlur, Igor is able to escape and to return to his court in Putivl, where he restores order after the shameful interregnum of his brother-in-law Galitsky. What happens next to Vladimir and Konchakovna is something we cannot tell from the opera itself, but only from Stasov's original scenario. They eventually marry in Putivl, with Igor's blessing. Igor had set his face firmly against a marriage that would take his son into the enemy camp, but drops his objections and accepts Konchakovna as his daughter-in-law when she becomes converted to Christianity and thus acknowledges the superiority of Russian culture. The scenario reflects the ideology designed to justify the eastward expansion of the Russian empire. Russian superiority was generally considered a legitimization of the military subjection of oriental nations. During the composition of *Prince Igor* that expansion was, in fact, proceeding apace. In this context *Prince Igor* amounts to an undisguised expression of aggressive nationalism, something that was supported by almost the entire Russian intelligentsia.

The opera plays on the continuous opposition between the Russian and oriental styles. The latter was given its classical form by Borodin, as the expression of languorous hedonism or barbarian splendor. The first aspect is apparent in the choruses of the Polovtsian maidens and in the famous Polovtsian Dances, with the help of which the khan tries to tempt Prince Igor into joining him in an alliance by offering him his ori-

ental slave girls. The height of Eastern sensuality is reflected in Konchakovna's role, where, in addition to the obbligato chromatic passing
notes and the ostinato patterns in the bass, there is the impact of the alto
voice. Borodin exploits all the sensual possibilities of the tessitura. In the
duet with Vladimir, Konchakovna's alto is constantly entwined with the
tenor part. In this manner Borodin gives musical expression to Khan Konchak's ultimate goal: paralyzing Vladimir into passivity, or as he puts it
in the original "Lay," "entoiling the falconet by means of a fair maiden."[20]

In *Prince Igor* Borodin distanced himself from the aesthetics of the
*kuchka*. Admitting openly that realistic declamation was not to his taste
(although his comical characters, the minstrels Skula and Yeroshka, come
close to Musorgsky's Varlaam and Missail), he looked upon opera as
preeminently a lyric genre, clearly divided into numbers and conceived
in broad musical gestures. By *kuchka* norms that approach was old-
fashioned. Yet all his associates stood by the score, because each could
find something to his taste in it. Borodin himself put it like this:

> Curiously enough, all the members of our circle seem to come together on my
> *Igor:* from the ultra-innovatory realist Modest Petrovich [Musorgsky], to the
> lyric-dramatic innovator César Antonovich [Cui], to the martinet with respect
> to outward form and musical tradition Nikolay Andreyevich [Rimsky-
> Korsakov], to the ardent champion of novelty and power in all things,
> Vladimir Vasil'yevich Stasov. Everyone is satisfied with *Igor,* strongly though
> they may differ about other things.[21]

### BORIS GODUNOV

Of all Rimsky-Korsakov's redactions, *Boris Godunov* received the
fiercest criticism. To keep matters in perspective, however, let us look at
its history: in 1882 *Boris Godunov* disappeared from the repertoire of
the Mariyinsky Theater. Between 1888 and 1890, the opera was occasionally performed in Moscow. We have seen that, the general impression to the contrary, little or no political pressure was put on the composer to alter the work. The opera was only outlawed for political reasons
during the reactionary reign of Alexander III, who personally removed
it from the list of works to be performed at the Imperial Theaters.[22]

In 1889 Rimsky-Korsakov reorchestrated the polonaise from the "Polish act" for a concert performance. He then conceived the idea of revising the whole opera and of stripping it of everything he considered to be
an imperfection. By 1896 his first revision was finished. In the preface
he explained that the purpose of his interventions was to stress the great

importance of the work and to silence the objections of those who had attacked Musorgsky for his lack of technical knowledge. The new version was substantially abridged. The last two scenes were changed around, so that the Kromy scene preceded Boris's death. The score was played in 1896 in the St. Petersburg Conservatory. On 7 December 1898, the full opera was performed by Savva Mamontov's Private Opera Company in Moscow. The performance made history because the role of Boris was sung for the first time by Fyodor Chaliapin, who was to set his inimitable stamp on the performance tradition of the work.

César Cui once again showed himself at his most unpredictable and intolerant. During the composition of *Boris Godunov* he had been the loudest in declaring that Musorgsky's talent was being ruined by his technical imperfections. Now he wrote:

> Recollecting and comparing the former *Boris* with the present "corrected" *Boris,* I admit that I sincerely miss the old version. Even if Mr. Rimsky-Korsakov's harmonies are smoother and more natural, they are not Musorgsky's harmonies and obviously not what he wanted. Even if Mr. Rimsky-Korsakov's voice-leading is flawless, while Musorgsky's occasionally sins against textbook rules, the latter often better suits the coarse and uncivilized scenes of the opera. Even if Mr. Rimsky-Korsakov's instrumentation is incomparably more perfect than Musorgsky's, it is nonetheless obvious that its coloration is not entirely what the author tried to achieve. The reorchestration of a work more normal, less off the beaten track, is a feasible thing, but the reorchestration of so extraordinary a work as *Boris*—hardly possible to consider as a rational act—only makes the opera insipid.[23]

This critique may seem surprisingly similar to the view of present-day music critics, but it sounds ironic in the light of Cui's devastating opinion of *Boris* expressed in 1874.

In 1906 Rimsky-Korsakov produced a second version, in which he restored the cuts he had made. Except for the switching around of the last two scenes and a few minor deletions, it was faithful to the version Musorgsky had recorded in his vocal score of 1874. The resulting score was intended to be the ultimate, ideal form of the opera, judged by Rimsky-Korsakov's standards.

Most of the changes in this version were technical. Rimsky-Korsakov improved the voice-leading, normalized the modulations, introduced transpositions, and provided a brighter orchestration. He also to some extent changed the content of the opera. It is often alleged that in switching the last scenes around he neutralized the ideological importance of the original. By ending the opera with Boris's death instead of with the revolutionary scene and the *yuródiviy*'s lament, Rimsky-Korsakov is said to have done away with the "folk drama" aspect.

This charge is rather sweeping and requires qualification. We must recall that it was Rimsky-Korsakov himself who restored the Kromy scene after it had been scrapped in 1876 with Musorgsky's express approval (and over Stasov's and Rimsky-Korsakov's protests). To meet the expectations of the public, for whom the drama was over with Boris's death, Rimsky-Korsakov, however, proposed changing the scenes around. As a result, both the function and the content of the Kromy scene were slightly altered. In the original *Boris*, it opened up the drama to a wider perspective: a reflection on history transcending Boris's personal fate. In Rimsky-Korsakov's version, by contrast, it served as the final nemesis: a kind of "Birnam Wood" in a *Macbeth*-like scenario. Rimsky-Korsakov's version is thus closer to Karamzin's original historical interpretation. The treatment of the coronation scene likewise brought about a change, this time with a more incisive ideological effect. By polishing up the instrumentation and discarding the clash of the bystanders with the police, Rimsky-Korsakov greatly increased the representative character of the scene. Whereas in Musorgsky's rendition the people reacted halfheartedly and with a lack of interest to Boris's installation as tsar, Rimsky-Korsakov's coronation ritual is an untroubled homage to the autocracy. Yet it would be wrong to attach too much ideological weight to that fact, since not much later Rimsky-Korsakov, with his *Golden Cockerel,* was to compose a satire on the autocracy that went a great deal further than Musorgsky's coronation scene.

In 1907 Diaghilev revealed his plan to stage the European première of *Boris Godunov* in Paris. Unfettered by our modern standards of authenticity, he aimed for maximum effect. Among his plans was the prolongation of the coronation scene, the better to stun the Parisians with its grandeur, and he asked Rimsky-Korsakov to make the necessary changes. The Parisian—and hence the European—première of *Boris* on 19 May 1908 presented the opera in an arrangement that reflected neither Musorgsky's nor Rimsky-Korsakov's version.[24] A number of constants in the performance history of the work originated at the time, including Rimsky-Korsakov's additions, which were incorporated into the vocal score published by Bessel & Co. in 1908. Chaliapin's protracted monopoly established the melodramatic, *quasi-parlando* interpretation of the title role. The emphasis on visual spectacle and the custom of scrapping, shortening, extending, or changing the sequence of scenes at will continue undiminished to this day.

## RIMSKY-KORSAKOV AND FOLKLORE

Rimsky-Korsakov revealed his most personal side in his approach to Russian folklore. The folklorism of Balakirev and of the *kuchka* had been largely modeled on the *protyazhnaya*. Since the composition of *May Night* (1878–79), Rimsky-Korsakov had felt attracted to a different category of folk song, namely "calendar songs," intended for particular ritual occasions. His fascination with them went beyond their purely musical appeal. Calendar songs were part of rural customs and contained echoes of old Slavic paganism. What most fascinated Rimsky-Korsakov in folk music was the pantheist world of folk rites. For him, folklore was less closely bound up with nationalism and ideology; even in his *kuchka* period, his view of the subject had differed from Balakirev's. He had this to say, for instance, about the composition of his *Serbian Fantasy:*

> In Balakirev's apartment I often met Czechs and other Slavic brethren who came and went. I listened to their conversations, but I confess that I understood them very little, taking a scant interest in the [pan-Slavic] movement. In the spring some Slavic guests were expected and a concert, which Balakirev was to conduct, was projected in their honour. Apparently this concert stimulated the composition of the overture on Czech themes and, contrary to his custom, this overture was written rather rapidly by Balakirev. I undertook, at Balakirev's suggestion, to write a fantasy on Serbian themes, for orchestra. In undertaking to compose the *Serbian Fantasy* I was not at all carried away by Slavism, but rather by the delightful themes Balakirev had selected for me.[25]

Rimsky-Korsakov's interest in pantheism was aroused by Alexander Afanasyev's folkloristic studies. That author's standard work, *The Slavs' Poetic Outlook on Nature,* became the composer's pantheistic bible. The first step in Rimsky-Korsakov's artistic development of Afanasyev's ideas was *May Night,* in which he complemented Gogol's tale with folk dances and calendar songs. In 1881 he followed this road further with *Snegurochka,* an opera based on Alexander Ostrovsky's play by the same name (Plate 11). The story is a parable of the transition from winter to spring, in which the author alluded to popular customs stretching from *maslenitsa* to *kupala:* the first, the Russian Shrovetide, represents the end of winter; the second represents midsummer, the moment when the sun god Yarilo takes control of the earth. The story centers on Snegurochka, a maiden of snow and ice. Her parents, King Winter and Fairy Spring, keep her hidden away from the fatal rays of the sun, where she is safe as long as she knows no passion. Love is represented by the shepherd girl Kupava and the shepherd boy Lel', the Slavic Eros. The story ends with

the marriage of Snegurochka to Mizgir—at which moment she melts and
Tsar Berendey's frozen land is freed from the grip of winter. Like the ritual destruction of an effigy representing winter, the sacrifice of the Snow
Maiden as a sign that winter is over reflects folk customs. By linking the
passage of the seasons to the human experience of love, moreover, Ostrovsky points to the link between procreative sexuality and the ever-
turning wheel of nature. Rimsky-Korsakov's score makes extensive use
of seasonal calendar songs and *khorovodi* (ceremonial dances) in the folk
tradition.

Rimsky-Korsakov also discovered pagan exuberance in the Orthodox
religion. This was the basis of his "Russian Easter" Overture, intended
as a summary of the colorful mixture of impressions evoked by the Easter
celebration:

> In this Overture were thus combined reminiscences of the ancient prophecy
> [Rimsky-Korsakov associated the ecclesiastical theme "Let God arise" with
> Isaiah's prophecy], of the Gospel narrative and also a general picture of the
> Easter service with its "pagan merry-making." The capering and leaping of
> the Biblical King David before the ark, do they not give expression to a mood
> of the same order as the mood of the idol-worshippers' dance? Surely the Rus-
> sian Orthodox chime is instrumental dance-music of the church, is it not? And
> do not the waving beards of the priests and sextons clad in white vestments
> and surplices, and intoning "Beautiful Easter" in the tempo of *Allegro vivo*,
> etc., transpose the imagination to pagan times? And all these Easter loaves
> and twists and the glowing tapers—how far a cry from the philosophic and
> socialistic teaching of Christ! This legendary and heathen side of the holiday,
> this transition from the gloomy and mysterious evening of Passion Saturday
> to the unbridled, pagan-religious merry-making on the morn of Easter Sun-
> day, is what I was eager to reproduce in my overture. . . . In any event, in or-
> der to appreciate my Overture even ever so slightly, it is necessary that the
> hearer should have attended Easter morning service at least once, and that,
> not in a domestic chapel, but in a cathedral thronged with people from every
> walk of life, with several priests conducting the cathedral service—something
> that many intellectual Russian hearers, let alone hearers of other confessions,
> quite lack nowadays. As for myself, I have gained my impressions in my child-
> hood, passed near the Tikhvin Monastery itself.[26]

In Russian folklore, Christian and pagan practices are often bound
up inseparably. Folk religiosity in fact constitutes a syncretic religion, referred to as *dvoyeveriye*, or "double faith." When Russia was converted
to Christianity, the Slavic rites, rather than disappearing, in many cases
were simply fitted into the new Christian rituals.

Rimsky-Korsakov devoted two operas to the *dvoyeveriye* theme:
*Christmas Eve* and *The Legend of the Invisible City of Kitezh and the*

*Maiden Fevroniya.* The first opera emphasized the pagan aspect, the second the Christian.

*Christmas Eve* (1894–95) is based on the short story by Gogol of the same name, which Chaikovsky also used in his *Vakula the Smith* and *Cherevichki.* After Chaikovsky's death in 1893, Rimsky-Korsakov considered the way clear for an alternative version. By focusing less on the love intrigue between Vakula and Oxana and by retaining the original dialogues, Rimsky-Korsakov tried to make his version more faithful to Gogol's. As far as the folkloristic aspects of the opera were concerned, however, he allowed his own viewpoints to prevail, expanding the mythological and ritual implications of the story. The episode in which the young people sing *kolyadki* (Christmas carols) is assigned a crucial role. The composer inserted a whole series of Ukrainian *kolyadki,* using them, moreover, as the inspiration for a brilliant ballet intermezzo in Act III. When Vakula flies to St. Petersburg on the Devil's back by night, the demonic characters Pachuk and Solokha gather together all the evil forces to chase away the gods Kolyada and Ovsen, who proclaim the equinoctial return of the sun after the storms and dark nights of winter. Christmas Eve is the evil spirits' last chance to rule over the earth. When Vakula comes back to Dikanka, the demons taste defeat and make way for the sun. At the end of the act, the Orthodox Christmas-morning hymn resounds, the festival of the rebirth of the sun coinciding with the celebration of Christ's birth.

The Christian aspect of Christmas is barely broached in *Christmas Eve.* Christian imagery is more patently present in *The Legend of the Invisible City of Kitezh and the Maiden Fevroniya,* though even then in little more than a superficial way: Orthodox chants set the general tone of the opera, but beyond that the Christian motif remains muted. The story is based on the sixteenth-century hagiography of Fevroniya of Murom, a text in which Christian and Slavonic mythological elements are fused. Vladimir Belsky, Rimsky-Korsakov's librettist, originally planned a dramatization of the hagiography as such, but that was not to the composer's taste. The final result was a profession of pantheistic faith.[27] The character of Fevroniya combines the ideal of Christian neighborly love with natural religion. In the first act we see her in the forest, where she instructs Prince Vsevolod in her faith:

> Is not God everywhere? You may think it is a deserted place; but it is not: there is a mighty church here. Look about with intelligent eyes. Day and night we have our service, day and night we have our thyme and frankincense; during the day the sun shines on us, a brilliant sun, and at night the stars begin

to gleam like little candles. Day and night we have tender singing, like jubilation in a multitude of voices: birds, beasts, everything that breathes, all glorify God's beautiful world. Glory to thee for ever more, radiant heaven, glory
to the Lord God and his lofty throne! And that same glory to thee, mother
earth, you are the solid pedestal of God![28]

When Fevroniya tries to convert the drunkard Grishka Kuterma in Act
IV, she teaches him to pray to the Earth. The supernatural elements in
the story are the work both of the Christian God and of Sirin and
Alkonost, the prophet-birds of Slavonic mythology.

The story is set at the time of the Mongol invasion in the thirteenth
century. Prince Vsevolod, the son of Prince Yuriy, the ruler of Kitezh, encounters the low-born maiden Fevroniya during a hunt and claims her
for his bride (Plate 12). Just before the wedding, the city of Lesser Kitezh,
the military outpost of Greater Kitezh, is overrun and sacked by the
Tatars. They carry off the drunkard Grishka and Fevroniya, who prays
for a miracle to save Greater Kitezh. A messenger carries the dreadful
news of the Tatar attack to the city. All able-bodied men go out under
the leadership of Prince Vsevolod, who will fall on the field of battle.
Meanwhile Prince Yuriy and the citizens who have stayed behind also
pray for a miracle. A golden mist descends. Guided by a coerced Grishka,
the Tatars find their way to the city, but because all they can see is the
mist, they accuse him of deceiving them and threaten to put him to death.
At night, however, they do see the city reflected in the lake, although
there is nothing on the land. In panic, they flee. We then see Grishka and
Fevroniya roaming exhausted through the forest. Grishka, tortured by
guilt, goes mad and runs away from her. Fevroniya is greeted by the spirit
of the slain Vsevolod. Sirin and Alkonost accompany the couple to the
city of Kitezh, which has left the earth for Paradise. There the interrupted
wedding is continued.

The opera betrays Wagner's influence with the murmur of the forest
from *Siegfried,* and the fight between the Tatar leaders recalls the rivalry
between Fasolt and Fafner. *Parsifal* also served as a model, though the
resemblance is superficial: in both cases we have a Christian legend, with
a city or stronghold lifted above earthly life. *The Legend of the Invisible City of Kitezh* is not a redemption play, however, unlike *Parsifal,* in
which liberation from weakness and guilt is obtained only with the utmost difficulty. *Kitezh,* in fact, is suffused with imperturbable optimism.
The Tatar invasion is no more than a brief interruption. When the inhabitants ask for help, they receive it; they have to do nothing to avert
the threat. The Tatars turn out to be harmless in the end: one sign from

God drives them away. The death they have sown makes no difference to the citizens of Kitezh. Even though Vsevolod has fallen on the field of battle, he is able to continue to celebrate his wedding to Fevroniya in the sacred city. *The Legend of the Invisible City of Kitezh* involves no true dramatic conflict; it is essentially an epic opera, in which a mythological folk tale is elaborated in a thoroughly folkloristic stylization. The libretto by Belsky is written in archaizing and neofolkloristic language, while the music involves every possible type of folk song. The wedding in the superterrestrial city is based on the model of the folk wedding ceremony. Indeed, a splendid new element, not found in his earlier folkloristic operas, is Rimsky-Korsakov's stylization of the folk church style in the wedding songs and supplications. The first scene of Act III, in which the inhabitants of the city commend their fate to God's mercy, is among the most beautiful moments of the opera, a touching picture of man renouncing action and delivering himself to a higher power.

*The Legend of the Invisible City of Kitezh and the Maiden Fevroniya* is a carefully constructed whole. The first and second acts have a sequel in the two scenes of the fourth act, the first of which repeats the meeting between Fevroniya and Vsevolod in Act I, and the second of which continues the wedding feast that was interrupted. The third act is the pivot around which the opera turns, involving the prayer of the people of Kitezh and the miracle of the vanished city. The entr'acte in Act III, the symphonic poem *The Battle of Kerzhenets,* is the centerpiece of the whole work.

In *The Legend of the Invisible City of Kitezh,* Rimsky-Korsakov continued the involvement with folklore that he had begun with *The Tale of Tsar Saltan,* an opera composed to celebrate the hundredth anniversary in 1899 of Pushkin's birth. Like the original poem, Rimsky-Korsakov's opera was a stylization of a *skazka,* a folk tale. The brief fanfare at the beginning of each act functions as a *priskazka,* a formula by which the storyteller seizes the listeners' attention. The plot transcends all realistic criteria, and the form follows folk-epic models.[29] Following rumors spread by three wicked women, Tsar Saltan has his wife and his son, Guidon, put into a barrel and cast into the sea. They are washed up on a magical island, where Guidon is appointed ruler and marries the swan princess. In order to visit his father unnoticed, the son turns himself into a bumblebee—the well-known "Flight of the Bumblebee." As some sailors are telling Saltan about the wonders of Guidon's realm, the bumblebee stings the eyes of the wicked women. Saltan decides to visit the island, and everything ends happily. Rimsky-Korsakov imposed folk stylization on the music in his use of children's songs, lullabies, the cries of street vendors and puppeteers, and urban airs.

## THE BELYAYEV CIRCLE

Belyayev turned into a patron after being deeply impressed with the achievements of the sixteen-year-old Alexander Glazunov. Glazunov emerged in public first as a symphonist and a little later as a string quartet composer. His First Symphony was chosen by Balakirev for a concert at the Free Music School. Belyayev took the promising young man under his wing, offered to publish his work, and invited him on a tour of western Europe. In Weimar, he introduced him to Franz Liszt. Glazunov became one of the key figures in the Belyayev circle, together with Rimsky-Korsakov and Rimsky's protégé, Anatoliy Lyadov. Other composers rallied around this nucleus, among them Blumenfeld, Vitols, Kalafati, Sokolov, Grechaninov, Cherepnin, Akimenko, Kopïlov, Antipov, Artsïbushev, and Steinberg.

The difference between the Belyayev circle and the former Balakirev circle, according to Rimsky-Korsakov, was that "Balakirev's circle was revolutionary, Belyayev's, on the other hand, was progressive."[30] That characterization, however, is somewhat misleading. Although Rimsky-Korsakov still tended to experiment (in combination with academic systematization), academicism had come to predominate in Belyayev's circle. The other Belyayev composers relied mainly on clichés and mannerisms, which they had distilled from the work of Balakirev and Rimsky-Korsakov. We must not be taken in by the modern appearance of some compositions by Lyadov or Cherepnin; in fact, they are based entirely on the use of Rimsky-Korsakov's octatonic technique. The harmonies of Musorgsky's coronation scene in *Boris,* the octatonicism of *Mlada* and *Sadko,* Balakirev's folk-song stylizations, Rimsky-Korsakov's colorful harmonization—all these served as a store of recipes for writing Russian national music. In the portrayal of the national character, indeed, these techniques prevailed over the subjects portrayed. National subjects are few and far between in Glazunov's oeuvre, the symphonic poem *Stenka Razin* (1885) being one of the rare exceptions. Lyadov imitated Rimsky-Korsakov's fantastic style, especially in his three orchestral works based on Russian fairy tales: *Baba Yaga* (1891–1904), *Kikimora* (1909), and *Volshebnoye ozero* (The magical [or enchanted] lake, 1909). Folklorism was not a great issue with the Belyayev composers, and when they produced folkloristic compositions, they simply imitated Balakirev's or Rimsky-Korsakov's style; they did not go to the countryside in active search of living folk songs. Orientalism was continued in the work of Ippolitov-Ivanov, a student of Rimsky-Korsakov's who spent some ten years in Tiflis in Georgia after his studies, and later worked in Moscow. His pupils included Vasilenko, Glière, and Yuliy Engel. Ippolitov-Ivanov wrote three operas with an oriental background and in Balakirev's style: *Ruth* (1883–86), *Azra* (1890), and *Izmena* (Treason, 1908–9). The last of these operas deals with the struggle between Christians and Moslems during the sixteenth-century occupation of Georgia by the Persians. *Caucasian Sketches* (1894) is an orientalist orchestral work modeled on Balakirev and Borodin.

It was clear to the actual members of the Belyayev circle what example they should follow. For those who did not belong to the immediate circle, the choice was more difficult. Anton Arensky is a good example. A pupil of Rimsky-Korsakov's, he finished his studies in 1882 at the St. Petersburg Conservatory. From 1882 to 1895 he lectured in Moscow, where he became an important link to the next generation, including Rachmaninoff and Glière. Despite his reputation as a Muscovite composer, he produced the major part of his oeuvre in St. Petersburg, where he followed Balakirev as director of the Imperial Court Chapel in 1895. In his instrumental work, Arensky considered himself Chaikovsky's heir—not of Chaikovsky the symphonist, but of the composer of songs and chamber music. In his compositions, however, we can see a dichotomy between the model of Rimsky-Korsakov and that of Chaikovsky. *Voyevode, ili Son na Volge* (The provincial governor, or a dream on the Volga, 1888) was intended as a remake of Chaikovsky's *Voyevoda*. Instead of Chaikovsky's recipe of concentrating on the love story line, however, Arensky developed the folkloristic aspect. In the dances, bridal songs, and other folkloristic choruses, he modeled himself on Glinka and Balakirev. The opera was warmly received by the Belyayev circle. Arensky's second opera was *Raphael* (1894), a saccharine fantasy about the famous painter, who, accused of seducing his model, unveils her portrait as the Mother of God and suddenly dispels all doubts about the purity of his intentions. In style and in many details, *Raphael* is based on Chaikovsky's *Iolanta*.

The most important composer outside the Belyayev circle was Sergey Taneyev, first Chaikovsky's pupil, then his successor at the Moscow Conservatory. His academic approach earned him the nickname of "the Russian Brahms." He was a keen advocate of form refinement and counterpoint. His musical idealism resulted, among other things, in a symphony in C minor (1898), six string quartets, and three quintets. In opera, he created a magnum opus with his *Oresteya* (The Oresteia, 1887–94). This work, however, had little chance of success in the context of Russian opera practice, not because of the non-Russian subject (a condensed version of Aeschylus's trilogy in three acts) but because Taneyev simply refused to compromise with the management. He saw the work as an organic whole and was hostile to Nápravník's habit of making cuts in every opera. Chaikovsky and Musorgsky had proved far more accommodating. Taneyev withdrew the opera after a few performances in 1895 and 1896.[31]

Rachmaninoff, who studied under Taneyev and Arensky, attracted Chaikovsky's attention with his symphonic poem *The Rock* (1893), inspired by Chekhov's short story "On the Road." Chaikovsky promised to conduct the first performance of the work, but his sudden death prevented that. Rachmaninoff composed a moving "In memoriam" in his *Trio élégiaque* (1893). In 1896 Belyayev received his First Symphony (1895) for performance as part of the series Russian Symphony Concerts. The implacable and unexpected critique by César Cui after the première on 17 March 1897 paralyzed Rachmaninoff's creativity for several years. Rachmaninoff blamed Glazunov, the conductor. The truth is more probably that Rachmaninoff, as a model student and protégé of Chaikovsky, Arensky, and Taneyev, and with a contract from the publisher Gutheil immediately upon obtaining his diploma, was unprepared for negative criticism. The First Symphony is well worth hearing, but anyone familiar with the later major works (such as the Second Symphony and the Second and Third Piano Concertos) can hardly help but conclude that the shock had a salutary effect.

From 1897 to 1906 Rachmaninoff was mainly active as an opera conductor in Moscow, first as assistant to Eugenio Esposito in Mamontov's company, then as conductor of Russian operas at the Bolshoy Theater. That experience and his friendship with Fyodor Chaliapin led him to consider writing his own operas. The results were *The Miserly Knight* (1904) and *Francesca da Rimini* (1905). The first is a word-for-word composition based on Pushkin's "little tragedy" by the same name. With it, Rachmaninoff completed the short list of operas based on the "little tragedies": Dargomïzhsky's *The Stone Guest*, Rimsky-Korsakov's *Mozart and Salieri*, and Cui's *A Feast in the Time of Plague* (1901). Rachmaninoff's work differs in style from the genre established by Dargomïzhsky—its texture is more symphonic. *Francesca da Rimini*, based on a libretto by Modest Chaikovsky, is an exercise in verismo. The prologue has the shape of a symphonic poem and is strongly influenced by Chaikovsky's orchestral work on the same subject. In 1907 Rachmaninoff composed an act for an opera based on Maeterlinck's *Monna Vanna*, but dropped the project because Maeterlinck had sold the exclusive rights to his oeuvre to the French composer Henry Février.

The composers of the Belyayev circle are often described as important links to, and pathbreakers for, the modernists of the years 1910 to 1920. This idea suggests that the transition toward the various expressions of modernism was a gradual process. In fact, however, it needed a radical break with the Belyayev aesthetic.

The modernist camp included Igor Stravinsky. Until 1910, he was a humble follower of the Belyayev circle. His work from that period (*The Faun and the Shepherdess* of 1906, the *Scherzo fantastique* of 1907–8, and *Fireworks* of 1908) only sounds modern to those insufficiently familiar with Rimsky-Korsakov's late oeuvre. The harmonic idiom is essentially Rimsky-Korsakov's octatonicism, completed with brilliant orchestral effects and borrowings from Richard Strauss and Debussy. At the time, Stravinsky's harmony went no further than the example of his teacher.

Rimsky-Korsakov's octatonicism was a gold mine for those bent on a modernist revolution. However, the renewing force had still to be liberated from the clichés and routines into which the Belyayev aesthetic had been pressed. For Stravinsky, the liberating experience came when Diaghilev commissioned him to write *The Firebird*. The performance in 1910 made Stravinsky an overnight Parisian celebrity. Whereas he had been no more than one among many in St. Petersburg—Rimsky-Korsakov rated his son-in-law Maximilian Steinberg more highly—he was suddenly the talk of the town in Paris, where he was considered a composer worthy to stand beside Debussy. That success was enough to cause Stravinsky to defect to the modernist camp, and to adopt the aesthetic of the Diaghilev circle, from which he had still held back when composing *The Firebird*. In the stage presentation, the music was much more traditional than the choreography and decor. The success of *The Firebird* came as a liberation for Stravinsky. From then on he worked in the spirit of the artists associated with the Ballets Russes, a group that had gathered together earlier around the journal *Mir iskusstva*. It was not long before Stravinsky drew the musical consequences from their aesthetic ideas.

## CHAPTER NINE

# Imagination and Renewal

## *The Silver Age*

Nadezhda von Meck bestowed her patronage in the strictest of secrecy. She acted from an aristocratic sense of duty, from the ideal of noblesse oblige. Only after her own death and that of Chaikovsky did the musical world learn of their correspondence, and only then did her generosity come to light. In the meantime, a different form of art patronage had emerged: no longer secret but, on the contrary, bent on attracting maximum attention. The new wealthy class of prosperous entrepreneurs vied openly with the aristocracy to sponsor the arts.

Capitalist entrepreneurs were a new phenomenon in Russian society. They constituted a nouveau riche class, sprung from the *kupechestvo,* the merchant estate established mainly in Moscow. Some became millionaires, thanks to their commercial and industrial enterprise. A wealthy "middle class," comparable to the rich bourgeoisie in the West, had been hitherto unknown in Russia, the autocracy having always opposed the rise of a class that would escape its direct control. Intellectuals, for their part, considered the middle class an unnecessary evil, equating the bourgeoisie with mercantilism and social careerism.

The disdain felt by the nobility and the intelligentsia for the Muscovite merchants in no way diminished as the financial power of these merchants grew and as the nouveaux riches endeavored to boost their social prestige through acts of charity and art sponsorship. The textile magnate Pavel Tretyakov was one of the first to take major initiatives in this field, setting himself up as patron of the *peredvizhniki,* the Russian realist painters.

Tretyakov's patronage was highly conservative and nationalistic. At around the turn of the century, other entrepreneurs also began to encourage contemporary movements. Their interest in modern art—a field especially chosen to avoid competition with the aristocracy, who concentrated on collecting old masters—laid the economic basis for the last cultural flowering of tsarist Russia: the so-called Silver Age.

Savva Mamontov's artists colony at Abramtsevo spurred the Moscow entrepreneurs on to follow his example. The rise of Russian symbolism was facilitated by such financiers as Nikolai Ryabushinsky, Genrietta Girshman, and Ivan Morozov, who also collected the work of modern Western artists. As a result, Russian painters became acquainted with impressionism, postimpressionism, symbolism, and the *Jugendstil*. A building boom was taking place, and through their construction and decoration of luxury villas the entrepreneurs encouraged the development of a Russian art nouveau.

Oddly enough, the new capitalists identified themselves above all with the transcendental, antimaterialistic art of the symbolists, whose Bohemian atmosphere, nocturnal revels, and occult séances they liked to share. They also organized literary salons and financed symbolist journals. *Iskusstvo* (Art) was founded in 1905 by Nikolai Tarovaty, survived for a mere year, and was succeeded by Nikolai Ryabushinsky's *Zolotoye runo* (The golden fleece). Artists and patrons would meet in art societies in Moscow, among them the Circle and the Society for Free Aesthetics. The entrepreneurs identified themselves with these artists, convinced that they, too, belonged to an avant-garde, albeit a social one.[1]

By about 1910, symbolism had passed its peak. The new radical avant-garde of the futurists or the supremacists (Malevich, Tatlin) could no longer rely on the support of the entrepreneurs, who clung to the earlier modernism of about 1905. From 1910, the artistic avant-garde and the financial elite drew apart.

Between 1881 and 1917 Russian society underwent sweeping changes as the effects of the reforms introduced by Alexander II made themselves felt. Commercial and industrial initiatives followed one another in quick succession. It was a time of great social and geographical mobility. As the social prestige of the entrepreneurs increased, so the influence of the aristocracy declined. The Emancipation—the abolition of serfdom—under Alexander II had undermined the economic status of the nobility, with only a few aristocrats strong enough to bow to the laws of early capitalism. In art patronage, too, the aristocracy felt threatened by the success of the entrepreneurs, although some members, accepting the challenge, endeavored to outdo the merchant class.

Princess Mariya Tenisheva set herself up as Mamontov's competitor. On the model of Abramtsevo, she founded her own center for neonationalist art on her estate at Talashkino. The artists she supported became the founders of a Russian form of *Jugendstil*. Her aristocratic idealism and lack of commercial acumen caused her many painful disappointments, not least in her dealings with those who had attuned their artistic activities to the laws of capitalism, Sergey Diaghilev among them.

Diaghilev knew better than anyone how to make capitalist methods serve art, channeling many different financial currents into his prestigious projects. He drew wide public attention with two successful exhibitions, the first of English, Scottish, and German watercolors (1897), the second devoted to Russian and Finnish artists (1898). Following these successes, Diaghilev learned that Mamontov and Tenisheva were prepared to finance an artistic journal, *Mir iskusstva* (World of art), which he launched in 1898. Although Mamontov's sponsorship came to an end the following year, and Tenisheva's in 1900, the journal survived until 1904, thanks to an annual subsidy from the tsar. Meanwhile, Diaghilev drew up other plans: in 1905 he organized an exhibition of Russian portraits in St. Petersburg; in 1906 he ventured abroad, organizing the Russian section of the Parisian Salon d'automne; in 1907 he ran a season of Russian music in the French capital, followed in 1908 by the historic European première of *Boris Godunov*. Diaghilev had been able to enlist the support not only of private sponsors but also of the Russian court for this last project. The production of *Boris Godunov* in Paris was a diplomatic coup, the Russian regime being anxious to restore its prestige following the catastrophic Japanese war and the loss of face during the 1905 Revolution. The actual stake was a French loan to stave off Russian bankruptcy. Produced in Rimsky-Korsakov's elaborate orchestration, with Fyodor Chaliapin in the title role and a spectacular decor, *Boris Godunov* was the ideal representation of Russia's status as a great power.[2]

The logical outcome of Diaghilev's exploitation of capitalist methods in the artistic sphere was the final transfer of his activities to the West. In Russia the capitalist base was still too narrow for him. Moreover, court intrigues had led to his losing the tsar's support. In 1911, therefore, he founded the Ballets Russes as a wholly Western enterprise, expressly designed for foreign consumption.

The Ballets Russes (1911–29) was a unique venture, representing artistic modernism in dance, music, and the visual arts. That the company managed to survive at all was a minor miracle, due entirely to Diaghilev's unique combination of artistic flair and commercial skill. It was a brilliant attempt to make the laws of the free market serve great art.

Ballet was not Diaghilev's first interest. He had earlier concentrated on opera productions, but during his first seasons in Paris he had come to appreciate that opera was not commercially viable. Ballet seemed to be the answer, though not in the form of an established company tied to a single theater. The Ballets Russes thus was established as a touring company, playing in existing opera houses. The company was also very flexible, so that the cast could be changed according to the circumstances.

Diaghilev knew to perfection how to trade on the taste of high society, satisfying the fashionable Parisian view of Russia with displays of exoticism and primitivism. Because he recruited his dancers largely from the Imperial Theaters, he was able to present the Ballets Russes as heirs to the classical imperial dance company. His productions even had a marked influence on fashion, design, and entertainment.

Commercially, the company always teetered on the verge of bankruptcy, but Diaghilev invariably found a way out of his difficulties. He sought his leading sponsors in diplomatic circles and among the Parisian nouveaux riches. Successful businessmen and their families, many of Jewish origin, had settled in Paris in order to join the upper strata of French society by means of suitable marriages. As a result, the new financial elite allied itself with the old social elite, giving rise to a new privileged class. It was precisely this latter group that provided the most prominent art sponsors outside the official, academic circuit, facilitating the rise of an alternative environment in which progressive art could develop.

The Ballets Russes took Russian art to *le tout Paris*—a metropolitan and cosmopolitan public of sponsors, collectors, art critics, artistic dilettantes, and reviewers. The public was above all interested in anything new, rare, or expensive, hence the main strategies of Diaghilev's artistic enterprise: constant innovation, exoticism, primitivism, and conspicuous luxury and refinement in the decorative aspects of the productions.[3]

The modernism of the Silver Age was an amalgam of divergent movements: neonationalism, symbolism, primitivism (also known by its Russian name of *Skiftsvo* or "Scythianism"), acmeism, and futurism. These movements had a common basis in their opposition to realism. Emerging in the 1860s, at the time of the Emancipation, realism had given expression to the social themes that were expected of art at the time. Ever since, Russian artists had had to put up with a double censorship, from the right and from the left. On the right, they were frustrated by the official, tsarist censors; on the left, the intelligentsia applied controls of their own to safeguard the seriousness and relevance of art. The ideal of "art for art's sake" did not have much of a chance in these circumstances— a few exceptions aside, such as the aristocratic aestheticism of Ivan Vsevolozhsky and Chaikovsky, which reached its peak during the prime of the imperial ballet.

Realism in Russian painting became bogged down in sterile academicism. The limited cultural background of the first entrepreneur-patrons, moreover, exerted a decidedly conservative influence on art. The merchant estate was not, as a rule, very highly educated. Its members were above all patriotic, Slavophile, and often Orthodox, which explains the pronounced nationalistic, almost xenophobic, nature of their patronage. Under the influence of Tretyakov—who was interested mainly in the national character of art, not in its social commitment (an attitude that the nationalistic art policy of Alexander III helped to promote)—the *peredvizhniki* developed from sociocritical artists into Russian genre painters. The same phenomenon emerged in music. Because Mitrofan Belyayev published and scheduled music by Russian composers only, the Belyayev circle fell into academicism and provincialism. When Igor Stravinsky later exaggerated his links with modern French music in Paris, he did so chiefly because of a sense of inferiority brought on by his provincial background as an ex-Belyayevist.[4]

This amalgam of academicism and realism came under attack during the Silver Age, the journal *Mir iskusstva* playing a prominent role in the dissemination of the new philosophy of art as serving aesthetic ends first and foremost. *Mir iskusstva* was the mouthpiece of an artistic circle that had emerged from a conversation society of dilettantes, the Nevsky Pickwick Club, of which Dmitry Filosofov, Walter Nouvel, and Alexander Benois were the leading members. The group was enlarged with the painters Léon Bakst and Konstantin Somov, the amateur musician Alfred Nurok, and Sergey Diaghilev, Filosofov's cousin, who encouraged the rest to break out of their private seclusion and to venture into the public arena.

The circle around *Mir iskusstva* advocated no particular style, but rather a certain attitude toward art. Their approach was retrospective and reactionary, their ideal being the restoration of the aristocratic perception of art. Socially no less than artistically, they identified themselves with the old nobility. Turning their backs on the socially committed art promoted under Alexander II and the rise of bourgeois art under Alexander III, they associated themselves with the cosmopolitan aristocratic art that had flourished from the reign of Catherine the Great to that of Nicholas I. The clearest expressions of this hankering after the past were Benois's predilection for neoclassical art and Diaghilev's prestigious exhibition of post-eighteenth-century Russian portraiture in the Tauride Palace in St. Petersburg—not by accident a building Catherine the Great had commissioned.

Inspired by the Western model of *l'art pour l'art, Mir iskusstva* advanced the idea that the artist's task was not to reflect existing reality but to create a new one: the autonomous world of the imagination. As Diaghilev put it, "The sole function of art is pleasure, its only instrument beauty. . . . For me, to demand social service from art on the basis of prescriptions established for it a priori is an incomprehensible blasphemy. The great strength of art lies precisely in the fact that it is self-sufficient, self-referential, self-purposeful, and above all, free."[5] Alexander Benois called nineteenth-century utilitarian art "one big slap in the face of Apollo."[6] The artistic approach of *Mir iskusstva* was instead apolitical, asocial, aphilosophical, and amoral. The artist's individuality was the measure of all artistic values.

The group's aestheticism was expressed in several ways: in the emphasis of the artist's individuality rather than of the content of his work; in the retrospectivism of Bakst and Benois; in the cult of form and technical discipline. When it came to folklore, the group championed neonationalism, as practiced at Abramtsevo and Talashkino—that is, folklore stripped of all nationalistic and social implications and transformed into a source of stylistic inspiration.

Such symbolists as Andrey Belïy and Vyacheslav Ivanov did not approve of the aestheticism of *Mir iskusstva.* Belïy called their aphilosophical, uncommitted art "the consequence of the philosophy of a dying century" and an "ideology of sleep."[7] In the wake of Nietzsche, the symbolists attributed a transforming force to art, which they called theurgy. They believed that art was able to change reality, that it had to assume the function of the divine creative force. The nurture of artistic individuals must culminate in the transcendence of the world. In folk art, therefore, they did not look for decorative patterns, but sought contact with the essence of reality, the pure vital force that had become obscured by cultural conventions and by artificial individuality. In painting, this trend culminated in the neoprimitivism of Goncharova and Laryonov. In literature, there was *Skiftsvo,* a term coined in reference to the collection of poems *The Scythians* (1918) by Alexander Blok. In about 1900, symbolism gave way to acmeism and futurism. In the wake of symbolist mysticism, acmeists—also referred to as neorealists or neoclassicists—stood for a return to reality, their poetry aiming at refinement of form and clarity of expression. Nikolai Gumilyov, Anna Akhmatova, and Osip Mandelstam were acmeism's leading exponents.

Futurism, too, rejected the mysticism of the symbolists. The idea of transforming the world through art, however, was something the two groups shared, although the ways in which they hoped to achieve that goal differed appreciably. The futurists believed that technological perfection would help to rid humans of all their shortcomings. The movement caused a stir, due primarily to its extreme violence: by destroying or distorting matter, they hoped to impose a new and perfected form upon it. The leading spokesman of futurism was the poet Vladimir Mayakovsky.

The impact of modernist movements on music in the Silver Age was limited. Until the October Revolution of 1917, the aesthetic of the Belyayev circle remained dominant, while romantic virtuosity lived on in the work of Sergey Rachmaninoff and Nikolai Medtner. In the end, only two composers can be said to have fully expressed the modernism of the Silver Age: Alexander Scriabin and Igor Stravinsky. The first was at the heart of symbolism; the second translated the aesthetics of *Mir iskusstva* and neonationalism into music. Other composers, even the most progressive among them, were not *au fait* with developments in different branches of art to more than a limited extent. Prokofiev was a typical case. Although he was called a musical futurist, that term was applied to him more as a general synonym for modernism than to indicate a specific stylistic direction. To be sure, Prokofiev set poems by Akhmatova to music, composed a "Scythian Suite," and turned a symbolist novel—Valeriy Bryusov's *The Fiery Angel*—into an opera, yet none of these artistic currents had a decisive influence on his music. Their impact remained confined to just a few of his works, and did not lead to a metamorphosis of his musical thought. The fact that Prokofiev was accused of having used "Mayakovskyisms" in his music since 1913 says more about the conservatism of the musical environment in which he worked than about his music. In fact, Prokofiev did not become acquainted with Mayakovsky and the futurist milieu until 1917.

The composer Arthur Lourié maintained closer contacts with the avant-garde. A friend of Alexander Blok who moved in futurist circles and wrote for their journal, *Strelets,* he was familiar with acmeism and was one of the first to set Anna Akhmatova's poetry to music. Vladimir Shcherbachov did likewise with the poems of Alexander Blok. Mikhaíl Gnesin passed through a brief symbolist phase, which he cut short as early as 1914. From then on he devoted himself to the creation of a Jewish style of music, encouraged by Rimsky-Korsakov's dictum that Jewish music urgently needed a Glinka of its own.

Of all the composers of the generation following that of Scriabin and Stravinsky, Nikolai Roslavets adopted the most progressive position, beginning to experiment with atonality as early as 1913. Nikolai Obukhov and Ivan Vishnegradsky tried to develop Scriabin's mysticism. Before the Revolution, however, there was little to encourage a musical avant-garde. Obukhov and Vishnegradsky were to emigrate soon after the Revolution. Yefim Golyshev and Leo Ornstein had done so even earlier, the first going to Berlin and the second to the United States.

Scriabin and Stravinsky were the dominant personalities of the Silver Age in music, and accordingly take pride of place in the discussion that follows. They were flanked by Sergey Rachmaninoff on the one hand—a composer who did not take part in the innovations but whose best-known work originated during this period—and, on the other hand, by Sergey Prokofiev, who set himself up from 1910 until the Revolution as a promising modernist and as Stravinsky's potential rival.

## "BRIGHT TONES DO NOT COME EASILY TO ME": SERGEY RACHMANINOFF

Songs to texts by Konstantin Balmont; a few to texts by Andrey Beliy and Valeriy Bryusov (in the Six Songs, op. 38); a choral symphony based on Edgar Allan Poe's *The Bells,* in Balmont's translation—these are the only points of contact between Rachmaninoff's music and symbolism. His preference for Balmont's poetry was in fact quite natural: ever since Arensky and Taneyev, Balmont had been a favorite of composers, less for the content of his verses than for their consciously pursued musicality. The symbolist current itself, however, had no musical consequences for Rachmaninoff. Together with Nikolai Medtner, he continued the nineteenth-century tradition of virtuoso composers. Thanks to its lyrical and often elegiac quality, Rachmaninoff's music represents the waning phase of romanticism in Russia. Rachmaninoff sometimes felt threatened by the success of such modernists as Scriabin and Prokofiev, which caused him to think from time to time that he should cease composing music.

In several ways, Rachmaninoff may be considered Chaikovsky's chief heir. Like his predecessor, he divided his time between long stays abroad and sojourns in the Russian countryside. He composed the choral symphony *The Bells* in Rome, at the same desk at which Chaikovsky had

worked. One difference was Rachmaninoff's busy agenda as conductor
and concert pianist. In 1906, as a consequence, he resigned from the Bolshoy Theater in Moscow so as to have more time to write music. Although he found no eccentric patron who would underwrite his existence
as a full-time composer, he did have a country estate in the southern Russian steppe: Ivanovka, the property of the family of Natalya Satina, his
wife. Ivanovka was for Rachmaninoff what Kamenka or Klin had been
for Chaikovsky: a haven of rest and inspiration, far from the pressures
of Moscow and St. Petersburg (Plate 13).

Compared with Chaikovsky's aesthetic, Rachmaninoff's was narrower.
He lacked the exuberant imagination and subtle aestheticism of his predecessor. The visionary power of a work such as *The Queen of Spades*
was quite beyond his reach. Only in the symphonic poem "The Isle of
the Dead," or in some pages of *The Bells,* did he achieve glimpses of it.
The fourth movement of *The Bells*—with the image of death as the demonic bell ringer—is reminiscent of the bedroom scene in *The Queen of
Spades.* With Rachmaninoff, the lyrical aspect prevails, as exemplified
in the broad themes of the Second and Third Piano Concertos. Rachmaninoff's music gave expression to the sentiments and musical values
of the lower strata of the aristocracy: the world of salon romances and
of the romantic character piece, combined with a display of virtuosity on
the concert platform. As for the Russian traits in Rachmaninoff's music,
they are based less on folklore than on the Orthodox liturgy. The opening melody of the Third Piano Concerto, for instance, has a close affinity
with Orthodox chants.

A central characteristic of the music Rachmaninoff wrote between
1906 and 1917 was its elegiac mood. In 1912, when he asked the poet
Marietta Shaginian to select early poems that would be suitable for composition, he stipulated that "the mood should be sad, rather than gay;
bright tones do not come easily to me."[8] A fatalistic spirit breathes in
Rachmaninoff's oeuvre, with an especially prominent part being played
by the *Dies Irae* motif—a motif from the Gregorian requiem mass that
recurs regularly in nineteenth-century works about death, for instance
in Berlioz's *Symphonie fantastique* and Liszt's *Totentanz.* In Rachmaninoff's work, the motif is found in, among others, the Cello Sonata, the
Second Symphony, the First Piano Sonata, and above all the evocative
symphonic poem "The Isle of the Dead."

In this work—based loosely on Arnold Böcklin's painting of the same
name, a mysterious representation of the transport of the souls in
Charon's ferry to the island of the dead—Rachmaninoff attained an ex-

pressive peak. The first section is directly linked to the painting. In an unrelenting pattern in quintuple meter, Rachmaninoff depicts the strokes of Charon's oars. The despondently falling melodies, the allusions to the *Dies Irae*, and the dark orchestral colors evoke an aura of sacredness and mystery. In the second passage the direct link to Böcklin's painting is abandoned, and Rachmaninoff contrasts the idea of death with the expression of life and of the vital urge. Passionate lyricism carries the work to a climax. After a return of the *Dies Irae* motif, the theme of life resounds once more, but this time in the minor. The quintuple pattern reappears, leaving no doubt about the fatalistic message of the whole.

Rachmaninoff shared Chaikovsky's ability to associate a spontaneous lyrical impression with a tightly knit structural context. In the Second Piano Concerto and the Second Symphony, the lyrical themes go hand in hand with great motivic unity. This characteristic probably reaches a peak in the Third Piano Concerto, a work loved for its melodies, and one that also has a structural refinement the genre had not known since Chaikovsky. The most important cohesive element already resounds in the beginning: the dotted rhythm constituting the accompaniment of the first theme. That rhythm is an important element of the whole work; it links the two themes of the first movement as well as those of the finale. The second themes of the first and last movement are also related, the central movement serving as an intermezzo between the thematically related outer movements.

In his best work, Rachmaninoff succeeded in combining a lyrical impulse with large structures. If we compare Rachmaninoff's symphonies once again with Chaikovsky's, Rachmaninoff's symphonic conception looks less complex and multifaceted. Chaikovsky used quite a few structural and stylistic devices: mottos, the juxtaposition of thematic or coloristic blocks, dramatic confrontations of distantly related tonalities, rhythmical complications, and the superposition of different meters. Rachmaninoff, for his part, relied entirely on the sheer momentum of his themes. The first movement of the Second Symphony is a good example. From the pulsating rhythm at the beginning of the allegro moderato, the lyrical construction of the whole movement flows with rare ease, culminating in carefully arranged climaxes in the development and in the splendid reprise. The development is based on the first theme and on the introduction. The process moves toward a climax that, however, does not coincide precisely with the return to the first theme. As a result, the reprise fits almost imperceptibly into the unfolding structure. The real climax is postponed until the end of the varied recapitulation of the first theme.

The special qualities of Rachmaninoff as a composer become clearest in his most outstanding achievement of all: the *Vsenoshchnoye bdeniye* (All-night vigil). No composition represents the end of an era so clearly as this liturgical work. Once Chaikovsky had broken the monopoly of the Court Chapel in St. Petersburg, Orthodox liturgical music enjoyed a brief blossoming period in Moscow, to disappear abruptly with the advent of the Revolution. Rachmaninoff's *Vsenoshchnaya* is generally considered one of the high points of Orthodox music; although many prefer to look on it as a concert piece rather than as a liturgical work, nothing stands in the way of its use for church services, except perhaps its length. The work satisfies all liturgical demands, but goes beyond them in the same way Bach's B Minor Mass and Beethoven's *Missa Solemnis* do. Johann von Gardner, one of the pioneers of the study of Orthodox church music, has bestowed the apt title of "liturgical symphony" on Rachmaninoff's *Vsenoshchnaya*.[9]

The all-night vigil is the combined service of vespers and matins held in the Orthodox church every Saturday night and on the eve of important liturgical feasts. In Rachmaninoff's composition, numbers 1–6 are part of the vespers, numbers 7–15, of the matins. The first part is a call to repentance and reflection. Rachmaninoff was even able to express the symbolism of light, which shines through much of the text, in musical terms, above all in the hymn "Svyete tikhi" (Radiant light), in which the setting sun is associated with the image of the everlasting light of Christ. The matins are a jubilant celebration of the Resurrection. The ninth part is the climax: the quasi-dramatized retelling of the Resurrection, based on the meeting of the women with the angel beside the empty tomb. The matins culminate in the monumental "Slava" (or "Gloria") of number 12. The two Resurrection hymns (numbers 13 and 14) are used alternately in liturgical practice. The concluding number 15 is a fragment of the so-called "Akathistos" hymn, an ancient Byzantine paean of praise to the Mother of God as patron of Constantinople. The "Akathistos," which is not part of the standard texts of the *Vsenoshchnaya*, bears witness to the great reverence in which the Russian church holds the Mother of God.

Rachmaninoff's *Vsenoshchnaya* has rightly been admired for its imaginative use of traditional chants: five melodies come from the oldest tradition (the *Znamen* chants, so called after the Russian word for "neume"), two from the Greek School (a tradition brought to Russia by Greek chorus-masters in the seventeenth century), and two from the School of Kiev. Rachmaninoff was able to fit these chants into a flexible structure in which every number involves a clear rise and fall of tension. The incorporation of dynamic, broad structures in unaccompanied choral song is a master stroke; unaccompanied choral music could hardly compete with most genres in the pursuit of the monumentality of form typical of that epoch. The reasons were purely technical. On the most general level, the nineteenth-century aesthetic of large forms rested on two technical factors: the extension of the range of frequencies and of harmonic modulation, on the one hand, and an increase in volume, on the other. In that respect, the unaccompanied choir is a strange paradox. The ensemble admittedly has great possibilities when it comes to varying the volume but is extremely limited in tonal range. Not only is the tessitura of the whole relatively small, but the tonal range of every separate voice is limited as well. Although Rachmaninoff was fortunate in being able to call on the famous deep basses found in so many Russian choirs, in this piece he made spare use of that facility. He deliberately reserved the extremes of the tessitura for structural climaxes. Successful choral composition is above all dependent on an ingenious play with relationships, balance, and gradation. Rachmaninoff was able to exploit the smallest distinctions in tonal range, volume, and sonority to the full. Thus he achieved the monumental form of the "Slava" by a deliberate emphasis of the middle register and of the alto voices, and as a result succeeded in postponing the climax until the very end.

Rachmaninoff's success as a choral composer was due to his disciplined use of tonal tessituras. It was exactly the same discipline that rendered the rest of his work so persuasive as well. Emotional and sentimental though his music may sound at times, its construction is the result of a precise feeling for relationships in the texture, of which a good example may be found in the first movement of the Second Symphony. In the coda, it is easy to see how Rachmaninoff portions out the final climax by the meticulous manipulation of the middle voices. This feeling for relationships is what also renders the development so convincing. The latter rests less on motivic work than on a sweeping climactic construction. Yet the climax does not coincide with the reprise, but has been subtly moved to the end of the recapitulation of the first theme.

## "THERE WILL BE A CELEBRATION! SOON!": ALEXANDER SCRIABIN

The cultivation of his own individuality was the hallmark of Alexander Scriabin's life. Remarkably enough, his extreme egoism—or solipsistic individualism—was not an end in itself. "He was convinced," his biographer and brother-in-law Boris de Schloezer wrote, "that he was destined to perform an important task in life, and he interpreted events in the outside world in such a way as to make his own actions appear not only entirely natural, but even inevitable."[10]

It was not the world that influenced Scriabin's art, but the opposite: he was certain that his music would transform the world. His final work was to be a *Mysterium,* an all-embracing apocalyptic ritual. Its purpose was to unleash a liberating Dionysian intoxication that would carry humankind to a higher state of consciousness; indeed, it was to be the culmination of world history.

At first sight, Scriabin's extreme egotism seems to have had all the characteristics of a mental aberration. People would sometimes mockingly refer to the grotesque contrast between his cosmic dream and his actual death, which could not have been more banal: he died on 27 April 1915 from gangrene, following an abscess on his upper lip. Icarus could not have fallen any farther.

There is a great temptation to look for explanations of Scriabin's eccentric personality in psychoanalytical factors, which is why his egocentrism is so often traced back to his unusual upbringing. Scriabin was raised by three women—his grandmother, his aunt, and his great-aunt—in the complete absence of a male role model. Although this fact is not irrelevant to the understanding of his personality, it is decidedly inadequate as an explanation of his work and thought.

The recourse to psychoanalysis in evaluating Scriabin's art is above all the result of a feeling of discomfort on the part of his critics. Present-day music critics tend to brush aside Scriabin's own views of his art as immaterial. "It would be a pity if appreciation of the music required us to follow Skryabin into this world of cosmic 'hocus pocus,'" runs a typical commentary.[11] The divorce of his music from his peculiar ideas is generally justified as follows:

> Over Scriabin's posthumous reputation hung the terrible accusations of Egotist, and Mystic, which more or less forbade actual examination of his work in strictly musical terms. If he had regarded himself as the new Messiah, his music could not possibly be real or good. The reasoning was false: if music is eloquent, the pretext for composing it, however unwelcome, is of no matter. . . . At this distance from the time when they were composed, Scriabin's works can be appreciated in the context of their own period, and strictly for the quality of their music, not for what Scriabin may have thought any of them represented.[12]

In other words, the music alone is what counts, regardless of its context and significance. Its standing is thus reduced to a purely technical level. In this manner Scriabin was assigned a place of honor among the musical innovators, beside Debussy and Schoenberg, musical innovation being equated with "material innovation" or new ways of arranging sounds.

Scriabin owes his present-day reputation above all to the strict logic he applied to his work. Rarely has a Dionysian art ideal been pursued in so sophisticated an Apollonian manner. As Boris de Schloezer puts it, "And yet in this poet, in this prophet there lived a refined, almost pedantic formalist who demanded accuracy in all that concerned his creative work."[13] This dualism linked Scriabin with the symbolist movement in Russia. Unlike the romantics, the symbolists did not reject rationalism and positivism. To them, in fact, the connection between rationalism and spirituality was essential. However, they did not indulge the romantic longing for the Beyond—the spiritual "other world" purged of all earthly commotion; rather, their goal was to bring the Beyond into the mundane sphere, which explains their peculiar and unique mixture of positivism and irrationality.

According to Leonid Sabaneyev, Scriabin abhorred the prospect of being remembered as a mere composer of sonatas and symphonies.[14] His example helps to remind us that musical innovation for the most part originates in ideas. The "material renewal" of music ushered in during the early twentieth century is generally considered the result of an autonomous musical process, an irreversible, necessary development of musical tone systems. However, judging Scriabin's music exclusively by his musical innovations is mistaking the content of his art. His oeuvre is first and foremost an artistic monument to a body of ideas, no matter how utopian and untenable. Scriabin's art leaves us torn between what fascinates us and what frightens us in his utopian vision. For his thinking did have sinister consequences. Perhaps most disturbingly, he welcomed the First World War with enthusiasm. To him it was a phase in a plan of salvation, based on the Nietzschean argument that struggle is the father of all things and on his own aristocratic aversion to social equality. To come to grips with Scriabin's music we have to bear this indissoluble tension in mind. That may not facilitate our appreciation of his work, but it certainly does more justice to Scriabin's personality than a reduction of his artistic significance to the neutral, sterile terrain of pure "material renewal."[15]

Scriabin was not the only one to believe that individual creativity exerts an influence on the world. It was the central theme of Russian symbolism: theurgy, or the belief that art, like God, had the power to transform creation and even to complete it. The task of art, in other words, was not to portray the world, but to transform it spiritually. For the symbolists, art was capable of "creating life," an idea enshrined in the concept of *zhiznetvorchestvo,* a term compounded of *zhizn* (life) and *tvorchestvo* (creative activity).

The theories of Russian symbolism go back to the philosophy of Vladimir Solovyov. Starting with a dualistic worldview, Solovyov saw the special task of art in the synthesis of opposites, such as heaven and earth, matter and spirit, ideal and real. In art these opposites must interpenetrate each other: "[The task of art] is the transformation of physical life into its spiritual counterpart, which . . . is capable of internally transfiguring, spiritualizing matter or truly becoming embodied in it."[16] According to Solovyov, art enables the material world to participate in the immortality of the spiritual world.

The symbolists extended this idea. They viewed art neither as the pure portrayal of the world nor as the imaginative conception of an ideal, spiritual existence. For them art had an active character: it was meant to create, not works of art, but life itself. According to Andrey Belïy, "Art is the creation of life."[17] That philosophy led to all sorts of utopian ideas, such as the achievement of immortality, the transcendence of sexuality in androgyny, and the transcendence of sexual reproduction by rebirth and resurrection. Incredible though all this may sound, it was taken seriously.[18] Life itself was endowed with the characteristics of an aesthetic project. Symbolism implied man's total pliability.

Music played a large role in symbolist thought. For Andrey Belïy, it was the final goal to which all art must aspire. That reverence did not necessarily benefit Scriabin, however. Not all poets were prepared to grant the highest status to a composer; indeed, Andrey Belïy felt contempt for Scriabin. For the symbolists, "music" was more a poetic picture of theurgy than a reference to a concrete form of art, and few were interested in Scriabin's attempt to translate symbolist ideas into music. The closest contacts Scriabin entertained with symbolism were with Jurgis Baltrushaitis, Konstantin Balmont, and above all Vyacheslav Ivanov. Margarita Morozova, hostess of a symbolist literary salon in Moscow, became Scriabin's patron, doing for him what Nadezhda von Meck had done for Chaikovsky. However, despite his contacts with symbolist circles, Scriabin reached his theurgic objective above all along a road of his own.

Scriabin began his musical career as a protégé of Mitrofan Belyayev. Between 1894 and 1903 Belyayev published Scriabin's music, organized his foreign concert tours as a virtuoso pianist, and lavished money on him. Although Belyayev acted on his own initiative, without Rimsky-Korsakov's blessing, Scriabin never joined the Belyayev circle. His early oeuvre consists almost exclusively of piano pieces, culminating in the Piano Concerto of 1897.

Philosophy was Scriabin's lifelong interest. Notes from 1894 give us some idea of his violent opposition to Christianity. In 1898 he fell under the influence of Prince Sergey Nikolayevich Trubetskoy, a professor at the philosophical faculty in Moscow, who ran a study group there, the Religious and Philosophical Society, meetings of which Scriabin regularly attended. Trubetskoy introduced him to Solovyov's philosophy.

Scriabin took a critical view of Solovyov's ideas, however. He rejected his religious mysticism, but was receptive to his theurgic conception of art. He wrote his First Symphony (op. 26) as a hymn to art. The finale, with solo parts and chorus, contains the following text:

> O, wonderful image of the Divine, pure art of harmonies, we praise thee fervently with ecstatic emotion. . . . Thy free and mighty spirit rules all over the earth. By exalting thee, man performs glorious deeds. Gather together, all ye nations of the earth, sing the praises of Art! Praise be to Art! Praise be forever!

Between 1900 and 1903 Scriabin planned to write a philosophical opera based on the myth of Eros and Psyche. The main character was a "young, unknown philosopher-musician-poet" who would raise up mankind by the force of celestial harmonies, miraculous and unbounded wisdom, and love. The idea of writing an opera with a philosophical subject suggests Wagner's influence, the fusion of eroticism and mysticism being reminiscent of *Tristan und Isolde*. Scriabin was almost the only Russian composer to take Wagner seriously. The role of Wagner in the development of Russian music had always been equivocal. His philosophical ideas did not reach Russia until about the turn of the century, and then they aroused the interest of poets and painters rather than of musicians. The symbolists and the *Mir iskusstva* artists were fascinated by the idea of the fusion of all the arts in a *Gesamtkunstwerk*. The younger generation of composers, by contrast, shared the dislike of Wagner expressed by Chaikovsky and by Taneyev, who had organized a few Wagner sessions at the Moscow Conservatory in 1894. The attitude of most students, including Rachmaninoff, ranged from indifferent to negative. Scriabin, too, was not greatly impressed at first. From the memoirs of Leonid Sabaneyev we know how conventional his first reaction was: he rebuked Wagner for his "lack of form."[19] His reserve, however, soon turned into enthusiasm.

Attempting to follow Wagner's example, Scriabin put his own opera project to one side. Yet the fusion of the arts advocated by Wagner struck Scriabin as being no more than a stopgap solution. To him, music was the highest stage of all art: it embraced all the others. The instrumental prelude to *Tristan und Isolde* provided Scriabin with so many musical ideas that he felt able to base his entire further oeuvre on it. Wagner had shown him how functional harmonic tension can be exploited to the full. The *Tristan* prelude convinced Scriabin that instrumental music could embody a metaphysical vision, and with a directness of which other arts could no more than dream.

At the start of Scriabin's Third Symphony, also known as *Le poème divin,* the Tristan model is unmistakably present. It is a reference to Wagner's famous opening: an unaccompanied preparatory melody makes way unexpectedly for an unusual dissonant chord, which leaves the listener guessing as to how it will be resolved. By analogy with Wagner's *Tristan* chord, Scriabin's chord also took a name of its own: the "Scriabin sixth," a German augmented sixth with one of its intervals expanded. The first resolution of this chord is to an unsullied consonant triad, announced by a trumpet motif, called a *"zov"* or "summons" motif in Scriabin's work and comparable to the shamanistic *zovï* (summonses) in Konstantin Balmont's poetry. In the subsequent structure, Scriabin further exploits the qualities of the chord. Typical of Scriabin is a tempering of the urge to come up with a harmonic solution by the linkage of chords with the bass note one tritone apart. This technique reflects Scriabin's aim of transcending the expression of desire. According to Scriabin's literary program—in fact written by his mistress, Tatyana de Schloezer—the *zov* motif in the trumpets proclaims a "joyful and intoxicated affirmation," which was to reach its climax in the last movement. The program continues: "The free, powerful man-god appears to triumph; but it is only the intellect which affirms the divine Ego, while the individual, still too weak, is tempted to sink into Pantheism."[20]

Scriabin extended his artistic ideal with borrowings from theosophy, an eclectic system that became very fashionable at the fin de siècle. Theosophy is an amalgam of elements of Christian mysticism and occult-esoteric and oriental religious concepts. One of the leading figures in the theosophical movement was Madame Hélène Blavatsky, whose writings

Scriabin discovered in about 1905. He was most enthusiastic about her *La clef de la théosophie* and *La doctrine secrète*. He also read such theosophists as C. W. Leadbeater and Annie Besant. He was less patient with their followers, whom he blamed above all for their lack of artistic interest and their superficial attitude to music. "Can you imagine, they adore Massenet!" was his comment about the theosophical circles in Moscow and St. Petersburg.[21]

It would not be true to say, however, that Scriabin was influenced by theosophy; rather, it merely helped to confirm and strengthen his own eschatological ideas. A central tenet of theosophy is that the universe is subject to a cycle in which Being passes from a subjective to an objective level. According to Blavatsky, this takes millions of years. While absorbing this view of the cosmic cycle into his own thought, Scriabin remained of the opinion that mankind should not have to wait so long for the ultimate ecstasy, but could attain the universal breakthrough into the highest spiritual level more immediately with the help of art. For the theosophists, redemption lay in the distant future; for Scriabin it was close at hand.

*Le poème de l'extase* (1905–8) reflects man's breakthrough to a new consciousness. As an extension of *Le poème divin,* this work, too, uses a trumpet as the Nietzschean protagonist. *Le poème de l'extase* represents the breakthrough of the transcendent in a single great musical gesture. The entire piece rests on a sustained dominant tension that is not resolved until the end. To attain his objective, Scriabin looked for a maximum number of sound gradations within the dominant function. He found the appropriate technical means in the extension of the Scriabin sixth with the so-called French sixth, which yields an aggregate of five notes. The addition of a single note then leads to a chord that comprises all the notes of the whole-tone scale. Because of the role that scale had played in Russian music, it is not surprising that Scriabin should have used it. Unlike his predecessors, he drew an important technical conclusion from the symmetrical structure of the whole-tone scale.

In music theory, symmetry means that the distance between all successive pitches is exactly the same. As a result, the same series of notes is obtained no matter where the scale begins. That is an important difference from the diatonic scales on which classical harmony is based, where asymmetrical structure is precisely what creates harmonic tension. Beyond that, the whole-tone scale has yet another symmetrical characteristic: it contains three tritones. A tritone is a symmetrical interval—it remains itself when it is inverted. All this sounds highly technical, but it explains the musical essence of Scriabin's technique: by the use of whole-tone scales he was able to reduce the tension of the dominant appreciably and at the same time vary its sonority. The numerous possibilities of sound gradations thus established lend his music a markedly sensual character. For that reason, it has sometimes been compared with Debussy's. Scriabin, however, although he shared Debussy's taste for voluptuous sonorities, could not tolerate the "passivity" and "essentially receptive sensuality" of Debussy's music.[22]

In *Le poème de l'extase,* because the whole-tone harmony has a dominant relationship with a diatonic tonic, the harmonic tension accumulates. The stunning resolution points to the ultimate spiritual breakthrough, the transition to a new consciousness.

The discovery of the symmetrical properties of the whole-tone scale was an important step toward a static harmony of endless shades of sound. For Scriabin, the reduction of functional tension coincided with a central idea in his philosophy. The transcendent transformation demands a surrender of individual personality, the ego—or, in Scriabin's terminology, the *malïy "ya"* (the "petty 'I'"). While Wagner achieved the closest possible portrayal of desire in his *Tristan* prelude, Scriabin was looking for the transcendence of desire. In the Fifth Piano Sonata, he returned to the scheme of *Le poème de l'extase,* even basing it on the same poem he had written as a guideline for *Le poème de l'extase.* Once the music had been composed, however, he considered the text superfluous and did not allow it to be used as a programmatic clarification of either *Le Poème* or the piano sonata.

From 1904 to 1910 Scriabin lived mainly in Switzerland and was not very well informed about musical developments in Russia. In 1909 he returned to attend the première of *Le poème de l'extase* in Moscow and St. Petersburg, once again coming into contact with the work of the Belyayev circle, and in particular with their octatonic technique in the footsteps of Rimsky-Korsakov. Just as from the whole-tone scale, Scriabin drew conclusions from octatonicism that left the clichés of the Belyayev composers far behind. The octatonic scale has as many as four tritones, making the potential of a nonfunctional, static harmony even greater than in the whole-tone scale. The combination of the whole-tone and octatonic scales therefore provides a continuously fluctuating harmony that no longer contains a functional—and hence emotional—tension. Scriabin developed this idiom in the orchestral work *Prométhée, le poème du feu* (1908–10).

The essential difference between *Prométhée* and *Le poème de l'extase* is the abandonment of the diatonic scale. In the absence of a tonic, *Prométhée* also had to abandon the dominant tension, meaning that any expression of longing disappears. The harmonic world of *Prométhée* represents the transcendence of the ego. The conclusion, too, is no longer a resolution of harmonic tension, but a sudden elevation—in symbolist terminology, a *poriv,* a transporting burst. The harmonic basis of *Prométhée* is a chord that Scriabin called the "chord of the pleroma." "Pleroma," or "plenitude," is a term borrowed from gnosticism; it designates the hierarchy of the divine world completely shorn of earthly reality. For Scriabin, "the chord of the pleroma" (usually referred to as the "mystic chord") was equivalent to a revelation of the supernatural. In *Prométhée,* he wanted to couple the gradations of sound visually with light and color. He marked two "light parts" in the score, but the technical realization left much to be desired, the color organs of Rimington and Moser in use at the time being unsatisfactory.

At first, Scriabin's harmony was not atonal. That idiom emerged from the step-by-step extension of the dominant function. Ultimately Scriabin was left with just one more step in his search for an all-embracing, immutable harmony: twelve-tone harmony. Chords that use the complete chromatic range of tones exceed the "pleroma chord" in fullness and immobility, conveying the impression of timelessness. Scriabin took this step in his late piano works, for instance in Sonatas Six to Ten, and in *Vers la flamme.* With these compositions, he told Sabaneyev, he had at last transcended human emotion.

To Scriabin, the victory over the "petty 'I'" opened the door to the "great 'I,'" or universal consciousness, liberated from the constraints of time and space. Anyone able to take that step could also create the universe: "Insofar as I am conscious of the world as my creation, everything must be the product of my free will, and nothing can exist outside me. I am an absolute being. All the rest are phenomena born in the rays of my consciousness."[23] As early as 1906 Scriabin was filled with dreams of his ultimate work. On the occasion of the 1905 Revolution he wrote to his patron Margarita Morozova:

> The political revolution in Russia in its present phase and the overthrow I want are different things, although, certainly, this revolution, as any unrest, hastens the approach of the desired moment. Using the word *overthrow* I err. It is *not the realization of anything whatever* that I desire, but the external exaltation of creative activity which will be called forth by my art. That means first of all my main work must be finished. . . . *My* moment has not yet come. But it's getting closer. There will be a celebration! Soon![24]

In about 1911 Scriabin began to gain a clearer picture of the ritual he aimed to establish. To begin with, the distinction between performers and listeners had to be removed: "There will not be a single spectator at this artistic event. All will be participants." In the fusion of the arts, Scriabin wanted to go even further than Wagner:

> The audience, the spectators, are separated by the stage instead of being joined [with the performers] in a single act. *I will not have any sort of theater.*
>
> Wagner (and he with all his genius) could never surmount the theatrical— the stage—never, because he didn't understand what was the matter. He didn't realize that all the evil in this separation lay in that there was no *unity*, no [genuine] experience, but only the representation of experience.

Scriabin envisioned a fusion of music and architecture: "The form of the temple in which the Mystery will always be taking place will not be monotonously fixed forever, but will be forever changing, together with the mood and movement of the Mystery." How was that to be done?

> I thought a long time about how to achieve fluidity and creativeness in the very structure of the temple. . . . And suddenly it came to me it was possible to have columns of incense. . . . They will be illuminated by the lights of the light-orchestra, and they will disperse and come back together again! They will be enormous fiery pillars. And the entire temple will consist of them.
>
> And the building will be fluid and changing, fluid like the music. And its forms will express the mood of the music and words.[25]

In the end, Scriabin did not get much beyond devising a general plan of the project and a number of musical sketches of a preparatory ritual, entitled *Acte préalable*. From this evidence it appears that he looked upon twelve-tone chords as the "harmony of a higher plane." His use of them was the logical result of his quest for the musical expression of superhuman experience. With victory over the ego, time and space would dissolve. *Mysterium* would lead to the transcendence of the world. Yet these sketches are all that remain of Scriabin's dream, fragments, together with such works as Schoenberg's *Jakobsleiter* and Ives's *Universe Symphony*, of the eschatological utopias of early-twentieth-century musicians.[26]

## FROM *MIR ISKUSSTVA* TO THE BALLETS RUSSES

The winding up of *Mir iskusstva* in 1904 did not mean the end of the circle around that journal. On the contrary, Diaghilev immediately threw himself into other projects: exhibitions and music, operas, and ballets in Paris. His most important activity was to channel the creativity of the *Mir iskusstva* artists into ballet. In this group Alexander Benois and Léon Bakst were the leading balletomanes, both having memories of the original production of *Sleeping Beauty* they had seen in their youth. (Not coincidentally, Ivan Vsevolozhsky, the man responsible for that ballet, served as an example to Diaghilev.) Alexander Benois maintained that of all the arts, ballet was the least tainted by realism and utilitarianism. As an uncommitted divertissement, the genre, according to him, had remained true to the principles of beauty and stylistic elegance. "Ballet is perhaps the most eloquent of all spectacles," Benois wrote, "since it permits the two most excellent conductors of thought—music and gesture—to appear in their full expanse and depth, unencumbered by words, which limit and fetter thought, bring it down from heaven to earth."[27]

Aestheticism and an antiliterary approach explained the interest of the *Mir iskusstva* artists in the ballet. The lack of words was considered an additional advantage of ballet over opera. Words tied opera to realism, which was now outdated. Moreover, opera hampered the complete fusion of the arts; ballet was thought to be more capable of achieving the Wagnerian *Gesamtkunst* ideal.

"Literature one reads. There is no need to hear it recited on the stage," Diaghilev declared in an interview.[28] The antiliterary tendency of the *Mir iskusstva* circle even influenced the Paris production of *Boris Godunov,* Diaghilev's willful rearrangement of the scenes having been motivated by an antiliterary conception of the role of the musical stage.[29] According to him, a *Gesamtkunstwerk* had above all to make a strong visual and auditory impact. Image and music had to create their own context, independent of any literary or narrative logic. It was a kind of musico-visual fresco technique, which had also been at the root of French *grand opéra*. With the exploitation of the visual aspect—for instance in the famous sets and costumes of Alexander Golovin, Alexander Benois, and Ivan Bilibin—Diaghilev introduced one of the main pillars of the future Ballets Russes.

For Benois and Diaghilev, ballet had yet another advantage: it was preeminently a cosmopolitan art. Originating as a French art form, it was the ideal expression of aristocratic "European" Russia. Benois's and Diaghilev's first ballet projects, accordingly, had a markedly French character. In 1907 Benois and the choreographer Mikhaíl Fokine staged *Le pavillon d'Armide,* a ballet with music by Nikolai Cherepnin. Based on Théophile Gautier's *Omphale,* "a tale in Rococo style," the ballet involves a dream about a tapestry that comes to life. The work had been shown first in the Imperial Theaters, but Diaghilev wanted to have a repeat performance in Paris. This was realized in 1909 at the Théâtre du Châtelet.

In 1909 Diaghilev presented five ballets and three operatic productions in Paris: the second act of *Prince Igor,* the complete *Ivan the Terrible* (that is, *Pskovityanka,* renamed so that Chaliapin could star in a title role once again), and a program with extracts from *Ruslan and Lyudmila* and from *Judith* (with Chaliapin as Holofernes). The *Prince Igor* fragment was actually more of a ballet than an opera, thanks to the predominant role of the Polovtsian Dances.

The Paris season of 1909 taught Diaghilev two clear lessons: first, that opera was not financially viable and that ballet did appreciably better; second, that the Parisian public manifestly had a taste for folklore and exotic spectacle. That fact emerged very plainly from the success of *Cléopâtre,* a ballet to music by Arensky, Glazunov, Glinka, Musorgsky, Rimsky-Korsakov, Taneyev, and Cherepnin, and of the Polovtsian Dances (Plate 14). Oriental fantasies appealed more to Parisian audiences than the rococo stylizations of *Le pavillon d'Armide.* From all this Diaghilev came to a double decision: his own preferences notwithstanding, he would go to Paris in 1910 with a program of ballets alone, and ballets, moreover, that satisfied the exotic and quasi-Asiatic image Parisians seemed to have of Russia. Thus neonationalism came to predominate in Diaghilev's aesthetic, and the concept of the Ballets Russes was born. Diaghilev asked Igor Stravinsky to give his brainchild musical expression.

## STRAVINSKY AND NEONATIONALISM

### THE FIREBIRD

The first great project of the Ballets Russes had to be a Slavic *Gesamtkunstwerk.* The choice of subject, *The Firebird,* amounted to the declaration of a program. The firebird was a well-known Russian fairy-tale motif, of great importance to both neonationalists and symbolists. Konstantin Balmont devoted a collection of poems to it, for which the *Mir iskusstva* artist Konstantin Somov designed the title page. To symbolists, the firebird represented the benign influence of the imagination. Alexander Blok called poetic inspiration "the light-winged, benevolent, free bird."[30] The symbol of the firebird was, moreover, close to that of the phoenix, the bird that rose from its ashes. Léon Bakst designed an emblem for *Mir iskusstva,* with an eagle on a snow-covered mountain, to show that "the 'World of Art' is above all earthly things, above the stars; there it reigns proud, secret, lonely as on a snowy peak."[31] The firebird embodied pure, unattainable beauty. The scenario of the ballet, then, was an amalgam of several fairy tales. In it, Tsarevich Ivan confronts the wicked sorcerer Kashchey the Deathless in an attempt to rescue a captive princess from his clutches. Ivan is victorious, thanks to the magical feather the firebird has given him.

Mikhaíl Fokine was put in charge of the choreography and Alexander Golovin of the decor. Stravinsky was commissioned to write the music, after Cherepnin, Lyadov, Glazunov, and possibly Nikolai Sokolov had declined to do so.

*The Firebird* was an unprecedented work (Plate 15). In a letter to Lyadov, Diaghilev called the project "the *first* Russian ballet, for there is no such thing as yet."[32] Russian subjects had never been part of the imperial ballet tradition. In transplanting the Russian fairy tale from the opera stage to the dance floor, *The Firebird* combined Rimsky-Korsakov's opera world with that of classical dance.

Stravinsky's score has all the ingredients of Russian fairy-tale operas, which go back by way of Rimsky-Korsakov to Glinka's *Ruslan and Lyudmila.* The main procedure is to divide the music into a diatonic and a chromatic style, so as to reflect the distinction between human and fantasy characters. The figure of Tsarevich Ivan is depicted by means of an old *kuchka* formula: the *protyazhnaya* stylization, or the style created by Balakirev and based on the lyrical type of Russian folk music. When Stravinsky wrote *The Firebird,* that formula was no longer in fashion. Even Rimsky-Korsakov thought it outdated and preferred to use ritual "calendar songs."

Rimsky-Korsakov's influence is never far away in *The Firebird.* The *Leitharmonie* with which Stravinsky characterizes the wicked sorcerer (Plate 16) and his henchmen is reminiscent of *Kashchey the Deathless.* The famous "Infernal Dance" is close to the dream scene in *Mlada,* which Stravinsky knew from the orchestral version, *Night on Mount Triglav.* The *Leitharmonie* of the firebird has a precedent in *Snegurochka.*[33]

The success of *The Firebird* in Paris transformed Stravinsky at a stroke from a provincial Russian composer into a European celebrity. The speed with which he took advantage of this development was amazing. Adopting Diaghilev's theory that opera was antiquated and ballet its modern substitute, he removed all references to opera from the ballets he wrote immediately after *The Firebird.* While still working on *The*

*Firebird*, moreover, he conceived the idea of a ballet based on pagan rites, with the working title of "The Great Sacrifice." This was the start of what would grow into the ballet *Vesna svyashchennaya* (literally, "Holy Spring"), better known in the West as *Le sacre du printemps* or *The Rite of Spring*. In the meantime, however, another work took his attention: *Petrushka,* originally begun as a concert piece for piano and orchestra, but on Diaghilev's advice expanded into a full-fledged ballet.

*Petrushka* and *The Rite of Spring* were not conceived as alternations of mime and dance, a scheme ballet had borrowed from the "recitative and aria" structure of operas. In *Petrushka,* the dramatic story is told in a continuous dance. *The Rite of Spring* goes even further. In it, the narrative element makes way for a radical ritualization: the ballet no longer tells a story about a pagan rite; it *is* the rite. This conception loosely reflected the symbolist idea of art as celebration. In interviews he gave in St. Petersburg in 1912, Stravinsky called his future ballet a kind of "mysterium"—in the purest Scriabin fashion.[34]

Stravinsky's membership in the circle around the Ballets Russes influenced his approach to folklore. Exploring the musical consequences of the neonationalist aesthetic—that is, using motifs from folk art as structural elements of a personal creation—he liberated folklore from the conventions of Balakirev and Rimsky-Korsakov. Rather than using their examples, moreover, he relied on the results of recent folk-song research. The fact that Rimsky-Korsakov had dismissed the songs transcribed by Yuliy Melgunov—and particularly the examples of folk polyphony—as "barbarous" shows how remote he had grown from actual folk music.[35] A great step forward in the study of Russian folk music was taken by Yevgeniya Linyova, who published three remarkable collections of folk songs and was the first to use a phonograph in field work, enabling her to obtain an accurate representation of folk harmonizations. Stravinsky was familiar with her work;[36] Linyova herself viewed her research as a step toward a musical form of neonationalism. The following exhortation found a ready ear with Stravinsky:

> It is probable that in spite of many unfavorable conditions, folk song, in the process of disappearing in the countryside, will be reborn, transformed, in the works of our composers. It will be reborn not only in the sense of borrowing melodies from the folk—that is the easiest and least gratifying means of using it; no, it will be reborn in the sense of *style:* free, broad, and lyric; in the sense of bold and complex voice leadings, the voices interlacing and separating, at times fused with the main melody, at times departing radically

from it. A rebirth of this kind . . . we await in bold and interesting compositions by musical innovators, both at home and abroad.[37]

## PETRUSHKA

Like *The Firebird, Petrushka* was the result of a collective effort. The choreography was once again the work of Fokine; Alexander Benois was responsible for the scenario, the decor, and the costumes; Vaslav Nijinsky danced the title role, supported by Tamara Karsavina and Alexander Orlov. Stravinsky's score, as we have seen, was originally not written for a ballet. He had been working on a concert piece for piano and orchestra, involving the character Petrushka as a point of departure—Petrushka being the harlequin of the traditional Russian puppet theater—when Diaghilev suggested that the idea be used for a ballet. For the scenario, he turned to Benois, who was an authority on the traditions of the Russian puppet theater.

*Petrushka* is a brilliant example of the combination of ethnographic details with free fantasy according to the neonationalist aesthetic. Scenically as well as musically, the ballet drew faithfully on folk traditions, albeit transformed into an aesthetic conception that transcended all forms of naturalism.

*Petrushka* takes up a theme Alexander Serov had elaborated in *The Power of the Fiend,* namely, the *maslenichnoye gulyaniye,* or *maslenitsa* in short: the Russian Shrovetide carnival, Butter Week Fair, the climax of urban festivities. Benois and Fokine placed the action very precisely in the years 1830 to 1840, through the use of visual details: peddlers, coachmen, gypsies, nursemaids, organ grinders, and the rest, all dressed in the fashion of the day; and decor that includes a merry-go-round, gingerbread stalls, and a table with a samovar from which tea is being sold.[38] Prominently on hand is the *balagannïy ded,* the carnival barker with his long beard. Fokine did not work with a corps de ballet; instead he endeavored to humanize and individualize his dancers. Thus, following the example of the stage director Konstantin Stanislavsky, he created the impression of the crowd as an aggregate of individuals rather than an impersonal mass.

*Petrushka* consists of four scenes. The first shows the crowd strolling among the booths. One of these is the little wooden theater booth in which a puppetmaster, the old magician, presents three puppets to the public: Petrushka, the Ballerina, and the Moor. In the second and third scenes we are introduced to the private world of these puppets, who are involved in a three-cornered relationship based on the commedia dell'arte model. The Petrushka of the ballet is not the real Petrushka. He has nothing in common with the impudent rogue of the Russian puppet theater, but is rather the unhappy Pierrot who fights the Moor for the love of Colombine (the Ballerina). In the fourth scene, we are back at the fair. A milling throng of various types passes us in review, including a bear trainer, nursemaids, and three masked figures: the devil, a pig, and a goat, borrowed from an old custom of the *ryazhenïye*, or Russian holiday mummers. Suddenly the quarrel between Petrushka and the Moor rises to such a pitch that Petrushka flees the little theater, pursued by the Moor, who strikes Petrushka down in the midst of the terrified crowd. "He's only a puppet," the magician tries to reassure his audience. But at night the magician is visited by Petrushka's ghost, who jeers at him from the roof of the little theater.

The ballet confronts the human world with the "inner" world of the puppets, who show that their emotional life is deeper than that of human beings. In pure *Mir iskusstva* style, they serve as symbols of the creative imagination, depicted as being more real and incisive than the world outside. In Petrushka's final grimace at the magician, fantasy proves superior to reality.

For a musical portrayal of the duality of these two worlds, Stravinsky fell back upon Glinka's familiar formula: diatonic folk-song style balanced against "fantasy" chromaticism. In the development, however, he followed new paths. In his choice of folk music for the first and fourth scenes, he abandoned the academic folklore of the Belyayev circle for good, substituting the crude, everyday ditties of urban life.

The first scene is a montage of folk songs, a *chansonette* (Emile Spencer's *polka populaire* about Sarah Bernhardt's wooden leg, "La jambe en bois"), a sentimental romance à la barrel organ (imitated by clarinets and flutes, complete with the simulation of a broken pin), and the cries of street vendors and stallholders.[39] The leaps by fourths at the beginning are based on the cries of charcoal vendors. The famous syncopated rhythms are echoes of the *pribautki* (nonsense verses of unequal length, recited at great speed and in a high tone) with which the *balagannïy ded* entices the public into the wooden carnival booths to attend the performances. In the third scene Stravinsky quotes two waltzes by Lanner; in the fourth, six folk songs.

The other facet, the "fantastic" chromaticism in *Petrushka,* was for a long time considered a crucial step toward polytonality, the simultaneous use of different keys. A closer study of Rimsky-Korsakov's technique, however, has shown that Stravinsky's harmony was in fact derived from

Rimsky-Korsakov's octatonicism—from which he drew the very conclusion his teacher had avoided, lest he lapse into "hyper-harmony." A splendid invention is the passage at the end of the whole work, in which octatonicism and diatonicism are brought together for the first time.

Despite all the naturalism in the choreography, music, and decor, the ballet as a whole does not make a realistic impression. *Petrushka* represents a "created world," as demanded by the *Mir iskusstva* ideal. Visually, that world is produced through the stylization of motifs and the interplay of colors. Musically, Stravinsky transcends the naturalism of his ethnographic sources with the help of his colorful orchestration.

### THE RITE OF SPRING

Like *Petrushka, The Rite of Spring* began with a detailed study of the ethnographic sources. Stravinsky had started with a sketchy idea about a pagan sacrificial rite during which a young girl dances until she falls dead before the assembled elders of her tribe. He called on Nikolai Roerich for help in turning this idea into a scenario. Roerich, who was known as an expert on Old Slavic myths and customs, belonged to the circle of neonationalists around Princess Tenisheva. At the time of his collaboration with Stravinsky, he was decorating her "neo-Russian" private chapel in Talashkino. He had by then devoted a large number of paintings to his visions of the ancient Slavic world, their titles indicating the direction he would follow in *The Rite of Spring: The Gathering of the Elders, Idols, The Stone Age (The North), The Sacred Spot, The Ancestors of Mankind,* and so on. According to Alexander Benois, Roerich was

> utterly absorbed in dreams of prehistoric, patriarchal and religious life—of the days when the vast, limitless plains of Russia and the shores of her lakes and rivers were peopled with the forefathers of the present inhabitants. Roerich's mystic, spiritual experiences made him strangely susceptible to the charm of this ancient world. He felt in it something primordial and weird, something that was intimately linked with nature—with that Northern culture he adored, the inspiration of his finest pictures.[40]

In August 1910, speaking of Stravinsky's new ballet, Roerich told the press: "The specifically choreographic part consists of ritual dances. This work will be the first attempt [in the theater] to give a reproduction of antiquity without any definite dramatic subject." He outlined the work as follows: "The new ballet will give a series of images of a holy night among the ancient Slavs. . . . The action begins with a summer night and finishes immediately before the sunrise, when the first rays begin to show."[41] From this statement it emerges that the ballet was originally planned as a summer, rather than a spring, ritual. In the terminology of Russian folk religion, that meant the celebration of *Kupala* (midsummer) instead of *Semik* (spring). The working title was *Velikaya zhertva*—"The Great Sacrifice." Later, when the *Semik* festival (also known as "the Green Week") took its place in the scenario, the title was changed: first to *Prazdnik vesnï* (The celebration of spring) and then to *Vesna svyashchennaya* ("Holy Spring").

The original plan differs from the definitive version in several respects, including the shift of the abduction scene from 5 to 3:[42]

| Original Scenario | | Definitive Titles | |
|---|---|---|---|
| | | | PART ONE |
| | | 1. | Introduction |
| 1. | Divination with Wands | 2. | Les Augures printanières |
| | | 3. | *Jeu du rapt* |
| 2. | Khorovod (ceremonial dance) | 4. | Rondes printanières |
| 3. | The Ritual of the Camps | 5. | Jeux des cités rivales |
| 4. | They Are Coming, They Are Bringing Him | 6. | Cortège du sage |
| 5. | *The Ritual of the Abduction* | | |
| | | 7. | Adoration de la Terre (le Sage) |
| 6. | Dance of the Earth (literally: Dancing-Out of the Earth) | 8. | Danse de la terre |
| | | | PART TWO |
| | | 9. | Introduction |
| 7. | Ceremonial Dances, Secret Rituals | 10. | Cercles mystérieux des adolescentes |
| 8. | Glorification, Wild Dance (Amazons) | 11. | Glorification de l'Elue |
| | | 12. | Evocation des ancêtres |
| 9. | The Act of the Elders | 13. | Action rituelle des ancêtres |
| 10. | Holy Dance | 14. | Danse sacrale (L'Elue) |

In a letter he wrote in 1912, Stravinsky described the project as follows:

"The first part, which bears the name 'The Kiss of the Earth,' is made up of ancient Slavonic rituals—the joy of spring. The orchestral introduction is a swarm of spring pipes [*dudki*]; later, after the curtain goes up, there are auguries, khorovod rituals, a game of abduction, a khorovod game of cities, and all of this is interrupted by the procession of the 'Oldest-and-Wisest,' the elder who bestows a kiss upon the earth. A wild stomping dance upon the earth, the people drunk with spring, brings the first part to its conclusion.

"In the second part the maidens at night perform their secret ritual upon a sacred hillock. One of the maidens is doomed by fate to be sacrificed. She wanders into a stone labyrinth from which there is no exit, whereupon all the remaining maidens glorify the Chosen One in a boisterous martial dance. Then the elders enter. The doomed one, left alone face to face with the elders, dances her last 'Holy Dance'—the Great Sacrifice. These last words are in fact the name of the second part. The elders are witness to her last dance, which ends in the death of the doomed one."

Throughout the whole composition I give the listener a sense of the closeness of the people to the earth, of the commonality of their lives with the earth, by means of lapidary rhythms.[43]

The ideas for Roerich's scenario came from a variety of sources, the most important of which was Alexander Afanasyev's book *The Slavs' Poetic Outlook on Nature,* a "reconstruction" of ancient Slavonic pagan life, objective observation being combined with romantic fantasy. Afanasyev's book describes the annual cycle of popular customs. The ballet itself follows two customs: the *Semik,* or Spring, celebration (held on the seventh Thursday after Easter) and the midsummer festival of *Kupala.* Together these two celebrations take the lion's share of the scenario. *Kupala* was a notorious and shameless erotic feast, as Afanasyev notes, quoting a sixteenth-century commentary by a monk from Pskov:

On this holy night, practically the whole town gathers in the countryside and goes wild. . . . They beat on tambourines, and raise their voices, and saw on fiddles, the women and the maidens flail about and dance, they roll their eyes, from their mouths come revolting howls and yelps, disgusting songs, they give rein to all sorts of mad devilry, they reel about leaping and stamping.[44]

Even more drastic is a comment in the eleventh-century *Nestor's Chronicle.* Roerich took the idea for the "Ritual of the Camps," followed by the "Ritual of the Abduction," from the following passage:

Living in the forests like the very beasts . . . there were no marriages among them, but simply games (*igry*) in between the villages. When the people gathered for games, for dancing, and for all other devilish amusements, the men on these occasions carried off wives for themselves, and each took any woman with whom he had arrived at an understanding. In fact, they even had two or three wives apiece.[45]

Some rituals during the *Kupala* feast, such as the burning of straw dolls, were reminiscent of pagan sacrifices. In some regions, a young girl was selected around whom the dances were performed, together with augural rituals.

The glorification of the elders is not taken from Russian folklore but from Herodotus's description of the Scythians (Book IV), whom the Russians viewed as their mythical ancestors. At about the turn of the century, they were a favorite symbol of an elementary vital force standing for a "new barbarism," which, at the time of the Revolution, would culminate in *Skifstvo*. Roerich included a Scythian burial mound in the decor, and the tableau of the divination with willow wands comes straight out of Herodotus, as does the wild dance of the Amazons.

The crucial theme in the scenario, the sacrifice of the maiden, however, has no equivalent in ancient Slavonic customs or fables. Most probably it was Stravinsky's, rather than Roerich's, idea. It was a fantasy element, indeed, a fin de siècle cliché. Dying young maidens are plentiful in the painting and literature of the French symbolists, the English Pre-Raphaelites, and the work of Edgar Allan Poe. Recall the sexual piquancy of Stravinsky's explanation that, in *The Rite of Spring*, the girls were adolescents with immature sexual characteristics.[46]

Stravinsky may have taken the link between the dying maiden and Slavonic paganism from the poems of Sergey Gorodetsky. In his collection of poetry entitled *Yar* (1907), this poet created a mythology of his own, inspired by mythical and anarchist ideas and the conviction that elementary forces must be helped to burst the shackles of civilization. Of particular relevance to *The Rite of Spring* is the bizarre poem in which a maiden is sacrificed to the sun god Yarila (or Yarilo). Tied to a sacred linden tree, she is hacked to death by an ax-wielding sorcerer, who is busy fashioning an idol from the tree.

The same attention Roerich paid to the ethnographic background of the scenario (Plate 17) is also apparent in Stravinsky's choice of folk music. All the identified folk tunes in the score belong to the genre of "calendar songs," songs associated with annual agrarian customs, some of which are explicitly represented in the scenario. A study of the sketches by Richard Taruskin has shown that the share of folk music in *The Rite of Spring* is greater than has been supposed, and that the folk songs underwent a complex metamorphosis during the process of composition.[47] Taruskin's conclusion that Stravinsky, although he set out with the old *kuchka* principle of ethnographic authenticity in mind, transformed the material while writing the score to suit his own imagination, is important. In that sense, Stravinsky showed himself to be a genuine neonationalist, one for whom ethnographic reality was but a spur to the free play of the imagination.

*The Rite of Spring* satisfies the neonationalist paradigm fully. First, it includes a combination of rites of different origin and function. The transposition of the whole—including the midsummer customs—to an imaginary celebration of spring is a primary form of artistic abstraction. The same process of stylization occurred in the utilization of folk-song material: not only did Stravinsky understand how to avoid direct references to the original songs by careful melodic and rhythmic manipulation, but he also allowed the folk-song material to influence the deepest layers of the musical structure. Most melodies and motifs in the score remain confined to a tonal range of just four notes: a minor tetrachord. From his training in Rimsky-Korsakov's octatonicism, Stravinsky discovered that two tetrachords one tritone apart jointly produce the octatonic scale. That principle had been put to use earlier in the prologue to Borodin's *Prince Igor* and in Rimsky-Korsakov's *Kashchey the Deathless,* but Stravinsky was the first to adapt it in vertical form, that is, in the construction of harmonies, and it constitutes the basis of the harmonic structure of *The Rite of Spring.* Whereas it was once thought that the score was based on a free application of polytonality, it now appears that the music has a clear rationale. The astonishing idiom springs from the combination of diatonic folk melodies with the principles of octatonicism; in other words, the two harmonic worlds, which remained separate until *Petrushka,* each with a function of its own, were synthesized in *The Rite of Spring* for the first time. *The Rite of Spring* uses few formal transitions and developments; instead the structure works with repetitions of the ostinato patterns of folk songs and folk dances, combined with bold juxtapositions and abrupt cuts.

In Chernïshevsky's theory, folk music was equated with pure emotion. Ethnographers at around the turn of the century, by contrast, took a different view. They were struck above all by the formal quality of folk music, by the "classical strictness of the style," as Linyova put it. According to them, no personal feelings were involved; there was an absence of sentimentality, an unemotional form of execution. "Could it be," Linyova wondered, "that the unselfconscious art of the people, in its purely classical simplicity of performance, surpasses even the highest level of training worked out by professional artists?"[48] This "classical strictness" was experienced as the musical equivalent of the primitivism of, for instance, Gauguin—an artist beloved of Stravinsky's circles. According to the dancer Serge Lifar, Diaghilev's appreciation of Gauguin was one of the motifs underlying the production of *The Rite of Spring.*[49]

The idea of impersonal art was extended radically in the ballet. Nijinsky's choreography allowed no room for the individual; the ballet represented a collectivity, a community following the rhythm of rituals without personal contributions or reactions. The original conception of *The Rite of Spring* involved no dramatic conflict. There was no antagonism between the community and the girl who sacrificed her life for the common good. Even in the music, aggressive though it may sound, there is no conflict; only ritual acts, represented by the obsessive ostinati, the harmony without dominant tension, and the montage technique.

*The Rite of Spring* is the preeminent artistic elaboration of *stikhya*, a concept the poet Alexander Blok defined as "the elementary spontaneity of the people" and as the very opposite of *kultura*, that is, "artificial, materialistic culture." Primitivism went a long way toward satisfying the dream of a restored unity of man with the elementary forces of nature.

Such impersonal primitivism can be alarming. The French reviewer Jacques Rivière saw the ballet, which he spoke of as a "biological ballet," as a reflection of "man at a time when he did not yet exist as an individual."[50] He worried about the consequences of its primitivism, as did the Russian critic Andrey Levinson, who described *The Rite of Spring* as an "icy comedy of this primeval hysteria."[51]

The tumultuous première on 29 May 1913 at the Théâtre des Champs Elysées has entered history as one of the most notorious scandals in twentieth-century art. Hostility was widespread, to be sure, but it was Nijinsky's choreography rather than Stravinsky's music that bore the brunt of the opprobrium. One year later, Stravinsky even scored the greatest triumph of his life with a concert performance of *The Rite of Spring* under Pierre Monteux, and meanwhile the work was performed in Moscow and St. Petersburg under Sergey Koussevitzky. Then, from 1914 to 1920, it disappeared from view. The orchestral score was not published until 1921.

The reaction in Russia to *The Rite of Spring* heralded the break between the Russian musical establishment and Stravinsky. Koussevitzky's concert performances were given a lukewarm reception, though the Parisian scandal was not repeated in St. Petersburg. Old César Cui, who dismissed *The Rite of Spring* as a further example of the advance of cacophony and ugliness, observed ironically: "This 'Rite' has been booed everywhere abroad, but among us it has found some applauders—proof that we are ahead of Europe on the path of musical progress."[52] The sharpest attack on Stravinsky came from an anonymous critic: "Stravinsky's music—or rather that sonic muddle [*sumbur*] he has given us in his 'Spring' instead of music [*vmesto muzïki*]—is a monstrosity through and through."[53] The expression "muddle [or chaos] instead of music" (*sumbur vmesto muzïki*) was to make history twenty-two years later, in connection with Stalin's reaction to Shostakovich.

The idea that there is a link between Stravinsky's music and the Russian national tradition is at the forefront of Russian comments on *The Rite of Spring*. While that aspect was overlooked in Paris, it was exaggerated in Russia. The critic Alexander Koptyayev, for example, called the Stravinsky of *Petrushka* "a modernized Serov." Another reviewer wrote, "It is particularly worth noting that *The Rite of Spring*, despite all its excesses, is nevertheless a purely Russian work." In presenting Stravinsky as the ultimate expression of the Russian past, the critic Boris Asafyev put it most clearly:

> Stravinsky is the last representative of an ultrarefined, yet fatigued and surfeited culture. The beauty of his tonal musings is a genuine beauty, but virtually devoid of insight into the future. There is no movement forward in Stravinsky's work, only an ultrarefined synthesis of previous achievements. Stravinsky remains wholly in the past. Despite his wondrous harmonic fancies, one feels that his strength lies in his weakness, that is, in his ability to grasp with an intuitive perspicacity the spirit and sense of any preceding epoch and to stylize it by means of the most ingenious techniques at his disposal today.

Asafyev saw Stravinsky's opposite in Sergey Prokofiev:

> But then Prokofiev's works appear, and the air is filled with freshness, good spirits, the self-assured tone of a man who knows his own strength. And above all, an immense creative will and an irrepressible creative impulse make themselves felt! . . . It would be a distortion to force Prokofiev's creativity into any framework for now, to measure it by any standard, because his work belongs to the future, and it ought to be judged by its own rules.[54]

## "SUCH A SWEET LITTLE SCYTH": SERGEY PROKOFIEV

Sergey Prokofiev revealed himself at the age of seventeen as the enfant terrible of Russian music. In particular, the young composer caused a stir at the St. Petersburg Evenings of Contemporary Music, a concert series set up by Alfred Nurok, Walter Nouvel, and Vyacheslav Karatïgin, opponents of the Belyayev circle.

When Prokofiev first played for Karatïgin, the latter called him the "antithesis to Scriabin—and thank God that the antithesis has appeared."[55] Prokofiev's metallic piano style, with its dry, assertive touch, contrasted with the Chopin tradition in which Scriabin had been trained. On 18 December 1908 Prokofiev made his sensational public debut at the Evenings of Contemporary Music with a number of piano pieces, including the invigorating *Suggestion diabolique*. On 21 February 1910 there followed his debut in Moscow with his First Sonata. Jurgenson published the work in 1911.

One year later the First Piano Concerto was ready, and Prokofiev performed it to great critical acclaim in Moscow on 25 July 1912. Next he wrote his Second Piano Sonata and the well-known *Toccata*, op. 11, a characteristic example of his sharp, caustic, and rhythmical style.

The critics were particularly impressed by the great wealth of unexpected ideas, which they took for the expression of unbridled and spontaneous inspiration. They also considered his music as international, because it showed no apparent connection to the Russian tradition, as exemplified by the composers of the Belyayev circle. Asafyev admired

> the colossal strength of the creative impulse, the intensity and expressiveness of the musical language, the mighty flights of fantasy, the inexhaustible wealth of themes, their individuality and their rhythmic and harmonic inventiveness, in a word, all of those things so difficult to come to terms with for the people who judge music from the viewpoint of its proximity to one or another school, circle or tendency.

Of Prokofiev's spontaneity he wrote: "One hears nothing that is labored, amorphous; on the contrary, one gets the impression that he is almost joking, playing the sonorous images that inhabit his soul, that beyond them much still remains unexpressed."[56]

A first peak of aggressive modernism was the Second Piano Concerto of 1913, which encountered a stormy reception at Pavlovsk on 23 August, the audience split between fierce opponents and fiery admirers. Prokofiev became associated with futurism in music, which does not, however, mean that he had links with the futurist movement. Rather, the term was used as a synonym for modernism, reflected in the high degree of dissonance and in the motoric rhythms.

Prokofiev made a particularly great impression on the followers of Scythianism: "There is a certain . . . sweet . . . barbarity in him," Alexey Podgayetsky, a theosophist in Scriabin's circle of friends, is said to have said in defense of Prokofiev to the skeptical Scriabin: "Such a sweet little Scyth."[57]

Characteristic of Prokofiev's music is the importance of polyphony. His linear approach differs from Scriabin's harmonically structured language. Scriabin's mobile, complex textures rested above all on his expansion of the traditional chord into a broad palette of harmonic colors, followed by the continuous rearrangement of those notes into an uninterrupted movement. Successive states of harmonic tension and relaxation characterized the structure. Prokofiev, for his part, continued to think tonally, but his diatonic system had been vastly expanded. The linear voice-leading that he favored breaches the traditional fifths hierarchy, meaning that the voices can move with marked independence of one another, to confirm the tonality only upon reaching the cadence. In the expanded tonality, ostinati play a clarifying role, for instance by emphasizing the tonic.

In 1914 Prokofiev called on Diaghilev in London. Although his arrogance and naïveté did not make the best impression on the impresario, Diaghilev was nevertheless prepared to give him a chance and commissioned a mythological ballet from him, based on a scenario by Sergey Gorodetsky. As an evocation of the legendary Scythian empire, *Ala and Lolli* was seen as a continuation of the primitivism of *The Rite of Spring*. While Prokofiev was at work on the score, however, Diaghilev, finding Prokofiev's music too obvious an imitation of Stravinsky's, had second thoughts. Prokofiev then recast the score of this now lost ballet into an independent orchestral work, the "Scythian Suite."

In the West, Prokofiev discovered that not everybody considered his music progressive. A performance of the Second Piano Concerto in Rome on 7 March 1915 split the audience into two factions, much as had happened in Pavlovsk. Prokofiev was particularly taken aback by the fact that the progressive critics thought his music was not new enough: they considered his concerto neither modern nor traditional, but placed it halfway in between.

Diaghilev gave him a new commission: *Chout* (The buffoon, 1915), a composition based on the Russian folk tales collected by Alexander Afanasyev. He expected more folklore than Prokofiev normally included in his work, Russian exotica still constituting the crux of Diaghilev's success with the Parisian public. The impresario warned Prokofiev against his suggestibility and against his eclectic tendencies: "In art you have to be able to hate—otherwise your own music will lose its personality."[58]

Diaghilev's fears were justified. Prokofiev was driven by his spontaneity in several directions. In the "Scythian Suite," he manifested his aggressive modernism, whereas in *Chout* he continued the neonationalistic principles of *Petrushka* and *The Rite of Spring*. Another "Scythian" work was the cantata *Semero ikh* (Seven, they are seven, 1917), based on an ancient Akkadian spell translated by Konstantin Balmont. With his *Five Poems by Anna Akhmatova* (1916), Prokofiev tried to prove that he had lyric talents as well. This work is a brittle, transparent composition in which careful attention is paid to the declamation. The same concern also went into the music for Hans Christian Andersen's "The Ugly Duckling." The caustic piano style of *Sarcasmes* was offset by the stylized and dreamy *Visions fugitives* of 1917. Between 1915 and 1917, Prokofiev wrote his First Violin Concerto, a work full of meditative lyricism. At the same time, he presented his *Classical* Symphony, a modernized evocation of a Haydn symphony.

Prokofiev considered all these divergent aspects as so many expressions of his wide-ranging musical talent. His international standing, however, did not improve as a result. The *Classical* Symphony can pass for an early example of neoclassicism, but Prokofiev never developed this aspect consistently into a style, as Stravinsky would do later. For him this kind of "classicism" remained a temporary phenomenon; it was merely one part of his multifaceted personality, not a dominant stylistic principle.

Prokofiev's greatest miscalculation on the international scene was his continued attachment to opera. In Diaghilev's view the opera genre had had its day, and Prokofiev was alone in his attempt to modernize it. He had first ventured when only eight years old to write a mini-opera, *The Giant*. As a student he had composed two versions of Pushkin's "little tragedy" *A Feast in Time of Plague*, modeled on Dargomïzhsky's *The Stone Guest*. *Maddalena* followed in 1911, based on a play by Magda Gustavovna Liven-Orlova that in turn was strongly influenced by Oscar Wilde's *A Florentine Tragedy*.

His discovery of Musorgsky's *Marriage* gave Prokofiev the idea of expanding that composer's radical realism. He launched the project with an ambitious opera based on Dostoyevsky's novel *The Gambler*. It was his response to the antagonism to opera shared by Diaghilev and his circle.

Prokofiev, under the spell of *Marriage,* saw the future of opera in a radical adaptation of Musorgsky's "dramatic music in prose." In interviews he gave in 1916 he paraphrased Musorgsky's aggressive attacks on opera conventions. In practice, however, Prokofiev's technique of *opéra dialogué* was less radical than that of his predecessor. He clung to Musorgsky's interest in naturalistic declamation, but underneath it all, musical structures played a greater role for him. This aspect made itself felt in his first version of *The Gambler*, but was intensified when he revised the score in 1928.

Prokofiev discovered for the first time with *The Gambler* how difficult the genre's position had become in the music market. He started on the work at the request of Albert Coates, then conductor at the Mariyinsky

Theater in St. Petersburg. The outbreak of the Revolution, however, caused preparations to be cut short, and the opera was never staged. After the Revolution, Vsevolod Meyerhold showed interest in a production in Moscow, but again without concrete results. The opera would not be produced until 29 April 1929, and then at the Théâtre Royal de la Monnaie in Brussels. With the translation into French, the work lost its links with the Russian vernacular that Prokofiev had maintained so carefully. The opera failed to hold its own in the international repertoire.

## A PROSPECTIVE AVANT-GARDE

Despite his reputation as the enfant terrible of Russian music, Prokofiev was by no means the most radical composer of his day. In combining expanded tonality and motoric rhythm, his friend and fellow student Nikolai Myaskovsky sometimes went further. The true, radical avant-gardists included Lourié, Roslavets, Obukhov, and Vishnegradsky.

Arthur Lourié owes his reputation as a futurist to his contacts with the futurist circle in Moscow, to a futurist march he composed in 1918 using a text by Mayakovsky, and to stage music for the poet Khlebnikov. His most daring compositions are the piano works *Synthèses* (1914) and *Formes en l'air* (1915). The first is a highly chromatic work, sometimes called an early example of twelve-tone music, though Lourié's technique failed to attach systematic equality to each of the twelve tones. *Formes en l'air* is a graphic score *avant la lettre*. The work consists of fragments without tempo, placed loosely all over the page. It was dedicated to Picasso, which may explain the visual appearance of the score.

Lourié's music is not always equally adventurous. His early piano works, such as the *Greek Songs* (1914), the *Suite japonaise* (1915), and the *Cinq rondeaux de Christine de Pisan* (1915), reflect above all his ultrarefined aestheticism, with a touch of Scriabin and Debussy. In the *Akhmatova* songs of 1914, Lourié used Russian modal effects. In about 1917 he abandoned chromatic experiments for a more diatonic style. Lourié also wrote a great deal of religious music, mostly of a modal character.

In the development of new tonal systems, Nikolai Roslavets went even further than Lourié. As early as 1915 he had perfected his own twelve-tone system. As his starting point, Roslavets took the "synthetic chord," a scale with an unvarying sequence of intervals: whole tones and semitones followed one another in regular succession. By the transposition of synthetic chords, Roslavets reached the chromatic total. He allowed the synthetic chord—which can be used both vertically and horizontally—to determine the entire harmonic structure of a composition. A departure from dodecaphony is the free succession of separate notes. The interval structure of the tone complexes, not the immutable pitch sequence, is the determining factor of the harmonic organization. Early applications of this harmonic approach can be found in *Trois compositions* (1914) and in *Deux compositions* (1915), both for piano.

In the footsteps of Scriabin, Ivan Vishnegradsky tried to give expression to a "cosmic consciousness." One of the first results was his oratorio *La journée de l'existence* (1916–17), intended to reflect the evolution of human consciousness from its most primitive form to its final stage in cosmic consciousness. To capture the development of consciousness musically, Vishnegradsky extended his harmony with quarter tones.

Nikolai Obukhov adopted the same starting point: Scriabin's mysticism. As early as 1914, he experimented with twelve-tone systems and electronic sounds. Like Scriabin, he considered the chromatic total as a reflection of tonality. *Les astrales parlent,* for piano (1915), and *Au sommet de la montagne,* for voice and piano (1915), are two early examples.

Finally we must mention Yefim Golyshev, who by 1909 had left Russia for Berlin, where he joined the dadaists as a composer and painter. One of the few of his extant works is a string trio published in 1925, which may have been composed as early as 1914.[59] If that is true, then Golyshev must be considered the first serialist: his trio includes twelve-tone complexes as well as a first attempt to order rhythmical durations in a serial fashion.

The Silver Age was an exceptional period in Russian culture. They were flourishing days, if unstable. The permanent emigration of Diaghilev and Stravinsky, the transfer of *Mir iskusstva*'s sphere of activity to the West, the creation of a Russian art for Western consumption in the Ballets Russes: all this shows that Russia's cultural and economic basis still lagged far behind that of the West. The social and political transformation of Russian society had only just begun; meanwhile, the sense of insecurity and instability was exploited by revolutionaries. The historian Sidney Monas has summed up the situation as follows:

> I do not wish to belittle the accomplishments of the Silver Age of Russian culture. Indeed, in terms of achievement, in terms of the richness of fulfilled talent in all branches of culture, it might well have been called a golden age, comparable even to the great flowerings of Periclean Athens and Renaissance

England. Although there was no Pushkin and no novelist of the stature of the great ones of the 1850s, 1860s, and 1870s, the arts and sciences—lyric poetry and lyric prose, and even the novel, to say nothing of drama, opera, the visual arts, architecture, the revival of native folk arts, medicine, science, music, mathematics, agronomy and engineering—flourished with a kind of renaissance richness that has few equals for such a brief period of time. . . . Yet most [historical studies] seem to conclude or to stop just short of concluding that all this was fragile and foredoomed and that although doom in fact took the shape of the Bolshevik revolution, even without that, the fate of this great flowering could go no further than permitted by the thinness of the social soil in which it grew. The beautiful purple twilight was evening, not morning; and the night was coming on.[60]

## CHAPTER TEN

# "The Cleansing Catastrophe"
## *Early Soviet Music*

In March 1917 an event with incalculable consequences took place: under pressure from the army command and from parliament, Tsar Nicholas II abdicated. The abdication led to the collapse of his entire regime. The bureaucracy crumbled, and the country was quickly plunged into a state of anarchy. The rebellion, which had started with the peasants, spread to the army, the workers, and the ethnic minorities, all of whom saw their chance to square accounts with the autocracy. Kerensky's provisional government was unable to stem the anarchic turmoil, its endeavors sabotaged by the soviets, workers' and soldiers' revolutionary councils led by radical intellectuals in the various socialist parties. The Bolsheviks, under the leadership of Vladimir Ilyich Lenin, added fuel to the flames. Lenin attempted to rally all the dissatisfied elements behind him, promising the various population groups that he would meet their demands: land for the peasants, trade unions for the workers, peace for the army, and national self-determination for the ethnic minorities.

Lenin's campaign was a stratagem; none of his promises was part of his party's platform. The aim of the Bolsheviks was to seize untrammeled power and to maintain it over the whole of Russian society.

The Russian Revolution broke out on 25 October 1917. It was presented by Party ideologists as the proletarian revolution predicted by Karl Marx, although in reality it was nothing but a classical coup d'état. In the Bolshevik seizure of power, ideology played no more than a secondary role. On 22 November, the Bolsheviks signed a truce with Germany at Brest-Litovsk. That treaty enabled Lenin to shift the struggle from the international to the national arena.

The Bolshevik party was marked by acts of extreme violence. It looked upon the subjection of the population in military terms. Leon Trotsky stated the case quite unequivocally: "Soviet authority is organized civil war."[1] First the Bolsheviks set out to suppress their political opponents; next they turned on the anti-Bolshevik White armies. The devastating civil war that followed was to continue until 1921. The ultimate victory of the Bolsheviks gave rise to an enormous wave of emigrants, which stripped the country of its social, professional, and intellectual elites.

In their policy of dominating the whole of Russian society, the Bolsheviks made no exception for culture, though they did not operate with the same thoroughness on the cultural plane as in the social and political arena: at least in the early years, scholars and artists continued to enjoy a fair measure of intellectual freedom. With the help of this laissez-faire policy, the Bolsheviks hoped to regain the confidence of the intellectuals, most of whom did not bother to disguise their distaste for Bolshevik vulgarity and brutality.

In an effort to turn the tide, Lenin appointed Anatoliy Lunacharsky as commissar for culture and education. Lunacharsky was a highly cultivated man who surrounded himself with leading artists and writers, Marc Chagall, Vasiliy Kandinsky, Vsevolod Meyerhold, Ilya Ehrenburg, and Alexander Blok among them. He relied on Arthur Lourié to look after the music.

## WAR COMMUNISM: ARTISTIC EUPHORIA AND BUREAUCRATIZATION

Because the civil war was still raging, the early years of the Communist regime are known as War Communism. During this time artists engaged in daring experiments, even though the regime did not actively encourage uninhibited artistic freedom. The apparent flowering of progressive art was not the most typical historical characteristic of the period, however. More important to the Bolsheviks, with their eye to the future, was the step-by-step bureaucratization of culture, which the regime viewed as a propaganda tool.

Lenin's intention was to force all spheres of public activity into mammoth institutions, modeled on capitalist cartels. Bureaucratization started with the establishment of the People's Commissariat of Public Education, or NARKOMPROS. NARKOMPROS was put in charge of all intellectual, artistic, and pedagogic life: science, literature, the visual arts, music, theater, film, education, and leisure. All private publishing houses were nationalized and handed over to NARKOMPROS. In 1922 censorship was systematized by the foundation of GLAVLIT, the central censorship authority of NARKOMPROS. While Lunacharsky was at the helm, NARKOMPROS acted with tolerance. When he was replaced in 1929, the exercise of tolerance went by the wayside.

Opinions were divided about the nature of revolutionary culture. Lenin believed that Soviet culture must continue to build on the achievements of the bourgeois era. In his view, however, the visual arts, music, and literature were of no more than secondary importance. What really mattered was science and technology. The idea of building on the past was contested by the PROLETKULT movement, which maintained that the new leading class, the proletariat, must develop a "proletarian" culture of its own. Historical progress, in their view, had rendered the heritage of the past obsolete.

PROLETKULT was based on the ideas of Alexander Bogdanov, Lunacharsky's brother-in-law. His philosophy was one of many fin de siècle attempts to come to grips with the Nietzschean idea "God is dead." Bogdanov, transferring the creative power of the divinity to the human collective, advocated "organization science," a practical philosophy tailored to the needs of the creators of the society of the future. Because of its close association with the proletarian class, Bogdanov considered machine production the highest type of organized human collective activity.

To Bogdanov, art, too, should be a form of collective activity. The proletariat would abolish the individualism of bourgeois culture for good, as the new art gave expression to a "collective perception of the world."[2]

The ambition of Bogdanov and his allies was nothing short of building a giant network of PROLETKULT organizations extending right across Russia. Their expectations were utopian in the extreme. PROLETKULT promised to abolish the boundary between the cultural elite and the underdeveloped masses once and for all, proclaiming the optimistic message that even the lowliest members of society could participate in cultural creativity.

In practice, PROLETKULT relied largely on workshops and studios, where artists would try to impart their skills to workers while joining them in a search for new forms of expression. The stage played an important role in this process. In music, revolutionary hymns took pride of place. PROLETKULT made particular use of choral singing, a form of music-making that had been developed for use in popular music education before the Revolution. The emphasis on choral singing and so-called mass songs does not, however, mean that PROLETKULT was the exclusive province of men of minor talent; such prominent musicians as Reinhold Glière, Grigoriy Lyubimov, and Arseniy Avraamov were also part of the movement. In Moscow, Alexander Kastalsky took the lead, having had wide experience in the choral and folk-song movement. Despite the participation of such luminaries, many PROLETKULT studios were indeed little more than popular art education classes. Music workshops, in particular, often did not go beyond running traditional courses in instrumental technique or in choral singing.

From 1920 Lenin turned against the PROLETKULT movement, though he had raised objections to Bogdanov's theories even earlier. Lenin was fundamentally opposed to Bogdanov's argument that culture was an autonomous sphere of human activity, on a par with politics and economics. To Lenin, culture was subordinate to politics. He accordingly took exception to the independence of PROLETKULT. In October 1920 he decreed that all PROLETKULT organizations were to be taken over by NARKOMPROS, whereupon PROLETKULT went into a steep decline.[3]

The PROLETKULT movement derived its strength from the revolutionary enthusiasm of some of the intelligentsia. The artistic avant-garde had welcomed the Revolution with open arms, their fervor closely bound up with their own apocalyptic expectations. Such diverse movements as symbolism, futurism, and communism shared at least one characteristic: a utopian conception of history, based on the belief that a new age was about to dawn, one that would raise humankind to a higher level. The symbolist Andrey Belïy put it as follows:

> The eternal appears in the line of time as the dawn of the ascending century. The fogs of grief are suddenly split asunder by the red dawn of completely new days. . . . The rupture of old ways is experienced like the End of the World, the tidings of a new epoch like the Second Coming. We felt the apocalyptic rhythm of time. We reached toward the Beginning through the End.[4]

The permanent atmosphere of crisis during the late tsarist phase had raised expectations to a feverish intensity. After the Revolution, the intelligentsia became divided; while some dwelled on the horrors of the civil war or on the totalitarian ambitions of the Bolsheviks, others placed all their hopes in the expected salvation of mankind. The second group felt euphoric, convinced that their hopes were about to be realized. Alexander Blok welcomed the Revolution with his poem *The Scythians,* in which he compared the revolutionary masses to the Asiatic hordes that had reduced Europe to ashes. The composer Nikolai Roslavets called the revolutionary process a "cleansing catastrophe" at the crossroads of the downward path of European decay and the upward course of communism, enlightenment, and rationality.[5]

A common characteristic of many currents in the Silver Age was the belief in *zhiznetvorchestvo*, "art as the creation of life." Much as the symbolists had pinned their hopes on the artistic individual, so the PRO-LETKULT movement extolled the human collective as the agent of creation and transformation of reality. They greeted the revolution as the turning point in the destruction of the old life and the beginning of the awaited renewal. The futurist poet Vladimir Mayakovsky even turned into a spokesman for the Bolsheviks, presenting himself as the "bard of the revolution." Although the Bolsheviks had great need of futurists for propaganda purposes, they nevertheless treated them with suspicion. Even so, the futurist dream colored the Bolshevist program. From his *Literature and Revolution* (1923), it appears that Trotsky, too, viewed the future in the light of a transformation of humankind through the absolute mastery of matter:

> Man will get used to regarding the world as an obedient clay for molding increasingly perfect forms of life. The wall between art and production will fall. The future monumental style will not be decorative, it will give form. In this the Futurists are right. . . . But not only the wall between art and production will fall; simultaneously the wall between art and nature will also fall. This is not meant in the sense of Jean-Jacques [Rousseau], that art will become closer to a state of nature; but on the contrary, nature will become more "artificial." The present position of mountains and rivers, of fields, of meadows, of steppes, of forests and seashores cannot be considered final. . . . If faith only promised to move mountains, then technology, which takes nothing "on faith," is able to lift up mountains and move them. Up till now this was done for industrial purposes; . . . in the future it will be done on an incomparably larger scale, in accordance with a general industrial-artistic plan. . . . In the end man will rebuild the earth, if not in his own image, then to his own taste.

Symbolist and futurist views combined in Trotsky's vision of the new socialist man: "Man will become immeasurably stronger, more intelligent and subtle; his body will become more harmonious, his movements more rhythmic, his voice more musical. The forms of every day life will take on dynamic theatricality. The average human type will rise to the heights of an Aristotle, a Goethe, or a Marx. And above this ridge new peaks will perpetually rise."[6]

The artistic vanguard, intent on playing the role of revolutionary pioneers, rallied under the banner of "left-wing culture." The journal *Lev* (Left) became the forum of futurists and their heirs: the constructivists and adherents of the "Production Art" movement. Vsevolod Meyerhold, for one, tried to attain "October in the theater," as he called his project—an extended program that would allow the theater to participate in the social transformations wrought by the October Revolution. In his view, the theater had to become a model of the new life. In concrete terms that meant, on the one hand, that the theater must imbue the masses with a new historical consciousness and, on the other, that acting style had to be renewed. Accordingly, he developed the so-called biomechanical method, a form of acting that emphasized body language as a means by which actors might develop a new mastery over their bodies as a means of expression. Biomechanics was an amalgam of a variety of influences: Dalcroze's eurhythmics, Pavlov's reflexology, Bogdanov's "techtology" (organization science), and Alexey Gastev's Taylorist models of the work process. The fundamental aim of Meyerhold's biomechanics was once again *zhiznetvorchestvo,* the aesthetic mastery of life itself. His experiments were widely used outside the theater as well, for instance in the "theatralization" of military training, in experiments with the use of rhythmic movements in the factory, and above all in the sports parades that became a distinctive feature of Soviet culture in the 1930s.[7]

Russian music was scarcely prepared for participation in the revolutionary movement. The academicism of the Belyayev circle still dominated musical life, while the most creative musicians had already moved abroad: Stravinsky in 1914 and Prokofiev in 1918. Scriabin left many followers and imitators behind, but none had anything like his creative powers.

Bureaucratization gradually took control of musical life. The first step was the nationalization of theaters. Next it was the turn of the court orchestras in Moscow and Petrograd, private music schools, music publishers, instrument makers, libraries, archives, and concert societies. Control of the musical repertoire was vested in a special committee, the GLAVREPERTKOM. The conservatories were handed over to NARKOMPROS. In Petrograd, the curriculum was reorganized in 1925, with ideological education becoming part of the program. Glazunov (who left the conservatory in 1928) tried to delay the general bureaucratization as long as possible and to guarantee the continued quality of musical instruction.

Petrograd and Moscow were given new theaters. In Petrograd, the

Malïy, or Malegot, Theater was established in the former Mikhailovsky Theater. In Moscow, the stage directors Konstantin Stanislavsky and Vladimir Nemirovich-Danchenko ran their own opera studios, which were combined in 1941 to form the Stanislavsky–Nemirovich-Danchenko Music Theater.

The musical section of NARKOMPROS took the name MUZO and was directed by Arthur Lourié. Lourié's fanatical modernism was opposed by many musicians, who—as members of VSERABIS, a new trade union (not a union of musicians but of people working in all spheres of the arts)—rose up en masse against MUZO. The Party then published a document, "Basic Policies in the Realm of the Arts," which stated unequivocally that all the arts fell under the control of the state. At the same time, the document condemned the excesses of the avant-garde, and especially their negative attitude to the art of the past.

THE NEP

Beginning in 1921, a succession of events rang in a new phase in Soviet history. On the political plane, there was the Kronstadt mutiny. In the cultural field, there was the death of Alexander Blok, the execution of the poet Nikolai Gumilyov for antirevolutionary activities, the emigration of Maxim Gorky, and the banishment of some 150 intellectuals in 1922. These events ended the War Communism phase and ushered in a new period, that of the NEP, or New Economic Policy, a change of tack introduced by Lenin in March 1921. It brought some measure of economic liberalization, but was no more than a stopgap designed to keep the Bolsheviks in power during the disastrous economic situation that had arisen.

The concessions made by the regime were purely economic; there was no question of any political climbdown. Trotsky declared in 1922: "As the ruling party we can allow the speculator in the economy, but we do not allow him in the political realm."[8] To prevent liberalization from getting out of hand, the regime tightened political repression even further. During the years 1921 to 1923, the Party launched a decisive attack against rival socialist parties and against the church, systematized the censor's grip, and strengthened the secret police.

On the cultural plane, the NEP is remembered as a time in which the modernist experiment was allowed to flourish, the country was open to international contacts, and cultural and intellectual pluralism was tolerated. It was also the time of the *poputchiki,* the "fellow travelers": writers or intellectuals who did not openly rally behind the Party but never-theless sympathized with the Revolution.

The NEP period is easily idealized. It has the aura of a time of hope, an example of what the Revolution might have become had it been spared Stalin's later excesses. In commentaries on culture in the twen-ties there is often a touch of nostalgia for "original, uncorrupted com-munism," communism without the show trials, mass deportations, gulags, or the Cold War. That nostalgia is misplaced. The relative liberalization had been ushered in by the regime itself and was carefully controlled. The NEP did not entail any decrease in the power of the Party, but was, on the contrary, a consolidation of that power and a preparation for even more drastic interventions. Cultural pluralism was only one side of the coin. The growing impact of the Party on cultural life was the other.

The NEP period is often considered a pause in the sovietization of cul-ture. There was room for experiment again, and links with the outside world became closer. Yet one could equally well say that it was precisely during the time of the NEP that the characteristic Soviet culture emerged. The artistic experiments of War Communism had been prepared by pre-revolutionary currents championed by Lunacharsky, Blok, Gorky, Male-vich, and Lourié. Although these men's work was revolutionary, it was not "Soviet" in the strict sense of the word. The prerevolutionary intel-ligentsia was simply co-opted by the regime as long as it provided use-ful propaganda tools. During the NEP, however, a new generation took over, which, unlike the prerevolutionary intelligentsia, was to shape the cultural profile of the whole of Soviet history. The key figures of Soviet art stepped into the limelight during this period. In literature, they were Konstantin Fedin, Leonid Leonov, and Valentin Katayev; in film, Gri-goriy Kosintsev and David Trauberg; and in music, Dmitry Shostakovich. The exponents of War Communism, meanwhile, left the country, died, or continued to work in Russia until they, too, came up against the wall of cultural repression and bureaucracy. Lourié and Gorky were among those who opted for emigration; Alexander Blok died in 1921; Lu-nacharsky was replaced as commissar in 1929; Mayakovsky committed suicide in 1930; Yevgeniy Zamyatin, the author of the depressing anti-Utopian novel We, was banished in 1931; Osip Mandelstam vanished into a gulag in 1938; and Meyerhold was arrested in 1939.

During the NEP, the Party's grip on culture tightened. Whereas un-der War Communism subsidies had been allocated by professionals, now the final say was with Party officials. NARKOMPROS was appropriated by the wives and relatives of the Bolshevik leaders. The NEP also put an end to the decentralization of cultural life practiced under War Communism. From 1918 to 1920 many provincial centers had blossomed, but under the NEP they lost their subsidies and the intellectuals returned to Moscow and Leningrad. That is how it would remain throughout Soviet history: the center would determine the face of Soviet culture. For all these reasons, it may be said that the NEP was not a temporary change in Soviet culture, but the very period during which the sovietization of culture had its real beginning.[9]

Music, too, received its Soviet stamp under the NEP, for it was during this period—the 1920s—that the protagonists of Soviet music stepped into the limelight. The conservatories, however, remained in the hands of the traditionalists: Glazunov (until 1928) and Maximilian Steinberg in Leningrad, Ippolitov-Ivanov in Moscow, and Glière in Kiev. As a result, the conservatories retained a direct link with the Belyayev aesthetic. Responsibility for the training of musicians was vested mainly in Vladimir Shcherbachov in Leningrad and in Nikolai Myaskovsky in Moscow. Both had been known as progressive composers before the Revolution, though after 1917 their modernistic élan gradually declined. Myaskovsky gained greatly in prestige thanks to the generous support he gave to young talent and to his insistence on technical mastery. His colleagues and students called him "the musical conscience of Moscow."

Soviet musicology was established with the help of Boris Asafyev, who in 1921 was put in charge of the music division of the Russian Institute of Arts History in Leningrad. (In Moscow, this discipline was practiced at the Moscow Academy for Arts Sciences.) One of the peaks of early Soviet musicology was the pioneering publication by Pavel Lamm of Musorgsky's work, beginning in 1928 and continuing until 1939, when the series was abruptly cut short. The impetus for this undertaking was the Paris performance of *Boris Godunov* in Rimsky-Korsakov's adaptation, which had aroused curiosity about the original. Paradoxically, Lamm's edition did not lead to any sweeping change in performance practice in the Soviet Union, where Rimsky-Korsakov's version of *Boris Godunov* held on at Moscow's Bolshoy Theater until the *glasnost* period.

Among performing musicians, too, the protagonists of Soviet music culture emerged during the NEP. From 1927, Soviet virtuosos began to flock to international music competitions. The Beethoven Quartet was formed in Moscow as one of many famous groups.

In the field of composition, it became clear as early as 1926 that the face of Soviet music would be shaped to a significant degree by Dmitry

Shostakovich. Shostakovich had finished his studies at the Leningrad Conservatory the previous year at the age of twenty. On 12 May 1926 his First Symphony enjoyed a triumphant première. The work made so deep an impression on the German conductor Bruno Walter that he performed it in Berlin on 6 February 1928. Shostakovich was fortunate in that he could profit from the close international contacts maintained by Russian musicians. During the NEP, leading foreign conductors, including Bruno Walter, Otto Klemperer, and Pierre Monteux, appeared in Leningrad and Moscow. Modern composers—Milhaud, Hindemith, Berg, and Schreker—also presented their work there. All this enabled Shostakovich to keep abreast of the latest trends in international music. The next generation of composers would have no such luck.

An example of the close international ties between Soviet and foreign musicians at the time was the joint publication of Russian scores by MUZGIZ—the state music publishing house—and the Viennese publishers Universal Edition. Soviet composers were also given the opportunity to participate in international festivals. Samuel Feinberg, Myaskovsky, Alexander Mosolov, and Lev Knipper, to name a few, represented their country at the festivals of the International Society for Contemporary Music (ISCM), for example.

An important institutional development during the NEP was the organization of all the arts into large coordinating societies. In 1923 the Association for Contemporary Music (ASM) was founded in Moscow. It promoted concerts of contemporary music and maintained close contacts with the ISCM in London. Its founders included Nikolai Myaskovsky, Victor Belyayev, Leonid Sabaneyev, and Pavel Lamm. The Moscow section published its own journal, *Sovremennaya muzïka* (Contemporary music).

In Leningrad, Boris Asafyev took the lead, founding a study group in 1922 devoted to the latest developments. He also wrote numerous articles on modern music under the pen name of Igor Glebov. His critical activities culminated in such pioneering publications as his *Book on Stravinsky* (1929)—still one of the classic works on this composer—and *Musical Form as a Process* (1930). As head of the music section of the Institute of Arts History, Asafyev, in collaboration with the Leningrad Philharmonic Orchestra, started his own concert series devoted to modern music. In 1926 the Leningrad branch of ASM (LASM) was established, splitting soon afterward into LASM and the Circle for New Music. Under the leadership of Asafyev and Shcherbachov, the Circle encouraged the most radical currents. In 1927 the two bodies merged again. Such modernists as Roslavets, Mosolov, Polovinkin, and Knipper were active in the administration of ASM.

The regime did not interfere directly in the affairs of ASM, but it did adopt a negative attitude toward it. The main opposition came from proletarian groups, which, although formally independent of the Communist Party, nevertheless had strong links with it. After the abolition of PROLETKULT, proletarian groups emerged in all artistic circles: the Russian Association of Proletarian Writers (VAPP, later renamed RAPP), the Association of Proletarian Musicians (RAPM), the Association of Revolutionary Russian Artists (AKHRR), and the Young Workers' Theater (TRAM). Unlike PROLETKULT, which still considered itself a broad cultural movement covering all the arts, ideology, and daily life, these groups specialized in separate branches of art. Demanding the continuing proletarization of culture, they believed that their efforts would help to consolidate the power of the working class.[10] On the whole, the proletarian groups of the 1920s proved more militant than their PROLETKULT predecessors. In literature, they actively opposed the *poputchiki,* the fellow travelers; in music they challenged ASM.

The Russian Association of Proletarian Musicians, or RAPM, was founded in 1923. The "Rapmovites" decried modernism as a product of bourgeois ideology. While ASM argued that the revolution necessitated new forms of expression, RAPM maintained that the Revolution had been made expressly for the working class. This meant that all culture must benefit the proletariat and be understood by them.

The Proletarian Musicians were not a united body. In 1925 a splinter group broke away under the name of ORKIMD (Organization of Revolutionary Composers and Musical Workers). This group, which concentrated on propaganda activities, was dissolved in 1929. Also in 1925 another proletarian group emerged, the PROKOLL (Production Collective of Student Composers), which was attached to the Moscow Conservatory. Its members collaborated on operas and oratorios, seeking a middle road between the extremes of ASM and of RAPM.

## ASM VERSUS RAPM

### THE ASMOVITES

The composers in ASM did not have a common program. They were a random collection of people with a variety of standpoints and styles, often no more than extensions of prerevolutionary currents. In the work of Myaskovsky and Shcherbachov, for instance, ASM maintained a close link with the modernism of the Silver Age. Vladimir Shcherbachov's massive Second Symphony (1925) for choir, soloists, and orchestra, the so-called *Blok* Symphony, was a late tribute to symbolism. Based on texts by Alexander Blok, the work reflects the spiritual search for the secret of life, with Dante as guide.

Nikolai Myaskovsky had been active in Russian music before the Revolution but enjoyed no real success until 1921, when he was discharged from the army and appointed professor of composition at the Moscow Conservatory. His Fourth and Fifth Symphonies (1917–18 and 1918) were conceived while he fought at the Austrian front. The première performance of the Fifth in 1920 earned the work the reputation of being the first Soviet symphony. The Sixth Symphony (1922–23) was intended as an expression of the revolutionary spirit, and included a finale replete with songs from the French Revolution. Yet the tone of the work was tragic rather than optimistic. In the finale the revolutionary songs were overshadowed by the *Dies Irae* and an Orthodox funeral hymn.

Myaskovsky's style was at first highly chromatic, subjective, and emotional. From the mid-1920s, however, he began to aim at simplification, objectivity, and direct communication with the Soviet public. His Seventh through Twelfth Symphonies bear traces of this search, which is reflected among other things in growing interest in folk themes. Some of the symphonies had a programmatic character. The Eighth, for example, was based on the story of the Russian folk hero Stenka Razin, and the Tenth was inspired by Pushkin's poem *The Bronze Horseman*.

While Myaskovsky gradually retreated from modernism, other Asmovites stuck to their progressive position, justifying their attitude with the argument that the Revolution demanded an appropriate musical expression. To them, musical modernism was the logical response to the social revolution. To defend that view, Leonid Sabaneyev recalled the dictum of the nineteenth-century aesthetician Hanslick that music was devoid of content. According to Sabaneyev, music did not become more revolutionary if it was labeled with a political message:

> Music as such has no ideology, and cannot have one; music does not express ideas, nor represent "logical" structures; it exists in its own world of musical sound and musical ideas, and purely musical logic. It is a world in itself, from which a breakthrough to logic and ideology normally involves force and artificiality. As a result, no single ideology, not even the most modern, can be considered the source of modern music, unless it has been absorbed into the musical element itself and has helped to organize the world of sound in a new way.

Sabaneyev ends with the claim that music can give expression to a new ideology only if it renews its own sound material:

> Modern music only begins the moment emotional or ideological progress affects the sound material itself, when that material is organized in a different way, but not while it remains conservative and has new texts "with a contemporary content" added to it. In a revolutionary age, "revolutionary art" is not art with revolutionary themes, but art that has transformed its technique under the influence of the times and of its ideas.[11]

The composer who took the call for material renewal most seriously was Nikolai Roslavets, who had developed his new tonal system even before the Revolution. Roslavets's "synthetic chords" were characterized by their specific and constant interval structure. By the transposition of tone complexes on all degrees of the chromatic scale, his system is close to Schoenberg's dodecaphonic music. The great difference is that whereas the pitch sequence is strictly determined with Schoenberg, Roslavets is more concerned with the interval structure, and consequently with the harmonic color, of the tone complex. Pitch sequences play no structural role in his music. Roslavets began to develop his ideas systematically in the 1920s, first in piano and chamber music, and later also in large orchestral works such as the Violin Concerto of 1925.

Roslavets held influential positions. From 1921 to 1923 he was director of the Kharkov Conservatory, a publisher in the official state music publishing house, and editor of *Muzïkalnaya kultura* (Music culture). In this journal, he defended his modernism against the skepticism of the proletarian groups.

Roslavets believed that modernism was justified by the Marxist principle of historical continuity. According to Marx, history follows a determined course and man need merely discover the underlying laws and act accordingly. Roslavets argued that the proletarian revolution would lead not only to the classless society, but also to a new consciousness. Music had to follow that development, had to be able to express the new consciousness. Hence it had constantly to evolve and be future oriented. Roslavets also believed that Soviet music must first appropriate the past achievements of bourgeois music to complete what bourgeois culture had left unfinished.

In his own work, Roslavets proved to be a musical positivist. He opposed anarchism in music, arguing that only a clear, rational system could be of any use. As he put it, "I believe that this system is destined to replace the classical system that we have at last outgrown and to place solid foundations under the 'intuitive' (actually anarchist) creative methods with which most contemporary composers are working nowadays." Roslavets considered his rational method an advance on bourgeois idealism, which looked for the origins of music in inspiration. "I know that the creative act is no mystical 'trance,' no 'divine discovery,' but a moment of the greatest concentration of the human intellect which aims to give conscious form to the 'unconscious.'" According to Roslavets, the emotional impact of music depends on the receptivity of the listener. He argued that there were no more or less emotional works of art, "but only people with a greater or smaller emotional compass who, on taking in a work of art, discover the 'sum of emotions' in it, which corresponds to the size of their emotional apparatus."[12]

Other composers extended the development of new tonal systems to the microtone sphere. Georgiy Rimsky-Korsakov founded the Society for Quarter-Tone Music in 1923, which gave concerts in Leningrad from 1925 to 1932. He wrote theoretical papers on the subject and produced several compositions. Other composers of microtone music included Alexander Kenel in Leningrad and Arseniy Avraamov in Moscow. Lev Termen, better known as Leon Theremin, did research into the possible application of electronics to music. He ran an electronic sound research laboratory in Leningrad and was the designer of "Termenvox," an early type of electronic instrument. Andrey Pashchenko wrote a *Symphonic Mystery* for Termenvox and orchestra in 1924, and Joseph Schillinger composed his *First Airphonic Suite* in 1929.

Constructivism was the Soviet successor to futurism. Like the futurists, the constructivists tried to break down the barrier between life and art. In music, constructivism stood for the abolition of traditional sounds by emphasizing industrial and urban acoustic effects. "Musical orgies" were staged, in which engines, turbines, and sirens served as instruments, and symphonies of factory whistles were performed. In 1922 a concert to celebrate the fifth anniversary of the October Revolution was given in Baku. The "instruments" were provided by the Caspian Fleet: foghorns, factory sirens, two artillery batteries, machine guns, and airplanes.[13]

When combined with more traditional music, constructivism led to the writing of such symphonic works as *Zavod* (The iron foundry), composed by Alexander Mosolov in 1926–27. This work caused a sensation at the Festival of Modern Music in Liège. It was planned as part of the ballet *Stal* (Steel) to a scenario by Inna Chernetskaya. Modeled on Honegger's *Pacific 231* and on Milhaud's *Machines agricoles*, *Zavod* is an attempt to capture industrial sound with a symphonic orchestra.

As might be expected, it is a noisy work, its texture built up from small ostinato cells.

In 1926 Vladimir Deshevov wrote the music for the play *Relsy* (Rails), an "industrial melodrama." The music was an imitation of industrial sounds by an ensemble of two violins, double bass, flute, clarinet, trombone, piano (with paper inserted between the strings), xylophone, cymbals, and bass drum. The only fragment to survive is a piano score, also called "Rails." The constructivist's attempt to bridge the gulf between art and daily life was reflected also in a collection of songs by Mosolov entitled *Newspaper Advertisements* (1926), in which banal advertisements from *Izvestia* were presented as art songs.

### OPPOSITION FROM THE RAPMOVITES

Sabaneyev's and Roslavets's arguments failed to impress the Rapmovites; indeed, they provided a great deal of ammunition with which the Rapmovites fired back. The fact that the Asmovites so openly claimed that their art was built on bourgeois achievements was reason enough to accuse them of a bourgeois mentality: "Everything comes down to this, that N. Roslavets's purest bourgeois essence hides under that quasi-Marxist phraseology."[14]

Roslavets tried to cover himself by playing on his "proletarian" origins (he came from Ukrainian peasant stock):

> By any social criteria, I am, so to speak, an "intellectual proletarian." . . . But I am no "proletarian composer" in the sense of writing bad music "for the masses" in the style of Bortnyansky or Galuppi. Far from it, I am so "bourgeois" that I consider the Russian proletariat—the rightful heir to all the culture that came before—worthy of the best in music, and that is precisely why my symphonies, quartets, trios, songs, and other "brain twisters," as my . . . critics label them in their blessed ignorance, are written for them, because I am firmly convinced that I shall still witness the time when music will be as intelligible and accessible to the proletariat as it now is to the best representatives of the progressive Russian musical community. And then, who knows, the moment may well arrive when the Russian proletariat will call my art their own.[15]

Under the pen name of Dialecticus, Roslavets wrote in 1924: "Asking the proletariat to ignore all the newest artistic achievements under the pretext that they are part of bourgeois culture is as senseless as wishing to proscribe chemistry because imperialism has invented chemical warfare."[16] Roslavets's opponents did not share this view: "N. Roslavets is a true apologist and 'theorist' of bourgeois decadence in music. . . . It is natural that the proletariat should neither approve nor comprehend these works. N. Roslavets realizes that and must therefore seek a theoretical justification for his work." The writer of this statement, L. Kaltat, considered it his duty "to unmask the bourgeois essence of Roslavets and his supporters, to isolate him ideologically from the musical community of the Soviet Union and thus to preserve the community from the pernicious influence of such 'theorists.'"[17]

The Proletarian Musicians were above all opposed to the "individualism" and elitist character of Roslavets's art. In their rejection of elitism they were considerably more militant than PROLETKULT, which had felt the mitigating influence of the prerevolutionary intelligentsia. Even the aims of the PROLETKULT movement had had a paternalistic objective: to take cultural life to the masses. Following a nineteenth-century tradition, the leaders of PROLETKULT had appealed to the *narod* ("the nation") and not explicitly to the proletariat.[18] All that was to change in the 1920s. The champions of proletarian culture took the *narod* concept far more literally and adopted a more radical view of the problem: "The proletariat seeks not only a political but also a cultural dictatorship. Proletarian culture and art tend to become human in the broadest senses."[19] They saw proletarian internationalism as the opposite of bourgeois cosmopolitanism. The difference, according to them, lay mainly in the importance the two attached to national culture, which played no part in bourgeois cosmopolitanism, but a considerable one in proletarian internationalism. The national element was considered the cornerstone of proletarian culture. In music, folk song was assigned the most important role once again. "Proletarian in content, national in form," was the new slogan.

Constructivism, too, was dismissed by the Rapmovites as a product of bourgeois decadence, as the last word of a dying culture that had emerged during the phase of capitalist industrialization:

> The industrial bourgeois class has . . . developed a philosophy of its own. It has "mechanized" the entire world, mankind included. For the capitalists of the industrial age man is simply an object for production, an object that produces surplus value for them. He is no more than an appendage of the machine. . . . Hence the "devitalization," the extirpation of "feelings," a-psychologization as one of the characteristics of "contemporary" art.

Instead, the same writer continued, the proletariat seeks a "new psyche": "The class whose human feelings have for a long time been mistaken and not given any opportunities to develop, demands of its artists in the first place no schemes or abstractions of 'constructions,' but works of art filled with living, too long suppressed, emotions, works that help them to fully unfold and develop their young emotions."[20]

## RAPM IN POWER

RAPM had been founded in June 1923 by Lev Shulgin, David Chernomordikov, and Alexey Sergeyev, employees of the Agitational Department (Agitotdel) of the State Press's Music Section. At first, it was meant as an advisory body and organizational aid to Agitotdel, the objective being to secure the hegemony of the proletariat in music. RAPM soon acquired a competitor when Shulgin and Sergeyev left the organization in 1924 to form ORKIMD, the Association of Revolutionary Composers and Musical Activists. The only composer of distinction to remain in RAPM was Alexander Kastalsky, who made his name before the Revolution as a composer of liturgical music, but who also had experience supervising a railway workers' choir and orchestra. Other members of RAPM were for the most part teachers and journalists. In 1926, the leadership was taken over by Lev Lebedinsky.

Because of the lack of composers in the group, as well as financial and organizational problems, RAPM found itself on the periphery of musical life. It was primarily a political group, more than a creative organization. The situation changed when the first Five-Year Plan was announced in 1928, putting an end to the liberal phase in Soviet culture. The internationalism of the NEP era was replaced by a xenophobic nationalism that was closer in spirit to RAPM than to the internationalist ASM. The first Five-Year Plan aimed to realize the definitive proletarization of Soviet society. Before Stalin began his megalomaniacal project of industrializing and collectivizing the entire Soviet Union at top speed, he first secured his political position, eliminating all forms of opposition within the party and seizing full control of the army and the secret police. The Five-Year Plan was intended to turn all workers on the land and in industry into state employees. It was a period of forced industrialization, collectivization, and unprecedented political violence. On the land, collectivization went hand in hand with the eradication of the richer peasants, the so-called kulaks, and with mass arrests and famine.

The whole process, which was presented as a Second Revolution, was to be completed by a revolution in culture. In December 1928, therefore, the Central Committee of the Communist Party placed all cultural bodies under the control of proletarian organizations. In music, this meant that RAPM gained an entry into the entire musical apparatus—a position that was bolstered when its most serious rival, ORKIMD, was disbanded in October 1929.

RAPM quickly consolidated its position. Its cells appeared in the conservatories and theaters, at radio stations and the State Music Press. Professionally trained composers joined its ranks, among others Alexander Davidenko, Boris Shekhter, Marian Koval, and Victory Beliy. The radicalism of RAPM now reached its peak. Its policy was militantly antimodernist, anti-Western, and anticlassical. On top of that, the organization launched a frontal assault on the composers of "light genres": it condemned most urban popular music because of its "narcotic" effect on listeners; the popular dance music of the 1920s—the fox-trot, tango, shimmy, and Charleston—was rejected because of its sensuality and eroticism; and jazz was censured as a product of the "slave culture of capitalism."

In their own compositions, RAPM composers favored short vocal pieces. The songs focused on revolutionary themes, such as paying homage to Lenin, the historic destiny of Soviet youth, the Soviet transformation of the countryside, and the glory of the armed forces. In their work, however, RAPM composers were seldom able to replace the music they condemned with viable alternatives. Amy Nelson characterizes their work thus:

> Pretension does distinguish these pieces. RAPM composers purported to write "music for millions." Yet many of the "mass songs" are not terribly easy to sing, and even the piano and accordion accompaniments are often moderately difficult. Even those with "hummable" melodies required practice and the ability to read music if they were to be thoroughly learned. RAPM composers refused to "write down" to their audience. Although they underwent constant soul-searching to identify the musical language that would deserve the designation "proletarian," their ideology convinced them that the form and content of this new music would have clear debts to the "best" of the nineteenth-century legacy.[21]

RAPM gained influence in the conservatories as well. The curriculum was radically revised, and such composers as Myaskovsky, Glière, and Gnesin were dismissed from their professorships. All entrance examinations were abolished; only proletarian students were admitted. Composers were expected to work in collectives. PROKOLL in Moscow commissioned operas and oratorios composed by groups that made use of mass songs alone. In 1931, the Moscow Conservatory was renamed the Felix

Kon School of Higher Musical Education, in honor of the editor of the
*Workers' Gazette.*[22]

## PERESTROYKA

The results of the Five-Year Plan were disastrous. As the economist Alec
Nove notes, "1933 was the culmination of the most precipitous peace-
time decline in living standards known in recorded history."[23] With its
notorious show trials, the Party leadership tried to shift the blame for
all the misery onto local officials and "saboteurs." To regain the support
of the intelligentsia, the power of the proletarian organizations was
curbed once more. In a decree dated 23 April 1932, the Central Committee of the Communist Party ordered a *perestroyka,* or "restructuring," of literary and artistic organizations. RAPM was dissolved, as were
comparable organizations in the other arts. Each artistic discipline was
given its own coordinating body. For music, that body was the Union of
Soviet Composers, organized first in Moscow and Leningrad, then
throughout the land. As a result, the whole of Soviet musical life became
centralized. From then on, the Union of Soviet Composers was the only
body entitled to commission and publish Soviet music or to present concerts. Composers were obliged to attend meetings at which their work
was discussed and criticized while it was still in progress, a practice that
gave rise to the typical Soviet phenomenon known as "Bolshevik self-
criticism." Composers were expected to allow their work to be constantly
examined by colleagues and to take account of their views. Refusal was
considered an unconstructive attitude and a sign of bourgeois individualism. From 1933 onward, the findings of such forums were published
in the union's journal, *Sovyetskaya muzïka* (Soviet music).

Significantly, the concentration of power in the Union of Soviet Composers lay in the hands of its bureaucrats. Nikolai Chelyapov was named
chairman of the Moscow branch and editor of *Sovyetskaya muzïka.* He
was not a musician, but a general-purpose bureaucrat who had to answer to the Committee on Artistic Affairs, a division of the Council of
People's Commissars. With his appointment, centralized control of music was complete.

At first, the *perestroyka* was greeted with acclaim, the Party resolution by which it was heralded generally praised as an event of historic
importance. Feeling that at long last they had been liberated from the
yoke of the hated RAPM, most composers viewed the establishment of
the Composers Union with optimism. The older ones were allowed to

resume their posts in the conservatories. Furthermore, they were given honorable positions in the union side by side with the youngest generation, that is, with the pupils of their pupils.

## SOCIALIST REALISM

At the First Congress of Soviet Writers, held in 1934, the official Soviet aesthetic was declared binding and normative. The Party's representative, Andrey Zhdanov, declared that socialist realism was now the common aesthetic of all Soviet writers. Their aim should henceforth be "to depict reality in its revolutionary development."[24] To lend these developments prestige, the authorities invited Maxim Gorky, one of the foremost *éminences grises* of Russian literature, to deliver an address. Gorky, who had just returned from abroad, said, among other things:

> We still do not see reality adequately. Even the landscape of our country has drastically changed: its particolored character has disappeared—a bluish strip of oats, a black patch of plowed land next to it, a golden ribbon of rye, a greenish one of wheat, strips of land overgrown with weeds, altogether—the multicolored sorrow of overall scatteredness [and] disunity. Today huge expanses of land are colored mightily, with one color.[25]

This passage is most revealing. Gorky claimed that Soviet writers still faltered in their perception of reality. A correct view would soon help them to detect the signs of the ideal state toward which reality evolves. That ideal state is characterized by uniformity, which must be seen as a victory over petty divisions. The monochrome landscape thus becomes a picture of heroic greatness, the picturesque and multicolored landscape, by contrast, a symbol of petit bourgeois self-interest.

Applied to art, Gorky's picture comprises two characteristics essential for socialist realism: first, the artist must see reality in its evolution toward the socialist ideal; second, individual creativity must make way for communal and comparable work. The first aspect reflects the difference between socialist realism and nineteenth-century realism: the critical view with which reality used to be observed has become outdated, because reality has moved positively ahead. The second aspect means the rejection of the "l'art pour l'art" principle. Every manifestation of autonomous aestheticism would henceforth be labeled "formalism."

Socialist realism is often seen as marking a definite break with avant-garde developments since the Silver Age. Insofar as it involves the rejection of artistic experiments and the underestimation of the creative personality, that view is correct. Yet a connection still exists with the earlier principle of *zhiznetvorchestvo:* the belief that art influences life. Gorky's picture bears traces of the futurist dream that the human will can shape the world. Such thinkers as Nikolai Chuzhak and Sergey Tretyakov constituted the links between symbolism and futurism, on the one hand, and socialist realism, on the other. Both had tried to combine Solovyov's theory with Marxism. They dethroned the artistic ego of the symbolists and futurists and assigned the role of artistic demiurge to the masses. Chuzhak called the Russian proletariat "the Pygmalion who brought to life the Galatea of Futurism and turned the evolutionary tasks of art into the task of creating revolution."[26] Tretyakov, for his part, specified the kind of reality the Soviet artist must come to grips with: "Not *bït* [life] in its inertia and dependence on an established pattern of things, but *bïtiye*—a dialectically perceived reality that is in a state of perpetual formation—reality understood as progress toward the commune, which is not to be forgotten for a single minute."[27] The vague symbolist idea of the future was now given a clear shape: that of communism.

Socialist realism was both the consequence and the negation of avant-garde trends. It held fast to the aesthetic utopia of Russian modernism, in which art played an active role in the creation of life; at the same time, it curbed the ambitions of art. At issue was a clear delimitation of the terrain in which art was allowed to operate. Artists were no longer permitted to concern themselves with the practical aspects of the construction of the new life. The Party had appropriated that role and brooked no competition. It alone was the supreme arbiter of what shape society must adopt, and by what means. What art could do was help the process along and pass the message on to the masses.

Since the time of PROLETKULT, the Party had been apprehensive about competition from artists. In his study of the totalitarian art of Stalinism, Boris Groys suggests that suspicion was the probable explanation for the artistic repression to come: "There would have been no need to suppress the avant-garde if its black squares and transrational poetry confined themselves to artistic space, but the fact that it was persecuted indicates that it was operating on the same territory as the state."[28] Art was now subordinated to the Party and was set the task of training the people along the right lines. Writers had to become "engineers of the human mind," in accordance with a slogan attributed to Stalin, but which in fact went back to Tretyakov's definition of the artist as "psycho-engineer" and "psycho-constructor."[29]

The subordination of art to the objectives of the Party was labeled *partiynost'*, while ideological correctness was given the name of *ideynost'*. These two criteria were combined with a third, *narodnost'*, close ties with the people, reflecting the demand that art must be understood by all. The insistence on direct accessibility involved a conservative element, which amounted in particular to a renewed bond with the national tradition. Stalin summed this ideal up with the slogan "National in form, socialist in content."

The combining of all aesthetic norms into a common denominator had typically Russian antecedents: it seemed like the sovietization of the Official Nationality of Nicholas I. The concepts of "autocracy" and "orthodoxy" were absorbed into the new ideology of socialism, and *narodnost'* was retained.

The similarity of socialist realism to Official Nationality was not its only link with the Russian past. The underlying theory also reflected Lev Tolstoy's aesthetic. In his later, moralizing, period, Tolstoy resolutely subordinated form and style to content, proclaiming that the unification of mankind was the real objective of art. According to him, beauty was naturally comprehensible and needed no explanation. Similarly, socialist realism evaluated art by its content and comprehensibility, rather than by its formal refinement or stylistic originality.

The application of socialist realism to music was a far from self-evident step. The relationship between music and reality has always been a thorny question. Originally, realism was projected into music in the most simplistic and lucrative manner by association and paraphrase. That state of affairs caused Shostakovich to protest vehemently in 1933 in his article "Soviet Music Criticism Is Lagging": "When a critic writes that in such-and-such a symphony, Soviet civil servants are represented by the oboe and the clarinet, and Red Army men by the brass section, then you want to scream!"[30] A more satisfactory relationship between musical expression and verbal explanation was put forward by Boris Asafyev. In his two main works, *Musical Form as a Process* (1930) and *Intonatsiya* (1947), he lays a useful theoretical basis for the verbal exegesis of music. Asafyev distinguishes two concepts for linking music to the phenomenal world: "*intonatsiya*" and "musical picture." The first signifies every possible sonorous effect in the phenomenal world, from the sound of raindrops to the thunderous noise of an explosion. A musical *intonatsiya* appears when such sound effects from the real world are used in a musical phrase: the music retains from the original effects precisely those qualities that convey a meaning or elicit an emotion. The combination of "intonations" into a coherent whole then determines the "musical pic-

ture" of a work. By means of an inner musical logic, the composer re-
arranges affective phenomena connected with the world of human emotions. The musical picture has the power to evoke feelings, ideas, and
associations in the listener. Asafyev's theory has retained its vitality.
Stripped of all the doctrinal implications of socialist realism, it is today
an important source of inspiration, even in Western musicology, for taking a fresh look at musical semantics.[31]

Yet references to reality were not the most important characteristics of
socialist realism in music. An adequate picture of Soviet reality called
above all for a monumental approach and an exalted rhetoric based in
optimism. In his first article as editor of *Sovyetskaya muzïka*, Nikolai
Chelyapov turned monumentality into the new criterion of Soviet music.
Wishing to distinguish the aesthetic of the new Union of Soviet Composers
from that of the former RAPM, he rejected the pettiness of mass songs in
favor of the monumentality of symphonies, program-symphonies, and
oratorios. The excesses of the avant-garde of the 1920s were rejected.
Composers were expected to return to "healthy and normal" values,
which meant chiefly to follow the classical Russian examples. The elevation of the "Russian Classics" to the status of models satisfied the first
part of the slogan "National in form, socialist in content." As for the
second part, Vladimir Iokhelson put it thus:

> Socialist realism is above all a style of profound optimism. The whole his-
> torical experience of the proletariat is optimistic in essence. And we can and
> must affirm that optimism is intended as an obligatory feature of this style,
> its very essence. It is a style that includes heroics, but a heroics that is not
> merely tied to narrow personal interests. Here we mean a heroics of an indi-
> vidual connected with the mass, and of a mass that is capable of bringing forth
> such a hero.[32]

Socialist realism resulted in a form of provincial conservatism that severed the link between Soviet music and international modernism. Soviet
compositions were judged first and foremost by "what," not by "how."
The stylistic and technical experiments that continued to flourish in the
West were dismissed in the Soviet Union as unnecessary. In their stead,
Soviet music kept the monumental forms of the nineteenth century
artificially alive, even as the traditional forms were being discarded by
the West.

An important aspect of socialist realism in music was the policy of es-
tablishing national music centers in the Caucasian and Central Asian republics of the Soviet Union. The project was launched in 1934, just when
*Sovyetskaya muzïka* adopted the slogan "National in form, socialist in

content." Soviet composers were expected to ensure the proper application of this formula. Only the external form, not the content, was allowed to be national, lest Soviet music lapse into nineteenth-century bourgeois nationalism.

According to the official ideology, the acceptance of national cultures was a strategic step toward the construction of a uniform Soviet culture. As Stalin stated,

> Under the conditions of a dictatorship of the proletariat within a single country, the rise of cultures national in form and socialist in content has to take place, so that when the proletariat wins in the whole world and socialism is a part of ordinary life, these cultures will merge into one culture, socialist both in form and in content, with a common language.[33]

This policy resulted in veritable artistic colonialism as Western musical institutes—conservatories, opera houses, symphony orchestras—were imported into the most remote republics. These were urged to set up their own national operas. Where local composers were not yet active, composers from Moscow and Leningrad were summoned into the breach. They wrote works in a style they deemed appropriate to the required national idiom, which generally meant producing copies of nineteenth-century models.

The results were often bizarre. Uzbek national operas were written by a group of three composers, two Russians and one Uzbek. The group became known under its composite name of Vlasov-Feré-Maldïbayev. Another composer, Sergey Balasanyan, though of Armenian descent and brought up in Turkmenistan, became the Tadzhik national composer. Reinhold Glière composed the first Azerbaijani opera and later placed his art in the service of Uzbekistan. Mosolov and Roslavets specialized in the development of Turkmen music.

The best-known composer to work on this nationalist project was Aram Khachaturyan, who became known as the leading composer of the Armenian nation. Khachaturyan, however, was born in Georgia, lived in Moscow, and based his style on nineteenth-century orientalism modeled on Glinka, Balakirev, and Borodin. Nevertheless, Moscow came gradually to look on Khachaturyan as the musical spokesman of the entire Soviet East.[34]

## DMITRY SHOSTAKOVICH: 1926–36

Although the 1920s may be called a decade of intense creativity in the Soviet Union, they yielded little music of lasting value. This was due in part to the repression that followed in the 1930s and led to the removal of the names of many composers from the annals of Soviet music. The music of such modernists as Roslavets and Mosolov has only recently been dusted off, and we still know very little about the musical activities of RAPM. Yet repression was not the sole cause of the limited impact Russian music made in the twenties. Musical creation was complicated by the extreme demands composers were expected to satisfy, which amounted to an irreconcilable clash in aesthetic points of view. In response, some composers resorted to artificial experiments or modernistic clichés, while others took refuge in an ideological message that they then labored hard to convey.

Attempts to give symphonic works an "actual" ideological content included Alexander Kastalsky's *Agricultural Symphony* (1923), Mikhaíl Gnesin's *Symphonic Monument 1905–1917* (1925), Alexander Krein's *Mourning Ode to Lenin* (1926), and the *Symphonic Dithyrambus* (1932) by the same composer, subtitled "The USSR—the Shock Brigade of the World Proletariat." The text of this hybrid work is in part derived from Stalin's speech "On the Tasks of Economists."[35]

Soviet opera had a difficult start. Even the best examples, such as Lev Knipper's *North Wind* and Vladimir Deshevov's *Ice and Steel*, did not convince the critics. *North Wind* deals with the execution of twenty-six commissars in Baku during the civil war; *Ice and Steel* with the Kronstadt mutiny of 1921. The reviewers were agreed that the music was not impressive enough to be worthy of such weighty subjects. A topical Soviet ballet was *The Football Players* by Victor Oransky, in which the difference between the Soviet Union and the decadent West was expressed in the musical distinction between revolutionary songs and jazz.

The most important creative work of this period was that of Dmitry Shostakovich. Together with Myaskovsky he wrote music of lasting significance during the first Soviet period, that is, the period between 1926—the year of his First Symphony—and 1936, when the Party leadership shackled his creativity. While Myaskovsky gradually retreated from his progressive, prerevolutionary style, Shostakovich persisted in his youthful enthusiasm. Myaskovsky became a link with the tradition, Shostakovich a passionate champion of Soviet modernism. In Shostakovich's early work, Soviet culture of the 1920s received its clearest musical expression, as witness the astonishing First Symphony, the daring symphonic experiments from the Second to the Fourth Symphonies, the ballets *The Golden Age, The Bolt,* and *The Limpid Stream,* and finally the two operas *The Nose* and *The Lady Macbeth of the Mtsensk District.*

We have mentioned the success of Shostakovich's First Symphony. The score on which he worked from October 1924 to July 1925 was the graduation piece with which he rounded off his study of composition at the Leningrad Conservatory. Considered by the conductor Nikolai Malko to be suitable for performance, the symphony was given a rousing première on 12 May 1926 by the Leningrad Philharmonic Orchestra. Malko recommended the work to Bruno Walter, who conducted it on 6 February 1928 in Berlin with the Berlin Philharmonic Orchestra, on 14 November 1930 in Vienna, and a month later in Mannheim.[36] In the United States, the symphony was performed under the baton of Stokowski in Philadelphia on 2 November 1928, Rodzinski in New York, and Toscanini, who made it part of his repertoire in 1931.

Shostakovich's First Symphony contains a great deal of contrasting material, with divergent characteristics arranged in various thematic blocks. The angular melodic contours are reminiscent of Prokofiev, the scherzo particularly so. The contrast between the combinations of sounds can be very marked, for instance in the transition of the tutti passage to the three piano chords at the end of the scherzo. The third movement is lyrical in character. In his First Piano Sonata (1926), Shostakovich continued on the same road of abstraction and dissonance.

In February 1927 Shostakovich received a commission from the propaganda section of the state publishing house to compose a symphonic work to celebrate the tenth anniversary of the October Revolution. The work, completed in August 1927, originally bore the title *To October;* this was fixed subsequently, the work ultimately being published under the title *To October, a Symphonic Dedication.* Now known as his Second Symphony, op. 14, it was christened a "symphony" considerably later.[37] It was based on a poem by Alexander Bezïmensky (the text of which is declaimed in the finale of the symphony), who glorified Lenin's role in the struggle of the proletariat in bombastic style. The composition has all the characteristics of the agitprop music of the time, as prescribed by the Rapmovites. The symphony's originality lies above all in its beginning. Shostakovich wanted to portray the advance from chaos—the symbol of the dark past—to protest, followed by the determination to fight back, and finally by the victory of the proletariat. To reflect the chaos, Shostakovich wrote a kind of "music in sonorous planes" reminiscent of the postwar aleatoric techniques.

In the summer of 1927 Shostakovich started on his first opera, *The*

*Nose,* based on Gogol's story by that name. With it he was trying not only to achieve a breakthrough in his own career but also to begin a characteristic Soviet opera tradition. He felt that this genre had become bogged down, and wanted to end the stagnation and to breathe new life into Soviet opera by bringing it into line with the spectacular innovations in the theater and film associated with such pioneering directors as Taïrov, Nemirovich-Danchenko, Meyerhold, and Eisenstein.

Shostakovich studied the foreign operas that could be seen in Leningrad at the time: Schreker's *Der ferne Klang;* Prokofiev's *The Love for Three Oranges,* first produced in the United States; Alban Berg's *Wozzeck;* and Křenek's *Der Sprung über den Schatten* and *Jonny spielt auf.*

The most decisive influence on his work, however, was Meyerhold's. Shostakovich observed theatrical life closely, and Meyerhold's interpretation of Gogol's *The Government Inspector* made a great impression on him. In it, Meyerhold adopted a grotesque and caricatural style, not purely for reasons of stagecraft, but in an attempt to show how classical works might be reinterpreted in a Soviet context.[38] Nikolai Malko introduced Meyerhold to Shostakovich's First Symphony, hoping to help the young composer to a post in Meyerhold's theater. (In order to support his impoverished family, Shostakovich was having to play the piano for silent films in movie theaters.) At first, Meyerhold was not interested in collaborating with him. In the winter of 1927, however, he engaged Shostakovich as a pianist in his Moscow theater, and he even put him up for two months in his own home. As a result, he was able to look over Shostakovich's shoulder during the composition of *The Nose.*

The opera was intended from the outset as a frontal attack on traditional opera conventions. In the spirit of Musorgsky's *Marriage,* Shostakovich based the work on Gogol—not a play, however, but a short story, and one that hardly lent itself to the stage. Major Kovalyov, a petty bureaucrat, discovers one morning that his nose has disappeared. He then sees it walking about in the cathedral, transformed into a personage of superior rank. Kovalyov places an announcement in the newspaper and also sends the police inspector in pursuit of the nose. Once recovered and reduced to its normal size, the nose miraculously resumes its former place.

Shostakovich wrote the libretto himself, aided by Georgiy Ionin, Alexander Preys, and Yevgeniy Zamyatin. To preserve Gogol's style as much as possible, he borrowed any missing material from other texts by Gogol, such as *Marriage, Taras Bulba,* "The Fair at Sorochintsï," and "A May Night." The words of the song sung by Kovalyov's servant Ivan are taken from Dostoyevsky's *Brothers Karamazov.*

Shostakovich used every musical device to emphasize the satirical nature of the opera: naturalism in the portrayal of such everyday matters as snoring and shaving; parodies of such dance forms as marches, waltzes, and galops; an angular style of writing that eschewed lyricism; and finally, the use of special vocal techniques, such as the nasal sound with which the character of the Nose is made to sing. Grotesquely clashing color combinations, earlier adumbrated in the First Symphony, are consistently exploited. The first entr'acte is scored for unpitched percussion alone, anticipating later efforts by Edgar Varèse and John Cage.

Shostakovich aimed at the optimum integration of the music into the play. He did not call *The Nose* an opera, but a "theater symphony." "The music is not arranged in separate numbers, but flows in a single symphonic stream, and there is no system of major motifs. Interruptions only occur between the acts. Every act is a movement of a symphony written for the musical stage."[39]

Apart from the pronounced modernism of its music, the dramatic rhythm of *The Nose* is its most striking characteristic. Typical is the quick succession of events, which in the professional literature has been referred to as a "cinematographic" effect. The climax is found in the two crowd scenes of the third act. In the first, the Nose is beaten so hard by the crowd that it resumes its original size; in the second, a throng of people appears, curious to have a look at the unusual spectacle of a walking nose.

The dimensions of the opera are cumbersome: as well as chorus and orchestra there are some seventy-eight singing and nine speaking parts. Even with the doubling of parts, thirty soloists are still needed. It was thus not until 1930 that the opera was staged. Meanwhile, Shostakovich wrote the music for Meyerhold's production of Mayakovsky's *The Bedbug*, in which he was able to develop his satirical idiom further.

In July 1929 Shostakovich started his Third Symphony, called *The First of May.* Like the Second Symphony, it is a propaganda work and culminates in a chorus singing bombastic lines by Semyon Kirsanov. At about that time, proletarian groups were given a free hand in Russian cultural life. Shostakovich joined TRAM, the Young Workers Theater, in which he remained active until 1931; there he made it known that he was working on a Soviet opera and that his involvement with TRAM would help him refine his ideas. He wrote the scores for three TRAM productions: *The Shot,* by Alexander Bezïmensky; *Virgin Soil,* by Nikolai Lvov and Arkadiy Gorbenko; and *Rule Britannia,* by Adrian Piotrovsky.

On 18 January 1930 *The Nose* premièred at the Leningrad Malïy Theater, with Nikolai Smolich as director, Vladimir Dimitriyev responsible for the decor, and Samuil Samosud conducting. Shostakovich and his supporters had begun promoting the opera in the press as early as 1928. In November of that year Malko conducted a suite from the opera in Moscow, and on 16 June 1929 they organized a concert performance of the opera. The controversy unleashed by the latter performance provided a foretaste of what was to come. Ranked in opposition were the Rapmovites, who severely criticized the opera for its complexity and lack of a proper Soviet theme. The critic Daniel Zhitomirsky warned Shostakovich that he was straying from the path of Soviet art. To take the edge off these attacks, Shostakovich and his collaborators decided to arrange a trial performance before a proletarian audience.

On 14 January 1930 three scenes were shown to an audience consisting entirely of Leningrad factory workers. Shostakovich, the critic Ivan Sollertinsky, and the scenic artist Vladimir Dimitriyev introduced the piece in some detail, and the performance proved a striking success. At the actual première, however, the followers of RAPM rejected the opera for lacking a theme based on Soviet reality, for its iconoclastic style, and for the absence of classical opera elements.

The staunchest defender of the opera was Ivan Sollertinsky. Calling *The Nose* "the first original opera written in the territory of the USSR by a Soviet composer," he stressed the promise the work held out for the future: "We shall feel the beneficial effects of the renewal of the techniques in *The Nose* in the future. *The Nose* is a long range canon." The critic S. Gres met Sollertinsky's militaristic metaphor with another: he called *The Nose* "the hand bomb of an anarchist."[40] In the charged cultural atmosphere of 1930, proletarian critics had the final say. After sixteen performances, *The Nose* disappeared from the repertoire.

Shostakovich did not allow himself to be discouraged. On 27 October 1930 a new work by him had its première, following a matinée preview on 25 October and a closed performance on 26 October: the ballet *The Golden Age*, which the Leningrad Theater Committee had commissioned him to write in 1929. The scenario for the ballet had been the result of a competition. The committee had offered a prize for the best subject for a modern Soviet ballet, and the scenario *Dinamiada,* submitted by Alexander Ivanovsky, won. The work was a merciless attack on bourgeois decadence, with a plot involving a soccer match between a Soviet team and a bourgeois-fascist squad.

*The Golden Age* can be considered the Soviet equivalent of the ballets on quotidian themes so fashionable in the West since the early twenties, Jean Cocteau being a leading champion of this type. Typical of the Soviet version was its dualistic approach: a healthy culture was contrasted with a degenerate one, and there was a clear moral message about where to draw the dividing line between good and evil. Western decadence is represented by a corrupt referee, a lascivious diva, a haughty maître d'ho-tel, VIPs, and caricature policemen. Musically, their degeneracy is indi-cated by parodies of such Western dance forms as the galop, the tango, tap dancing, the polka, and the foxtrot (for the foxtrot in *The Golden Age*, Shostakovich orchestrated "Tea for Two" from *No, No, Nanette* by Vincent Youmans). The entire third act is one long fight between work-ers and capitalists relating to the release of the falsely arrested Soviet soc-cer players.

On 8 April 1931 Shostakovich's second ballet, *The Bolt*, was staged, a tale of industrial sabotage—a subject typical of the period of the first Five-Year Plan. Despite the success of the music, neither *The Golden Age* nor *The Bolt* could maintain its place in the repertoire. Shostakovich blamed the failure on a lack of coordination between the choreography and the score.

Ever since the Second Symphony, Shostakovich's compositions had been geared to the defense of the Revolution. In *The Nose* he had cre-ated a biting satire of the prerevolutionary era; in *The Golden Age* he portrayed a confrontation between a healthy culture and a decadent one in the light of the Marxist class struggle. By about 1930, he had devel-oped a full arsenal of musical techniques for expressing satire and his antibourgeois attitude. At the end of that year he started a work in which he would drive both of these aspects home: the opera *The Lady Mac-beth of the Mtsensk District*.

The opera ostensibly concerns the fate of Katerina Izmailova, a woman who fights against the suffocating influence of her surroundings. She seeks an escape in adultery and murder, but is finally found out and banished to Siberia, where she is, into the bargain, deceived by her lover, who has also been sent to Siberia. In utter despair, she drags her lover's sweetheart with her into the ice-cold waters of the Volga. The real significance of the work becomes apparent, however, only when we com-pare it with its literary source, the nineteenth-century story of the same name by Nikolai Leskov.

"In our part of the world one sometimes comes across people of such character that one cannot recall them without a shudder," Leskov starts his story. "The Lady Macbeth of the Mtsensk District" is the nickname

of Katerina Izmailova, a merchant's wife who commits adultery with the
worker Sergey, murders her father-in-law and her husband, and then—
so as not to lose her inheritance—does away with her husband's little
nephew. This murder is discovered by the villagers, who happen to be
returning from church the very moment the crime is committed. The
crowd breaks into the house. Katerina and her lover are sentenced to a
public flogging, banishment, and forced labor. On the way to Siberia,
she commits a fourth murder. This final victim is Sonyetka, the new fancy
woman of her faithless Sergey. She drags Sonyetka with her into the Volga,
and is drowned together with her rival.

Leskov's Katerina is a monster. His tale is a horror story, a painfully
detailed analysis of aberrant behavior. The hair-raising effect is magnified
by the detached style in which the story is told: Leskov presents it in the
form of an official summary of evidence for a court.

It was this Katerina Izmailova, of all people—inhumanity personified—
whom Shostakovich chose to paint in a positive light, aiming to humanize her and to justify her behavior. He portrayed her as a victim of
her milieu, a fascinating woman whose life is destroyed by the nightmare of the cruel, heartless, environment of the merchant estate in which
she lives. Hence she seeks solace in extramarital love, which, under the
relentless pressure of her surroundings, is bound to lead her to murder.

To what extent can a monster like Katerina really be excused? Mstislav
Rostropovich hit the nail on the head when he said in an interview in
1981,

> Who is Katerina Izmailova? Is she, if you will excuse me, a swine or not a
> swine? Of course, a swine. She murdered one man, then another. And there's
> basically no room for sympathy for her. But Shostakovich is constantly
> sympathizing with Katerina. She has committed murder, she's being driven
> into hard labour, and the choir sings about "heartless gendarmes." . . .
> Shostakovich calls on us to pity the killer. . . . Did Shostakovich hate the so-
> cial system so much that he justified a murderer? . . . The way I look at it,
> Shostakovich showed us a human anomaly.[41]

Shostakovich defended his choice with the argument that "Leskov was
unable to come up with the correct interpretation of the events taking
place in his story. My role as a Soviet composer consists in retaining the
power of Leskov's narrative while using a critical approach to explain
these events from our Soviet point of view."[42] In other words, Shostakovich viewed the events through the spectacles of the Marxist ideal of
progress. All human misery springs from the social order and will disappear when mankind reaches a higher stage of historical development.

In the program written for the original production, Shostakovich stated the case clearly and plainly. He explained that "there is no work of Russian literature that more vividly or expressively characterizes the position of women in the old prerevolutionary time," that "Leskov, as a brilliant representative of prerevolutionary literature, could not correctly interpret the events that unfold in his story," and that he considered it his task "in every way to justify Katerina so that she would impress the audience as a positive character." He called Katerina "a ray of light in the dark kingdom," harking back to an essay by that name written by the nineteenth-century critic Nikolai Dobrolyubov.[43] That essay, however, did not deal with Leskov's story but with Alexander Ostrovsky's play *The Storm,* well known by music lovers through Janáček's opera *Kát'a Kabanová.*

Leskov's short story and *The Storm* are vaguely related. Both portray Muscovite merchant life. The main character of both is a young woman called Katerina who enters into extramarital relations. However, Ostrovsky's approach is quite different from Leskov's. His Katerina is indeed vulnerable, the innocent victim of her tyrannical environment. She has a pure heart and is plunged into despair by her feelings of guilt. Ostrovsky's play is a classic example of critical realism, an analysis of social injustice by means of a character who commands unquestioning sympathy. Dobrolyubov treated Ostrovsky's play as a protest against the suffocating patriarchal state of the merchant class, an interpretation that Shostakovich projected into Leskov's *Lady Macbeth.* He tried to render his Katerina as innocent as possible, and for that reason omitted the murder of the child, saying in justification that "the murder of a child, no matter how it may be explained, always makes a bad impression."[44] Next he took over several elements of Ostrovsky's play, among them the scene in which Katerina swears fidelity at her husband's departure, with the difference that, with Ostrovsky, she does so of her own accord, and with Shostakovich, under pressure from her father-in-law, Boris Timofeyevich. Shostakovich also expanded the role of the latter, a sexually possessive tyrant who interferes in the marital life of his passive son and whose character is based on that of the mother-in-law Kabanikha in Ostrovsky.[45] Shostakovich portrays the father-in-law in a particularly bad light, as having designs on his daughter-in-law during his son's absence.

Shostakovich's chief means of defense of Katerina is his caustically satirical view of her surroundings. Everyone except for Katerina is portrayed negatively or ironically. The last murder is not discovered by a crowd of church worshipers, but by a drunkard, "a shabby peasant," as he is called in the libretto. The police, who are busy hunting nihilists, arrest Katerina and Sergey not because of their crimes, but because they are incensed at not having been invited to Katerina's wedding feast. The priest assisting the dying Boris Timofeyevich is likewise a cruel caricature.

The contrast between Katerina's positive character and the depravity of her environment is carefully reflected in the music. Katerina's aria is full of emotion, with splendid broad phrases and snatches of Russian folk-music intonations. For the other characters, Shostakovich deploys all the variations of his satirical idiom—circus music, operetta, vaudeville songs—all parodied with hard, clashing colors and mechanical ostinati. Apart from Katerina, there is nothing human in the opera. The murder of her husband, for instance, is justified by the music. After the lyrical passage portraying a bedroom scene between Katerina and Sergey, her husband suddenly appears. His musical portrait is so heartless and base that the listener is almost bound to approve of his murder.

The division of operatic characters into real people and caricatures is not uncommon in twentieth-century music. A classic example is Alban Berg's *Wozzeck*, an opera with which Shostakovich was familiar. Less radically, this approach is also used in Britten's *Peter Grimes*—also in order to humanize a criminal literary character, remarkably enough. No one, however, went as far as Shostakovich. As Richard Taruskin puts it:

> In his second opera [Shostakovich] proves himself a genius of the genre, fully able to create a world in tone that carries complete conviction. And he used his awesome powers to perpetrate a colossal moral inversion. In one of the most pernicious uses to which music has ever been put, he gave the lie to formalists who would deny music the ethical and expressive powers of which the ancients speak. In the hands of a genius the art of music is still the potent, dangerous thing about which Plato warned.[46]

*The Lady Macbeth of the Mtsensk District* is both a brilliant opera and a horrifying historical document. As a manifest expression of the belief in the pitiless class struggle, the opera bears witness to an age in which humanistic values were stifled by high-flown idealist propaganda. Taruskin sees the hate campaign against the prerevolutionary bourgeoisie in *Lady Macbeth* as an illustration of the manner in which the eradication of the kulaks in real life was ideologically justified.[47]

The opera was a great success. It had its première in the Maliy Thea-

ter in Leningrad on 22 January 1934, and two days later in Moscow. It
was also quick to go abroad. Before the end of 1935, it had been performed in Cleveland, New York, Argentina, Czechoslovakia, and Swe-
den. With success, Shostakovich grew more ambitious. He dreamed about
a tetralogy of operas:

> I want to write a Soviet *Ring of the Nibelungs*. It will be an operatic tetral-
> ogy about women, in which *Lady Macbeth* will take the place of *The Rhine-
> gold*. The driving image of the next opera will be a heroine of the People's
> Will movement. Next, a woman of our century. And, finally, I will portray
> our Soviet heroine, embracing collected features of women from the present
> and the future, from Larisa Reysner to Zhenya Romanko, the best female con-
> crete worker on the Dneprostroy Dam project.[48]

Shostakovich was well on the way to becoming the most influential twentieth-century opera composer. His success, however, proved short-lived—
as we shall see in chapter 12.

In *The Lady Macbeth of the Mtsensk District,* Shostakovich's art
reached its most radical ideological phase. In the Fourth Symphony,
again, he went to musical extremes. He started on the composition in
October 1935, completing it in April 1936. The demands of the work
are huge. The orchestra is extravagantly large, with a scoring of twenty
woodwinds, seventeen brass, and large complements of percussion and
strings.

The Fourth Symphony has three movements. The use of traditional
forms is purely schematic, the music unfolding in a loose concatenation
of episodes, with nothing of the conventional symphonic structure. The
orchestration is reminiscent of Mahler, but with Shostakovich there is
none of the purposive buildup of tension that Mahler still shared with
Beethoven's symphonies. Monumentality in Shostakovich's Fourth is
the result not of an underlying structural plan, but of the enthusiasm
with which the composer develops his exuberant ideas. It seems as if
Shostakovich takes all the time in the world for every single musical idea,
without wishing to force the result into a preconceived plan. Rather than
culminating in a symphonic climax, each movement ends in a fade-out.
The combination of unbridled fantasy and unconventional structure
makes Shostakovich's Fourth perhaps the most original post-Mahlerian
symphony in the repertoire.

In light of the incisive events in Shostakovich's life at about the time of
the composition of the Fourth Symphony—events discussed in Chapter
12—this symphony has sometimes been called a pessimistic work. But

while dark colors and great tensions are doubtless present in it, the whole does not make a gloomy impression. The symphony can equally well be heard as an expression of the extreme self-confidence of an intrepid young composer, of his faith in the compelling power of his musical gifts. This self-confidence was, however, to be sorely tested. After 28 January 1936 musical life in the Soviet Union was never to be the same again.

Plate 18.   Rachmaninoff and his daughter Irina at Le Bourget airport, Paris,
March 1934.

Plate 19.   Rehearsal of the reprise of Stravinsky's *Svadebka* (*Les noces*),
choreographed by Bronislava Nijinska, on the roof of the Monte Carlo
Casino in 1923.

# BALLETS RUSSES

### DE

# SERGE DE DIAGHILEW

# GAÎTÉ LYRIQUE

## 1923

Plate 20.   Cover of program for *Pulcinella* at the Gaîté Lyrique Theater
in 1923, with Picasso's original set design.

Plate 21.   Serge Lifar and Alice Nikitina in Stravinsky's *Apollon Musagète,*
choreographed by George Balanchine, 1928. Musically and choreographi-
cally, this work served as a manifesto of the classicist and Apollonian
reorientation of the Ballets Russes.

Plate 22.   Leonid Massine and Alexandra Danilova in Prokofiev's
*Le pas d'acier*, choreographed by Leonid Massine, 1927.

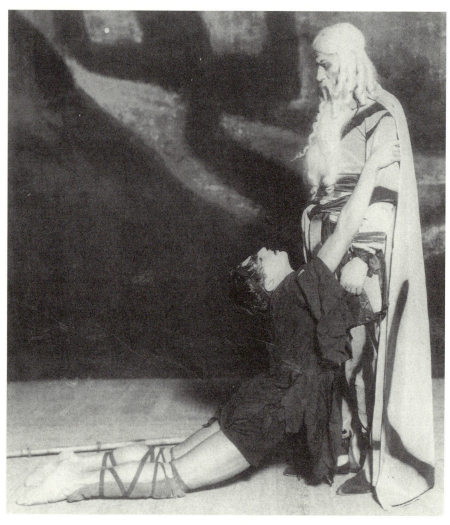

Plate 23.   The return of the prodigal son: Serge Lifar and Mikhaíl Fyodorov
in Prokofiev's *Prodigal Son*, choreographed by George Balanchine, 1929.

Plate 24.   Sergey Prokofiev and Boris Asafyev at Asafyev's house
outside Moscow during Prokofiev's first tour of the Soviet Union
in 1927.

Plate 25.   The First All-Union Congress of Soviet Composers in 1948.

Plate 26.    Dmitry Shostakovich during the conference at the Waldorf-Astoria
hotel, New York, 1949.

Plate 27.   Reception at the Kremlin on the occasion of the Third All-Union Congress of Soviet Composers in 1962; in the center, by the table, are Khrushchev and Khrennikov. Shostakovich is third from left.

Plate 28.   Shostakovich with the Glazunov Quartet during a performance of the Piano Quintet in Leningrad in December 1940.

Plate 29.   Concert in Moscow in honor of Shostakovich's sixtieth birthday on 25 September 1966.

Plate 30.  Shostakovich, Kiril Kondrashin, and Yevgeny Yevtushenko
after the première of the Thirteenth Symphony (*Babi Yar*) in Moscow
on 18 December 1962.

Plate 31.  Dmitry Shostakovich with his son Maxim during a rehearsal
of the Fifteenth Symphony, conducted by Maxim, in January 1972.

## CHAPTER ELEVEN

# "Russia's Loss"
## *The Musical Emigration*

"For seventeen years, since I lost my country, I have felt unable to compose. When I was on my farm in Russia during the summers, I had joy in my work. Certainly I still write music—but it does not mean the same to me now," Sergey Rachmaninoff said in an interview in 1933.[1] For him, emigration effectively put a brake on his creative activity (Plate 18). For twenty-five years after leaving Russia in 1917, he composed no more than six major works. Of these, only the Rhapsody on a Theme of Paganini and the Symphonic Dances enjoyed the popularity of his earlier contributions. The Fourth Piano Concerto never fared well, and Rachmaninoff finally abandoned it as a failure. Music lovers missed the lyricism that had made the Second and Third Concertos such favorites.

The reasons for this decline were practical as well as emotional. Rachmaninoff was already in his forties when, to support his family, he was forced to start a new career as a concert pianist. To do so called for courage and discipline. He was admittedly familiar with concert life, but even so he had quickly to acquire a repertoire of his own and to adapt himself to the demanding tempo of Western stage appearances. The resulting stress was an important reason for his diminished creativity, although the emotional factors, too, should not be underestimated. With his departure from Russia, the original framework of his musical activity collapsed: the concert circuit of St. Petersburg and Moscow, and the peace, solitude, and financial security of his Ivanovka estate. Rachmaninoff's music is closely bound up with the Russia the Bolsheviks destroyed: the Russia of the landowning aristocracy, with their love of European culture, the rural ambience of landed estates, the sentimentality of the salon romance, and the emotional link with the Orthodox Church. Rachmaninoff looked back nostalgically on this world in his Third Symphony and in his Symphonic Dances.

Rachmaninoff was one of many Russian composers to go into exile. His friend Nikolai Medtner did likewise, as did Ivan Vishnegradsky, Nikolai Obukhov, Arthur Lourié, Alexander Grechaninov, Nikolai and Alexander Cherepnin, Vladimir Ussachevsky, Vladimir Fedorov, Nicolas Nabokov, Sergey Lyapunov, Nikolai Lopatnikoff, and Joseph Schillinger. Alexander Glazunov joined their company in 1928. The list of émigré performing musicians was more impressive still: apart from the operatic bass singer Fyodor Chaliapin, these ranks included the conductors Alexander Siloti, Serge Koussevitzky, Nikolai Malko, and Isaiah Dobrowen; the pianists Alexander Borovsky, Nikolai Orlov, and Vladimir Horowitz; the violinists Jascha Heifetz, Joseph Achron, Nathan Milstein, and Leopold Auer; and the cellists Gregor Piatigorsky, Nikolai Graudan, and Raya Garbuzova. Among musicologists and critics, the exiles included Leonid Sabaneyev, Nicolas Slonimsky, and Boris de Schloezer. The composer Vladimir Dukelsky turned to writing light music in Hollywood, changing his name to Vernon Duke on Gershwin's advice. In Paris, Vishnegradsky and Obukhov continued their experiments with post-Scriabinesque mysticism. Russian emigrants founded their own conservatory in that city, named after Sergey Rachmaninoff, their honorary president.

Koussevitzky's publishing house, the Edition Russe de Musique, played an important part in the life of exiled Russian musicians. Although the Russian branch had been nationalized by the Soviet authorities, the company continued to publish music through its offices in Paris and Berlin. Once appointed conductor of the Boston Symphony Orchestra in 1924, Koussevitzky became a leading champion of Russian music. The lasting results of his efforts include Ravel's famous orchestration in 1922 of Musorgsky's *Pictures at an Exhibition*. Ravel was not the only one to orchestrate that work—at about the same time, Leo Funtek, conductor of the Finnish Opera, was working independently on the same project, and earlier, Mikhaíl Tushmalov and Sir Henry Wood had tried their hand at it. Because Koussevitzky reserved Ravel's orchestration for his own use until 1929, and then demanded impossibly high royalties, other conductors were forced to rely on alternatives, provided by Lucien Cailliet, Leopold Stokowski, and Walter Goehr. However, none of these orchestrations was a match for Ravel's. Recently, the "French filter" of the work has on occasion been considered an impediment, and interest in the original piano version has accordingly revived. In 1982, for instance, Vladimir Ashkenazy produced a new orchestration, one more in keeping with Musorgsky's own style. However, Ravel's version will probably always maintain its place on the concert stage as a masterpiece sui generis.[2]

In 1921 Arthur Lourié failed to return to Russia from an official visit to Berlin. In 1922 he settled in Paris, where he became Stravinsky's assistant and spokesman. Between 1924 and 1931 he was part of Stravinsky's inner circle, providing piano arrangements of the *Concertino,* the *Octuor,* and the *Symphonies d'instruments à vent.* He defended Stravinsky's neoclassicism and his renewed interest in religion—for which Lourié was, in fact, largely responsible. In particular, he had introduced Stravinsky to the work of the neo-Thomist philosopher Jacques Maritain, whose views helped to consolidate Stravinsky's antimodernism. Lourié's *Concerto spirituale* of 1929 can even be considered the model for Stravinsky's *Symphony of Psalms.* The fact that Lourié resigned his post as head of MUZO, the musical section of NARKOMPROS, and then emigrated was taken very badly in the Soviet Union, where he was regarded as a traitor and his work was subsequently ignored.

The reasons for emigration were numerous: dissatisfaction with the regime, the economic hardships of the civil war, and class and career considerations. This last was certainly the reason for Sergey Prokofiev's departure in 1918.

The exodus of Russian musicians to the West had in fact been occurring even before the Revolution. Such composers as Chaikovsky, Rachmaninoff, and Scriabin had long had one foot in the West. Diaghilev's enterprise was entirely attuned to the Western market. Stravinsky wrote his most indicatively Russian music for a non-Russian public. The legendary bass singer Fyodor Chaliapin was helped to enter the Western commercial circuit by Diaghilev. In Russia the status of a singer depended on his rank in the Imperial Theaters; in the West the leading singers were chosen for their audience appeal. The fees Chaliapin commanded in the West were unimaginable in Russia.

Most émigré composers followed in the conservative footsteps of the Belyayev circle. Only Stravinsky and Prokofiev strayed from that path, playing an important role in the development of modern music. In Stravinsky's work, the effects of leaving Russia went deepest of all—his entire postwar career was strongly affected by it. As the most influential émigré musician, he was considered the renegade-in-chief in the Soviet

Union, a situation that would last until his historic reconciliation with the regime in 1962.

For Prokofiev the cards were stacked differently. During his stay in the West from 1918 to 1932, he continued to compose with both a Western and a Soviet public in mind. His exile was temporary only, and as soon as his Western career began to falter, he made plans to return to Russia.

## AN IMAGINARY RUSSIA: STRAVINSKY'S "SWISS PERIOD"

Stravinsky said his final farewell to Russia at the beginning of World War I, in 1914. Forced into exile, he lost touch with Russian musical life, a fact that may be considered surprising, since Stravinsky was still to write his most characteristically Russian works: his collections of songs to Russian folk texts, the ballet *Baika pro lisu, petukha, kota da barana* (The fable of the fox, the cock, the cat, and the ram, known as *Renard*), and *Svadebka* (The wedding, better known as *Les Noces*). Strange though it may sound, Stravinsky's Russian music from his "Swiss period"—so called because he spent the war years in Switzerland—was completely unconnected with the music then being played in St. Petersburg and Moscow. In his "Swiss" works, Stravinsky reflected a very particular Russia. Like Rachmaninoff's, his music was a nostalgic look, not at the Russia he had known and left behind, but at the Russia that lived on in his imagination.

In 1914 Stravinsky visited the land of his birth for the last time. He returned to Switzerland armed with all the available standard works on Russian folklore, of which the most important were the collections of folk tales by Alexander Afanasyev, wedding songs by Pyotr Kireyevsky, popular legends by Ivan Sakharov, and *The Everyday Life of the Russian People* by A. V. Tereshchenko. Stravinsky was interested in particular in the most original, the most primitive expressions of popular Russian culture: wedding rites, stories, sayings, children's nursery rhymes, and nonsense verses, often in dialect. The very choice of the material reflected a break with the St. Petersburg musical milieu. The Belyayev composers had no interest in such subjects. The material, collected in the nineteenth century, had never been put to music.

The distance from St. Petersburg grew greater still when Stravinsky finally came to the decision that ballet rather than opera was the ideal art form. The influence of Diaghilev and Benois was crucial here, persuading Stravinsky to turn his back on the remnants of the *kuchka* aesthetic. The experience that ultimately convinced him to reject opera as a modern art form was the 1914 Parisian production of Rimsky-Korsakov's *The Golden Cockerel,* staged by Diaghilev in ballet form. The singers performed offstage, while mimers and dancers portrayed the characters onstage. With this production, which was considered a milestone, Diaghilev's antiliterary aesthetic reached a new height. Concrete content made way for the direct impact of visual impression. The production was, moreover, a new climax in neonationalism: the choreographer, Mikhaíl Fokine, took his cue from the style of Russian woodcuts, while the designer, Natalya Goncharova, based the decor on woodcuts, homespun fabrics, folk ornaments, and icons.

In Russia, news of the production was greeted with indignation. Rimsky-Korsakov's widow threatened to go to court. Diaghilev was accused of destroying the operatic character of the work—which was, of course, his declared intention. He viewed the association of music with words as more artificial than that of music with movement. For Alexander Benois, the result exceeded all expectations: "Who knows, perhaps the union of the arts Wagner dreamed about has been realized at last by us."[3]

The Parisian *Golden Cockerel* became the model for Stravinsky's own stage works. In *Baika* and *Svadebka* he, too, would separate the singers from the mime artists or dancers on the stage. His last operatic work for some time to come was the completion of the fragment *The Nightingale* for Alexander Sanin, the founder of the Free Theater in Moscow. When, after just one season, the theater went bankrupt, *The Nightingale* was taken over by Diaghilev, who put on the work together with *The Golden Cockerel.* In the newly composed second and third acts of *The Nightingale,* Stravinsky downplayed any operatic character and stylized the action in ballet form. Words were kept to a minimum. The result was Stravinsky's first sung ballet. In 1917 he rearranged the two new acts into a wordless ballet score, *Chant du rossignol.*

The Rimsky-Korsakov family broke with Stravinsky in the wake of what they considered an attack on the authority of his teacher: his collaboration in Diaghilev's plan to restore Musorgsky's *Khovanshchina.* Diaghilev asked Ravel and Stravinsky to complete the work in a version that reflected Musorgsky's intention more closely than Rimsky-Korsakov had done. Stravinsky wrote a new final chorus—a fade-out of the Old Believers' hymn used by Musorgsky. Even though Diaghilev did not succeed in this restorative attempt and still had to rely largely on Rimsky-Korsakov's orchestration, the breach was past healing.

With *Petrushka* and *The Rite of Spring*, Stravinsky had gained a leading position among Western modernists, which he was now anxious to
retain. Becoming indistinguishable from the bulk of his fellow musicians
was the last thing he wanted. Stravinsky had a keen eye for cultural trends
and heeded the wishes of the progressive critics. French reviewers thus
had a decisive influence on his development.

Anti-German sentiment had dominated French cultural policy since
the turn of the century. Both Wagner's extreme romanticism and Brahms's
traditionalism, dismissed as neoclassical academicism, were rejected by
French composers, who felt that they must seek a clear alternative. The
nationalist journal *La Nouvelle Revue Française* played a pioneering role
in this development. Its aim was to link modern French with seventeenth-
century classical culture, thereby liberating France from the subjectivity
and "emotional morphine" of romanticism. Objectivity and respect for
the material became the key concepts in the new orientation of French
art. The critics at *La Nouvelle Revue Française* saw their ideal reflected
in the Ballets Russes, Henri Ghéon welcoming Diaghilev's productions
as a realization of the French dream. In 1910 he said about *The Firebird*:
"How Russian it all is, what these Russians have made, but also how
French!"[4] Among the qualities that made *The Firebird* a model for French
artistic aspirations, he placed respect for the material first and foremost.

Jacques Rivière developed this theme at some length. His program for
French art was largely antiromantic; he pleaded for objectivity instead
of subjectivity, arguing that art had to be classical in its absolute intrinsic beauty and freed of all utilitarian, moral, or theoretical prejudice. To
Rivière, classical art was always positivistic in essence, consisting as it
did of purely aesthetic objects. He saw that ideal attained for the first
time in *Petrushka* and perfected in *The Rite of Spring*. About the second
work he wrote:

> The great novelty of *Le sacre du printemps* is its renunciation of "sauce."
> Here is a work that is absolutely pure. Bitter and harsh, if you will; but a
> work in which no gravy deadens the taste, no art of cooking smooths or smears
> the edges. It is not a "work of art," with all the usual attendant fuss. Noth-
> ing is blurred, nothing is mitigated by shadows; no veils and no poetic sweet-
> eners; not a trace of atmosphere. The work is whole and tough, its parts re-
> main quite raw.[5]

Rivière replaced Debussy with Stravinsky as the leader of French music:

> Stravinsky has not simply amused himself by taking the opposite path from
> Debussy. If he has chosen those instruments that do not sigh, that say no more
> than they say, whose timbres are without expression and are like isolated

words, it is because he wants to enunciate everything directly, explicitly, and concretely. That is his chief obsession. That is his personal innovation in contemporary music. . . . His voice becomes the object's proxy, consuming it, replacing it; instead of evoking it, he utters it. He leaves nothing out; on the contrary, he goes after things; he finds them, seizes them, brings them back.[6]

Rivière made no mention whatsoever of the folkloristic or Russian aspects of Stravinsky's work. In their stead he extolled its "objectivity": the music is no more than what it is. Stravinsky took the hint. Never again would he speak of the neonationalistic origins of *The Rite of Spring*. Instead he adopted Rivière's point of view in his famous declaration that *The Rite of Spring* was "une oeuvre architectonique et non anecdotique."[7]

In the view of *La Nouvelle Revue Française*, aesthetic avant-gardism was coupled with a reactionary ideology, a point of view underlined by the journal *Montjoie!*, which set itself up as "l'organe de l'Impérialisme artistique française."[8] *Montjoie!* stood openly for racism, anti-Semitism, and antidemocratic ideas, and upheld the art of an elite whose task it was to impose its culture upon the world. Stravinsky worked for the journal and was even upheld in it as the messiah of the new elitist, antibourgeois art. Florent Schmitt, Stravinsky's chief link with *Montjoie!*, put it like this: "Igor Stravinsky, I firmly believe, is the Messiah we have awaited since Wagner, for whom Musorgsky and Claude Debussy, as well as Richard Strauss and Arnold Schoenberg, now seem to have prepared the way."[9] It is odd that Stravinsky, a foreigner, should have been honored in this way, by a declared chauvinist avant-garde. In reality, of course, the leading lights on *La Nouvelle Revue Française* and on *Montjoie!* were simply hijacking Stravinsky's art to boost their own extreme right-wing politics. The fact that he did not protest may be explained by the awe in which he held his champions and also by his own elitist, aristocratic origins.

For a time, Stravinsky still clung to the Russian character of his music. Exoticism continued to be an important formula for his success. In his Swiss period he linked Russian folklore to a new program of objectification and abstraction, a trend that had been heralded in *The Rite of Spring*. He now needed a fresh motive, and found it in a new ideology: Eurasianism.

Eurasianism was the successor of nineteenth-century Slavophilism and of *pochvennichestvo* (the ideology of "the soil"), two currents that placed Russia and Europe at opposite poles. Eurasianism applied this distinction radically: Russia was a world of her own, the antithesis of both Europe and Asia. This radically anti-Western ideology was opposed to every

conceivable aspect of European culture: Catholicism, Protestantism, sec-
ularism, atheism, materialism, decadence. In their place, the Eurasianists put the Orthodox Church, obedience to an absolute authority, and
the Slavophile idea of an "organic society." Their ideology was an amalgam of Slavophilism and Scythianism, the glorification of mythical, primitive Russia.

This radicalization was a direct consequence of the Revolution and
of the emigration of a large part of the Russian intelligentsia. The
Eurasianists considered the Bolshevik seizure of power the ultimate step
in the Europeanization of Russia. According to them, the Western
influence, which had begun with Peter the Great, had destroyed Russia;
the introduction of atheist communism had simply been the coup de
grâce. Detesting the Europe in which they were forced to live, they therefore created a fictitious Russia, one that preserved all its typical traits.
The historian Nicholas Riasanovsky observes: "In a sense, Eurasianism
constituted a desperate bid to reestablish vanished Russia, to transmute
fragmented and rootless existence in a foreign society into an organic
and creative life at home. The scope of the dream corresponded to that
of the loss."[10] The tone was set by Prince Nikolai Trubetskoy in his pam-
phlet "Europe and Humanity" (1920). He called the enlightened cosmopolitanism of the West a form of chauvinism, for which he coined the
term "panromanogermanic chauvinism." The movement took off with
the publication of Pyotr Suvchinsky's *Exodus to the East* in 1921. Stravinsky was in close contact with such advocates of Eurasianism as Suvchinsky and Lev Platonovich Karsavin (the brother of Diaghilev's ballerina Tamara Karsavina). Karsavin was the leading religious thinker of
the movement. His dream was of a "symphonic society," a protofascist
social utopia.

The Eurasianists welcomed Stravinsky as their musical representative.
In their eyes he had adopted their ideals even before the movement came
into the open. Thanks to his friendship with Karsavin, whose ideas had
been clearly formed as early as 1911, he had adopted Eurasianism early
on, a fact that is reflected in a number of his statements. Romain Rolland, for example, recorded the following anti-German declaration by
Stravinsky in his *Journal:*

> It is . . . in the highest common interest of all nations that still feel the need
> to breathe the air of their healthy and age-old culture to come down on the
> side of Germany's enemies and to remove themselves once and for all from
> the intolerable spirit of that enormous, bloated Teutonic Order that is men-
> aced by deadly symptoms of moral decay.[11]

Anti-German sentiment was widespread in France. Debussy's anti-Germanism was intense, but Stravinsky went even further. In his first reaction to the February Revolution, he had welcomed "the new liberated Russia," stripped of all pernicious European influences:

> Finally the true Russia will reveal herself to the world, a new Russia, but one that is also the old—finally burgeoning, opening up, waking from her long sleep, aroused from her own death. . . . The Holy Russia of the Orthodox, a Russia rid of her parasites: the bureaucracy imported from Germany, a certain kind of English liberalism that had found favor with the aristocracy, her scientism (alas!), her "intellectuals," with their foolish and purely theoretical belief in progress—the Russia before Peter the Great and before Europeanism, the Russia that will first take a step backward the better to advance because her foundations have been restored; a peasant Russia, but above all a Christian one, and truly the only Christian country in Europe.[12]

Stravinsky's Russia did not exist in reality. A greater contrast than that between his exalted vision and the liberal constitutional republic envisaged by the Provisional Government is hardly conceivable. The Bolshevik seizure of power shattered the dream completely. Stravinsky's ideal could be kept alive only in his music. *Svadebka* (*Les Noces*) would be the ultimate expression of his Eurasianist dream. Planned in 1914 but not finished until 1923, *Svadebka* kept Stravinsky busy throughout the period during which Russia was finally lost to him.

In his attitude to folklorism he proved to be more radical than he had been during his earlier neonationalistic phase. He was looking for Russian music that could serve as an adequate alternative to the Western tradition, and considered the music of the *kuchka* no more than pseudonationalistic because it had tried to adapt Russian folklore to Western genres and forms. He even came to look upon his own *Petrushka* and *Rite of Spring* as unsatisfactory, for in them he had still made use of the symphony orchestra, the preeminent Western medium. In his Swiss period, Stravinsky no longer composed for traditional European ensembles, except when completing *The Nightingale*. The usual argument that he resorted to small, unusual ensembles because of the privations of war is not tenable. He had ample opportunity to work with the Montreux Kursaal Orchestra, the Geneva Symphony Orchestra, or the Suisse Romande Orchestra. Stravinsky's abandonment of the symphony orchestra was a deliberate choice. Instead he established his own ensembles, the better to turn his back on Western sounds. He was aiming his shafts not only at Western ensembles but also at the music associated with them, that is, at music as the expression of subjective emotion. Now, for Stravinsky that expression was bound up mainly with the predominant role of string instruments in romantic music, which is why he chose wind instruments (*Symphonies d'instruments à vent*), piano and percussion (*Svadebka*), or unusual ensembles (*L'histoire du soldat*). The only compositions he wrote for an established ensemble during this period were Three Pieces for String Quartet and *Concertino*. In them, however, Stravinsky upset all established ideas connected with these genres. Rejecting expressivity and thematic development, characteristic of the string quartet since Beethoven, he instead used ostinati and juxtaposed musical blocks and mechanical passages. Adorno's indignant reaction proves how well Stravinsky attained his aim: "Of the Concertino for String Quartet, that is, of that combination of instruments more purely suited than any other to musical humanism, to the absolute enspiritualization of the instrumental medium, the composer insisted that it should hum along like a sewing machine."[13]

Between work on his two greatest folkloristic projects, *Svadebka* and *Baika,* Stravinsky wrote various collections of songs based on Russian folk poetry. For a long time the ethnographical background of these songs remained obscure, a matter since researched in detail by Richard Taruskin.[14] It appears that Stravinsky had studied the sources carefully. He was familiar with the subtlest characteristics of Russian folk culture—at least during his Swiss period, since later on he often issued inaccurate or mistaken information on the subject.

In *Expositions and Developments,* Stravinsky describes his *Pribautki* as being based on a popular type of word game in which the text is passed from one person to the next at great speed, each uttering a single word. His account, however, was mistaken. *Pribautki* are witty sayings, aphorisms, or even nonsense verses. Quite often they contain references to old pagan rites. This link to the oldest layers of Russian folk culture was precisely what appealed to Stravinsky.

The collection *Kolïbel'nïye* (Lullabies) is known by the French title of the 1917 edition prepared by Ramuz: *Berceuses du chat.* The title was later translated into English as *Cat's Cradle Songs,* which appeared for the first time on Stravinsky's recording of the songs of 1964. The image of the cat slipped into the title because of an article that the original collector of the texts, V. Passek, had written in the 1850s about the songs, in which he associated the tenderness of the mother and the safekeeping of the child with the image of a purring cat. Stravinsky was familiar with the article through a reprint in Kireyevsky's collection of ritual songs. The image is unfortunate, however, because it gives the impression that the lullabies in Stravinsky's set are sung to or by a cat. At the time of their composition in 1915, Stravinsky intended simply to call the songs "lullabies," which would convey their meaning more clearly.

Three songs in *Quatre chants russes,* a collection published in 1919, are associated with children's games. The fourth is a *sektanskaya,* a ritual song of the *khlïst* sect, in which the text expresses a yearning for the *radeniye,* the ecstatic whirling dance of the *khlïst* liturgy, and conveys a sense of isolation from one's brothers and sisters in the sect.[15]

Confusion also surrounds the collection called *Podblyudnïye.* In the first edition (by Schott in 1930), the term was translated as *Unterschale,* saucer. Later, Stravinsky suggested the English title of "Saucer Readings" or "Saucer Riddles." The literal translation of the Russian term is "songs sung beside a bowl"—a reference to a fortunetellers' practice in which the participants sit in a circle around a matchmaker and a bowl. Each person places an object in the bowl; songs are then sung that foretell, say, a marriage or riches. With every song, the matchmaker removes one object from the bowl. The prophecy then applies to its owner. We have already encountered one of the *podblyudnïye:* the "Slava" in Musorgsky's *Boris Godunov.*

The Russian songs Stravinsky wrote in his Swiss period reflect his antisubjective program in two ways: they are ritual, collective songs, and they are "verbal music." In other words, the music in them is not bound up with the expression of a concrete verbal content, but makes free with the sound material of the text. Stravinsky then expanded both aspects, "verbal music" and "ritualism," the first forming the basis of *Baika* and the second of *Svadebka.*

*Baika pro lisu, petukha, kota da barana* was the original title of the "merry performance with song and music" that today is known by its French title, *Renard.* Intended for a Western audience, this title elicits associations with fables about Reynard, Renard, or Reineke Fuchs. Stravinsky's composition, however, has nothing to do with these associations. Its origins lie entirely in Russian folklore, and more particularly in Afanasyev's nineteenth-century collection of folk tales.

The text can hardly be called a tale, however. It tells of a cock that is attacked twice by a vixen, only to be saved by the cat and the ram, who finally drive the vixen off and kill her. This meager plot, though, is of minor importance. What matters is the "verbal music." The text is a collage of some fifteen different fragments taken from Afanasyev's collection, which are by and large *pribautki,* or nonsense rhymes. The sketches indicate that the composition began as an arrangement of children's songs and nonsense rhymes in the spirit of Stravinsky's other song collections from the Swiss period. Gradually, he expanded the material into the collage we know today.[16] The result is an entirely new *skazka*, or folk tale, with all the authentic characteristics: it is prose on the verge of nonsense, with unpredictable digressions and a "story-within-a-story" structure. The same is true of the music: the phrases all sound like authentic folk-song fragments, but they were in fact all newly composed.

*Baika* marks the climax of Stravinsky's treatment of the "verbal music" of Russian folklore. Yevgeniya Linyova had shown that Russian folk songs could differ markedly from the prosody of the spoken language. For Stravinsky, that was an important discovery. It justified his attempt to detach the music from the form and meaning of the words, and was the decisive step in his revolt against realism, which had turned correct prosody into a dogma.

In its scenic aspects, *Baika* continues the idea behind Diaghilev's production of *The Golden Cockerel*: singers offstage, dancers or mimers onstage—though Stravinsky radically extended this idea. In *Baika*, the singers even ceased to represent separate characters; rather, their roles intermingled, and the four voices were turned, so to speak, into an integral part of the instrumental group, which consisted of flute, oboe, clarinet, bassoon, two horns, trumpet, percussion, timpani, string quintet, and a Hungarian cimbalom. This last instrument was intended to add an authentic touch, as a replacement for the *gusli* (the Russian psaltery).

The *gusli*'s range of sound was linked to the visual content of the work. On the stage, the various parts were played by clowns, dancers, or acrobats—references to the *skomorokhi*, Russian minstrels before the time of Peter the Great, who used to sing stories to the accompaniment of the *gusli* and entertain the crowd and the aristocracy as acrobats, tightrope walkers, jugglers, conjurers, or dancers. Theater historians like to think of them as precursors of the Russian theater, but however plausible this view may be, there is no hard evidence in the historical sources that they acted out their stories. Stravinsky, however, had no need of historical corroboration. On his own authority, he linked the performances of the *skomorokhi* to the oral narrative tradition. As a result, *Baika* is a capricious fantasy based on authentic folkloristic material. Richard Taruskin has called it "the dazzling evocation of an ancient Russia that never was, but that in its intense artistic imagining was far 'realer-than-the-real,' as art alone could be."[17]

A wedding in the Russian countryside demanded elaborate rituals. As a complex collection of traditional customs, in which Christian and pagan elements were intimately interwoven, the *svadebka* (the term is the rural form of the more common *svadba*, "wedding") attracted the particular attention of nineteenth-century Slavophiles. Stravinsky accordingly found his sources chiefly in the work of Slavophile ethnographers from Pushkin's day, Ivan Sakharov, Vasiliy Tereshchenko, and Pyotr Kireyevsky.

Russian peasant marriages were arranged by matchmakers, who struck a settlement between the two families concerned. The "contract" between the bridegroom's matchmaker and the bride's father was sealed with a slapping of hands (*rukobitiye*). The marriage ritual itself is above all a *rite de passage* for the bride, the transition "from girl to woman" being a key event in her life. Not only is she being prepared for her reproductive role, but she also exchanges the familiarity of her own family background for that of her husband's family, which is often completely alien to her. She enters her new family on the lowest rung of the hierarchy, a subordinate of her mother- and sisters-in-law.

The first phase of the ritual consists mainly of the bride's lamentations: from the moment the agreement is reached she laments her break with her youth, her family, and her girlfriends, cursing the matchmaker and her bridegroom, and imploring her parents to stop the marriage. The climax of this stage is the *devichnik*: the meeting of the bride with her girlfriends, at which her transformation from girl into woman is denoted ritually by a change in her hairstyle. The girlish single braid is undone, divided into two, and wound around her head. This act is accompanied by the bitter lamentations of the bride, while her girlfriends try to console her.

The church ceremony marks a turning point as lamentation (*plach*) makes way for joy and pleasure. During the actual wedding feast (*krasniy stol*, literally "beautiful table"), bride and bridegroom are escorted to the bedroom by the matchmakers. Outside, the *druzhko* (the bridegroom's witness and chief master-of-ceremonies) keeps guard on horseback with his saber drawn.

Stravinsky started on his ballet version of the Russian wedding with the help of a detailed scenario. The sequence of tableaux had a narrative structure, and the singers were intended to interpret individual roles. However, Stravinsky abandoned that plan. It was not feasible musically: too many scenes relied on the same sort of musical accompaniment, and the bride's lamentations were too dominant. He therefore opted ultimately for a nonnarrative rendering of the material events.

He divided the work into two sections. The First Part consists of three

tableaux, of which the first represents the bride, the second the bridegroom, and the third their meeting. The first two tableaux, which are developed in parallel, both revolve around the dressing of the bride's and
groom's hair. The union of the two is indicated symbolically by their meeting before the wedding procession leaves for church. The entire Second
Part consists of one tableau, the wedding feast. It culminates in the true
aim of the proceedings, the procreative act.

Stravinsky's sketchbook reveals his familiarity with a vast quantity
of ethnographic sources. In this work, however, he goes beyond reality.
The folklore of *Svadebka* is not copied from life, but created by the imagination. As a result, the score may be considered a late flowering of the
*Mir iskusstva* ideal of independent creative work with Russian folklore
as its basis.

In the Russian wedding ritual, the participants do not behave as their
hearts dictate but as tradition demands. Stravinsky took this idea one
step further: in his version, he has done away with individuals. The singers
do not represent particular characters; rather, all the roles merge. The
separation of performer and character is absolute. This interpretation
symbolizes a world in which humans do not act as individuals, but are
organically bound up with their community. Stravinsky called the work
"perfectly homogeneous, perfectly impersonal, and perfectly mechanical."[18] The musical effect is the result of a radical abstraction. All the
melodies sound authentic, and yet, with two exceptions, they were composed by Stravinsky himself.

The music is all strictly diatonic. A considerable proportion is even
anhemitonic (without the use of semitones), the share of anhemitony being strikingly greater than is usual in Russian folk music. That was
Stravinsky's deliberate choice. Its significance becomes clearer when we
look at the Eurasianist conception of music. Prince Trubetskoy called
the absence of semitones the most important characteristic of Turanian
music—"Turan" being an old-fashioned term for the Eurasian steppe. (For
what used to be called the "Turanian people," we nowadays use the linguistic term "Ural-Altaic.") According to Trubetskoy, the psychological,
social, and artistic characteristics of the Russians can be traced back to
the pre-Slavic—that is, Turanian—period. Since anhemitony was a feature of Turanian music, it was an anti-Western characteristic. This interpretation was admittedly more fantasy than reality, but Stravinsky applied it consistently in *Svadebka*.

The absence of leading notes renders tonal development impossible.
Stravinsky achieved harmony by various interactions of anhemitonic

melodies with pentatonic, diatonic, and octatonic scales. He arranged the overall composition in a strictly hierarchical and symmetrical manner by means of a binding *"complexe sonore."*[19] The overall structure thus contained no tonal movement; it was a musical picture of an all-embracing, hierarchical, and immutable universe.

The instrumentation was the last step in the process of abstraction. At first, Stravinsky thought of using a symphony orchestra. He then planned to imitate folk instruments by scoring the work for pianola, harmonium, percussion, and two Hungarian cimbaloms—an impractical choice that made Diaghilev despair. He finally decided on four pianos and percussion. This choice of instruments helped to stylize all manner of sounds that are part of the tradition: the chiming of bells, the noise made by percussive instruments as a magical protection from evil. Moreover, it brought out something for which Stravinsky was aiming: sound that is homogeneous, impersonal, and mechanical.

The choreographer, Bronislava Nijinska, embraced the idea, rejecting the folkloristic costumes that had been designed, with great attention to detail, by Natalya Goncharova (Plate 19). Diaghilev supported the designer and released Nijinska from her contract. A year later, however, he changed his mind and gave the choreographer a free hand. Nijinska settled on functional costumes with no folkloristic frills; she also omitted all folkloristic references in the decor, and even banished what little anecdotal material had remained in Stravinsky's outline (the bride's house, the rearrangement of the coiffure, and so on). In her choreography there was no place for individuality. All movements were collective, the anonymous mass moving in abstract geometrical patterns. The brown color of Goncharova's new costumes emphasized the association with the soil.[20]

*Svadebka* marked the climax of Stravinsky's antihumanism. The Eurasianists welcomed the use of their ideas on the subordination of the individual to the community, the organic link with religious traditions, and the superiority of Eurasian traditions over those of the decadent, individualistic West. *Svadebka* was the ultimate artistic expression of the totalitarian nostalgia of uprooted Russians. "At a time of upheaval and ruin," Richard Taruskin writes, "it offered a restorative view of the only eternity humans can know—the eternity of customs. At a time of existential trauma it offered the solacing prospect of life as liturgy."[21]

Liturgy is the basis of a purely instrumental composition, the *Symphonies d'instruments à vent* (1920). Written in memory of Claude Debussy, it is a fairly faithful rendering of the *panikhida,* the Orthodox funeral service. The mosaic structure, which juxtaposes the music seamlessly in blocks, is based on the imitation of the sequence of prayers and chants in that ritual. The liturgical orientation and the detached sound of the winds are part of the Turanian aesthetic. Another telling element is the particular form of the title. The work is not, in fact, a "symphony for wind instruments"; the word "symphonies" in the title is a reference to the Greek-Byzantine term *simfonia*—a synonym for harmony and coordinated activity. The choice of this title goes back to Karsavin, who used the term in his conception of the "symphonic personality," by which he meant the subordination of the individual to the organic community.[22]

*L'histoire du soldat* holds a special place in Stravinsky's oeuvre. It was the only theatrical work he produced without Diaghilev, the concept of a folk tale set to music running counter to Diaghilev's antiliterary tendency. Not only that, but the narrative and linear structure of the project (the idea for which came from the poet Charles-Ferdinand Ramuz and not from Stravinsky himself, as Stravinsky was later to claim) contradicted Stravinsky's own then-prevailing aesthetic of abstraction and timelessness. He took on the project, however—on which he and Ramuz worked to some extent independently—because he desired a composition that could lead its own life as a separate concert suite.

The source of the text is a Russian folk tale in Afanasyev's collection, "The Deserter and the Devil." Ramuz eradicated all Russian characteristics, moving the setting to Switzerland and injecting into the text modern, contemporary references: the troika became an automobile, and the traditional Russian merchant a modern entrepreneur who conducts business over the telephone and deals on the stock exchange. He also added a lofty tone to the text, which culminates in the moral that "wishing to have everything leads to ruin." The Soldier's violin playing is an important part of the original tale, though, and Ramuz gave particular emphasis to this feature, turning the Soldier's violin into an ambiguous symbol of the human soul.

Stravinsky's score calls for an unusual combination of instruments: violin, double bass, clarinet, bassoon, cornet, trombone, and percussion. Later, Stravinsky attributed the choice to the influence of jazz. However, this combination is anything but a jazz ensemble. It seems more likely that Stravinsky was inspired by the Jewish village orchestras of eastern Europe, known as klezmer bands, which he had come to know during the time he had spent on the Ustilug estate. The standard instruments of the klezmer band are violin, double bass, clarinet, and drums, sometimes combined with trumpet and trombone. Stravinsky's emphasis on brass was related to the military character of the story.

The stylization of the folk music is rendered brilliantly in a rich peasant style of playing the violin. Stravinsky achieved this effect by exploiting the low register of the instrument, double stops, and the sonority of the open strings. True to the modern touches in Ramuz's treatment of the story, Stravinsky also introduced contemporary elements such as ragtime, the tango, and the waltz.

## THE DICTATOR OF THE REACTION

After *Svadebka*, Stravinsky took his leave of Russia even in his music, becoming transformed from Russian composer into the leader of cosmopolitan neoclassicism, a turnabout that poses one of the greatest riddles in recent music history. In any event, with the loss of the real Russia at the end of the civil war, Stravinsky abandoned the Turanian dream.

The year 1923 brought an incisive change in Stravinsky's music. In the Octet, the Concerto for Piano and Winds, and the *Sonate* for piano, he completely severed his links with the Russian tradition and, by openly quoting Bach and Handel, resolutely entered the Western mainstream.

Stravinsky suddenly came out as an opponent of prewar modernism. In 1925 he declared: "The modernists set out to shock the bourgeoisie, sometimes they succeed only in pleasing the Bolshevists. I am not interested in either the bourgeoisie or the Bolshevists."[23] Arthur Lourié characterized Stravinsky as follows (a characterization that Stravinsky approved): "After beginning on the extreme left flank of the modernists, he went through a complex evolution and appeared on the extreme right of the position. In recent years he has been the dictator of the reaction against the anarchy into which modernism degenerated."[24] In France, "modernist degeneration" was a label openly attached to Schoenberg, who was described as the representative of the decadent decline of German music. The contrast between Schoenberg and Stravinsky became part of an aggressive nationalistic rhetoric. Stravinsky did not hesitate in referring to Germans as "human caricatures," whereas the qualities attributed to Stravinsky's music—objectivity, simplicity, purity, and clarity—were presented as French characteristics by the postwar French avant-garde. Georges Auric, for instance, wrote that Stravinsky forced French composers to follow a path that had, in fact, been theirs all along.[25] The contrast between German and French music was seen as the distinction between psychologizing music, on the one hand, and autonomous, purely "architectural," music, on the other.

Stravinsky's new style, referred to variously as *nouveau classicisme, objectivisme,* or *style dépouillé,* ultimately entered music history as neoclassicism.

The origins of Stravinsky's neoclassicism are not simple and unequivocal. First of all, there was his determination to remain the leader of the avant-garde. Stravinsky was aware of the direction in which French aesthetics were moving, and he tried not only to follow that direction but to seize the lead in it. The direction underpinned the musical autonomy that Jacques Rivière had applauded in Stravinsky's earlier work. A new radical element was the theory of "les choses en soi" (things in themselves), Jean Cocteau's antiromantic aesthetics first articulated in the manifesto *Le coq et l'arlequin.* In it Cocteau had praised Satie as the pioneer of the new ideal. In 1926, when he republished this text under the telling title of *Le rappel à l'ordre* (The call to order), he added a lengthy tribute to Stravinsky.

The retrospective element in Stravinsky's neoclassicism—the evocation of historical styles—was not the main reason for the prestige he enjoyed among young French composers. Together with Cocteau, the members of the group Les Six applauded his "new simplicity," his "purified style," and his classical clarity and directness. At first, in fact, they had been opposed to retrospective tendencies. By dissociating themselves from all prewar styles, for example, they rejected the retrospective elements in the work of Debussy and Ravel, which they dismissed as a pastiche of the French harpsichordists, such as Couperin and his contemporaries.[26] Nor did they consider references to historical French music a national characteristic. Objectivism was all that mattered.

Stravinsky's neoclassicism was closely connected with a new type of social elitism. It was part of the reaction of the social upper crust to the chaos of the war. The underlying objective of neoclassicism was to safeguard culture from the masses and from the nouveaux riches. It was art for the educated, which in the rhetoric of the time meant people of good breeding.

The link between neoclassicism and social privilege can be found, for instance, in the testimony of Nikolai Medtner. While he himself experienced Stravinsky's Concerto for Piano and Winds as a terrible shock, the public remained, in his eyes, surprisingly loyal to its idol:

> The public, who had filled the Grand Opéra to overflowing, this public who takes it as an insult if someone should appear in its midst in anything but tails or a smoking jacket (for which reason I had to hide myself and my little grey

jacket in the highest loges)—this public steadfastly withstood every slap in the face and every humiliation, and what is more, rewarded the author with deafening applause.[27]

Social elitism was not confined to Stravinsky. We must not be misled by the recourse of Cocteau and Les Six to "lower" forms of culture—jazz, circus, and cabaret. This had nothing to do with democratic ideas, let alone with populism, but was part of the pleasure-round of *le tout Paris.* Cocteau knew how to render the radical left-wing art of the war years serviceable to the postwar right-wing restorative ideology. His attitude toward these forms of "popular art" was, however, thoroughly paternalistic. He did not look upon them as art, but merely as raw material that a real artist might use to advantage.[28]

Stravinsky came down openly on the side of the social elite. He sought out the company of the emigrant titled nobility, became a staunch follower of the Romanovs, and cultivated his aristocratic status. His political sympathies became totalitarian and fascist. He called Mussolini the hope of the world.

Stravinsky's identification with aristocratic Russia influenced his change of style. In this Diaghilev had set the example. The impresario had never been tempted into Eurasianism, but had always identified himself with the Russia that was nearest to his heart: the cosmopolitan and European culture of St. Petersburg. At the beginning of the war, he had turned his back on exoticism, orientalism, and folklore. His change of tack began with a series of ballets set to Italian music: *Les femmes de bonne humeur* (The good-humored ladies; Scarlatti, orchestrated by Tommasini), *La boutique fantasque* (The fantastic toyshop; Rossini, orchestrated by Respighi), and *Le astuzie femminili* (Women's wiles; Cimarosa, orchestrated by Respighi). With these Italian ballets, Diaghilev played up French ideas on elitism, according to which the Germans were corrupt and decadent, and the "Latin spirit" superior. At the same time, the ballets served him as a link with the early musical tradition of imperial Russia—Italian opera had been the first musical form cultivated at the Russian court. The Cimarosa project was especially significant: Cimarosa had worked from 1787 to 1791 in the service of Catherine the Great. The opera *Le astuzie femminili*, composed in 1794 for the court of Naples, ended with a *ballo russo.* (Diaghilev thought mistakenly that the work had been meant for Catherine, and accordingly treated it as a St. Petersburg court spectacle.) The *ballo russo* was, moreover, based on the *kamarinskaya,* the dance tune that, in Glinka's hands, had served as the "acorn from which the oak of the Russian symphonic tradition has grown," to use Chaikovsky's famous phrase. Cimarosa's *kamarinskaya* showed that there was also another Russia: that of the Europeanized aristocracy.

At Diaghilev's request, Stravinsky orchestrated music by Pergolesi for the ballet *Pulcinella* (Plate 20), music that has since turned out to be not so much by Pergolesi as by Gallo, Van Wassenaar, Parisotti, and Martini. *Pulcinella* is little more than an arrangement, Stravinsky's own contribution being small. This experience therefore entailed no change of course for him, the less so as he was still working on *Svadebka*. His real break with music based on Russian folklore came only with the chamber opera *Mavra*.

With his greatest postwar project, the revival of Chaikovsky's *Sleeping Beauty*, Diaghilev tried to shake off the folkloristic image of the Ballets Russes once and for all. Contemporaries saw the project as a betrayal of the modernism of the Ballets Russes, but for Diaghilev it was the fulfillment of his ambition to succeed Ivan Vsevolozhsky, the director of the Imperial Theaters in the days of Chaikovsky and Petipa.

Diaghilev asked Stravinsky to make a few changes to the score and to promote the production. Stravinsky did so with great energy, as if his publicity for *The Sleeping Princess*—as Diaghilev rechristened the ballet—were at one and the same time a proclamation of his own change of style. Stravinsky defended Chaikovsky as the spokesman of the lost Russian empire. In an open letter to the London *Times* of 1 October 1921, he wrote: "This work seems to me to be the most authentic expression of the epoch in our Russian life that we call the 'Petersburg period,' engraved in my memory by the matutinal vision of the horse-drawn carriage of Alexander III, the enormous Emperor and his enormous coachman, and with the boundless joy that awaited me in the evening: the spectacle of *The Sleeping Beauty*."[29] Stravinsky extolled Chaikovsky's melodic gifts, which he saw as a Franco-Slavic characteristic free of any German taint, and presented Chaikovsky as a Russian composer who managed to express the soul of his people without resorting to folk music: "Without specifically cultivating the 'Russian peasant soul' in his art, Chaikovsky imbibes subconsciously the true national sources of our race"—an echo of Laroche's review of *The Sleeping Beauty*.[30] Stravinsky spoke out bluntly against the exotic picture of Russian music common among the Western public:

A few years ago, people appreciated Russian music as if it were a sort of Negro music. No critic spoke of it without using the term "sauvage et raffiné." In those days the picturesqueness of the Five was something one valued. It is time to have done with it. Russian stage designs are no longer obliged to be Oriental tapestries. And Russian music can speak to us of other things besides the Russia that existed before Peter the Great.[31]

*The Sleeping Princess* did not enjoy the hoped-for success. The première at the Alhambra Theatre, London, on 2 November 1921 proved a financial disaster. The performances planned for Paris were abandoned, except for a presentation in highly fragmentary form under the title *Le mariage d'Aurore.* Diaghilev finally decided to desist from putting on spectacles that lasted the entire evening.

The production had a decisive effect on Stravinsky. From then on he exalted the aristocratic and Apollonian character of the classical ballet (Plate 21). In his statements, he also made efforts to gloss over his historical links with Rimsky-Korsakov and the *kuchka* and to draw closer to Chaikovsky.

He developed the relationship between imperial Russia and European music in the chamber opera *Mavra* (1922), the only genuine fiasco in his entire career. This time it did not even turn out to be a *succès de scandale; Mavra* was simply ignored or dismissed as a mistake. Yet it formed Stravinsky's pivotal attempt to forge a link between his work and Europeanized Russia. Boris Kochno's libretto is based on Pushkin's poem "The Little House in Kolomna." As in *Eugene Onegin,* the way it is told is more important than the tale itself (about a mother, a daughter, and a lover who joins the household as a cook). Like Chaikovsky's famous Pushkin opera, Stravinsky's, too, is based on music from Pushkin's day: the salon romance, the *rossiyskaya pesnya,* and the so-called *zhestokiy romans* ("cruel romance"), a genre that is generally associated with chanting gypsy women and plaintive, passionate recitation. *Mavra* originated in a sketch with separate musical numbers, modeled on the revues of the popular cabaret group Chauve-Souris. Stylistically, Stravinsky once again linked up with Western cadencing melodies and with dominant harmony replete with leading tones. By means of this detour into Europeanized Russian music, Stravinsky found the way back to Western styles after many years of exploring the harmonic possibilities of tetrachords in Russian folk music.

With his neoclassicist work Stravinsky turned his back on Russian music, although he would at times return to his roots, for instance in the *Scherzo à la russe* (1943–44) and *Le baiser de la fée* (1928), which is based on short pieces by Chaikovsky. In his arrangement, Stravinsky stayed far closer to Chaikovsky's own style and orchestration than he had in his editorial work on *The Sleeping Beauty.* His treatment was even devoid of the irony with which he generally distanced himself from the styles he quoted. *Le baiser de la fée* is a downright pastiche of *The Sleeping Beauty*. There is no question of stylization or disguise; it is a deliberate, calculated imitation. In his antimodernism, Stravinsky clung to "good old Uncle Petya," the time-honored representative of aristocratic Russia.

## "OUR MUSICAL ADVANCE POST" IN THE WEST: SERGEY PROKOFIEV

When Prokofiev left Russia in 1918, he had no intention of remaining abroad; his sole purpose in venturing to the West was to advance his career. He reached San Francisco by way of Vladivostok and Tokyo, then moved on to New York and Chicago. His piano playing, in particular, caused a sensation, though his reputation as a "Bolshevist pianist" elicited suspicion as well as curiosity. Cleofonte Campanini, director of the Chicago Opera, found him a commission for a new opera. Prokofiev chose Meyerhold's adaptation of a commedia dell'arte play by Carlo Gozzi (1720–1806), *The Love for Three Oranges*. Following a delay of two years, the opera was staged in Chicago.

Gozzi's aim had been to parody Goldoni's bourgeois realism and the melodramatic work of Abbé Chiari. With the help of commedia dell'arte conventions, he dramatized an absurd story about a prince's pursuit of three oranges, an illusive quest forced upon him by the witch Fata Morgana. In the second act, three characters argue about dramatic criteria. This aspect was seized upon by Meyerhold, who had the action commented on by jesters representing three aesthetic standpoints: comedy, tragedy, and opera fanaticism. Prokofiev extended the list with lyrical poetry and empty-headed ignorance.

Prokofiev exploited the satirical side of his style to the full, adhering to the declamatory type he had developed in *The Gambler*. New, however, were the instrumental numbers, which he combined into an independent orchestral suite.

In 1920 Prokofiev moved back to Europe, commuting until 1923 between Paris, the United States, and the Bavarian hamlet of Ettal, where he tried to work without distractions on his new opera, *The Fiery Angel*. Because the opera is set in sixteenth-century Germany, Prokofiev thought it essential to soak up the atmosphere in situ. However, he did not try to make contact with German composers and, in general, continued to concentrate on developments in Paris and America. Following his marriage to the Spanish-born singer Lina Llubera (whose real name was Carolina Codina) in 1923, he made Paris his permanent residence.

In Paris, Prokofiev renewed his acquaintanceship with Diaghilev, and on 17 May 1921 the ballet *Chout* (The buffoon) was given its first performance. Sharing the program with Stravinsky's *The Firebird,* the work was bound to elicit comparisons. These came down in favor of Stravinsky, and Diaghilev dropped *The Buffoon* after two seasons with no immediate plans to bring it back.

In 1919 Prokofiev had started on an opera with which he had hoped to break into the international opera circuit, *The Fiery Angel,* based on Valeriy Bryusov's novel by the same name. The book is a roman à clef that, using a sixteenth-century background, examines the stormy three-cornered relationship between the author himself and Andrey Belïy and Nina Petrovskaya, a trio of poets who tried to live in the purest symbolist style according to their artistic ideals. Bryusov told their story in a romance about a young woman called Renata (Petrovskaya), Count Heinrich (Belïy), and Ruprecht, a knight newly returned from his travels (Bryusov). As a child, Renata had visions of a "fiery angel" called Madiel, whom she thinks she recognizes in Count Heinrich. She begs Ruprecht to help her search for Heinrich, to which end he uses black magic. Renata ultimately withdraws into a convent, where she infects the nuns with her hysteria. The Inquisitor is called in and condemns her to death at the stake. In the novel, Ruprecht and Renata meet again in the convent dungeon, where she dies in his arms. Prokofiev ends the opera with the scene of mass hysteria in the convent and the Inquisitor's condemnation of Renata.

The most interesting aspect of the novel is the continuous conflict between spiritual and sexual longing. Prokofiev used that subject not for its metaphysical significance but for its dramatic elements—passion, hysteria, magic, and black art—concentrating instead on the outward manifestations of the religious perversity portrayed in the story. This placed the opera on shaky foundations, for the psychological basis of the various actions remains obscure. The development of Ruprecht's behavior—from rational adventurer to a compulsive practitioner of black magic—seems in particular to have no motive. Prokofiev sacrificed everything to the colorful portrayal of Renata's hysteria.

He worked on this opera from 1919 to 1923, and revised the score in 1926 and 1927. His hopes of demonstrating his mastery as a dramatic and lyric composer with *The Fiery Angel* proved to have been misplaced. Plans for productions in Paris, Berlin (under Bruno Walter), and New

York came to nothing. On 14 June 1928 Serge Koussevitzky gave a concert performance of excerpts from the second act in Paris. The public
was moderately enthusiastic, but the avant-garde around Diaghilev was
unanimously hostile. For them the modern impression given by the music failed to disguise the conservatism of the general concept. In *The Fiery
Angel*, Prokofiev rescinded the radical naturalism of *The Gambler*.

The total loss of the investment of seven years of his life caused
Prokofiev seriously to doubt if he still had a role to play, a feeling reinforced by new disappointments. His Violin Concerto was found to be
old-fashioned, even "Mendelssohnian."[32] Prokofiev's revision of his
Second Piano Concerto (1924) did not fare much better, being judged
not modern enough by the Parisian public.

The greatest disappointment came with the Second Symphony (1925),
with which Prokofiev hoped to restore his reputation as a modernist. He
had planned a symphony of "iron and steel." The music was strikingly
aggressive, the orchestration extravagant. The structure was based on
Beethoven's Piano Sonata, op. 111: an allegro ben articolato, followed
by a theme with variations, of which the last brings back the thematic
material of the first movement. The critics did not know quite what to
make of it, although in general they found the symphony vulgar and
brash. As far as most of them were concerned, it in any case failed to
add anything new to the genre.

The Third Piano Concerto (1921), in contrast, brought a ray of hope.
With it, Prokofiev earned himself a permanent place in the international
concert repertoire. He dedicated the score to Konstantin Balmont, who
happened to be staying near the composer in Brittany at the time it was
being written. (Prokofiev interrupted his work on the concerto to compose Five Songs to Poems by Konstantin Balmont, op. 36.) The Third
Piano Concerto is one of Prokofiev's most balanced works, in which light-
heartedness and depth go harmoniously hand in hand and piano and orchestra are brilliantly matched. Prokofiev never saw any need to revise
the work, which was created with the same spontaneity as the *Classical*
Symphony.

His greatest public successes came with two new commissions from
Diaghilev. The first was *Le pas d'acier* (1925; first performance 1927).
Its subject, daily life in the Soviet Union, was something about which the
West was very curious, especially after the 1925 Exposition Internationale
des Arts Décoratifs, and Diaghilev was quick to exploit that curiosity.
He entrusted the mise-en-scène to Georgiy Yakulov, a Soviet postfutur-

ist artist, and the music to Prokofiev. It turned out to be a harsh, dissonant score for Yakulov's constructivist tableaux of the joys of collectivist industrial labor (Plate 22).

The other commission was a ballet on the biblical theme of the Prodigal Son. *Le fils prodigue* was premièred on 21 May 1929 to a scenario by Diaghilev's right-hand man, Boris Kochno, choreographed by the promising George Balanchine, and with the dancer Serge Lifar in one of his star roles (Plate 23). The ballet was centered on the adventures of the Prodigal Son, complete with carousals and temptations by a siren. Prokofiev captured the moving reunion of father and son particularly evocatively, the emotional character of the music not escaping the audience. Prokofiev was to recycle music from the ballet in his Fourth Symphony, having previously imported music from *The Fiery Angel* into his Third. The success of *Le fils prodigue* opened up new horizons, but on 19 August 1929 Diaghilev died and the fate of the Ballets Russes was sealed.

With Diaghilev, Prokofiev's chief guide to Western tastes disappeared. Prokofiev had, however, heard the call of another musical world in the meantime—Russia—and in 1927 he went on a triumphant concert tour that took in Leningrad, Moscow, and the Ukraine. His friends Myaskovsky, Pavel Lamm, and Asafyev (Plate 24) did their best to prepare a warm welcome for him and to promote his work. Prokofiev gave concerts with, among others, the PERSIMFANS (First Symphonic Ensemble), a well-known orchestra that played without a conductor as an experiment in collectivism. Anatoliy Lunacharsky, as head of NARKOMPROS, showered Prokofiev with attentions and honors. All his Soviet colleagues did their best to present musical life in the Soviet Union in its most glowing colors, in the hope that he might be tempted to return home permanently.

Prokofiev immediately made plans for a second tour. In 1929, however, the situation in the Soviet Union changed radically. The tolerant Anatoliy Lunacharsky was dismissed as head of NARKOMPROS, and power shifted into the hands of the RAPM, the organization for proletarian music. The Rapmovites were openly hostile to Prokofiev and tried to boycott his concert tour, attacking the content of *Le pas d'acier* in particular. They argued that as a traitor to his country, Prokofiev had no right to speak about life in the Soviet Union. In an interview at the Bolshoy Theater he was forced to defend the ideological content of the ballet before representatives of the RAPM. He had the support of Meyerhold, who spoke out for him as "our musical advance post in the West."[33] Oddly enough, Prokofiev failed to read the writing on the wall. He treated his harassment by the RAPM as just another case of unfair criticism, not as an indication of the harsh repression that was still to come.

Prokofiev was especially mindful of the success of his music with the Russian public. In Russia, he did not have to worry about the unpredictable reactions of sophisticated Parisian audiences, nor did he have to fret about his constant rivalry with Stravinsky, whose supreme position he could never hope to attain. He was not at the time considering returning permanently to the Soviet Union, but he wanted to keep a foot in both camps. Even so, he was no longer afraid of presenting himself to the West as a traditionalist, and during his 1930 concert tour of the United States he tried to undo his earlier image as a rebel composer. In an interview with the *New York Times* he complained: "Why do they continue to speak of me only as a satirist or a sarcastic composer, or an *enfant terrible* of discord, etc.? Perhaps this was true fifteen years ago, when that was my spirit, and somewhat my style. But I have left that period behind." Prokofiev declared openly that the time of experiments was over:

> We want a simpler and more melodic style for music, a simple, less complicated emotional state, and dissonance again relegated to its proper place as one element of music. . . . I think we have gone as far as we are likely to go in the direction of size, or dissonance, or complexity in music. Music, in other words, has definitely reached and passed the greatest degree of discord and complexity that can be attained in practice. I want nothing better, more flexible or more complete than the sonata form, which contains everything necessary for my structural purposes.[34]

The tendency to simplify was already present in the Fifth Piano Sonata (1923). Prokofiev wrote his First String Quartet (1930) with Beethoven in mind. Inasmuch as he elaborated the traditional tendency further— as in the ballet *On the Dneper* (1930–31), a story about the sentimental love of a Red Army soldier for a peasant girl—his music spontaneously drew closer to the Soviet aesthetic.

There were two new disappointments: the Concerto for the Left Hand (1931), written for Paul Wittgenstein, who had lost his right arm in World War I, was rejected by that pianist without commentary; and Prokofiev himself was dissatisfied with his Fifth Piano Concerto. These setbacks confirmed his decision to exchange the unpredictable Western milieu for the certainty of the Russian musical world. In 1932, the main obstacle to his return seemed to have been removed: the RAPM had been scrapped and replaced by the Union of Soviet Composers. Prokofiev was not the only one to see the foundation of this new organization as a liberation from the strict dogmatism of the RAPM. Nothing now seemed to stand in the way of his homecoming. He drew no conclusions from the suicide of his friend Mayakovsky in 1930. During his third visit to the Soviet Union in the fall of 1932, he openly demonstrated his loyalty to the regime and planned to write the music for a Soviet satirical film, *Lieutenant Kije*. He departed with the promise, issued through the press, that he would be returning very soon.

## CHAPTER TWELVE

# From *Yezhovshchina* to *Zhdanovshchina*

In about 1930 the source of modernism in Soviet music began running dry. Composers such as Roslavets and Mosolov were coming under fire from the RAPM. Roslavets tried to cover himself by writing agitprop songs, and from 1931 to 1933 he withdrew from the musical scene in Leningrad and Moscow, spending the years in Tashkent as conductor and composer at the Uzbek National Theater and as director of the Uzbek broadcasting station. On returning to Moscow in 1933, he was given such unimportant jobs as radio producer, instructor of military bandmasters, and leader of a gypsy ensemble. Mosolov came off even worse: he was sentenced to hard labor in the years 1937 and 1938, although his sentence was eventually commuted to exile. He was then barred from living in Moscow, Leningrad, or Kiev, and devoted himself to research into folk song.

Folkloristic studies or unimportant bureaucratic posts were indeed typical outlets for modernist composers who had been active in the 1920s. Deshevov went to Uzbekistan to study folk music; Schillinger went to Georgia and then emigrated to the United States in 1928; Gnesin practically gave up composing in the 1930s for a career in education and public administration.

The modernism of the twenties was now labeled "formalism," and intense pressure from the regime helped to silence most modernists. Soviet historiographers expunged their names from the records, and it was not until the 1980s that an official attempt was made to reappraise the contributions of Roslavets, Mosolov, and Lourié.

The regime's unrelenting grip on Soviet composers was revealed with particularly dramatic effect on 28 January 1936, when *Pravda,* the Party paper, published the following anonymous article:

CHAOS INSTEAD OF MUSIC:
ON THE OPERA *THE LADY MACBETH OF THE MTSENSK DISTRICT*

Along with the general cultural development in our country, the demand for good music has also grown. Never before and nowhere else have composers had such appreciative audiences. The masses expect not only good songs, but also good instrumental works, and good operas.

Some theaters are offering Shostakovich's opera *The Lady Macbeth of the Mtsensk District* as a novelty, as a work of art, to the new, culturally developed Soviet public. Obliging critics praise the opera to the skies and enthusiastically commend it. Instead of an objective and serious critique that might prove helpful to him in his further work, the young composer receives nothing but glowing compliments.

The listener is stunned from the first moment by a deliberately discordant and chaotic stream of sound. Snatches of melody and embryonic musical phrases appear, fade away, reappear, and disappear again in the blaring, the grating, and the jarring. It is difficult to follow this "music," impossible to remember it.

Virtually the whole opera proceeds in the same way. Singing gives way on the stage to bawling. Whenever the composer chances upon a simple and comprehensible melody, he immediately—as if appalled by such a disaster—plunges back into the maze of musical chaos, which in places degenerates into cacophony. The expressive force for which the listener is waiting makes way for a furious rhythm. This musical racket can only whip up passion.

All this is due not to the composer's lack of talent, nor to his inability to express ordinary and strong feelings in music. This is music "stood on its head," written deliberately so as not to echo classical opera, to have nothing in common with symphonic sounds, or with simple, universally accessible music. This music is constructed as a denial of opera, with which "leftist" art in general rejects simplicity, realism, and intelligible spectacle, as well as the natural clarity of the spoken word on the stage. Thus the most negative features of "Meyerholdism" are carried to the nth degree and applied to opera, to music. This is "leftist" deformation instead of natural, human music. The ability of good music to captivate the masses is sacrificed here to petit bourgeois and formalistic exertions, and to sham originality achieved by cheap and extravagant means. This is a meaningless game that may well come to a very bad end.

The danger of this trend to Soviet music is clear. "Leftism" in opera stems from the same source as "leftism" in painting, poetry, teaching, and science. Petit bourgeois "innovations" lead to a break with genuine art, genuine science, and genuine literature.

To endow his heroes with "passion," the author of *The Lady Macbeth of the Mtsensk District* has had to borrow his nervous, frenetic, and epileptic music from jazz.

While our critics—including our music critics—swear by socialist realism, the scene created by Shostakovich presents us with the crudest naturalism. All the characters—the merchants no less than the people—are drawn in an oversimplified and bestial manner. The avaricious merchant's wife, who has been able to acquire riches and power by murderous means, is depicted as a kind of "victim" of bourgeois society. As a result, Leskov's moral tale has a significance imposed upon it that it does not possess.

And all this is coarse, primitive, and vulgar. The music quacks and groans and puffs and pants, in order to portray love scenes as naturally as possible. And "love" is plastered all over the opera in the most vulgar manner. The merchant's double bed takes center stage. On that bed, all "problems" are solved. In the same naturalistic style, death by poisoning is presented on the stage almost like a slaughter.

The composer has clearly not made it his business to heed what the Soviet public looks for in music and expects of it. As if by design, he has encoded his music and jumbled up all the sounds in such a way that it can only appeal to aesthetes and formalists who have lost all touch with good taste. He has ignored the determination of Soviet culture to banish crassness and crudeness from every corner of Soviet daily life. Some critics have described the acclamation of mercantile lust as satirical. But there can be no question of satire here. With all the means of musical as well as of dramatic expression at his disposal, the author has tried to elicit the sympathy of the audience for the coarse and vulgar yearnings and doings of the merchant's wife, Katerina Izmailova.

*Lady Macbeth* enjoys success with the bourgeois public abroad. Is that audience not full of praise for this opera precisely because it is chaotic and wholly apolitical? Is it not because, with his convulsive, blaring, and neurasthenic music, the author is gratifying the degenerate tastes of the bourgeoisie?

Our theaters have tried hard to be scrupulous in their staging of this opera by Shostakovich. The actors have exhibited great skill in overcoming the stridency, the shrillness, and the raucousness of the orchestra. They have tried to offset the melodic poverty of the opera with their dramatic talents. Alas, the coarse naturalistic traits of the work have only been rendered more obvious as a result. Talented play deserves recognition; wasted ability—compassion.[1]

What had happened? In January 1936 no fewer than three productions of *The Lady Macbeth of the Mtsensk District* were showing in Moscow: one directed by Nemirovich-Danchenko in his own theater; a new production on the Bolshoy Theater's second stage; and a series of guest performances by the Leningrad Maliy Theater. On 26 January Stalin attended a performance at the Bolshoy's affiliated theater. Shostakovich was also present. The performance was a great success, but Stalin refused to receive Shostakovich in his box and ostentatiously left the theater with his entourage before the last act. Shostakovich went home filled with dark premonitions.

On 28 January the bomb exploded: *Pravda* published "Chaos instead of Music." With unprecedented venom, Shostakovich's opera was labeled vulgar, formalistic, and unworthy of the Soviet people. The expression "chaos instead of music" had been used earlier, almost word for word, by an anonymous critic of Stravinsky's *Rite of Spring.* The phrase is typical of a philistine faction that had come to wield considerable influence since the Silver Age over Russian music. Shostakovich was accused of encouraging "leftist" tendencies. And paradoxically enough, it was his ideologically committed *Lady Macbeth of the Mtsensk District,* of all things, that was accused of being apolitical. That accusation shows clearly that the political element in Soviet art had to satisfy very specific criteria. The required music had to be "healthy," accessible, able to move the masses, and was expected to help eradicate "coarseness and shamelessness" from all aspects of Soviet life.

For Stalin the most offensive aspect of the opera was probably its marked erotic naturalism. That aspect also disconcerted several foreign critics. The first love scene between Katerina and Sergey is a musical evocation of the sexual act. Trombone glissandi accompany Sergey's movements with a suggestiveness that leaves little to the imagination, and for which, indeed, the term "pornophony" was coined. Objections to the vulgarity of some of the scenes were made the most of in the *Pravda* article, not least because, in the thirties, the regime was attempting to restore the mores that had been discarded as petit bourgeois during the permissive, sexually liberated twenties.

Stalin's indignation at the opera's overt sexuality was perhaps the immediate cause of the article, but its aim was wider than that. The article fit into the cultural policy of the Party leadership, which aimed to make it clear once and for all that artists would not be allowed to stray unpunished from the Party line. Was there a better way of driving that point home than hitting out at the most successful Soviet composer of the day? With the enormous, worldwide success of *Lady Macbeth* to his credit, Shostakovich, not yet thirty, was the unchallenged star of Soviet composers. In "Chaos instead of Music," the Party made it clear that no one was allowed to ignore its directives, that public success offered no protection, and that the higher they climbed the harder they could fall.

To gain some idea of the effect of the *Pravda* article, we must place it in the context of the political denunciations common in the Soviet press prior to the show trials of 1937 and 1938. The article was written in much the same terms as were being used to topple such political leaders as Zinoviev and Kamenev. The attack on Shostakovich was full of veiled threats. The suggestion that this "meaningless game may well come to a very bad end" was an unmistakable warning that Shostakovich could suffer the same fate as the politicians fallen from grace.

The text was part of the pattern of the great Party purges of its own members and of the Soviet army command, supplemented by the mass arrest of ordinary citizens. The terror soon spread to the entire population, reaching its height in 1937 and 1938. This period is generally referred to as the *Yezhovshchina,* so called after the then head of the People's Commissariat for Internal Affairs, Nikolai Yezhov.

In 1932, Shostakovich had applauded the establishment of the Union of Soviet Composers. That organization had struck him as being a welcome discussion forum and a body capable of safeguarding the interests of composers against zealots like the RAPM. By 1936, however, it had become quite clear what the real aim of the union was. Being directly answerable to the Party leadership, it was the chosen instrument for exerting central control over Soviet music. The union's administrative structure offered musicians no protection whatsoever from the dictatorial whims of Stalin and the Party leadership. The purpose of the organization was total domination.

The events of 1936 demonstrate the efficiency with which the Party leadership had tightened its grip on composers. Instead of defending Shostakovich, the Union of Soviet Composers turned on him. Everyone now tried to save his own skin by proving his loyalty to the regime. The attack on Shostakovich was strongly endorsed by *Sovyetskaya muzïka,* which not only repeated the *Pravda* attack on *Lady Macbeth* but also reprinted a second article from *Pravda* of 6 February entitled "Balletic Falsehood." It was aimed at Shostakovich's ballet *The Limpid Stream,* which had been premièred in the Malïy Theater in Leningrad on 4 June 1935 and dealt with life on a collective farm. *The Limpid Stream* was blasted not so much for its decadent formalism as for its deliberate failure to set off the subject matter with folk music. *Sovyetskaya muzïka* also reprinted a third document: a TASS (official news service) report of a friendly chat between Stalin, Molotov, and Ivan Dzerzhinsky, the composer, conductor, and director of the opera *The Quiet Don.* This work, a so-called "song opera," with music reminiscent of mass songs and based on folkloristic idiom, had been officially approved and was said to be a model for all good Soviet operas.

The discussions of the Union of Soviet Composers turned into a blatant smear campaign against Shostakovich, in which nearly all his colleagues joined. For many, it was an ideal opportunity to work off their jealousy at Shostakovich's phenomenal success. The administrative posts in the Composers Union had deliberately been placed in the hands of the oldest and the youngest generations—for reasons that quickly became apparent as the Party proceeded to play both groups against the truly creative generation of the day, of which Shostakovich was the leading protagonist. The older composers, including Maximilian Steinberg, dissociated themselves from his modernism, while the younger ones declared that Shostakovich's music was alien to them. The composer Tikhon Khrennikov, barely twenty-two, declared:

> How did the youth react to *Lady Macbeth?* In the opera there are some big melodic numbers that opened up for us some creative vistas. The entr'actes and a lot of other things called forth total antipathy. In general, our youth is healthy. A certain faction has succumbed to formalist influences, but this is being overcome; it does not represent any principal objective on our part.[2]

Although most of Shostakovich's former allies turned against him in a panic—Boris Asafyev, for example, to whom Shostakovich had wanted to dedicate the score of *Lady Macbeth,* rejected the opera out of hand— there were exceptions. On 14 March, Vsevolod Meyerhold delivered a lecture in Leningrad, speaking boldly in defense of his colleague. The composer Andrey Balanchivadze also defended Shostakovich in public. Vissarion Shebalin put up a brave front in Moscow as well, but as a result was left without a living, his music no longer performed.

Shostakovich sought the protection of Marshal Tukhachevsky, one of the highest-ranking officers of the Red Army and since 1925 a patron to the composer, but the marshal himself fell victim to the terror. Shostakovich saw many friends and relatives arrested and disappear: the musicologist Nikolai Zhilyayev; Shostakovich's brother-in-law Vsevolod Frederiks; his mother-in-law, Sofiya Varzar; his uncle Maxim Kostrikin; the writers Boris Kornilov, Adrian Piotrovsky (the Malïy Theater's dramaturg), and Galina Serebryakova; and the stage director Vsevolod Meyerhold. For a whole year Shostakovich lived with the sword of Damocles hanging over his head. He completed his Fourth Symphony in April 1936, but was bullied during rehearsals into withdrawing the work. In April 1937 Shostakovich started work on his Fifth Symphony, a work with which he was hoping to rehabilitate himself, and which, accordingly, came up to Party expectations, at least in its outward expression. The Fifth could pass for an example of the heroic classicism demanded by Stalin's cultural policy.

The première of the Fifth Symphony took place on 21 November 1937,

under the baton of the still relatively unknown thirty-four-year-old Yevgeniy Mravinsky. It proved a tumultuous success, so much so that the
last bars were lost in the unprecedented ovation. This triumph was followed by months of public tributes to the composer. The authorities took
the opportunity to stress their own role in Shostakovich's artistic growth:
"See where justified criticism by the Party can lead" was the crux of their
message.

They treated the work as a turning point in Shostakovich's career, the
official critics presenting the symphony as a personal *perestroyka,* or "restructuring," by the composer. A few days before the first Moscow performance on 29 January 1938, the composer himself declared that the
symphony was his "creative response" to the criticism he had endured.
An article in the Moscow newspaper *Vechernyaya Moskva* proclaimed
that "the Fifth Symphony is a Soviet artist's creative response in practice to justified criticism." Whether Shostakovich wrote that declaration
himself is difficult to ascertain. In any case, it coincided with the official
promotion of the work. Shostakovich's rehabilitation was as carefully
calculated as his fall and, like the *Pravda* attack, was part and parcel of
the Party's strategy to make artists bow to its dictates. The regime had
to demonstrate that it could not only smite, but also anoint with balm.

After the extraordinary tributes Shostakovich received for his Fifth,
it was only to be expected that official critics would once again bare their
teeth at the unveiling of his Sixth Symphony. Written in 1939, the work
was first performed on 5 November of that year. Because the structure
again diverged from the classical model—just three instead of four movements, with a strikingly static largo as the opening movement, and with
trite circus music at the end instead of a grandiose finale—the Sixth was
rejected by the official critics. The Union of Soviet Composers needed to
demonstrate that they remained vigilant, no matter how successful a composer might be.

## THE "LIBERATING" WAR

The subjection of art came to a sudden end with the German attack on
the Soviet Union on 22 June 1941. By the end of that year, Kiev had fallen,
Leningrad was besieged, and the Germans were approaching Moscow.
Cultural institutions were evacuated, and so were most composers:
Prokofiev went to Nalchik in the Caucasus and then to Alma Ata;
Myaskovsky traveled via Nalchik to Tiflis and later to Frunze. Only a
few artistic institutions, such as the radio orchestras and Moscow's

Stanislavsky–Nemirovich-Danchenko Theater, stayed behind. Shostakovich endured the horrifying siege of Leningrad until he was evacuated
to Moscow on 1 October 1941. Influenced by the misery he had wit-
nessed, he composed his Seventh Symphony, known as the *Leningrad*.
He started on the work in that city but finished it in Kuybïshev. "Never
in my life," he wrote, "have I dedicated my compositions to anyone.
But this symphony—if I succeed in its realization—I shall dedicate to
Leningrad. For all that I wrote into it, all that I expressed in it, is tied up
with that beloved native city of mine, is connected with the historic days
of its defense against fascist oppressors."[3]

The first performance of the Seventh Symphony was given in Kuybïshev on 5 March 1942, with Samuil Samosud conducting the Bolshoy
Theater Orchestra. The symphony then went to Moscow and after that
abroad, traveling around the world before it was heard in Leningrad.
On 22 June 1942, Henry Wood conducted it in London; on 19 July
Toscanini gave a radio performance, which served as its American première. In 1942 and 1943 the work was performed no fewer than sixty-
two times in the United States. Leningrad was finally given the chance
to hear "her symphony" on 9 August 1942 in a performance by the Radio Orchestra under Karl Eliasberg. The effect of this concert on the starving city can scarcely be exaggerated. The orchestra had been reduced by
the war to a mere fourteen players, and for this occasion their ranks were
filled with retired players. Musicians who were fighting at the front were
given special leave to participate in the performance. Laurel Fay describes
the situation thus:

> The obstacles to performance in the devastated city were enormous. Over-
> coming them became a matter of civic, even military, pride. In early July, the
> score of Shostakovich's symphony was flown by night to the blockaded city.
> A team of copyists worked day and night—despite shortages of paper, pen-
> cils, and pens—to prepare the parts. More serious was the insufficiency of
> brass players to tackle Shostakovich's score; most had to be tracked down at
> the front. By the end of July the orchestra was rehearsing full time. The con-
> cert hall on 9 August 1942 was packed, and the audience applauded with all
> the strength they could muster. The concert was also broadcast on loud-
> speakers throughout the city and, in psychological warfare, to the German
> troops stalled outside the city. They had been targets of an intensive artillery
> bombardment in advance ordered by the commander of the Leningrad front
> to ensure their silence during the performance of Shostakovich's Seventh.[4]

The authorities were well aware of the psychological impact of art,
and supported every form of artistic endeavor that might rally the people
behind the fight for their country. Stalin's propaganda played on the en-

tire gamut of nationalistic sentiments. He called the war "the Great Patriotic War," adopting the popular name of the defensive campaign against Napoleon. The Stalin cult reached its apogee at the beginning of the Second World War. All history was presented as an inevitable progression to Stalin's regime, and all important historical figures, including Alexander Nevsky, Ivan the Terrible, and Marshal Kutuzov, as prefigurations of the "consummator of Russian history." The regime ordered all these revisions of history to be shown artistically in a Stalinist light, above all in the popular medium of the film. Thus Prokofiev was commissioned to write the music for *Alexander Nevsky* and for *Ivan the Terrible,* by Sergey Eisenstein. At the same time, he also started work on an opera based on Tolstoy's *War and Peace.* As he himself explained, he saw this work as a reaction to contemporary historical events.

The government relied on the patriotism of Soviet artists and so left them largely in peace. With the subjection of art no longer a priority, the war period was a time of relative freedom and great creativity for Russian composers. During the war years, Shostakovich wrote the Eighth Symphony; the Second Piano Sonata; the Six Romances, op. 62; the Piano Trio; and the Second String Quartet. In addition, he started on a new opera project along the lines of *The Nose,* called *The Gamblers,* based on a play by Gogol. Shostakovich's decision to write an opera was the more remarkable in the face of the negative experiences with the genre he had undergone with *Lady Macbeth.* It may be that he thought the repressive period was over for good. In *The Gamblers,* he planned to deploy the old *kuchka* realism of Dargomïzhsky and Musorgsky more closely than he had in *The Nose,* and to include every word of Gogol's text. He started on the work in December 1941, but put it to one side at the end of 1942, having come to realize that without drastic cuts in the text the opera would assume unwieldy proportions.[5]

For Sergey Prokofiev and Nikolai Myaskovsky, too, the war years were a fruitful period. In addition to film·music and the *War and Peace* project, Prokofiev wrote the Second String Quartet and the Fifth Symphony, and sketched out his Sixth Symphony, which he would complete in 1947. Myaskovsky, for his part, wrote, among many other works, a cello concerto and Symphonies Nos. 22, 23, and 24. The Twenty-third Symphony was based on Caucasian folklore, with which Myaskovsky and Prokofiev had become acquainted during their stay in Nalchik in 1941. Symphonies Nos. 22 and 24 were more direct responses to war experiences. In his original plan for the Twenty-second, Myaskovsky gave each movement a programmatic title: the first, "Peaceful Life, Overshadowed Occasionally by Threats"; the second, "Harkening to the Horrors of War"; and the third, "And the Enemy Trembled."[6]

The war filled Soviet artists with the hope that the repressive days of the 1930s had been relegated to the past, although only too soon it became apparent that these hopes were vain. The first indication was the cool reception accorded Shostakovich's Eighth Symphony. The work was a counterpart of the Seventh, or *Leningrad,* Symphony, in which Shostakovich had painted the war in a heroic light. The Eighth provided a deeper and artistically more profound reaction to the war: besides heroism and patriotism, it also gave voice to suffering and tragedy. The performance on 4 November 1943 came too late to drive this point home, however, because the fortunes of war had just then begun to turn in favor of the Soviet Union; what the authorities were looking for now was above all the optimistic strains accompanying the imminent victory. At a meeting of the Composers Union in March 1944 the Eighth Symphony was mercilessly taken to task. Mravinsky conducted the work in December 1944 in liberated Leningrad, but after that the work disappeared from the repertoire, not to be rehabilitated until 1957.

Prokofiev must have read the writing on the wall as early as May 1942, when his opera *War and Peace* was returned by the Committee for Artistic Affairs in Moscow with a list of required revisions. Although he had chosen the opera because of its relevance to the war, Prokofiev stuck to the realism he had developed in *The Gambler* and *The Fiery Angel,* concentrating less on the great historical tableaux than on the individual fate of such characters as Pierre Bezukhov, Andrey Bolkonsky, and Natasha Rostova. The committee, however, insisted on unequivocal emphasis on the novel's patriotism and on a larger part for Marshal Kutuzov, whom they presented as embodying Stalin's role as Russian commander-in-chief. With that, the tortured path of the opera began, the work being dragged for ten years through one revision after another. It did not achieve its definitive form until 1952.

Following the rejection of his Eighth Symphony, Shostakovich also encountered opposition to his Ninth, composed in 1945. Everyone had been expecting a "real Ninth," with soloists, chorus, and the rest, and for it to be the musical crowning of the victory gained in the Great Patriotic War—an impression created by Shostakovich himself when he declared in October 1943, on the eve of the première of the Eighth Symphony, that his Ninth would be dedicated to the theme of the victory and the greatness of the Russian people. In the issue of the newspaper *Sovetskoye Iskusstvo* published on 7 November 1944, the anniversary of the

October Revolution, he wrote: "What are my dreams today, reflecting on the future of our creative art? Undoubtedly, like every Soviet artist, I harbor the tremulous dream of a large-scale work in which the over-powering feelings ruling us today would find expression. I think that the epigraph to all our work in the coming years will be the single word 'Victory.'"[7]

During the winter of 1945 musical circles were aware of the progress Shostakovich had made on his monumental symphony. Izaak Glikman tells us that the composer played the beginning to him at the end of April: "Majestic in scale, in pathos, in its breathtaking motion."[8] We can only guess, therefore, at why Shostakovich stopped working on the symphony and, indeed, apparently changed his plans dramatically. The Ninth Symphony he actually composed in no way resembles the monumental choral symphony he had planned. It turned out to be a purely instrumental, lightly orchestrated symphony full of satire and irony. Most of Shostakovich's colleagues reacted positively to the musical qualities of the work and to the joie de vivre it exudes. That the authorities nevertheless took a stand against it emerges among other things from the fact that the symphony did not gain him a Stalin Prize.

## THE IRON GRIP RESTORED

The years after the war's end were a period of severe trial for artists and intellectuals. The regime was determined to restore its grip on the intelligentsia. Stalin himself set the tone of postwar cultural policy in his speeches of 24 May 1945 and 9 February 1946. Following the defeat of fascism, he proclaimed Western capitalism the new enemy. National pride and anti-Western sentiment dominated postwar Soviet propaganda. In art, all traces of decadent formalism were once again to be eradicated, the ideological reorientation of intellectual life being entrusted by the regime to Andrey Zhdanov, secretary of the Central Committee. Zhdanov was no unknown in cultural circles: in 1934 he had presided over the First All-Union Congress of Soviet Writers, where socialist realism had been formally proclaimed. His assignment after the war was to oversee nothing short of the total reindoctrination of artists and intellectuals. The period of his notorious campaign of repression has entered history under the name of *Zhdanovshchina*.

Zhdanov set to work with unsparing thoroughness. On the model of the prewar campaign against Shostakovich, he aimed his shafts at prominent figures in particular, inciting the younger generation against them.

He started by turning his attention to literature, publishing his first resolution, the "Resolution on the Journals *Zvezda* and *Leningrad*," on 14 August 1946. He accused the two journals of having published "works which cultivated a non-Soviet spirit of servility before the contemporary bourgeois culture of the West." He decreed that Soviet journals could never be nonpolitical: "Any preaching of 'art for art's sake' . . . is harmful to the interests of the Soviet people and the Soviet state." Alexander Fadeyev, a militant disciple of Stalin, was appointed head of the Writers Union. He accused Boris Pasternak of upholding a form of individualism that is "profoundly alien to the spirit of our society." Zhdanov himself chose the poet Anna Akhmatova and the satirist Mikhaíl Zoshchenko as his pet scapegoats, accusing them of individualism and formalism. His crude personal attack on Anna Akhmatova has become notorious. He accused her of being "not exactly a nun, not exactly a harlot, but rather nun and harlot, with whom harlotry is mixed with prayer." As for Zoshchenko, he bluntly called him a "scum of literature."[9]

On 26 August, Zhdanov turned his attention to the theater, with a resolution entitled "On the Repertoire of the Dramatic Theaters and Measures for Its Improvement." According to Zhdanov, too many plays served the propaganda of reactionary bourgeois ideology. Film was dealt with in the resolution of 4 September 1946 entitled "On the Film *Bolshaya Zhizn* [*The Great Life*]." Unforgivable in this film was the "backwardness, vulgarity, and ignorance" of its portrayal of the Soviet people. Also condemned were the second part of Eisenstein's film *Ivan the Terrible* and Pudovkin's *Admiral Nakhimov*. Eisenstein was told that he "exhibited ignorance of historical facts by portraying the progressive army of *Oprichniki* as a band of degenerates, similar to the American Ku Klux Klan, and Ivan the Terrible, a man of strong will and character, as weak and spineless, something like Hamlet."[10]

On 10 February 1948 Zhdanov turned his attention to music with the resolution "On the Opera *Velikaya Druzhba* [*The Great Friendship*] by Muradeli." By way of an attack on musical formalism, he paradoxically enough directed his gibes at an opera that, intended for the thirtieth anniversary celebration of the October Revolution, had been deliberately written to satisfy all the criteria of socialist realism. Vano Muradeli, a Georgian composer of Shostakovich's generation, had chosen a nationalist theme, with the Georgian commissar Ordzhonikidze as his hero. What Muradeli did not realize at the time was that Stalin had probably had a hand in Ordzhonikidze's death during the 1937 purges. Moreover, Muradeli had portrayed the people of the northern Caucasus

(Georgians, Ossets, and Lesghians) as enemies of Russia during the civil war. Stalin thought otherwise, holding that these people had always been allies of the Russians and had helped them to victory. The gravest accusation leveled at the composer was therefore that he had been guilty of "falsification of the historical facts."

The resolution of 10 February was not confined to Muradeli. Every prominent musician came under fire, including Myaskovsky, Prokofiev, Shostakovich, Khachaturyan, Shebalin, and Popov. Dmitry Kabalevsky, a composer who had taught at the Moscow Conservatory since 1932, was originally named as well, but his contacts in official circles were sufficient to have his name quickly removed from the list. All these composers were accused of "formalistic distortions and anti-democratic tendencies which are alien to the Soviet people and its artistic taste."[11]

Before he published his resolution, Zhdanov convened an informal meeting with the members of the Composers Union. Once again the antagonism of 1936 was reenacted, with the older and the younger composers joining forces against the middle generation, which in creative respects was the most influential. Zhdanov exploited this antagonism. As the older and the younger generations poured out all their frustrations in a long campaign of innuendo, the targeted leading composers had no other option than to accuse themselves, repent, and accept the Party's guidance. Muradeli, for one, tried to blame the influence of his teachers and colleagues. He made great play of the pernicious effect of Shostakovich, and of *The Lady Macbeth of the Mtsensk District* in particular. This charge hit Shostakovich all the harder because it offered Zhdanov an opportunity to remind the composer that the objections to the formalism of *Lady Macbeth* still held, and that he had repeated his old mistakes in his Eighth Symphony.

Following the publication of the 1948 resolution, the Composers Union convened special meetings to ratify that "historic document" formally (Plate 25). The younger generation seized on the opportunity to gain a privileged position in the hierarchy. The composer Tikhon Khrennikov, then aged thirty-four and author of the "song opera" *Into the Storm* (1939), was handpicked to assume the leadership of the union. The old administrative body, the ORGKOMITET (Organizational Committee), was dissolved, and Khrennikov was appointed general secretary. The rest of the administration was entrusted to Party followers—in contrast to the dissolved ORGKOMITET, on which such prominent composers as Glière, Shostakovich, Kabalevsky, and Khachaturyan had still served. The sole artistic figure of any renown in the new body was Boris Asafyev, who became chairman of the new directorate of the Composers Union—a purely honorary post. He was, in fact, but a shadow of the influential figure he had been in the 1920s, and when he died on 27 January 1949, Khrennikov took complete charge of the Composers Union.

Zhdanov died six months after the promulgation of his resolution, though not before he was able to sully Soviet science as well with his official endorsement of the untenable genetic theories of Trofim Lysenko. Zhdanov's death did not mean the end of *Zhdanovshchina*, for the bureaucrats continued his ideological attack on the intelligentsia. In the Composers Union, Khrennikov ensured the implementation of Party decisions. The condemned composers confessed their guilt and went on to write nothing but simplistic, accessible works, including Shostakovich's oratorio *The Song of the Forests*, Prokofiev's cantata *On Guard for Peace*, and Myaskovsky's Twenty-seventh Symphony. As in 1937, the Party let it be known that those toeing the line would be rewarded. For the above-mentioned works, each of the composers received a Stalin Prize.

*Soviet Music Is Forging Ahead* was the title of a collection of essays the Composers Union published in 1950 with the intention of demonstrating that the 1948 resolution had benefited Soviet music. At a meeting of the Moscow section of the union, the most recent works of Shostakovich (the film score for *Molodaya Gvardia*) and of Khachaturyan (*Symphonic Dithyramb in Memory of Lenin*) were, without much enthusiasm, judged "acceptable." Muradeli was extolled for his recent choral works. The main attack was reserved for Prokofiev's latest opera, *The Story of a Real Man*: "Formalism still lives in the music of Soviet composers. This is demonstrated by the new opera of Prokofiev. . . . In the modernistic, anti-melodic music of his opera, in the treatment of the Soviet people, the composer remains on his old positions, condemned by the Party and by Soviet Society."[12] As if that charge were not enough, Prokofiev was reproached as well for not having presented his opera to the union for "constructive criticism" while working on it.

Myaskovsky was deeply upset by these accusations and made special efforts to turn his last works into direct, clear, and accessible compositions. His rehabilitation began with the positive reception of his Cello Sonata, first performed by Mstislav Rostropovich on 5 March 1949. At the end of 1948 he was allowed to resume his post and continue teaching composition at the Moscow Conservatory. His last symphony, the Twenty-seventh, enjoyed immense success, the critics greeting this retrospective work as proof of the composer's final reorientation. Myaskovsky was no longer there to witness its reception, however, for he died on 9 August 1950. The première took place on 5 December.

Vissarion Shebalin was removed from the Moscow Conservatory in 1948 and not rehabilitated until 1951, when he had his posts as director and teacher restored. Khachaturyan blamed his own temporary deviation from socialist realism on the noxious influence of critics and musicologists who had urged him to overcome the limitations of his strict Armenian national style. He accordingly returned to the folkloristic and heroic style he had developed in his ballet *Gayaneh* (1942).

For Shostakovich the story of 1936 was repeated, with the difference that this time he was not alone. Yuriy Abramovich Levitin, an eyewitness and composer who had been studying under Shostakovich at the Leningrad Conservatory since 1938, described his situation as follows:

> Nina Vasilyevna, Dmitri Dmitriyevich's first wife, together with his close friend, the cinema director Leo Oskarovich Arnshtam, and myself went by car to the Sanatorium outside Moscow, where Dmitri Dmitriyevich stayed for some days. He was in a terrible state. We calmed him down as best we could. I reminded him how he had succeeded in overcoming all the difficulties which had been created by the article "Muddle Instead of Music" in 1936, and how he had composed so many marvellous works afterwards. But, quite honestly, our persuasions were of little effect. Nina Vasilyevna went for a walk in the garden with Dmitri Dmitriyevich, while Leo Arnshtam and I sat on a bench and waited, our hearts saddened. After a while Nina Vasilyevna returned in tears and said it would probably be best to take Dmitri Dmitriyevich home.
> "You cannot imagine our position. Mitya is on the verge of suicide."
> We have often heard talk of the incredible force of Shostakovich's spirit, of his great willpower. This was indeed so, but who knows what it cost him, this man who put kindness and justice above all else, and who was himself so unjustly insulted and humiliated. Fortunately, Dmitri Dmitriyevich was able to overcome these blows of fortune on this occasion as well, and before long he rebounded on his feet.[13]

Shostakovich acknowledged his lapses publicly. He admitted his mistakes and expressed gratitude to the Party, in accordance with Stalinist protocol, for its clear directives. While the harassment in the Composers Union continued, Shostakovich was charged by the authorities with representing the Soviet Union abroad. He went on his first trip to the United States in 1949, where he was obliged to attend the first World Peace Congress in New York from 25 to 28 March. This placed him in a highly visible but equivocal position. At home the regime tried to keep him on a short leash, but abroad it exploited his international reputation and expected him to show the Soviet Union in the best possible light.

Shostakovich's arrival in New York brought the tension between Soviet composers and émigrés to a head. Stravinsky refused to sign a telegram by American composers welcoming Shostakovich. His reply to Olin Downes was quoted in the press: "Regret not to be able to join welcomers of Soviet artists coming this country. But all my ethic and esthetic convictions oppose such gesture." That was grist to the mills of the Soviet press, who rounded on Stravinsky as a "traitor and enemy of our fatherland." To journalists, Stravinsky explained why he would rather not engage in a public debate with Shostakovich: "How can you talk to them? They are not free. There can be no public discussion with people who are not free."[14]

Shostakovich was ordered to deliver a speech written by Party bureaucrats (Plate 26). The émigré composer Nicolas Nabokov has told us what happened:

> When, after several trying and ludicrous speeches, his turn came to speak he began to read his prepared talk in a nervous and shaky voice. After a few sentences he broke off, and the speech was continued in English by a suave radio baritone. In all the equivocation of that conference, Shostakovich's speech was at least direct. Written in the standard style of Agitprop speeches, it was quite obviously prepared by the "party organs" in charge of the Waldorf-Astoria conference, on the Soviet side of the picture. In it these "organs" through their mouthpiece, the composer Shostakovich, condemned most Western music as decadent and bourgeois, painted the glories of the rising Soviet music culture, attacked the demon Stravinsky as the corruptor of Western art (with a dig at Prokofiev) and urged upon the "progressive Americans" of the conference the necessity of fighting against reactionaries and warmongers in America . . . and admitted that the "mouthpiece" (Mr Shostakovich) had itself often erred and sinned against the decrees of the Party. I sat in my seat petrified by this spectacle of human misery and degradation.[15]

During the conference, protests against the presence of the Soviet delegation erupted all over the United States, so much so that their tour of the country was called off. The international public relations campaign, however, continued. In November 1950 Shostakovich attended the Peace Congress in Warsaw, and in December 1952, the one held in Vienna.

Soviet attacks on composers were unpredictable and arbitrary, not least because of the vague nature of the theory of socialist realism. Marina Frolova-Walker summed it up:

> "Socialist Realism" was never worked out as a coherent theory, although enormous efforts were expended in attempting to create the illusion of one. Rather, it amounted only to a range of slogans with obscure gray valleys between them. In truth, officials found this vagueness and lack of coherence far too useful

to be sacrificed, for it allowed them unlimited flexibility in manipulating artists. Given two works of similar character, one might be praised and the other condemned, according to some momentary official whim. Attacks on composers were sometimes based on nothing more than fear that the absence of criticism might attract unwelcome attention to the critic concerned: no one wanted to march out of step.[16]

Perhaps the most tragic victim of *Zhdanovshchina* was Prokofiev. In 1948 it became clear beyond question that he had misread the signs on his return to the Soviet Union in 1932. He had adopted Soviet nationality in that year, although he kept his apartment in Paris until 1936, when he took the final step of leaving the West. At first he held a privileged position in the Soviet Union. Unlike his colleagues, he did not have to teach to earn a living; he could live by his pen. He was also offered the opportunity of going on foreign tours and had just left the Soviet Union when the storm burst around Shostakovich's *Lady Macbeth of the Mtsensk District*. However, the full impact of his return home did not make itself felt until 1939, with the arrest and execution of Meyerhold. The stage director had been not only Prokofiev's close friend but also one of his artistic partners; together they had launched Pushkin's *Boris Godunov,* with music by Prokofiev, and the opera *Semyon Kotko,* both of which proved unsuccessful. By 1939, however, it was already too late for Prokofiev to leave the Soviet Union. That year all foreign travel was banned.

For Prokofiev the war was a time of evacuation and travel, and also of undisturbed creativity. In Nalchik, in the Caucasus, he started work on *War and Peace,* on the Second String Quartet, and on the orchestral suite *The Year 1941.* Friends who visited him in Nalchik, including Myaskovsky and the Lamm family, mentioned the carefree impression Prokofiev then made. "We were astonished," Olga Lamm wrote. "What had happened to the carelessly condescending attitude toward others? He was simple and kind with everyone, received guests in his room with the greatest pleasure—sharing everything he had on his table—and was concerned and welcoming."[17] From Nalchik, Prokofiev moved on to Tiflis, the Georgian capital. There he continued to work on *War and Peace* and wrote his Seventh Piano Sonata. Olga Lamm relates: "In his creative inspiration, Prokofiev had exerted a joyful influence on all of us, and forced others—through his wonderful music and robust, energetic presence—to face the trials of the time more courageously."[18]

In May 1942, Prokofiev joined Sergey Eisenstein in Alma Ata, the capital of Kazakhstan, where the Soviet film studios had been moved in 1941.

Eisenstein was working on his film *Ivan the Terrible* and asked Prokofiev to write the score. Once in Alma Ata, Prokofiev was also approached for other film projects, such as the war films *Tonya, Kotovsky,* and *Partisans in the Ukrainian Steppe,* and *Lermontov,* a biography of the Russian romantic poet. His collaboration with the film director Albert Gendelstein, however, quickly went awry.

In 1943, Prokofiev was awarded his first Stalin Prize, which was followed by a series of official honors, including the Order of the Red Banner of Labor and the title of Honored Artist of the Russian Soviet Socialist Republic. In Alma Ata, Prokofiev also started work on *Khan Buzay,* an opera based on Kazakh folklore. He did not complete the work. Meanwhile, his music was being played with great success in Moscow, where he enjoyed the support of the critics.

On 13 January 1945 Prokofiev's Fifth Symphony had its première. The performance had to be delayed when suddenly cannon salvos were heard in the streets, fired to pay tribute to the Red Army soldiers setting out on their triumphant advance on Germany. Partly because of the great expectations of the audience, the concert was a triumph. The Fifth earned Prokofiev another Stalin Prize, as did the Eighth Piano Sonata and the first part of *Ivan the Terrible.* His fifty-fifth birthday on 23 April 1946 was the occasion of a series of concerts in his honor.

After this wave of recognition, the sabotage of the production of the second part of *War and Peace* by Party officials came as a great blow. Prokofiev looked upon this opera as his greatest work and was impatient to see it staged. The production in the Leningrad Malïy Theater had been carefully rehearsed under the conductor Samuil Samosud and the director Boris Pokrovsky, but the opera did not progress beyond the dress rehearsal. "Errors in the historical concept," was the gist of the authorities' objections. In other words, the scenes were not heroic and nationalistic enough. With *War and Peace,* Prokofiev suffered the same frustration as he had earlier with his *Fiery Angel.* His hopes that a return to the Soviet Union would further his career as an opera composer, which had been thwarted in the West, proved idle.

As his response to official criticism, Prokofiev wrote two safe works for the thirtieth anniversary of the October Revolution: *A Festive Poem* ("Thirty Years") and the cantata *Flourish, O Mighty Land,* using verses by Yevgeny Dolmatovsky, a state-approved poet. He also completed his Sixth Symphony, which was warmly acclaimed at its première on 11 October 1947, the musicologist Grigoriy Shneerson writing: "This great work shows once again how immeasurably superior Soviet music is to the music of the capitalist West, where symphonism has long ceased to be an art of lofty ideas and high emotionalism, and is now in a state of profound decadence and degeneration."[19]

Following Zhdanov's resolution, however, opinions were radically revised. The Sixth was declared a model of formalism and disappeared from the repertoire. At Zhdanov's notorious informal meeting with the Composers Union in January, Prokofiev's name cropped up time and again. The younger members rounded on him because they resented his international standing and the privileges he enjoyed in the Soviet Union. Illness prevented Prokofiev from attending the meetings that followed the publication of the resolution. In a letter he declared that he had made a deliberate effort after his return to the Soviet Union to discover an accessible but artistically responsible style, and that he thought he had succeeded in finding it in his *Alexander Nevsky, Romeo and Juliet,* and the Fifth Symphony. "The Resolution is valuable," he continued loyally, "precisely in that it pointed out how alien the formalistic movement is to the Soviet people. This movement leads to the impoverishment and decline of music. At the same time the Resolution has shown us the goals toward which we need to strive to better serve the Soviet people."[20]

Official criticism of his work was not the only trial Prokofiev had to endure. He was also hit hard personally by the arrest of his first wife, Carolina (Lina) Codina, though he had been separated from her for years, having started a new relationship in 1939 with Mira Mendelson. In March 1941 he left his family, and although there was never an official divorce, he nevertheless married Mira on 13 January 1948, relying on the legal argument that his marriage to Lina had not been officially registered in accordance with Soviet law.

Lina had followed Prokofiev to Moscow, but she did not have her husband's links with Russia. The daughter of a Spanish father and a mother who was part Polish and part Huguenot, from Alsace, she had originally been of Spanish nationality. When Prokofiev left her, she felt imprisoned in a country in which, apart from her children, she had no family and had to forgo the luxuries to which she had been used in the West. However, this awkward situation was as nothing compared with the trials that lay in store for her.

On 20 February 1948 she was arrested on charges of espionage. There is no evidence whatsoever that this accusation had any substance; it was a lot that fell to thousands of foreigners that year. Lina was sentenced to hard labor and spent eight years in Siberia. She was not released until 1956.

Lina's arrest was an indirect attack on Prokofiev, the authorities using it to demonstrate that being a leading artist was no guarantee of personal safety. Prokofiev was never officially notified of the arrest, but heard
the news from his two sons, Oleg and Svyatoslav. Nothing is known about
any attempt by Prokofiev to help Lina—the arrest came, and not by
chance, at a time when Prokofiev himself was in a weak position. His
friends advised him not to go out of his way to intercede, lest he be arrested himself. Be that as it may, this tragic event was to becloud the rest
of his life. Not only did it touch him personally, but it saddled him with
enormous moral responsibility for his wife's tragedy. It had been for him
and for his art, after all, that Lina had moved to Moscow. She had been
made to pay the price for Prokofiev's naive belief that an artist of his
renown had nothing to fear from the regime.

## CHAPTER THIRTEEN

# "Prokofiev Must Return to Us"

While Sergey Prokofiev's talent is beyond question, his career as a composer was a succession of misjudgments. There are many examples, large and small. The first mistake was his dismissal of the American musical scene as conservative and narrow-minded. In 1926 he told a journalist: "You all ride in automobiles, and yet you lag behind in music. I would prefer you rode in horse-drawn carriages, but were more up-to-date in music."[1] America had been the first planned stage in Prokofiev's international career, but he returned from the United States with the belief that the future of music lay in Europe. All his actions from 1918 to 1932 can be seen as a step-by-step return, first to western Europe, and then to Moscow. This road led in the opposite direction from that taken by the musical avant-garde: toward the end of the thirties the leading composers were on the other side of the Atlantic, while Prokofiev was locked away in Russia.

Another mistake was his disagreement with Balanchine over the staging of *The Prodigal Son*. Prokofiev completely failed to appreciate Balanchine's creative contribution. In a discussion of royalties, Prokofiev is said to have brushed the choreographer aside arrogantly: "Why should you get money? Who are you? You're nothing but a lousy ballet master."[2] Plainly Prokofiev did not foresee that Balanchine would become Diaghilev's artistic heir and a mainstay of Stravinsky's career after the disbandment of the Ballets Russes.

Prokofiev misjudged also the importance and the tenacity of the modernist movement. In an interview with Olin Downes of the *New York Times* during his 1930 American tour, Prokofiev stated that modernism in music had gone as far as it could. Yet at the time that he himself was returning to a melodic style and traditional forms, the most radical consequences of modernism were still to come.

Opera was yet another miscalculation in Prokofiev's career. The genre had noticeably lost ground in the West, where avant-garde circles had come to consider it outdated. Modern operas had great difficulty in keeping their place in the repertoire, a trend that continues to this day. The fundamental cause of the trouble was not so much the absence of interest or skill among composers as the lack of economic viability. Under twentieth-century market conditions, opera had become a commercial absurdity. Given the huge rise in wages and the discrepancy between costs and revenue, it could simply no longer pay its way, let alone make a profit. Diaghilev realized this during his first Paris seasons and drew his own conclusions.

Prokofiev was heedful only of the artistic aspect of the situation and felt capable of modernizing the genre. His understanding of the international opera circuit was found wanting, however, so much so that he concluded from the debacle of his *Fiery Angel* that his career in the West was over.

All these miscalculations, however, pale into insignificance compared with Prokofiev's greatest mistake: his return to the Soviet Union. Had he returned in the 1920s, his choice could perhaps have been explained by the promising artistic climate in Russia at the time. But Prokofiev returned in the middle of the thirties, when Stalin had already launched his campaign of political repression and the regime was preparing to shackle the arts. Prokofiev's decision is generally attributed to nostalgia and political naïveté—an explanation that does not take us very far. Nostalgia is barely discernible in his correspondence, and a patent readiness to work in the service of a regime that was shocking the world with its brutality is hard to characterize as political naïveté. The real explanation for his decision is most likely to be sought in a combination of several factors.

The foremost of these was the great success his music enjoyed in the Soviet Union. The production of *The Love for Three Oranges* in Leningrad's Mariyinsky Theater in 1926 was given an enthusiastic reception. Prokofiev's 1927 tour of the Soviet Union was a triumph. At that time, Anatoliy Lunacharsky tried to coax him into staying on: "To realize his full potential, Prokofiev must return to us," he declared.

Myaskovsky, too, Prokofiev's fellow student and loyal champion, tried to talk him into remaining in the Soviet Union. In 1932 he wrote to Prokofiev: "If a *pied-à-terre* could be found for you here, it would be just delightful to have you in the midst of Soviet composers. . . . It would really refresh and shake up our pedagogical and creative existence. Soviet musical life needs fresh air—we have argued with each other too much and have forgotten about music."[3]

By the time he went on his first tour of the Soviet Union in 1927, Prokofiev's fame in the West had begun to falter. The successful production in 1929 of *The Prodigal Son* by the Ballets Russes gave him the impression that he might still be on the right track, but when Diaghilev died soon afterward, Prokofiev lost his most important link with Parisian circles. Like no one else, Diaghilev had sensed what Paris expected of artists. After his death, the critics were quick to observe that his guiding spirit was absent from Prokofiev's new work. Of the first performance on 16 December 1932 of the ballet *On the Dnepr* (choreographed by Serge Lifar and with costumes by Natalya Goncharova and sets by Mikhaíl Larionov), Robert Brussel wrote in *Le Figaro*: "M. Prokofiev has presented a score that the late Serge Diaghilev would probably not have wanted, and with which in any case he should not have been satisfied."[4] After 1924, Prokofiev could also no longer count on the steady support of Serge Koussevitzky, who had moved to the United States to take up his appointment as conductor to the Boston Symphony Orchestra.

In the West, Prokofiev found it hard to maintain his modernist status. Comparisons with Stravinsky invariably redounded to Prokofiev's disadvantage. His art lacked a clear direction, a consistent approach. The leading modernists in Western music were those who could present their own work as milestones in musical development. Schoenberg and Stravinsky in particular laid down the criteria by which modernism was judged. Although Prokofiev avoided a confrontation with Schoenberg, he had all the greater a clash with Stravinsky. The difference between Stravinsky and Prokofiev becomes most obvious when we compare the role of neoclassicism in their work. For Prokofiev, it was just one of many facets of his music. The *Classical* Symphony and the Fifth Piano Sonata were examples of neoclassicism, to be sure, but these two works existed side by side with the aggressive "Scythian" music of the "Scythian Suite" and the Second Symphony. Stravinsky, in contrast, developed neoclassicism as a consistent style: from the moment he made the change from neonationalism to neoclassicism he was undeviating in his course. He defended neoclassicism as the most up-to-date current and as the inevitable response to the chaos in which he thought modernism must end. So much directness was alien to Prokofiev, and the difference did not escape the critics. A characteristic reaction, for instance, was that of Dominique Sordet: "The action of a strong will appears in the successive self-denials of M. Stravinsky. There is nothing of the sort in M. Prokofiev, who floats wherever the wind blows him."[5] Olin Downes of the *New York Times* put it as follows:

> One still wonders what on earth Serge Prokofieff will evolve into. He is a born virtuoso. He appears to be a temperament and a mind very symptomatic of his age. He is also a very gifted composer, but of what category, and what future? . . . Perhaps, until recently the very abundance of his ideas and his eager temperament, by denying him a deep-breathing repose, have delayed the accomplishment of his deepest purposes as a composer.[6]

Prokofiev believed that a return to the Soviet Union would free him from the pressures of Western modernism. In about 1930 he began to simplify his style. He advocated a new look at the traditional elements of music, such as tonality, melody, and classical forms, and spoke of the need to create "a new simplicity." This move brought him closer to the criteria of Soviet music than to those of the Western avant-garde. It used to be thought that the simplification of Prokofiev's style was a consequence of his adaptation to the Soviet aesthetic. However, Prokofiev had shown himself to be a traditionalist even before he contemplated a permanent return to the Soviet Union. Hence it is more likely that his decision to go back to Russia was in part the result of his musical development. His "new simplicity" fell on more fertile soil in the Soviet Union than it did in Paris or New York.

Finally, there was his frustrated opera career. The failure of *The Fiery Angel,* the result of seven years of intensive work, made it clear to Prokofiev that he could no longer expect to attain a leading position in the West. Following the concert performance of the second act in Paris on 14 June 1928 under Koussevitzky, the Diaghilev circle loudly voiced its disapproval. Nor did others' appreciation satisfy Prokofiev. He wrote to Myaskovsky: "[Leonid] Sabaneyev and [Alexander] Grechaninov came up to me and started to praise the act. But I felt rather ashamed of it and concluded that the piece was probably no more than mediocre." According to Richard Taruskin, the fiasco of *The Fiery Angel* was one of the causes of Prokofiev's return:

> The antipathy of the fashionable moderns coupled with the enthusiasm of two of the most conservative musical members of the Russian emigré community

(the one an unreconstructed partisan of Scriabin, the other a latter-day Rim-skian, and both rabid anti-Stravinskians), should have tipped Prokofiev off that he had fallen behind the march of chic. He would never recapture his former standing with the Paris tastemakers. For one as addicted as Prokofiev to prestige, it was an intolerable situation that would lead him inexorably back to Russia and, eventually, to the tragic Stalinist finale of his career.[7]

However, *The Fiery Angel* did not stand a chance in the Soviet Union, the erotic and mystical decadence of the subject having been taboo since the thirties. Even so, Prokofiev saw greater prospects for his operas at home than in the West. In the Soviet Union, the genre did not have to square up to any avant-garde anti-opera campaigns. Moreover, there were pioneering stage directors who did not consider opera unworthy of their talent, among them Nemirovich-Danchenko, Radlov, Taírov, and Meyerhold. The last had always been an influential champion of Prokofiev's music and had repeatedly shown interest in collaborating with him. In particular, he encouraged Prokofiev to revise *The Gambler* for a production he proposed to direct.

Nothing came of the planned performance in the Mariyinski Theater, however, due to obstruction by the RAPM. Nevertheless, this bad omen did not deflect Prokofiev from his decision to transfer his field of activity, any more than had the boycott by the RAPM of his second tour of the Soviet Union in 1929, the removal of Anatoliy Lunacharsky, and the attacks by the press on the ideological content of the ballet *Le pas d'acier,* which the Rapmovites thought insulting.

When Prokofiev was granted Soviet citizenship in 1932, the situation appeared brighter. The RAPM had been dissolved and the Union of So-viet Composers established. For a while, Prokofiev commuted between Paris and Moscow, not giving up his Paris apartment and making the final move to Moscow until 1936. Three years later, Meyerhold would be arrested, to die in prison. But by that time Prokofiev had burned all his bridges.

Summing up, it may be said that Prokofiev returned to the Soviet Union for the sake of his career. Stravinsky was probably close to the truth when he declared:

Prokofiev was always very Russian-minded and always primitively anticleri-cal. But in my opinion these dispositions had little to do with his return to Russia. The latter was a sacrifice to the bitch goddess, and nothing else. He had had no success in the United States or Europe for several seasons, while his visit to Russia had been a triumph. . . . He was politically naive, however, and learned nothing from the example of his good friend Miaskovsky. He returned to Russia, and when finally he understood his situation there, it was too late.[8]

By 1938 Prokofiev had become so adjusted to the new phase in his career that he even rejected a handsome offer from Hollywood. Through Vladimir Dukelsky's agent, a movie studio had offered him $2,500 a week. Dukelsky (who had changed his name to Vernon Duke) told the story:

> I showed Serge the telegram exultantly; there was a flicker of interest for a mere instant, then, his face set, his oversize lips petulant, he said gruffly: "That's nice bait, but I won't swallow it. I've got to go back to Moscow, to my music and my children. And now that that's settled, will you come to Macy's with me? I've got to buy a whole roomful of things you can't get in Russia—just look at Lina's list."
>
> The list was imposing, and we went to Macy's department store, another sample of capitalistic bait designed by the lackeys of Wall Street to be swallowed by oppressed workers. Although he wouldn't admit it, Serge enjoyed himself hugely in the store—he loved gadgets and trinkets of every description. Suddenly he turned to me, his eyes peculiarly moist, his voice even gruffer than usual: "You know, Dima, it occurred to me that I may not be back for quite some time. . . . I don't suppose it would be wise for you to come to Russia, would it?" "No, I don't suppose it would," I answered, smiling bravely, my happiness abruptly gone. I never saw Prokofiev again.[9]

## A LOYAL SOVIET CITIZEN

Prokofiev had no qualms about collaborating with a dictatorial regime. From 1936 on, he did everything he could to convince the authorities of his loyalty. Examples of the resulting "political" works are his Six Songs, op. 66—including two propagandist "mass songs"—about Ukrainian partisans in the civil war, about new educational opportunities for peasants, about Marshal Voroshilov, the hero of the civil war, and about the collectivization of farms. The song "Beyond the Hill" conveys some idea of Prokofiev's ideological adaptation. "I became a man when I joined the *kolkhoz*" is how the text trivializes the brutality of the megalomaniacal collectivization process.

In 1937 Prokofiev wrote the *Cantata for the Twentieth Anniversary of October,* based on texts by Marx, Engels, Lenin, and Stalin. However monumental in conception, the cantata did not please the authorities, who did not think the work heroic enough. In *Songs of Our Days,* Prokofiev came closer to the required nationalism and optimism. The last song, "The Golden Ukraine," a text that eulogizes the wonders of farming, conveys an impression of the tendentious simplism of the entire cycle: "And now my spacious land is decked with flowers; I have been plowing the earth in the wide fields with tractors."

Prokofiev found just the right tone for heroic nationalism in 1938 in his music for Sergey Eisenstein's propaganda film *Alexander Nevsky*. Party bureaucrats exerted a strong influence on the execution of the film, the leading role being given to a prominent Party member, Nikolai Cherkasov, an actor with a seat in the Supreme Soviet. The film proved a great success. Stalin is said to have complimented Eisenstein, telling him that he was "a good Bolshevik after all!"[10]

In his Seven Songs, op. 79, Prokofiev continued his Stalinist propaganda. Mira Mendelson's lyrics extol the bravery of the Red Army and sing the praises of the Soviet system. For Stalin's sixtieth birthday, Prokofiev wrote the cantata *Zdravitsa* (known in English as "Hail to Stalin").

## THEATER, FILM, AND BALLET

Prokofiev's return was not marked by the composition of propaganda music alone. Adapting himself to conditions in the Soviet Union meant in particular writing music for film, the stage, and the ballet. Prokofiev's first film project was *Lieutenant Kije* (1933), directed by Alexander Faintsimmer. Based on the Gogolian tale of the same name by Yuriy Tinyanov, it revolved around a nonexistent lieutenant whose name, through a clerical error, turns up in military documents. Tsar Paul (1796–1801) bestows a number of special favors upon him, his bureaucrats being too terrified to contradict his orders. Lieutenant Kije enjoys a classical military career, complete with disgrace, banishment to Siberia, amnesty, and promotion to general. When he "dies," he is buried in an empty coffin with appropriate military honors. For the music, Prokofiev relied on his own satirical idiom. He also paid careful attention to the period style: all the songs in the film are based on the eighteenth-century urban song. In 1934 he rewrote the music to turn it into a suite.

In 1933 Prokofiev came up with an orchestral work with which he hoped to consolidate his reputation as a Soviet composer: the *Symphonic Song,* a work in three movements with vague programmatic titles. The andante assai corresponds to "darkness," the allegro to "struggle," and the andante to "achievement." Things did not turn out as the composer had hoped. The performance on 14 April 1934 in Moscow was a fiasco, critics calling the work "a symphonic monologue for the few, a sad tale of the decline of the fading culture of individualism."[11] Myaskovsky drew Prokofiev's attention to the lack of grandeur in the work and advised

him to provide something "monumental, with definite personality and—
don't be angry, o horrors—even cheerful." [12]

From 1934 to 1937 Prokofiev wrote scores for three stage productions: *Egyptian Nights,* a project by Alexander Taírov for the Moscow
Chamber Theater that was pieced together from plays by Shakespeare,
Shaw, and Pushkin; *Eugene Onegin* (another of Taírov's initiatives); and
Pushkin's *Boris Godunov,* directed by Meyerhold. Of these three works,
only *Egyptian Nights* was ever staged, the other two being dropped following pressure from the authorities.

*Eugene Onegin* and *Boris Godunov* were both attempts to rid the
literary sources of the classical musical interpretations proffered by Chaikovsky and Musorgsky. For *Onegin,* Prokofiev concentrated on scenes
Chaikovsky had not set to music, such as the wandering by Tatyana
through Onegin's house as she tries to fathom the mystery of the man.
Meyerhold saw *Boris Godunov* as a portrait of a barbaric age. He wanted
above all to depict the violence and brutality of the Time of Troubles,
and asked Prokofiev to contribute music in the spirit of his earlier "Scythian" works. Prokofiev obliged, but the work was never performed. In
1937 Meyerhold became persona non grata, and in 1939 he disappeared
behind prison walls.

A film project based on Pushkin's "Queen of Spades" and directed
by Mikhaíl Romm also came to nothing, even though the director had
interpreted the story in the approved Soviet manner, as a social skit on
the decaying aristocracy. Prokofiev had again tried to come up with an
alternative to Chaikovsky's classical version, wishing to discard Chaikovsky's melodramatic approach and match the music more closely to
Pushkin's dry style. He was not given the chance: in 1938 the authorities
decided to give preference to films dealing with contemporary themes.

Prokofiev was more fortunate with his incidental music for *Hamlet,*
which was performed in Sergey Radlov's Theater Studio in Leningrad
on 15 May 1938. Compared with the other, abandoned, projects, however, Prokofiev's contribution was small, music playing no more than a
minor part in the work.

In 1934, Radlov had commissioned Prokofiev to write a ballet based
on Shakespeare's *Romeo and Juliet* for the Mariyinsky Theater in
Leningrad. That would turn out to be one of Prokofiev's best-loved
scores, but before it came to that, numerous obstacles had first to be
cleared. Among the first of these was the radical change in the administration of the Mariyinsky Theater at the end of 1934. The name was
changed to Kirov Theater, in honor of Sergey Kirov, the Leningrad Party

leader who had been assassinated shortly before, probably on Stalin's orders, and who was replaced by Andrey Zhdanov, the later architect of *Zhdanovshchina*. The reorganization also entailed the abandonment of Radlov's projects. He took them to Moscow, where the Bolshoy Theater offered him a new contract for *Romeo and Juliet*. While Radlov worked on the scenario, Prokofiev began to write the music. However, the Bolshoy Theater administrators went back on their word soon afterward.

So as not to lose time, Prokofiev turned the music into two suites. The First Suite was premièred in Moscow on 24 November 1936, the Second in Leningrad on 15 April 1937. In December 1938, *Romeo and Juliet* was given its first performance in ballet form, although strangely enough not in either Moscow or Leningrad but at the provincial theater in Brno, Czechoslovakia.

In 1938 the board of the Kirov Theater appointed a new choreographer, Leonid Lavrovsky, who took charge of the production of *Romeo and Juliet*. He was given the green light in 1939, but it was not until 11 January 1940 that the Russian première could take place.

Lavrovsky and the playwright Adrian Piotrovsky adapted Radlov's scenario, making their most important change to the ending. Radlov had rewritten Shakespeare's tragic conclusion to allow Romeo to find Juliet alive and well beside the grave. "The reasons that led us to such a barbarism were purely choreographic," Prokofiev later explained. "Living people can dance, but the dead cannot dance lying down."[13]

The preparations went anything but smoothly. The dancers had profound reservations about Prokofiev's score, finding it too subtle, too rhythmically complex, and often too much like chamber music. They missed the steady rhythmical beat of traditional ballet music. Reluctantly, Prokofiev was forced to make further changes. Lavrovsky, for his part, showed little respect for the composer, making cuts and additions on his own initiative without consulting Prokofiev—an approach that was reminiscent of the circumstances in which Chaikovsky had written his ballets. For Prokofiev, who had learned the trade from Diaghilev, such willfulness was new and unexpected. Tensions ran high.

A few weeks before the première, the ballet troupe threatened a boycott of the production, demanding that the work be dropped lest the public laugh them off the stage. However, matters were smoothed over and the performance went ahead as planned. Its success exceeded the wildest expectations. Even the official critics spoke of a great occasion for Soviet ballet. For Galina Ulanova, the prima ballerina, Juliet was the greatest role of her career.

*Romeo and Juliet* is a world away from the ballets Prokofiev composed for Diaghilev, its literary and narrative character being incompatible with Diaghilev's aesthetic. The scenario follows the play faithfully, and the dancers are expected not only to dance but also to act. The structure is not divided in the traditional way into mime and dance, the first portraying actions and the second sublimating emotions or simply serving as a divertissement. In *Romeo and Juliet,* the action pervades the dance numbers. The work enabled Prokofiev to carry through an impressive synthesis of his art. For the violent scenes—the clashes between the Capulets and the Montagues—he was able to use his "Scythian" idiom; for the court dances he drew on the "classicism" he had developed in his *Classical* Symphony. The score includes such dazzling numbers as the characteristic "Folk Dance" and the "Dance with Mandolins." The famous "Dance of the Knights" depicts the ceremonial splendor and unbending severity of the Capulet court. *Romeo and Juliet* also contains a good share of lyrical melodies. For the balcony scene in Act I, Prokofiev composed his most emotional music since *The Prodigal Son.*

Prokofiev's most frequently performed work, *Peter and the Wolf,* dates from 1936. The initiative came from Natalya Satz, the director of the Moscow Children's Musical Theater. It is a work about animals and people for symphonic orchestra and narrator, with each animal represented by a particular instrument or set of instruments in the orchestra: the bird by the flute, the cat by the clarinet, the duck by the oboe, and the wolf by four horns. The main character, Peter, is represented by the string quintet, the grumpy grandfather by the bassoon, and the group of hunters by the kettledrums.

Prokofiev himself wrote the simple and direct text. The story is about a boy who goes against his grandfather's advice, captures a wolf, and takes him to a zoo with the help of some hunters. It is not a typical Soviet story, except for one detail: Peter is a Pioneer, a member of the Communist youth movement. The moral is accordingly a "Pioneer moral," namely that the young must rely on their own wits, if necessary against the advice of their elders. Prokofiev's composition took the world by storm as an educational guide to the orchestra—a task this work shares with Benjamin Britten's *A Young Person's Guide to the Orchestra.*

In 1938 Prokofiev began his collaboration with the film director Sergey Eisenstein. Their first project was *Alexander Nevsky,* a virulent anti-German account of the thirteenth-century struggle of Novgorod against the Teutonic knights. Alexander Nevsky, prince of Novgorod, is a central figure in the Russian nationalist pantheon. In both cinematographic and musical respects, *Alexander Nevsky* is marked by extreme dramatic contrasts. All the film and musical material is designed to impress the spectator with the unequivocal polarization of Good and Evil. The Russians are shown as sensitive beings, as individuals, an image best expressed in the scene of the girl roaming over the battlefield in search of her lover's body. The Teutons, by contrast, are depicted as devoid of all human qualities. They appear at all times in groups, in armor, unrecognizable behind their invariably closed visors—they are literally "faceless." Prokofiev uses the same contrast in his music. The Russians sing snatches of diatonic folk songs, the Teutons a dissonant and inflexible version of the Catholic pilgrims' hymn "Peregrinus expectavi." In the recording studio, Prokofiev emphasized the difference even more by having the brass blow straight into the microphones, producing a threatening, sinister sound.

*Alexander Nevsky* met all official expectations. Only during the brief alliance of Stalin and Hitler did the film disappear temporarily from the screen.

In the wake of the success of *Romeo and Juliet*, the Kirov Theater commissioned Prokofiev to write a new ballet, *Cinderella*, with a scenario by Nikolai Volkov. Prokofiev started work on it in 1941, but put the project to one side for a composition that had closer links with the current situation, *War and Peace*. The Kirov planned to stage *Cinderella* in Perm in 1943, however, so Prokofiev was under pressure to finish the score. In fact, the ballet was never produced there, for practical reasons: the small theater in Perm was not suited to so large a spectacle and too few dancers were available. Prokofiev completed the work in 1944; in 1945 it was staged in Moscow's Bolshoy Theater.

In *Cinderella*, Prokofiev drew on the lesson he had learned from the production of *Romeo and Juliet*, when the dancers had been unprepared for the unconventional and dramatic style of his Shakespeare ballet. This time, he stuck more closely to the tradition. He was determined to compose music that was above all *dansante*, which meant paying closer attention to the individual dance numbers. Wherever the story allowed, he introduced dances in which the dancers could excel, each character having his or her own variation. Like *Romeo and Juliet*, *Cinderella* is also a long way from the earlier ballets Prokofiev wrote for Diaghilev, thanks in this case to the number of purely balletic divertissements and character dances. This time he had Chaikovsky in mind. The eighteenth-century setting of this *Cinderella* brings the atmosphere of the ballet close to that of *The Sleeping Beauty*, the period style playing a large part in the music, particularly in the ballroom scene. The positive characters—

Cinderella, the Prince, and the Fairy Godmother—are characterized by lyrical music. For the Wicked Stepmother, Prokofiev drew on his satirical idiom, though less pointedly than he had done in his earlier works.

The success of *Alexander Nevsky* led to a new collaboration between Prokofiev and Eisenstein: the film *Ivan the Terrible*. Eisenstein received the commission from Mosfilm in January 1941, at the very moment when *Izvestia*, the Party newspaper, was preparing an article justifying Ivan's rule. The author was the novelist Valentin Kostilev, who was working on a three-volume biography of the sixteenth-century tsar. Kostilev's work fit well into Stalin's revisionist historiography. Kostilev described Ivan as a forward-looking statesman who fought against Russia's internal and external enemies. He dismissed the negative portrayal of Ivan "the Terrible" (*Ivan Groznïy*) introduced by the nineteenth-century historian Nikolai Karamzin as nothing short of a foreign smear campaign, and blamed boyar opposition to the tsar on the intrigues of foreign powers. The subjection of the Baltic countries was in accordance with the wishes of the people concerned and not an act of brute force—an argument that soon served to justify the annexation of the Baltic states by the Soviet Union. A revision of the importance given to the *oprichniki* was considered to be of essential importance, the gruesome methods of Ivan's secret police being only too reminiscent of Stalinist brutalities. The *oprichniki* were accordingly portrayed as a weapon that was turned exclusively on the old feudal aristocrats and never on the common people. Moreover, as Kostilev and his followers, the historians Vipper and Smirnov, explained, the cruelties of the *oprichniki* went against the tsar's express wishes. Ivan himself had had nothing to do with their excesses. On the contrary, Kostilev portrayed him as a fair-minded opponent who treated his enemies justly and never spilled blood without good reason.

It fell to Eisenstein to present this tendentious view on the screen. The film was planned in three parts, of which only two were ever completed. Lacking the dramatic contrasts of *Alexander Nevsky, Ivan the Terrible* is a more subtle work. Prokofiev drew his music from several sources: patriotic choruses, the Orthodox liturgy, folk songs, and his own satirical and Scythian idioms.

Eisenstein by and large adopted the new standard image of Ivan, but he deviated from it in a number of notable respects. In Part Two, he did not provide the expected portrayal of Ivan's glorious campaign against the Baltic nations, concentrating instead on palace intrigues. His portrait of Ivan had many harrowing features. Moreover, he presented the establishment of the *oprichnina* not as historically necessary, but as a tragic episode, an opportunist reaction to the web of palace intrigues that threatened to engulf Ivan. Part Two of the film was condemned by a resolution of 4 September 1946 for betraying "ignorance of historical facts."[14]

## INSTRUMENTAL MUSIC

During the first phase of his career as a Soviet composer, Prokofiev completed just one concert piece, the Second Violin Concerto, which was also the last commission he received in the West. He wrote the concerto for the French violinist Robert Soetens. It was first performed in 1935, in Madrid, and immediately made its way into the international repertoire. In the Second Violin Concerto, Prokofiev exploited his special talent for composing diatonic, melodic music that nevertheless sounded surprising and fresh. In 1933 he started on a Cello Concerto, but he put it to one side and did not complete it until 1938, when it earned him nothing but adverse criticism.

In 1939, following a long period during which he wrote mainly theater and program music, Prokofiev returned to nonprogrammatic instrumental music with his Sixth, Seventh, and Eighth Piano Sonatas. He sketched out all ten movements of the three works at one time, assigning them to the three sonatas only later—used as he was to thinking in separate movements rather than in coherent cycles. The sonatas were completed over the course of several years: the Sixth in 1940, the Seventh in 1942, and the Eighth in 1944. Mira Mendelson tells us that his reading of Romain Rolland's book on Beethoven had rekindled his interest in this genre.[15]

After a gap of sixteen years following the composition of the Fifth Piano Sonata, Prokofiev reverted to his earlier piano style. The composer of *Suggestion diabolique* and *Toccata* was back in harness. For the fast movements, he drew entirely on his rhythmical and energetic style, using ostinati, dry staccato passages, and caustic accents. In the slow movements he used his expanded-tonality technique. Meditative lyricism and subtle textures characterize the tempo di valzer lentissimo of the Sixth Sonata, the andante caloroso of the Seventh, and the first (andante dolce) and second (andante sognoso) movements of the Eighth. In the last of these sonatas the lyrical character predominates. In the andante sognando, Prokofiev reused extracts from the stage music for *Eugene Onegin* and from the film score for *The Queen of Spades*.

Prokofiev gave the première of the Sixth Piano Sonata in 1940 at the Composers Union, assuming once more his former status of virtuoso pianist. Svyatoslav Richter's own successful interpretation, however, dissuaded Prokofiev from continuing to perform his music himself. Richter gave the première of the Seventh Sonata in 1943, and Emil Gilels that of the Eighth in 1944.

While working on the piano sonatas, Prokofiev also rediscovered chamber music. In 1938 he began a violin sonata, though he soon put it to one side. In 1941 he wrote his Second String Quartet, the result of his evacuation to Nalchik and of the call by the authorities to make use of local folklore. The score is considerably simpler than that of the First String Quartet.

In 1942 and 1943 Prokofiev wrote a Sonata for Flute and Piano, wanting to compose something light as a diversion from such major and serious projects as *War and Peace* and *Ivan the Terrible*. As he put it, he was looking for "bright and transparent classical tones."[16] The work, which is along the lines of the *Classical* Symphony and the Fifth Piano Sonata, was given its first performance in December 1943 by the flutist N. Kharkovsky and the pianist Svyatoslav Richter. David Oistrakh then asked the composer for a transcription for violin and piano, and presented him with a list of possible variations. Choosing from among these, Prokofiev composed his Second Violin Sonata—which thus actually preceded the First Violin Sonata, a work he had planned out but that remained in draft form. Not until 1946 did Prokofiev find the time to complete the First Violin Sonata. One of his most emotionally charged works, it differs radically in character from the optimistic Second, being comparable instead with the First String Quartet by virtue of its Beethovenian touches. It is one of the greatest pieces of music Prokofiev composed, at least if it is judged by its expressive power and emotional tension. The confrontation of violin and piano is striking, the tense relationship between the two instruments contributing to the Beethovenian weight of the sonata.

In 1944 Prokofiev returned to the symphony, a genre he had put aside sixteen years earlier. In the West, symphonic music was encumbered with so weighty a tradition that progressive composers had come to disdain it. Prokofiev, too, had had little success with his symphonies there. In the Soviet Union, however, the traditional profile of the symphony was held in high regard, Shostakovich having shown that a composer could use it to brilliant effect. Prokofiev, however, had lagged considerably behind Shostakovich in the symphonic field. With his Fifth and Sixth Symphonies he took up the challenge and became Shostakovich's rival.

Like Shostakovich's Fifth, Prokofiev's Fifth Symphony goes back to the great Romantic tradition. Apart from the slow tempo of the first movement (andante), the work has all the contours of a traditional symphony. The form, the tonal relationships, and the phrase structure all hark back to the classical models. Prokofiev reserved the technique of expanded tonality for the internal development of the themes. The Fifth Symphony has an epic character; with it, Prokofiev translated the monumental style he had elaborated in *Alexander Nevsky, Zdravitsa,* and *Ivan the Terrible* into autonomous orchestral music. The music shows a feeling for symphonic drama and continuity, something that distinguishes the Fifth Symphony from the more fragmented "montage structure" of the Third and the Fourth. The overall character of the Fifth Symphony is one of hope and life-affirmation. The work was greeted as an expression of optimism following the Russian victory in the Second World War.

In 1945 Prokofiev began his Sixth Symphony, completing it in 1947. This work is less uniform in character than the Fifth; in it one finds the warm lyricism of *Romeo and Juliet* as well as melancholy themes and sharply orchestrated sound blocks. Only in the concluding vivace does Prokofiev find the way back to the optimism of the Fifth Symphony. The Sixth is rich in contrasts and intense entanglements of motifs. Thanks to *Zhdanovshchina,* however, the work was dismissed as an example of formalism.

In the autumn of 1947 Prokofiev completed his Ninth Piano Sonata. The score is deliberately simple and melodic. In it, Prokofiev demonstrates to the full his mastery in the imaginative treatment of diatonic tone material. The general sense of simplicity and melodic charm has sometimes been compared with that of Schubert.

## OPERA

With his first Soviet opera, *Semyon Kotko* (1939), Prokofiev played for safety, choosing a literary source that was above all suspicion: Valentin Katayev's novel *I Am a Son of the Working People.* This was a typical Soviet bildungsroman, a very popular genre during the Stalinist era, exemplified, for instance, by Nikolai Virtá's *Loneliness* and Nikolai Ostrovsky's *How the Steel Was Tempered.* These novels center on the growth of a new consciousness; taught in the hard school of life, the leading characters come to recognize that the revolutionary ideals are the best. Semyon Kotko, a Ukrainian soldier returning home from the First World War, is one of these honest seekers. Back home, he is drawn into the clash between the Bolsheviks and the counterrevolutionaries supported by the German inter-

ventionists. Kotko finds his love for the girl Sofia obstructed by her father, a kulak and a sworn enemy of the Bolsheviks. He wants to have
Kotko put to death so that he can marry his daughter off to a big
landowner. At the last moment, the luck of the Bolsheviks changes, and
Semyon Kotko learns once and for all how to tell the good from the bad.

Ideologically, the subject was safe. Stylistically, it involved great dramatic contrasts: good and evil, love and hate, new ideals and past injustices. Prokofiev underlined the story with musical contrasts.

In the aftermath of the events surrounding *The Lady Macbeth of the
Mtsensk District,* it had been brought home to him that what the authorities expected from an opera was that it be allied to the classical Russian tradition. Dramatic contrast had been the principle underlying such
works as *A Life for the Tsar* and *Prince Igor,* and the influence of *A Life
for the Tsar* could be clearly seen in *Semyon Kotko.* Both works hinge
on the confrontation of positive, simple people with a hateful enemy. The
link between the two operas is underlined in the scene in which the Germans arrive and ruin the celebration of the betrothal of Semyon and Sofia,
just as the Poles had done in the home of Ivan Susanin.

Like Susanin, the character of Semyon Kotko is intended to reflect the
ideals of an entire people. Susanin cannot be happy while Russia is in
danger. For Semyon Kotko, similarly, personal gratification appears to
be bound up with the Bolshevik victory. The bridal choruses at his betrothal sing of the dawn of Soviet power, much as Susanin glorified
tsarism in his family circle. (Shortly before Prokofiev started on *Semyon
Kotko, A Life for the Tsar* had been ideologically revised: the poet Sergey
Gorodetsky had rewritten the libretto, replacing all references to tsarism
with tributes to the Russian soil and the Russian nation. The new version had its première on 21 February 1939.)

The ties between the individual and the collective are reflected in the
music of both works as well. Susanin expresses his feelings through folk
song, while Semyon's musical motifs return in the revolutionary choruses.
In both cases, the music attempts to typify the characters less as individuals than as representatives of the people. Prokofiev thus returned to
the musical-drama devices that the early *kuchka*—and he himself, in the
footsteps of Musorgsky—had rejected in favor of realism and the indi-
vidualization of the musical portraits. Musical generalization, in contrast,
was one of the hallmarks of socialist realism in opera.

Operatic dramaturgy based on contrasts was new to Prokofiev, in
whose earlier operas contrast had played no part. *The Gambler* and
*The Fiery Angel* had both been conceived as a single great buildup of

dramatic tension—of "dramatic crescendos," as Prokofiev himself called it. In *Semyon Kotko*, he relied on a sharp contrast between the dissonant, marchlike music of the German enemy, on the one hand, and diatonic melodies involving snatches of folk song to signify the good characters, on the other. Despite adhering to a number of basic principles of his earlier opera approach—continuing to use prose and a fluid *parlando* style in the vocal parts, for example—he nonetheless rendered the recitative more lyrical than had been his custom, and came closer to the use of self-contained numbers characteristic of the traditional opera structure. In every respect, Soviet criteria were adhered to.

No matter how carefully Prokofiev tried to weigh up the prospects of his new opera, however, *Semyon Kotko* proved a fiasco. The work appeared at the worst possible moment, the Nazi-Soviet pact of 1940 rendering an opera in which Germans were the enemy an uncertain enterprise. When the critics objected to the project, it was saved by changing the Germans into Austrians. More serious was the arrest of Vsevolod Meyerhold, which put an end to Prokofiev's hopes of collaborating with this legendary director. Serafima Birman, new to the job, took over the stage production. The greatest setback Prokofiev had to face, however, was competition from a work the authorities preferred, the song opera *Into the Storm* by Tikhon Khrennikov, which had been produced in 1939—and in the same house, the Stanislavsky Theater in Moscow. Despite all the trouble Prokofiev had taken to adapt himself, he continued to apply musico-dramatic criteria that proved too exalted for Soviet audiences. He could never hope to outdo Khrennikov in naive simplism.

In 1940 Mira Mendelson drew Prokofiev's attention to an eighteenth-century libretto of an English comic opera, *The Duenna; or, The Double Elopement* (1775) by Richard Brinsley Sheridan, a comedy full of masquerades, misunderstandings, and amorous intrigues that culminate in a triple wedding at a monastery. Prokofiev felt the libretto might lend itself to a musical comedy in the style of Rossini. Moreover, the subject was politically neutral.

He wrote the opera in 1940 under the title *Betrothal in a Monastery*. In contrast to *The Love for Three Oranges*, he paid less attention to the satire than to the romantic intrigue. The opera contains numerous self-contained numbers. The vocal score is also noticeably more lyrical than that of the earlier comedy.

Prokofiev now started on the most ambitious work of his entire oeuvre, an opera based on Tolstoy's monumental novel *War and Peace*. The idea had first occurred to him in 1935. In 1941 he sketched out a first scenario, without, however, proceeding to the actual composition. The German invasion of Russia under Hitler, in which Prokofiev saw a clear parallel with Tolstoy's account of the French invasion under Napoleon, provided a fresh impetus. He expanded the original outline into eleven scenes. Among the multiplicity of interesting set pieces in Tolstoy's novel, Prokofiev concentrated on two story lines: the betrothal of Natasha to Prince Andrey Bolkonsky and the seduction and attempted abduction of Natasha by Anatol Kuragin; and the invasion of Russia by the French army and the ultimate Russian victory. In the martial scenes, Pierre Bezukhov is the central figure. The two lines of the plot combine in the penultimate scene, where the badly wounded Andrey is reunited with Natasha on his deathbed.

Prokofiev finished the opera within eight months. True to his habit of not allowing anything he had composed to fall by the wayside, he reused themes and motifs from his incidental music for Pushkin's *Eugene Onegin*. The theme of Tatyana's declaration of love for Onegin, for example, was transposed to Pierre's realization that he feels a deep affection for Natasha. The theme of Lensky's love for Olga now accompanied Andrey's musings about spring, good fortune, and Natasha's beauty in the first scene. The growth of Andrey's feelings for Natasha was related to the theme of Tatyana's passion for Onegin. The passage in which Onegin pays court to Olga lent itself to Anatol's attempt to seduce Natasha.

The production of the opera had to wait, however. When he presented it to the Soviet Committee on Artistic Affairs in Moscow, he was handed a list of essential revisions. The committee voiced two types of objection: the military scenes were not heroic enough, and the vocal style needed to be more lyrical and rely less on the rendering of the words. To remedy the first complaint, the committee asked for a significant extension of the role of the people and for an appreciable reduction of the genre episodes with which Prokofiev had portrayed the social milieu. As far as the second complaint was concerned, Prokofiev demonstrated that he had taken great care to be as faithful as possible to Tolstoy's language. The dialogue was close to the original, and Prokofiev declared that virtually all phrases in the libretto had come straight from Tolstoy. Nevertheless, the critics found, the lyrical side of opera had been neglected and needed to be improved.

To emphasize the heroic and patriotic character of the opera, Prokofiev then deleted much anecdotal detail. A disarming, unaffected scene with Field Marshal Kutuzov, the Russian commander-in-chief, at the battlefield of Borodino, had to go, and the field marshal's bantering address to the partisans in the last scene was put into the mouth of another character, Colonel Denisov. The last scene of the opera now ended in a grand apotheosis. Prokofiev also added a grandiloquent patriotic epigraph: "The forces of a dozen European nations burst into Russia"—though Prokofiev was never able to decide where, precisely, this chorus should appear: at the beginning of the whole opera or as a prologue to the battle scenes.

In his revision, Prokofiev also strengthened the lyrical element, replacing recitative with arioso in several places. Kutuzov was even given an aria to sing on the battlefield.

As a consequence of the dismissal of Samuil Samosud as chief conductor of the Bolshoy Theater, the revised version was not performed in Moscow. Samosud had always been a champion of Prokofiev's project, and as soon as he was appointed to the Maliy Theater in Leningrad, a production there became a real possibility.

Samosud at first insisted on staging the revised version without cuts, but that plan was thwarted by the opera's immense length. The conductor's solution was to urge Prokofiev to make the work even longer, so that it could be spread over two evenings. He himself suggested two new scenes: the ball at which Andrey and Natasha meet for the first time, and the war council at Fili at which Kutuzov makes the historic decision not to defend Moscow, thus saving the Russian army from certain destruction. Prokofiev agreed at once to the addition of the first scene, which gave him the opportunity to expand on the glittering background of ballroom music. That first meeting, moreover, had the advantage that it could be recalled musically in the penultimate scene, when Andrey and Natasha are together for the last time.

As for the second scene Samosud suggested—a military discussion involving technical details—Prokofiev was rather hesitant. In the end, Samosud persuaded him to use the scene in order to expand Kutuzov's role. Kutuzov would have to be given an aria that could vie with the arias of Ivan Susanin or Prince Igor—"central, eloquent, crucial," as Samosud put it. Prokofiev drew on his film score for *Ivan the Terrible* when writing Kutuzov's aria; the motifs in the aria recur in the apotheosis at the end of the opera. With this treatment, the field marshal becomes the central figure of the war scenes, at the expense of Pierre Bezukhov. Kutuzov is turned into a near-mythical character, representing the Russian nation and serving, wholly in line with the official propaganda, as a precursor of Stalin in the role of supreme commander of the Russian people.

Part One of *War and Peace* was premièred on 12 June 1946. It was a resounding success, the first eight scenes being shown no fewer than 105 times over two seasons. Part Two, in contrast, proceeded no further than the dress rehearsal. Faceless bureaucrats feared inaccuracies in its interpretation of history. The 1946 Party decrees had just been issued, and no one dared shoulder the responsibility for the ideological correctness of an important theater production.

All this made Prokofiev nervous, afraid that his complete *War and Peace* would go the same way as his *Fiery Angel*. He was prepared to make all sorts of concessions and cuts in order to see the opera staged. He again reduced *War and Peace* to an opera that could be shown on a single evening, excising everything that might have been considered difficult from an ideological point of view. The result was a stunted version in ten scenes, whose production, incidentally, Prokofiev would not live to see. Not until 1953 would this version be staged, and then not in Russia, but in Florence.

When Prokofiev wrote the final version in 1952, he returned to the thirteen scenes he had composed for the two-part version, and even added several passages. He no longer had in mind a work that would be shown on two evenings. *War and Peace* was clearly conceived as a single great opera, not as a diptych.

For the second time, Prokofiev had to face a failure, this time with a work he considered his most representative, his magnum opus. The parallel with *The Fiery Angel* did not escape him. Mira Mendelson has said that "during his last few years Sergey spoke almost daily of how he longed for a production of *War and Peace;* it was constantly, incessantly in his thoughts."[17]

In Tolstoy's *War and Peace*, the personal fate of the characters is closely bound up with the historical events. The family history of the Rostovs has parallels with the history of Russia. The abortive attempt to seduce Natasha illustrates the sense of solidarity of the Russian family in the face of the unscrupulous interloper Anatol—not by chance a man who frequents French circles. In the same way, the Russian people are united against Napoleon.

With this parallel in mind, Prokofiev chose the scenes for his opera. Tolstoy forges a symbolic bond between Natasha and the Russian people. Her character constitutes the central point of the overall structure of the opera. "Natasha/Russia" betrays her true love, "Andrey/the people," for the intruder, "Anatol/France." In the personal sphere, Pierre Bezukhov must restore the balance; in the historical realm that task falls to Field Marshal Kutuzov.

Prokofiev draws this parallel by joining the two strands of the plot in a double denouement: the dying Andrey becomes reconciled with Natasha, and the struggling nation succeeds in freeing Russia from the French. These two aspects of the novel are brought out by a rich network of musical references. The first two scenes present the basic material of the relationship between Andrey and Natasha, in two motifs that are finally brought together in the death scene. Prokofiev also brings back the waltz music from the ballroom scene, an intervention he did not use until the third version. In the battle scene, Kutuzov's aria provides the central motif, underlining the heroism of the Russian people.[18]

*War and Peace* is in several respects the high point in the history of Russian opera, for with it Prokofiev achieved a synthesis of the influence of Chaikovsky and Musorgsky. Part One is close to the world of *Eugene Onegin* and *The Queen of Spades*. *War and Peace* in fact shares several details with the latter opera, such as the polonaise in the "wrong" time of 4/4, which is similar to the use by Chaikovsky of a saraband in 4/4 time in *The Queen of Spades*. In both cases, the aberrant rhythm creates an unreal atmosphere of dreams and intoxication. In his last revision of the score, Prokofiev introduced a duet for Sonya and Natasha in the first scene. For the text, he chose a passage from a poem by Zhukovsky—the same poem Chaikovsky had used for the duet of Pauline and Liza in *The Queen of Spades*. Similarly, the importance attached to characterization at the expense of the dramatic development is comparable with what happens in *Eugene Onegin*.

The war scenes hark back to Musorgsky. When Matveyev, a man of the people, tries with great difficulty to read a French edict in occupied Moscow, we are reminded of Varlaam's struggle with the warrant of arrest in the inn scene of *Boris Godunov*. The greatest similarity with Musorgsky, however, lies in the nonnarrative nature of the scenes. The occupation of Moscow is portrayed in one great panoramic tableau that seethes with life and action but remains static when viewed in its dramatic entirety, lacking a clear narrative thread. The prototype is Musorgsky's Kromy scene, the parallel between the two scenes being most evident in the role of Platon Karatayev. The simple peasant, whom Tolstoy turned into the unforgettable personification of integrity and sincerity, has assumed the role of the *yuródivïy* in Musorgsky's Kromy scene.

In 1947, following the failure to see Part Two of *War and Peace* staged, Prokofiev started on an opera he felt would get him back in the good graces of the authorities, probably also hoping that it might help to pave the way for the production of his magnum opus. He chose a subject that concerned the Second World War, thereby following the Stalinist propaganda line. During the war, the Party ideologists had persisted in referring to historical precedent in Russia's fight with foreign powers. Following victory, such references were no longer needed: Stalin had emerged as the ultimate victor, compared with whom all predecessors paled into insignificance. The authorities lost interest in other historical subjects—the Great Patriotic War had become the most important theme of Soviet art.

Prokofiev based his latest opera on Boris Polevoy's novel *The Story of a Real Man*. A Soviet fighter pilot loses both his legs, but with enormous strength of will and a double prosthesis he manages to struggle on. The climax is a scene in which an old commissar inspires him to continue the good fight with the declaration "But you're a Soviet man!"

Prokofiev did what he could to play by the rules. The score made extensive use of propagandist mass songs and self-contained numbers. Yet *The Story of a Real Man* was another miscalculation. After listening to it behind closed doors on 3 December 1948 in Leningrad's Kirov Theater, the Committee on Artistic Affairs called the première off. The head of the committee, Vasiliy Kukharsky, attacked Prokofiev virulently in the official press. He called the opera "a striking example of the artist's detachment from real life."[19] Prokofiev's music was still not heroic enough.

The only work Prokofiev did on an opera after *The Story of a Real Man* was his final revision of *War and Peace*. With that, the most dedicated opera composer of the twentieth century—not to say the Don Quixote of the genre—called a halt.

## AFTER 1948

Zhdanov's campaign had seriously weakened Prokofiev's position. He no longer enjoyed the prestige among Soviet composers on which he had been able to rely from 1939 to 1948. The accusation of formalism hung like a sword of Damocles over every one of his new compositions. Meanwhile, his health declined. The years from 1948 to 1953 marked an anything but glorious end to Prokofiev's career.

With *The Story of a Real Man*, Prokofiev had hoped to find favor with the authorities. Though that hope proved to be vain, he immediately tried again. Together with the co-authors of the scenario, Leonid Lavrovsky and Mira Mendelson, he had seen great possibilities for a ballet in a story included in a collection of folk tales from the Urals chronicled and adapted by Pavel Bazhov and set in the world of stonecutters. The scenario of the ballet *The Stone Flower* (also called *The Tale of the Stone Flower*) combines two tales about the stonecutter Danilo and his sweetheart, Katerina. In his quest for artistic perfection, Danilo enters the realm of the Mistress of the Copper Mountain, who shows him the secret of absolute beauty, the Stone Flower. Anyone beholding the Stone Flower is held a prisoner in the stone room. The Mistress wants to keep Danilo for herself, but Katerina, who has gone in search of him, begs for his release. The Mistress then turns him into stone, but the strength of Katerina's love melts the stone. The Mistress yields, and they all live happily ever after.

In the ballet, the story is pushed into the background, drama and characterization being of secondary importance. The greater part of the ballet consists of folkloristic dances of varied origin: *khorovods* (ceremonial dances), bridesmaids' dances, gypsy dances, Russian dances, and so on. A "Ural Rhapsody" accompanies a scene at a country fair. The handling of folklore here is a far cry from the neonationalism of Stravinsky and Diaghilev. In Prokofiev's ballet, folklore is again brought back to a decorative role.

The simple, decorative, and nationalistic score did not, however, stand up to official criticism. When the music was played to the management of the Bolshoy Theater in 1949, the bureaucrats repeated their hurtful criticisms of the composer. Lavrovsky describes the incident:

> Voices were raised sharply criticizing the music. It was thought that the music poorly corresponded to the artistic imagery of Bazhov's tales, that it was somber, heavy, undanceable. Many thoughtless, careless (and even sometimes tactless) things were said. Sergei Sergeevich took the postponement of the theater's work very hard, and became offended. Around this time, his health began to noticeably deteriorate. There were long periods when he was categorically forbidden to work. Unfortunately, I could do nothing to cheer him up—in fact, I had to hide a great deal from Sergei Sergeevich, protecting his health and well-being. It was especially difficult then for Mira Alexandrovna, who, aware of everything that was going on, tried to calm Sergei Sergeevich, using her characteristic sensitivity and caution.[20]

Prokofiev found a fresh incentive to compose in his friendship with Mstislav Rostropovich, the young cello virtuoso, whom he had met at Rostropovich's performance in 1947 of the First Cello Concerto, written in 1938. In 1949 Prokofiev wrote a cello sonata for Rostropovich, which turned out to be Prokofiev's most nostalgic composition. While the First Violin Sonata is reminiscent of Beethoven, the Cello Sonata sounds more like a tribute to Brahms, above all in the relationship between the two instruments, not least the combination of lyrical melodies in the cello with a texture of broad chords in the piano. The second movement (moderato–andante dolce) sounds more like a Brahmsian character piece than a sarcastic Prokofiev scherzo. Very close to the Brahmsian model is the flowing main theme of the third movement (allegro ma non troppo). All this is the more remarkable when we consider that, throughout his career, Prokofiev tried to stay clear of the influence of the German Romantics.

With Rostropovich's help, he also decided to rewrite his earlier Cello Concerto. He at first called the result of the revision his Second Cello Concerto, but remained dissatisfied with it and, in 1952, decided to undertake an even more thorough revision. In its final form, the work was given the title of Sinfonia Concertante for Cello and Orchestra. It is a major concert piece, calling for considerable virtuosity and tailored to Rostropovich's talent.

Prokofiev wrote his last symphony, the Seventh, in 1951–52. He deliberately kept it very simple, and the work may be said to lack a clear character. The authorities could ask for no more. In 1957, Prokofiev was posthumously awarded a Lenin Prize (so renamed after Stalin's death in 1953) for this work.

He devoted the rest of his time to official compositions, such as the oratorio *On Guard for Peace* and *Winter Bonfire* (1949), a simplistic suite that tells the story of an outing to the forest by a group of boys from Moscow. "There is no irony in Prokofiev's approach to this saccharine material," Harlow Robinson comments. "If Peter from *Peter and the Wolf* had disobeyed his grandfather in this setting, the other boys might have turned him in to the Party officials for punishment."[21] The most important composition in Prokofiev's last period was the orchestral work he wrote in 1951 to celebrate the completion of the canal between the Volga and the Don. Prokofiev himself had this to say, in the spirit of the purest Stalinist optimism, about this *Festive Poem—The Meeting of the Volga and the Don:* "As I work, I remember the endless expanse of our great rivers, I remember the songs which our people have sung about them, and the lines by Russian classical and contemporary poets devoted to them. I am striving in this poem to write music that is melodious, reflecting the joy of construction that now seizes our entire people."[22]

Prokofiev died on 5 March 1953, on the same day as Joseph Stalin. It took some time for his music to return to the concert halls, and the rehabilitation of his entire oeuvre in the Soviet Union took even longer.

*War and Peace*, for instance, had to wait until 15 December 1959 before a more or less complete performance was given in the Bolshoy Theater in Moscow, following two severely cut performances in 1955 and 1957 at the Malïy Theater in Leningrad and the Stanislavsky–Nemirovich-Danchenko Theater in Moscow, respectively. *The Fiery Angel* had to wait even longer, until 1987, for its Russian première, at the Perm provincial theater. Leningrad did not see the opera until December 1991, shortly before the dissolution of the Soviet Union on 1 January 1992 and the formal end of Soviet history.

## CHAPTER FOURTEEN

# "The Secret Diary of a Nation"

## *The Works of Shostakovich*

Shostakovich has managed more successfully than any other Soviet composer to maintain his place in the international repertoire. Apart from Prokofiev—who can be considered "Soviet" for half his career at the most—Shostakovich is the only Soviet composer of his generation to have made a strong and consistent international impact.

Shostakovich is held in particularly high esteem today, but fame is no guarantee of the validity of the prevailing historical picture. As in all cases in which art is closely linked to incisive historical events, the present-day response to Shostakovich's work is influenced to a large extent by ideological considerations and irrational reactions. A critical study of the contemporary evaluation of Shostakovich is essential to determine his true self. This process has only just begun and does not yet admit of any concrete conclusions. Discussion of Shostakovich therefore remains largely problematic.

Shostakovich's image has been radically transformed since the time of *glasnost*. For years, Soviet ideologists characterized him as the preeminent representative of socialist realism and as a loyal Communist (Plate 27). It was not difficult in the West to see through the political manipulation behind this image: the official critics did little more than paraphrase Shostakovich's music simplistically in socialist terms. It proved far harder to fathom the true historical circumstances in which Shostakovich's oeuvre was created.

In 1979 the whole issue seemed suddenly to grow clearer with the publication of Shostakovich's alleged memoirs under the title *Testimony*, "as related to" Solomon Volkov, an émigré Soviet musicologist who claimed that Shostakovich had dictated the book to him in person. *Testimony* set the tone for the greater part of the Shostakovich literature that followed. The portrayal of Shostakovich as a convinced Communist and apologist for the Soviet regime was turned upside down, and he was now seen as an embittered dissident who, in the line of the old Russian tradition of the *yuródiviy*—the "holy fool" who had the privilege of telling the tsar the truth with impunity, as in *Boris Godunov*—proclaimed his real and devastating opinion of the pernicious regime through hidden codes in his music. The revelations in *Testimony* fundamentally changed the interpretation of Shostakovich's music. However, this did not mean that the new picture was any more subtle than the old. A negative simply took the place of the old print; white became black and black became white.

The picture that emerged from *Testimony* was taken up and applied to the music most radically by Ian MacDonald in his book *The New Shostakovich*. The writer minced neither his words nor his opinions:

> Was it [Shostakovich's Fifteenth Symphony] written by the sterling orthodox Communist buried in Novodevichy Cemetery on 14 August 1975? It was not. That figure, a ghost created by Soviet propaganda, certainly did not exist after 1931 and in all probability was as much of a mirage beforehand. Was it, then, written by the embittered secret dissident introduced to the world in 1979 via Solomon Volkov's *Testimony*? It was. Is the new Shostakovich the real Shostakovich? Of course.[1]

Not all writers rely on such rudimentary rhetoric; Shostakovich's music has also been subjected to detailed analyses. However, when it comes to interpreting the meaning of the music, *Testimony* continues to serve as a basic reference work. A clear example is Karen Kopp's *Form und Gehalt der Symphonien des Dimitrij Schostakowitsch* (Form and content of Dmitry Shostakovich's symphonies, 1990), which includes detailed technical and stylistic analyses but, for an explanation of meaning, cites *Testimony*.

Yet for a long time now the authenticity of *Testimony* has been a matter of dispute. In 1980 Laurel Fay subjected the book to a critical examination. She summed up her findings in a particularly striking article entitled "Shostakovich vs. Volkov: Whose Testimony?" that, however, went largely unnoticed.[2] Her conclusions were damning. She demonstrated that the book is not what it claims to be: an account of interviews, of orally transcribed memories. In at least seven places in the text she discovered copies—word for word or slightly adapted—of articles that Shostakovich had published earlier in Soviet journals, subtly altered so as to circumvent references to the past. Even more disturbing was the fact that all the copied passages appear at the beginning of chapters. This arrangement considerably weakens Volkov's claim about the authenticity of the document, which rests mainly on his assertion that Shostakovich had signed the beginning of every chapter with the inscription "Read. D. Shostakovich." Neither Volkov nor the publisher has been prepared to produce the original documents, with the exception of a group photograph that includes both Shostakovich and Volkov and that refers specifically to conversations about Meyerhold, Glazunov, and the Soviet writer Mikhaíl Zoshchenko, as we learn from an inscription by the composer. In consequence, the photograph offers no proof of conversations about the material that has been controversial or held to be revelatory.

Instead of submitting the document to the relevant scholars for validation, then, Volkov produced a manuscript that was impossible to authenticate. It is often argued that the negative reaction of the Soviet authorities to the text, who dismissed the whole affair as a smear campaign, is proof enough of its authenticity, but that is farfetched at best. Today, while there is general agreement in the professional literature that *Testimony* should be treated critically and with circumspection, such reservations do not stop most writers about Shostakovich from relying on it in many details. In her biography of the composer published in 2000, Laurel Fay concludes:

> Whether *Testimony* faithfully reproduces Shostakovich's confidences, and his alone, in a form and context he would have recognized and approved for publication, remains doubtful. Yet even were its claim to authenticity not in doubt, *Testimony* would still furnish a poor source for the serious biographer. The embittered, "deathbed" disclosures of someone ravaged by illness, with festering psychological wounds and scores to settle, are not to be relied upon for accuracy, fairness, or balance when recreating the impact of the events of a lifetime as they actually occurred.[3]

## SHOSTAKOVICH AND THE MODERN MUSIC MARKET

With *Testimony,* however, the public was given precisely what it seemed to have been waiting for. The book filled a need. To understand that, we must recall the structure of modern music on the international scene. At the end of the 1970s, the music market set out to make Shostakovich's oeuvre part of the general repertoire. The reason is simple: Shostakovich wrote music for two of the most important institutions of modern concert life, the symphony and the string quartet. I speak of "institutions" rather than "genres" because both forms of music-making are part of an institutionalized framework—an "institution" implying a complex system of organization, finance, commerce, and marketing. Aesthetic values are an integral part of the operation of such musical institutions. They determine the norms on which the prestige and success of the wider production and reproduction system rests. Since the end of the nineteenth century, symphonies and string quartets have been developing into the hub around which the musical and commercial circuits revolve. In both cases the machinery—the symphony orchestra and the string quartet respectively—is closely linked to a specific type of music. A symphony orchestra is a complex and expensive enterprise. Investment in so large a group of players can only be justified by music of "the greatest weight": expansive forms, with a substantial content, aimed at the largest possible target group. The functioning of the string quartet as a separate, institutionalized ensemble rests on the enormous prestige Beethoven bestowed on this genre.

Both institutions have their roots in the bourgeois, capitalist music culture of the late nineteenth century. The so-called New Music that emerged after 1910 was in many ways a deliberate attempt to discard existing institutions. The avant-garde aimed not only at technical and stylistic innovation, but also at a transformation of the entire musical apparatus. While the Western avant-garde aspired to dismantle the traditional institutions, however, Soviet culture clung to them.

The difference between the two music cultures was greatest during the postwar period. The Cold War was reflected in the musical sphere by a radical split between an institution-supporting form of music with an emphasis on ideological importance, on the Soviet side, and an institution-transcending aesthetic stressing the transformation of the musical material, on the Western side.

Nor was that all. Although the avant-garde enjoyed great critical prestige in the postwar West, the traditional musical apparatus remained untouched and was still supported by the majority of music audiences. Symphony orchestras continued to exist, as did string quartets and opera houses. Indeed, they dominated the music market. However, like every commercial sector, the music market has a regular need for fresh impetus. Following the Mahler revival in the sixties, the search for additions to the repertoire was on. When all the great orchestras and conductors had played and adopted Mahler's entire oeuvre, Shostakovich's symphonies seemed to provide the ideal way forward.

Like Mahler's symphonies, they offer a link with both tradition and a new sound.

The situation of the string quartet is similar. When all the great ensembles had made integral recordings of Beethoven and Bartók, they began to explore Shostakovich's corpus of fifteen quartets. All this, of course, says nothing about the value of Shostakovich's music; it means only that market mechanisms play a large role in the present-day success of his work.

In order to draw attention to the work of Shostakovich in the West, it was essential to rid him of his negative image as an official Soviet composer. He had to be unequivocally "on the right side." Because *Testimony* removed all doubts on that score, it was welcomed with open arms and a general determination to take it at face value. Volkov's portrait of Shostakovich was exactly what the Western music market needed: that of a lifelong dissident, who behind the official façade of his music had been making ironic comments about the Soviet regime the whole time. Shostakovich could henceforth be counted among the opponents of Soviet ideology. Even his most propagandist works, such as the Second and Third Symphonies, could now be heard as covert anti-Soviet manifestos.

Once the final settling up with the Soviet state began during the *glasnost* period, Shostakovich's status grew spectacularly. His work was heard and praised in anticipation of the ever-louder anti-Soviet message that was everywhere to be proclaimed. When it was no longer dangerous for them to do so, Shostakovich adherents suddenly came out into the open—including some of the critics who had previously accused him of formalism. The height of this dubious and cheap revisionism was the publication in 1990 of Ian MacDonald's *The New Shostakovich*, in which the author randomly projected all the implications of *Testimony* onto the musical plane. Although the book was discredited in academic circles for the evidently unfounded way in which it turned the former official value judgments upside down, *The New Shostakovich* is a symptom of a more profound phenomenon: the settling of scores with the Soviet past from the understandable, but unproductive and misleading, need to make a clear distinction between the criminals and their victims. A black-and-white picture of a complex reality simply will not help us to come to terms with so momentous a historical period. As Richard Taruskin puts it:

*Poshlost'*—smug vulgarity, insipid pretension—had always lived and thrived in such accounts. Risking nothing, we excoriate the past to flatter ourselves.

Our high moral dudgeon comes cheap. It is sterile. In fact it is nostalgic. We look back upon the Stalin period romantically, as a time of heroism. We flay the villains, as we define them, and enjoy an ersatz moral triumph. We not only pity the victims, as we define them, but we envy them and wishfully project on to them our own idealised identities. Nor have we even given up our investment in personality cults, it seems; all we have done is install new worshipped personalities in place of the old. The new idolatry is as blinding as the old, just as destructive of values, just as crippling to our critical faculties. Shostakovich remains just as hidden from view as he was before.[4]

## SHOSTAKOVICH AND HIS CRITICS

The biographical portrayal of Shostakovich, the depiction of his life and personality, has been, until recently, determined largely by the reception of his work and opinions about his compositions. The emphasis is almost invariably laid on the political and moral message he is supposed to have preached, and not on his real character. Even the recent biography by Krzysztof Meyer, published in 1995, has uncritically included problematic passages from *Testimony*.[5] The first persistent attempt at writing a more critical and objective biography appeared in 2000 and was written by Laurel Fay. Her *Shostakovich: A Life* is based on a thorough and detailed study of the sources and scrupulously eschews the customary ideological viewpoints. Her study by no means closes the debate, but makes it possible to conduct it henceforth on the basis of solid facts instead of suppositions, fabrications, and half-truths.

Interpretation of Shostakovich's music is generally based on verbal paraphrases of the underlying thought content. However, instrumental music is an intangible form of art, and the "meaning" of music is hard to establish. By looking for a specific and exclusive thought content, the critics tend to ignore the subtlety and elusiveness of all great instrumental music. The urge to lay down an irrefutable and unassailable meaning in fact follows the method used by the Soviet aesthetic. In socialist-realist theory the content, the message of a work, plays a more important role than its aesthetic effect. In addition, Soviet critics insisted that there could be only one correct content. The same method was now being applied, albeit in reverse, by the revisionist Shostakovich exegetes, Ian MacDonald being the most obvious example. We have already seen how Shostakovich distanced himself from such simplistic, anecdotal interpretations; in his article "Soviet Music Criticism Is Lagging," published in 1933, he wrote: "When a critic . . . writes that in such-and-such a symphony Soviet civil servants are represented by the oboe and the clarinet, and Red Army men by the brass section, then you want to scream!"[6] His recent analysts do exactly as did the Soviet critics to whom Shostakovich was objecting; they merely changed the dramatis personae and the plot.

The same aim as Ian MacDonald's underlies Karen Kopp's study *Form und Gehalt der Symphonien des Dimitrij Schostakowitsch:* "[Volkov's] *Testimony* puts forward sociocritical interpretations of various symphonies that clearly demand verification by analysis. In this way, one could also contribute something to the discussion about the authenticity of *Testimony*—which is denied by the Soviet side."[7] Kopp's analysis is a great deal more meticulous than MacDonald's. Her work is a model of detailed structural analysis and reflects a thorough knowledge of the scores she discusses. As regards the content, however, Kopp's arguments undermine the value of her analysis.

The discussion of the Eleventh Symphony is a good example. The work, written in 1957, was described by the composer himself as a programmatic symphony about the revolution of 1905. In the preface to *Testimony,* Solomon Volkov tells us that the work has a hidden meaning, namely an indictment of the Soviet intervention in Hungary in 1956. Karen Kopp promises to clarify that issue by an analysis of the work. The structure is painstakingly dissected and the revolutionary songs on which Shostakovich based the symphony—most of which have a direct connection with the 1905 Revolution—are identified. The analysis accordingly fails to show in any way that Shostakovich was thinking explicitly of Hungary. Yet he did just that, Karen Kopp avers, and she gives two reasons, one general and one based on a specific detail. The first is that the musical treatment of these songs "generalizes" their significance:

> Generalization on the musical plane allows the transposition or incorporation of tyranny into any epoch whatsoever. Even if the songs are directly bound up with the revolution of 1905, the handling of this song repertoire shows that its topicality is by no means confined to that event, but that because of the general validity of their subject matter—opposing tyranny and violence and upholding freedom and self-determination—these songs were sung time and again in different situations. For that reason, the confinement of the subject of the symphony to the outlined historical situation is not tenable.[8]

The belief that a work of art has the power of generalizing its content, or of endowing it with a symbolic function, is nothing new. If we can take Shostakovich's rendering of the revolution of 1905 as a *general* treatment of the theme "tyranny against longing for freedom," it does plead for the wider significance of the work. But how can we justify a *concrete* assignment of that significance to the anti-Soviet reaction to the Hungarian intervention? To render this interpretation plausible, Karen Kopp has a single trump card: the "Warshavyanka," a song of the Polish Workers Party, at least in its 1883 version, which she uses as the basis of her second argument. The melody derives from well before 1883 and had originally been sung to a text about the Polish fight for freedom from Russia. Shostakovich, Karen Kopp concludes, was familiar with the original significance and used the song to voice his objection to Russian domination. This interpretation is speculative and based on an arbitrarily chosen detail, and even then fails to link the work demonstrably to the Hungarian uprising. The author makes this ultimate mental leap, however, on the principle that *Testimony* is authentic.

This sort of interpretation does not rest on the probative strength of the analysis but on the author's a priori image of Shostakovich. Karen Kopp states that she cannot imagine that a man like Shostakovich would compose a tribute to the revolutionary ideal, not even during the de-Stalinization period following the Twentieth Party Congress: "Attributing so much political naïveté and inflexibility to a society and to a man like Shostakovich, who had felt the effects of 'crude power' so strongly and knew the system inside out, seems untenable and guided by the attempt to justify or excuse Shostakovich's apparent adherence to the Party line with somewhat blind idealism and confidence in the new course."[9]

Analysis can serve as an element in the debate, but not as decisive proof. The step from structural analysis to an explanation of the contents must be supported with concrete data. Like MacDonald, Karen Kopp treats *Testimony* as if it were an authenticated source. The result is in both cases a circular argument.

## A DISSIDENT?

Do critical reservations about MacDonald's and Kopp's studies imply that the picture of Shostakovich as an opponent of the regime is wholly mistaken? Or indeed that his work is nothing more than the message of affirmation the Soviet authorities had always heard in it? Far from it. Yet a too narrow revisionism ignores the nuances and passes over the richness of his music.

Shostakovich's entire oeuvre is often reduced to a single denominator. Of some of his works it can be shown that this kind of projection of a presupposed ideological content is an anachronism. Two of his operas, *The Nose* and *The Lady Macbeth of the Mtsensk District,* are generally assumed to be anti-Stalinist works. This view rests on an obvious projection: since both works are sociocritical satires, it is taken for granted that the satire must be directed at the Stalinist regime. Yet in both cases the satire can easily be explained in terms of the Marxist theory of the class struggle, and hence as a justification of communist ideology.

In that respect, *Lady Macbeth* can even be said to be an extreme case. The opera became a cause célèbre because it was responsible for Shostakovich's fall from grace with Stalin. The status of "forbidden work" immediately suggests that it must be an anti-Stalinist manifesto. The character of Katerina Izmailova can then be seen as a symbol for the suffering Soviet citizen, and the caricature of the policeman as a caricature of Stalin himself. Because the opera ends in Siberia, a connection with the gulag is easily made. Indeed, the opera owes its recent revival entirely to this revisionist view. However, such a view is inadequate if we bear in mind the circumstances set out in Chapter 10. Above all, the tendentious changes made to the literary source lend considerable weight to the arguments for considering the opera an extreme expression of fanatical Marxism. As Richard Taruskin puts it:

> So ineluctably has the opera come to symbolize pertinacity in the face of despotism that it is almost impossible to see it clearly now as an embodiment of that very despotism. The fate of *Lady Macbeth of Mtsensk* opened Shostakovich's eyes to the nature of the regime under which he was condemned to live. It could be argued that the work's martyrdom humanized its creator. And yet the opera remains a profoundly inhumane work of art. Its chilling treatment of the victims amounts to a justification of genocide.[10]

The idea that Shostakovich was a lifelong dissident is anachronistic. Dissidence did not exist under Stalin: all his opponents were either dead or in the gulag. Malcontents kept quiet and tried not to draw attention to themselves. The terror was so great that no one could openly distance himself from the regime. Dissidence only raised its head in the Soviet Union after Stalin's death, and then but gradually, as one result of the relaxation of control and repression. The conflict between the regime and dissidents surfaced perceptibly under Brezhnev, who did not succeed in restoring Stalinist control. Until the advent of Gorbachev, however, explicit anticommunism could only be preached from abroad. In view of the omnipresent repression during the Stalinist period, it is inconceivable that Shostakovich should have acted openly as a dissident. According to *Testimony*, however, he did precisely that. On the subject of the Fifth Symphony, we are told:

> I think that it is clear to everyone what happens in the Fifth. The rejoicing is forced, created under threat, as in *Boris Godunov*. It's as if someone were beating you with a stick and saying, "Your business is rejoicing, your business is rejoicing," and you rise, shakily, and go marching off, muttering, "Our business is rejoicing, our business is rejoicing." What kind of apotheosis is that? You have to be a complete oaf not to hear that.[11]

Were the strains of revolt in the Fifth Symphony indeed as clearly audible as the author of *Testimony* alleges, they must have been heard by everyone who listened. In that case, how could Shostakovich possibly have withdrawn his Fourth Symphony for fear of repression and at the same time have openly declared his dissent in the Fifth?

Ian MacDonald claims that we can understand music only if we bear the composer's intentions in mind:

> All that the West (or at least the majority of musical opinion leaders in the West) has heard of Shostakovich's music so far is the noise it makes. The music itself, being beyond the notes, can only be heard if the listener is in tune with the composer's *intentions*—for to attribute inappropriate meaning to a piece of music is to experience not the music itself, but a sort of self-hypnotic dream one is having about it.[12]

The belief that we can have a complete grasp of a composer's intentions is an illusion. To deduce meanings from the composer's intentions, moreover, amounts to a denial of the expressive power of his music. Contact with a work of art is always an interaction between what that work has to offer and what the spectator or listener sees or hears in it. Great art has the power of living a life of its own, regardless of what its creator may have wanted it to signify. This is true of all forms of art, but most particularly of instrumental music, precisely because here an unequivocal semantic meaning is generally lacking. Shostakovich's music cannot be divorced from its influence. Richard Taruskin summarizes this succinctly:

> "I always sensed intuitively in [Shostakovich's music] a protest against the regime," Volkov attests. Of course he did; he and millions of his countrymen. They needed to sense it; and music, with its blessed multivalence, afforded them a consolation no other art could provide under conditions of Soviet thought control. That is why music was valued in the Soviet Union so much more highly than it has ever been in countries that have taken a laissez-faire attitude toward the arts—and Shostakovich's music above all, which exploited with such mastery the rhetoric of post-Beethovenian instrumental music, so full of tension and catharsis, so richly laden with symbols and portents, but

carrying no explicit key to interpretation. It became the secret diary of a nation. But what made it so was due not only to what the composer put into it, but what it enabled listeners to draw out.[13]

## THE TURNING POINT: THE FIFTH SYMPHONY

To gauge the significance of Shostakovich's art we must try to grasp the effect of a turning point in his life: his fall from favor because of *The Lady Macbeth of the Mtsensk District* and his personal *perestroyka,* or "restructuring," that followed. The tangible result of this turning point was the Fifth Symphony of 1937.

Following his censure in 1936, Shostakovich was under pressure to simplify his style and to adapt it to that of the classical models. We have seen that socialist realism in music was defined first of all as a form of heroic classicism. With its division into four movements, the Fifth Symphony is a clear example of Stalinist neoclassicism. Orchestration and sound patterns are less exuberant than in the groundbreaking Fourth. The harmonic experiment has been curbed.

With his Fifth Symphony, Shostakovich scored an unprecedented triumph. Remarkably, the symphony appealed equally to two different parties: the official critics no less than the public reacted ecstatically. The authorities found everything they had looked for restored in the symphony. The public, for its part, heard it as an expression of the suffering to which it had been subjected by the Stalinist terror. One and the same work was therefore received in two distinct ways.

The official critics held the work up as Shostakovich's public apology. For the authorities, it was also an opportunity to extol their own role, to allow it to appear as if they had helped to purge a great artist of his errors and to impose on the Fifth Symphony the official status of "a Soviet artist's creative response to justified criticism." Shostakovich openly endorsed this interpretation in an article published in a Moscow paper, although whether he actually wrote the article himself is difficult to tell. In any event, the interpretation was sanctioned by the official critics and supported by Shostakovich in self-defense against any possible new charges.

The tone of the official critics was set in an influential review by Alexey Tolstoy, who associated the symphony with the literary model of the Soviet bildungsroman, the genre in which simple people learn from experience to appreciate the justice of revolutionary ideals. In similar terms, Tolstoy described the Fifth as "the formation of a personality"—that is, of a Soviet personality. In the first movement, the composer-hero suffers a psychological crisis that gives rise to a burst of energy. The second movement provides a breather. In the third movement, the personality begins to take shape: "Here the personality submerges itself in the great epoch that surrounds it, and begins to resonate with the epoch." In the finale, Tolstoy saw victory, "an enormous optimistic lift." As for the ecstatic reaction of the public, it showed that Shostakovich's *perestroyka* was sincere: "Our audience is organically incapable of accepting decadent, gloomy, pessimistic art. Our audience responds enthusiastically to all that is bright, optimistic, life-affirming."[14]

Shostakovich was quick to concur: "Very true were the words of Alexey Tolstoy, that the theme of my symphony is the formation of a personality. At the center of the work's conception I envisioned just that: a man in all his suffering. . . . The symphony's finale resolves the tense and tragic moments of the preceding movements in a joyous, optimistic fashion." Optimism was the crucial element in the socialist-realist interpretation of the work: "I think that Soviet tragedy, as a genre, has every right to exist; but its content must be suffused with a positive idea, comparable, for example, to the life-affirming ardor of Shakespeare's tragedies." In his public statements Shostakovich identified himself with the personality alleged to be speaking through his symphony: "If I have really succeeded in embodying in musical images all that I have thought and felt since the critical articles in *Pravda*, if the demanding listener will detect in my music a turn toward greater clarity and simplicity, I will be satisfied."[15]

The audience included people who heard something different in the Fifth Symphony, as we know from subsequent statements. Alexander Fadeyev, the head of the Writers Union, wrote in his diary (published in 1957): "A work of astonishing strength. The third movement is beautiful. But the ending does not sound like a resolution (still less like a triumph or victory), but rather like a punishment or vengeance on someone. A terrible emotional force, but a tragic force. It arouses painful feelings."[16] The musicologist Genrikh Orlov declared after his emigration to the West that the symphony must be seen as an artistic portrayal of the time in which it originated: "In the years preceding the creation of the Fifth Symphony, Shostakovich had grown not only as a master but as a thinking artist-citizen. He grew up together with his country, his people, sharing their fate, their aspirations and their hopes, intently scrutinizing the life around him, sensing with all his being its inner pulse."[17] According to those attending the memorable première on 21 November

1937, during the largo members of the audience wept. The music was steeped in an atmosphere of mourning, and even contained echoes of the *panikhida*, the Russian Orthodox requiem. It also harked back to a genre of Russian symphonic preludes written in memory of the dead—pieces composed by, among others, Glazunov, Steinberg, and Stravinsky. Typical of these pieces is the use of tremolo in the strings as a reference to the hallowed ambience of the requiem. In addition to this allusion, Shostakovich's largo also recalls Mahler's *Das Lied von der Erde,* particularly the last movement, "Der Abschied" (The farewell). In an audience that had lost friends and relatives on a massive scale to the Stalinist terror, these references were bound to evoke intense emotional reactions. This explains why the Fifth Symphony was received and cherished by the Soviet public like no other work as an expression of the ineffable grief they endured during the Stalinist period.

The grandiose finale has been the subject of interminable discussion: is it a Stalinist victory hymn or a parody of one? In the second case the bombast of the coda would have been deliberately pitched so as to sound ridiculous, thus revealing the hypocrisy of the synthetic, obligatory tribute. Leo Mazel has provided more convincing analysis. In his study of Shostakovich's symphonies he links the dissonant passages in the finales of the Fifth and Seventh Symphonies to the suffering accompanying the struggle for the progress of mankind.[18] And indeed, toward the conclusion of the finale of the Fifth Symphony, the stereotypical outburst of rejoicing makes way for a dissonant passage, reminiscent of other works by Shostakovich that deal explicitly with the theme of suffering. At the conclusion of the Fifth, therefore, personal grief supplants the valedictory nature of the finale.

Shostakovich's ability to please the authorities with his Fifth Symphony, and at the same time give the audience an outlet for their sorrow, shows how effectively he had mastered the essence of the Romantic symphony. In the wake of Beethoven's Ninth, the symphony had developed via Bruckner and Mahler into a genre that works specific musical images and allusions into a network that each listener can evaluate and interpret on personal grounds. Its very transcendence of concrete content thus allows for varied—and opposite—readings, and at the same time renders a definitive account of its meaning impossible. Shostakovich owes his artistic survival to the successful way in which he made this genre his own. It satisfied the Soviet demand for monumentality and classicism while leaving room for individual expression. The ambiguous content of the symphony was the very salvation of Shostakovich's art. He was to remain faithful to the paradigm of heroic classicism in the symphonic field for the rest of his life.

## AFTER THE FIFTH:
## SHOSTAKOVICH'S OTHER SYMPHONIES

The about-face that came with the Fifth Symphony was enduring. In the rest of Shostakovich's symphonic oeuvre we can see that he tried constantly to relax the prevailing norms. The Sixth Symphony (1939) abandoned the classical scheme of four movements. It has only three, which are, moreover, of disparate lengths. The first movement is slow (largo) and lasts longer than the other two put together. The second movement is an allegro and the third a presto. The music has several distinguishing features. The first movement is static in character, in stark contrast to the dynamic structure with which symphonies traditionally begin. The first theme lacks a definitive form; it consists of three motifs that recur in ever-different combinations. There is no proper development in the middle of the movement; instead, instrumental recitatives hold the movement up and convey a sense of expectation and timelessness. Another feature is the absence of a triumphant finale. The lighthearted presto culminates in circus music, Shostakovich once again engaging in the satirical idiom of *The Golden Age* and *The Nose*.

The official critics were vigilant and let Shostakovich know that deviations from the rule would not go unnoticed. One reviewer called the Sixth a "headless symphony" because of the absence of an opening allegro.

The Seventh Symphony (1941) once more met official expectations. Shostakovich had at first intended to write a single-movement symphony, including a chorus and a requiemlike passage, but in the end opted for the classical four-movement structure. He considered titles for the individual movements—"War," "Remembrance," "The Vastness of the Fatherland," and "Victory"—but later dropped them. The Seventh Symphony (the *Leningrad*) may be considered a model of socialist realism in music, the message of the work outweighing its craftsmanship. The music relies on concrete images—stylized fanfares, folkloristic themes, and pastoral passages—of the Russian people on the one hand and of the German invasion on the other, complete with march rhythms, an aggressive use of timpani, and obsessive ostinati. The portrayal of the German advance unfolds in eleven variations in the middle of the first movement, the buildup of tension reflecting the German war machine, the terror of the bombardment, and the wail of the air-raid sirens.

The composition lays greater emphasis on the effect of the musical images than on symphonic coherence and development. Western commentators have always criticized the rudimentary nature of the work, its simple texture and a structure that relies on excessive repetition. The American critic Virgil Thomson wrote about the *Leningrad* Symphony: "Whether one is able to listen [to it] without mind-wandering . . . depends on the rapidity of one's musical perceptions. It seems to have been written for the slow-witted, the not very musical and the distracted."[19] The Soviet audience, however, did not come to the work with the same expectations as Western listeners. What mattered to them above all was the message and the seriousness of its moral content. The *Leningrad* Symphony maintained its leading position in the esteem of the Soviet public because its content was so momentous: the Great Patriotic War, which lived on in the nation's consciousness as the event that had united the Soviet people.

The Eighth Symphony (1943) is generally considered a richer composition than the Seventh. The war theme is handled with greater structural rigor. The fourth movement, for example, is based on the strict theme of a passacaglia (that is, of variations played over a continually repeated bass). By virtue of the greater structural tension, the combination of drama with emotional expression is more marked than in the Seventh. The symphony comes to a close, not with a bombastic finale, but with a pastorale that ends pianissimo. For the Soviet public, however, the Eighth was unable to displace the Seventh as a musical memorial to the war.

In the Ninth Symphony (1945), Shostakovich broke openly with the paradigm of heroic classicism, opting for "classicism *tout court*," for music that, using the model of a Haydn symphony, was in line with Prokofiev's *Classical* Symphony. Like no other work, the Ninth is a plea for artistic freedom. At a time when the audience was expecting a "genuine Ninth" in celebration of the heroic victory, complete with final chorus à la Beethoven, Shostakovich came up with a deliberately lighthearted work. He defended his choice as a return to normal life after the exceptional circumstances of the war. However, the Ninth is not as "normal" as all that. Shostakovich makes extensive use of his satirical idiom and of the parody techniques he had developed during his first period. In the conditions prevailing at the end of the war, the abundant satirical elements were bound to shock. We can only guess at Shostakovich's intentions. The work—especially the parodic-bombastic passages in the finale—is generally greeted as an exposure of the hypocrisy of the officially promulgated flush of victory. All that can be said with certainty, however, is that the composer had once again joined the ranks of the satirical modernists. The Ninth reflects the hopes nurtured during the war that a more liberal era would follow. *Zhdanovshchina*, the repression that followed in 1948, was to extinguish any such hopes.

The first symphony Shostakovich wrote following the *Zhdanovshchina* period was his Tenth (1953). Because the work was composed shortly after Stalin's death, most commentators have looked for some connection between the two events. In *Testimony*, for instance, the uncommonly abrasive scherzo is identified as a sarcastic portrait of the tyrant. That claim, though perhaps accurate enough, is hard to substantiate, however. Certainly no hard evidence exists for such a program during the composition or early reception of the work. Maxim Shostakovich, moreover, has stated that his father never said the scherzo was a portrait of Stalin.[20]

By and large, the Tenth is a return to the model of heroic classicism and can be considered the successor of the Fifth. It, too, is divided into four movements and is of comparable monumentality. The reaffirmation of the official aesthetic can be explained by the great pressure to which Shostakovich had been subjected during the preceding years. Accusations of formalism and decadence had not yet lost their edge in the early fifties. Shostakovich was, for instance, attacked for his Twenty-four Preludes and Fugues (1950–51), a collection modeled on *Das wohltemperierte Klavier* and, as such, an impressive homage to Bach. There were discussions in the Composers Union about these piano pieces and whether music of such complexity was really needed at the time, or whether it should be rejected as part and parcel of the hated formalism. Only a few people dared to come out publicly in Shostakovich's defense, among them especially his students, including Georgiy Sviridov and Yuriy Levitin, and the pianist Tatyana Nikolayeva. As far as Shostakovich was concerned, the Tenth Symphony was simply a return to safer ground.

Shostakovich's recent experience with the polyphonic style had a favorable impact on the structural logic of the symphony. The first movement of the Tenth—which is related to the last fugue (in D minor) of the Preludes and Fugues, op. 87—is deemed by many to be the composer's most convincing symphonic structure, while the scherzo is an unprecedentedly aggressive, compact piece of music. In the third movement, Shostakovich introduces his musical monogram: the initials of his name, DSCH (in the German transliteration), are rendered by the notes D, E-flat, C, B (= H). Shostakovich had previously used motifs resembling this monogram, for instance in the First Violin Concerto (composed in 1948 but not performed until 1955), but it was in the Tenth Symphony that he first used it openly as a personal signature. Yet another monogram is hidden in the score: the notes E, la, mi, re, and A form the name Elmira, an allusion to his pupil Elmira Nazirova, with whom Shostakovich was conducting an intense correspondence at the time. (The relationship was of short duration; he broke with her after completing the symphony.)The music also includes a reference to a song Shostakovich had based on Pushkin's poem "What Is in My Name for You?" We can only guess at the specific significance of these various codes. The Tenth Symphony was condemned at meetings of the Composers Union. Shostakovich was accused of modernism, of gloomy introspection, and of a lack of positive ideas. With the public, by contrast, the symphony swiftly proved a great success. The work was immediately perceived as a settling of accounts with the past, and as an expression of the hope that things would change for the better.

Both the Eleventh Symphony ("The Year 1905," 1957) and the Twelfth Symphony ("The Year 1917," 1961) are programmatic works. The Eleventh Symphony belongs to the Soviet genre of "song symphonies," which flourished in the thirties in particular. Shostakovich based its musical development on nine revolutionary songs; the structure resembles a collage of song quotations. The first movement portrays the Palace Square before the bloody clash there in 1905; the second depicts "January the Ninth," or Bloody Sunday—the day when the tsarist guard opened fire on an unarmed crowd. The third movement is entitled "Eternal Memory," and the fourth, called "The Tocsin," heralds the Revolution of 1917. The composer's real aims with his Eleventh Symphony have been the subject of debate, though Shostakovich himself was unequivocal in his official explanation of the content of this work: "I am now writing my Eleventh Symphony, dedicated to the First Russian Revolution, to its unforgettable heroes. And I would like in this work to reflect the soul of the people who first paved the way to socialism."[21] As discussed above, the symphony is regularly interpreted as an allusion to the Soviet invasion of Hungary in 1956, but there are no concrete indications that Shostakovich intended it as such.

The Twelfth Symphony, a sequel to the Eleventh, was written in homage to Lenin. The first movement is called "Revolutionary Petrograd," the second "Razliv" (the site of Lenin's retreat before the October Revolution); the third movement, "Aurora," incorporates the historic cannon shot with which the Revolution was ushered in on 24 October 1917. The finale is called "The Dawn of Humanity." The Twelfth Symphony met with a cooler response than the Eleventh. The latter retained its appeal because of its suspected hidden meaning (the assumed allusion to the Hungarian uprising), whereas it was more difficult to read secondary meanings into the Twelfth.

The Thirteenth and Fourteenth Symphonies are song cycles rather than traditional symphonies and will be discussed below. Only with the Fifteenth Symphony (1971) did Shostakovich return to the classical symphonic mold (Plate 31). The first movement, a lighthearted allegretto, is in keeping with the Ninth Symphony. The quotations from Rossini's *William Tell* Overture are striking. The tense adagio of the second movement contrasts with the carefree character of the first, the music here being reminiscent of the first movement of the Sixth Symphony. There follows a scherzo on a dodecaphonic theme. The finale contains a quotation from Wagner's *Walküre,* the passage that, in Wagner, accompanies Brünnhilde's words "Nur Todgeweihten taugt mein Anblick: wer mich erschaut, der scheidet vom Lebenslicht" (The doomed alone can bear my glance: those who behold me surrender the spark of life). This is followed by the two themes of the finale, continued by a passacaglia, functioning as a development section. The bass theme of the passacaglia is a reference to the invasion theme in the *Leningrad* Symphony.


THE THAW

After Stalin's death on 5 March 1953, the writers Ilya Ehrenburg and Vladimir Pomerantsev published a number of articles in which they challenged the Party's right to lay down the law to artists. Aram Khachaturyan and Dmitry Shostakovich were quick to back them up, emphasizing the artist's right to "independence, boldness, and originality." In February 1954 the minister of culture, the Party ideologist Panteleymon Ponomarenko, was replaced by Georgiy Alexandrov, who had been Zhdanov's opponent. The hope entertained during this period by artists and intellectuals was symbolized by the publication of Ehrenburg's novel *The Thaw.*

However, the ideological and political thaw did not progress very fast. At the Second Congress of Soviet Writers, official voices were still admonishing those present not to break with Party ideology. Signs could be seen of a freeze as well as a thaw. In March 1955, Alexandrov was dismissed.

At the Twentieth Party Congress in February 1956, the new Party leader, Nikita Khrushchev, delivered his "secret address," in which he exposed a number of Stalin's crimes, among them the murder of loyal Party leaders. Although he contended that Stalin had rendered great service to the international labor movement, Khrushchev called for an end to the personality cult, for the restoration of collective leadership, and for a return to the "Leninist principles of Soviet socialist democracy."

Khrushchev gave his address because he had come to the conclusion that Stalin—whom he had served faithfully—was anything but loved by the majority of the population. Khrushchev's form of de-Stalinization was above all an attempt to ensure the continued existence of the Soviet regime.

Following this "secret address," several writers felt brave enough to speak out about Soviet life. Vladimir Dudintsev published the novel *Not by Bread Alone,* and Boris Pasternak wrote *Doctor Zhivago,* for which he was awarded the Nobel Prize, an honor Khrushchev forced him to turn down. A mild thaw set in after 1959. Yevgeniy Yevtushenko attacked anti-Semitism in his poem *Babi Yar,* and Alexander Solzhenitsïn published *One Day in the Life of Ivan Denisovich,* a book set in a Stalinist concentration camp.

In 1963 Khrushchev launched a counterattack. He criticized Ehrenburg and Yevtushenko and declared that untrammeled creative freedom would not be tolerated in the Soviet Union. Some writers, including Valeriy Tarsis and Alexander Esenin-Volpin, were arrested on a charge of "mental instability." Joseph Brodsky was banished under the "antiparasite" laws. In general, however, things went no further than verbal threats, and the arts enjoyed slightly greater leeway than they had under Stalin.

In the Composers Union little changed at first. Khrennikov was reelected general secretary. In 1958, however, a decree was passed acknowledging errors in the resolution of 1948. The decree was entitled "On Rectifying Errors in the Evaluation of the Operas *The Great Friendship, Bogdan Khmelnitsky,* and *From All My Heart,*" a reference to three operas that had been censured in 1948. Although the decree stated unequivocally that formalism alienated the art of the people and must therefore be disowned, it recognized that the criticism leveled at some composers had been undeserved. From the memoirs of the soprano Galina Vishnevskaya we know that Shostakovich was astounded by the decree. He is supposed to have said, "A historical decree, mark you, a historical decree to annul a historical decree. . . . It's as simple as that—just as simple as that."[22]

The thaw was reflected in Shostakovich's career by the performance of works that he had written earlier but that had stood no chance of being played. These included the Fourth String Quartet (1949), the song cycle *From Jewish Folk Poetry* (1948), and the First Violin Concerto (1947–48). The first two, as the composer expressly stated, had not been written for immediate publication. In both works Shostakovich made use of Jewish folklore as a protest against the anti-Semitism rife during the late Stalinist period. This "Jewish theme" became important in Shostakovich's compositions from the Second Piano Trio (1944) onward, a work in which he quoted a Jewish dance in order to express his abhorrence of the Nazi atrocities. Ever since, the Jewish element had been present in all his work.

The first performance of the Violin Concerto came at a bad moment. Shostakovich ran the risk of being accused once more of formalism, not least because he had made use of the strict form of a passacaglia in the third movement. The violinist David Oistrakh, however, was most anxious to perform the concerto. About to go on tour in the United States, he had been asked to bring the work with him. Because the Soviet regime was keen to improve relations with the West, Oistrakh was given permission to present the concerto, first in Leningrad and then in America. The performance in Leningrad on 29 October 1955 was hardly mentioned by the reviewers, except for one notice by Marina Sabinina. Unhappy about this silence, Oistrakh himself wrote an apologia for the work, under the title of "A Great Idea Takes Shape."[23] The performance on 29 December 1955 at Carnegie Hall in New York, conducted by Dimitri Mitropoulos, was a triumph.

The performance of these works raised Shostakovich's hopes that there might be a rehabilitation of the work with which the whole smear campaign against him had begun, namely *The Lady Macbeth of the Mtsensk District*. He started revising the opera at the end of 1954, the death of his wife, Nina Vasilyevna, to whom he had dedicated the work, perhaps providing the impetus. Shostakovich wrote to Isaak Glikman:

> I noticed many errors there [in the part of Boris Timofeyevich]. Besides which, the part is inconvenient for the singer. The second and third acts I am leaving untouched. I want to talk with you about the finale of the opera. However, I am not doing this for the theater. The question of whether the opera will be staged again or not is of little concern to me.[24]

From this we may take it that Shostakovich began his revision for personal and artistic reasons. New documentation does indeed show that the traditional view of the revision as being due to political pressure is inadequate.

The new version was at least in part the consequence of Shostakovich's artistic development. He had in fact begun the revision before the opera was banned, and in the piano version that he published in 1935 he had already deleted the crudest and earthiest sections and had played down the seduction scene. In short, he had curbed his acute naturalism even before being attacked for it. In the definitive revision he went further still in neutralizing the work's shock effects. The opera was given a new title, *Katerina Izmailova*, and a new opus number, 114. As well as writing two new interludes, Shostakovich changed the character of the main protagonist, replacing Katerina's sexual hunger with a more general and poetic expression of desire, thus carrying the justification of her actions one step further. The character of Boris, too, had some of his sharp edges smoothed off. The rape scene no longer occurred onstage—with the notorious glissandos in the trombones—but was left to the spectator's imagination.

All in all, it is impossible to tell to what extent the accusations leveled at him in the *Pravda* article were at the back of his mind when he made these adjustments. It is entirely possible that in his middle age he was himself somewhat shocked by his youthful excesses.

Plans to stage the opera had to be shelved for some time, however, and it was not until 1963 that the revised version was premièred in the Stanislavsky–Nemirovich-Danchenko Music Theater in Moscow. Shostakovich was emphatically opposed to Western performances of the original version, responding unfavorably, for example, to plans for a La Scala staging in 1964. Through his agent Nicolas Benois he announced, "I have been able to make many corrections and improvements in the new version and I beg you to tell them to produce my opera in the new version by all means, or to leave it alone. . . . And one more thing: I categorically object to any cuts or rearrangement of episodes."[25]

To the definitive version of the opera Shostakovich added a passage that was not present in the original. In the last scene, on the road to Siberia, he has an old prisoner sing: "Ach, why is this life of ours so dark, so fearful? Is man really born for such a life?" This addition can be considered a personal aside by Shostakovich on the inhumanity of his age and the suffering that so many of his compatriots had to undergo; with it, the scene alludes unmistakably to the tragic history of the Soviet gulag.[26]

A great event in Shostakovich's life was the long-postponed première of the Fourth Symphony on 30 December 1961, a highly emotional affair for both the public and the composer. Isaak Glikman reported that Shostakovich was so impressed on hearing the work performed that he said, "It seems to me that for many reasons the Fourth Symphony is more interesting than all my later symphonies."[27]

THE JEWISH THEME

From 1943 the "Jewish theme"—Jewish music, Jewish poetry, and Jewish subjects—played a prominent role in Shostakovich's work. Such positive treatment of Jewish culture was new in the history of Russian music. The great composers of the previous generation had all been antiSemites, with the exception of Nikolai Rimsky-Korsakov and, of course, of such Jewish composers as Steinberg and Gnesin. Glinka, Balakirev, Musorgsky, Chaikovsky, and Stravinsky had all made offensive remarks. When music with a Jewish coloring was used at all, it was usually treated as part of the orientalist mode.

Shostakovich's interest in Jewish subjects surfaced in 1943, when he orchestrated an opera by a Jewish composer, Venyamin Fleishman's *Rothschild's Violin*. This work had the typical characteristics of what was to become Shostakovich's Jewish idiom: Jewish modes (the Phrygian mode with an augmented third and the Dorian mode with an augmented fourth), the so-called iambic prime (that is, a series of primes—two notes of the same pitch—in an iambic rhythm, or with the first note of each group on an upbeat), and the typical accompaniments to Jewish klezmer music. After his work on that opera, Shostakovich used this Jewish idiom in a work of his own, the Second Piano Trio, op. 67. In its finale, he included a macabre Jewish dance, reflecting his horror on hearing the first news of the Holocaust, then reaching Russia.

From 1948 to 1952 Shostakovich composed a whole series of works in which the Jewish idiom played a part: the First Violin Concerto (1947–48), the Fourth String Quartet (1949), the song cycle *From Jewish Folk Poetry* (1948), the Twenty-four Preludes and Fugues (1951), and the *Four Monologues on Texts by Pushkin* (1952).

He returned to Jewish themes in 1959. Between that year and 1963 he included them in the First Cello Concerto (1959), the Eighth String Quartet (1960), the Thirteenth Symphony (1962), and the orchestral version of *From Jewish Folk Poetry*. In 1970, finally, he contributed to the publication of a collection of Jewish songs.

The social significance of Shostakovich's use of the Jewish idiom becomes clear when it is viewed in relation to the virulent anti-Semitism of the Soviet regime. It was during the years 1948–52 that the regime set out to destroy Jewish culture, as part of the anti-Western propaganda campaign of *Zhdanovshchina*. The Soviet people were told that Jews had an innate tendency to glorify the West and that they had therefore to be excluded from Soviet life. Jewish institutions were shut down and Jewish intellectuals persecuted. The works by Shostakovich mentioned above thus came quickly to be seen as indicators of resistance to the regime.

That does not necessarily mean, however, that Shostakovich composed the First Violin Concerto and the song cycle *From Jewish Folk Poetry* in explicit opposition to the regime. The fact that it took a long time before these works could be performed in public persuaded many commentators that Shostakovich meant to keep them "on hold," that they were written not for public performance but as a matter of conscience. Laurel Fay's studies have, however, cast fresh light on the matter.

Shostakovich completed *From Jewish Folk Poetry* on 24 October 1948. At that time, the intelligentsia had no inkling of Stalin's plans to wage a postwar anti-Semitic campaign. Shostakovich could therefore not have known during the composition of the work that he was courting danger. Recently, after all, a new Sinfonietta on Jewish themes by the composer Moisey Vainberg had been well received by the Composers Union. That work was even performed in public and praised by Khrennikov as proof that music based on folk themes could triumph over the bad influence of modernism.

When he was composing *From Jewish Folk Poetry,* Shostakovich was under heavy pressure to become rehabilitated. It is hence perfectly possible that he planned the song cycle as a "safe" work, in keeping with the resolution of February 1948. For without a doubt, *From Jewish Folk Poetry* satisfies all official demands: it is intelligible; text and music are based on folklore; its content is realistic, portraying as it does ordinary people. The composition even ushered in a new trend: the so-called New Folklore Wave, a movement that dwelled on national and ethnic elements. The socialist-realist aspect, meanwhile, is clearly present in the optimistic songs at the end: "The Good Life" and "A Girl's Song," paeans of praise to the joys of Soviet life from which the Jewish idiom has almost disappeared. Character and expression remain neutral in these last songs, in comparison with the other songs, which are all sharply defined and deal with poverty or grief.

At the end of January 1949 Stalin's virulent campaign against Jewish culture and Zionism was launched in the Soviet press. There could no longer be any question of a public unveiling of *From Jewish Folk Poetry;* Shostakovich's new work thus fell victim to extremely bad timing. Even so, the songs were performed at private concerts within a small circle. Students and composers were familiar with them.

Finally, on 15 January 1955, the long-awaited première took place in Leningrad, performed by Nina Dorliak, Zara Dolukhanova, and Alexey Maslennikov, with the composer at the piano. It was then that the cycle received its Aesopian connotation: the telling of the truth in covert form. Soviet anti-Semitism had all but unleashed another Holocaust since the completion of the composition. For the audience, the cycle assumed a tragic and horrifying significance.

The music of *From Jewish Folk Poetry,* as we have seen, includes typical Jewish phrasing, and two songs (numbers two and five) are related to original Jewish folk melodies. In most of the songs, however, Shostakovich's language, as well as the structure, meter, and rhythm, expresses a more general character typical of the folk music of various East European peoples.

In some of his instrumental works the Jewish idiom is used in purer form. In the Fugue in F-sharp Minor included in the Twenty-four Preludes and Fugues, for instance, Shostakovich makes use of Jewish liturgical music. The Jewish theme, with its Aesopian connotation, is thus raised in this work to the most abstract musical level.

The link between the Jewish theme and protests against the regime was most pronounced in the Thirteenth Symphony, called *Babi Yar.* In this work, Shostakovich dispensed with the Jewish coloring; the text was perfectly clear without it. The symphony includes five poems by Yevgeniy Yevtushenko. The first is the renowned *Babi Yar,* a poem that turns the mass murder by Nazis of Jews in Babi Yar, near Kiev, into an outspoken protest against all forms of anti-Semitism. Although the Soviet authorities refused permission for a monument to be put up at Babi Yar, it nevertheless became an unofficial place of pilgrimage for Soviet Jews.

The theme of the suffering of the Jewish people is complemented in the Thirteenth Symphony with Yevtushenko's verses about other Soviet abuses. "Humor" denounces the vain attempts of tyrants to shackle wit. "At the Store" is a tribute to the women who have to stand in line for hours to buy the most basic foods. "Fears" evokes the terror under Stalin. "Career" is an attack on bureaucrats and a tribute to genuine creativity.

Shostakovich set the poem *Babi Yar* to music as soon as he heard it. At first, he thought of a single-movement composition. Then he discovered three other poems, in Yevtushenko's collection *Vzmakh ruki* (A wave of the hand), which caused him to change his plans and to proceed to a choral symphony of several movements, including "At the Store," "Humor," and "Career." Yevtushenko wrote the poem "Fears" at the composer's request.

Yevtushenko was a controversial figure. His poem *Babi Yar* set in motion a smear campaign against him in which he was accused of having placed the suffering of the Jewish people above that of the Russians. The intelligentsia also called him a "boudoir poet," or a moralist. In a letter to his pupil Boris Tishchenko on 26 October 1965, Shostakovich defended Yevtushenko in the following words:

> As for what "moralizing" poetry is, I didn't understand. Why, as you maintain, it isn't "among the best." Morality is the natural sister of conscience. And because Yevtushenko writes about conscience, God grant him all the very best. Every morning, instead of morning prayers, I reread, well, recite from memory, two poems by Yevtushenko, "Boots" and "A Career." "Boots" is conscience. "A Career" is morality. One should not be deprived of conscience. To lose conscience is to lose everything.[28]

In the Thirteenth Symphony Shostakovich takes his critique of the regime to its furthest point, although even then it does not betoken outright dissent. The symphony broaches subjects that could be discussed more or less freely, provided only that the basis of the Soviet regime was not brought into question. "Let the Internationale resound when the last anti-Semite is buried for ever"—that sort of verse still reflects faith in communism. Soviet heroism, too, is not absent. The greatness of Russia is, for instance, evoked in the lines "We are not demoralized or corrupted, and not without reason Russia, having conquered her own fears, fills her enemies with even greater fear." On the whole, the dissent to which the work bears witness remains within the bounds that were tolerated at the end of Khrushchev's regime.

When performed at a public concert with symphonic backing, however, critical texts have a greater public impact than when they are simply read at home. No wonder, then, that the authorities were doubly concerned. The conductor, Yevgeniy Mravinsky, and the bass singer, Boris Gmïrya, foresaw difficulties and refused their collaboration. Shostakovich then asked Kyril Kondrashin to conduct the work. Two singers were engaged, Viktor Nechipailo and Vitaliy Gromadsky. The first was expected to sing at the première, but he too withdrew at the last moment. Kondrashin was then put under official pressure to omit the first movement of the symphony. The concert nevertheless went ahead on 18 December 1962 in the great hall of the Moscow Conservatory, the work being performed in full with Gromadsky as soloist (Plate 30). Although the planned live television broadcast of the 18 December performance was canceled, the concert was repeated two days later.

It was a real triumph for both Shostakovich and Yevtushenko. However, the press carried only the briefest of notices. In addition to Kondrashin's enthusiastic defense of the work, the most important comment was an anonymous editorial that reproved the composer, without mentioning him by name, for devoting a great work to minor aspects of Soviet life and hence conveying a mistaken and inaccurate picture of it.[29]

Yevtushenko was now put under pressure to change his poem so as to make it clear that Jews had not been the only people to be murdered at Babi Yar, that Russians and Ukrainians had also perished. He therefore replaced eight of the original verses with a politically correct version.[30] Kondrashin persuaded Shostakovich to include the new verses in his score, in the hope of saving the symphony. Shostakovich agreed to the performance of the new version, but never added the new verses to the manuscript of the symphony.

These verses were heard during performances of the Thirteenth Symphony under Kondrashin on 10 and 11 February 1963. In March there followed two performances in Minsk, with the original text. Silence then descended upon the work. No official edict against it was ever issued, but pressure by the Party cadres was enough to prevent further performances. *Babi Yar* was the last composition in which Shostakovich expressed a clear public message. Thereafter he confined himself to introspective works.

## SHOSTAKOVICH AND MUSORGSKY

Of all his Russian predecessors, Musorgsky was the composer to whom Shostakovich referred most widely, both in new orchestrations of works by Musorgsky himself and, less directly, in his own oeuvre.

In 1939 Shostakovich started on a commission from the Bolshoy Theater for a new orchestration of *Boris Godunov.* The publication of the original, by Pavel Lamm, had aroused keen interest, but had failed to remove the doubts of many as to whether Musorgsky's own orchestration was playable. Shostakovich shared these reservations:

> The deeply Russian national opera *Boris Godunov* is the crown of Musorgsky's creative work. However its orchestration leaves a great deal to be desired. Musorgsky achieved splendid individual orchestral successes, but on the whole his technique of orchestration was inadequate. In the composer's score, for instance, scenes of enormous symphonic tension, such as the bell peals, the coronation, and the polonaise, sound poorly.[31]

In Shostakovich's judgment, Musorgsky did extremely well with solo timbres in soft passages but fell short with loud passages for the full orchestra. Shostakovich based his orchestration on the critical edition of the vocal score and orchestrated the hypersaturated conflation Lamm had compiled from the 1869 and 1872 versions of the opera. However, the war prevented its production in the Bolshoy Theater, which in fact reverted to the use of the Rimsky-Korsakov orchestration after 1945. Not until 4 November 1959 was Shostakovich's score premièred, at the Kirov Theater in Leningrad.

The composition by Shostakovich closest to Musorgsky's model is "Antiformalist *Rayok*," a composition for four basses, mixed choir, piano, and narrator. As mentioned in the discussion of Musorgsky's songs in Chapter 5, it was based on a folkloristic custom: a peepshow display (*rayok*) of various tableaux, with a narrator providing a satirical commentary. Musorgsky's song poked fun at the opponents of the *kuchka*, Shostakovich's at the antiformalistic campaign of 1948. Shostakovich compiled his "*Rayok*" from addresses by Zhdanov, Stalin, Zakharov, Dimitry Shepilov, and other ideologists. The work dates back to about 1957. Some writers claim that it was composed as early as 1948, but in view of the extreme danger such a work entailed for the composer—even though it was not intended for the concert platform—the earlier date, at the height of *Zhdanovshchina*, does not seem very probable.

In 1958 Shostakovich started on an orchestration of *Khovanshchina* for a film of the opera. He restored the cuts Rimsky-Korsakov had made and completed the unfinished score with music of his own. The film came out in 1959, and the opera was staged with Shostakovich's orchestration in 1960 in Leningrad. In his revision of the chaotic score, Shostakovich kept to Rimsky-Korsakov's melioristic interpretation. He retained Rimsky-Korsakov's final chorus, but extended it with a recapitulation of the "Dawn" theme from the prelude. The reforms of Peter the Great and the end of Old Russia are presented in an even more positive light in his version than they were in Rimsky-Korsakov's. Shostakovich's orchestration has proved its worth and forms the basis of most modern performances.

In 1962 Shostakovich produced his third Musorgsky orchestration, the song cycle *Songs and Dances of Death*. The orchestration is highly imaginative, Shostakovich adding a further visionary dimension to the last song, "The Field Marshal."

These orchestrations had an important bearing on Shostakovich's late work. The greater part of his vocal music was written after his immersion in the works of Musorgsky: the Thirteenth and Fourteenth Symphonies (1962 and 1969), which may be taken for orchestral song cycles; the cantata *The Execution of Stepan Razin* (1964); Seven Romances to the Poems of Alexander Blok (1967); *Six Poems by Marina Tsvetayeva* (1973); Suite to the Poems of Michelangelo Buonarroti (1974); and *Four Verses of Captain Lebyadkin to Texts by Dostoyevsky from "The Devils"* (1975). Shostakovich's method of writing for the voice in small intervals, with much tonal repetition and with attention to natural declamation, was taken directly from Musorgsky.

The Fourteenth Symphony (1969) is a creative response to Musorgsky's *Songs and Dances of Death*. Like Musorgsky, Shostakovich brings back the theme of death in different situations and in various images. He found, however, that Musorgsky did not go far enough and that his cycle was too short. To expand the idea of death in different guises, Shostakovich selected eleven poems by García Lorca, Apollinaire, Küchelbecker, and Rilke. The score is sober and designed for two soloists (soprano and bass), string orchestra, and percussion. Shostakovich attached great importance to this symphony, observing in a letter to Glikman: "Everything that I have written until now over these long years has merely served as a preparation for this work."[32] He added that he wanted to provide a counterweight to the positive presentation of death in the music literature:

> In part, I am trying to polemicize with the great classics who touched upon the theme of death in their work. . . . Remember the death of Boris Godunov. When . . . he dies, then a kind of brightening sets in. Remember Verdi's *Otello*. When the whole tragedy ends and Desdemona and Otello die, we also experience a beautiful tranquillity. Remember *Aida*. When the tragic demise of the hero and heroine occurs, it is softened with radiant music.[33]

In Musorgsky's song cycle Shostakovich found a model that spoke out against death. In his own Fourteenth Symphony he expanded this protest further still.

### THE STRING QUARTETS

Shostakovich came to string quartets relatively late in life. His First Quartet appeared in 1938, following the composition of the Fifth Symphony. It was an unambitious work, as Shostakovich himself explains:

> For a whole year after the completion of the 5th Symphony I did almost nothing. I wrote only a quartet, consisting of four short movements. I began to write it without special ideas and feelings, thinking that it wouldn't work out. After all, the quartet is one of the most difficult musical genres. I wrote the first page as a sort of original musical exercise in the quartet form, not think-

ing about subsequently completing and publishing it. . . . But then work on
the quartet captivated me and I finished it rather quickly.[34]

After the First Quartet, Shostakovich left the genre alone until 1944, when
his quartet output increased as his interest in symphonies waned. According
to Dmitry Tsïganov, first violin in the Beethoven Quartet—the ensemble for which Shostakovich wrote most of his quartets—Shostakovich
had planned to write a cycle of twenty-four quartets, one for each key.
The fifteen quartets he completed seem to bear this out: each is in a different key.

The history of Shostakovich's string quartets is closely bound up with
the career of the Beethoven Quartet ensemble (consisting of Vasiliy Shirinsky, Vadim Borisovsky, and Sergey Shirinsky, in addition to Tsïganov),
and we may speak of an exceptional musical partnership. The Beethoven
Quartet gave thirteen of the fifteen premières of Shostakovich's quartets,
six of which were dedicated to the ensemble or to individual members.
Moreover, Shostakovich took specific qualities of the players into account
when he composed the works.

Shostakovich's string quartets are usually considered the composer's
private preserve, the sanctuary to which he withdrew to escape from the
pressures of official music life. This distinction is, however, too sharply
drawn. The private and elitist character of Shostakovich's string quartets is fully in keeping with the tradition of the genre, and there is certainly no stylistic gulf between them and his other work—few elements
of the musical language of the quartets are absent from the rest of his
oeuvre. Thus the "classicism" of the first movement of the Third Quartet (1946) is related to the Ninth Symphony, and the satirical idiom of
the third movement can, as we have seen, be found in various other works
by Shostakovich. As an expressive movement, Shostakovich uses a passacaglia, by analogy with the First Violin Concerto. In the finale of the
Fourth String Quartet (1949) he makes use of his Jewish idiom. The Fifth
String Quartet (1952) is closely bound up with the Tenth Symphony,
among other reasons because of the persistent structural use of the C-D-
E♭-B-C♯ motif, which foreshadows the DSCH monogram Shostakovich
would deploy in the Tenth Symphony.

The last four quartets often sound like musical reflections on the theme
of suffering and death, the clearest example being the desolate and uncompromising Thirteenth String Quartet (1970). Although the theme of
death is not confined to the quartets, as witness the Fourteenth Symphony,
it is perhaps more prominent in the quartets since during his last years

Shostakovich was faced with the departure of two members of the Beethoven Quartet: Borisovsky had to retire in 1964 for health reasons and died in 1972; Vasiliy Shirinsky died in 1965. The Twelfth String Quartet (1968) begins accordingly with a long passage without the second-violin part, to give symbolic expression to Shirinsky's absence. In the second movement of the Fourteenth String Quartet (1973) there is an extended duet for first violin and cello—by then the only two musicians of the original quartet who were still alive. During rehearsals of the Fifteenth String Quartet in 1974 the cellist, Sergey Shirinsky, also died.

The remarkable quality of Shostakovich's quartets lies in his stunning mastery of the sound of the string instruments, in the structural depth and refinement, and above all in the quantity of expressive means and musical characters. Shostakovich's development did not proceed along straight lines, however. After arriving at a new means of expression, he invariably returned to tried-and-true elements. In his late work, for instance, we can see a marked condensation of chromatic writing. In the Twelfth, Thirteenth, and Fifteenth String Quartets he uses twelve-tone sequences, as he had done earlier in the Seven Romances to the Poems of Alexander Blok (1967) and the Second Violin Concerto (1967). For Shostakovich, a limited use of dodecaphony by no means involved the wholesale adoption of that system; it remained for him a means of chromatic concentration and special coloration. He might, for instance, use twelve-tone passages in order to disrupt the tonality. In the Fourteenth String Quartet he abandoned the twelve-tone sequences to return to a more tonal style. The Fifteenth Quartet (1974) is essentially tonal, exploiting the chromatic possibilities explored in the Twelfth and Thirteenth String Quartets only to a limited extent.

As far as their structure is concerned, Shostakovich's string quartets differ markedly one from the other. The First, Second, Fourth, and Sixth Quartets have four movements, the Third has five, and the Fifth and the Seventh have three. In the later quartets the structure becomes less rigid and more original. The seven-movement Eleventh String Quartet (1966), for example, is indebted to the complex and startling structures of Beethoven's last quartets. In the Eighth, Ninth, Eleventh, and Fifteenth String Quartets the movements are joined into a continuous whole. This process is accompanied by the ever-increasing coherence of the motivic content of the different movements. The Thirteenth String Quartet consists of a single, long, freely structured movement. Only the Tenth String Quartet (1964) keeps to the traditional four-movement scheme.

The Eighth String Quartet, written in 1960 following a visit to devastated Dresden, holds a special place in Shostakovich's oeuvre. According to the official version, it is dedicated to the victims of fascism and war. Thanks to the testimony of his daughter Galina and a letter to Isaak Glikman, however, we know that Shostakovich in fact dedicated the work to himself. Its autobiographical character is unmistakable: the DSCH monogram-motif constitutes the core of the motivic material, and throughout the work Shostakovich quotes amply from his own oeuvre— the First Symphony, the Eighth Symphony, the finale of the Second Piano Trio, the First Cello Concerto, and the aria "Seryozha, my dearest" from the last act of *The Lady Macbeth of the Mtsensk District*. In addition to these quotations from his own work, we can also hear the Russian revolutionary song "Tortured by Grievous Bondage." The precise meaning of the quotations is hard to reconstruct, but in this quartet Shostakovich was probably trying to come to terms with his own eventful life. To Isaak Glikman he wrote:

> I had to remember that after my death no one would probably compose a work in my memory. That is why I decided to write such a work myself. You could well write on the title page: "In memory of the composer of this quartet." The main theme of the quartet is made up of the notes D-ES-C-H, my initials (D. Sch.). In the quartet I use themes from my works and the revolutionary song "Tortured by Grievous Bondage." . . . There are also allusions to Wagner's funeral march from *Götterdämmerung* and to the second theme in the first movement of Chaikovsky's Sixth Symphony—not to forget a theme from my Tenth Symphony. In other words a medley. The pseudo-tragedy of this quartet is so great that on writing it my tears streamed as copiously as urine after half a dozen glasses of beer. When I came home, I tried to play it twice and again I wept. This time, however, not because of the pseudo-tragedy, but from amazement at the wonderful unity of form. Perhaps a kind of intoxication with one's own person was involved here, which tends to pass quickly and leaves a hangover in the form of self-criticism.[35]

Dmitry Shostakovich died on 9 August 1975. *Pravda* did not announce his death until forty-eight hours later, printing a stock tribute to a "faithful son of the Communist Party," who "had devoted his entire life to the struggle for peace and brotherhood among nations."[36]

Shostakovich's music is more alive today than ever before. Like no other, it bears witness to the work of a great artist forced to develop under stifling conditions. Shostakovich has grown into the symbol of the fate of art under a totalitarian regime. The full significance of that fate, with all the nuances and imperfections characteristic of mankind, is, however, not yet entirely clear. This subject is of the utmost importance, because only the full truth can enable us to come to terms with the most tragic aspects of the last century. Laurel Fay's long-awaited biography is an important step toward a critical and nuanced account of Shostakovich's life and work. The fact that despite his terrible ordeals the composer managed to carry on working as an artist bears witness in any case to an admirable strength of will and indisputable mastery.

In the meantime, the Soviet Union has ceased to exist and the institutions Shostakovich had to serve have been dismantled. A new generation of composers has emerged. Some have already made their way onto the international concert platform, among them Galina Ustvolskaya, Alfred Schnittke, Arvo Pärt, and Sofia Gubaydulina. They had built bridges to the West even before the permanent demise of the Soviet Union. An evaluation of their work falls outside the period covered by this book, and it is in any case probably too early for one. For the young composers in Russia itself, the winding-up of the Composers Union has led to the disappearance of the artificial security that, despite everything, the Soviet system offered. How the musical life that is replacing the musical culture of the Soviet Union will look is impossible to predict in the prevailing chaotic conditions.

# Notes

CHAPTER ONE

1. L. N. Tolstoy, *War and Peace,* trans. Rosemary Edmonds (Harmondsworth, Eng., 1978), 604.

2. Ibid., 605.

3. Edward Garden, "Tchaikovsky and Tolstoy," *Music and Letters* 55 (1974): 307–16.

4. Quoted in Richard Taruskin, "Realism as Preached and Practiced: The Russian Opera Dialogué," *Musical Quarterly* 56 (1970): 436.

5. Quoted in Alexander Poznansky, *Tchaikovsky: The Quest for the Inner Man* (New York, 1991), 288; and Richard Taruskin, *Defining Russia Musically: Historical and Hermeneutical Essays* (Princeton, 1997), 293.

6. Michael Russ, *Musorgsky: Pictures at an Exhibition* (Cambridge, 1992), 8.

7. "Das Fallenlassen bürgerlicher Themen zugunsten episch-volkstümlicher erscheint so als unvermeidlicher Ausweg des 'Russisten' Musorgskij, als seine utopische und aussenseiterische kulturelle Entscheidung, die es verschmäht, sich mit der europäischen Kultur Petersburgs zu identifizieren, mit ihrer klassischen- und Salonmelodik, mit jener Entwicklungslinie, die von Glinka zu Čaikovskij führte und in *Eugen Onegin* ihr Paradewerk sieht. . . . Der Gegensatz ist der zwischen dem Russland der Millionen Seelen und dem der Million Gebildeter." Gioacchino Lanza Tomasi, "*Der Jahrmarkt von Soročincyj* und sein Beitrag zur Suche des spezifisch Russischen in der Musik," in Heinz-Klaus Metzger and Rainer Riehn, eds., *Modest Musorgskij: Aspekte des Opernwerks,* Musik-Konzepte, Heft 21 (Munich, 1981), 97.

8. "Ich habe mich bemüht, den nationalen Charakter und auch die Rolle der Folklore in der Kunstmusik ernst zu nehmen und herauszuarbeiten als ein zentrales Phänomen der musikalischen Entwicklung im Russland des 19. Jahrhunderts. . . . Nur so kann deutlich werden, daß die Komponisten des 'mächtigen

Häufleins,' insbesondere Musorgskij, eben nicht jene 'Klassiker' waren, zu de-
nen die sowjetische Musikgeschichtsschreibung sie machte; vielmehr haben nationale Sujets und Folklore etwa in der Zeit zwischen 1860 und 1880 eine
gesellschaftskritische, aufrührerische und politische Dimension, die vom zaristi-
schen Staat als bedrohlich empfunden wurde." Dorothea Redepenning, *Geschichte
der russischen und der sowjetischen Musik*, vol. 1: *Das 19. Jahrhundert* (Laaber,
1994), 13.

9. For the quotations from letters, see Richard Taruskin, "How the Acorn
Took Root: A Tale of Russia," *19th-Century Music* 6 (1983): 205–7.

10. Richard Taruskin, *Musorgsky: Eight Essays and an Epilogue* (Princeton,
1993), 329.

11. Richard Taruskin, "'Entoiling the Falconet': Russian Musical Orientalism in Context," *Cambridge Opera Journal* 4 (1992): 279.

CHAPTER TWO

1. For the three quotations, see Taruskin, "How the Acorn Took Root,"
191, 189, 190.

2. Andrzej Walicki, *The Slavophile Controversy: History of a Conservative Utopia in Nineteenth-Century Russian Thought* (Notre Dame, Ind., 1989),
177.

3. Gerald Abraham, "The Operas of Alexei Verstovsky," *19th-Century Music* 7 (1984): 326–35.

4. Taruskin, *Musorgsky*, 38–54.

5. Quoted ibid., 328–29.

6. Ibid., 330.

7. Quoted in Nicholas V. Riasanovsky, *Nicholas I and Official Nationality
in Russia, 1825–1855* (Berkeley, 1961), 91.

8. Quoted in Richard Taruskin, "Glinka's Ambiguous Legacy and the Birth
Pangs of Russian Opera," *19th-Century Music* 1 (1977): 143.

9. For a detailed analysis, see Taruskin, "How the Acorn Took Root,"
189–212.

CHAPTER THREE

1. Quoted in Richard Taruskin, "Glinka, Mikhail (Ivanovich)," in Stanley
Sadie, ed., *The New Grove Dictionary of Opera* (London, 1992), 2:448.

2. Quoted in Robert C. Ridenour, *Nationalism, Modernism, and Personal
Rivalry in Nineteenth-Century Russian Music* (Ann Arbor, 1981), 90.

3. Quoted in Taruskin, *Defining Russia Musically*, 197.

4. Quoted in Ridenour, *Nationalism, Modernism, and Personal Rivalry*, 32.

5. Quoted ibid., 68.

6. Nikolay Andreyevich Rimsky-Korsakov, *My Musical Life* (London,
1989), 19–28.

7. Quoted in Ridenour, *Nationalism, Modernism, and Personal Rivalry*, 81.

8. Quoted ibid., 83.

9. The reappraisal of Serov is of recent date. In the West, Richard Taruskin took the initiative with his dissertation of 1975, published in revised form in 1981 as *Opera and Drama as Preached and Practiced in the 1860s* (republished in 1993). In the Soviet Union a study by A. Stupel was published in Leningrad in 1981 under the title *Alexander Nikolayevich Serov.*

10. Quoted in Ridenour, *Nationalism, Modernism, and Personal Rivalry,* 113.

11. Quoted ibid., 133; italics added.

12. Rimsky-Korsakov, *My Musical Life,* 125.

13. The rumors that he made this revision under pressure from the censors, and that the theaters directorate refused to accept the work once again, are part of the mythology that has been woven around *Boris Godunov* over the years. For a detailed discussion of the myth and reality, see Caryl Emerson and Robert William Oldani, *Modest Musorgsky and "Boris Godunov": Myths, Realities, Reconsiderations* (Cambridge, 1994), 67–90.

14. Quoted in Ridenour, *Nationalism, Modernism, and Personal Rivalry,* 201.

15. For Stasov's tendentious distortion of Musorgsky's image, see Taruskin, *Musorgsky,* 3–37.

## CHAPTER FOUR

1. Quoted in Taruskin, "Glinka's Ambiguous Legacy," 159.

2. Ibid., 145–46.

3. Quoted bid., 151.

4. Quoted ibid., 153.

5. Ridenour, *Nationalism, Modernism, and Personal Rivalry,* 26.

6. Ibid., 43.

7. Quoted ibid., 150.

8. Quoted ibid., 183.

9. Taruskin, "Glinka's Ambiguous Legacy," 160.

10. Quoted in David Brown, *Tchaikovsky: A Biographical and Critical Study,* vol. 1: *The Early Years (1840–1874)* (London, 1979), 180–81, 183–84.

11. Quoted in Taruskin, "Realism as Preached and Practiced," 434.

12. Quoted ibid., 436.

13. Quoted ibid., 437–38.

14. Quoted ibid., 445.

15. Quoted in Richard Taruskin, *Opera and Drama in Russia, as Preached and Practiced in the 1860s* (Ann Arbor, 1981), 346.

16. Ibid., 324.

17. Quoted in Taruskin, "Opera and Drama in Russia: The Case of Serov's 'Judith,'" *Journal of the American Musicological Society* 32 (1979): 81.

18. Quoted ibid., 82.

19. Quoted ibid., 83.

20. Quoted ibid., 95, 96.

21. Quoted in Taruskin, *Musorgsky,* 337.

22. From *Moskvityanin*, August 1854; quoted in Taruskin, *Opera and Drama in Russia*, 144.

23. Quoted ibid., 152.

CHAPTER FIVE

1. Taruskin, "How the Acorn Took Root," 198.

2. Quoted ibid., 205.

3. Quoted ibid., 206.

4. Edward Garden, *Balakirev: A Critical Study of His Life and Music* (London, 1967), 195.

5. Quoted in Rimsky-Korsakov, *My Musical Life*, 61.

6. For Rubinstein's offensive reaction, see Poznansky, *Tchaikovsky*, 161–66.

7. James Friskin, "The Text of Tchaikovsky's B-flat-minor Concerto," *Music and Letters* 50 (1969): 246–51; Jeremy Norris, *The Russian Piano Concerto*, vol. 1: *The Nineteenth Century* (Bloomington, 1994), 114–51.

8. Eric Blom, "Works for Solo Instrument and Orchestra," in Gerald Abraham, ed., *Tchaikovsky: A Symposium* (London, 1945), 51.

9. See J. Norris, *The Russian Piano Concerto*, 1:114–51.

10. See for instance Redepenning, *Geschichte der russischen und der sowjetischen Musik*, 1:289: "dennoch scheinen Orientalismen . . . eine zentrale Bedeutung für die russische Musik zu besitzen: Erstens sind sie ein Spezifikum der russischen Musik—durch diese Elemente unterscheidet sie sich als nationale russische Kunst von der westeuropäischen; zweitens sind Orientalismen nicht nur an östliche Inhalte geknüpft" (yet orientalisms . . . seem to have a central significance in Russian music: first, they are specific to it—thanks to these elements national Russian art can be distinguished from the West European; second, orientalisms are not merely bound up with eastern contents). This opinion is based on a sweeping underestimate of the importance of orientalism in Western music.

11. For a detailed discussion, see Richard Taruskin, "'Entoiling the Falconet': Russian Musical Orientalism in Context," *Cambridge Opera Journal* 4 (1992): 253–80.

12. An example on CD is RCA 09026 613542: London Symphony Orchestra/Claudio Abbado.

13. This passage was quoted in chapter 4, p. 55. For a discussion of orientalism in Chaikovsky's *Romeo and Juliet*, see Richard Taruskin, "Russian Musical Orientalism: A Postscript," *Cambridge Opera Journal* 6 (1994): 81–84.

14. Richard Taruskin, "Chernomor to Kashchei: Harmonic Sorcery; or, Stravinsky's 'Angle,'" *Journal of the American Musicological Society* 38 (1985): 79–88.

15. Taruskin, "Serov and Musorgsky," in *Musorgsky*, 106–7.

16. Edward R. Reilly, "The First Extant Version of 'Night on Bare Mountain,'" in Malcolm Hamrick Brown, ed., *Musorgsky: In Memoriam, 1881–1981* (Ann Arbor, 1982), 148.

17. It must be stressed that we are referring to Musorgsky's original composition, not to the radical revision by Rimsky-Korsakov which is usually heard.

The two have little in common. For an illustration on CD, see RCA Victor 09026 613542, London Symphony Orchestra/Claudio Abbado.

18. Quoted in Reilly, "First Extant Version of 'Night on Bare Mountain,'" 141.

19. Taruskin, *Musorgsky,* 382.

20. Ibid., 100–101.

21. For a detailed discussion, see ibid., 13–33 and 383–90.

## CHAPTER SIX

1. Quoted in Taruskin, "Glinka's Ambiguous Legacy," 143.

2. Taruskin, *Opera and Drama in Russia.*

3. Ibid., 267.

4. Quoted ibid., 270.

5. Ibid., 290.

6. Quoted in Taruskin, *Musorgsky,* 73–74.

7. Quoted ibid., 92.

8. Although the opera is seldom performed, a rare recording of the work can give an idea of its musical language: Chant du Monde, LDC 288035–36.

9. Quoted in Taruskin, *Opera and Drama in Russia,* 85.

10. Ibid., 154–56.

11. From *Kriticheskiye stati i retsenzii* 100; quoted ibid., 199.

12. Quoted in Taruskin, *Musorgsky,* 127.

13. Ibid., 237–39.

14. Emerson and Oldani, *Modest Musorgsky and "Boris Godunov,"* 63–65.

15. Taruskin, *Musorgsky,* 220.

16. Ibid., 300–312.

17. Quoted ibid., 251.

18. Quoted in Emerson and Oldani, *Modest Musorgsky and "Boris Godunov,"* 74.

19. Quoted in Taruskin, *Musorgsky,* 250.

20. For details, see Robert William Oldani, "Boris Godunov and the Censor," *19th-Century Music* 2 (1979): 245–53; and Emerson and Oldani, *Modest Musorgsky and "Boris Godunov,"* 67–90. For the relevant documents, see ibid., 127–33.

21. Taruskin, *Musorgsky,* 262.

22. Ibid., 194–99.

23. Quoted ibid., 177.

24. Ibid., 281.

25. A recording of the two versions, combined in one boxed CD, finally appeared in 1998: Philips 462 230-2, with Valery Gergiev conducting the ensembles of the Mariyinsky Theater.

26. Quoted in Taruskin, *Musorgsky,* 314.

27. For a discussion and the quotations, see ibid., 323.

28. See for instance Redepenning, *Geschichte der russischen und der sowjetischen Musik,* 1:233–40.

29. Emerson, "Musorgsky's Libretti on Historical Themes: From the Two 'Borises' to 'Khovanshchina,'" in A. Groos and R. Parker, eds., *Reading Opera* (Princeton, 1988), 259.

30. Taruskin, *Musorgsky*, 361.

31. For an example on CD: Wiener Staatsoper, under Claudio Abbado (DG 429 758-2).

32. Quoted in Taruskin, *Musorgsky*, 348–49.

33. Quoted ibid., 338.

34. "Wahre Kultur ist für Musorgskij vor allem Volkstum, das zur Einheit geballte Handeln einer Gemeinschaft, die rituell ihre eigenen, vielfältigen, geschichtlichen Neuablagerungen hervorbringt und nur Kraft solcher liturgischen Bewahrung und Fixierung die Identität ihrer Art erreicht. 'Ich würde es vorziehen, weniger zu fingieren und mehr die Wahrheit zu sagen', schreibt er der Sängerin Ljubova Ivanovna Karmalina über den *Jahrmarkt von Soročincyj*." Tomasi, "*Der Jahrmarkt von Soročincyj*," 95.

35. Redepenning, *Geschichte der russischen und der sowjetischen Musik*, 1:242–43.

36. Nikolai Gogol, *The Complete Tales*, trans. Constance Garnett, rev. and ed. Leonard J. Kent (Chicago, 1985), 1:106.

37. Quoted in Taruskin, *Musorgsky*, 373.

38. Quoted ibid., 388.

39. Quoted ibid., 351–52.

40. Ibid., 350–51.

41. Pyotr Chaikovsky, diary note for 23 July 1888; quoted in Taruskin, "Realism as Preached and Practiced," 454.

42. For an analysis, see Richard Taruskin, "*Yevgeny Onegin*," in Sadie, ed., *New Grove Dictionary of Opera*, 4:1193–94.

43. Ibid.

CHAPTER SEVEN

1. Quoted in Poznansky, *Tchaikovsky*, 214.

2. Ibid., 211.

3. Vladimir Fédorov, "Čajkovskij, musicien type du XIXe siècle?" *Acta Musicologica* 42 (1970): 62.

4. David Brown, *Tchaikovsky: A Biographical and Critical Study*, vols. 1–4 (London, 1979–91).

5. Alexandra Orlova, "Tchaikovsky: The Last Chapter," *Music and Letters* 62 (1981): 125–45; David Brown, *Tchaikovsky: A Biographical and Critical Study*, vol. 4: *The Final Years (1885–1893)*, 478–88; André Lischke, *Piotr Ilyitch Tchaikovski* (Paris, 1993), 309–35.

6. Alexander Poznansky, "Tchaikovsky's Suicide: Myth and Reality" *19th-Century Music* 11 (1988): 199–220. Poznansky, a historian, came to his study of Chaikovsky through his investigation of sexual mores in nineteenth-century Russia.

7. The relevant information can be found in Alexander Poznansky, *Tchaikovsky's Last Days: A Documentary Study* (Oxford, 1996).

8. For a detailed discussion of the problems raised by the various suicide theories, see Malcolm Hamrick Brown, Review of *Tchaikovsky: The Quest for the Inner Man* by Alexander Poznansky, *Journal of the American Musicological Society* 47 (1994); and particularly Taruskin, "Pathetic Symphonist: Chaikovsky, Russia, Sexuality, and the Study of Music," *New Republic* (6 February 1995): 26–40.

9. Poznansky, *Tchaikovsky*.

10. Quoted ibid., 271.

11. Abraham, ed., *Tchaikovsky*, 20 and 34.

12. These three quotations are from Poznansky, *Tchaikovsky*, 155, 156, 228.

13. Quoted ibid., 449.

14. Quoted ibid., 564.

15. Quoted ibid., 181.

16. Quoted ibid., 497.

17. Quoted ibid., 167.

18. Quoted ibid., 509.

19. Quoted ibid., 608.

20. Quoted ibid., 279.

21. From a letter of 7 March 1877, quoted ibid., 201.

22. See Richard Taruskin, "Tchaikovsky, Pyotr Il'yich," in Sadie, ed., *New Grove Dictionary of Opera*, 4:663–69.

23. Letter of 13 June 1879, quoted in Thomas Kohlhase, "Tschaikowsky als Kirchenmusiker: Die 'Vsenoščnaja' und ihre liturgischen Vorlagen," in Thomas Kohlhase and Volker Scherliess, eds., *Dadelsen Festschrift* (Stuttgart, 1978), 194.

24. Ibid., 194–95.

25. Quoted ibid., 201.

26. From a letter to Modest Chaikovsky of 14 May 1881, quoted ibid., 203.

27. From Laroche's review of *Swan Lake*, quoted in Roland John Wiley, *Tchaikovsky's Ballets* (Oxford, 1985), 54.

28. Quoted ibid., 1.

29. Quoted ibid., 8.

30. For a detailed discussion of the differences between the two versions, see ibid., 321–27 and 337–41.

31. These three critical marks are quoted in ibid., 53.

32. For a detailed discussion, see ibid., 109–10 and 354–70.

33. For the changes made for the first production, see ibid., 151–92.

34. Margarita Mazo, Review of *Tchaikovsky's Ballets* by Roland John Wiley, *Journal of the American Musicological Society* 42 (1989): 194–203.

35. Quoted in Poznansky, *Tchaikovsky*, 557.

36. Taruskin, "Tchaikovsky," in Sadie, ed., *New Grove Dictionary of Opera*, 4:668.

37. Quoted in Poznansky, *Tchaikovsky*, 557.

38. Letter of 16 April 1884, in Pyotr Chaikovsky, *Polnoye sobranië sochineniy*, vol. 12 (Moscow, 1981), 352.

39. Edward Garden, *Tchaikovsky* (London, 1973), 82, 120.

40. Susan McClary, *Feminine Endings: Music, Gender, and Sexuality* (Minneapolis, 1991), 69–79.

41. D. Brown, *Tchaikovsky,* 4:459.

42. Quoted ibid., 2:166–67.

43. Quoted in Poznansky, *Tchaikovsky,* 270.

44. Quoted ibid., 490.

45. Ibid., 556–57.

46. Quoted in Poznansky, *Tchaikovsky's Last Days,* 27.

47. Ibid.

48. Ibid., 27–28.

49. Quoted in Wiley, *Tchaikovsky's Ballets,* 191–92.

CHAPTER EIGHT

1. Quoted in Taruskin, "How the Acorn Took Root," 207.

2. Quoted ibid.

3. Letter from 19 June 1873, quoted in Taruskin, *Musorgsky,* 388–89.

4. Ibid., 384–85.

5. Quoted ibid., 23.

6. Even in recent publications: see for instance Redepenning, *Geschichte der russischen und der sowjetischen Musik,* vol. 1.

7. Rimsky-Korsakov, *My Musical Life,* 28, 33.

8. Ibid., 116–17.

9. Quoted in Richard Taruskin, "Rimsky Korsakov, Nikolay Andreyevich," in Sadie, ed., *New Grove Dictionary of Opera,* 3:1334.

10. Quoted in Taruskin, *Musorgsky,* 392.

11. Rimsky-Korsakov, *My Musical Life,* 270.

12. *Mir iskusstva* (1899), 79; quoted in Pasler, ed., *Confronting Stravinsky: Man, Musician, and Modernist* (Berkeley, 1986), 19.

13. Taruskin, "Rimsky-Korsakov," 1335–36.

14. Gerald Seaman, *Nikolai Andreevich Rimsky-Korsakov: A Guide to Research* (New York, 1988), 20–21.

15. Quoted in Taruskin, "Rimsky-Korsakov," 1335–36.

16. From a letter to E. M. Petrovsky (librettist of *Kashchey the Deathless*); quoted in Taruskin, "Chernomor to Kashchei," 98.

17. From a letter to Yastrebtsev; quoted ibid., 116–17.

18. Rimsky-Korsakov, *My Musical Life,* 249.

19. Such an alternative is available on CD: Philips 442 537-2, with Valery Gergiev conducting the forces of the Mariyinsky Theater in a new redaction using additional music by Yuri Faliek. For a discussion of the problems and the choices made, see the liner notes by Marina Malkiel and Anna Barry.

20. Taruskin, "'Entoiling the Falconet,'" 254.

21. Quoted in Richard Taruskin, *"Prince Igor,"* in Sadie, ed., *New Grove Dictionary of Opera,* 3:1102.

22. Emerson and Oldani, *Modest Musorgsky and "Boris Godunov,"* 107.

23. Quoted ibid., 110–13.

24. The plan of Diaghilev's production:

| | | |
|---|---|---|
| Act 1. | Scene 1: | Novodevichy monastery |
| | Scene 2: | Pimen's cell (abridged) |
| | Scene 3: | Coronation (expanded) |
| Act 2. | Scene 1: | Garden by the fountain (abridged) |
| | Scene 2: | Kremlin scene (abridged) |
| Act 3. | Scene 1: | Kromy |
| | Scene 2: | Death of Boris |

For a detailed discussion, see ibid., 114–24. The authors rightly point out that Diaghilev's version has a logical content of its own. It is based on a radical confrontation of the Pretender and Boris. After the opening scene, the two appear alternately in a regular pattern, the first in his growing success, the second in his decline. The people provide the background for their clash.

25. Rimsky-Korsakov, *My Musical Life,* 70–71.

26. Ibid., 294–96.

27. See Richard Taruskin, "*The Legend of the Invisible City of Kitezh and the Maiden Fevroniya,*" in Sadie, ed., *New Grove Dictionary of Opera,* 2:1123–26.

28. Translation by Philip Taylor in liner notes to Philips 462 225-2, 44.

29. See Richard Taruskin, "*The Tale of Tsar Saltan,*" in Sadie, ed., *New Grove Dictionary of Opera,* 4:635–37.

30. Rimsky-Korsakov, *My Musical Life,* 286.

31. Richard Taruskin, "Taneyev, Sergey Ivanovich," in Sadie, ed., *New Grove Dictionary of Opera,* 4:645.

## CHAPTER NINE

1. John E. Bowlt, "The Moscow Art Market," in Edith W. Clowes et al., eds., *Between Tsar and People: Educated Society and the Quest for Public Identity in Late Imperial Russia* (Princeton, 1991), 108–28.

2. Lynn Garafola, *Diaghilev's Ballets Russes* (Oxford, 1989), 172.

3. Ibid., 273–99.

4. Taruskin, "Revising Revision," *Journal of the American Musicological Society* 46 (1993): 114–38.

5. *Mir iskusstva* 7 (1902); quoted in John E. Bowlt, *The Silver Age: Russian Art of the Early Twentieth Century and the "World of Art" Group* (Newtonville, Mass., 1982), 74.

6. *Mir iskusstva* 10 (1903): 40; quoted in Taruskin, *Stravinsky and the Russian Traditions: A Biography of the Works through "Mavra"* (Berkeley, 1996), 428.

7. Quoted in Bowlt, *Silver Age,* 82.

8. Letter of 15 March 1912; quoted in Barrie Martyn, *Rachmaninoff: Composer, Pianist, Conductor* (Aldershot, Hant., Eng., 1990), 235.

9. Johann von Gardner, "Russland; Kirchenmusik," in Friedrich Blume, ed., *Die Musik in Geschichte und Gegenwart,* 17 vols. (Kassel, 1949–86), 11:1144.

10. Boris de Schloezer, *Scriabin: Artist and Mystic* (Berkeley, 1987), 235.

11. Hugh Macdonald, *Skryabin* (London, 1978), 10.

12. William Mann, "Scriabin: Icarus or Eros?" inserted in CD (Philips) 420 786-2–788-2, 4.

13. De Schloezer, *Scriabin*, 57.

14. Statement by Leonid Sabaneyev, quoted in Sigfried Schibli, *Alexander Skrjabin und seine Musik: Grenzüberschreitungen eines prometheischen Geistes* (Munich, 1983), 345.

15. For a detailed discussion, see Taruskin, "Scriabin and the Superhuman." My thanks to Professor Taruskin for putting his typescript—since published in *Defining Russia Musically*—at my disposal.

16. From *The General Meaning of Art* (1890), quoted in Irina Paperno and Joan Delaney Grossman, eds., *Creating Life: The Aesthetic Utopia of Russian Modernism* (Stanford, 1994), 14.

17. Quoted ibid., 16.

18. For a detailed discussion, see Olga Matich, "The Symbolist Meaning of Love: Theory and Practice," ibid., 22–40.

19. Leonid Sabaneyev, *Vospominaniia o Skriabine* (Moscow, 1925), 14; quoted in Malcolm Brown, "Skriabin and Russian 'Mystic' Symbolism," *19th-Century Music* 3 (1979): 45.

20. Quoted in Taruskin, *Defining Russia Musically*, 333.

21. Quoted in De Schloezer, *Scriabin*, 69.

22. Quoted ibid., 321.

23. Quoted ibid., 125.

24. Quoted in M. Brown, "Skriabin and Russian 'Mystic' Symbolism," 48.

25. For all quotations, see ibid.

26. For a detailed description of *Mysterium* and the *Acte préalable*, see Simon Morrison, "Skryabin and the Impossible," *Journal of the American Musicological Society* 51 (1998): 283–330. A performance version of *Acte préalable* has been made by the twentieth-century composer Alexander Nemtin, who worked on it from 1970 to 1996. The work is available on CD in a recording from 1999, Decca 466 329-2, with Vladimir Ashkenazy conducting the Deutsches Symphonie-Orchester Berlin. Although this version is interesting, one wonders whether any hypothetical reconstruction could possibly do justice to Scriabin's utopian dream.

27. From *Teatr* (St. Petersburg, 1908), 103; quoted in Taruskin, *Stravinsky and the Russian Traditions*, 540–41.

28. *New York Post*, 24 January 1916; quoted ibid., 532.

29. For Diaghilev's rearrangement, see Chapter 8, note 24.

30. Quoted in D. S. Mirsky, *A History of Russian Literature* (New York, 1947), 457.

31. Quoted in Taruskin, *Stravinsky and the Russian Traditions*, 440.

32. Quoted ibid., 576.

33. For a detailed analysis, see ibid., 586–614.

34. Richard Taruskin, "The *Rite* Revisited: The Idea and the Source of Its Scenario," in Edmond Strainchamps and Maria Rika Maniates, eds., *Music and Civilization: Essays in Honor of Paul Henry Lang* (New York, 1984), 185.

35. Taruskin, *Stravinsky and the Russian Traditions*, 725.

36. For Stravinsky's knowledge of Linyova's work, see ibid., 733.

37. Quoted ibid., 730.

38. Garafola, *Diaghilev's Ballets Russes*, 24.

39. For a detailed list of the quotations and their sources, see Taruskin, *Stravinsky and the Russian Traditions*, 695–717.

40. Alexandre Benois, *Reminiscences of the Russian Ballet* (London, 1941), 347.

41. *Petersburgskaya gazeta*, no. 235 (28 August 1910); quoted in Taruskin, "*Rite* Revisited," 186, 188.

42. Ibid., 189.

43. Quoted in Taruskin, *Stravinsky and the Russian Traditions*, 874 (the quotation marks are Stravinsky's).

44. Quoted in Taruskin, "*Rite* Revisited," 195.

45. Ibid., 195–96.

46. "Ce ne sont pas des êtres déjà formés; leur sexe est unique et double, comme celui de l'arbre" (These are not yet fully formed beings; their sex is unique and dual, like a tree's); in Igor Stravinsky, "Ce que j'ai voulu exprimer dans 'Le Sacre du Printemps,'" *Montjoie!*, 29 May 1913. For a provocative comment on the text, see Richard Taruskin, "A Myth of the Twentieth Century: *The Rite of Spring*, the Tradition of the New, and 'The Music Itself,'" *Modernism/Modernity* 2 (1995): 1–26.

47. Richard Taruskin, "Russian Folk Melodies in *The Rite of Spring*," *Journal of the American Musicological Society* 33 (1980): 501–43.

48. Quoted in Taruskin, *Stravinsky and the Russian Traditions*, 732.

49. Taruskin, "*Rite* Revisited," 186.

50. Jacques Rivière, "Le Sacre du Printemps," *La Nouvelle Revue Française*, November 1913; quoted in Taruskin, "Myth of the Twentieth Century," 15.

51. A. Levinson, "Russkiy balet v Parizhe," *Rech'* 3 (1913); quoted in Taruskin, *Stravinsky and the Russian Traditions*, 1012.

52. Quoted ibid., 1024.

53. Quoted ibid., 1024–25.

54. Quoted in M. Brown, "Stravinsky and Prokofiev: Sizing Up the Competition," in Pasler, ed., *Confronting Stravinsky*, 43–44.

55. Quoted in Harlow Robinson, *Sergei Prokofiev: A Biography* (New York, 1987), 57–58.

56. Quoted in M. Brown, "Stravinsky and Prokofiev," 43, 44.

57. From Sabaneyev's *Reminiscences of Scriabin*, quoted in Taruskin, *Stravinsky and the Russian Traditions*, 856.

58. Quoted in Robinson, *Sergei Prokofiev*, 111.

59. Larry Sitsky, *Music of the Repressed Russian Avant-Garde, 1900–1929* (Westport, Conn., 1994), 323–24.

60. Sidney Monas, "The Twilit Middle Class of Nineteenth-Century Russia," in Clowes et al., eds., *Between Tsar and People*, 35.

CHAPTER TEN

1. Quoted in Richard Pipes, *Russia under the Bolshevik Regime* (New York, 1995), 6.

2. Irina Gutkin, "The Legacy of the Symbolist Aesthetic Utopia: From Futurism to Socialist Realism," in Paperno and Grossman, eds., *Creating Life*, 172–73.

3. For the PROLETKULT movement, see Lynn Mally, *Culture of the Future: The Proletkult Movement in Revolutionary Russia* (Berkeley, 1990).

4. Quoted in Alexander Lavrov, "Andrei Bely and the Argonauts' Mythmaking," in Paperno and Grossman, eds., *Creating Life*, 100.

5. Dialecticus, "On Reactionary and Progressive Aspects of Music," *Muzïkalnaya kultura* 1 (1924); quoted in Detlef Gojowy, *Neue sowjetische Musik der 20er Jahre* (Laaber, 1980), 402. Dialecticus was most probably the pen name of Nikolai Roslavets, although this cannot be proved except possibly by style and content.

6. Quoted in Gutkin, "Legacy of the Symbolist Aesthetic Utopia," 174–77.

7. Ibid., 183–84.

8. Quoted in Pipes, *Russia under the Bolshevik Regime*, 370.

9. This idea is discussed at length in Katerina Clark, "The 'Quiet Revolution' in Soviet Intellectual Life," in Sheila Fitzpatrick et al., eds., *Russia in the Era of NEP: Explorations in Soviet Society and Culture* (Bloomington, 1991), 210–30.

10. For a detailed discussion, see ibid., 220–23.

11. Leonid Sabaneyev, "Sovremennaya muzika," *Muzïkalnaya kultura* 1 (1924): 9–12; quoted in Gojowy, *Neue sowjetische Musik der 20er Jahre*, 409–10.

12. From *Sovremennaya muzïka* 5 (1924), 135; quoted ibid., 397, 398, 399.

13. Pipes, *Russia under the Bolshevik Regime*, 313.

14. L. Kaltat, "On the True Bourgeois Ideology of Citizen Roslavets," *Muzïkalnoye obrazovaniye*, 1927, nos. 3–4: 42; quoted in Gojowy, *Neue sowjetische Musik der 20er Jahre*, 387.

15. Quoted ibid., 399–400.

16. Dialecticus, "On Reactionary and Progressive Aspects of Music," *Muzïkalnaya kultura* 1 (1924): 51; quoted ibid., 406. For the identification of Dialecticus with Roslavets, see ibid., 407; and note 5 above.

17. L. Kaltat, "On the True Bourgeois Ideology," quoted ibid., 387–88.

18. The Russian *narod* is the antithesis of *obshchestvo*, or "society," a term that by and large coincided with the aristocracy after the reforms by Peter the Great. For a discussion of Russian sociological terms, see Abbott Gleason, "Terms of Russian Social History," in Clowes et al., eds., *Between Tsar and People*, 15–17.

19. L. Kaltat, "On the True Bourgeois Ideology," quoted in Gojowy, *Neue sowjetische Musik der 20er Jahre*, 382.

20. E. M., "'The Last Word' of a Decrepit Culture," *Muzïka i revolyutsia* 9 (1927): 3; quoted ibid., 389, 394.

21. Amy Nelson, "The Struggle for Proletarian Music: RAPM and the Cultural Revolution," *Slavic Review* 59 (2000): 125–26.

22. For recent studies about RAPM, see ibid.; and Neil Edmonds, "Music and Politics: The Case of the Russian Association of Proletarian Musicians," *Slavonic and East European Review* 78 (2000): 66–89.

23. Alec Nove, *An Economic History of the USSR* (London, 1980), 207.

24. Quoted in Boris Schwarz, *Music and Musical Life in Soviet Russia* (Bloomington, 1983), 110.

25. Quoted in Gutkin, "Legacy of the Symbolist Aesthetic Utopia," 194.

26. Quoted ibid., 188.

27. Quoted ibid., 191.

28. Boris Groys, *The Total Art of Stalinism: Avant-Garde, Aesthetic Dictatorship, and Beyond* (Princeton, 1992), 35.

29. Gutkin, "Legacy of the Symbolist Aesthetic Utopia," 190.

30. *Sovyetskaya muzïka,* 1933, no. 3: 120–21; quoted in Taruskin, "Shostakovich and the Inhuman," in *Defining Russia Musically,* 480–81.

31. M. Brown, "The Soviet Russian Concepts of 'Intonazia' and 'Musical Imagery,'" *Musical Quarterly* 60 (1974): 557–67.

32. Vladimir Iochelson, "The Creative Discussion in Leningrad," *Sovyetskaya muzïka,* 1936, no. 4: 5–15; quoted in Richard Taruskin, "Public Lies and Unspeakable Truth: Interpreting Shostakovich's Fifth Symphony," in David Fanning, ed., *Shostakovich Studies* (Cambridge, 1995), 33.

33. I. V. Stalin, *Marksizm i natsional'no-kolonial'nïy vopros* (Moscow, 1934), 195; quoted in Marina Frolova-Walker, "'National in Form, Socialist in Content': Musical Nation-Building in the Soviet Republics," *Journal of the American Musicological Society* 51 (1998): 334.

34. For a detailed discussion of this type of musical colonialism, see ibid., 331–71.

35. Schwarz, *Music and Musical Life in Soviet Russia,* 84–85.

36. "Most sources incorrectly list 27 May 1927 as the day of the first Western performance of the symphony"; Laurel E. Fay, *Shostakovich: A Life* (Oxford, 2000), 295.

37. Ibid., 40.

38. For the link between Meyerhold's aesthetic and Shostakovich, see Marina Tcherkashina, "Gogol and Leskov in Shostakovich's Interpretation," *International Journal of Musicology* 1 (1992), 229–44.

39. "After the Première of 'The Nose,'" *Rabochii i teatr,* no. 24 (16 June 1929): 22; quoted in Laurel Fay, "The Punch in Shostakovich's Nose," in M. Brown, ed., *Russian and Soviet Music: Essays for Boris Schwarz* (Ann Arbor, 1984), 232.

40. For both quotations and the critical controversy surrounding *The Nose,* see ibid., 236–39.

41. Interview with Solomon Volkov, quoted in Caryl Emerson, "Back to the Future: Shostakovich's Revision of Leskov's 'Lady Macbeth of Mtsensk District,'" *Cambridge Opera Journal* 1 (1989): 71.

42. From the introduction to an edition of the libretto (Moscow, 1934), quoted in Elizabeth Wilson, *Shostakovich: A Life Remembered* (Princeton, 1994), 96.

43. For these quotations, see Taruskin, "The Opera and the Dictator: The Peculiar Martyrdom of Dimitri Shostakovich," *New Republic,* 20 March 1989, 34–40.

44. Quoted in Emerson, "Back to the Future," 63.

45. Ibid.

46. Taruskin, "The Opera and the Dictator," 37.
47. Ibid., 39–40.
48. Quoted in Fay, *Shostakovich*, 78.

CHAPTER ELEVEN

1. From an interview by H. E. Wortham, *Daily Telegraph*, 29 April 1933; quoted in Martyn, *Rachmaninoff*, 26.
2. Ravel's version has several differences from the original. For instance, he omitted the fifth *Promenade*, and made several minor changes to *Baba Yaga*, *The Ballet of the Unhatched Chicks*, and *Kiev*. The crescendo in *Bydlo* differs from Musorgsky's idea of starting the scene immediately in fortissimo. The misunderstanding is due to the use of the Rimsky-Korsakov edition: at the time, the original version was unobtainable. For a detailed discussion, see Russ, *Musorgsky*, 76–86.
3. Quoted in Taruskin, *Stravinsky and the Russian Traditions*, 1071.
4. *Nouvelle Revue Française* 4 (1910): 210–11; quoted ibid., 990. "Que cela est donc russe, que des Russes créèrent, mais que cela est donc aussi français!"
5. Quoted ibid., 992. "La grande nouveauté du *Sacre du Printemps*, c'est le renoncement à la 'sauce.' Voici une oeuvre absolument pure. Aigre et dure, si vous voulez; mais dont aucun jus ne ternit l'éclat, dont aucune cuisine n'arrange ni ne salit les contours. Ce n'est pas une 'oeuvre d'art,' avec tous les petits tripotages habituels. Rien d'estampé, rien de diminué par les ombres; point de voiles ni d'adoucissements poétiques; aucune trace d'atmosphère. L'oeuvre est entière et brute, les morceaux en restent tout crus."
6. Quoted ibid., 993. "Strawinsky ne s'est pas simplement amusé à prendre le contrepied de Debussy. S'il a choisi des instruments qui ne frémissent pas, qui ne disent rien de plus que ce qu'ils disent, dont le timbre est une expansion et qui sont comme des mots abstraits, c'est parce qu'il veut tout énoncer directement, expressément, nommément. Là est sa préoccupation principale. Là est son innovation personnelle dans la musique contemporaine. . . . Sa voix se fait pareille à l'objet, elle le consomme, elle le remplace; au lieu de l'évoquer, elle le prononce. Il ne laisse rien en dehors; au contraire, il revient sur les choses; il les trouve, il les saisit, il les ramène."
7. Quoted in Taruskin, "*Rite* Revisited," 183 ("An architectonic work, not anecdotal").
8. Quoted in Taruskin, *Stravinsky and the Russian Traditions*, 995 ("The organ of French artistic imperialism").
9. Quoted ibid., 1001. "Igor Strawinsky est, je crois bien, le Messie que nous attendions depuis Wagner et dont Moussorgsky et Claude Debussy, comme aussi Richard Strauss et Arnold Schoenberg semblent avoir préparé les voies."
10. Nicholas Riasanovsky, "The Emergence of Eurasianism," *California Slavic Studies* 4 (1967): 71.
11. Quoted in Taruskin, *Stravinsky and the Russian Traditions*, 1132–33. "Il est . . . du plus haut intérêt commun de toutes les nations qui sentent encore le besoin de respirer l'air de leur saine et ancienne culture de se mettre du côté des ennemis de l'Allemagne et de se soustraire une fois pour toujours à l'intolérable

esprit de cette colossale et obèse Germania qui est menacée de funestes symptômes de décomposition morale."

12. Quoted in C. F. Ramuz, "Souvenirs sur Igor Strawinsky," in *Oeuvres complètes*, vol. 14 (Lausanne, 1941), 68. "La vraie Russie allait paraître enfin à la face du monde, une Russie nouvelle, mais qui serait en même temps l'ancienne—éclose enfin, épanouie, tirée de son long sommeil, ressuscitée de sa propre mort. . . . La Sainte Russie des Orthodoxes, une Russie débarrassée de ses végétations parasites: sa bureaucratie venue d'Allemagne, certain libéralisme anglais fait à la mode dans la noblesse, son scientisme (hélas!), ses 'intellectuels', leur croyance assez niaise et tout livresque au progrès—celle d'avant Pierre le Grand et d'avant l'européanisme, qui ainsi irait d'abord en arrière, mais pour mieux aller de l'avant, ayant retouché à ses bases; une Russie paysanne, mais avant tout chrétienne, et véritablement la seule terre chrétienne de l'Europe."

13. "Von dem *Concertino für Streichquartett*, also für jene Besetzung, die einmal dem musikalischen Humanismus, der absoluten Durchseelung des Instrumentalen, am reinsten sich angemessen hatte, verlangte der Autor, es solle abschnurren wie eine Nähmaschine." Theodor W. Adorno, *Philosophie der neuen Musik* (Frankfurt am Main, 1978), 150; for the English translation, see Taruskin, *Defining Russia Musically*, 424 and note.

14. This following description of the songs is based on Taruskin's account in *Stravinsky and the Russian Traditions*, 1136–62.

15. Cf. ibid., 1151–52.

16. The process is discussed in detail in ibid., chap. 16, "A Pair of Minstrel Shows."

17. Richard Taruskin, "Notes on the Program: *Baika*," in *The Russian Stravinsky* (Brooklyn, N.Y., 1994), 52.

18. Quoted in Taruskin, *Stravinsky and the Russian Traditions*, 1320.

19. The technical explanation involves the central role of the sequence of intervals of three minor thirds in the octatonic scale. The matrix / o 3 6 9 / comprises precisely the degrees on which the octatonic ladder is repeated; tranposition of these degrees yields the identical pitch series. This matrix determines the overall structure of *Svadebka*. For a detailed analyis, see ibid., chap. 17, "The Turanian Pinnacle (*Svadebka*)."

20. For a discussion of Nijinska's choreography, see Garafola, *Diaghilev's Ballets Russes*, 122–29.

21. Taruskin, *Defining Russia Musically*, 390–91.

22. Ibid., 404.

23. Igor Stravinsky, *An Autobiography* (New York, 1962), 99–100; translation of *Chroniques de ma vie*, 2 vols. (Paris, 1935–36).

24. Arthur Lourié, *Sergei Koussevitzky and His Epoch* (New York, 1931), 196.

25. Scott Messing, *Neoclassicism in Music: From the Genesis of the Concept through the Schoenberg/Stravinsky Polemic* (Ann Arbor, 1988), 130.

26. Jean Cocteau, "Fragments d'une conférence sur Eric Satie," *Revue Musicale*, March 1924, 223.

27. Letter to Sergey Rachmaninoff dated 28 May 1924; quoted in Taruskin, *Stravinsky and the Russian Traditions*, 1516.

28. Garafola, *Diaghilev's Ballets Russes*, 98–105.

29. Quoted in Taruskin, *Stravinsky and the Russian Traditions*, 1529. "Cette oeuvre me semble être l'expression la plus authentique de l'époque de notre vie russe que nous appelons la 'période de Petersbourg', gravée dans ma mémoire avec la vision matinale des traîneaux impériaux d'Alexandre III, l'énorme Empéreur et son énorme cocher, et la joie immense qui m'attendait le soir: le spectacle de *La Belle au Bois Dormant*."

30. Quoted ibid., 1532. "Ne cultivant pas spécialement dans son art 'l'âme paysanne russe', Tchaïkovsky puisait inconsciemment dans les vraies sources populaires de notre race."

31. "Une Lettre de Stravinsky sur Tchaikovsky," *Figaro*, 18 May 1922; quoted ibid., 1534. "Il y a quelques années, on appréciait la musique russe comme une musique nègre. Pas un critique qui ne parlât d'elle en se servant du terme 'sauvage et raffiné'. A cette époque, le pittoresque des *cinq* était de mise. Il est temps d'en finir. Les décors russes ne sont plus obligatoirement des tapis d'Orient. Et la musique russe peut nous parler d'autre chose que de la Russie d'avant Pierre le Grand."

32. Robinson, *Sergei Prokofiev*, 179.

33. Quoted ibid., 240.

34. Quoted ibid., 243.

CHAPTER TWELVE

1. From *Pravda*, 28 January 1936. Slightly amended English version based on Dutch translation by Xavier Verbeke.

2. From *Sovyetskaya muzïka*, 1936, no. 3: 45; quoted in Taruskin, "Public Lies and Unspeakable Truth," 23.

3. Quoted in Schwarz, *Music and Musical Life in Soviet Russia*, 178.

4. Fay, *Shostakovich*, 133.

5. A stage version of *The Gamblers* was completed by the Polish composer Krzysztof Meyer in 1980–81.

6. Schwarz, *Music and Musical Life in Soviet Russia*, 201.

7. Quoted in Fay, *Shostakovich*, 145–46.

8. Quoted ibid., 146.

9. All quotations are from Schwarz, *Music and Musical Life in Soviet Russia*, 207.

10. Quoted ibid., 208.

11. Quoted ibid., 219.

12. Quoted ibid., 229.

13. Yuri Abramovich Levitin, "The Year 1948"; quoted in Wilson, *Shostakovich*, 210–11.

14. All three quotations ibid., 239.

15. Nicholas Nabokov, *Old Friends and New Music* (London, 1951), 203–5.

16. Marina Frolova-Walker, "'National in Form, Socialist in Content,'" 368.

17. Quoted in Robinson, *Sergei Prokofiev*, 392.

18. Quoted ibid., 401.
19. Quoted ibid., 462.
20. Quoted ibid., 474.

CHAPTER THIRTEEN

1. Quoted in Robinson, *Sergei Prokofiev*, 193.
2. Quoted ibid., 231.
3. Quoted ibid., 263–64.
4. Quoted ibid., 272.
5. Quoted ibid., 274.
6. Quoted ibid.
7. Taruskin, "To Cross That Sacred Edge: Notes on a Fiery Angel," in booklet accompanying the CD *Prokofiev: The Fiery Angel*, Deutsche Grammophon 431 669-2, 13–19 (including Prokofiev's comment to Myaskovsky).
8. Quoted in Robinson, *Sergei Prokofiev*, 318.
9. Vernon Duke, *Passport to Paris* (Boston, 1955), 367; quoted ibid., 346.
10. Quoted ibid., 357.
11. Quoted ibid., 288.
12. Quoted ibid., 282.
13. Quoted ibid., 302.
14. For a detailed discussion, see Bernd Uhlenbruch, "The Annexation of History: Eisenstein and the Ivan Grozny Cult of the 1940s," in Hans Günther, ed., *The Culture of the Stalin Period* (London, 1990), 266–87.
15. Robinson, *Sergei Prokofiev*, 366.
16. Quoted ibid., 421.
17. Quoted in M. Brown, "Prokofiev's War and Peace: A Chronicle," *Musical Quarterly* 63 (1977): 298.
18. This interpretation is based on Richard Taruskin, "*War and Peace*," in Sadie, ed., *New Grove Dictionary of Opera*, 4:1100–1105.
19. Quoted in Richard Taruskin, "*The Story of a Real Man*," ibid., 556–57.
20. Quoted in Robinson, *Sergei Prokofiev*, 484.
21. Ibid., 487.
22. Quoted ibid., 490.

CHAPTER FOURTEEN

1. Ian MacDonald, *The New Shostakovich* (Boston, 1990), 244.
2. Laurel E. Fay, "Shostakovich versus Volkov: Whose Testimony?" *Russian Review* 39 (1980): 484–93.
3. Fay, *Shostakovich*, 4.
4. Taruskin, "Public Lies and Unspeakable Truth," 18.
5. Krzysztof Meyer, *Schostakowitsch: Sein Leben, sein Werk, seine Zeit* (Bergisch Gladbach, 1995).
6. *Sovyetskaya muzïka*, 1933, no. 3: 120–21; quoted in Taruskin, *Defining Russia Musically*, 480–81. Cf. Chapter 10, p. 257.

7. "In der *Zeugenaussage* werden gesellschaftskritischen Deutungen verschiedener Symphonien vorgestellt, die eine Überprüfung durch die Analyse geradezu herausfordern. Auf diesem Weg lässt sich auch zu der Frage der Autentizität der *Zeugenaussage*—die von sowjetischer Seite bestritten wurde—einiges beitragen." Karen Kopp, *Form und Gehalt der Symphonien des Dmitrij Schostakowitsch* (Bonn, 1990), 12.

8. "Die Verallgemeinerung auf der musikalischen Ebene lässt eine Übertragung oder Einordnung der Gewaltherrschaft in jede beliebige Epoche zu. Auch wenn die Lieder in direktem Zusammenhang mit der Revolution des Jahres 1905 stehen, zeigt die Pflege dieses Liedgutes, dass ihre Aktualität keineswegs auf dieses Ereignis beschränkt bleibt, sondern sie aufgrund der Allgemeingültigkeit ihrer Thematik: Parteinahme gegen Tyrannei und Gewalt und für Freiheit und Selbstbestimmung, in verschiedenen Situationen immer wieder gesungen wurden. Von daher ist eine Festlegung des Sujets der Symphonie auf die umrissene historische Situation nicht haltbar." Ibid., 355.

9. "So viel politische Naivität und Unflexibilität einer Gesellschaft und einem Mann wie Schostakowitsch zuzuschreiben, der die 'grobe Macht' so sehr gespürt hat und der das System von innen her kannte, erscheint unhaltbar und von dem Versuch geleitet, Schostakowitschs scheinbare Linientreue mit ziemlich blindem Idealismus und Vertrauen in den neuen Kurs zu rechtfertigen oder zu entschuldigen." Ibid., 330.

10. Taruskin, "The Opera and the Dictator," 40.

11. Solomon Volkov, ed., *Testimony: The Memoirs of Dimitri Shostakovich* (New York, 1979), 183.

12. MacDonald, *New Shostakovich*, 15.

13. Richard Taruskin, Review of *The New Shostakovich* by Ian MacDonald, *Slavic Review* 52 (1993): 397.

14. Quoted in Taruskin, "Public Lies and Unspeakable Truth," 32.

15. Quoted ibid., 33.

16. Quoted ibid., 35.

17. Quoted ibid.

18. Lev Abramovich Mazel, *Simfonii D. D. Schostakovicha* (Moscow, 1960), 8–9; quoted in Taruskin, *Defining Russia Musically*, 541.

19. Quoted in Taruskin, "Molchanov's 'The Dawns Are Quiet Here'" *Musical Quarterly* 62 (1976): 110.

20. Cf. Fay, *Shostakovich*, 327.

21. D. Shostakovich, "Nash sovremennik," *Izvestiya*, 14 February 1956, 3; quoted ibid., 199.

22. Quoted in Meyer, *Schostakowitsch*, 390.

23. Fay, *Shostakovich*, 196.

24. Quoted in Laurel E. Fay, "From *Lady Macbeth* to *Katherina*: Shostakovich's Versions and Revisions," in David Fanning, ed., *Shostakovich Studies* (Cambridge, 1995), 178.

25. Quoted ibid., 185.

26. Ibid., 187.

27. Quoted in Meyer, *Schostakowitsch*, 444.

28. Quoted in Fay, *Shostakovich*, 229.

29. Ibid., 235.
30. Ibid., 236. Here are the eight original verses:

> I imagine now that I am a Jew.
> Here I wander through ancient Egypt.
> And here, I am crucified on the cross and die,
> And still bear the marks of the nails.
>
> And I become like a long, soundless scream
> Above the thousand thousands here interred.
> I am each old man shot dead here,
> I am each child shot dead here.

These verses replaced them:

> I stand there as if at a wellspring,
> That gives me faith in our brotherhood.
> Here lie Russians and Ukrainians,
> With Jews they lie in the same earth.
>
> I think about Russia's heroic feats,
> In blocking fascism's path.
> To the very tiniest dewdrop,
> Her whole essence and fate is dear to me.

31. Quoted in Laurel E. Fay, "Musorgsky and Shostakovich," in Malcolm Hamrick Brown, ed., *Musorgsky in Memoriam, 1881–1981* (Ann Arbor, 1982), 216.
32. Quoted in Wilson, *Shostakovich,* 412.
33. Quoted in Fay, "Musorgsky and Shostakovich," 220.
34. From *Izvestiya,* 29 September 1938; quoted in Laurel Elizabeth Fay, "The Last Quartets of Dimitrii Shostakovich: A Stylistic Investigation" (Ph.D. diss., Cornell University, 1978), 9.
35. Quoted in Meyer, *Schostakowitsch,* 402–3.
36. Quoted ibid., 525.

# Bibliography

Abraham, Gerald. "Arab Melodies in Rimsky-Korsakov and Borodin." *Music and Letters* 56 (1975): 313–18.

———. *Essays on Russian and East European Music.* Oxford, 1985.

———. "The Operas of Alexei Verstovsky." *19th-Century Music* 7 (1984): 326–35.

———. "Pskovityanka: The Original Version of Rimsky-Korsakov's First Opera." *Musical Quarterly* 54 (1968): 58–73.

———. "Rimsky-Korsakov as Self-Critic." In Anna Amalie Abert and Wilhelm Pfannkuch, eds., *Festschrift Friedrich Blume zum 70. Geburtstag,* 16–21. Kassel, 1963.

———. "Satire and Symbolism in 'The Golden Cockerel.'" *Music and Letters* 52 (1971): 46–54.

———. *Slavonic and Romantic Music: Essays and Studies.* London, 1968.

———, ed. *Tchaikovsky: A Symposium.* London, 1945.

Acocella, Joan, et al. "'The Rite of Spring' Considered as a Nineteenth-Century Ballet." *Ballet Review* 20 (1992): 68–71.

Asaf'yev, Boris. *A Book about Stravinsky.* Ann Arbor, 1982.

Baker, James M. *The Music of Alexander Scriabin.* New Haven, 1986.

Berger, Karol. Review of *A Book about Stravinsky* by Boris Asaf'yev. *Journal of Music Theory* 28 (1984): 294–302.

Blume, Friedrich, ed. *Die Musik in Geschichte und Gegenwart.* 17 vols. Kassel, 1949–86.

Bobeth, Marek. *Borodin und seine Oper "Fürst Igor": Geschichte—Analyse—Konsequenzen.* Munich, 1982

Bowlt, John E. *The Silver Age: Russian Art of the Early Twentieth Century and the "World of Art" Group.* Newtonville, Mass., 1982.

Braun, Joachim. "The Double Meaning of Jewish Elements in Dimitri Shostakovich's Music." *Musical Quarterly* 71 (1985): 68–80.

Brown, David. *Mikhail Glinka. A Biographical and Critical Study.* London, 1974.

———. *Tchaikovsky: A Biographical and Critical Study.* 4 vols. London, 1979–91.

———. "Tchaikovsky, Pyotr Il'yich." In Stanley Sadie, ed., *The New Grove Dictionary of Music and Musicians,* 18:606–36. London, 1980.

Brown, Malcolm Hamrick. "Prokofiev's War and Peace: A Chronicle." *Musical Quarterly* 63 (1977): 297–326.

———. Review of *Tchaikovsky: The Quest for the Inner Man* by Alexander Poznansky. *Journal of the American Musicological Society* 47 (1994): 359–64.

———. "Skriabin and Russian 'Mystic' Symbolism." *19th-Century Music* 3 (1979): 42–51.

———. "The Soviet Russian Concepts of 'Intonazia' and 'Musical Imagery.'" *Musical Quarterly* 60 (1974): 557–67.

———. "Stravinsky and Prokofiev: Sizing Up the Competition." In Jann Pasler, ed., *Confronting Stravinsky: Man, Musician, and Modernist,* 39–50. Berkeley, 1986.

———, ed. *Musorgsky: In Memoriam, 1881–1981.* Ann Arbor, 1982.

———, ed. *Russian and Soviet Music: Essays for Boris Schwarz.* Ann Arbor, 1984.

Clark, Katerina. "The 'Quiet Revolution' in Soviet Intellectual Life." In Sheila Fitzpatrick, Alexander Rabinowitch, and Richard Stites, eds., *Russia in the Era of NEP: Explorations in Soviet Society and Culture,* 210–30. Bloomington, 1991.

Clowes, Edith W., et al., eds. *Between Tsar and People: Educated Society and the Quest for Public Identity in Late Imperial Russia.* Princeton, 1991.

Edmunds, Neil. "Music and Politics: The Case of the Russian Association of Proletarian Musicians." *Slavonic and East European Review* 78 (2000): 66–89.

Emerson, Caryl. "Back to the Future: Shostakovich's Revision of Leskov's 'Lady Macbeth of Mtsensk District.'" *Cambridge Opera Journal* 1 (1989): 59–78.

———. *Boris Godunov: Transpositions of a Russian Theme.* Bloomington, 1986.

———. "Musorgsky's Libretti on Historical Themes: From the Two 'Borises' to 'Khovanshchina.'" In A. Groos and R. Parker, eds., *Reading Opera,* 235–66. Princeton, 1988.

———. Review of *Sergei Prokofiev* by Harlow Robinson. *Russian Review* 47 (1988): 323–24.

Emerson, Caryl, and Robert William Oldani. *Modest Musorgsky and "Boris Godunov": Myths, Realities, Reconsiderations.* Cambridge, 1994.

Fanning, David. *The Breath of the Symphonist: Shostakovich's Tenth.* London, 1989.

———, ed. *Shostakovich Studies.* Cambridge, 1995.

Fay, Laurel Elizabeth. "From *Lady Macbeth* to *Katerina*: Shostakovich's Versions and Revisions." In David Fanning, ed., *Shostakovich Studies,* 160–88. Cambridge, 1995.

———. "The Last Quartets of Dmitrii Shostakovich: A Stylistic Investigation." Ph.D. diss., Cornell University, 1978.

———. "Musorgsky and Shostakovich." In Malcolm Hamrick Brown, ed., *Musorgsky in Memoriam, 1881–1981*, 215–26. Ann Arbor, 1982.

———. "The Punch in Shostakovich's Nose." In Malcolm Brown, ed., *Russian and Soviet Music: Essays for Boris Schwarz*, 229–43. Ann Arbor, 1984.

———. *Shostakovich: A Life*. Oxford, 2000.

———. "Shostakovich versus Volkov: Whose Testimony?" *Russian Review* 39 (1980): 484–93.

Fédorov, Vladimir. "Čajkovskij, musicien type du XIXe siècle?" *Acta Musicologica* 42 (1970): 59–70.

Feuchtner, Bernd. *"Und Kunst geknebelt von der groben Macht." Dimitri Schostakowitsch: Künstlerische Identität und staatliche Repression*. Frankfurt, 1986.

Fiess, Stephen C. E. *The Piano Works of Serge Prokofiev*. Metuchen, N.J., 1994.

Fink, Robert. "'Rigoroso (♩ = 126)': *The Rite of Spring* and the Forging of a Modernist Performing Style." *Journal of the American Musicological Society* 52 (1999): 299–362.

Fitzpatrick, Sheila, ed. *Cultural Revolution in Russia, 1928–1931*. Bloomington, 1978.

Fitzpatrick, Sheila, Alexander Rabinowitch, and Richard Stites, eds. *Russia in the Era of NEP: Explorations in Soviet Society and Culture*. Bloomington, 1991.

Friskin, James. "The Text of Tchaikowsky's B-flat Minor Concerto." *Music and Letters* 50 (1969): 246–51.

Frolova-Walker, Marina. "'National in Form, Socialist in Content': Musical Nation-Building in the Soviet Republics." *Journal of the American Musicological Society* 51 (1998): 331–71.

———. "On *Ruslan* and Russianness." *Cambridge Opera Journal* 9 (1997): 21–45.

Garafola, Lynn. *Diaghilev's Ballets Russes*. Oxford, 1989.

Garden, Edward. *Balakirev: A Critical Study of His Life and Music*. London, 1967.

———. *Tchaikovsky*. London, 1973.

———. "Tchaikovsky and Tolstoy." *Music and Letters* 55 (1974): 307–16.

———. "Three Russian Piano Concertos." *Music and Letters* 60 (1979): 166–79.

Gojowy, Detlef. *Arthur Lourié und der russische Futurismus*. Laaber, 1993.

———. *Neue sowjetische Musik der 20er Jahre*. Laaber, 1980.

Groys, Boris. "The Birth of Socialist Realism from the Spirit of the Russian Avant-Garde." In Hans Günther, ed., *The Culture of the Stalin Period*, 122–48. London, 1990.

———. *The Total Art of Stalinism: Avant-Garde, Aesthetic Dictatorship, and Beyond*. Princeton, 1992.

Günther, Hans, ed. *The Culture of the Stalin Period*. London, 1990.

Gutkin, Irina. "The Legacy of the Symbolist Aesthetic Utopia: From Futurism to Socialist Realism." In Irina Paperno and Joan Delaney Grossman, eds., *Creating Life: The Aesthetic Utopia of Russian Modernism*, 167–96. Stanford, 1994.

Haimo, Ethan, and Paul Johnson, eds. *Stravinsky Retrospectives*. Lincoln, Neb., 1987.

Ho, Allan B., and Dmitry Feofanov, eds. *Shostakovich Reconsidered*. London, 1998.

Joseph, Charles M. "Stravinsky's Piano Scherzo (1902) in Perspective: A New Starting Point." *Musical Quarterly* 67 (1981): 82–93.

Karlinsky, Simon. "Russian Comic Opera in the Age of Catherine the Great." *19th-Century Music* 7 (1984): 318–25.

———. "Stravinsky and Russian Pre-Literate Theater." *19th-Century Music* 6 (1983): 232–40.

Kaschkin, Nikolai. *Meine Erinnerungen an Peter Tschaikowski*. Berlin, 1992.

Kohlhase, Thomas. "Tschaikowsky als Kirchenmusiker: Die 'Vsenoščnaja' und ihre liturgischen Vorlagen." In Thomas Kohlhase and Volker Scherliess, eds., *Dadelsen Festschrift*, 189–299. Stuttgart, 1978.

Kopp, Karen. *Form und Gehalt der Symphonien des Dmitrij Schostakowitsch*. Bonn, 1990.

Lemaire, Frans C. *La musique du XXe siècle en Russie et dans les anciennes Républiques soviétiques*. Paris, 1994.

Lischke, André. *Piotr Ilyitch Tchaikovski*. Paris, 1993.

Lvov, Nikolai, and Ivan Prach. *A Collection of Russian Folk Songs*. Ann Arbor, 1987.

Macdonald, Hugh. *Skryabin*. London, 1978.

MacDonald, Ian. *The New Shostakovich*. Boston, 1990.

Macquere, Gordon D., ed. *Russian Theoretical Thought in Music*. Ann Arbor, 1983.

Maes, Francis. "Modern Historiography of Russian Music: When Will Two Schools of Thought Meet?" *International Journal of Musicology* 6 (1997): 377–94.

Mally, Lynn. *Culture of the Future: The Proletkult Movement in Revolutionary Russia*. Berkeley, 1990.

Martyn, Barrie. *Nicolas Medtner: His Life and Music*. Aldershot, Hant., Eng., 1995.

———. *Rachmaninoff: Composer, Pianist, Conductor*. Aldershot, Hant., Eng., 1990.

Mazo, Margarita. Review of *Tchaikovsky's Ballets* by Roland John Wiley. *Journal of the American Musicological Society* 42 (1989): 194–203.

———. "Stravinsky's 'Les Noces' and Russian Village Wedding Ritual." *Journal of the American Musicological Society* 43 (1990): 99–142.

McClary, Susan. *Feminine Endings: Music, Gender, and Sexuality*. Minneapolis, 1991.

Messing, Scott. *Neoclassicism in Music: From the Genesis of the Concept through the Schoenberg/Stravinsky Polemic*. Ann Arbor, 1988.

Metzger, Heinz-Klaus, and Rainer Riehn, eds. *Modest Musorgskij, Aspekte des Opernwerks*. Musik-Konzepte, Heft 21. Munich, 1981.

Meyer, Krzysztof. *Schostakowitsch: Sein Leben, sein Werk, seine Zeit*. Bergisch Gladbach, 1995.

Monas, Sidney. "The Twilit Middle Class of Nineteenth-Century Russia." In Edith W. Clowes et al., eds., *Between Tsar and People: Educated Society and the Quest for Public Identity in Late Imperial Russia*, 28–37. Princeton, 1991.

Morrison, Simon. "Skryabin and the Impossible." *Journal of the American Musicological Society* 51 (1998): 283–330.

Nelson, Amy. "The Struggle for Proletarian Music: RAPM and the Cultural Revolution." *Slavic Review* 59 (2000): 101–32.

Niemöller, Klaus Wolfgang, et al., eds. *Bericht über das Internationale Dmitri-Schostakowitsch-Symposion Köln 1985*. Regensburg, 1986.

Norris, Christopher, ed. *Shostakovich: The Man and His Music*. Boston, 1982.

Norris, Geoffrey. "Tchaikovsky and the Eighteenth Century." *Musical Times* 118 (1977): 715–16.

Norris, Jeremy. *The Russian Piano Concerto*. Vol. 1: *The Nineteenth Century*. Bloomington, 1994.

Oldani, Robert William. "Boris Godunov and the Censor." *19th-Century Music* 2 (1979): 245–53.

Orlova, Alexandra. *Musorgsky Remembered*. Bloomington, 1991.

———. "Tchaikovsky: The Last Chapter." *Music and Letters* 62 (1981): 125–45.

Paperno, Irina, and Joan Delaney Grossman, eds. *Creating Life: The Aesthetic Utopia of Russian Modernism*. Stanford, 1994.

Pasler, Jann. "Stravinsky and the Apaches." *Musical Times* 123 (1982): 403–7.

———, ed. *Confronting Stravinsky: Man, Musician, and Modernist*. Berkeley, 1986.

Pipes, Richard. *Russia under the Bolshevik Regime*. New York, 1995.

Poznansky, Alexander. "The Man behind the Myth." *Musical Times* 4 (1995): 175–82.

———. *Tchaikovsky: The Quest for the Inner Man*. New York, 1991.

———. *Tchaikovsky's Last Days: A Documentary Study*. Oxford, 1996.

———. "Tchaikovsky's Suicide: Myth and Reality." *19th-Century Music* 11 (1988): 199–220.

Prokofiev, Sergei. *Soviet Diary 1927 and Other Writings*. London, 1991.

Redepenning, Dorothea. *Geschichte der russischen und der sowjetischen Musik*. Vol. 1: *Das 19. Jahrhundert*. Laaber, 1994.

Reilly, Edward R. "The First Extant Version of 'Night on Bare Mountain.'" In Malcolm Hamrick Brown, ed., *Musorgsky: In Memoriam, 1881–1981*, 135–49. Ann Arbor, 1982.

Reise, Jay. "Late Skriabin: Some Principles behind the Style." *19th-Century Music* 6 (1983): 220–31.

Riasanovsky, Nicholas V. "The Emergence of Eurasianism." *California Slavic Studies* 4 (1967).

———. *A History of Russia*. Oxford, 1969.

———. *Nicholas I and Official Nationality in Russia, 1825–1855*. Berkeley, 1961.

Ridenour, Robert C. *Nationalism, Modernism, and Personal Rivalry in Nineteenth-Century Russian Music*. Ann Arbor, 1981.

Rimsky-Korsakov, Nikolay Andreyevich. *My Musical Life*. London, 1989.

Roberts, Peter Deane. *Modernism in Russian Piano Music: Skriabin, Prokofiev, and Their Russian Contemporaries*. Bloomington, 1993.

Robinson, Harlow. "Flirting with Decadence: Sergei Prokofiev and 'Ognennyi angel.'" *Opera Quarterly* 8 (1991): 1–7.

———. *Sergei Prokofiev: A Biography*. New York, 1987.

Russ, Michael. *Musorgsky: Pictures at an Exhibition*. Cambridge, 1992.

Sadie, Stanley, ed. *The New Grove Dictionary of Music and Musicians*. 20 vols. London, 1980.

———, ed. *The New Grove Dictionary of Opera*. 4 vols. London, 1992.

Schibli, Sigfried. *Alexander Skrjabin und seine Musik: Grenzüberschreitungen eines prometheischen Geistes*. Munich, 1983.

Schloezer, Boris de. *Scriabin: Artist and Mystic*. Berkeley, 1987.

Schwarz, Boris. *Music and Musical Life in Soviet Russia*. Bloomington, 1983.

Seaman, Gerald. *History of Russian Music*. Vol. 1. New York, 1967.

———. *Nikolai Andreevich Rimsky-Korsakov: A Guide to Research*. New York, 1988.

Seehaus, Lothar. *Dmitrij Schostakovitsch: Leben und Werk*. Wilhelmshaven, 1986.

Seibert, Donald C. "The Dramaturgy of Tchaikovsky's *Mazeppa*: An Interview with Mark Elder." *Music Review* 49 (1988): 272–88.

———. "The Tchaikovsky Fifth: A Symphony without a Programme." *Music Review* 51 (1990): 36–45.

Sitsky, Larry. *Music of the Repressed Russian Avant-Garde, 1900–1929*. Westport, Conn., 1994.

Stravinsky, Igor. *An Autobiography*. New York, 1962.

Taruskin, Richard. "Back to Whom? Neoclassicism as Ideology." *19th-Century Music* 16 (1993): 286–302.

———. "Chernomor to Kashchei: Harmonic Sorcery; or, Stravinsky's 'Angle.'" *Journal of the American Musicological Society* 38 (1985): 72–142.

———. "*Chez Petrouchka*: Harmony and Tonality *chez* Stravinsky." *19th-Century Music* 10 (1987): 265–86.

———. "Christian Themes in Russian Opera: A Millennial Essay." *Cambridge Opera Journal* 2 (1990): 83–91.

———. "To Cross That Sacred Edge: Notes on a Fiery Angel." In *Prokofiev: The Fiery Angel* (liner notes, Deutsche Grammophon 431 669-2), 13–19. 1991.

———. *Defining Russia Musically: Historical and Hermeneutical Essays*. Princeton, 1997.

———. "'Entoiling the Falconet': Russian Musical Orientalism in Context." *Cambridge Opera Journal* 4 (1992): 253–80.

———. "From Fairy Tale to Opera in Four Moves (Not So Simple)." In Thomas Bauman and Marita Petzoldt McClymonds, eds., *Opera and the Enlightenment*, 299–307. Cambridge, 1995.

———. "From *Firebird* to *Rite*." *Ballet Review* 10 (1982): 72–88.

———. "Glinka's Ambiguous Legacy and the Birth Pangs of Russian Opera." *19th-Century Music* 1 (1977): 142–62.

———. "How the Acorn Took Root: A Tale of Russia." *19th-Century Music* 6 (1983): 189–212.

———. "Molchanov's 'The Dawns Are Quiet Here.'" *Musical Quarterly* 62 (1976): 105–15.

———. *Musorgsky: Eight Essays and an Epilogue*. Princeton, 1993.

———. "Musorgsky vs. Musorgsky: The Versions of *Boris Godunov*." *19th-Century Music* 8 (1984–85): 91–118, 245–72.

———. "A Myth of the Twentieth Century: *The Rite of Spring*, the Tradition of the New, and 'The Music Itself.'" *Modernism/Modernity* 2 (1995): 1–26.

———. "Notes on the Program: *Baika.*" In *The Russian Stravinsky.* Brooklyn, N.Y., 1994.

———. *Opera and Drama in Russia, as Preached and Practiced in the 1860s.* Ann Arbor, 1981.

———. "Opera and Drama in Russia: The Case of Serov's 'Judith.'" *Journal of the American Musicological Society* 32 (1979): 74–117.

———. "The Opera and the Dictator: The Peculiar Martyrdom of Dmitri Shostakovich." *New Republic,* 20 March 1989, 34–40.

———. "Pathetic Symphonist: Chaikovsky, Russia, Sexuality, and the Study of Music." *New Republic* (6 February 1995): 26–40.

———. "The Present in the Past: Russian Opera and Russian Historiography, ca. 1870." In Malcolm H. Brown, ed., *Russian and Soviet Music: Essays for Boris Schwarz,* 74–143. Ann Arbor, 1984.

———. "Public Lies and Unspeakable Truth: Interpreting Shostakovich's Fifth Symphony." In David Fanning, ed., *Shostakovich Studies,* 17–56. Cambridge, 1995.

———. "Realism as Preached and Practiced: The Russian Opera Dialogué." *Musical Quarterly* 56 (1970): 431–54.

———. Review of *A Collection of Russian Folk Songs* by Nikolai Lvov and Ivan Prach'. *Journal of the American Musicological Society* 43 (1990): 162–74.

———. Review of *The New Shostakovich* by Ian Macdonald. *Slavic Review* 52 (1993): 396–97.

———. "Revising Revision." *Journal of the American Musicological Society* 46 (1993): 114–38.

———. "*The Rite* Revisited: The Idea and the Source of Its Scenario." In Edmond Strainchamps and Maria Rika Maniates, eds., *Music and Civilization: Essays in Honor of Paul Henry Lang,* 183–202. New York, 1984.

———. "Russian Folk Melodies in *The Rite of Spring.*" *Journal of the American Musicological Society* 33 (1980): 501–43.

———. "Russian Musical Orientalism: A Postscript." *Cambridge Opera Journal* 6 (1994): 81–84.

———. *Stravinsky and the Russian Traditions: A Biography of the Works through "Mavra."* Berkeley, 1996.

———. "Stravinsky's 'Rejoicing Discovery' and What It Meant: In Defense of His Notorious Text Setting." In Ethan Haimo and Paul Johnson, eds., *Stravinsky Retrospectives,* 162–99. Lincoln, Neb., 1987.

———. "The Traditions Revisited: Stravinsky's *Requiem Canticles* as Russian Music." In C. Hatch and D. Bernstein, eds., *Music Theory and the Exploration of the Past,* 391–406. Chicago, 1993.

Taylor, Philip. *Gogolian Interludes: Gogol's Story "Christmas Eve" as the Subject of the Operas by Tchaikovsky and Rimsky-Korsakov.* London, 1984.

Tcherkashina, Marina. "Gogol and Leskov in Shostakovich's Interpretation." *International Journal of Musicology* 1 (1992): 229–44.

Tolstoy, L. N. *War and Peace.* Translated by Rosemary Edmonds. Harmondsworth, Eng., 1978.

Tomasi, Gioacchino Lanza. "*Der Jahrmarkt von Soročincyj* und sein Beitrag zur Suche des spezifisch Russischen in der Musik." In Heinz-Klaus Metzger and Rainer Riehn, eds., *Modest Musorgskij: Aspekte des Opernwerks,* Musik-Konzepte, Heft 21. Munich, 1981.

Treadgold, Donald W. *Twentieth-Century Russia.* Boulder, Colo., 1995.

Tumanov, Alexander N. "Correspondence of Literary Text and Musical Phraseology in Shostakovich's Opera 'The Nose' and Gogol's Fantastic Tale." *Russian Review* 52 (1993): 397–414.

Uhlenbruch, Bernd. "The Annexation of History: Eisenstein and the Ivan Grozny Cult of the 1940s." In Hans Günther, ed., *The Culture of the Stalin Period,* 266–87. London, 1990.

Van den Toorn, Pieter C. *The Music of Igor Stravinsky.* New Haven, 1983.

———. "Stravinsky: Reflections on Context and Analytical Method." *International Journal of Musicology* 1 (1992): 161–200.

Volkov, Solomon, ed. *Testimony: The Memoirs of Dmitri Shostakovich.* New York, 1979.

Walicki, Andrzej. *The Slavophile Controversy: History of a Conservative Utopia in Nineteenth-Century Russian Thought.* Notre Dame, Ind., 1989.

Walker, James. "Mussorgsky's Sunless Cycle in Russian Criticism: Focus of Controversy." *Musical Quarterly* 67 (1981): 382–91.

Walter, Günter. *Dmitri Schostakowitsch: Eine sowjetische Tragödie—Rezeptionsgeschichte.* Frankfurt, 1991.

Warrack, John. *Tchaikovsky.* London, 1973.

———. *Tchaikovsky: Symphonies and Concertos.* London, 1974.

———. *Tchaikovsky Ballet Music.* London, 1979.

Weber-Bockholdt, Petra. *Die Lieder Mussorgskijs: Herkunft und Erscheinungsform.* Munich, 1982.

Wiley, Roland John. *Tchaikovsky's Ballets.* Oxford, 1985.

Wilson, Elizabeth. *Shostakovich: A Life Remembered.* Princeton, 1994.

Yastrebtsev, V. V. *Reminiscences of Rimsky-Korsakov.* New York, 1985.

Zajaczkowski, Henry. "The Function of Obsessive Elements in Tchaikovsky's Style." *Music Review* 63 (1982): 24–30.

———. *Tchaikovski's Musical Style.* Ann Arbor, 1987.

# Index

Ablesimov, Alexander, *The Miller Who Was a Wizard, a Cheat, and a Matchmaker*, 16
Abramtsevo artists colony, 174, 197, 198
abstraction, Stravinsky and, 284–85, 286
academicism: of Belyayev circle, 192, 200, 241, 244; French rejection of, 276; opponents of, 8, 38, 39, 41, 44, 67; Rimsky-Korsakov's conversion to, 127, 169–71; Russian painting, 200; War Communism and, 241. *See also* education
Achron, Joseph, 272
acmeism, 199, 201–2
Adorno, Theodor W., 280
aesthetics: ballet, 217; Belyayev circle, 192–95, 202, 244; Chaikovsky, 73, 137–39, 141, 147, 165, 200; Diaghilev, 195, 218, 231, 274–75, 289, 327; French, 276–77, 288; Golenishchev-Kutuzov, 89–92, 168; *kuchka*, 8–9, 38, 43–44, 49, 55–56, 61, 73, 151, 184; Lourié's ultrarefined, 233; opera, 93, 95–96, 100–101, 104–5, 184; pre-Romantic, 156; Rachmaninoff, 204; Russian earliest, 139; Soviet, 5–6, 238–41, 255–60, 264–68, 296, 301, 321, 323, 346–48, 358; Stravinsky, 274–87; Vsevolozhsky, 139, 146, 147, 200. *See also* art; conservatism; formalism label; modernism; neonationalism; progressivism; realism; symbolism

Afanasyev, Alexander, 231, 274, 281, 286; *The Slavs' Poetic Outlook on Nature*, 187, 225
Agitational Department (Agitotdel), 252
Akhmatova, Anna, 202, 231–32, 309
Alexander II, 19, 35, 197, 200; and assassination, 48, 87, 178; orientalism during expansion by, 80, 81; serfdom abolished by, 91, 197
Alexander III, 140, 200, 290; and *Boris Godunov*, 184; as Chaikovsky patron, 141, 144, 156
Alexandrov, Georgiy, 360
Alexandrovich, Vladimir, Grand Duke, 175, 178
All-Union Congress of Soviet Composers: First, 310, *Plate 25;* Third, *Plate 27*
All-Union Congress of Soviet Writers: First, 255, 308; Second, 360
Alyabyev, Alexander, 17, 65
amateurism, Rubinstein vs., 34, 36, 41
Ambros, August Wilhelm, *Culturhistorische Bilder aus dem Musikleben der Gegenwart*, 49–50
Andersen, Hans Christian, "The Ugly Duckling," 232
anhemitony, 284–85
Anne, Empress, 14
anti-Semitism, 129, 142; of *Montjoie!*, 277; of Musorgsky, 39, 86–87, 129, 364; against Rubinstein, 39, 40; Shostakovich vs., 361–62, 363–68; Stalinist, 361–62, 364–66; Yevtushenko vs., 361, 366–67

|  |  |
|---|---|
| Compositor: | Integrated Composition Systems |
| Text: | 10/13 Sabon |
| Display: | Sabon |
| Printer/Binder: | Edwards Brothers, Inc. |
| Indexer: | Barbara Roos |